CIPS-SIGHAN Joint Conference on Chinese Language Processing

(CLP 2010)

Beijing, China
28-29 August 2010

Editors:

Le Sun **Keh-Jiann Chen**

ISBN: 978-1-62748-364-3

Printed from e-media with permission by:

Curran Associates, Inc.
57 Morehouse Lane
Red Hook, NY 12571

Some format issues inherent in the e-media version may also appear in this print version.

Printed by Curran Associates, Inc. (2013)

For permission requests, please contact the Association for Computational Linguistics at the address below.

Association for Computational Linguistics
209 N. Eighth Street
Stroudsburg, Pennsylvania 18360

Phone: 1-570-476-8006
Fax: 1-570-476-0860

acl@aclweb.org

Additional copies of this publication are available from:

Curran Associates, Inc.
57 Morehouse Lane
Red Hook, NY 12571 USA
Phone: 845-758-0400
Fax: 845-758-2634
Email: curran@proceedings.com
Web: www.proceedings.com

Preface

With the rapid of expansion of Chinese language materials on the Internet, the use of natural language technology as a way of harnessing Chinese language content is drawing growing interest from researchers around the globe. The rise of China as a global power with increasing influence on the world stage is only fanning this interest. The Chinese language also has a number of characteristics that make Chinese language processing particularly challenging and intellectually rewarding. To meet the challenge, the first CIPS-SIGHAN Joint Conference on Chinese Language Processing (CLP2010) is organized under the auspices of CIPS (Chinese Information Processing Society of China) and SIGHAN, a Special Interest Group of the ACL.

The goal of CLP2010 is to bring together both established and aspiring researchers around the globe and provide a unified forum for them to showcase their research achievements, share their ideas, and frame research problems that are crucial in advancing the state-of-the-art in Chinese language processing.

There have been four successful international Chinese word segmentation bakeoffs sponsored by SIGHAN that have greatly advanced the state-of-the-art in this area. This year, in addition to the Chinese word segmentation task, the conference will include tasks in Chinese parsing, Chinese personal name disambiguation and Chinese word sense induction, hence attracting wider participation.

The proceedings includes 5 invited papers from senior researchers and 20 regular papers carefully reviewed and selected out of 31 submissions from different areas of Chinese language processing. The four bakeoff tasks have attracted more than 68 groups to submit their results. The proceedings also includes 4 overview papers that introduce the bakeoff tasks as well as the 44 bakeoff papers.

Last but not least, we would like to thank professors Chu-Ren Huang, Dan Jurafsky, Youqi Cao, and Chenqing Zong for initiating and proposing to hold this conference. We are also deeply indebted to the reviewers for their tireless and generous work.

We wish you all an enjoyable and thought-provoking conference.

Le Sun and Keh-Jiann Chen — CLP2010 General Co-Chairs
Qun Liu and Nianwen Xue — CLP2010 Program Co-Chairs

General chairs:

Le Sun, Institute of Software, Chinese Academy of Sciences
Keh-Jiann Chen, Institute of Information Science, Academia Sinica

Program chairs:

Qun Liu, Institute of Computing Technology, Chinese Academy of Sciences
Nianwen Xue, Brandeis University

Local arrangements chair:

Erhong Yang, Beijing Language and Culture University

Bakeoff chairs:

* Chinese Word Segmentation:

Qun Liu, Institute of Computing Technology, Chinese Academy of Sciences
Hongmei Zhao, Institute of Computing Technology, Chinese Academy of Sciences

* Chinese Parsing:

Qiang Zhou, Tsinghua University
Jingbo Zhu, North East University

* Chinese Personal Name disambiguation:

Maggie Li, The Hong Kong Polytechnic University
Chu-Ren Huang, Institute of Linguistics, Academia Sinica

* Chinese Word Sense Induction :

Le Sun, Institute of Software, Chinese Academy of Sciences
Zhendong Dong, Chinese Information Processing Society of China

Publications chair:

Tiejun Zhao, Harbin Institute of Technology

Publicity chair:

Bin Wang, Institute of Computing Technology, Chinese Academy of Sciences

Reviewers:

Pi-Chuan Chang
Wanxiang Che
Keh-Jiann Chen
Jinying Chen
Jiajun Chen
Boxing Chen
Xuanjing Huang
Heng Ji
Yumei Li
Maggie Li
Sujian Li
Hongfei Lin
Ting Liu
Qun Liu
Yang Liu
Zhanyi Liu
Yajuan Lv
Shaoping Ma
Haitao Mi
Jianyun Nie
Keh-Yih Su
Le Sun
Maosong Sun
Bing Sun
Huihsin Tseng
Xiaojun Wan
Houfeng Wang
Haifeng Wang
Xiaojie Wang
Bin Wang
Kam-Fai Wong
Yunfang Wu
Hua Wu
Fei Xia
Yunqing Xia
Deyi Xiong
Jinan Xu
Nianwen Xue
Muyun Yang
Erhong Yang
Guan Yi
Kun Yu
Dongdong Zhang
Min Zhang
Min Zhang
Weidong Zhan
Zhenzhong Zhang
Honemei Zhao
Guodong Zhou
Ming Zhou
Qiang Zhou
Jingbo Zhu
Chengqing Zong

Location: 311B+C, 2nd floor, BICC

CLP-2010 Program

Day-1 (August 28 Saturday)

Morning

Time		*Outline*	*Chair*	*Speaker & Title*
8:30-8:40		**Opening**	**Le Sun**	
8:40-9:00		**Invited Paper**	**Keh-Jiann Chen**	**Zhendong Dong, Qiang Dong and Changling Hao, Word Segmentation needs change**
9:00 - 10:20	9:00 - 9:20	**Overview of All tasks**	**Qun Liu**	Hongmei Zhao and Qun Liu, The CIPS-SIGHAN CLP 2010 Chinese Word Segmentation Bakeoff
	9:20 - 9:40			Qiang Zhou and Jingbo Zhu, Chinese Syntactic Parsing Evaluation
	9:40 - 10:00			Ying Chen, Peng Jin, Wenjie Li and Chu-Ren Huang, The Chinese Persons Name Disambiguation Evaluation: Exploration of Personal Name Disambiguation in Chinese News
	10:00 - 10:20			Le Sun Zhenzhong Zhang and Qiang Dong, Overview of the Chinese Word Sense Induction Task at CLP2010
10:20 10:50		**Coffee Break**		
10:50-11:10		**Invited Paper**	**Nianwen Xue**	**Chu-Ren Huang, Ying Chen, Sophia Yat Mei Lee, Textual Emotion Processing From Event Analysis**
11:10 - 12:10	11:10 - 11:25	**Bakeoff Paper: Task1**	**Hongmei Zhao**	Qin Gao and Stephan Vogel, A Multi-layer Chinese Word Segmentation System Optimized for Out-of-domain Tasks
	11:25 - 11:40			Degen Huang, Deqin Tong and Yanyan Luo, HMM Revises Low Marginal Probability by CRF for Chinese Word Segmentation
	11:40 - 11:55			Chongyang Zhang, Zhigang Chen and Guoping Hu , A Chinese Word Segmentation System Based on Structured Support Vector Machine Utilization of Unlabeled Text Corpus
	11:55 - 12:10			Yu-Chieh Wu, Jie-Chi Yang and Yue-Shi Lee, Chinese Word Segmentation with Conditional Support Vector In-spired Markov Models

12:10-12:30	**POSTER 1**		1. Yali Li, Weiqun Xu and Yonghong Yan, Semantic class induction and its application for a Chinese voice search system
			2. Shih-Hung Wu, Yong-Zhi Chen, Ping-che Yang, Tsun Ku and Chao-Lin Liu, Reducing the False Alarm Rate of Chinese Character Error Detection and Correction
			3. Ling-Xiang Tang, Shlomo Geva, Andrew Trotman and Yue Xu, A Boundary-Oriented Chinese Segmentation Method Using N-Gram Mutual Information
			4. Wenjun Gao, Xipeng Qiu and Xuanjing Huang, Adaptive Chinese Word Segmentation with Online Passive-Aggressive Algorithm
			5. Kun Wang, Chengqing Zong and Keh-Yih Su, A Character-Based Joint Model for CIPS-SIGHAN Word Segmentation Bakeoff 2010
			6. Hua-Ping Zhang, Jian Gao, Qian Mo and He-Yan Huang, Incorporating New Words Detection with Chinese Word Segmentation
			7. Xiaoming Xu, Muhua Zhu, Xiaoxu Fei and Jingbo Zhu, High OOV-Recall Chinese Word Segmenter
			8. Baobao Chang and Mairgup Mansur, Chinese word segmentation model using bootstrapping
			9. Xiao Qin, Liang Zong, Yuqian Wu, Xiaojun Wan and Jianwu Yang, CRF-based Experiments for Cross-Domain Chinese Word Segmentation at CIPS-SIGHAN-2010
			10. Tian-Jian Jiang, Shih-Hung Liu, Cheng-Lung Sung and Wen-Lian Hsu Hsu, Term Contributed Boundary Tagging by Conditional Random Fields for SIGHAN 2010 Chinese Word Segmentation Bakeoff
			11. Jianping Shen, Xuan Wang, Hainan Zhao and Wenxiao Zhang, Chinese Word Segmentation based on Mixing Multiple Preprocessor and CRF
			12. Guo Jiang, A domain adaption Word Segmenter
			13. Huixing Jiang and Zhe Dong, An Double Hidden HMM and an CRF for Segmentation Tasks with Pinyin's Finals
			14. Jiangde Yu, Chuan Gu and Wenying Ge, Combining Character-Based and Subsequence-Based Tagging for Chinese Word Segmentation
12:30-14:00	**Lunch**		

Afternoon				
14:00-14:20		**Invited Paper**	**Rou Song**	**Hen-Hsen Huang, Chuen-Tsai Sun and Hsin-Hsi Chen, Classical Chinese Sentence Segmentation**
14:20 - 16:00	14:20-14:40	**Research Papers**	**Jingbo Zhu**	Liou Chen and Qiang Zhou, Automatic Identification of Chinese Event Descriptive Clause
	14:40-15:00			Lidan Zhang and Kwok-Ping Chan, Bigram HMM with Context Distribution Clustering for Unsupervised Chinese Part-of-Speech tagging
	15:00-15:20			Bin LU, Benjamin K. Tsou, Tao Jiang, Oi Yee Kwong and Jingbo Zhu, Mining Large-scale Parallel Corpora from Multilingual Patents: An English-Chinese example and its application to SMT
	15:20-15:40			Hongying Zan, Junhui Zhang, Xuefeng Zhu and Shiwen Yu, Studies on Automatic Recognition of Common Chinese Adverb's usages Based on Statistics Methods
	15:40-16:00			Xiaona Ren, Qiaoli Zhou, Chunyu Kit and Dongfeng Cai, Automatic Identification of Predicate Heads in Chinese Sentences
16:00-16:30		**Coffee Break**		
16:30-16:50		**Invited Paper**	**Wenjie Li**	**Rou Song, Yuru Jiang and Jingyi Wang, On Generalized-Topic-Based Chinese Discourse Structure**
16:50 - 17:35	16:50-17:05	**Bakeoff Paper: Task2**	**Qiang Zhou**	Weiwei Sun, Rui Wang and Yi Zhang, Discriminative Parse Reranking for Chinese with Homogeneous and Heterogeneous Annotations
	17:05-17:20			Qiaoli Zhou, Wenjing Lang, Yingying Wang, Yan Wang and Dongfeng Cai, The SAU Report for the 1st CIPS-SIGHAN-ParsEval-2010
	17:20-17:35			Xuezhe Ma, Xiaotian Zhang, Hai Zhao and Bao-Liang Lu, Dependency Parser for Chinese Constituent Parsing
17:35 - 18:20	17:35-17:50	**Bakeoff Paper: Task3**	**Ying Chen**	Huizhen Wang, Haibo Ding, Yingchao Shi, JI Ma, Xiao Zhou and Jingbo Zhu, A Multi-stage Clustering Framework for Chinese Personal Name Disambiguation
	17:50-18:05			Ruifeng Xu, Jun Xu, Xiangying Dai and Chunyu Kit, Combine Person Name and Person Identity Recognition and Document Clustering for Chinese Person Name Disambiguation
	18:05-18:20			Yang Song, Zhengyan He, Chen Chen and Houfeng Wang, A Pipeline Approach to Chinese Personal Name Disambiguation

18:20-18:40	**POSTER 2**		1. Xingjun Xu, Guanglu Sun, Yi Guan, Xishuang Dong and Sheng Li, Selecting Optimal Feature Template Subset for CRFs
			2. Zhen Hai, Kuiyu Chang, Qinbao Song and Jung-jae Kim, A Statistical NLP Approach for Feature and Sentiment Identification from Chinese Reviews
			3. Guangfan Sun, Technical Report of the CCID System for the 2th Evaluation on Chinese Parsing
			4. Yong Cheng and Chengjie Sun, CRF tagging for head recognition based on Stanford parser
			5. Zhiguo Wang and Chengqing Zong, Treebank Conversion based Self-training Strategy for Parsing
			6. Wenzhi Xu, Chaobo Sun and Caixia Yuan, A Chinese LPCFG Parser with Hybrid Character Information
			7. ZhiPeng Jiang, Yu Zhao, Yi Guan, Chao Li and Sheng Li, Complete Syntactic Analysis Based on Multi-level Chunking
			8. Xiang Zhu, Xiaodong Shi, Ningfeng Liu, YingMei Guo and Yidong Chen, Chinese Personal Name Disambiguation: Technical Report of Natural Language Processing Lab of Xiamen University
			9. Hua-Ping Zhang, Zhi-Hua Liu, Qian Mo and He-Yan Huang, Chinese Personal Name Disambiguation Based on Person Modeling
			10. Yu Hong, Fei Pei, Yue-hui Yang, Jian-min Yao and Qiao-ming Zhu, Jumping Distance based Chinese Person Name Disambiguation
			11. Erlei Ma and Yuanchao Liu, Research of People disambiguation by combining multiple knowledges
			12. Dongliang Wang and Degen Huang, DLUT: Chinese Personal Name Disambiguation with Rich Features
			13. Jiashen Sun, Tianmin Wang, Li Li and Xing Wu, Person Name Disambiguation based on Topic Model
			14. Zhang Jiayue, Cai Yichao, Li Si, Xu Weiran and Guo Jun, PRIS at Chinese Language Processing --Chinese Personal Name Disambiguation

CLP-2010 Program

Day-2 (August 29 Sunday)

Morning				
8:30 - 10:10	8:30-8:50	**Research Papers**	**Nianwen Xue**	Yu Chen, Wenjie Li, Yan Liu, Dequan Zheng and Tiejun Zhao, Exploring Deep Belief Network for Chinese Relation Extraction
	8:50-9:10			Yulan He, Harith Alani and Deyu Zhou, Exploring English Lexicon Knowledge for Chinese Sentiment Analysis
	9:10-9:30			Youzheng Wu and Hisashi Kawai, Exploiting Social Q&A Collection in Answering Complex Questions
	9:30-9:50			Andi Wu, Treebank of Chinese Bible Translations
	9:50-10:10			Jiang Yang and Min Hou, Using Topic Sentiment Sentences to Recognize Sentiment Polarity in Chinese Reviews
10:10-10:40		**Coffee Break**		
10:40-11:00		**Invited Paper**	**Chu-Ren Huang**	**Lei Wang and Shiwen Yu, Semantic Computing and Language Knowledge Bases**
11:00 - 11:45	11:00-11:15	**Bakeoff Paper: Task4**	**Le Sun**	Yuxiang Jia, Shiwen Yu and Zhengyan Chen, Chinese Word Sense Induction with Basic Clustering Algorithms
	11:15-11:30			Zhao Liu, Xipeng Qiu and Xuanjing Huang, Triplet-Based Chinese Word Sense Induction
	11:30-11:45			Bichuan Zhang and Jiashen Sun, Word Sense Induction using Cluster Ensemble

11:45-12:05	**POSTER 3**		1. Shan-Bin Chan and Hayato Yamana, The Method of Improving the Specific Language Focused Crawler
			2. Hongyan Song and Tianfang Yao, Active Learning Based Corpus Annotation
			3. Chongyang Zhang, Zhigang Chen and Guoping Hu, Improving Chinese Word Segmentation by Adopting Self-Organized Maps of Character N-gram
			4. Min Hou, Yu Zou, Yonglin Teng, Wei He, Yan Wang, Jun Liu and Jiyuan Wu, CMDMC: A Diachronic Digital Museum of Chinese Mandarin
			5. Gulila Altenbek and Xiao-long Wang, Kazakh Segmentation System of Inflectional Affixes
			6. Rongzhou Shen, Claire Grover and Ewan Klein, Space characters in Chinese semi-structured texts
			7. Peng Jin, Yihao Zhang and Rui Sun, LSTC System for Chinese Word Sense Induction
			8. Hao Zhang, Tong Xiao and Jingbo Zhu, NEUNLPLab Chinese Word Sense Induction System for SIGHAN Bakeoff 2010
			9. Ke Cai, Xiaodong Shi, Yidong Chen, Zhehuang Huang and Yan Gao, Chinese Word Sense Induction based on Hierarchical Clustering Algorithm
			10. Zhenzhong Zhang, Le Sun and Wenbo Li, ISCAS: A System for Chinese Word Sense Induction Based on K-means Algorithm
			11. Hua Xu, Bing Liu, Longhua Qian and Guodong Zhou, Soochow University: Description and Analysis of the Chinese Word Sense Induction System for CLP2010
			12. Lisha Wang, Yanzhao Dou, Xiaoling Sun and Hongfei Lin, K-means and Graph-based Approaches for Chinese Word Sense Induction Task
			13. Zhengyan He, Yang Song and Houfeng Wang, Applying Spectral Clustering for Chinese Word Sense Induction
12:05-12:15	**Closing**	**Chu-Ren Huang**	

Table of Contents

Invited Papers:

Research Papers:

Bakeoff Papers:

Task 1: Chinese word segmentation

Task 2: Chinese parsing

Task 3: Chinese personal name disambiguation

Task 4: Chinese word sense induction

Word Segmentation needs change

— From a linguist's view

Zhendong Dong
Research Center of Computer
& Language Engineering, CAS
dzd@keenage.com

Qiang Dong
Canada Keentime Inc.
dongqiang@keenage.com

Changling Hao
Canada Keentime Inc.
support@keenage.com

Abstract

The authors propose that we need some change for the current technology in Chinese word segmentation. We should have separate and different phases in the so-called segmentation. First of all, we need to limit segmentation only to the segmentation of Chinese characters instead of the so-called Chinese words. In character segmentation, we will extract all the information of each character. Then we start a phase called Chinese morphological processing (CMP). The first step of CMP is to do a combination of the separate characters and is then followed by post-segmentation processing, including all sorts of repetitive structures, Chinese-style abbreviations, recognition of pseudo-OOVs and their processing, etc. The most part of post-segmentation processing may have to be done by some rule-based sub-routines, thus we need change the current corpus-based methodology by merging with rule-based technique.

1 Introduction

Chinese word segmentation seems to be an old grandma's story. We very often hear some contradictory remarks about its advance. Most of reports from the evaluation tasks always gave us positive, or even impressive results, such as over 96% accuracy, but some reports were rather negative and expressed their deep concern. They claimed that word segmentation was still entangled in a difficult situation and no breakthrough in real applications. By careful and longtime observation, the incompetence is usually caused by the coarseness in the currently prevalent technology.

We carefully observed some Chinese-English MT systems and found some errors were caused even in the very early stage of the processing, that is, in the stage of word segmentation. No matter the MT is statistics-based or rule-based, they have their Achilles' heel in the segmentation stage. Can today's prevalent technology effectively cope with the problem? Or do we need some change? The present technology is characterized by its "trilogy", that is, "corpora + statistics (ML) + evaluation". We regret to say that many researchers today may be indulged in methodology itself rather than the language they have to target. They are enchanted by the scores and ranks, but they forget the object they are processing.

Therefore we propose that a Chinese morphological processing (CMP) should be taken to replace the current Chinese word segmentation. CMP includes the following components:

- Chinese character processing (CCP)
- Initial combination of Chinese multi-character expressions (CMEs)
- Morphological structure processing (MSP)

2 Chinese character processing

2.1 "Word" in Chinese

"Word or no word" may be an even older story in Chinese linguistic circle. One assertion about Chinese words may be quite popular, even to most of western researchers in the NLP circle, that is, different from English or other western languages, there is no space between Chinese words and thus segmentation of a running text into words is necessary for Chinese processing. However, do words really exist in Chinese? It is still a vexing and controversial issue. Some Chinese grammarians argue that in Chinese there are no words at all, but there are only characters instead and some express their strong objection.

What is a Chinese "word"? It was reported that the concept of "word" had not been introduced into China until the very beginning of the last century. In fact word is alien to Chinese. At least the concept of word in Chinese is rather vague. In Chinese there are no clear-cut distinction between characters and so-called word, either between multi-character words and those that are similar to English MWE. Ordinary English people may be surprised if they are told that even in popular Chinese dictionaries there are no entries equivalent to English "pork (猪肉)", "beef 牛肉)", "egg (鸡蛋)", "rain (verb 下雨)", "snow (verb 下雪)", but there are entries equivalent to English "lower limbs(下肢)", "give orders (下令)", "appendicitis (盲肠炎)". There is somewhat arbitrariness in recognition of Chinese "words", so the vocabulary in different Chinese dictionaries may vary very greatly. Does a dictionary take usage frequency into account when it decides on its entries? Let's compare their occurrence with the following entries in the dictionary as shown in Table 1. Let's compare the occurrence with the following entries in different dictionaries and in reference to Google's results. In Table 1, "-" indicates that the entry does not occur and "+" indicates the entry occurs.

Entries	3 Popular dictionaries	Results in Google
身为	- 现汉[1] - 规范[2] - 新时代汉英[3]	32,500,000
身亡	- 现汉 + 规范 - 新时代汉英	24,300,000
身居	- 现汉 +规范 - 新时代汉英	16,600,000
身故	+ 现汉 - 规范 + 新时代汉英	6,760,000
身教	+ 现汉 + 规范 + 新时代汉英	497,000
身历	- 现汉 + 规范 + 新时代汉英	409,000
身受	+ 现汉 + 规范 + 新时代汉英	900,000

Table 1. Comparison of entry occurrence in dictionaries

In a word, since "word" in Chinese is rather vague, what is a better tactics we should take then? The present word segmentation is burdened too heavily. In comparison with English tokenization, it goes too far. Does English tokenization deal with MWEs, such as "United nations", "free of charge", "first lady"? Why does Chinese word segmentation have to deal with Chinese multi-character "word"?

2.2 Chinese character processing (CCP)

We propose that the real task of so-called Chinese word segmentation is to segment a running text into single characters with spaces between. We call this processing Chinese character processing (CCP). CCP is in parallel with English tokenization. In most cases CCP can achieve 100% accuracy. The most important task for CCP is not only to segment a text, but also to obtain various kinds of information (syntactic, semantic) of every character. What will be followed depends on the tasks to be designated. Usually a demand-led morphological processing will be taken.

3 Initial combination

In most cases, what we called initial combination of Chinese multi-character expressions (CMEs) should be followed indispensably. It may be either shallow or deep, and may be done either with the help of a lexical database or a corpus, and the longest matching may be the frequently-used technique.

[1] Modern Chinese Dictionary
[2] Modern Chinese Standard Dictionary
[3] New Age Chinese-English Dictionary

4 Morphological structure processing (MSP)

4.1 Pseudo-OOVs

The first task of MSP is to recognize and process Chinese OOVs. What are OOVs in English? Normally if a string between two spaces in a running text does not exist in the lexical database or the corpus the processing system is using, this string is taken as an OOV. However, what is an OOV in Chinese then? It is really not so easy to define an OOV in Chinese as in English. The recognition of English OOVs may be done in the phase of tokenization, but the recognition of Chinese OOVs should, in a strict sense, not be done in so-called word segmentation. It should be regarded as a special phase of the morphological processing. It is commonly acknowledged that OOV recognition is the most serious factor that impairs the performance of current Chinese word segmentation.

We may first look at some instances of machine translation results and find the actual problems. The reason why we use MT systems to test and evaluate segmentation is because this will make it explicit and easy for human to assess. One error in segmentation makes a 100% failure in translation. In our examples, the translation (a) is done by a statistical MT system and the translation (b) by a rule-based MT system. (C) is human translation, which may help make comparison and find the errors made by MT.

1. 美国民众**力挺**南京申办2020年奥运会。

(a) Americans even behind the bid to host the 2020 Olympic Games in Nanjing.

(b) American people's strength holds out in Nanjing and bids for the 2020 Olympic Games.

(c) Americans fully backed up Nanjing's bid to host the 2020 Olympic Games.

Chinese OOVs can be roughly categorized into two classes, one is true OOVs and the other is pseudo-OOVs. The recognition and processing of true OOVs can be done as English OOVs are treated in English. However, the recognition and processing of Chinese pseudo-OOVs should be done by a special processing module. Chinese pseudo-OOVs includes two types: plain pseudo-OOVs, such as "力挺", "洁肤", "野泳", "浴宫", "首胜", "完胜", and abbreviated pseudo-OOVs, such as "二炮", "世博", "严打", "婚介", "疾控中心", "驻京办", "维稳办", "园博会", "中老年", "事病假", "军地两用".

- **Plain pseudo-OOVs**

A pseudo-OOV is a combinatory string of Chinese characters in which each character carries one of its original meanings and the way of combination conforms to Chinese grammatical pattern. In the above Chinese sentence the word "力挺" is a typical pseudo-OOV. "力挺" is a combination of two characters, "力" and "挺". "力" has four meanings, one of which is "do one's best". "挺" has six meanings, one of which is "back up". Originally in Chinese dictionaries we can find the following expressions similar to the pattern of "力挺", such as "力避", "力持", "力促", "力挫", "力荐", "力戒", "力克", "力拼", "力求", "力图", "力争", "力主". In all these expressions the character "力" carries the same meaning as that in "力挺", and the second characters in the combinations are all actions. Therefore the expression "力挺" is a grammatical and meaningful pseudo-OOV. It should be noticed that this kind of pseudo-OOV is highly productive in Chinese. In addition to all the dictionary entries that we listed above, we found "力陈(to strongly state)"and "力抗(to strongly resist)" are already used in the web. Its highly occurrence in real texts calls our special attention. Let's see how MT will tackle them poorly.

2. 辩护人**力陈**多处疑点。

(a) Chen multiple defense of human doubt.

(b) Many old doubtful points of the manpower of pleading.

(c) The pleader argued and showed many doubtful points.

We wonder how the current technique of segmentation tackles the problem. We are not sure how one error in a segmentation effect the score in Bakeoff.

Let's look at two more examples and have a brief discussion of them.

3.据邻居反映，案发当天中午有一个快餐**外卖郎**来过被害人家中。

(a) According to neighbors reflected the incident that day at noon there is a fast food take-Lang came to the victim's home.

(b) According to the information of neighbour's, a fast food takes out the my darling to been to victim's home at noon on the day when the case happened.

(c) According to the neighbors, at noon on the same day a fast food takeout boy came to the victim's house.

4. 一个官员被**修脚女**刺死了。

(a) One officer was stabbed to death the women pedicure.

(b) An officer is trimmed the foot daughter and assassinated.

(c) An official was stabbed to death by the girl pedicurist.

All the four erroneous MT translations above originate from the so-called recognition of OOVs "外卖郎" and "修脚女" in the segmentation. The MT systems might make out "外卖"and "郎" or "修脚" and "女" separately, but fail to recognize their combinations. The combination pattern of these two plain pseudo-OOVs is a very typical and popular one in Chinese, just similar to the suffix "-er" or "-or" in English to derive a noun of a doer. "外卖郎" is a combination of "外卖"(takeout) and "郎"(boy). When a MT failed to tackle it, the translation would be so poor.

- **Abbreviated pseudo-OOVs**

Different from English abbreviations or acronyms, Chinese abbreviations in essence are contracted forms of words and expressions. The contraction is mainly related to three factors: (1) maximal preservation of the original meaning; (2) possible maintenance of Chinese grammatical structural pattern; (3) consideration of acceptableness of rhythm. Let's take "维稳办" for example. "维稳办" is the contraction of "维护稳定办公室". The literal translation of the expression is "maintain stability office". Thus the first part of the expression "维护稳定" is contracted to "维稳", and the second part is contracted to "办". "维护稳定" grammatically is a "verb + object" structure while "维稳" can be regarded as the same grammatical structure. Grammatically "办公室" is modified by "维护稳定", and in the contraction the word "办" is also modified by the contraction "维稳". As for acceptableness of rhythm, "维稳办" is a three-character expression, in which the first two are a "verb + object structure and the last is single. The structure of "2-character verb + 1-character noun" is a highly-productive pattern of noun expression in Chinese. So it is desirable to process this type of structures before syntactic processing. As the structure can usually be patternized, it is possible to have them well-processed. We propose that we should deal with it in the morphological processing stage.

4.2 Repetitive structures

First let's look at a MT translation and see what has happened when a Chinese repetitive structure is ill-processed.

5. 你来**穿穿看**，太小了。

(a) Come see Chuan Chuan, too small.

(b) You come to wear looking, it is too small.

(c) Come and try on, it is too small.

The above two erroneous MT translations (a) and (b) originate from the failure in dealing with a typical verb structural pattern for expression to urge someone to have a try. This pattern is: "VV看", its actual meaning is "have a try" and "to see if …". The literal translation of the above instance "穿穿看" may be "put on, put on and let's have a look". Similarly we can have "吃吃看" (which can be literally translated as "taste, taste, and let's see").

Chinese is unique with its various types of repetitive structures. They are by no means rare phenomena in real texts. Any negligence or failure in the processing of repetitive structures will surely spoil the succedent tasks. Unfortunately this problem has not caught enough attention of researchers and developers of word segmentation tools. Most of neglecters usually leave the problem to the vocabulary that they collect. Let's compare the following two groups of translations:

Group A

你再仔细听一听，是不是哪里漏水了。

他看了看停在旁边的火车。

Group B

你再仔细嚼一嚼，是不是有薄荷味。

他坐了下来，又向后靠了靠。

Group A1

You listen carefully, is not where the leak was.

He looked at the stop next to the train.

Group B1

Carefully you chew a chewing is not a mint flavor.

He sat down, then back by the by.

The English translations of the repetitive structures in Group A1 are acceptable for the structures "听一听" and "看了看" are no doubt in the vocabulary. And the translations of Group B are messy enough to show that the repetitive structures become OOVs and are not well-processed.

Generally most of Chinese repetitive structures originate from three word classes:

- Verb repetitive patterns:

AA	听听, 想想, 谈谈
ABAB	商量商量, 研究研究
A一/了A	嚼一嚼, 看了看
AA看	穿穿看, 吃吃看
A了一/又A	闻了一闻, 按了一按,摸了又摸

- Adjective repetitive patterns:

AA	大大, 轻轻, 红红, 胖胖
AABB	漂漂亮亮, 大大方方,斯斯文文
ABAB	白胖白胖, 焦黄焦黄

- Classifier repetitive patterns:

AA	个个（是好汉）, 件件（是稀世珍宝）
一AA	一辆辆, 一只只, 一碗碗, 一床床
一A一A	一件一件, 一套一套,一块一块
一A又一A	一张又一张, 一朵又一朵, 一条又一条

All these patterns are highly productive in Chinese. It will be impracticable for any Chinese parsing or MT systems to leave all the resolutions of them to the vocabulary rather than special processing module.

4.3 Plain classifier and unit structures

Chinese is featured by its plenty of classifiers. In many cases a concrete noun occurs idiomatically with its particular classifier especially when modified a numeral, for example, "一个人"(a person), "两辆车"(two cars), "三公斤苹果"(3 kilos of apples). The processing of this type of structures will surely benefit the succeeding parsing and even word sense disambiguation. Besides the processing is comparatively easy even in the early stage.

4.4 Chinese verb aspect processing

The verb aspect in Chinese is different from that in English. In general, by using Chinese aspects, we add some procedural tune to a verb rather than relating to time. In other words Chinese verb aspects give hints of the developmental phases or results, or the capability or possibility of the events. Chinese verb aspects are expressed by the aspect markers, such as simple markers "上", "下", "进", "出", "回", "过", "起", "开", "到" and compound markers "上来", "下去", etc.

Again let's look at two pair of Chinese-to-English MT translations.

(6) 要干的工作太多了，一个人实在是干不过来了。

(a) To dry too much work, a person indeed dry However come.

(b) The ones that should do have too much work, one can not really be dry.

(c) I have too much work to do, I can hardly cope with it.

(7) 姑娘说着说着哭起来了。

(a) Said the girl spoke to cry.

(b) The girl has cried saying.

(c) The girl began to weep while talking.

The messy translations tell us how serious the impairment of the translation will be if we fail to process the Chinese verb aspects.

Table 2 shows the meanings conveyed by most Chinese aspect and its corresponding "aspect markers" and examples. Finally, when speaking about Chinese aspect, one point we would like to invite readers' attention that different from the aspect of English. It is known that English aspect is usually closely related to tenses, for example, English verbs can be used in progressive aspect with various tenses, such as present progressive, progressive and future progressive tenses. However, Chinese aspects are related to the development of the event itself, but not related to the time when the event happens.

5 Conclusion

Is it time for Chinese NLP circle to rethink what we have actually achieved in the word segmentation and consider some radical change? How much room left is there for the current trilogy to improve? We propose that we should have morphological processing to replace the so-called word segmentation. We have designated new tasks for the processing. In addition, we hope that we should design and use a new evaluation method. The general idea of new evaluation is to use a post-segmentation, or post-morphological-processing task, say, chunking, to evaluate, rather than the present method of isochronous self-testing.

sememe in HowNet	meaning	marker	examples
{Vsuppose|假定}	presupposing	起来	读~流畅
{Vstart|发端}	inceptive	起来	双方对骂~
		上	在一旁聊~了
{Vgoingon|进展}	progressive	在	~发言呢
		正	~睡觉呢
		正在	~干活
		着	说~说~动手了
{Vcontinue|延续}	protractive	下去	谈~会有结果
{Vend|完结}	terminative	过	吃~饭再走吧
{Vachieve|达成}	perfective	出	做~新成绩
		出来	算~了吗
		到	接~人了吗
		得	饭做~了
		过来	错的地方改~
		过去	被我蒙~了
		好	功课做~了
		见	听~了但看不~
		上	吃~一顿饱饭
		下	谈~那笔生意
		着	见~要见的人
{Vable|能力}	capable	得到	办~
		得过	信~
		得过来	忙~
		得了	一个人干~
		得起	买~
		得下	装~
		起	输~输不~
		下	可以睡~3 个人
{Vincapable|没能力}	incapable	不得	动也动~
		不过	说~你
		不过来	一个人忙~
		不了	一个人可干~
		不起	负担~
		不下	吃~
{Vpossible|可能}	possible	得	这菜吃~吃不~
{Vtry|试试}	Trying	看	穿穿~

Table 2. Chinese aspect markers and their meanings

References

Hai Zhao and Chunyu Kit, 2008. Unsupervised Segmentation Helps Supervised Learning of Chinese Tagging for Word Segmentation and Named Entity Recognition. In Prceedings of the Sixth SIGHAN Workshop on Chinese Language Processing, 2008, Hyderbad, India.

Hwee Tou Ng and Jin Kiat Low, 2004. Chinese Part-of-speech Tagging: One-at-a-Time or All-at-once? Word-Based or Character-Based? In Proceedings EMNLP.

Nianwen Xue, 2003. Chinese Word Segmentation as Character Tagging. International Journal of Computational Lnguistics and Chinese Language Processing, 8(1):29-48

Wenbin Jiang and Haitao Mi and Liang Huang and Qun Liu, 2008b. Wird Lattice Reranking for Chinese Word Segmentation and Part-of-speech Tagging. In Proceedings of COLING

Xinnian Mao, Yuan Dong and Saike He, Sencheng Bao and Haila Wang, Chinese Word Segmentation and Name Entity Recognition Based on Condition Random Fields, In Prceedings of the Sixth SIGHAN Workshop on Chinese Language Processing, 2008, Hyderbad, India.

Zhendong Dong and Qiang Dong, 2006. HowNet and the Computation of Meaning, World Scientific Publishing Co. Pte. Ltd., Singapore

黄昌宁, 赵海, 2007, 中文分词十年回顾. 中文信息学报, 2007, 21(3):8-20.

黄居仁, 2009, 瓶颈, 挑战, 与转机: 中文分词研究的新思维. In Proceedings of CNCCL-2009, Yantai

Textual Emotion Processing From Event Analysis

Chu-Ren Huang[†], Ying Chen[*†], Sophia Yat Mei Lee[†]
[†]Department of Chinese and Bilingual Studies
The Hong Kong Polytechnic University
* Department of Computer Engineering
China Agricultural University
{churenhuang, chenying3176, sophiaym}@gmail.com

Abstract

Textual emotion recognition has gained a lot of attention recent years; it is however less developed due to the complexity nature of emotion. In this paper, we start with the discussion of a number of fundamental yet unresolved issues concerning emotion, which includes its definition, representation and technology. We then propose an alternative solution for emotion recognition taking into account of emotion causes. Two pilot experiments are done to justify our proposal. The first experiment explores the impact of emotion recognition. It shows that the context contains rich and crucial information that effectively help emotion recognition. The other experiment examines emotion cause events in the context. We find that most emotions are expressed with the presence of causes. The experiments prove that emotion cause serves as an important cue for emotion recognition. We suggest that the combination of both emotion study and event analysis would be a fruitful direction for deep emotion processing.

1 Introduction

The study of emotion attracts increasingly greater attention in the field of NLP due to its emerging wide applications, such as customer care (Gupta et al., 2010), and social information understanding (Lisa and Steyvers, 2010). In contrast to sentiment, which is the external subjective evaluation, emotion mainly concentrates on the internal mental state of human (Ortony et al., 1987). Emotion is indeed a highly complicated concept that raises a lot of controversies in the theories of emotion regarding the fundamental issues such as emotion definition, emotion structure and so on. The complexity nature of emotion concept makes automatic emotion processing rather challenging.

Most emotion studies put great effort on emotion recognition, identifying emotion classes, such as *happiness*, *sadness*, and *fear*. On top of this surface level information, deeper level information regarding emotions such as the experiencer, cause, and result of an emotion, needs to be extracted and analyzed for real world applications. In this paper, we discuss these two closely related emotion tasks, namely emotion recognition and emotion cause detection and how they contribute to emotion processing.

For emotion recognition, we construct an emotion corpus for explicit emotions with an unsupervised method. Explicit emotions are emotions represented by emotion keywords such as e.g., "*shocked*" in "*He was shocked after hearing the news*". In the course of emotion recognition, the keyword in an explicit emotion expression is deleted and only contextual information remains. In our pilot experiments, the context-based emotion identification works fairly well. This implies that plenty of information is provided in the context for emotion recognition. Moreover, with an in-depth analysis of the data, we observe that it is often the case that emotions co-occur and interact in a sentence. In this paper, we deal with emotion recognition from a dependent view so as to capture complicated emotion expressions.

Emotion is often invoked by an event, which in turn is very likely to elicit an event (Descartes 1649, James 1884, Plutchik 1980, Wierzbicka

1999). Despite the fact that most researches recognize the important role of events in emotion theories, little work, if not none, attempts to make explicit link between events and emotion. In this paper, we examine emotion constructions based on contextual information which often contains considerable relevant eventive information. In particular, the correlations between emotion and cause events will be explored based on empirical data. Emotion causes refer to explicitly expressed propositions that evoke the corresponding emotions.

To enhance emotion recognition, we examine emotion causes occurring in the context of an emotion. First, we manually annotate causes for emotions in our explicit emotion corpus. Since an emotion cause can be a complicated event, we model emotion cause detection as a multi-label problem to detect a cross-clause emotion cause. Furthermore, an in-depth linguistic analysis is done to capture the different constructions in expressing emotion causes.

The paper is organized as follows. Section 2 discusses some related work regarding emotion recognition and emotion cause detection. In Section 3, we present our context-based emotion corpus and provide some data analysis. Section 4 describes our emotion recognition system, and discusses the experiments and results. In Section 5, we examine our emotion cause detection system, and discuss the performances. Finally, Section 6 concludes our main findings for emotion processing from the event perspective.

2 Related Work

Most current emotion studies focus on the task of emotion recognition, especially in affective lexicon construction. In comparison with emotion recognition, emotion cause detection is a rather new research area, which account for emotions based on the correlations between emotions and cause events. This section discusses the related research on emotion recognition and emotion cause detection.

2.1 Emotion Recognition

Although emotion recognition has been intensively studied, some issues concerning emotion remain unresolved, such as emotion definition, emotion representation, and emotion classification technologies.

For the emotion definition, emotion has been well-known for its abstract and uncertain definition which hinders emotion processing as a whole. Ortony et al., (1987) conducted an empirical study for a structure of affective lexicon based on the ~500 words used in previous emotion studies. However, most of the emotion corpora in NLP try to avoid the emotion definition problem. Instead, they choose to rely on the intuition of annotators (Ren's Blog Emotion Corpus, RBEC, Quan and Ren, 2009) or authors (Mishne's blog emotion corpus, Mishne, 2005). Therefore, one of the crucial drawbacks of emotion corpora is the problem of poor quality. In this paper, we explore emotion annotation from a different perspective. We concentrate on explicit emotions, and utilize their contextual information for emotion recognition.

In terms of emotion representation, textual emotion corpora are basically annotated using either the enumerative representation or the compositional representation (Chen et al., 2009). The enumerative representation assigns an emotion a unique label, such as *pride* and *jealousy*. The compositional representation represents an emotion through a vector with a small set of fixed basic emotions with associated strength. For instance, *pride* is decomposed into "*happiness* + *fear*" according to Turner (2000).

With regard to emotion recognition technologies, there are two kinds of classification models. One is based on an independent view (Mishne, 2005; Mihalcea and Liu, 2006; Aman and Szpakowicz, 2007; Tokuhisa et al., 2008; Strapparava and Mihalcea, 2008), and the other is a dependent view (Abbasi et al, 2008; Keshtkar and Inkpen, 2009). The independent view treats emotions separately, and often chooses a single-label classification approach to identify emotions. In contrast, the dependent view takes into account complicated emotion expressions, such as emotion interaction and emotion co-occurrences, and thus requires more complicated models. Abbasi et al. (2008) adopt an ensemble classifier to detect the co-occurrences of different emotions; Keshtkar and Inkpen (2009) use iteratively single-label classifiers in the top-down order of a given emotion hierarchy. In this paper, we examine emotion recognition as a multi-label problem and investigate several multi-label classification approaches.

2.2 Emotion Cause Detection

Although most emotion theories recognize the important role of causes in emotion analysis (Descartes, 1649; James, 1884; Plutchik, 1962; Wierzbicka 1996), yet very few studies in NLP explore the event composition and causal relation of emotions. As a pilot study, the current study proposes an emotion cause detection system.

Emotion cause detection can be considered as a kind of causal relation detection between two events. In other words, emotion is envisioned as an event type which triggers another event, i.e. cause event. We attempt to examine emotion cause relations for open domains. However, not much work (Marcu and Echihabi, 2002; Girju, 2003; Chang and Choi, 2006) has been done on this kind of general causal relation for open domains.

Most existing causal relation detection systems contain two steps: 1) cause candidate identification; 2) causal relation detection. However, Step 1) is often oversimplified in real systems. For example, the cause-effect pairs are limited to two noun phrases (Chang and Choi, 2005; Girju, 2003), or two clauses connected with selected conjunction words (Marcu and Echihabi, 2002). Moreover, the task of Step 2) often is considered as a binary classification problem, i.e. "causal" vs. "non-causal".

With regard to feature extraction, there are two kinds of information extracted to identify the causal relation in Step 2). One is constructions expressing a cause-effect relation (Chang and Choi, 2005; Girju, 2003), and the other is semantic information in a text (Marcu and Echihabi, 2002; Persing and Ng, 2009), such as word pair probability. Undoubtedly, the two kinds of information often interact with each other in a real cause detection system.

3 Emotion Annotated Sinica Corpus (EASC)

EASC is an emotion annotated corpus comprising two kinds of sentences: emotional-sentence corpus and neutral-sentence corpus. It involves two components: one for emotion recognition, which is created with an unsupervised method (Chen et al. 2009), and the other is for emotion cause detection, which is manually annotated (Chen et al. 2010).

3.1 The Corpus for Emotion Recognition

With the help of a set of rules and a collection of high quality emotion keywords, a pattern-based approach is used to extract emotional sentences and neutral sentences from the Academia Sinica Balanced Corpus of Mandarin Chinese (Sinica Corpus). If an emotion keyword occurring in a sentence satisfies the given patterns, its corresponding emotion type will be listed for that sentence. As for emotion recognition, each detected keyword in a sentence is removed, in other words, the sentence provides only the context of that emotion. Due to the overwhelming of neutral sentences, EASC only contains partial neutral sentences besides emotional sentences. For experiments, 995 sentences are randomly selected for human annotation, which serve as the test data. The remaining 17,243 sentences are used as the training data.

In addition, in the course of creating the emotion corpus, Chen et al. (2009) list the emotion labels in a sentence using the enumerative representation. Besides, an emotion taxonomy is provided to re-annotate an emotion with the compositional representation. With the taxonomy, an emotion is decomposed into a combination of primary emotions (i.e. *happiness*, *fear*, *anger*, *sadness*, and *surprise*).

From this corpus, we observe that ~54% emotional sentences contain two emotions, yet only ~2% sentences contain more than two emotions. This implies emotion recognition is a typical multi-label problem. Particularly, more effort should be put on the co-occurrences of two emotions.

3.2 The Corpus for Emotion Cause Detection

Most emotion theories agree that the five primary emotions (i.e. *happiness*, *sadness*, *fear*, *anger*, and *surprise*) are prototypical emotions. Therefore, for emotion cause detection, we only deal with the emotional sentences containing a keyword representing one of these primary emotions. Beyond a focus sentence, its context (the previous sentence and the following sentence) is also extracted, and those three sentences constitute an entry. After filtering non-emotional and ambiguous sentences, 5,629 entries remain in the emotion cause corpus.

Each emotion keyword is annotated with its corresponding causes if existing. An emotion keyword can sometimes be associated with more than one cause, in such a case, both causes are marked. Moreover, the cause type is also identified, which is either a nominal event or a verbal event (a verb or a nominalization).

From the corpus, we notice that 72% of the extracted entries express emotions, and 80% of the emotional entries have a cause, which means that causal event is a strong indicator for emotion recognition.

Furthermore, since the actual cause can sometimes be so complicated that it involves several events, we investigate the span of a cause text as follows. For each emotion keyword, an entry is segmented into clauses with some punctuations, and thus an entry becomes a list of cause candidates. In terms of the cause distribution, we find ~90% causes occurring between 'left_2' and 'right_1'. Therefore, our cause search is limited to the list of cause candidates which contains five text units, i.e. <left_2, left_1, left_0, right_0, right_1>. If the clause where emotion keyword locates is assumed as a focus clause, 'left_2' and 'left_1' are the two previous clauses, and 'right_1' is the following one. 'left_0' and 'right_0' are the partial texts of the focus clause, which locate in the left side of and the right side of the emotion keyword, respectively. Finally, we find that ~14% causes occur cross clauses.

4 Emotion Processing with multi-label models

4.1 Multi-label Classification for Emotion recognition

Based on our corpus, two critical issues for emotion recognition need to be dealt with: emotion interaction and emotion co-occurrences. Co-occurrence of multiple emotions in a sentence makes emotion recognition a multi-label problem. Furthermore, the interaction among different emotions in a sentence requires a multi-label model to have a dependent view. In this paper, we explore two simple multi-label models for emotion recognition.

The Binary-based (BB) model: decompose the task into multiple independent binary classifiers (i.e., "1" for the presence of one emotion; "0" for the absence of one emotion), where each emotion is allocated a classifier. For each test instance, all labels (emotions) from the classifiers compose a vector.

The label powset (LP) model: treat each possible combination of labels appearing in the training data as a unique label, and convert multi-label classification to single-label classification.

Both the BB model and the LP model need a multi-class classifier. For our experiment, we choose a Max Entropy package, Mallet[1]. In this paper, we use only words in the focus sentence as features.

4.2 Emotion Recognition Experiments

To demonstrate the impact of our context-based emotion corpus to emotion recognition, we compare EASC data to Ren's Blog Emotion Corpus (RBEC). RBEC is a human-annotated emotion corpus for both explicit emotions and implicit emotions. It adopts the compositional representation with eight emotion dimensions (*anger*, *anxiety*, *expect*, *hate*, *joy*, *love*, *sorrow*, and *surprise*). For each dimension, a numerical value ranging in {0.0, 0.1, 0.2... 1.0} indicates the intensity of the emotion in question. There are totally 35,096 sentences in RBEC. To fairly compare with the EASC data, we convert a numerical value to a binary value. An emotion exists in a sentence only when its corresponding intensity value is greater than 0.

For RBEC data, we use 80% of the corpus as the training data, 10% as the development data, and 10% as the test data. For EASC, apart from the test data, we divide its training data into two sets: 90% for our training data, and 10% for our development data. For evaluation of a multi-label task, three measures are used: accuracy (extract match ratio), Micro F1, and Macro F1. Accuracy is the extract match ratio of the whole assignments in data, and Micro F1 and Macro F1 are the aver-

[1] http://mallet.cs.umass.edu/

Table 1: The overall performances for the multi-label models

	EASC		RBEC	
	BB	LP	BB	LP
Accuracy	21.30	28.07	22.99	28.33
Micro F1	41.96	46.25	44.77	44.74
Macro F1	34.78	35.52	36.48	38.88

age scores of F scores of all possible values for all variables. Micro F1 takes the emotion distribution into account, while Macro F1 is just the average of all F scores. Note that due to the overwhelming percentage of value 0 in the multi-label task, during the calculating of Micro F1 and Macro F1, most previous multi-label systems take only value 1 (indicating the existence of the emotion) into account.

In Table 1, we notice that the emotion recognition system on our context-based corpus achieves similar performance as the one on human-annotated corpus. This implies that there is rich contextual information with respect to emotion identification.

5 Emotion Cause Detection

Most emotion theories agree that there is a strong relationship between emotions and events (Descartes 1649, James 1884, Plutchik 1980, Wierzbicka 1999). Among the rich information in the context of an emotion, cause event is the most crucial component of emotion. We therefore attempt to explore emotion causes, and extract causes for emotion automatically.

5.1 Emotion Cause Detection

Based on the cause distribution analysis in Section 3.2, in contrast to binary classification used in previous work, we formalize emotion cause detection as a multi-label problem as follows.

Given an emotion keyword and its context, its label is the locations of its causes, such as "left_1, left_0". Then, we use the LP model to identify the cause for each sentence as well as an emotion keyword. With regard to emotion cause detection, the LP model is more suitable than the BB model because the LP model can easily capture the possible label combinations.

In terms of feature extraction, unlike emotion recognition, emotion cause detection relies more on linguistic constructions, such as "*The BP oil spill makes the country angry*", "*I am sad because of the oil spill problem*" and so on.

According to our linguistic analysis, we create 14 patterns to extraction some common emotion cause expressions. Some patterns are designed for general cause detection using linguistic cues such as conjunctions and prepositions. Others are designed for some specific emotion cause expressions, such as epistemic markers and reported verbs. Furthermore, to avoid the low coverage problem of the rule-based patterns, we create another set of features, which is a group of generalized patterns. For details, please refer to Chen et al. (2010).

5.2 Experiments

For EASC, we reserve 80% as the training data, 10% as the development data, and 10% as the test data. For evaluation, we first convert a multi-label tag outputted from our system into a binary tag ('Y' means the presence of a causal relation; 'N' means the absence of a causal relation) between the emotion keyword and each candidate in its corresponding cause candidates. We then adopt three common measures, i.e. precision, recall and F-score, to evaluate the result.

A naive baseline is designed as follows: The baseline searches for the cause candidates in the order of <left_1, right_0, left_2, left_0, right_1>. If the candidate contains a noun or a verb, this clause is considered as a cause and the search stops.

Table 2 shows the overall performances of our emotion cause detection system. First, our system based on a multi-label approach as well as powerful linguistic features significantly outperforms the naïve baseline. Moreover, the greatest improvement is attributed to the 14 linguistic patterns (LP). This implies the importance of linguistic cues for cause detection. Moreover, the general patterns (GP) achieve much better performance on the recall and yet slightly hurt on the precision.

The performances (F-scores) for ‘Y’ and ‘N’ tags separately are shown in Table 3. First, we notice that the performances of the ‘N’ tag are much better than the ones of ‘Y’ tag. Second, it is surprising that incorporating the linguistic features significantly improves the ‘Y’ tag only (from 33% to 56%), but does not affect ‘N’ tag. This suggests that our linguistic features are effective to detect the presence of causal relation, and yet do not hurt the detections of ‘non_causal’ relation. Furthermore, the general feature achieves ~8% improvements for the ‘Y’ tag.

Table 2: The overall performance with different feature sets of the multi-label system

	Precision	Recall	F-score
Baseline	56.64	57.70	56.96
LP	74.92	66.70	69.21
+ GP	73.90	72.70	73.26

Table 3: The separate performances for ‘Y’ and ‘N’ tags of the multi-label system

	‘Y’	‘N’
Baseline	33.06	80.85
LP	48.32	90.11
+ GP	56.84	89.68

6 Discussions

Many previous works on emotion recognition concentrated on emotion keyword detection. However, Ortony et al. (1987) pointed out the difficulty of emotion keyword annotation, be it manual or automatic annotation. Emotion keywords are rather ambiguous, and also contain other information besides affective information, such as behavior and cognition. Therefore, contextual information provides important cues for emotion recognition. Furthermore, we propose an alternative way to explore emotion recognition, which is based on emotion cause. Through two pilot experiments, we justify the importance of emotion contextual information for emotion recognition, particularly emotion cause.

We first examine emotion processing in terms of events. Context information is found to be very important for emotion recognition. Furthermore, most emotions are expressed with the presence of causes in context, which implies that emotion cause is the crucial information for emotion recognition. In addition, emotion cause detection also explores deep understanding of an emotion. Compared to emotion recognition, emotion cause detection requires more semantic and pragmatic information. In this paper, based on the in-depth linguistic analysis, we extract different kinds of constructs to identify cause events for an emotion.

To conclude, emotion processing is a complicated problem. In terms of emotion keywords, how to understand appropriately to enhance emotion recognition needs more exploration. With respect to emotion causes, first, event processing itself is a challenging topic, such as event extraction and co-reference. Second, how to combine event and emotion in NLP is still unclear, but it is a direction for further emotion studies.

References

Abbasi, A., H. Chen, S. Thoms, and T. Fu. 2008. Affect Analysis of Web Forums and Blogs using Correlation Ensembles”. In *IEEE Tran. Knowledge and Data Engineering*, vol. 20(9), pp. 1168-1180.

Aman, S. and S. Szpakowicz. 2007. Identifying Expressions of Emotion in Text. In *Proceedings of 10th International Conference on Text, Speech and Dialogue*, Lecture Notes in Computer Science 4629, 196--205

Chang, D.-S. and K.-S. Choi. 2006. Incremental cue phrase learning and bootstrapping method for causality extraction using cue phrase and word pair probabilities. *Information Processing and Management*. 42(3): 662-678.

Chen, Y., S. Y. M. Lee and C.-R. Huang. 2009. Are Emotions Enumerable or Decomposable? And Its Implications for Emotion Processing. In *Proceedings of the 23rd Pacific Asia Conference on Language, Information and Computation.*

Chen, Y., Y. M. Lee, S. Li and C.-R. Huang. 2010. Emotion Cause Detection with Linguistic Constructions. In *Proceedings of the 23rd International Conference on Computational Linguistics.*

Descartes, R. 1649. *The Passions of the Soul*. USA: Hackett Publishing Company.

Ghazi, D., D. Inkpen and S. Szpakowicz. 2010. Hierarchical versus Flat Classification of Emotions in Text. In Proceedings of *NAACL-HLT 2010 Workshop on*

Computational Approaches to Analysis and Generation of Emotion in Text. Los Angeles, CA: NAACL.

Girju, R. 2003. Automatic Detection of Causal Relations for Question Answering. In the 41st Annual Meeting of the Association for Computational Linguistics, Workshop on Multilingual Summarization and Question Answering - Machine Learning and Beyond, Sapporo, Japan.

Gupta, N., M. Gilbert, and G. D. Fabbrizio. Emotion Detection in Email Customer Care. In *Proceedings of NAACL-HLT 2010 Workshop on Computational Approaches to Analysis and Generation of Emotion in Text*.

James, W. 1884. What is an Emotion? *Mind*, 9(34): 188–205.

Keshtkar, F. and D. Inkpen. 2009. Using Sentiment Orientation Features for Mood Classification in Blog Corpus. In *Proceedings of IEEE International Conference on Natural Language Processing and Knowledge Eng. (IEEE NLP-KE 2009)*, Sep. 24-27.

Marcu, D. and A. Echihabi. 2002. An Unsupervised Approach to Recognizing Discourse Relations. In *Proceedings of ACL*.

Mihalcea, R., and H. Liu. 2006. A Corpus-based Approach to Finding Happiness. In *Proceedings of AAAI*.

Mishne, G. 2005. Experiments with Mood Classification in Blog Posts. In *Proceedings of Style2005 – the 1st Workshop on Stylistic Analysis of Text for Information Access*, at *SIGIR 2005*.

Ortony, A., G. L. Clore, and M. A. Foss. 1987. The Referential Structure of the Affective Lexicon. *Cognitive Science*, 11: 341-364.

Pang B., L. Lee and S. Vaithyanathan. 2002. Thumbs up? Sentiment Classification Using Machine Learning Techniques. In *Proceedings of EMNLP02*, 79-86.

Pearl, L. and M. Steyvers. 2010. Identifying Emotions, Intentions, and Attitudes in Text Using a Game with a Purpose. In *Proceedings of NAACL-HLT 2010 Workshop on Computational Approaches to Analysis and Generation of Emotion in Text*. Los Angeles, CA: NAACL.

Persing, Isaac and Vincent Ng. 2009. Semi-Supervised Cause Identification from Aviation Safety Reports. In *Proceedings of ACL*.

Plutchik, R. 1980. *Emotions: A Psychoevolutionary Synthesis*. New York: Harper & Row.

Quan, C. and F. Ren. 2009. Construction of a Blog Emotion Corpus for Chinese Expression Analysis. In Proceedings of *EMNLP*.

Strapparava, C. and R. Mihalcea. 2008. Learning to Identify Emotions in Text. In *Proceedings of the ACM Conference on Applied Computing ACM-SAC*.

Tokuhisa, R., K. Inui, and Y. Matsumoto. 2008. Emotion Classification Using Massive Examples Extracted from the Web. In *Proceedings of COLING*.

Turner, J. H. 2000. *On the Origins of Human Emotions: A Sociological Inquiry into the Evolution of Human Affect*. California: Stanford University Press.

Wierzbicka, A. 1999. *Emotions across Languages and Cultures: Diversity and Universals*. Cambridge: Cambridge University Press.

Classical Chinese Sentence Segmentation

Hen-Hsen Huang†, Chuen-Tsai Sun‡ and Hsin-Hsi Chen†
†Department of Computer Science and Information Engineering, National Taiwan University, Taipei, Taiwan
‡Department of Computer Science, National Chiao Tung University, Hsinchu, Taiwan
hhhuang@nlg.csie.ntu.edu.tw ctsun@cis.nctu.edu.tw hhchen@csie.ntu.edu.tw

Abstract

Sentence segmentation is a fundamental issue in Classical Chinese language processing. To facilitate reading and processing of the raw Classical Chinese data, we propose a statistical method to split unstructured Classical Chinese text into smaller pieces such as sentences and clauses. The segmenter based on the conditional random field (CRF) model is tested under different tagging schemes and various features including n-gram, jump, word class, and phonetic information. We evaluated our method on four datasets from several eras (i.e., from the 5th century BCE to the 19th century). Our CRF segmenter achieves an F-score of 83.34% and can be applied on a variety of data from different eras.

1 Introduction

Chinese word segmentation is a well-known and widely studied problem in Chinese language processing. In Classical Chinese processing, sentence segmentation is an even more vexing issue. Unlike English and other western languages, there is no delimiter marking the end of the word in Chinese. Moreover, not only is there a lack of delimiters between the words, almost all pre-20th century Chinese is written without any punctuation marks. Figure 1 shows photocopies of printed and hand written documents from the 19th century. Within any given paragraph, the Chinese characters are printed as evenly spaced characters, with nothing to separate words from words, phrases from phrases, and sentences from sentences. Thus, inside a paragraph, explicit boundaries of sentences and clauses are lacking. In order to understand the structure, readers of Classical Chinese have to manually identify these boundaries during the reading. This process is called Classical Chinese sentence segmentation, or *Judo* (句讀).

For example, the opening lines of the Daoist classic *Zhuangzi* originally lacked segmentation:

北/north 冥/ocean 有/have 魚/fish 其/it 名/name 爲/is 鯤/Kun (a kind of big fish) 鯤/Kun 之/of 大/big 不/not 知/know 幾/how 千/thousand 里/mile 也/exclamation

The meaning of the text is hard to interpret without segmentation. Below is the identical text as segmented by a human being. It is clearly more readable.

北冥有魚/in the north ocean there is a fish
其名爲鯤 /its name is Kun
鯤之大/the size of the Kun
不知幾千里也/I don't know how many thousand miles the fish is

However, sentence segmentation in Classical Chinese is not a trivial problem. Classical Chinese sentence segmentation, like Chinese word segmentation, is inherently ambiguous. Individuals generally perform sentence segmentation in instinctive ways. To identify the boundaries of sentences and clauses, they primarily rely on their experience and sense of the language rather than on a systematic procedure. It is thus difficult to construct a set of rules or practical procedures to specify the segmentation of the infinite variety of Classical Chinese sentences.

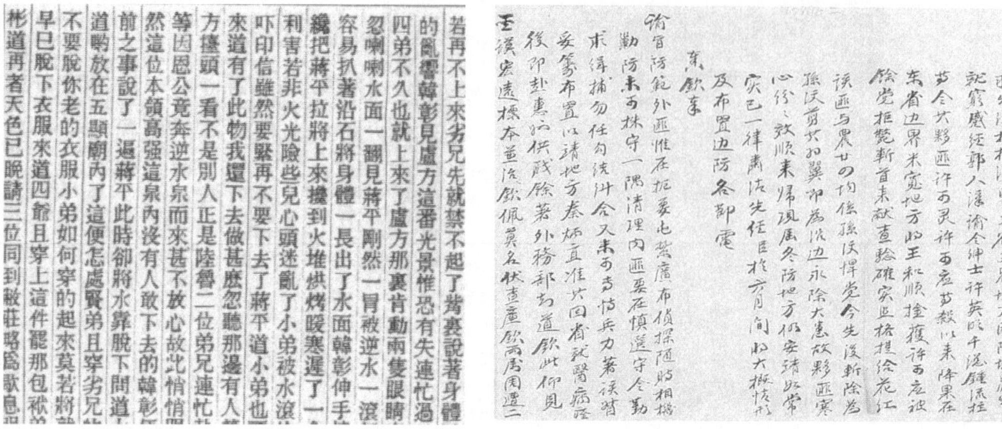

Figure 1. A Printed Page (Left) and a Hand Written Manuscript (Right) from the 19th Century.

Because of the importance of sentence segmentation, beginning in the 20th century, some editions of the Chinese classics have been labor-intensively segmented and marked with modern punctuation. However, innumerable documents in Classical Chinese from the centuries of Chinese history remain to be segmented. To aid in processing these documents, we propose an automated Classical Chinese sentence segmentation approach that enables completion of segmentation tasks quickly and accurately. To construct the sentence segmenter for Classical Chinese, the popular sequence tagging models, conditional random field (CRF) (Lafferty et al., 2001), are adopted in this study.

The rest of this paper is organized as follows. First, we describe the Classical Chinese sentence segmentation problem in Section 2. In Section 3, we review the relevant literature, including sentence boundary detection (SBD) and Chinese word segmentation. In Section 4, we introduce the tagging schemes along with the features, and show how the sentence segmentation problem can be transformed into a sequence tagging problem and decoded with CRFs. In Section 5, the experimental setup and data are described. In Section 6, we report the experimental results and discuss the properties and the challenges of the Classical Chinese sentence segmentation problem. Finally, we conclude the remarks in Section 7.

2 Problem Description

The outcomes of Classical Chinese sentence segmentation are not well-defined in linguistics at present. In general, the results of segmentation consist of sentences, clauses, and phrases. For instance, in the segmented sentence "野馬也 / 塵埃也 / 生物之以息相吹也", "野馬也" ("the mists on the mountains like wild horses") and "塵埃也" ("the dust in the air") are phrases, and " 生物之以息相吹也" ("the living creatures blow their breaths at each other") is a clause. A sentence such as "吾以是狂而不信也" ("I do not believe it because it is ridiculous.") is a short sentence itself, and does not require any segmentation. For a given text, there is no strict rule to determine at which level the segmentation should be performed. For instance, the opening lines of the Daoist classic *Daodejing* is "道可道非常道名可名非常名" ("The way that can be spoken is not the eternal way. The name that can be given is not the eternal name.") which is usually segmented as "道可道 / 非常道 / 名可名 / 非常名", but may also be segmented as "道 / 可道 / 非常道 / 名 / 可名 / 非常名". Either segmentation is reasonable.

In this paper, we do not distinguish among the three levels of segmentation. Instead, our system learns directly from the human-segmented corpus. After training, our system will be adapted to perform human-like segmentation automatically. Further, we do not distinguish the various outcomes of Classical Chinese sentence segmentation. Instead, for the sake of convenience, every product of the segmentation process is termed "clause" in the following sections.

3 Related Work

Besides Classical Chinese, sentence boundary detection (SBD) is also an issue in English and other western languages. SBD in written texts and speech represents quite different problems. For written text, the SBD task is to distinguish periods used as the end-of-sentence indicator (full stop) from other usages, such as parts of abbreviations and decimal points. By contrast, the task of SBD in speech is closely related to the task of Classical Chinese sentence segmentation. In speech processing, the outcome of speech recognizers is a sequence of words, in which the punctuation marks are absence, and the sentence boundaries are thus lacking. To recover the syntactic structure of the original speech, SBD is required.

Like Classical Chinese sentence segmentation, the task of SBD in speech is to determine which of the inter-word boundaries in the stream of words should be marked as end-of-sentence, and then to divide the entire word sequence into individual sentences. Empirical methods are commonly employed to deal with this problem. Such methods involve many different sequence labeling models including HMMs (Shriberg et al., 2000), maximum entropy (Maxent) models (Liu et al., 2004), and CRFs (Liu et al., 2005). Among these, a CRF model used in Liu et al (2005) offered the lowest error rate.

Chinese word segmentation is a problem closely related to Classical Chinese sentence segmentation. The former identifies the boundaries of the words in a given text, while the latter identifies the boundaries of the sentences, clauses, and phrases. In contrast to sentences and clauses, the length of Chinese words is shorter, and the variety of Chinese words is more limited. Despite the minor unknown words, most of the frequent words can be handled with a dictionary predefined by Chinese language experts or extracted from the corpus automatically. However, it is impossible to maintain a dictionary of the infinite number of sentences and clauses. For these reasons, the Classical Chinese sentence segmentation problem is more challenging.

Methods of Chinese word segmentation can be mainly classified into heuristic rule-based approaches, statistical machine learning approaches, and hybrid approaches. Hybrid approaches combine the advantages of heuristic and statistical approaches to achieve better results (Gao et al., 2003; Xue, 2003; Peng et al., 2004).

Xue (2003) transformed the Chinese word segmentation problem into a tagging problem. For a given sequence of Chinese characters, the author applies a Maxent tagger to assign each character one of four positions-of-character (POC) tags, and then coverts the tagged sequence into a segmented sequence. The four POC tags used in Xue (2003) denote the positions of characters within a word. For example, the first character of a word is tagged "left boundary", the last character of a word is tagged "right boundary", the middle character of a word is tagged "middle", and a single character that forms a word by itself is tagged "single-character-word". Once the given sequence is tagged, the boundaries of words are also revealed, and the task of segmentation becomes straightforward. However, the Maxent models used in Xue (2003) suffer from an inherent the label bias problem. Peng et al (2004) uses the CRFs to address this issue. The tags used in Peng et al (2004) are of only two types, "start" and "non-start", in which the "start" tag denotes the first character of a word, and the characters in other positions are given the "non-start" tag.

The closest previous works to Classic Chinese sentence segmentation are Huang (2008) and Zhang et al. (2009). Huang combined the Xue's tagging scheme (i.e., 4-tag set) and CRFs to address the Classical Chinese sentence segmentation problem and reported an F-score of 80.96% averaged over various datasets. A similar work by Zhang et al. reported an F-score of 71.42%.

4 Methods

Conditional random field is our tagging model, and the implementation is CrfSgd 1.3[1] provided by Léon Bottou. As denoted by the tool name, the parameters in this implementation are optimized using Stochastic Gradient Descent (SGD) which convergences much faster than the common optimization algorithms such as L-BFGS and conjugate gradient (Vishwanathan, et al., 2006). To construct the sentence segmenter on

[1] http://leon.bottou.org/projects/sgd

CRF, the tagging scheme and the feature functions play the crucial roles.

4.1 Tagging Schemes

In the previous works (Huang, 2008; Zhang et al., 2009), POC tags used in Chinese word segmentation (Xue, 2003) are converted to denote the positions of characters within a clause. The 4-tag set is redefined as L ("the left boundary of a clause"), R ("the right boundary of a clause"), M ("the middle character of a clause"), and S ("a single character forming a clause"). For example, the sentence "北冥有魚其名爲鯤鯤之大不知幾千里也" should be tagged as follows.

北/L 冥/M 有/M 魚/R 其/L 名/M 爲/M 鯤/R 鯤/L 之/M 大/R 不/L 知/M 幾/M 千/M 里/M 也/R

We can easily split the sentence into clauses by making a break after each character tagged R and S and obtain the final outcome "北冥有魚 / 其名爲鯤 / 鯤之大 / 不知幾千里也".

In this work, more tagging schemes are experimented. The basic tagging scheme for segmentation is 2-tag set in which only two types of tags, "start" and "non-start", are used to label the sequence. The segmented fragments (clauses) for sentence segmentation are usually much longer than those for word segmentation. Thus, we add more middle states into the 4-tag set to model the nature of long fragments. The Markov chain of our tagging scheme is shown in Figure 2, where L2, L3, …, Lk are the additional states to extend Xue's 4-tag set. In our experiments, various k values are tested. If the k value is 1, the scheme is identical to the one used in the two previous works (Zhang et al., 2009; Huang, 2008). The 2-tag set, 4-tag set, 5-tag set and their corresponding examples are listed in Table 1. With the tagging scheme, the Classical Chinese sentence segmentation task is transformed into a sequence labeling or tagging task.

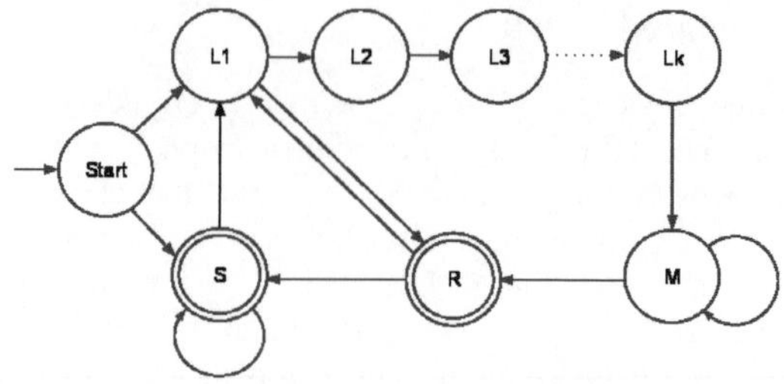

Figure 2. Markov Chain of Our Tagging Scheme.

Tag set	Tags	Example
2-tag	S: Start	不**不**知其幾千里也
	N: Non-Start	不**知其幾千里也**
4-tag (k=1)	L1: Left-end	不**不**知其幾千里也
	M: Middle	不**知其幾千里**也
	R: Right-end	不知其幾千里**也**
	S: Single	性**性**猶鰥柳也
5-tag (k=2)	L1: Left-end	不**不**知其幾千里也
	L2: Left-2nd	不**知**其幾千里也
	M: Middle	不知**其幾千里**也
	R: Right-end	不知其幾千里**也**
	S: Single	性**性**猶鰥柳也

Table 1. Examples of Tag Sets.

4.2 Features

Due to the flexibility of the feature function interface provided by CRFs, we apply various feature conjunctions. Besides the n-gram character patterns, the phonetic information and the part-of-speech (POS) are also included. The pronunciation of each Chinese character is labeled in three ways. The first one is Mandarin Phonetic Symbols (MPS), also known as Bopomofo, which is a phonetic system for Modern Chinese. The initial/final/tone of each character can be obtained from its MPS label.

However, Chinese pronunciation varies in the thousands of years, and the pronunciation of Modern Chinese is much different from the Classical Chinese. For this reason, two Ancient Chinese phonetic systems, Fanqie (反切) and Guangyun (廣韻), are applied to label the characters. The pronunciation of a target character is represented by two characters in the Fanqie system. The first character indicates the initial of the target character, and the second character indicates the combination of the final and the tone. The Guangyun system is in a similar manner with a smaller phonetic symbol set. There are 8,157 characters in our phonetic dictionary and the statistics are shown in Table 2.

The POS information is also considered. It is difficult to construct a Classical Chinese POS

System	#Initials	#Finals	#Tones
MPS	21	36	5
Fanqie	403	1,054	
Guangyun	43	203	

Table 2. Phonetic System Statistics.

POS	# Characters	Examples
Beginning	60	蓋, 唯, 雖
Middle	50	是, 或
End	45	乎, 者, 也, 矣
Interjection	20	呼, 嗟, 噫, 唉

Table 3. Four Types of POS.

tagger at this moment. Instead, we collected three types of particles that are usually placed at the beginning, at the middle, and at the end of Classical Chinese clauses. In addition, the interjections which are usually used at the end of clauses are also collected. Some examples are given in Table 3. The five feature sets and the feature templates are shown in Table 4.

5 Experiments

There are three major sets of experiments. In the 1st set of experiments, we test different tagging schemes for Classical Chinese sentence segmentation. In the 2nd set of experiments, all kinds of feature sets and their combinations are tested. The performances of the first two sets of experiments are evaluated by 10-fold cross-validation on four datasets which cross both eras and contexts. In the 3rd set of experiments, we train the system on one dataset, and test it on the others. In last part of the experiments, the generality of the datasets and the toughness of our system are tested (Peng et al., 2004). The cut-off threshold for the features is set to 2 for all the experiments. In other words, the features occur only once in the training set will be ignored. The other options of CrfSgd remain default.

5.1 Datasets

The datasets used in the evaluation are collected from the corpora of the Pre-Qin and Han Dynasties (the 5th century BCE to the 1st century BCE) and the Qing Dynasty (the 17th century CE to the 20th century CE). Chinese in the 19th century is fairly different from Chinese in the era before 0 CE. In ancient Chinese, the syntax is much simpler, the sentences are shorter, and the words are largely composed of a single character. Those are unlike later and more modern Chinese, where word segmentation is a serious issue. Given these properties, the task of segmenting

Feature Set	Template	Function
Character	$C_i, -2 \le i \le 2$	Unigrams
	$C_i C_{i+1}, -2 \le i \le 1$	Bigrams
	$C_i C_{i+1} C_{i+2}, -2 \le i \le 0$	Trigrams
	$C_i C_{i+2}, -2 \le i \le 0$	Jumps
POS	$POS\_B(C_0)$	Current character serves as a clause-beginning particle.
	$POS\_M(C_0)$	Current character serves as a clause-middle particle.
	$POS\_E(C_0)$	Current character serves as a clause-end particle.
	$POS\_I(C_0)$	Current character serves as an interjection.
MPS	$M\_I(C_0)$	The initial of current character in MPS.
	$M\_F(C_0)$	The final of current character in MPS.
	$M\_T(C_0)$	The tone of current character in MPS.
	$M\_F(C_{-1})M\_T(C_{-1})M\_I(C_0)$	The connection between successive characters.
Fanqie	$F\_I(C_0)$	The initial of current character in Fanqie.
	$F\_F(C_0)$	The final and the tone of current character in Fanqie.
	$F\_F(C_{-1})F\_I(C_0)$	The connection between successive characters.
Guangyun	$G\_I(C_0)$	The initial of the current character in Guangyun.
	$G\_F(C_0)$	The final and the tone of current character in Guangyun.
	$G\_F(C_{-1})G\_I(C_0)$	The connection between successive characters.

Table 4. Feature Templates.

Corpus	Author	Era	# of data entries	# of characters	Size of character set	Average # of characters/clause
Zuozhuan	Zuo Qiuming	500 BCE	3,381	195,983	3,238	4.145
Zhuangzi	Zhuangzi	300 BCE	1,128	65,165	2,936	5.183
Shiji	Qian Sima	100 BCE	4,778	503,890	4,788	5.049
Qing Documents	Qing Dynasty Officials	19th century	1,000	111,739	3,147	7.199

Table 5. Datasets and Statistics.

ancient Chinese sentences is easier than that of segmenting later Chinese ones. Thus, we collected texts from the pre-Qin and Han period, and from the late Qing Dynasty closer to the present, to show that our system can handle Classical Chinese as it has evolved across a span of two thousand years.

A summary of the four datasets is listed in Table 5. The *Zuozhuan* is one of earliest historical works, recording events of China in the Spring and Autumn Period (from 722 BCE to 481 BCE). The book *Zhuangzi* was named after its semi-legendary author, the Daoist philosopher Zhuangzi, who lived around the 4th century BCE. The book consists of stories and fables, in which the philosophy of the Dao is propounded. The *Shiji*, known in English as *The Records of the Grand Historian*, was written by Qian Sima in the 1st century BCE. It narrates Chinese history from 2600 BCE to 100 BCE. The *Shiji* is not only an extremely long book of more than 500,000 characters, but also the chief historical work of ancient China, exerting an enormous influence on subsequent Chinese literature and historiography.

The three ancient works are the most important classics of Chinese literature. We fetched well-segmented electronic editions of these works from the online database of the Institute of History and philology of the Academia Sinica, Taiwan.[2] Each work was partitioned into paragraphs forming a single data entry, which acted as the basic unit of training and testing. The dataset of Qing documents is selected from the Qing Palace Memorials (奏摺) related to Taiwan written in the 19th century. These documents were kindly provided by the Taiwan History Digital Library and have also been human-segmented and stored on electronic media (Chen et al., 2007). We randomly selected 1,000 paragraphs from them as our dataset.

[2]http://hanji.sinica.edu.tw

5.2 Evaluation Metrics

For Classical Chinese sentence segmentation, we define the precision P as the ratio of the boundaries of clauses which are correctly segmented to all segmented boundaries, the recall R as the ratio of correctly segmented boundaries to all reference boundaries, and the score F as the harmonic mean of precision and recall:

$$F = \frac{P \times R \times 2}{P + R}$$

Dataset	Precision	Recall	F-Score
Zuozhuan	100%	32.80%	42.73%
Zhuangzi	100%	19.84%	29.83%
Shiji	100%	14.11%	20.63%
Qing Doc.	100%	33.08%	41.42%
Average	100%	24.96%	33.65%

Table 6. Performance of Majority-Class Baseline.

Tag Set	Precision	Recall	F-Score
2-tag set	85.00%	82.16%	82.92%
4-tag set	85.11%	82.13%	82.95%
5-tag set	85.26%	82.36%	83.18%
7-tag set	84.47%	82.18%	82.74%
Baseline	100%	24.96%	33.65%

Table 7. Comparison between Tagging Schemes.

Features	Precision	Recall	F-Score
Character	85.26%	82.36%	83.18%
POS	61.04%	40.35%	43.93%
MPS	65.31%	54.00%	56.31%
Fanqie	80.96%	76.80%	77.95%
Guangyun	73.11%	69.13%	69.59%
POS + Fanqie	81.07%	74.91%	76.77%
Character + Fanqie	85.43%	82.52%	83.34%
Character + POS + Fanqie	85.67%	81.70%	82.98%

Table 8. Comparison between Feature Sets.

Dataset	Precision	Recall	F-Score
Zuozhuan	92.83%	91.56%	91.79%
Zhuangzi	81.02%	78.87%	79.34%
Shiji	80.79%	78.10%	78.99%
Qing Doc.	87.07%	81.53%	83.24%
Average	85.43%	82.52%	83.34%

Table 9. Performance on Four Datasets.

6 Results

Our baseline is a majority-class tagger which always regards the whole paragraph as a single sentence (i.e., never segments). In Table 6, the performance of the baseline is given. In the 1st set of experiments, four tagging schemes are tested while the feature set is Character. The results are shown in Table 7. In the table, each of the precision, the recall, and the F-score are averaged over the four datasets for each scheme. The results show that the CRF with the 5-tag set is superior to the 4-tag set used in previous works. However, the performance is degraded when the k is larger.

In the 2nd set of experiments, the tag scheme is fixed to the 5-tag set and a number of feature set combinations are tested. The results are shown in Table 8. The performance of MPS is significantly inferior to the other two phonetic systems. As expected, the pronunciation of Classical Chinese is much different from that of Modern Chinese, thus the Ancient Chinese phonetic systems are more suitable for this work. The Fanqie has a surprisingly performance close to the Character. However, performance of the combination of Character and Fanqie is similar to the performance of Character only model. This result indicates that the phonetic information is an important clue to Classical Chinese sentence segmentation but such information is mostly already covered by the characters. Besides, the simple POS features do not help a lot. The higher precision and the lower recall of the POS features show that the particles such as 之/乎/者/也 is indeed a clue to segmentation, but does not catch enough cases.

The best performance comes from the combination of Character and Fanqie with the 5-tag set. We use this configuration as our final tagger. The performances of our tagger for each dataset are given in Table 9. The result shows that our tagger achieves fairly good performance on the Zuozhuan segmentation, while obtaining acceptable performance overall. Because the 19th century Chinese is more complex than ancient Chinese, what we had assumed was that segmentation of the Qing documents would more difficult. However, the results indicate that our assumption does not seem to be true. Our tagger performs the sentence segmentation on the Qing documents well, even better than on the Zhuangzi and on the Shiji. The issues of longer clauses and word segmentation described earlier in this paper do not significantly affect the performance of our system.

In the last experiments, our system is trained and tested on different datasets, and the results are presented in Table 10, where the training datasets are in the rows and the test datasets are in the columns, and the F-scores of the segmentation performance are shown in the inner entries. As expected, the results of segmentation tasks across datasets are significantly poorer than the segmentation in the first two experiments.

These results indicate that our system maintains its performance on a test dataset differing from the training dataset, but the difference in written eras between the test dataset and training dataset cannot be very large. Among all datasets, Shiji is the best training dataset. As training on Shiji and testing on the two other ancient corpora Zuozhuan and Zhuangzi, the performances of our CRF segmenter are not bad.

Training Set	Testing Set				
	Zuozhuan	Zhuangzi	Shiji	Qing doc.	Average
Zuozhuan		72.04%	59.12%	38.85%	56.67%
Zhuangzi	63.70%		52.51%	42.75%	52.99%
Shiji	76.27%	75.46%		44.11%	65.28%
Qing doc.	52.68%	53.13%	42.61%		49.47%
Average	64.22%	66.88%	51.41%	41.90%	

Table 10. F-score of Segmentation cross the Datasets.

7 Conclusion

Our Classical Chinese sentence segmentation is important for many applications such as text mining, information retrieval, corpora research, and digital archiving. To aid in processing such kind of data, an automatic sentence segmentation system is proposed. Different tagging schemes and various features are introduced and tested. Our system was evaluated using three sets of experiments. Five main results are derived. First, the CRF segmenter achieves an F-score of 91.79% in the best case and 83.34% in overall performance. Second, a little longer tagging scheme improves the performance. Third, the phonetic information, especially sourced from Fanqie, is an important clue for Classical Chinese sentence segmentation and may be useful in the related tasks. Fourth, our method performs well on data from various eras. In the experiments, texts from both 500 BCE and the 19th century were well-segmented. Last, the CRF segmenter maintains a certain level of performance in situations which the test data and the training data differ in authors, genres, and written styles, but eras in which they were produced are sufficiently close.

References

Chen, Szu-Pei, Jieh Hsiang, Hsieh-Chang Tu, and Micha Wu. 2007. On Building a Full-Text Digital Library of Historical Documents. In *Proceedings of the 10th International Conference on Asian Digital Libraries, Lecture Notes in Computer Science, Springer-Verlag 4822*:49-60.

Gao, Jianfeng, Mu Li, and Chang-Ning Huang. 2003. Improved Source-Channel Models for Chinese Word Segmentation. In *Proceedings of the 41st Annual Meeting of the Association for Computational Linguistics*, 272-279.

Huang, Hen-Hsen. 2008. *Classical Chinese Sentence Division by Sequence Labeling Approaches*. Master's Thesis, National Chiao Tung University, Hsinchu, Taiwan.

Lafferty, John, Andrew McCallum, and Fernando Pereira. 2001. Conditional Random Fields: Probabilistic Models for Segmentation and Labeling Sequence Data. In *Proceedings of the 18th International Conference on Machine Learning*, 282-289.

Liu, Yang, Andreas Stolcke, Elizabeth Shriberg, and Mary Harper. 2004. Comparing and Combining Generative and Posterior Probability Models: Some Advances in Sentence Boundary Detection in Speech. In *Proceedings of the Conference on Empirical Methods in Natural Language Processing.*

Liu, Yang, Andreas Stolcke, Elizabeth Shriberg, and Mary Harper. 2005. Using Conditional Random Fields for Sentence Boundary Detection in Speech. In *Proceedings of the 43rd Annual Meeting of the Association for Computational Linguistics*, 451-458. Ann Arbor, Mich., USA.

Peng, Fuchun, Fangfang Feng, and Andrew McCallum. 2004. Chinese Segmentation and New Word Detection using Conditional Random Fields. In *Proceedings of the 20th International Conference on Computational Linguistics*, 562-568.

Shriberg, Elizabeth, Andreas Stolcke, Dilek Hakkani-Tür, and Gökhan Tür. 2000. Prosody-Based Automatic Segmentation of Speech into Sentences and Topics. *Speech Communication*, 32(1-2):127-154.

Vishwanathan, S. V. N., Nicol N. Schraudolph, Mark W. Schmidt, and Kevin P. Murphy. 2006. Accelerated training of conditional random fields with stochastic gradient methods. In *Proceedings of the 23th International Conference on Machine Learning*, 969–976. ACM Press, New York, USA.

Xue, Nianwen. 2003. Chinese Word Segmentation as Character Tagging. *Computational Linguistics and Chinese Language Processing*, 8(1):29-48.

Zhang, Hel, Wang Xiao-dong, Yang Jian-yu, and Zhou Wei-dong. 2009. Method of Sentence Segmentation and Punctuating for Ancient Chinese. *Application Research of Computers*, 26(9):3326-3329.

On Generalized-Topic-Based Chinese Discourse Structure *

Song Rou[1] Jiang Yuru[2,4] Wang Jingyi[3]
Beijing Language and Culture University[1]
Beijing University of Polytechnic Technology[2]
Beijing Forest University[3]
Beijing University of Information Science and technology[4]

Abstract: Due to the lack of external formal marks, components in Chinese discourse can hardly be categorized into the traditional syntactic system. In fact, Chinese is a typical topic-prominent language, so it should rather be analyzed from the point of topic. This paper, targeting at computer processing, raises the concepts of punctuation clause, generalized topic, discourse structure and topic clause, and reveals the properties of Chinese discourse structure based on generalized topic. The applicability of this theory has been validated in an initial experiment.
Keywords: Punctuation Clause, Generalized Topic, Discourse Structure, Topic Clause.

1. Punctuation Clause, Generalized Topic and Discourse Structure

The traditional study on syntax is based on individual sentences and the formal marks of syntactic components. But due to the lack of external formal marks, the concept of sentence in Chinese is not clear and the boundary of sentences is difficult to be defined. What's more, there are no formal means to discriminate variant types of syntactic structures. Therefore, the traditional parsing often meets difficulty when it comes to Chinese. This paper does not intend to provide a comprehensive analysis of the achievements and deficiency of the work done by the scholars in this field before. The study is rather based on the factual language phenomena in Chinese and oriented to computer processing of the language. In this paper, some concepts, including punctuation clause, generalized topic, discourse structure and topic clause, are defined, and some properties of Chinese discourse structure are raised, and initial verification done in practical application.

The basic unit of a Chinese discourse is punctuation clause (PClause). A PClause is a string of words separated by comma, semicolon, period, exclamation mark, question mark or quotation marks. Since PClauses can be identified with formal marks, and their internal structure and their relations with each other are restrained, therefore the basic conditions of processing them with computers are satisfied.

E.g. 1.1. (Adopted from newspaper news)

①突然，②他听到洗手间有流水声，③警官与特警踢开门，④将洗手间内的人猛地摔倒在地并铐住，⑤经辨认，⑥正是叶成坚。

(①Suddenly，②he heard the sound of water in the washroom.③the police officers and the special policemen kicked the door open，④wrestled the man in the washroom on the floor and handcuffed him，⑤after identifying，⑥was nobody but Ye Chengjian.[1])

This is a discourse fragment composed of 6 punctuation clauses.

E.g. 1.2. (Adopted from newspaper news)

①叶成坚对在珠海杀人、诱赌勒索台商游某，②以及在澳门实施的四宗持枪抢劫案的犯罪事实供认不讳，③并将私藏枪支的地点一一指认。

(①Ye Chengjian confessed murders in Zhuhai, seducing and blackmailing a Taiwan businessman named You, ② and the four armed robbery in Macao，③ and identified the places where he illegally hid

* This study is supported by National Natural Science Foundation of China, subject No. 60872121
[1] With a purpose to show the structure of PClauses in Chinese, the translation of Chinese works may not appear very standard in English. The same applies hereinafter.

the guns.)

This is a discourse fragment composed of 3 punctuation clauses.

The discourse structure in Chinese is a kind of syntactic structure of a PClause sequence, which is composed of a generalized topic and a number of comments. Generalized topic refers to a syntactic component of a PClause. The subsequent parts of the punctuation clause after it and the neighbor PClauses may be comments about it. Usually a generalized topic is nominal, functioning as the subject, object or attributive in the clause in traditional grammar. In this case, the comments answer "what" and "how" about the topic. The generalized topic can also be verbal, playing the part of the central component of a verb phrase. In some cases, the generalized topic can even be adverbial or an individual preposition. That's why the word "generalized" is adopted. For sake of simplicity, generalized topic will simply be referred to as topic in later sections.

E.g. 1.3. (Adopted from *A Tale of Old Man Xing and His Dog*, by Zhang Xianliang)

她收起了手中的针线，进到屋里，把炕扫了扫，上炕跪坐在炕头，低着脑袋，两手垂在两膝之间，像一个犯人在审讯室里一样静等着。

(She collected her needlework, went into the house, swept the kang[2], got on it and sat down, lowered her head, let her hands dangle between her knees and waited quietly like a prisoner in the hearing room.)

In this example, each of the seven PClauses has the topic "她(she)" as appears in the first PClause, and make comment about "她(she)", answering the questions about her behavior and what she is like. They compose a discourse structure. The first PClause is composed of one topic and one comment, while the rest have comment only but no topic. This discourse structure can be expressed below.

{她[收起了手中的针线，	{She [collected her needlework,
进到屋里，	went into the house,
把炕扫了扫，	swept the kang,
上炕跪坐在炕头，	got on it and sat down,
低着脑袋，	lowered her head,
两手垂在两膝之间，	let her hand dangle between her knees,
像一个犯人在审讯室里一样静等着。]}	waited quietly like a prisoner in the hearing room.]}

For sake of visual cognition, the PClauses are put in different lines and are indented after the topic that they comment. This way of expression is called indented new-line representation. What is quoted by the "[]"marks is some comments, the left of which is the topic. And what is quoted by the "{}"marks is the discourse structure.

E.g. 1.4. (Adopted from *Fortress Besieged* by Chien Chung-Shu)

{她[{只穿[绯霞色抹胸，	{She [{was wearing only [a scarlet top,
海蓝色贴肉短裤，]}]}	and navy blue, skin-tight shorts,]}]}

These two PClauses both comment on what "她只穿(she was wearing only)". "只穿(was wearing only)" is one topic, and "绯霞色抹胸(a scarlet top)", and "海蓝色贴肉短裤(navy blue, skin-tight shorts)" are two comments, answering the question of what was being worn only. The topic and its two comments, when combined together, constitute a discourse structure, which is in turn the comment of "她(she)", answering the question of what she was like. In other words, this discourse structure and "she" constitute an external discourse structure.

E.g. 1.5. (Adopted from *Fortress Besieged* by Chien Chung-Shu)

{鸿渐{吓得[头颅几乎下缩齐肩，
眉毛上升入发，]}}

[2] a kind of bed in some parts of China

{Hung-chien[{was so horrified that[his forehead nearly shrank into his eyebrows,

(as) his eyebrows rose up to his hairline,]}]}

These two PClauses both comment on the extent of his being horrified. The verbal structure of verb + auxiliary "吓得[3]（was so horrified）" is the topic. The topic and its two comments constitute a discourse structure, which is in turn the comment of "鸿渐(Hung-chien)".

E.g. 1.6. (Adopted from *A Tale of Old Man Xing and His Dog*, by Zhang Xianliang)

{全队三百多口子[{都[张着嘴要吃，
伸起手要穿。]}]}

{More than 300 people of the team [{all [need feeding,
need clothing.]}]}

The two PClauses comment on what "全队三百多口子(more than 300 people all)". The generalized topic "都(all)" has two comments "张着嘴要吃(need feeding)" and "伸起手要穿(need clothing)". They both answer "all" what. "都(all)" and the two comments constitutes a discourse structure, commenting on what "全队三百多口子(more than 300 people all)" were like. The two form external discourse structure.

E.g. 1.7. (Adopted from Preamble of CONSTITUTION OF THE PEOPLE'S REPUBLIC OF CHINA)

{本宪法[{以法律的形式[确认了中国各族人民奋斗的成果，

规定了国家的根本制度和根本任务，]}

是国家的根本法，

具有最高的法律效力。]}

{This Constitution, [{in legal form, [affirms the achievements of the struggles of the Chinese people of all nationalities,

(and) defines the basic system and basic tasks of the state;]}

(it) is the fundamental law of the state,

(and) has supreme legal authority.]}

The adverbial "以法律的形式(in legal form)" in the first PClause is the generalized topic. The section after it "确认了中国各族人民奋斗的成果(affirms the achievements of the struggles of the Chinese people of all nationalities)" and the second PClause "规定了国家的根本制度和根本任务(defines the basic system and basic tasks of the state)" are its two comments, answering what is done "in legal form". These three constitute a discourse structure. This structure, together with the third and the fourth PClauses, are all comments on the subject of the first PClause "本宪法(this Constitution)", answering what "本宪法(this Constitution)" is about. These three comments, together with "本宪法(this Constitution)" form the external discourse structure.

E.g. 1.8. (Adopted from *Fortress Besieged* by Chien Chung-Shu)

{学生[{把[分数看得太贱，
功课看得太容易]}]}

{The students[{took[grades as too cheap,
courses as too easy]}]}

The preposition "把[4]" in the first PClause is the generalized topic. "分数看得太贱(took grades as too cheap)" and "功课看得太容易(took courses as too easy)" comment on what and its result. These three then constitute a discourse structure, making comments on "学生(the students)". They form the external discourse structure.

E.g. 1.9. (Adopted from *Royal Tramp (Lu Ding Ji)* by Louis Cha)

顾炎武在城中买了{一份邸报，

[上面详列明史一案中获罪诸人的姓名。]}

Gu Yanwu bought at the town{a piece of court bulletin,

3 the word "得" in Chinese is an auxiliary, indicating result.

4 the word "把" in Chinese is a preposition. It is used in transitive structure, introducing the object.

[(it) listed in detail the names of the criminals accused in the case of Ming Dynasty history.]}

The discourse structures in other examples of this section are embedding, while this example is of overlapping type. The first PClause "顾炎武在城中买了一份邸报(Gu Yanwu bought at the town a piece of court bulletin)" is a discourse structure. The object "一份邸报(a piece of court bulletin)" is not the topic in this PClause, but it is the topic of the second PClause "上面详列明史一案中获罪诸人的姓名(it listed in detail the names of the criminals accused in the case of Ming Dynasty history)" and the two form another discourse structure. The two structures are overlapping, they share one component "一份邸报(a court bulletin)".

2. The static property of Chinese discourse structure

From the examples in the previous section, we can notice the characteristics of Chinese discourse structure:

(1) A generalized topic and a comment group constitute a discourse structure. A comment group is composed of a number of comments.

(2) A comment can be the part of a PClause that follows the topic, or a whole PClause, or another discourse structure. Therefore, the discourse structure is embedded in a recursive way to the right.

Using Context-Free Grammar, the rules are

① DiscourseStructure→GeneralizedTopic CommentGroup
② CommentGroup→Comment
③ CommentGroup→Comment CommentGroup
④ Comment→PClauseTail
⑤ Comment→PClause
⑥ Comment→DiscourseStructure
⑦ GeneralizedTopic→
⑧ PClauseTail→
⑨ PClause→

Here PClauseTail is the tail of the PClause where the generalized topic appears. In these rules, ①-⑥ are generating rules for discourse structure, comment group and comment respectively. ⑦⑧⑨ are the generating rules for generalized topic, PClause tail and PClauses. The right part of these rules is related to terminal symbols and is not listed here.

Statistics on the corpora show that in genuine Chinese texts, there are a large number of PClauses whose subject is missing. This phenomenon is regarded as zero anaphora or elision in traditional language study. But as a matter of fact, the nature of this phenomenon is that there is more than one comment that corresponds to a topic. Since it is a topic, it is natural that there are a lot of comments. There are pauses between the comments and the result is that several PClauses are formed. Neither is this phenomenon zero anaphora nor ellipses, but topic sharing.

Take 1.8 as an example. The following is its generating process (the numbers following the arrow are rule ID).

DiscourseStructure
→①GeneralizedTopic CommentGroup
→⑦本宪法 CommentGroup
→③本宪法 Comment CommentGroup
→⑥本宪法 DiscourseStructure CommentGroup
→①本宪法 GeneralizedTopic CommentGroup CommentGroup

→⑦本宪法 以法律的形式 CommentGroup CommentGroup

→③本宪法 以法律的形式 Comment CommentGroup CommentGroup

→④本宪法 以法律的形式 PClauseTail CommentGroup CommentGroup

→⑧本宪法 以法律的形式 确认了中国各族人民奋斗的成果，CommentGroup CommentGroup

→②本宪法 以法律的形式 确认了中国各族人民奋斗的成果，Comment CommenrGroup

→⑤本宪法 以法律的形式 确认了中国各族人民奋斗的成果，PClause CommenrGroup

→⑨本宪法 以法律的形式 确认了中国各族人民奋斗的成果，规定了国家的根本制度和根本任务，CommentGroup

→③本宪法 以法律的形式 确认了中国各族人民奋斗的成果，规定了国家的根本制度和根本任务，Comment CommentGroup

→⑤本宪法 以法律的形式 确认了中国各族人民奋斗的成果，规定了国家的根本制度和根本任务，PClause CommentGroup

→⑨本宪法 以法律的形式 确认了中国各族人民奋斗的成果，规定了国家的根本制度和根本任务，是国家的根本法，CommentGroup

→②本宪法 以法律的形式 确认了中国各族人民奋斗的成果，规定了国家的根本制度和根本任务，是国家的根本法，Comment

→⑤本宪法 以法律的形式 确认了中国各族人民奋斗的成果，规定了国家的根本制度和根本任务，是国家的根本法，PClause

→⑨本宪法 以法律的形式 确认了中国各族人民奋斗的成果，规定了国家的根本制度和根本任务，是国家的根本法，具有最高的法律效力。

This nature describes the internal relations of a discourse structure. Therefore it is termed static nature.

This nature can cover most examples in the preceding section except example 1.9. This is because the overlapping type of the discourse structure in the example 1.9 can not be represented by Context-Free Grammar.

3. Dynamic Property of Chinese Topic Clause

3.1. Topic Structure and Topic Clause

In this paper, the structure formed by a comment and its topic is called a topic structure. A topic structure as comment can be combined with an external topic and form an external topic structure. If the topic of a comment is the outmost layer of a discourse structure, it is then called the topic clause. In most cases, every PClause corresponds to a topic clause.

E.g.3.1. (Adopted from the Biology Section of China Encyclopedia)

c_1 澳洲肺鱼产卵期很长，(the spawning season of neoceratodus forsteri is quiet long)

c_2 一般以 9 ~ 10 月为旺期。(usually September and October are most productive period)

c_3 卵大，(eggs are big)

c_4 卵径 6 ~ 7 毫米，(eggs are 6-7 mm in diameter)

c_5 具胶质膜，(have gelatinous membrane)

c_6 无粘性。(are not sticky)

c_7 卵产于植物中间，(the eggs are laid among plants)

c_8 一部分沉入水底。(some sink deep in the water)

Here, the outmost topic is "澳洲肺鱼(neoceratodus forsteri)".

The topic clause of c_1 is c_1 itself. The comment is "产卵期很长(the spawning season of is quiet long)".

c_2"一般以 9～10 月为旺期(usually September and October are most productive period)"is a comment, and its topic is"产卵期(the spawning season)". The topic structure composed of the two is the comment on "澳洲肺鱼(neoceratodus forsteri)", therefore "澳洲肺鱼产卵期一般以 9～10 月为旺期" is the topic clause of c_2。

c_3"卵大(eggs are big)"is the comment on the topic "澳洲肺鱼(neoceratodus forsteri)". The topic clause of c_3 is "澳洲肺鱼卵大".

c_4"卵径 6～7 毫米(eggs are 6-7 mm in diameter)" is the comment on the topic "澳洲肺鱼(neoceratodus forsteri)". The topic clause of c_4 is "澳洲肺鱼卵径 6～7 毫米"。

c_5"具胶质膜(have gelatinous membrane)"is the comment on the topic "卵(eggs)". The topic structure "卵具胶质膜(eggs have gelatinous membrane)" composed of the two is the comment on "澳洲肺鱼(neoceratodus forsteri)". And the topic clause of c_5 is "澳洲肺鱼卵具胶质膜"。

c_6"无粘性(are not sticky)" is the comment on the topic "卵(eggs)". The topic structure "卵无粘性(eggs are not sticky)" composed of the two is the comment on "澳洲肺鱼(neoceratodus forsteri)". And the topic clause of c_6 is "澳洲肺鱼卵无粘性"。

c_7"卵产于植物中间(the eggs are laid among plants)" is the comment on the topic "澳洲肺鱼(neoceratodus forsteri)". The topic clause of c_7 is "澳洲肺鱼卵产于植物中间"。

c_8"一部分沉入水底(some sink deep in the water)"is the comment on the topic "卵(eggs)", The topic structure "卵一部分沉入水底(eggs some sink deep in the water)" composed of the two is the comment on the topic "澳洲肺鱼(neoceratodus forsteri)". And the topic clause of c_8 is "澳洲肺鱼卵一部分沉入水底"。

The purpose of analyzing a PClause sequence is to find out its discourse structure. If the topic clause of every PClause is constructed, the topic of each comment at every layer is then found out, and consequently the entire discourse structure will be clear. The next section provides an approach to finding out the topic clause of PClauses.

3.2. Stack Model of Dynamic Generation of the Topic Clause

The topic clause of PClause c_i of Ex.3.1 is marked as c_i'. They are listed below.

c_1' . 澳洲肺鱼产卵期很长, (the spawning season of neoceratodus forsteri is quiet long)

c_2' . 澳洲肺鱼产卵期一般以 9～10 月为旺期。(the spawning season of neoceratodus forsteri usually September and October are most productive period)

c_3' . 澳洲肺鱼卵大, (neoceratodus forsteri' s eggs are big)

c_4' . 澳洲肺鱼卵径 6～7 毫米, (neoceratodus forsteri' s eggs are 6-7mm in diameter)

c_5' . 澳洲肺鱼卵具胶质膜, (neoceratodus forsteri' s eggs have gelatinous membrane)

c_6' . 澳洲肺鱼卵无粘性。(neoceratodus forsteri' s eggs are not sticky)

c_7' . 澳洲肺鱼卵产于植物中间, (neoceratodus forsteri' s eggs are laid among plants)

c_8' . 澳洲肺鱼卵一部分沉入水底。(some eggs of neoceratodus forsteri sink deep in the water)

The generation of each ci′ is exemplified below.

$c_1'=c_1$;

The topic of c_2 is "产卵期(the spawning season)" in c_1'. Delete the part of c_1' right to the topic and replace it with c_2, and we will have c_2';

The topic of c_3 is "澳洲肺鱼(neoceratodus forsteri')" in c_2'. Delete the part of c_2' right to the topic and replace it with c_3, and we will have c_3'.

The topic of c_4 is "澳洲肺鱼(neoceratodus forsteri')" in c_3'. Delete the part of c_3' right to the topic and replace it with c_4, and we will have c_4'.

The topic of c_5 is "卵(eggs)" in c_4'. Delete the part of c_4' right to the topic and replace it with c_5, and we will have c_5'.

The topic of c_6 is "卵(eggs)" in c_5'. Delete the part of c_5' right to the topic and replace it with c_6, and we will have c_6'.

The topic of c_7 is "澳洲肺鱼(neoceratodus forsteri')" in c_6'. Delete the part of c_6' right to the topic and replace it with c_7, and we will have c_7'.

The topic of c_8 is "卵(eggs)" in c_7'. Delete the part of c_7' right to the topic and replace it with c_8, and we will have c_8'.

Generally, given a PClause sequence $\{c_1, \ldots, c_n\}$, if the first PClause is a complete structure of topic-comment, then

(1) the topic clause of the first PClause is the PClause itself;

(2) if the topic of a subsequent PClause is missing, then the topic should be in the topic clause of its previous PClause;

(3) the topic clause of every subsequent PClause can be generated recursively by stack operation.

Note the topic clause of c_i as c_i', and the topic clause of c_{i+1} as c_{i+1}',

(3.1) if the topic of c_{i+1} is missing, and $c_i' = \alpha A \beta$, where A is the topic of c_{i+1}, then $c_{i+1}' = \alpha A c_{i+1}$。

(3.2) if the topic of c_{i+1} is not missing, then $c_{i+1}' = c_{i+1}$.

If we regard the beginning and the end of a topic clause as the bottom and the top of a stack respectively, then the removal and connection of the components in the generation process of topic clause are typical stack operations. Therefore the recursive law of such generation can be called the stack model

The stack model can not only applied to embedded discourse structure, but also some overlapping structures such as instance 1.4. Details are not given here. Our investigation into corpora (about 340,000 Chinese characters) of different registers shows that more than 95% PClauses meet the model.

From the stack model, it can be seen that the key to generate the topic clause of a PClause is to identifying which component of the topic clause of the previous PClause is its topic. This would require to uncover the constraints for forming the discourse structure.

4. Constraints on Discourse Structure

4.1. Acceptability and completeness of Topic Clause

A topic structure is composed of a topic and its comments. Therefore mostly it is acceptable. A topic clause is not only acceptable, but also complete with necessary syntactic and semantic components. Taking advantage of this nature, the filtering of topic-seeking for a PClause can be boiled down to the judgment of the acceptability and completeness of a single clause. For example, the topic clause of PClause 7 in example 3.1 is:

c_7'.澳洲肺鱼卵产于植物中间，(neoceratodus forsteri' s eggs are laid among plants)

and PClause c_8 is

一部分沉入水底。(some sink deep in the water)

According to the stack model, the options for the topic clause of c8 are:

(1) 一部分沉入水底。(some sink deep in the water)
(suppose that the topic of c_8 is not missing)

(2) 澳洲肺鱼一部分沉入水底。(neoceratodus forsteri some sink deep in the water)
(suppose that the topic of c_8 is "澳洲肺鱼(neoceratodus forsteri)")

(3) 澳洲肺鱼卵一部分沉入水底。(neoceratodus forsteri' eggs some sink deep in the water)

（suppose that the topic of c_8 is "卵(eggs)"）

(4) 澳洲肺鱼卵产于一部分沉入水底。(neoceratodus forsteri' eggs some are laid sink deep in the water)

（suppose that the topic of c_8 is "产于(be laid)"）

(5) 澳洲肺鱼卵产于植物一部分沉入水底。(neoceratodus forsteri' eggs some are laid plant sink deep in the water)

（suppose that the topic of c_8 is "植物(plant)"）

(6) 澳洲肺鱼卵产于植物中间一部分沉入水底。(neoceratodus forsteri' eggs some are laid among plant sink deep in the water)

(suppose that the topic of c_8 is "中间(middle)")

Chinese intuition tells us that (1) is not complete, and (4)(5)(6) are not acceptable, so the candidates are (2) and (3) only. We see that if we can formalize our intuition, we can considerably narrow down the scope of options.

The topic and the comment of a topic clause are often from different PClauses, and the components in a topic clause that have discourse functions (such as discourse conjunctions) can affect the acceptability of the topic clause. This problem needs to be addressed in separate study.

4.2. Semantic Constraints

E.g. 4.1.他买了一个钱包，是名牌产品。(He bought a wallet, (it) is a brand product.)

The topic of the second PClause could be "他(he)" or "钱包(a wallet)". We can eliminate the first possibility by using semantic constraints, because a person can not be a product.

4.3. Syntactic Constraints

An investigation into corpora shows that the syntactic relations of the topic and the comments are of the following types:

(1) If the relation of a topic and its comment in the same PClause is subject-predicate, then the same relation is true of it with its comments in other PClauses (see example 1.3);

(2) If the relation of a topic and its comment in the same PClause is predicate-object, preposition-object or attribute-central, then the relation of it and its comment in other PClauses is of the same type or subject-predicate type (see example 1.4 and 1.8).

(3) If the relation of a topic and its comment in the same PClause is adverbial-central or predicate-complement, then its relation with its comment in other PClauses is the same (see example 1.5, 1.6 and 1.7).

(4) If a component is not the topic of the PClause where it is appears, but is the topic of other PClauses, then it must be the object or attribute in the PClause where it appears and its relation with the comments in other PClauses is subject-predicate (see example 1.9).

In addition, adjectives, numbers in partition in respect of quantity and some adverbs (such a adverbs indicating degree) cannot function as general topics.

4.4 Context Constraints

E.g. 4.2.他有个朋友，很阔气。(He has a friend, (who is)very generous with money.)

The topic of the second PClause could be "他(he)" or "个朋友(a friend)". Whether it is "he is generous with money" or "his friend is generous with money", it will present no problem either semantically or syntactically. However, abundant instances and analyses show that if

(1) the structure of the topic clause of the previous PClause is SVO;

(2) the core verb of the topic clause of the previous PClause has a sense of "owing" or "introducing"; and

(3) the second PClause is an adjective phrase but does not fall into the category of mental state

then the topic of the second PClause is the object rather than the subject of the topic clause.

According to this constraint, the topic of the second PClause is "个朋友(a friend)"

4.5. Cognition Constraints

Theoretically, there is no limit to the size of a discourse structure. Countless layers could be embedded or overlapped. For example, we could have the following discourse structure.

E.g. 4.3 圆周率整数部分是 3,

小数部分第一位是 1,

后面是 4,

再后面是 1,

再后面是 5,

……

(The circumference ratio's

integer part is 3,

the first number in the fraction part is 1,

followed by 4,

followed by 1,

followed by 5

…)

Here "圆周率(circumference ratio)", "1", "4", "1", "5" all are topics. They could go on with no limit.

But the study on factual corpora have discovered that the maximum layer of embedding or overlapping is 5, and if we shall return from the deeper layers, the maximum number of the layers that can be jumped back is 3. This has much to do with people's cognition ability. The following is an example of 5 layers of embedding and overlapping with 3 layers of maximum return. The underlined words are the generalized topics. The numbers in the brackets to the right of the PClauses indicating the depth of the embedding and overlapping. PClause "行销于外(release them)" reaches the fifth layer in depth, but the next PClause "官府追究之时(when the authorities started investigating)" returns to layer2, retreating 3 layers.

Ex. 4.4. (Adopted from *Royal Tramp* by Louis Cha)

程维藩从杭州坐船到南浔之时,(0) (Cheng Weifan, on the long boat journey from Hangzhou to Nanxun)

反覆推考,(1) (thought things over)

已思得良策,(1) (had come up with a good plan.)

心想这部《明书辑略》流传已久,(1)(thought the book had already been in circulation for some time)

隐瞒是瞒不了的,(2) (It was therefore too late for concealment)

惟有施一个釜底抽薪之计,(2) (the only expedient left was to play a trick)

一面派人前赴各地书铺,(3) (on one hand, send people to go to the bookshops all over the country)

将这部书尽数收购回来销毁,(4) (buy back and then destroy all copies of the book)

一面赶开夜工,(3) (on the other hand, work day and night)

另镌新版,(4) (make a new printing mould)

删除所有讳忌之处,(4) (remove all the offensive bits)

重印新书,(4) (reprint the book)

行销于外。(5) (release them)

官府追究之时,(2) (when the authorities started investigating)

将新版明史拿来一查,(3) (inspect the new edition of Ming History)

发觉吴之荣所告不实,(3) (find Wu's charges to be groundless)

便可消一场横祸了。(2) (can avert a hideous disaster)

5. Initial Application of Discourse Structure based on General Topic

5.1. Discourse Structure in Encyclopedia

The herein discussed Chinese discourse structure based on general topic has been initially applied and tested in the analyses of encyclopedia texts.

The entries in encyclopedia are expository, covering people, places, species, events, devices and terms etc. in various subjects. Because the different aspects of an object must be exposed, the leading role of the topic is very obvious. It frequently occurs that many PClauses are used to comment on one topic, and the comments on different aspects of an object are often presented as embedded or overlapping structures. In order to mine the information of the object described, it is necessary to analyze the governing scope of a topic. In other words, it is necessary to locate the object commented by every PClause. Therefore the discourse structure must be analyzed. Take 3.1 for example, we must be clear about for "what" September and October are the active period, the eggs of "what" are big, the eggs of "what" are 6-7 mm in diameter, "what" has gelatinous membranes and so on.

5.2. An Experiment on Discourse Structure in Encyclopedia

The experiment object of the paper is the entries about various fishes in the biology volume of China Encyclopedia. The objective is the find the topic clause of every Pclause.

There are 224 entries about fishes in this volume, each one with a title, viz. the name of the order, family, genera and species of a fish. The first PClause in the text does not mention the name, but introduces the genera information of it. The name is not necessarily mentioned in later Pclauses. For example,

澳洲肺鱼

Neoceratodus forsteri; Queensland lungfish

角齿鱼目角齿鱼科新角齿鱼属的 1 种(见图澳洲肺鱼外形),是现代肺鱼中最大的种类。体长约 125 厘米,重达 10 千克。体呈长梭形,覆盖大而薄的圆鳞。……

(A member of the family Ceratodontidae and order Ceratodontiformes (see picture of Neoceratodus forsteri). (It) is the biggest extant lungfish species in the world. (Its)Body length (is) about 125 centimeters, (it) weighs as much as 10 kilograms. (Its) Body is elongated, covered with big and thin round scales …)

In the experiment, the entry names (both in Chinese and English) and bracketed information are deleted. But the entry title is added to the left of the first PClause, connected by a "是(is) ". For example, the first PClause of the above example of neoceratodus forsteri is changed into "澳洲肺鱼是角齿鱼目角齿鱼科新角齿鱼属的 1 种，", the rest remains unchanged.

The experiment selected 3999 PClauses of 86 entries as training data, and 577 PCauses of 13 entries as open-test data. The input of the experiment is the topic clause of a PClause and its next PClause, and the output is the topic clause of the second PClause. In other words, the target of the experiment is to decide the topic of the PClause within a limited scope under the scheme of stack model.

For the training data, each PClause is replenished manually into a topic clause, and then the words are segmented. In this way, the training topic clause set G is obtained. The principle of testing is described below. For each tested PClause c and the topic clause d of its proceeding PClause, word segmentation is done separately. String d is cut at different places, the tails are replaced with c every time. Thus a number of candidate topic clauses of c are obtained. Then the similarity reckoning is made about the candidate topic clauses and the topic clauses in G. The one with the maximum similarity is chosen as the result for output.

In order to solve the problem of data sparse in the calculation, semantic generalization is made about related words. The semantic categories employed are： subjects of fishes (e.g. neoceratodus forsteri, alopias), part (e.g. head, scale, fin), position (e.g. back, abdomen), location (e.g. front, upper), shape (e.g. fusiformis, cylindrical), size (e.g. big, short), color (e.g. red, light blue). environment (e.g. pond, near sea), geographical region(e.g. the Pacific, Huanghai), season(e.g. early spring, autumn), number (e.g. 3, 1-3) etc. Verbs are rarely generalized.

The result of the initial experiment showed the accuracy rate for open test was 78%. If add the title of a text to the beginning of every PClause in the text, 66% accuracy rate can be got as a baseline. The result of the experiment is not high indeed and there is room for improvement. Since the experiment principle was the similarity of the topic clauses, in essence only the stack model and the acceptability of topic clause are used. Semantic constraints, syntactic constraints, context constraints and cognitive constraints are not employed. In addition, word segmentation is not entirely correct, and the semantic generalization is quite rough. 78% accuracy rate of under such rough conditions has initially proved the applicability of the theoretical system.

6. Discussion

This paper employs discourse structure of topic-comment in analyzing Chinese, takes PClauses as the basic discourse unit, and extends the concept of topic to generalized topic. As a result, the properties of Chinese discourse structure are proposed. Investigations into large amount of language data have proved that this theoretical system is natural and applicable to Chinese, which is also backed up by initial experiment. Of course, the theory need to be improved, and the various types of constraints under the theory framework need to be further uncovered. More and detailed study needs to be done along this path.

References

[1] CHEN Ping（1987）, Discouse Analysis of Zero anaphora in Chinese, *Zhongguo Yuwen*, No.5,1987.

[2] CHU Chauncey C.（1998）, A Discourse Grammar of Mandarin Chinese, Peter Lang Publication Inc. New York.

[3] HUANG He yan, CHEN Zhao xiong（2002）, The Hybrid Strategy Processing Approach of Complex Long Sentence, *Journal of Chinese Information Processing*, Vol.16, No.3.

[4] HOU min, SUN Jian-jun（2005）, Zero Anaphora in Chinese and How to Process it in Chinese-English MT, *Journal of Chinese Information Processing*, Vol.19, No.3.

[5] HUANG Jian-cuan, SONG Rou（2008）,A Research on the Annotation of Punctuated Clauses, *Frontiers of Content Computing*, Edited by SUN Mao-song and CHEN Qun-xiu, Tsinghua University Press, Beijing.

[6] LI Xing; ZONG Cheng-qing（2006）, A Hierarchical Parsing Approach with Punctuation Processing for Long Chinese Sentences, Journal of Chinese Information Processing, Vol.20, No.4.

[7] MAO Qi, LIAN Le-xin, ZHOU Wen-cui, YUAN Chun-fang（2007）, Chinese Syntactic Parsing Algorithm Based on Segmentation of Punctuation, *Journal of Chinese Information Processing*, Vol.21, No.2.

[8] SONG Rou（1992）, The Delesion of the Fronts of Clauses in Chinese Narratives, *Journal of Chinese Information Processing*, Vol.6, No.3.

[9] SONG Rou（2008）, Research on Properties of Syntactic RelationBetween P-Clauses in Modern Chinese, *Chinese Teaching in the World*, No.2, 2008.

[10] SONG Rou, WANG Jingyi（2008）, Syntactic Relation Between P-Clauses in Modern Chinese and Annotated Corpus, CCID & Lancaster University Joint Workshop on Corpus Linguistics & Machine Translation Applications, 2008. Beijing.

[11] XING Fu-yi（1997）, Chinese Gramma, Northeast Normal University Press, Changchun.

[12] XU Yu-long（2004）, Towards a Functional-Pragmatic Model of Discourse Anaphora Resolution, Shaihai Foreign Language Education Press, Shaihai.

Semantic Computing and Language Knowledge Bases[1]

Lei Wang
Key Laboratory of Computational Linguistics of Ministry of Education
Department of English, Peking University
wangleics@pku.edu.cn

Shiwen Yu
Key Laboratory of Computational Linguistics of Ministry of Education,
Peking University
yusw@pku.edu.cn

Abstract

As the proposition of the next-generation Web – semantic Web, semantic computing has been drawing more and more attention within the circle and the industries. A lot of research has been conducted on the theory and methodology of the subject, and potential applications have also been investigated and proposed in many fields. The progress of semantic computing made so far cannot be detached from its supporting pivot – language resources, for instance, language knowledge bases. This paper proposes three perspectives of semantic computing from a macro view and describes the current status of affairs about the construction of language knowledge bases and the related research and applications that have been carried out on the basis of these resources via a case study in the Institute of Computational Linguistics at Peking University.

1 Introduction

Semantic computing is a technology to compose information content (including software) based on meaning and vocabulary shared by people and computers and thereby to design and operate information systems (i.e., artificial computing systems). Its goal is to plug the semantic gap through this common ground, to let people and computers cooperate more closely, to ground information systems on people's life world, and thereby to enrich the meaning and value of the entire life world. (Hasida, 2007) The task of semantic computing is to explain the meaning of various constituents of sentences (words or phrases) or sentences themselves in a natural language. We believe that semantic computing is a field that addresses two core problems: First, to map the semantics of user with that of content for the purpose of content retrieval, management, creation, etc.; second, to understand the meanings (semantics) of computational content of various sorts, including, but is not limited to, text, video, audio, network, software, and expressing them in a form that can be processed by machine.

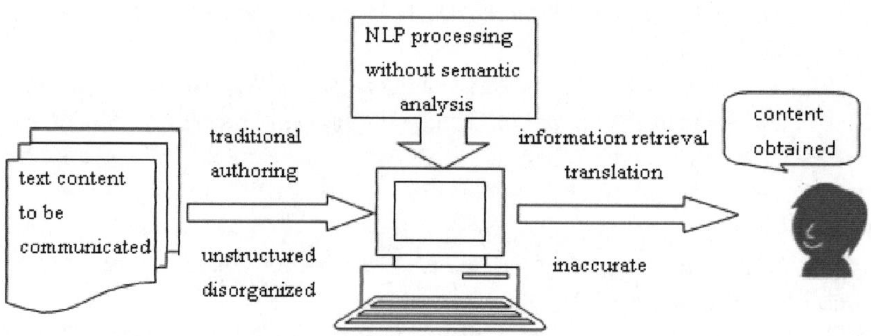

Figure 1. Human-computer interaction is handicapped without semantic computing.

[1] This work is supported by the National Natural Science Foundation of China (No. 60970083) and Chiang Ching-kuo Foundation for International Scholarly Exchange (2009).

But the way to the success of semantic computing is not even and it has taken a quite long time for researchers to make some progress in this field. The difficulties of semantic computing involve many aspects: ambiguity, polysemy, domain of quantifier, metaphor, etc. Different individuals will have different understanding of the same word or the same sentence. Research on the theory and methodology of semantic computing still has a long way to go.

Now we provide an example in a search engine to show how difficult for the computer to understand the meaning of a word. We input two sentences into Google.com Translate and the following results were returned:

Example 1

I bought a table with three dollars.（20091016 Google: 本人买了3 美元一表）

I bought a table with three legs.（20091016 Google: 本人买了3 条腿的表）

We know that the word "table" has two common meanings in English (a wooden object and a structured data report). But in Chinese they correspond to two different words (表 biǎo and 桌子 zhuō zi[2]). From Example 1, we can see that the search engine cannot distinguish the two senses and translate them both as 表. Thus, without semantic analysis queries in a search engine may result in very poor performance. The first principle of a search engine is based on shallow Natural Language Processing (NLP) techniques, for instance, string matching, while future direction of search engines should aim at content index and the understanding of user's intention. Semantic computing becomes applicable only with the development of deep NLP techniques. Machine Translation (MT) is the first application of digital computers in the non-digital world and semantic information is indispensable in MT research and applications. However, there has been no breakthrough to the extent of Natural Language Understanding (NLU) and semantic computing may serve as the key to some success in this field.

2 Related Work on Semantic Computing

Semantics is an interesting but controversial topic. Many a theory has been proposed in attempt to describe what meaning really means. But up until now there has not been a theory that can describe the meaning of various language units (words, phrases and sentences) so perfectly that was accepted universally, even though Fillmore's proposition of Framework semantics (1976) is successful enough. Since Gildea et al. (2002) initiated the research on automatic semantic role labeling, many evaluations have been conducted internationally, such as Senseval-3 and SemEval 2007, as well as CoNLL SRL Shared Task 2004, 2005 and 2008. Word Sense Disambiguation (WSD) is also a very important research subject and a lot of work has been done in this regard, such as Lesk (1986), Gale et al. (1998), Jin et al. (2007) and Qu et al. (2007) as the Chinese counterpart. As to the research on computing word sense relatedness, Dagan et al (1993) did some pilot work and Lee (1997) and Resnik (1999) contributed to the research on semantic similarity.

In recent years, semantics-based analysis such as data and web mining, analysis of social networks and semantic system design and synthesis have begun to draw more attention from researchers. Applications using semantics such as search engines and question answering (Li et al., 2002), content-based multimedia retrieval and editing, natural language interfaces (Yokoi et al., 2005) based on semantics have also been attracting attentions. Even semantic computing has been applied to areas like music description, medicine and biology and GIS systems and architecture. The whole idea is how to realize human-centered computing.

---

[2] Pinyin is currently the most commonly used Romanization system for standard Mandarin. The system is now used in mainland China, Hong Kong, Macau, parts of Taiwan, Malaysia and Singapore to teach Mandarin Chinese and internationally to teach Mandarin as a second language. It is also often used to spell Chinese names in foreign publications and can be used to enter Chinese characters on computers and cell phones.

3 The Theory and Methodology of Semantic Computing

3.1 Important Questions That Need to Be Asked about Semantic Computing

In the past few years there has been a growing interest in the field of semantics and semantic computing. But there are questions that have been always lingering on researchers' minds. What on earth semantics is? What is the best way to describe the meaning of a language unit? How can natural languages be processed so that we are able to benefit from human-computer interaction, or even interpersonal communication? It seems that no one can give satisfactory answers to these questions. But it is now commonly agreed that the study of semantic computing or knowledge representation is a central issue in computational linguistics. The major contributions on this topic are collected in *Computational Linguistics* (1987-2010) and *International Journal of Semantic Computing* (2007-2010). Research in computing semantics is, however, rather heterogeneous in scope, methods, and results. The traditional "wh" and "how" questions need to be asked again to understand the consequences of conceptual and linguistic decisions in semantic computing:

What? What should be computed in terms of semantics? Each word is a world and its meaning can be interpreted differently. Despite the interest that semantics has received from the scholars of different disciplines since the early history of humanity, a unifying theory of meaning does not exist, no matter whether we view a language from a lexical or a syntactic perspective. In practice, the quality and type of the expressed concepts again depend upon the one who uses it: any language speaker or writer, a linguist, a psychologist, a lexicographer, or a computer. In psycholinguistics and computational linguistics, semantic knowledge is modeled with very deep and formal expressions. Often semantic models focus on some very specific aspect of language communication, according to the scientific interest of a researcher. In natural language processing, lexical entries or semantic attributes typically express linguistic knowledge as commonsensically understood and used by humans. The entries or attributes are entirely formatted in some knowledge representation and can be manipulated by a computer.

Where? What are the sources of semantic knowledge? Traditionally, individual introspection is often a source of obtaining word senses. However, individual introspection brings about both theoretical and implementation problems. Theoretically, it is because "different researchers with different theories would observe different things about their internal thoughts..." (Anderson 1989). With regard to implementation, it is because consistency becomes a major problem when the size of the lexicon or the syntactic tree bank exceeds a few thousands entries or annotation tags. Despite the scientific interest of such experiments, they cannot be extensively repeated for the purpose of acquiring mass word sense definitions. On-line corpora and dictionaries are widely available today and provide experimental evidence of word uses and word definitions. The major advantage of on-line resources is that in principle they provide the basis for very large experiments, even though at present the methods of analysis and application are not fully developed and need further research to get satisfactory results.

How? Semantic computing can be realized at various levels. The hard work is to implement a system in a real domain, or the more conceptual task of defining an effective mathematical framework to manipulate the objects defined within a linguistic model. Quite obviously the "hows" in the literature about semantic computing are much more important than the "whats" and "wheres". The methodology that really works in semantic computing is deeply related to the ultimate objective of NLP research, which still cannot be defined adequately so far.

3.2 The Perspectives of Semantic Computing from a Macro View

Why semantic computing (or NLU) has posed so great a challenge? We may attribute this to two major reasons: First, it is based on the knowledge of human language mechanism. If fully-developed complicated brains are often seen as a crowning achievement of biological evolution, the interpersonal communication is no simpler than human biological mechanism. Language has to be a crucial part of the evolutionary process, which has not been fully understood by scientific research. Second, in NLP research the language is both the target and the tool. Current NLP research focuses on either speech or written texts only. However, in the real world scenario, reading and interaction between humans are multi-dimensional (through different forms of information such as text, speech, or images and utilizing our different senses such as vision, hearing). It is necessary to rely on the advancements of brain science, cognitive science and other related fields and work in collaboration to produce better results. Linguistics, especially computational linguistics, has made its own contribution, and semantic computing will play an important role in NLP.

There are complex many-to-many relations between the form and the meaning of a language. Semantic computing is not only the way but also the ultimate goal of natural language understanding. Although it is hard, we should not give up. Here we propose that the main contents of semantic computing include the following three aspects:

- semantic computing on the ontological perspective
- semantic computing on the cognitive perspective
- semantic computing on the pragmatic perspective

As for ontologies, much progress has been made worldwide. The remarkable achievements in English include: WordNet by Princeton University, PropBank by University of Pennsylvania, etc. Also there are quite a number of efforts made on building ontologies in Chinese, which will be elaborated in Section 5.

In the last few years, the main direction of semantic computing is to disambiguate language units and constructions. In the following Example 2, the word 仪表 yí biǎo has two meanings in different contexts. In Chinese, word segmentation is also a problem that needs to be addressed. In Example 3, segmenting the word 白天鹅 bái tiān é as 白/天鹅 or 白天/鹅 can result in different understanding of the sentences.

Example 2

她的仪表很端庄。 tā de yí biǎo hěn duān zhuāng (*She has a graceful appearance.*)
她的仪表很精确。 tā de yí biǎo hěn jīng què (*Her meters are very accurate.*)

Example 3

白天鹅飞过来了。bái tiān é fēi guò lái le (*A white swan flies toward us.*)
白天鹅可以看家。bái tiān é kě yǐ kān jiā (*A goose can guard our house at daytime.*)

As to WSD tasks on the word level, some problems can be solved when ontology is applied. But ambiguity can also appear on the syntactic level. For this, it is usually difficult for ontologies to do much, so we may seek help from language knowledge bases (See Section 5). The following examples of syntactic semantic analysis will illustrate how different syntactic structures will change the meaning of sentences:

Example 4

这样的电影不是垃圾是什么?	--该电影是垃圾。
zhè yàng de diàn yǐng bú shì lā jī shì shén me?	-- gāi diàn yǐng shì lā jī
If a movie as such is not rubbish, what is it?	-- It is rubbish.
这样的电影怎么能说是垃圾呢?	-- 该电影不是垃圾。
zhè yàng de diàn yǐng zěn me néng shuō shì lā jī ne?	-- gāi diàn yǐng bú shì lā jī
How can a movie as such be rubbish?	-- It is not rubbish.

Example 5

蚂蚱是蚂蚱，蛐蛐是蛐蛐。 -- 蚂蚱不是蛐蛐。
mà zhà shì mà zhà , qū qū shì qū qū -- mà zhà bú shì qū qū
A grasshopper is a grasshopper, while a cricket is a cricket. -- A grasshopper is not a cricket.
Rule：A is A, while B is B. ——〉A is not B.
丁是丁，卯是卯。dīng shì dīng, mǎo shì mǎo
Ding is ding, while mao is mao. — being conscientious

With respect to semantic computing on cognitive level, we will use metaphor as an example. For a long time, NLP research has focused on ambiguity resolution. Can NLU be realized after ambiguity resolution? Metaphor, insinuation, pun, hyperbole (exaggeration), humor, personification, as well as intended word usage or sentence composing, pose a great challenge to NLU research. If the computer can deal with metaphors, it will greatly improve the ability of natural language understanding.

First, let's discuss the rhetorical function of a metaphor. Metaphor is extensively and skillfully used in the Chinese classic "Book of Songs" to boost expressiveness.

Example 6

Simile: 自伯之东，首如飞蓬[3]；岂无膏沐？谁适为容。 --（卫风·伯兮）
zì bó zhī dōng ，shǒu rú fēi péng ；qǐ wú gào mù ? shuí shì wéi róng。--（wèi fēng ·bó xī）
(Your hair is like disordered grass.)
Metaphor：它山之石，可以攻玉。 --（小雅·鹤鸣）
tā shān zhī shí ，kě yǐ gōng yù。 --（xiǎo yǎ· hè míng）
(Rocks from another mountain can be used to carve jade. Metaphorically this phrase means a change of method may solve the current problem.)

Also, many Chinese idioms are metaphorical expressions: 同舟共济 tóng zhōu gòng jì (Literally, to cross the river in the same boat; metaphorically, to work together with one heart while in difficulty), 铜墙铁壁 tóng qiáng tiě bì (Literally, walls of brass and iron; metaphorically, impregnable). The Chinese language makes use of lots of idioms or idiomatic expressions that are derived from ancient Chinese stories and fables. These idioms and idiomatic expressions are often used metaphorically and reflect historical and cultural background of the language. They are the most precious relics to the Chinese language and culture. Therefore the Chinese Idiom Knowledge Base (CIKB) was also built in 2009. CIKB consists of 38,117 entries and describes many attributes of Chinese idioms. Among the attributes, "literal translation", "free translation" and "English equivalent" are very valuable.

The linguistic function of metaphor is also important. Metaphor is the base of new word creation and polysemy production (sense evolution), for example, 垃圾箱 lā jī xiāng (recycle) and 病毒 bìng dú (virus) are used in a computer setting and words like 高峰 gāo fēng (peak), 瓶颈 píng jǐng (bottleneck) and 线索 xiàn suǒ (clue) are endowed with new meanings which have not been included in traditional Chinese dictionaries. Besides, metaphor creates new meanings in sentence level, for instance, in 地球是人类的母亲。dì qiú shì rén lèi de mǔ qīn (The earth is the mother of humanity.), the word 母亲 (mother) has a different meaning. So, metaphor understanding is beyond the scope of ambiguity resolution. Metaphor, linguistics, and human cognitive mechanisms are inextricably interlinked. So metaphor becomes a fort that must be conquered in NLU research.

From an NLP perspective, metaphors can be summarized into the following categories as in Table 1. As for the NLP tasks of metaphor computing, we can conclude that there are three tasks to be accomplished: First, metaphor

[3] For the purpose of conciseness, only the underlined parts that contain metaphors are translated.

recognition. For instance, how can we distinguish 知识的海洋 from 海洋资源考察 hǎi yáng zī yuán kǎo chá (investigation of ocean resources); Second, metaphor understanding and translation. For instance, 知识的海洋 actually means 知识像海洋一样丰富。zhī shí xiàng hǎi yáng yí yàng fēng fù (Knowledge is as rich as the ocean.). Third, metaphor generation. For instance, how phrases such as 信息的海洋 xìn xī de hǎi yáng (ocean of information) and 鲜花的海洋 xiān huā de hǎi yáng (ocean of flowers) can be generated successfully by computer?

Perspective of grammatical properties		Perspective of language unites of metaphorical expressions	
Nominal	祖国的花朵 zǔ guó de huā duǒ (flower of the country), 生命的旅程 shēng mìng de lǚ chéng (life journey)	Word-formation level	卵石 luǎn shí(egg-like stone), 杏仁眼 xìng rén yǎn (apricot-like eyes)
Verb	心潮澎湃 xīn cháo péng pài (heart wave), 放飞理想 fàng fēi lǐ xiǎng (let f dream fly)	Word level	潮流 cháo liú (tide), 朝阳 zhāo yáng (morning sun)
Adjective	这篇文章写得干巴。zhè piān wén zhāng xiě de gān bā(This article is written drily), 这篇文章清汤寡水。zhè piān wén zhāng qīng tāng guǎ shuǐ (This article is like plain soup and water.)	Phrase level	知识的海洋 zhī shí de hǎi yáng (ocean of knowledge), 播种幸福的种子 bō zhǒng xìng fú de zhǒng zi (to sow the seeds of happiness)
Adverb	纯粹胡说 chún cuì hú shuō(absolute nonsense)	Sentence level	汽车喝汽油。qì chē hē qì yóu (Cars drink gasoline.), 女人是水 nǚ rén shì shuǐ (A woman is water.)
		Discourse level	打起黄莺儿，莫叫枝上啼。啼时惊妾梦，不得到辽西。dǎ qǐ huáng yīng ér, mò jiào zhī shàng tí。tí shí jīng qiè mèng, bù dé dào liáo xī 。 (To scare away the nightingales for their noise has my dream in which I went to the west to meet my dear husband.)

Table 1. Categories of metaphors from NLP perspective.

Currently we focus on recognition and understanding of metaphors on phrase and sentence level. The automatic processing methods of metaphors can be summarized as two: First, rule (or logic)-based method, i.e., finding the conflicts between the target and the source, and search their common properties.

Example 7

这个人是一头狮子。zhè gè rén shì yī tóu shī zi (This man is a lion)
— only the target and the source

那个人是老狐狸。nà gè rén shì lǎo hú li (That man is an old fox.)
— only the target and the source

森林里既有勇猛的狮子，也有狡猾的狐狸。sēn lín lǐ jì yǒu yǒng měng de shī zi, yě yǒu jiǎo huá de hú li (In the forest, there are both brave lions and sly foxes.)
--- find out properties of the sources

这个人是勇猛的，那个人是狡猾的。zhè gè rén shì yǒng měng de, nà gè rén shì jiǎo huá de (This man is brave, while that man is sly.)

The utterance 河北有个老太太吃土块。hé běi yǒu gè lǎo tài tài chī tǔ kuài (An old lady in Hebei eats clay.) is not in conformity with common sense, but it is not a metaphor; whereas 男人都是动物。nán rén dōu shì dòng wù (All men are animals.) is logical but it may be a metaphor in certain context and may not be in another context.

Second, empirical (statistical) method i.e., providing machine with a large number of samples and training a model. Yu Shiwen presided over the national 973 project "Database for text content understanding" (2004-2009), which includes a subtask named "Analysis of Metaphorical Expressions and Their Pointed Contents in Chinese Texts". In this project, various machine learning methods have been applied to do semantic analyses from the token level. Among them, Wang Zhimin completed her doctoral thesis "Chinese Noun Phrase Metaphor Recognition" in 2006. Jia Yuxiang studied verb metaphor recognition and "X is Y" type metaphor understanding and generation. Qu Weiguang presided over the National Natural Science Fund Project "Research on Key Technologies in Chinese Metaphor Understanding" (2008-2010).

From a statistical point of view, metaphor recognition can be seen as a problem to compute the conditional probability $p(m|c)$ to decide whether 海洋 is a metaphor in context c. The reversed order of two variants m and c will not change the value of unified probability of $p(m|c)$ and $p(c|m)$, while the relation between unified probability and conditional probability can be written as:

$$p(c)p(m \mid c) = p(m)p(c \mid m) \qquad (1)$$

Then,

$$p(m \mid c) = p(m)p(c \mid m) / p(c) \qquad (2)$$

Given c，$p(c)$ is a constant. Then,

$$p(m \mid c) \propto p(m)p(c \mid m) \qquad (3)$$

Given a threshold δ , if $p(m)p(c \mid m) > \delta$, then we can deem this 海洋 is a metaphor.

Then the problem becomes how to compute $p(m)p(c \mid m)$. We can compute it based on large-scale annotated corpus and get

$$p(m) = N_m / N \qquad (4)$$

N_m — the times of 海洋 as a metaphor in the corpus;

N — the total times of 海洋 in the corpus.

Then we simplify 海洋 and its context c into: W_{-k} … W_{-1} 海洋 W_1 … W_i, where W_{-k}, …, W_{-1}, W_1,…, W_i represent the n-gram of 海洋 and its syntactic and semantic attributes respectively.

$$p(c \mid m) = p(W_{-k} \mid m) \cdots p(W_{-1} \mid m) p(W_1 \mid m) \cdots p(W_i \mid m) \qquad (5)$$

$$p(W_s \mid m) = N(W_s) / N_w, \quad (s = -k, \cdots, -1, 1, \cdots, i) \qquad (6)$$

$N(W_s)$ stands for the times of co-occurrence of 海洋 as a metaphor and word W with designated attributes at position. Here an important hypothesis of independence is: words at different position s is not correlated with the word 海洋.

Last, we will discuss semantic computing on the pragmatic perspective, which is more or less unique of Chinese language. First, the change of construction in Chinese will affect the meaning of a sentence even though the words themselves are not changed. The emphasized meaning of the construction is not equal to the combination of the underlying meaning from each element in the construction. The meaning reflects the distribution of quantity of entities and the relative locations among entities. Although the underlying syntactic relationship among the main verb, the agent and the object(s) still exists, such syntactic relationship is only secondary. As in the sentence 这张床可以睡三个人。zhè zhāng chuáng kě yǐ shuì sān gè rén (This bed can sleep three people.) is different in meaning from the sentence 三个人可以睡这张床。(Three people can sleep on this bed.). Second, the semantic direction of the complement in verb-complement constructions and the adverbial phrase in verb-adverbial constructions also change the semantic roles of each constituent. For instance, （文章）写完了。（ wén zhāng ） xiě wán le ((The article) is completed.) or （老师）写累了。（ lǎo shī ） xiě lèi le ((The teacher) is tired for writing.) or 香喷喷地炸了一盘花生米。xiāng pēn pēn dì zhà le yī pán huā shēng mǐ(aromatically fried a plate of peanuts). Here the ontology cannot provide enough information to reflect the process and result of change in semantic roles. Thus the Generalized Valence Mode (GVM) is proposed to describe not only participants of the action, but also the change of participants' states. Third, our ultimate goal will be to achieve "semantic harmony". For instance, in both English and Chinese we can say 拔出来 bá chū lái (pull out) or 插进去 chā jìn qù (thrust into), but we never say 插出来 (thrust out) or 拔进去 (pull into). It is alright to say 那个大苹果他都吃了。nà gè dà pín guǒ tā dōu chī le (That big apple he eats it all.) , but it is awkward to say 那颗小核桃他都吃了。nà kē xiǎo hé táo tā dōu chī le (That small chestnut he eats it all.). In fact we can say 那颗小核桃松鼠都吃了。nà kē xiǎo hé táo sōng shǔ dōu chī le (That small chestnut the squirrel eats it all.).

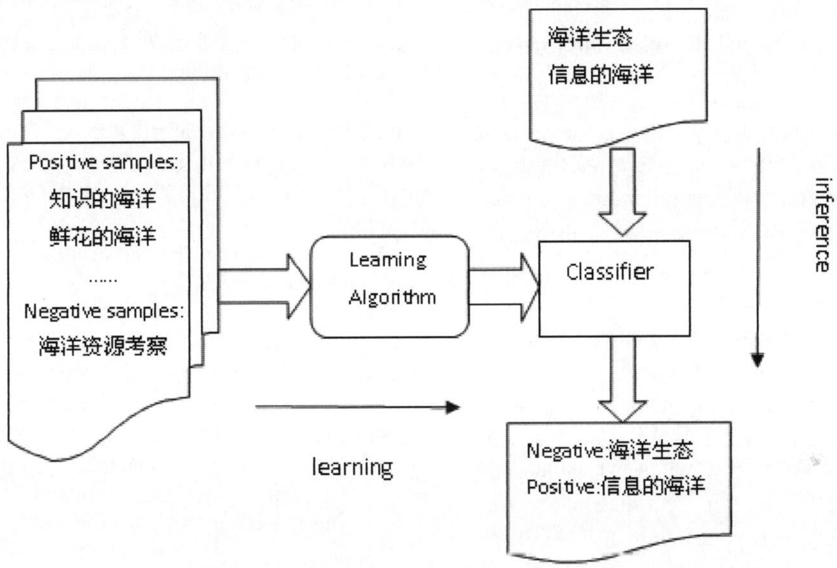

Figure 2. Empirical (statistical) method of metaphor processing.

Professor Lu Jianming (2010) remarked on the realization of semantic harmony. The principle of semantic constraint of words essentially requires that the words in sentences should be harmonic in terms of meaning. Analysis of ill-formed sentences and automatic language generation will benefit from the research in semantic harmony. Semantic computing on the pragmatic level has unique characteristics with respect to Chinese language. The solution of these problems poses a great challenge and will make great contribution to the understanding of the essence and universality of languages.

4 Potential Applications of Semantic Computing – a Case Study on Automatic Metaphor Processing in Search Engines

Nowadays, search engines are developing very rapidly and some of them have won great economic success. In terms of semantic computing, Baidu.com takes the lead and has unveiled the search concept "Box computing" which introduces semantic analysis. The precision and recall of a search engine are always the essential issue that a user is concerned. Therefore we will find the value of semantic computing first in a search engine.

Certainly, if metaphor can be understood properly by a computer, the precision of search engines will be improved. Let's take the phrase 起飞 qǐ fēi(take off) as an example. Literally 起飞 means an aircraft takes off such as in 航班起飞时间 háng bān qǐ fēi shí jiān (the time for the airplane to take off). Sometimes we also use it in phrases like 经济起飞 jīng jì qǐ fēi (economic take-off) or 东方美女歌坛起飞 dōng fāng měi nǚ gē tán qǐ fēi (Oriental beauties take off in the music arena.) to mean metaphorically. If the literal sense and its metaphorical sense can be distinguished successfully, we will find the exact information that we need. Meanwhile, we hope that through this the recall of search engine will also be improved. For example, in Chinese we often use the phrase 祖国的花朵 zǔ guó de huā duǒ (flowers of the country) metaphorically to refer to 儿童 ér tong (children). So web pages describing 祖国的花朵 should also be related to the query word 儿童.

We also observe that the phrases 金融风暴 jīn róng fēng bào (financial storm) and 金融海啸 jīn róng hǎi xiào(financial tsunami) metaphorically refer to 金融危机 jīn róng wēi jī (financial crisis). But when we input the query 金融危机 into a search engine, the results were only web pages with 金融危机 or 金融//危机. But when we use the query 金融风暴 or 金融海啸, there were no web pages with the results 金融危机. We know that the phrase 炒鱿鱼 chǎo yóu yú has literal usage (to fry squids) and metaphorical usage (to fire sb. from his/her job). When we input the phrase into the search engine, we find the result with metaphorical usage takes up 65% while other usage only accounts for 35% (Wang, 2006). Therefore we may conclude that whether metaphor is understood will seriously affect precision and recall.

Another important application lies in machine translation and cross-lingual search. Correct metaphor recognition and understanding is the precondition of correct translation. Machine translation can be a framework to evaluate the performance of metaphor recognition and understanding, and also is a tool to realize cross-lingual search. For instance, a well-known Chinese female volleyball player got a nickname as 铁榔头 tiě láng tou. Shall we translate it literally as "iron hammer" or more metaphorically as "iron fist" in order to let a user of search engine have a better sense of what it actually means? Translation is culture-bound. When we see the sentence 该电影是鸡肋。gāi diàn yǐng shì jī lèi, how should we translate the word 鸡肋 (a chicken's rib) here? And how shall we distinguish its literal meaning with its metaphorical meaning (食之无味弃之可惜。shí zhī wú wèi qì zhī kě xī, tasteless to eat but a waste to cast away) in order to understand better the sentence "The movie is a chicken's rib"?

Therefore when we investigate the feasibility analysis of applications of automatic metaphor recognition, we propose there are still three solutions to the above-mentioned problems:

- To overcome the limitedness of source domain words
- To recognize metaphors in web pages and build metaphor indexes. Offline processing often makes good use of the advantages of a search engine.
- Before realizing query understanding, let users choose metaphorical or literal meaning of the query through human-computer interaction.

5 Language Knowledge Bases as the Foundation of Semantic Computing

As the foundation of semantic computing, language knowledge bases are in great demand. The achievements on language knowledge bases for Chinese-centered multilingual information processing include: Chinese LDC, Comprehensive Language Knowledge Base (CLKB) by ICL at Peking University, HowNet by Zhendong Dong, Chinese Dependency Tree Bank by Harbin Institute of Technology, etc.

Language knowledge base is an indispensable component for NLP system, and its quality and scale determines the failure or success of the system to a great extent. For the past two decades, a number of important language knowledge bases have been built through the effort of people in Institute of Computational Linguistics (ICL) at Peking University. Among them, the Grammatical Knowledge Base of Contemporary Chinese (GKB) (Yu et al., 2000) is the most influential.

Based on GKB, various research projects have been initiated. For instance, a project on the quantitative analysis of "numeral-noun" construction of Chinese was conducted by Wang (2009) to further analyze the attributes of Chinese words. A project aiming at the emotion prediction of entries in CIKB was completed by Wang (2010) to further understand how the compositional elements of a fossilized construct like an idiom function from the token level.

Offset	Synset	Csyncet	Hypernym	Hyponym	Definition	Cdefinition
07632177	teacher instructor	教师 教员 老师 先生 导师 老板 孩子王 臭老九 …	07235322	07086332 07162304 07209465 07243767 07279659 07297622 07341176 07401098 …	a person whose occupation is teaching	以教学为职业的人

Offset	Synset	Csyncet	Hypernym	Hyponym	Definition	Cdefinition
07331418	husband hubby married_ man	丈夫 先生 夫君 夫婿 爱人 老公 郎君 驸马 驸马爷 …	07391044	071094820 719596807 255726073 28008	a married man; a woman's partner in marriage	已婚男子； 婚姻中女性一方的伴侣

Offset	Synset	Csyncet	Hypernym	Hyponym	Definition	Cdefinition
07414666	Mister Mr.	先生 师傅 同志 大哥 老兄 老弟	07391044		a form of address for a man	对男子的一种称呼

Table 2. The Synset of the word 教师 jiào shī and its related Synsets.

Following GKB, language knowledge bases of large scale, high quality and various type (words and texts, syntactic and semantics, multi-lingual) have been built, such as the Chinese Semantic Dictionary (CSD) for Chinese-English machine translation, the Chinese Concept Dictionary (CCD) for cross-language text processing, the multi-level Annotated Corpus of Contemporary Chinese, etc. The projects as a whole won the Science and Technology Progress Award issued by Ministry of Education of China in 2007.

As mentioned in Section 3, the word 病毒 (virus) has two senses in both English and Chinese: one is in biology and the other is in computer science. When we want to do cross-lingual information retrieval, the two senses need to be distinguished. Hence, CCD can serve as a useful tool to complete the task for it organizes semantic knowledge from a different angle. Concepts in CCD are represented by Synsets, i.e. sets of synonyms as in Table 2. For instance, the concept 教师 is in a Synset {教师 教员 老师 先生 导师 老板 孩子王 臭老九 …} and all the concepts form a network to associate the various semantic relations between or among the concepts: hypernym-hyponym, part-whole, antonym, cause and entailment, by which we can retrieve information in either an extensive or a contractive way so as to improve the precision or recall of a search engine. It can also provide support for WSD tasks.

In 2009, the various knowledge bases built by ICL were integrated into the CLKB. The integration of heterogeneous knowledge bases is realized by a resolution of "a pivot of word sense". Three basic and important knowledge bases, GKB, CSD and CCD have been integrated into a unified system which includes language processing module, knowledge retrieval module and knowledge exploration module.

Although there are some fundamental resources on semantic computing, it needs further improvement, updating, integration and specification to form a collective platform to perform more complicated NLP tasks. To further improve the result of semantic computing, innovative projects for new tasks should also be launched, for instance:

- metaphor knowledge base
- ultra-ontology dynamic knowledge base (generalized valence mode)
- the integration of information based on multi-lingual translation

6 Concluding Remarks

Why semantics is so useful in the first place? Linguists and psychologists are interested in the study of word senses to shed light on important aspects of human communication, such as concept formation and language use. Lexicographers need computational aids to analyze in a more compact and extensive way word definitions in dictionaries. Computer scientists need semantics for the purpose of natural language processing and understanding. Therefore, the significance of semantic computing in NLP is obvious and more research needs to be done with this respect.

All in all, we may conclude that the methods of semantic computing can be summarized as the following:

- The research of applicable language model
- The research of effective algorithms
- To build language knowledge bases as its foundation

Semantic computing is a long-term research subject. We hope more progress can be made if a clearer view can be provided for the direction of its development and the pavement for future research can be constructed more solidly with more work done.

Acknowledgements

Our work is based on the long-term accumulation of the language resources that have been built by the colleagues of ICL and it is their contributions that make our achievement possible today. Parts of the content in this paper were presented by Shiwen Yu on the conferences in Hangzhou (International Workshop on Connected Multimedia 2009) and Suzhou (the 11th Chinese Lexical Semantics Workshop 2010), and many thanks should be given to those who offered valuable thoughts and advice. The authors also want to extend their gratitude toward CIPS-Sighan for this valuable opportunity to demonstrate our viewpoints and work.

References

Anderson, J. R. 1989. A Theory of the Origins of Human Knowledge. *Artificial Intelligence*. 40(1-3): 313-351.

Carreras, X. and Marques L. 2004. Introduction to the CoNLL-2004 Shared Task: Semantic Role Labeling. *Proceedings of the CoNLL 2004:* 89-97.

Dagan, I. et al. 1993. Contextual Word Similarity and Estimation from Sparse Data. In *Proceedings of the 31st Annual Meeting on the Association for Computational Linguistics (ACL):*164-171

Fillmore, C. J.. 1976. Frame Semantics and the Nature of Language. In *Annals of the New York Academy of Sciences: Conference on the Origin and Development of Language and Speech*:20-32

Gale, William A., Kenneth W. Church, and David Yarowsky. 1993. A Method for Disambiguation Word Senses in a Large Corpus. *Computers and the Humanities*. 26(5-6): 415-439

Gildea, Denial and Denial Jurafsky. 2002. Automatic Labeling of Semantic Roles. *Computational Linguistics,* 28(3): 245-288.

Hasida, K. 2007. Semantic Authoring and Semantic Computing. Sakurai, A. et al. (Eds.): JSAI 2003/2004, LNAI 3609, 137–149.

Ide, Nancy and Jean Véronis. 1998. Introduction to the Special Issue on Word Sense Disambiguation: The State of the Art, *Computational Linguistics*, 24(1) : 2-40.

Jin, Peng, Wu Yunfang, Yu Shiwen. SemEval-2007 Task 05: Multilingual Chinese-English Lexical Sample. In *Proceedings of SemEval-2007*: 19-23.

Johansson, Richard and Pierre Nugues. 2008. Dependency-based Syntactic-semantic Analysis with PropBank and NomBank. In *Proceedings of the Twelfth Conference on Computational Natural Language Learning:* 183-187.

Lee, Lillian. Similarity-Based Approaches to Natural Language Processing. Ph.D. thesis. Harvard University.

Lesk, Michal. 1986. Automatic Sense Disambiguation: How to Tell a Pine from an Ice Cream Cone. In *Proceedings of the 5th Annual International Conference on Systems Documentation:* 24-26.

Li, Sujian, Zhang Jian, Huang Xiong and Bai Shuo. 2002. Semantic Computation in Chinese Question-Answering System, *Journal of Computer Science and Technology,* 17(6) : 993-999.

Lu, Jianming. 2010. Foundations of Rhetoric -- The Law of Semantic Harmony. *Rhetoric Learning,* 2010(1): 13-20.

Qu, Weiguang, Sui Zhifang, et al. 2007. A Collocation-based WSD Model: RFR-SUM. In *Proceedings of the 20th International Conference on Industrial, Engineering, and Other Applications of Applied Intelligent Systems*:23-32.

Schutze, Hinrich. 1998. Automatic Word Sense Discrimination. *Computational Linguistics*, 24(1):97-124.

Resnik, Philip. 1999. Semantic Similarity in a Taxonomy: An Information-Based Measure and its Application to Problems of Ambiguity in Natural Language, *Journal of Artificial Intelligence Research 11*: 95-130.

Wang, Lei and Yu Shiwen. Forthcoming 2010. Construction of Chinese Idiom Knowledge Base and Its Applications. In *Proceedings of Coling 2010 Multi-word Expressions Workshop*.

Wang, Meng et al. 2009. Quantitative Research on Grammatical Characteristics of Noun in Contemporary Chinese. *Journal of Chinese Information Processing*, 22(5): 22-29.

Wang, Zhiming. 2006. Recent Developments in Computational Approach to Metaphor Research. *Journal of Chinese Information Processing*, 20(4): 16-24.

Xue, Nianwen and Martha Palmer. 2005. Automatic Semantic Role Labeling for Chinese Verbs. In *Proceedings of the 19th International Joint Conference on Artificial Intelligence:* 1160-1165

Yu, Shiwen et al.. 2003. *Introduction to Grammatical Knowledge Base of Contemporary Chinese* (Second Edition) (in Chinese), Tsinghua University Press, Beijing, China.

Semantic class induction and its application for a Chinese voice search system

Yali Li
ThinkIT laboratory, Institute of Acoustics, Chinese Academy of Sciences
liyali@hccl.ioa.ac.cn

Weiqun Xu
ThinkIT laboratory, Institute of Acoustics, Chinese Academy of Sciences
xuweiqun@hccl.ioa.ac.cn

Yonghong Yan
ThinkIT laboratory, Institute of Acoustics, Chinese Academy of Sciences
yyan@hccl.ioa.ac.cn

Abstract

In this paper, we propose a novel similarity measure based on co-occurrence probabilities for inducing semantic classes. Clustering with the new similarity measure outperformed that with the widely used distance measure based on Kullback-Leibler divergence in precision, recall and F1 evaluation. We then use the induced semantic classes and structures by the new similarity measure to generate in-domain data. At last, we use the generated data to do language model adaptation and improve the result of character recognition from 85.2% to 91%.

1 Introduction

Voice search (e.g. Wang et al., 2008) has recently become one of the major foci in spoken dialogue system research and development. In main stream large vocabulary ASR engines, statistical language models (n-grams in particular), usually trained with plenty of data, are widely used and proved very effective. But for a voice search system, we have to deal with the case where there is no or very little relevant data for language modeling. One of the conventional solutions to this problem is to collect and use some human-human or Wizard-of-Oz (WOZ) dialogue data. Once the initial system is up running, the performance can be further improved with human-computer data in a system-in-the-loop style. Another practical approach is to handcraft some grammar rules and generate some artificial data. But writing grammars manually is tedious and time-consuming and requires some linguistic expertise.

In this paper, we introduced a new similarity measure to induce semantic classes and structures. We then generated a large number of data using the induced semantic classes and structures to make language model adaptation. At the end, we give the conclusion and implied the future work.

2 Semantic Class Induction

The studies on semantic class induction in spoken language (or spoken language acquisition in general) have received some attention since the middle 90's. One of the earlier works is carried out by Gorin (1995), who employed an information -theoretic connectionist network embedded in a feedback control system to acquire spoken language. Later on Arai et al. (1999) further studied how to acquire grammar fragments in fluent speech through clustering similar phrases using Kullback-Leibler distance. Meng and Siu (2002) proposed to semi-automatically induce language structures from unannotated corpora for spoken language understanding, mainly using Kullback-Liebler divergence and mutual information. Pargellis et al. (2004) used similar measures (plus three others) to induce semantic classes for comparing domain concept independence and porting concepts across domains. Potamianos (2005, 2006, 2007) and colleagues conducted a series of studies to further improve semantic class induction, including combining wide and narrow context similarity measures, and adopting a soft-clustering algorithm (via a probabilistic class-membership function).

2.1 Clustering

In general, words and phrases which appear in similar context usually share similar semantics. E.g., 清华大学(Tsinghua University) and 北京大学(Peking University) in the following two utterances (literal translations are given in brackets) are both names of place or organisation.

请 找 **清华大学** 附近 的 银行。
Please/look for/Tsinghua University/near//bank
(Please look for banks near Tsinghua University.)

请 找 **北京大学** 附近 的 体育馆。
Please/look for/Peking University/nearby//gym
(Please look for gyms near Peking University.)

To automatically discover that the above two words have similar semantics from unannotated corpus, we try unsupervised clustering based on some similarity measures to induce semantic classes. Further details about similarity measures are given in section 2.2.

Before clustering, the utterances are segmented into phrases using a simple maximum matching against a lexicon. Clustering are conducted on phrases, which may be of a single word.

2.2 Similarity Measures

For lexical distributional similarity, several measures have been proposed and adopted, e.g., Meng and Siu (2002), Lin(1998), Dagan et al. (1999), Weeds et al. (2004).

We use two kinds of similarity measures in the experiments. One is similarity measure based on distance, and the other is a new similarity measure directly using the co-occurrence probabilities.

2.3 Distance based similarity measures

The relative entropy between two probability mass functions $p(x)$ and $q(x)$ is defined by (Cover and Thomas, 2006) as:

$$D(p \| q) = \sum_{x \in X} p(x) \log \frac{p(x)}{q(x)} = E_p \log \frac{p(x)}{q(x)} \quad (1)$$

The relative entropy, as an asymmetric distance between two distributions, measures the inefficiency of assuming that the distribution is q when the true distribution is p.

It is commonly used as a statistical distance and can be symmetry as follows:

$$div(p,q) = D(p \| q) + D(q \| p) \quad (2)$$

For two words in a similar context, e.g., in the sequence $\{\ldots, w_{-1}, w, w_1, \ldots\}$, where w can be word a or b, the right bigram $D_1(a^R \| b^R)$ and $D_1(b^R \| a^R)$ are defined as:

$$D_1(a^R \| b^R) = \sum_{w_1 \in W} p(w_1 | a) \log \frac{p(w_1 | a)}{p(w_1 | b)} \quad (3)$$

and

$$D_1(b^R \| a^R) = \sum_{w_1 \in W} p(w_1 | b) \log \frac{p(w_1 | b)}{p(w_1 | a)} \quad (4)$$

where W is the set of words or phrases.

And the symmetric divergence is

$$div_1(a^R, b^R) = D_1(a^R \| b^R) + D_1(b^R \| a^R) \quad (5)$$

The left bigram symmetric divergence can be similarly defined.

Using both left and right symmetric divergences, the distance between a and b is

$$d_1(a,b) = div_1(a^L, b^L) + div_1(a^R, b^R) \quad (6)$$

So the KL distance becomes:

$$\begin{aligned} KL(a,b) &= div(a^L, b^L) + div(a^R, b^R) \\ &= \sum_{w_{-1} \in W} p(w_{-1} | a) \log \frac{p(w_{-1} | a)}{p(w_{-1} | b)} \\ &+ \sum_{w_{-1} \in W} p(w_{-1} | b) \log \frac{p(w_{-1} | b)}{p(w_{-1} | a)} \quad (7) \\ &+ \sum_{w_1 \in W} p(w_1 | a) \log \frac{p(w_1 | a)}{p(w_1 | b)} \\ &+ \sum_{w_1 \in W} p(w_1 | b) \log \frac{p(w_1 | b)}{p(w_1 | a)} \end{aligned}$$

This is the widely used distance measure for lexical semantic similarity, e.g., Dagan et al. (1999); Meng and Siu (2002); Pargellis et al (2004). We can also see the IR distance and L1 distance below:

$$IR(a,b) = \sum_{w_{-1} \in W} p(w_{-1} \mid a) \log \frac{2p(w_{-1} \mid a)}{p(w_{-1} \mid a) + p(w_{-1} \mid b)} + \sum_{w_{-1} \in W} p(w_{-1} \mid b) \log \frac{2p(w_{-1} \mid b)}{p(w_{-1} \mid a) + p(w_{-1} \mid b)} + \sum_{w_1 \in W} p(w_1 \mid a) \log \frac{2p(w_1 \mid a)}{p(w_1 \mid a) + p(w_1 \mid b)} + \sum_{w_1 \in W} p(w_1 \mid b) \log \frac{2p(w_1 \mid b)}{p(w_1 \mid a) + p(w_1 \mid b)} \quad (8)$$

We can see from the IR metric that it is similar to the KL distance. Manhattan-norm (L1) distance :

$$L1(a,b) = \sum_{w_{-1} \in W} | p(w_{-1} \mid a) - p(w_{-1} \mid b) | + \sum_{w_1 \in W} | p(w_1 \mid a) - p(w_1 \mid b) | \quad (9)$$

In Pargellis et al. (2004), the lexical context is further extended from bigrams to trigrams as follows. For the sequence:

$..., w_{-2}, w_{-1}, w, w_1, w_2, ...$

where w can be word a or b, the trigram KL between a and b is:

$$KL_2(a,b) = \sum_{w_{-2}, w_{-2} \in W} p(w_{-2}w_{-1} \mid a) \log \frac{p(w_{-2}w_{-1} \mid a)}{p(w_{-2}w_{-1} \mid b)} + \sum_{w_{-2}, w_{-2} \in W} p(w_{-2}w_{-1} \mid b) \log \frac{p(w_{-2}w_{-1} \mid b)}{pw_{-2}w_{-1} \mid a)} + \sum_{w_1, w_2 \in W} p(w_1w_2 \mid a) \log \frac{p(w_1w_2 \mid a)}{p(w_1w_2 \mid b)} + \sum_{w_1, w_2 \in W} p(w_1w_2 \mid b) \log \frac{p(w_1w_2 \mid b)}{p(w_1w_2 \mid a)} \quad (10)$$

Since more information is taken into account in $KL_2(a,b)$, more constraints are imposed on the similarity measure. This is expected to improve the precision of clustering but may lead to a lower recall.

2.4 Co-occurrence Probability based similarity measures

After a close investigation of the corpus, we came up with an intuitive similarity measure directly based on the co-occurrence probability. The key idea is that the more common neighbouring words or phrases any two words or phrases in question share, the more similar they are to each other. Therefore, for each left or right neighboring word or phrase, we take the lower conditional probability into account.

Thus we have the following similarity measures:

Similarity using the bigram context

$$S_1(a,b) = \sum_{w_{-1} \in W} \min(p(w_{-1} \mid a), p(w_{-1} \mid b)) + \sum_{w_1 \in W} \min(p(w_1 \mid a), p(w_1 \mid b)) \quad (11)$$

Similarity using the trigram context

$$S_2(a,b) = \sum_{w_{-2}, w_{-1} \in W} \min(p(w_{-2}w_{-1} \mid a), p(w_{-2}w_{-1} \mid b)) + \sum_{w_1, w_2 \in W} \min(p(w_1w_2 \mid a), p(w_1w_2 \mid b)) \quad (12)$$

Similarity extending $S_1(a,b)$, taking both left and right contexts into account simultaneously

$$S_3(a,b) = S_1 + \sum_{w_{-1}, w_1 \in W} \min(p(w_{-1}w_1 \mid a), p(w_{-1}w_1 \mid b)) \quad (13)$$

After pairs of words or phrases are clustered above, those pairs with common members are further merged.

2.5 Comparison of measures

The KL distances emphasize on the difference of two probability but the new measure take the probability itself into account. Take the right bigram context the similarity measure for example:

$$KL_R(a,b) = \sum_{w_1 \in W} (p(w_1 \mid a) \log \frac{p(w_1 \mid a)}{p(w_1 \mid b)} + p(w_1 \mid b) \log \frac{p(w_1 \mid b)}{p(w_1 \mid a)}) \quad (14)$$

seeing $P(w_1 \mid a)$ as x and seeing $P(w_1 \mid b)$ as y, the equation changed to:

$$KL_R(x, y) = \sum (x \log \frac{x}{y} + y \log \frac{y}{x}) \quad (15)$$

and $S_R(x,y)$ becomes to:

$$S_R(x, y) = \sum \min(x, y) \quad (16)$$

We can also get the $IR_R(x,y)$ and $L1_R(x,y)$

$$IR_R(x, y) = \sum (x \log \frac{2x}{x+y} + y \log \frac{2y}{x+y}) \quad (17)$$

and $L1_R(x,y) = | x - y |$ (18)

We can see the space distribution in Figure.1.

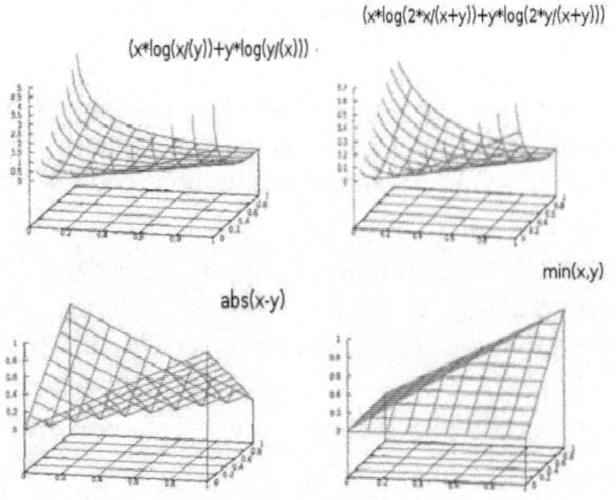

Figure 1. Space distribution of different metrics

$$\begin{aligned} x &= y \\ z &= 0 \end{aligned} \quad (19)$$

$$x = y = z \quad (20)$$

We can see from the four figures (the space distribution of four bigram metrics) that four curve surface are all symmetric. The curve surface of the three distance (KL,IR, L1) all contain the curve of (19), and curve surface of the minimum similarity contains the curve of (20). We say that the KL distances, IR distances and L1 distances all emphasize only on the distances and don't take the probability itself into account.

We take the right context of two pairs (a_1, b_1) and (a_2, b_2) for example. If

$p(w|a_1) = 0.1, \quad p(w_1|a_1) = 0.9$

$p(w|b_1) = 0.1, \quad p(w_2|b_1) = 0.9$

$p(w'|a_2) = 0.9, \quad p(w_3|a_2) = 0.1$

$p(w'|b_2) = 0.9, \quad p(w_4|b_2) = 0.1$

The calculation is shown as follows:

$$\begin{aligned} KL_R(a_1,b_1) &= p(w \mid a_1) \log \frac{p(w \mid a_1)}{p(w \mid b_1)} \\ &+ p(w \mid b_1) \log \frac{p(w \mid b_1)}{p(w \mid a_1)} \\ &= 0.1 * \log \frac{0.1}{0.1} + 0.1 * \log \frac{0.1}{0.1} \\ &= 0 \end{aligned}$$

$$\begin{aligned} KL_R(a_2,b_2) &= p(w' \mid a_2) \log \frac{p(w' \mid a_2)}{p(w' \mid b_2)} \\ &+ p(w' \mid b_2) \log \frac{p(w' \mid b_2)}{p(w' \mid a_2)} \\ &= 0.9 * \log \frac{0.9}{0.9} + 0.9 * \log \frac{0.9}{0.9} \\ &= 0 \end{aligned}$$

$$\begin{aligned} S_R(a_1,b_1) &= \min(p(w|a_1), p(w|b_1)) \\ &= \min(0.1, 0.1) \\ &= 0.1 \end{aligned}$$

$$\begin{aligned} S_R(a_2,b_2) &= \min(p(w'|a_2), p(w'|b_2)) \\ &= \min(0.9, 0.9) \\ &= 0.9 \end{aligned}$$

The KL calculation result of two pairs is the same but the new similarity calculated that (a_2, b_2) is more similar than (a_1, b_1) because they have more similar context probability 0.9.

3 Experiments and Results

3.1 Data

In our experiments, four types of corpora are exploited in different stages and different ways.

- T: A large collection of text corpus is used to train a general n-gram language model.
- H: Some WOZ dialogues were collected before the system is built, using a similar scenario where users talked in Chinese to a service provider (human) via telephone to search for local information, or information about some local points of interest (POI). These dialogues were manually transcribed and used for language model training. This is the best data we could get before the

system is built though it is not the real but near in-domain data.

- C: After the initial system was up running, some real human-computer dialogues were collected and transcribed. These dialogues were split into three sets. One (C1) is used for semantic class and structure induction. One (C2) is used as test data. The other (C3) is reserved.
- A: Domain information (domain entities) is used in conjunction with the induced semantic classes and structures from C1 to generate a large amount of in-domain corpus for language model adaptation. In Table 1, we give some statistics in terms of the number of utterances(no. u) and Chinese characters(no. c) for the above corpora.

corpus	no. u	no. c
T	38, 636	8, 706, 340
H	6, 652	151, 460
C1	658	15, 434
C2	1, 000	19, 284
C3	411	8, 014
A	14, 205	365, 576

Table 1. statistics of different corpus

3.2 Semantic Clustering

We conducted clustering with the above similarity measures on the data set C1.
During the clustering, it is required that all the probabilities involved in calculating similarity be larger than 0. We have no threshold except this constraint.

The outcomes are pairs of phrases.

It is noticed that most of the clustered words and phrases are domain entities.

In our experiments, we merged the induced similar pairs into large clusters. For example, if a is similar to b and b is similar to c, then (a, b, c) are merged into one category. In the end we use the categories to replace those words and phrases in corpus C1 and obtained templates.

Examples of the results are given below.

$ask $toponym $near $wh-word $sevice
[麻烦] $ask $toponym $near 有 $sevice 吗
我 在 $toponym $ask 怎么去 $poi
where:

$ask = 请问 | 问一下| 查询一下 | ...
$toponym = 清华大学 | 知春路 | ...
$sevice = 银行 | 加油站 | 体育馆 |...
$near = 附近 | 周围 | ...
$wh-word = 有没有 | 有什么 | 有哪些 | ...
$poi = 北京饭店 | 国家体育馆 | ...

To evaluate the induction performance, we compare the induced word pairs against manual annotation. We manually annotated each phrase with a tag like $toponym, $poi and so on. If a and b are calculated as a pairs and the annotation is the same, we see that they are correctly induced which is referred to Pangos (2006).

We compute the metrics of precision P, recall R and f-score F_1 as follows:

$$P = \frac{m}{M} \times 100\% \quad (21)$$

where m is the number of correctly induced pairs, and M is the number of induced pairs.

$$R = \frac{n}{N} \times 100\% \quad (22)$$

where n is the number of correctly induced words and phrases, and N is the number of words and phrases in the annotation.

$$F_1 = \frac{2 \times P \times R}{P + R} \times 100\% \quad (23)$$

which is a harmonic mean of P and R.

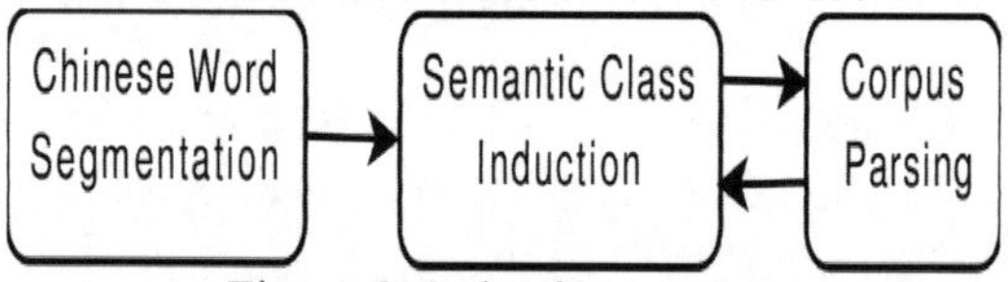

Figure 2. Induction process

The iterate process we adopted is as in Pargellis et al. (2004). In the first iteration, we calculated the similarity and use the largest similarity pairs to generate large classes which can be called semantic generalizer. Then we use these semantic classes to replace the corpus, and obtained new corpus just as the example presented above. Then we duplicate this process for the second iteration and so on.

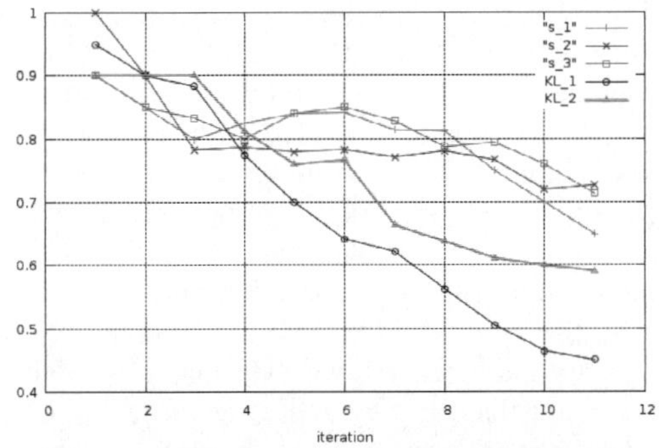

Figure 3. Precision according to iterations induced by KL and S1 similarity measure

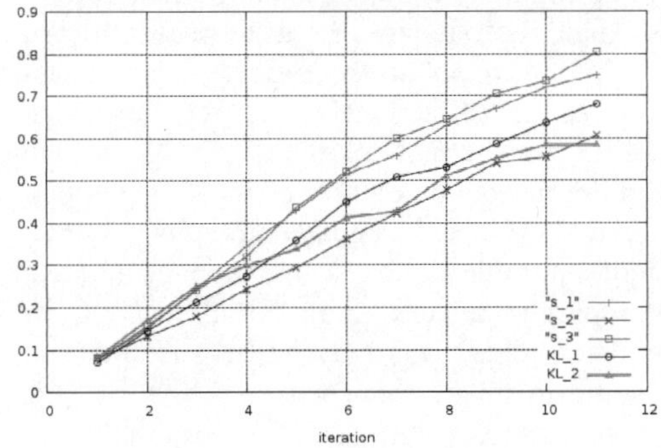

Figure 4. Recall according to iterations induced by KL and S1 similarity measure

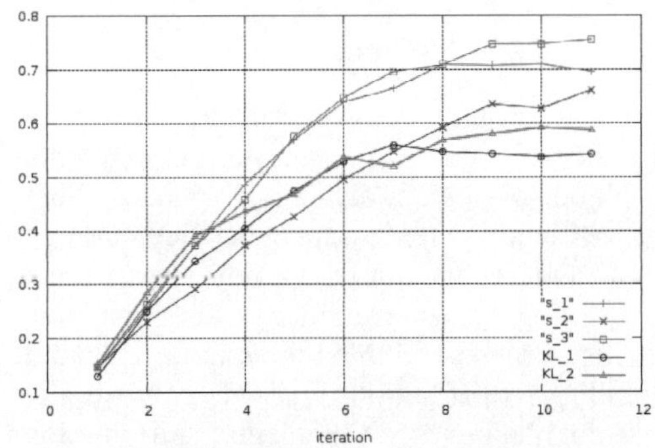

Figure 5. F1 according to iterations induced by KL and S1 similarity measure

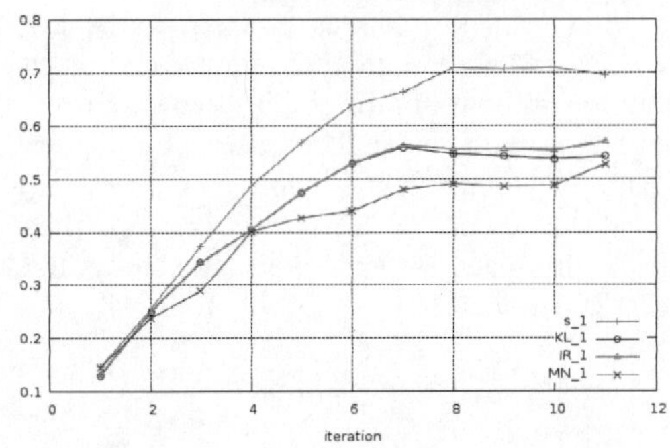

Figure 6. F1 according to iterations induced by all bigram similarity measure

From figures (Figure 3-6), we can see that clustering with our new co-occurrence probability based similarity measures outperforms that with the widely used relative entropy based distance measure consistently for both bigram and trigram contexts. This confirms the effectiveness of our new and simple measure. Regarding the context size, the results from using the bigram context outperforms that from using the trigram context in precision. But recall and F_1 drops a lot. This is due to that larger contexts bring more constraints. The context size effect holds for both types of similarity measures. And the best performance is achieved with the similarity measure S_3. It is based on S_1 and takes both left and right contexts into account at the same time.

3.3 Corpus Generation

Since the number of the domain entities (terminals) we can collect from the dialogues is very limited, we have to expand those variables (non-terminals) in the induced templates with domain information from the application database and relevant web sites. For example, we used all the words and phrases in the toponym cluster, e.g., ``清华大学 | 知春路 | ...", to replace $toponym in the templates above. Then we generated a large collection of artificial data which has a good coverage in both the utterance structures (the way people speak) and the domain entities. This resulted in the generated corpus A in Table 1. In generation we used the semantic classes and structures induced with S_3 and manually corrected some obvious errors. In the generated data, there are 14,205 utterances and 365,576 Chinese characters.:

3.4 Language Model Adaptation

There are some language model adaptation (LMA) work oriented to the dialogue systems e.g. Wang et al(2006), Hakkani-Tür et al.(2006), Bellegarda(2004). So far major effort has been spent on adaptation for large vocabulary speech recognition or transcription tasks. But recently there have been a few studies that are oriented toward dialogue systems, e.g. Wang et al(2006), Hakkani-Tür et al.(2006). In our experiments, three trigram language models were built, each trained separately on the large text collection (T), on the WOZ data (H) and on the artificially generated data (A). These trigram models were then combined through model interpolation as follows: We used the linear interpolation to adapt language model. The formula is shown as follows. T is the out-of-domain data, H is the humane-to-humane dialogues, and A is the corpus generated by grammars

$$P(w_i \mid w_{i-1}w_{i-2}) = \lambda_T P_T(w_i \mid w_{i-1}w_{i-2}) + \lambda_H P_H(w_i \mid w_{i-1}w_{i-2}) + \lambda_A P_A(w_i \mid w_{i-1}w_{i-2}) \quad (24)$$

where $0 < \lambda_T, \lambda_H, \lambda_A < 1$ and $\lambda_T + \lambda_H + \lambda_A = 1$.

The weights were determined empirically on the held-out data (C3 in Table 1}).

All the language models were built with the Stolcke(2002)'s {SRILM} toolkit.

Why we did not use the C corpus directly is that it does't have a good covering on the domain-entities and other users usually say utterances similar to C in structures but different domain entities. So we use the good covering generated data to make LMA.

We evaluated the different language models with both intrinsic and extrinsic metrics. For intrinsic evaluation, we computed the perplexity. For extrinsic evaluation, we ran speech recognition experiments on the test data C2 and calculated the character error rate (CER).

We can see that corpus A is useful to make model adaptation and it is closer to the in-domain data than the human-human data for human-computer dialogues. By using these generated sentences, our domain-specific Chinese speech recognition have a growth from 85.2% to 91.4%.

λ_T, λ_H, λ_A	1, 0, 0	0. 2, 0. 8, 0	0. 2, 0, 0. 8	0. 2, 0. 4, 0. 4
PP	984	95. 4	33. 6	23. 3
CER (%)	32. 3	14. 8	10. 7	9. 0

Table 2. perplexity and character error rate according to model interpolation

The optimized weights (0.2,0.4,0.4) is obtained from the develop sets C3. From Table 2, we can see that language models built using additional dialogue related data, either human-human/WOZ dialogues or data generated from human-computer dialogues, shows significant improvement in both perplexity and speech recognition performance over the one built with the general text data only. For the two dialogue related data, the generated data is better than the WOZ data or closer to the test data, since perplexity further drops from 103.5 to 38.1 and CER drops from 14.8 to 10.7. This confirms our conjecture that human-human WOZ dialogue data is near in-domain and not very proper for human-computer dialogues. Therefore, to effectively improve language modeling for human-computer dialogues, we need more in-domain data, even if it is generated or artificial. The best language model is obtained through interpolation of both language models from dialogue related data with the one from general text data. This may be because there is still some mismatch between data sets C1 (for induction and generation) and C2 (for test).

And some of the missing bits in C1 appeared in the WOZ data (corpus A).

4 Related Works

The most relevant work to ours is done by Wang et al. (2006), who generated in-domain data through out-of-domain data transformation. First some artificial sentences are generated through parsing and reconstructing out-of-domain data and the illegal ones are filtered out. Then the synthetic corpus is sampled to achieve a desired probability distribution, based on either simulated dialogues or semantic information extracted from development data. But we used a different approach in producing more in-domain data. First semantic classes and structures are induced from limited human-computer dialogues. Then large amount of artificial in-domain corpus is generated with the induced semantic classes and patterns augmented with domain entities.

The main difference between the two works lies in how the data is generated and how the generated data helped.

5 Conclusions and Future Work

In this paper, we described our work on generating in-domain corpus using the auto-induced semantic classes and structures for language model adaptation in a Chinese voice search dialogue system. In inducing semantic classes we proposed a novel co-occurrence probability based similarity measure. Our experiments show that the simple co-occurrence probability based similarity measure is effective for semantic clustering which is used in our experiment. For interpolation based language model adaptation, the data generated using the induced semantic classes and structures enhanced with domain entities helped a lot for human-computer dialogues. Despite that we dealt with the language of Chinese, we believe that that approaches we employed are language independent and can be applied to other languages as well.

In our experiment we noticed that the performance of semantic clustering was affected quite a lot by the noises in the data. For future work, we would like to investigate how to further improve the robustness of semantic clustering in noisy spoken language. The semantic structures induced above are very shallow. We would like to investigate how to find deep semantics and relations in the data.

Acknowledgement

This work is partially supported by The National Science & Technology Pillar Program (2008BAI50B03), National Natural Science Foundation of China (No. 10925419, 90920302, 10874203, 60875014).

References

Arai, K. J. H., Wright, G. Riccardi, and Gorin, A. L. "Grammar fragment acquisition using syntactic and semantic clustering," *Speech Communication*, vol. 27, iss. 1, pp. 43–62, 1999

Bellegarda, J. R. Statistical language model adaptation: review and perspectives, *Speech Communication*, vol. 42, iss. 1, pp. 93–108, 2004

Cover, T. M. and Thomas, J. A., *Elements of Information Theory*. Wiley-Interscience, 2006

Dagan, I., Lee, L. and Pereira, F. C. N. "Similarity-Based Models of Word Cooccurrence Probabilities," *Machine Learning*, 1999

Gorin, A. L. "On automated language acquisition," *Acoustical Society of America Journal*, vol. 97, pp. 3441–3461, 1995

Hakkani-Tür, D. Z., Riccardi, G. and Tur, G. An active approach to spoken language processing, *ACM Transactions on Speech and Language Processing (TSLP)*, vol. 3, iss. 3, pp. 1–31, 2006

Lin, D. "An information-theoretic definition of similarity," in *Proc. ICML '98: Proceedings of the Fifteenth International Conference on Machine Learning*, 1998

Meng, H. M. and Siu, K.-C. "Semiautomatic Acquisition of Semantic Structures for Understanding Domain-Specific Natural Language Queries," *IEEE Trans. Knowl. Data Eng.* 2002

Pargellis, A. N., Fosler-Lussier, E., Fosler-Lussier, Lee, C.-H., Potamianos, A. and Tsai, A. "Auto-induced semantic classes," *Speech Communication*, vol. 43, iss. 3, pp. 183–203, 2004

Pangos, A Combining statistical similarity measures for automatic induction of semantic classes, 2005

Pangos, A., Iosif, E. and Tegos, A. Unsupervised combination of metrics for semantic class induction, *SLT 2006*, 2006

Pangos, A. and Iosif, E., A Soft-Clustering Algorithm for Automatic Induction of Semantic Classes, *interspeech07*, 2007

Stolcke, A. SRILM – an extensible language modeling toolkit, in *Proc. ICSLP*, 2002

Wang, C. Chung, G. and Seneff, S. Automatic induction of language model data for a spoken dialogue system, *Language Resources and Evaluation*, vol. 40, iss. 1, pp. 25–46, 2006

Wang, Y.-Y. and Dong Yu, E. A., An introduction to voice search, *Signal Processing Magazine, IEEE*, vol. 25, iss. 3, pp. 28–38, 2008

Weeds, J., Weir, D. and McCarthy, D. "Characterising measures of lexical distributional similarity," in *Proc. in Proc. COLING '04*, 2004,

Reducing the False Alarm Rate of Chinese Character Error Detection and Correction

Shih-Hung Wu, Yong-Zhi Chen
Chaoyang University of Technology, Taichung Country
shwu@cyut.edu.tw

Ping-che Yang, Tsun Ku
Institute for information industry, Taipei City
maciaclark@iii.org.tw, cujing@iii.org.tw

Chao-Lin Liu
National Chengchi University, Taipei City
chaolin@nccu.edu.tw

Abstract

The main drawback of previous Chinese character error detection systems is the high false alarm rate. To solve this problem, we propose a system that combines a statistic method and template matching to detect Chinese character errors. Error types include pronunciation-related errors and form-related errors. Possible errors of a character can be collected to form a confusion set. Our system automatically generates templates with the help of a dictionary and confusion sets. The templates can be used to detect and correct errors in essays. In this paper, we compare three methods proposed in previous works. The experiment results show that our system can reduce the false alarm significantly and give the best performance on f-score.

1 Introduction

Since many Chinese characters have similar forms and similar or identical pronunciation, improperly used characters in Chinese essays are hard to be detectted. Previous works collected these hard-to-distinguish characters and used them to form confusion sets. Confusion sets are critical for detecting and correcting improperly used Chinese characters. A confusion set of a Chinese character consists of characters with similar pronunciation, similar forms, and similar meaning. Most Chinese character detection systems were built based on confusion sets and a language model. Ren et.al proposed a rule-based method that was also integrated with a language model to detect character errors in Chinese (Ren, Shi, & Zhou, 1994). Chang used confusion sets to represent all possible errors to reduce the amount of computation. A language model was also used to make decisions. The confusion sets were edited manually. Zhang et al. proposed a way to automatically generate confusion sets based on the Wubi input method (Zhang, Zhou, Huang, & Sun, 2000). The basic assumption was that characters with similar input sequences must have similar forms. Therefore, by replacing one code in the input sequence of a certain character, the system could generate characters with similar forms. In the following work, Zhang et al. designed a Chinese character detection system based on the confusion sets (Zhang, Zhou, Huang, & Lu, 2000). Another input method was also used to generate confusion sets. Lin et al. used the Cangjie input method to generate confusion sets (Lin, Huang, & Yu, 2002). The basic assumption was the same. By replacing one code in the input sequence of a certain character, the system could generate characters with similar forms. Since the two input methods have totally different representations of the same character, the confusion set of any given character will be completely different.

In recent years, new systems have been incorporating more NLP technology for Chinese character error detection. Huang et al. proposed that a word segmentation tool can be used to detect character error in Chinese (Huang, Wu, & Chang, 2007). They used a new word detection function in the CKIP word segmentation toolkit to detect error candidates (CKIP, 1999). With the help of a dictionary and confusion set, the system can decide whether a new word is a character error or not. Hung et al. proposed a system that can detect character errors in student essays and then suggest corrections (Hung & Wu, 2008). The system was based on common error templates which were manually edited. The precision of this system is the highest, but the recall remains average. The main drawback of this approach is the cost of editing common error templates. Chen et al. proposed an automatic method for common error template generation (Chen, Wu, Lu, & Ku, 2009). The common errors were collected from a large corpus automatically. The template is a short phrase with one error in it. The assumption is the frequency of a correct phrase must be higher than the frequency of the corresponding template, with one error character. Therefore, a statistical test can be used to decide weather there is a common error or not.

The main drawback of previous systems is the high false alarm rate. The drawback is found by comparing the systems with sentences without errors. As we will show in our experiments, the systems in previous works tent to report more errors in an essay than the real ones, thus, cause false alarms.

In this paper, we will further improve upon the Chinese character checker using a new error model and a simplified common error template generation method. The idea of error model is adopted from the noise channel model, which is used in many natural language processing applications, but never on Chinese character error detection. With the help of error model, we can treat the error detection problem as a kind of translation, where a sentence with errors can be translated into a sentence without errors. The simplified template generation is based on given confusion sets and a lexicon.

The paper is organized as follows. We introduce briefly the methods in previous works in section 2. Section 3 reports the necessary language resources used to build such systems. Our approach is described in section 4. In section 5, we report the experiment settings and results of our system, as well as give the comparison of our system to the three previous systems. Finally, we give the conclusions in the final section.

2 Previous works

In this paper, we compare our method to previous works. Since they are all not open source systems, we will reconstruct the systems proposed by Chang (1995), Lin, Huang, & Yu (2002), and Huang, Wu, & Chang (2007). We cannot compare our system to the system proposed by Zhang, Zhou, Huang, & Sun (2000), since the rule-based system is not available. We describe the systems below.

Chang's system (1995) consists of five steps. First, the system segments the input article into sentences. Second, each character in the sentence is replaced by the characters in the corresponding confusion set. Third, the probability of a sentence is calculated according to a bi-gram language model. Fourth, the probability of the sentences before and after replacement is compared. If the replacement causes a higher probability, then the replacement is treated as a correction of a character error. Finally, the results are outputted. There are 2480 confusion sets used in this system. Each confusion set consists of one to eight characters with similar forms or similar pronunciation. The system uses OCR results to collect characters with similar forms. The average size of the confusion sets was less than two. The language model was built from a 4.7 million character news corpus.

The system proposed by Lin, Huang, & Yu (2002) has two limitations. First, there is only one spelling error in one sentence. Second, the error was caused by the Cangjie input method. The system also has five steps. First, sentences are inputted. Second, a search is made of the characters in a sentence that have similar input sequences. Third, a language model is used to determine whether the replacement improves the probability of the sentence or not. Fourth, the three steps for all input sentences are repeated. Finally, the results are outputted. The confusion sets of this system were constructed from the Cangjie input method. Similarity of characters in a confusion set is ranked according to the similarity of input sequences. The language model was built from a 59 million byte news corpus.

The system by Huang, Wu, & Chang (2007) consists of six steps. First, the input sentences are segmented into words according to the CKIP word segmentation toolkit. Second, each of the characters in the new words is replaced by the characters in the confusion sets. Third, a word after replacement checked in the dictionary. Fourth, a language model is used to assess the replacement. Fifth, the probability of the sentence before and after replacement is compared. Finally, the result with the highest probability is outputted. The confusion set in this system, which also consists of characters with similar forms or similar pronunciation, was edited manually.

Since the test data in the papers were all different test sets, it is improper to compare their results directly, therefore; there was no comparison available in the literature on this problem. To compare these systems with our method, we used a fixed dictionary, independently constructed confusion sets, and a fixed language model to reconstruct the systems. We performed tests on the same test set.

3 Data in Experiments

3.1 Confusion sets

Confusion sets are a collection of sets for each individual Chinese character. A confusion set of a certain character consists of phonologically or logographically similar characters. For example, the confusion set of "辦" might consist of the following characters with the same pronunciation "半伴扮姅拌絆瓣" or with similar forms "辨辧辮辯避僻辣梓辭鋅辟滓辛宰癖莘辜薜薛闢". In this study, we use the confusion sets used by Liu, Tien, Lai, Chuang, & Wu (2009). The similar Cangjie (SC1 and SC2) sets of similar forms, and both the same-sound-same-tone (SSST) and same-sound-different-tone (SSDT) sets for similar pronunciation were used in the experiments. There were 5401 confusion sets for each of the 5401 high frequency characters. The size of each confusion set was one to twenty characters. The characters in each confusion set were ranked according to Google search results.

3.2 Language model

Since there is no large corpus of student essays, we used a news corpus to train the language model. The size of the news corpus is 1.5 GB, which consists of 1,278,787 news articles published between 1998 and 2001. The n-gram language model was adopted to calculate the probability of a sentence $p(S)$. The general n-gram formula is:

$$p(S) = p(w_n \mid w_{n-N+1}^{n-1}) \quad (1)$$

Where N was set to two for bigram and N was set to one for unigram. The Maximum Likelihood Estimation (MLE) was used to train the n-gram model. We adopted the interpolated Kneser-Ney smoothing method as suggested by Chen & Goodman (1996). As following:

$$p_{interpolate}(w \mid w_{i-1}) = \lambda p_{bigram}(w \mid w_{i-1}) + (1-\lambda) p_{unigram}(w) \quad (2)$$

To determine whether a replacement is good or not, our system use the modified perplexity:

$$Perplexity = 2^{-\log(p(S))/N} \quad (3)$$

Where N is the length of a sentence and $p(S)$ is the bigram probability of a sentence after smoothing.

3.3 Dictionary and test set

We used a free online dictionary provided by Taiwan's Ministry of Education, MOE (2007). We filtered out one character words and used the remaining 139,976 words which were more than one character as our lexicon in the following experiments.

The corpus is 5,889 student essays collected from a primary high school. The students were 13 to 15 years old. The essays were checked by teachers manually, and all the errors were identified and corrected. Since our algorithm needed a training set, we divided the essays into two sets to test our method. The statistics is given in Table 1. There are less than two errors in an essay on average. We find that most (about 97%) of characters in the essays were among the 5,401 most common characters, and most errors were characters of similar forms or pronunciation. Therefore, the 5,401 confusion sets constructed according to form and pronunciation were suitable for error detection.

Table 2 shows the error types of errors in students' essays. More than 70% errors are characters with similar pronunciation, 40% errors are characters with similar form, and there are 20% errors are characters with both similar pronunciation and similar form. Only 10% errors are in other types. Therefore, in this study, our system aimed to identify and correct the errors of the two common types.

Table 1. Training set and test set statistics

	# of Essays	Average length of essay	Average # of errors	% of common characters
Training set	5085	403.18	1.76	96.69%
Test set	804	387.08	1.2	97.11%

Table 2. Error type analysis

	Similar form	Similar pronunciation	Both	Other
Training set	41.54%	72.60%	24.24%	10.10%
Test set	40.36%	76.98%	27.66%	10.30%

4 System Architecture

4.1 System flowchart

Figure 1 shows the flowchart of our system. First, the input essays are segmented into words. Second, the words are sent to two different error detection modules. The first one is the template module, which can detect character errors based on the stored templates as in the system proposed by Chen, Wu, Lu, & Ku, (2009). The second module is the new language model module, which treats error detection as a kind of translation. Third, the results of the two modules can be merged to get a better system result. The details will be described in the following subsections.

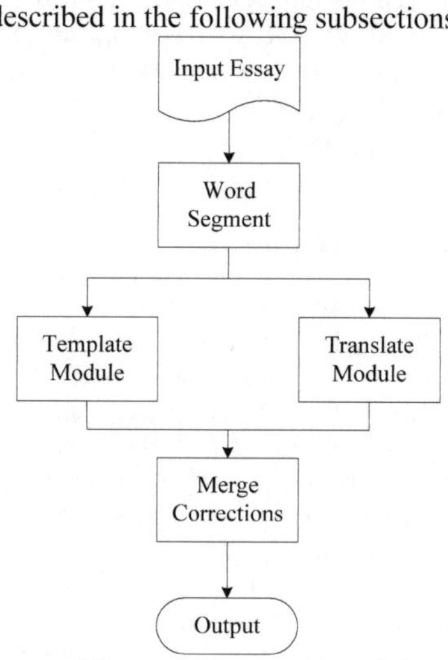

Figure 1. System flowchart

4.2 Word segmentation

The first step in our system uses word segmentation to find possible errors. In this study, we do not use the CKIP word segmentation tool (CKIP, 1999) as Huang, Wu, & Chang (2007) did, since it has a merge algorithm that might merge error charactersto form new words (Ma & Chen, 2003). We use a backward longest first approach to build our system. The lexicon is taken from an online dictionary (MOE, 2007). We consider an input sentence with an error, "它總會變成放大鏡讓我關看世界", as an example. The sentence will be segmented into "它|總會|變成|放大鏡|讓|我|關|看|世界". The sequence of single characters will be our focus. In this case, it is "**讓我關看**". These kinds of sequences will be the output of the first step and will be sent to the following two modules. The error character can be identified and corrected by a "關看"-"觀看" template.

4.3 Template Module

The template module in this study is a simplified version of a module from a previous work (Chen, Wu, Lu, & Ku, 2009), which collects templates from a corpus. The simplified approach replaces one character of each word in a dictionary with one character in the corresponding confusion set. For example, a correct word "辦公" might be written with an error character "辨公" since "辨(bian4)" is in the confusion set of "辦(ban4)"'. This method generates all possible error words with the help of confusion sets. Once the error template "辨公" is matched in an essay, our system can conclude that the character is an error and make a suggestion on correction "辦公" based on the "辨公"-"辦公" template.

4.4 Translate module

To improve the n-gram language model method, we use a statistical machine translation formula (Brown, 1993) as a new way to detect character error. We treat the sentences with/without errors as a kind of translation. Given a sentence *S* that might have character errors in the sentence in the source language, the output sentence $\widetilde{C}$ is the sentence in the target language with the highest probability of different replacements *C*. The replacement of each character is treated as a translation without alignment.

$$\widetilde{C} = \arg\max_{c} p(C \mid S) \qquad (4)$$

From the Bayesian rule and when the fixed value of *p(w)* is ignored, this equation can be rewritten as (5):

$$\widetilde{C} = \arg\max_{c} \frac{p(S \mid C)p(C)}{p(S)}$$

$$\approx \arg\max_{c} p(S \mid C)p(C) \qquad (5)$$

The formula is known as noisy channel model. We call $p(S|C)$ an "error model", that is, the probability which a character can be incorrect. It can be defined as the product of the error probability of each character in the sentence.

$$p(W \mid C_j) = \prod_{i=1}^{n} p(s_i \mid c_{ij}) \qquad (6)$$

where *n* is the length of the sentence *S*, and s_i *i*th character of input sentence *S*. *Cj* is the *j*th replacement and c_{ij}.is the *i*th character at the *j*th replacement. The error model was built from the training set of student essays. Where $p(C)$ is the n-gram language model as was described in section 3.2. Note that the number of replacements is not fixed, since the number of replacements depends on the size of all possible errors in the training set.

For example, consider a segmented sentence with an error: "就|像是|在|告|訢|我們", we will use the error model to evaluate the replacement of each character in the subsequence: "在告訢". Here *p*(再|在) and *p*(訴|訢) are 0.0456902 and 0.025729 respectively, which are estimated according to the training corpus. And in training corpus, no one write the character 告, therefore, there is no any replacement. Therefore, the probability of our error model and the n-gram language model can be shown in the following table. Our system then multiplies the two probabilities and gets the perplexity of each replacement. The replacement "在告訴" gets the lowest perplexity, therefore, it is the output of our system and is both a correct error detection and correction.

Table 3. An example of calculating perplexity according the new error model

	Error Model	LM	multiply	Perplexity
在告訴	0.025728988	1.88E-05	4.83E-07	127.442812
再告訴	0.001175563	1.05E-04	1.24E-07	200.716961
在告訢	1	2.09E-09	2.09E-09	782.669809
再告訢	0.045690212	1.17E-08	5.34E-10	1232.6714

4.5 Merge corrections

Since the two modules detect errors using an independent information source, we can combine the decisions of the two modules to get a higher precision or a higher recall on the detection and correction of errors. We designed two working modes, the Precision Mode (**PM**) and the Detection Mode (**DM**). The output of PM is the intersection of the output of the template module and translation module, while the output of DM is the union of the two modules.

5 Experiment Settings and Results

Since there is no open source system in previous works and the data in use is not available, we reproduced the systems with the same dictionary, the same confusion set, and the same language model. Then we performed a test on the same test set. Since the confusion sets are quite large, to reduce the number of combinations during the experiment, the size must be limited. Since Liu's experiments show that it takes about 3 candidates to find the correct character, we use the top 1 to top 10 similar characters as the candidates only in our experiments. That is, we take 1 to 10 characters from each of the SC1, SC2, SSST, and SSDT sets. Thus, the size of each confusion set is limited to 4 for the top 1 mode and 40 for the top 10 mode.

The evaluation metrics is the same as Chang's (1995). We also define the precision rate, detection rate, and correction rate as follows:

$$\text{Precision} = C / B * 100\% \qquad (7)$$

$$\text{Detection} = C / A * 100\% \qquad (8)$$

$$\text{Correction} = D / A * 100\% \qquad (9)$$

where A is the number of all spelling errors, B is the number of errors detected by be system, C is the number of errors detected correctly by the system, and D is the number of spelling errors that is detected and corrected. Note that some errors can be detected but cannot be corrected. Since the correction is more important in an error detection and correction system, we define the corresponding f-score as:

$$\text{F}-\text{score} = \frac{2 * \text{Precision} * \text{Correction}}{\text{Precision} + \text{Correction}} \quad (10)$$

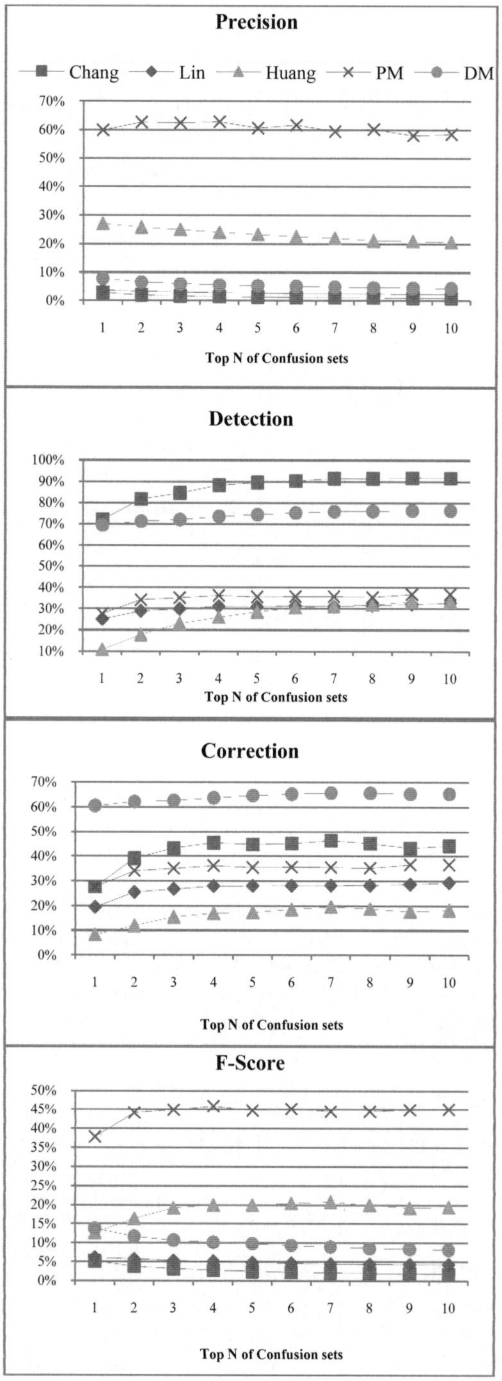

Figure 2. The comparison of different methods on full test set

5.1 Results of our initial system

Table 4 shows the initial results of the template module (TM), the translation module (LMM) and the combined results of the precision mode (PM) and detection mode (DM). We find that the precision mode gets the highest precision and f-score, while the detection mode gets the highest correction rate, as expected. The precision and detection rate improved dramatically. The precision improved from 14.28% to 61.68% for the best setting and to 58.82% for the best f-score setting. The detection rate improved from 58.06% to around 72%. The f-score improved from 22.28% to 43.80%. The result shows that combining two independent methods yield better performance than each single method does.

5.2 Results of our system when more knowledge and enlarged training sets are added

The templates used in the initial system were the simplified automatic generated templates, as described in section 4.3. Since there were many manually edited templates in previous works, we added the 6,701 manually edited templates and the automatically generated templates into our system. The results are shown in Table 5. All the performance increased for both the template module and the translation module. The best f-score increased from 43.80% to 45.03%. We believe that more knowledge will increase the performance of our system.

5.3 Results of methods in previous works

We compared the performance of our method to the methods in previous works. The result is shown in Table 6. Chang's method has the highest detection rate, at 91.79%. Note that the price of this high detection rate is the high false alarm. The corresponding precision is only 0.94%. The precision mode in our method has the highest precision, correction, and f-score. The comparison is shown in Figure 2. The horizontal axis is the size of confusion sets in our experiment. We can find that the performances converge. That is, the size of confusion sets is large enough to detect and correct errors in students' essays.

5.4 Comparison to methods in previous works related to sentences with errors

The numbers in Table 6 are much lower than that in the original paper. The reason is the false alarms in sentences without any errors, since most previous works tested their systems on sentences with errors only. In addition, our test set was built on real essays, and there were only one or two errors in an essay. Most of the sentences contained no errors. The previous methods tend to raise false alarms.

To clarify this point, we designed the last experiment to test the methods on sentences with at least one error. We extracted 949 sentences from our test set. Among them, 883 sentences have one error, 61 sentences have two errors, 2 sentences have three errors, and 3 sentences that have four errors. The result is shown in Table 7. All the methods have better performance. The precision of Chang's method rose from 3% to 43%. The precision of Lin's method rose from 3.5% to 61%. The precision of Huang's method rose from 27% to 84%, while PM's precision rose from 60% to 97% and DM's precision rose from 7% to 62%. The detection mode of our system still has the highest f-score.

The differences of performances in Table 7 and Table 6 show that, systems in previous works tent to have false alarms in sentences without errors.

5.5 Processing time comparison

Processing complexity was not discussed in previous works. Since all the systems require different resources, it is hard to compare the time or space complexity. We list the average time it takes to process an essay for each method on our server as a reference. The processing time is less than 0.5 second for both our method and Huang's method. Lin's method required 3.85 sec and Chang's method required more than 237 seconds.

6 Conclusions

In this paper, we proposed a new Chinese character checker that combines two kinds of technology and compared it to three previous methods. Our system achieved the best F-score performance by reducing the false alarm significantly. An error model adopted from the noisy channel model was proposed to make use of the frequency of common errors that we collected from a training set. A simplified version of automatic template generation was also proposed to provide high precision character error detection. Fine tuning of the system can be done by adding more templates manually.

The experiment results show that the main drawback of previous works is false alarms. Our systems have fewer false alarms. The combination of two independent methods gives the best results on real world data. In the future, we will find a way to combine the independent methods with theoretical foundation.

Acknowledgement

This study is conducted under the "Intelligent Web - enabled Service Research and Development Project" of the Institute for Information Industry which is subsidized by the Ministry of Economy Affairs of the Republic of China.

References

Brown, Peter F., Stephen A. Della Pietra, Vincent J. Della Pietra, and Robert L. Mercer. (1993). The mathematics of statistical machine translation: Parameter estimation. Computational Linguistics 19 (pp. 263-311).

Chang, C.-H. (1995). A New Approach for Automatic Chinese Spelling Correction. In Proceedings of Natural Language Processing Pacific Rim Symposium, (pp. 278-283). Korea.

Chen, S. F., & Goodman, J. (1996). An Empirical Study of Smoothing Techniques for Language Modeling. Proc. of the 34th annual meeting on Association for Computational Linguistics, (pp. 310-318). Santa Cruz, California.

Chen, Y.-Z., Wu, S.-H., Lu, C.-C., & Ku, T. (2009). Chinese Confusion Word Set for Automatic Generation of Spelling Error Detecting Template. The 21th Conference on Computational Linguistics and Speech Processing (Rocling 2009), (pp. 359-372). Taichung.

CKIP. (1999). AutoTag. Academia Sinica.

Huang, C.-M., Wu, M.-C., & Chang, C.-C. (2007). Error Detection and Correction Based on Chinese Phonemic Alphabet in Chinese Text. Proceedings of the Fourth Conference on Modeling Decisions for Artificial Intelligence (MDAI IV), (pp. 463-476).

Hung, T.-H., & Wu, S.-H. (2008). Chinese Essay Error Detection and Suggestion System. Taiwan E-Learning Forum.

Lin, Y.-J., Huang, F.-L., & Yu, M.-S. (2002). A CHINESE SPELLING ERROR CORRECTION SYSTEM. Proceedings of the Seventh Conference on Artificial Intelligence and Applications (TAAI).

Liu, C.-L., Tien, K.-W., Lai, M.-H., Chuang, Y.-H., & Wu, S.-H. (2009). Capturing errors in written Chinese words. Proceedings of the Forty Seventh Annual Meeting of the Association for Computational Linguistics (ACL'09), (pp. 25-28). Singapore.

Liu, C.-L., Tien, K.-W., Lai, M.-H., Chuang, Y.-H., & Wu, S.-H. (2009). Phonological and logographic influences on errors in written Chinese words. Proceedings of the Seventh Workshop on Asian Language Resources (ALR7), the Forty Seventh Annual Meeting of the Association for Computational Linguistics (ACL'09), (pp. 84-91). Singapore.

Ma, W.-Y., & Chen, K.-J. (2003). A Bottom-up Merging Algorithm for Chinese. Proceedings of ACL workshop on Chinese Language Processing, (pp. 31-38).

MOE. (2007). MOE Dictionary new edition. Taiwan: Ministry of Education.

Ren, F., Shi, H., & Zhou, Q. (1994). A hybrid approach to automatic Chinese text checking and error correction. In Proceedings of the ARPA Work shop on Human Language Technology, (pp. 76-81).

Zhang, L., Zhou, M., Huang, C., & Lu, M. (2000). Approach in automatic detection and correction of errors in Chinese text based on feature and learning. Proceedings of the 3rd world congress on Intelligent Control and Automation, (pp. 2744-2748). Hefei.

Zhang, L., Zhou, M., Huang, C., & Sun, M. (2000). Automatic Chinese Text Error Correction Approach Based-on Fast Approximate Chinese Word-Matching Algorithm. Proceedings of the 3rd world congress on Intelligent Control and Automation, (pp. 2739-2743). Hefei.

Table 4. Results of our initial system

	Top	1	2	3	4	5	6	7	8	9	10
TM	P	5.74%	5.63%	5.21%	5.02%	4.90%	4.65%	4.36%	4.12%	4.06%	3.95%
	D	29.23%	41.25%	45.36%	49.17%	52.00%	53.47%	54.94%	55.13%	56.79%	57.09%
	C	26.00%	36.75%	40.08%	43.40%	45.65%	46.33%	46.92%	46.82%	48.00%	48.58%
	F	9.40%	9.76%	9.23%	8.99%	8.85%	8.46%	7.99%	7.58%	7.49%	7.31%
LMM	P	14.28%									
	D	58.06%									
	C	50.63%									
	F	22.28%									
PM	P	55.52%	60.03%	60.60%	61.58%	60.65%	**61.68%**	60.51%	61.19%	58.82%	59.03%
	D	21.60%	29.52%	31.28%	32.74%	34.21%	34.31%	34.31%	33.91%	35.19%	34.79%
	C	21.60%	29.42%	31.18%	32.64%	34.01%	34.11%	34.01%	33.62%	34.89%	34.50%
	F	31.10%	39.49%	41.17%	42.67%	43.58%	43.93%	43.55%	43.40%	**43.80%**	43.55%
DM	P	7.32%	6.15%	5.64%	5.33%	5.11%	4.87%	4.62%	4.42%	4.30%	4.19%
	D	62.75%	65.59%	67.44%	69.40%	70.38%	71.06%	71.94%	72.23%	72.62%	**72.72%**
	C	54.05%	56.69%	58.16%	59.62%	60.60%	60.99%	61.68%	61.77%	61.58%	**61.68%**
	F	12.89%	11.10%	10.28%	9.79%	9.43%	9.02%	8.60%	8.25%	8.04%	7.85%

Table 5. Results of our system after adding more knowledge and enlarged the train set

	Top	1	2	3	4	5	6	7	8	9	10
TM	P	7.31%	6.45%	5.73%	5.41%	5.12%	4.83%	4.51%	4.26%	4.20%	4.08%
	D	37.93%	47.70%	50.15%	53.18%	54.45%	55.62%	56.89%	57.09%	58.75%	59.04%
	C	34.70%	43.21%	44.87%	47.41%	47.70%	48.48%	48.88%	48.78%	49.95%	50.54%
	F	12.08%	11.23%	10.17%	9.70%	9.25%	8.79%	8.26%	7.84%	7.74%	7.55%
LMM	P	14.03%									
	D	63.14%									
	C	55.52%									
	F	22.40%									
PM	P	59.95%	62.72%	62.50%	**62.88%**	60.66%	61.72%	59.51%	60.29%	58.08%	58.54%
	D	27.66%	34.21%	35.19%	36.26%	35.58%	35.77%	35.77%	35.48%	36.85%	36.85%
	C	27.66%	34.11%	35.09%	36.16%	35.48%	35.67%	35.58%	35.28%	36.65%	36.65%
	F	37.85%	44.19%	44.95%	45.92%	44.77%	45.21%	44.53%	44.51%	44.94%	**45.08%**
DM	P	7.76%	6.46%	5.85%	5.51%	5.28%	5.04%	4.78%	4.57%	4.45%	4.33%
	D	69.50%	71.26%	72.04%	73.50%	74.48%	75.26%	75.95%	76.05%	**76.34%**	**76.34%**
	C	60.50%	62.17%	62.65%	63.73%	64.71%	65.29%	65.78%	65.68%	**65.39%**	**65.39%**
	F	13.76%	11.70%	10.70%	10.14%	9.76%	9.36%	8.91%	8.55%	8.33%	8.12%

Table 6. Results of methods in previous works

	Top	1	2	3	4	5	6	7	8	9	10
Chang	P	2.82%	1.95%	1.63%	1.43%	1.25%	1.13%	1.07%	0.98%	0.94%	0.91%
	D	72.04%	81.72%	84.55%	88.27%	89.54%	90.32%	91.50%	91.50%	**91.79%**	91.59%
	C	27.66%	39.10%	43.30%	45.45%	44.77%	45.16%	**46.33%**	45.26%	43.30%	44.28%
	F	5.11%	3.71%	3.14%	2.77%	2.43%	2.21%	2.08%	1.92%	1.83%	1.77%
Lin	P	3.59%	3.19%	2.93%	2.82%	2.60%	2.51%	2.39%	2.35%	2.32%	2.31%
	D	25.12%	28.93%	29.91%	31.18%	30.98%	31.37%	31.18%	31.57%	32.16%	32.74%
	C	19.45%	25.51%	26.78%	27.95%	28.05%	28.15%	28.25%	28.25%	28.73%	29.42%
	F	6.06%	5.67%	5.28%	5.12%	4.76%	4.61%	4.41%	4.34%	4.29%	4.28%
Huang	P	**27.02%**	25.81%	25.02%	24.05%	23.30%	22.54%	22.04%	21.16%	20.98%	20.62%
	D	10.75%	17.79%	23.06%	26.00%	28.54%	30.49%	31.37%	31.86%	33.33%	33.43%
	C	8.30%	12.02%	15.54%	17.00%	17.39%	18.57%	19.64%	18.76%	17.69%	18.27%
	F	12.70%	16.40%	19.17%	19.92%	19.92%	20.36%	**20.77%**	19.89%	19.20%	19.37%

Table 7. Results of methods in previous works on sentences with errors

	Top	1	2	3	4	5	6	7	8	9	10
Chang	P	**42.94%**	37.21%	33.30%	31.18%	29.31%	27.19%	25.98%	24.48%	23.61%	23.14%
	D	72.33%	81.62%	84.55%	88.26%	89.63%	90.51%	91.78%	91.79%	**92.08%**	91.89%
	C	27.95%	39.58%	43.98%	46.23%	45.65%	46.04%	**47.31%**	46.14%	44.28%	45.26%
	F	33.86%	**38.36%**	37.90%	37.24%	35.70%	34.19%	33.54%	31.99%	30.80%	30.62%
Lin	P	**60.59%**	59.33%	57.32%	57.19%	55.10%	55.35%	54.27%	53.88%	53.80%	53.97%
	D	25.70%	29.52%	30.59%	31.86%	31.67%	32.35%	32.25%	32.55%	33.13%	**33.82%**

	C	19.55%	25.80%	27.37%	28.64%	29.03%	29.52%	29.61%	29.52%	30.00%	**30.69%**
	F	29.56%	35.96%	37.05%	38.17%	38.03%	38.50%	38.32%	38.14%	38.52%	**39.13%**
Huang	P	**84.16%**	76.99%	78.51%	76.11%	73.66%	74.07%	73.21%	70.19%	66.23%	66.66%
	D	9.87%	16.03%	20.72%	23.36%	25.70%	27.37%	28.05%	28.54%	**29.91%**	**29.91%**
	C	7.62%	10.85%	14.17%	15.64%	15.83%	16.71%	**17.79%**	17.20%	16.12%	16.61%
	F	13.97%	19.02%	24.01%	25.95%	26.06%	27.27%	**28.62%**	27.63%	25.93%	26.59%
PM	P	96.72%	96.66%	**96.76%**	96.57%	96.51%	96.54%	96.54%	96.23%	96.11%	96.10%
	D	25.90%	31.09%	32.16%	33.04%	32.45%	32.75%	32.75%	32.45%	**33.82%**	33.72%
	C	25.90%	30.98%	32.06%	32.94%	32.36%	32.65%	32.55%	32.26%	**33.63%**	33.53%
	F	40.86%	46.92%	48.16%	49.13%	48.46%	48.80%	48.69%	48.32%	**49.82%**	49.71%
DM	P	**61.83%**	58.45%	56.46%	54.75%	54.21%	53.48%	52.80%	51.53%	51.15%	50.45%
	D	69.20%	70.97%	71.74%	73.22%	74.19%	74.98%	75.66%	75.76%	**76.05%**	**76.05%**
	C	55.62%	57.28%	57.77%	58.84%	59.82%	60.41%	**60.90%**	60.80%	60.51%	60.51%
	F	**58.56%**	57.86%	57.11%	56.72%	56.88%	56.73%	56.56%	55.78%	55.44%	55.03%

Automatic Identification of Chinese Event Descriptive Clause

Liou Chen
Department of Computer Science and technology
Tsinghua University

chouou@foxmail.com

Qiang Zhou
National Laboratory for Information Science and Technology,
Tsinghua University

zq-lxd@mail.tsinghua.edu.cn

Abstract

This paper gives a new definition of Chinese clause called "Event Descriptive Clause" and proposes an automatic method to identify these clauses in Chinese sentence. By analyzing the characteristics of the clause, the recognition task is formulated as a classification of Chinese punctuations. The maximum entropy classifier is trained and two kinds of useful features and their combinations are explored in the task. Meanwhile, a simple rule-based post processing phase is also proposed to improve the recognition performance. Ultimately, we obtain 81.32% F-score on the test set.

1 Introduction

An important task in natural language processing (NLP) is to identify the complete structure of a sentence. However, the ambiguities of the natural language make full parsing difficult to become a practical and effective tool for NLP applications. In order to solve this problem, "partial parsing" is proposed to divide complex sentences into simple units, and then the complex full-parsing task can be simplified to be the analysis of single units and relations among them. Ejerhed(1998) once found that a parser can benefit from automatically identified clause boundaries in discourse, and he showed the partial parsing method called "clause identification" is useful for full parsing.

For example, given a Chinese sentence as follows:

- 沿途，我们见到因为更新伐倒的树木，因为建筑伐倒的树木，都是有用之材；运送树木的货车、拖拉机，南来北往。
- Along the way, we see the trees have been cut down for regeneration, and the trees needed to be cut for building. All of them are useful building material. We also see several freight trucks and tractors going south and north.

The illustrative sentence is a long one that is difficult to parse with a one-step full parsing and will suffer from the error propagation from the previous wrong parsing results.

However, if the sentence is segmented into several independent clauses which can be parsed separately, the shortening of sentence length will make each sub-parsing much easier and the independent of each clause can also prevent the error-propagation. For example, the above sentence can be divided into four parts which are labeled with dashed borders shown in Figure 1. Each segment can be parsed solely as a sub tree and the whole parse tree can be easily built through analyzing the event relationships among them. Moreover, the parse errors occurring in each sub tree have little effect on the whole tree as they are parsed independently in each segment region.

The key issue is how to select a suitable segmentation unit. It is not a trivial question because it must be based on the characteristics of language itself. In English, a clause is a closely related group of words that include both a subject and a verb. The independent sentence is usually ended by punctuation and the dependent one is often introduced by either a subordinating conjunction or a relative pronoun. The structural trait of English language is the basic to define English clause and clause recognition task, like CoNLL-2001 (Erik F et al., 2001).

However in Chinese, there is no obvious conjunction between two clauses, especially the dependent clauses. The separators used often are just punctuations, like commas and periods. Therefore the characteristics of Chinese sentence call for a new clause identification scheme to spit a sentence into clause segments.

To meet this need, we define a new clause unit called "Event Descriptive Clause (EDC)" in the Chinese sentence. It mainly considers the punctuation separators so as to skip the difficulty in identifying different subordination clauses without any obvious separating tags.

```
[D 沿途 (along the way) ]
,
[S 我们 (we)]
[P 见到 (see)]
[C
    [H
        [D 因更新 (for regeneration)]
        [P 伐倒 (cut down)]
        的 (-)
        [H 树木 (trees)]
    ]
    ,
    [H
        [D 因建筑 (for building)]
        [P 伐倒 (cut down)]
        的 (-)
        [H 树木 (trees)]
    ]
]
,
[D 都 (all)]
[P 是 (are)]
[O 有用之材 (useful)]
,
[S
    [P 运送树木 (freight)]
    的 (-)
    [H 货车\拖拉机
    (trucks and tractors)]
    ,
]
[P 南来北往 (going south and north)]
。
```

Figure 1. Parsing result of the example sentence.

According to the definition, we proposed an EDC recognition method based on punctuation classification. Experimental results show that the new definition of Chinese clause identification task is reasonable and our feature set is effective to build a feasible EDC recognition system.

2 EDC Recognition Task

2.1 Definition of Chinese Clause

As we discussed before, '*clause identification*' is a useful step in language processing as it can divide a long complex sentence into several short meaningful and independent segments. Therefore the definition of a clause should satisfy two basic requirements: 'meaningful' and 'independent'. The previous restriction requires each clause to make sense and express a full meaning, and the latter one insures that each clause can be parsed alone.

We firstly give the definition of '*Event*'. An event is expressed by several functional chunks (Zhou and Li, 2009) which are controlled by a certain predicate. The functional chunks are defined as the subject, predicate, object and adverbial parts of a clause. According to different event level, the complex components of a high level event may contain some low level events.

Let us take the second part of Figure 1 as an example. The high level event dominated by the verbal predicate '见到/see' is : "[S 我们/ We] [P 见到/ see] [C 因为更新伐倒的树木，因为建筑伐倒的树木/ the trees have been cut down for regeneration, and the trees needed to be cut for building]". The event is composed of three high level functional chunks.

The complement of above event also contains two nested events controlled by the predicate '伐倒/cut down'. Which are '[D 因为更新(for regeneration)] [P 伐倒(cut down)] 的 [H 树木(trees)]' and '[D 因为建筑(for building)] [P 伐倒(cut down)]的[H 树木(trees)]'. The chunks in these two events are low level ones.

Next, we consider the characteristics of Chinese sentences. Because the punctuations, like commas, semicolons, question marks, etc. are commonly-used obvious independent event separators. We can use them to segment a word sequence as a possible clause in a sentence.

Then based on the overall consideration of the definition of 'Event' and the characteristics of Chinese sentence, we define the Event Descriptive Clause (EDC) as a word sequence separated by punctuations, the sequence should contain either a simple high level event or a complex main event with its nested low level events.

Taking some special conditions into consideration, the adverbials to describe common time or space situations of several events, and the independent components to describe sentence-level parenthesis, can also be regarded as special EDCs though sometimes they do not contain any predicates.

In the Chinese language, many events can share subject and object with the adjacent events so that the subject or object can be omitted. We differentiated them with different tags in our EDC definition schemes.

In summary, three types of EDCs are considered as follows:

(1) E1: an EDC that includes at least one subject in the event it contains.

(2) E2: an EDC that has no subject.

(3) D/T: an EDC acted as sentence-level adverbial or independent composition.

Then the above example sentence can be divided into following four EDCs:

- [D 沿途]，[E1 我们见到因更新伐倒的树木，因建筑伐倒的树木]，[E2 都是有用之材]；[E1 运送树木的货车、拖拉机，南来北往] 。
- [D Along the way], [E1 we see the trees have been cut down for regeneration, and the trees needed to be cut for building]. [E2 All of them is useful building material]. [E1 We also see several freight trucks and tractors going south and north].

2.2 Task Analyses

According to the EDC definition, we define the Chinese clause identification as a task that recognizing all types of EDCs in an input sentence after word segmentation and POS tagging. Like the example in section 2.1, each EDC is recognized and enclosed between brackets. The task consists of two subtasks. One is to recognize suitable EDC boundaries in a sentence. The other is to assign suitable tags for each recognized EDCs. We only focus on the first subtask in the paper. Comparing with CoNLL-2010 task, our task only recognizes the EDCs that contain the highest level events without identifying its internal nested structures.

Since EDC is defined as a word sequence separated by certain punctuations. The identification problem can be regarded as a classification task to classify the punctuations as one of two classes: boundary of an EDC (Free Symbol), or not an EDC boundary (Non-Free Symbol). Then the words sequence between two Free Symbols is an EDC.

By analysis, we found only several types of punctuations could be used as EDC separator commonly, including period, question mark, exclamatory mark, ellipsis, comma, semicolon , colon and brackets. The previous four types of punctuations always appear at the end of a sentence so we simply name them as 'End Symbol'. The following four types are called 'Non-End Symbol' accordingly. The Free-Symbols are recognized from these special punctuations.

3 EDC Recognition System

3.1 Recognition Process

Statistical data from the EDC-annotated corpus provided by CIPS-ParsEval-2009 task (Zhou and Li, 2009) show that 99.87% End Symbols act as the boundaries of EDCs. So we can simply assume them as Free Symbol. But for Non-End Symbols, the linguistic phenomena are complex. If we present a baseline system that regards every Non-End Symbol as a Free Symbol rough, only 61% symbols can be correctly recognized and the remaining 39% are wrongly treated.

To solve this problem, we implement a classifier for Non-End Symbol specially. First of all, we propose several features that might be useful to determine whether a Non-End Symbol is free or not. Then, the performance of each feature is tested on a maximum entropy classifier to find the most effective features and form the final feature set. We will discuss them detailed in the following sections.

3.2 Features

Features are very important in implementing a classifier. We consider two types of features:

As EDC is a word sequence, the word and part of speech (POS) features are the most intuitional information for clause boundary recognition. We call the word level features 'basic features' as Table 1 shows.

However, the structural characteristics of a sentence cannot be completely reflected by words it contains. As the events in an EDC are expressed by functional chunks as section 2.1 presents, the functional chunk (FC) might be effective in recognition. They can provide more syntactic structure features than the word sequences. We consider four types of FC-related features as in Table 2.

Those two major types of features are tested and the final feature set will be selected through experiments

Feature	
Current POS	
Word$_n$/POS$_n$	
Adjacent Non-End Symbols	distance
	current word
	adjacent word
Left verb	
Left preposition	
Adjacent brackets	distance
	adjacent POS

Table 1. Basic Features

Feature	Description
Location	if current punctuation is in a functional chunk, the feature is 1, else is 0
Chunk$_n$	functional tags in different positions of local context windows
Chunk sequence	functional tags between current punctuation and first left Non-End Symbol
Predicate number	the number of predicates between current punctuation and first left Non-End Symbol

Table 2. Extended Features

3.3 Feature Selection Strategy

The features listed in Table 1 and Table 2 are considered to be useful but whether there are actually effective are unknown. Therefore we should select the most useful ones through experiments using certain strategy.

In the paper, we try a greedy strategy. Firstly, each feature is used alone to get its '*contribution*' to the classification system. Then after all features are tested, they are sorted by their contributions. At last, features are added one by one into classifier according to their contribution ranks and then pick out the features that can improve the performance and take out those features that have no effect on performance or even lead to the degradation. Eventually, we get a proper feature set.

As shown in Table 1 and Table 2, Word$_n$/POS$_n$ and Chunk$_n$ tags are used and their positions (n) are important. In this paper, we let the position window change from [0, 0] to [-5, 5] to select the proper position area.

4 Experimental results

All data we use in this paper are provided by CIPS-ParsEval-2009 task (Zhou and Li, 2009). They are automatically extracted from Tsinghua Chinese Treebank/TCT (Zhou et al., 1997), including 14,248 Chinese sentences as training material and 3,751 sentences as test data. We used the sentences annotated with Gold-standard word segmentation and POS tags as the input data for EDC recognition.

4.1 Feature Selection

We use the 14,248 training sentences to judge the contribution of each feature and get final feature set. The training corpus is divided into two parts with the ratio of 80% and 20%. 80% data is used to train classifiers and the remaining 20% for feature selection.

The maximum entropy toolbox[1] is chosen for classification due to its training efficiency and better performance. A functional chunk parser (Yu, 2007) trained on the same CIPS-ParsEval-2009 FC bank (Zhou and Li, 2009) are used to provide extended features. Its F-score is 85%. The parser could only provide the lowest level functional chunks. For example, given the input sentence "运送树木的货车、拖拉机，南来北往/ the freight trucks and tractors going south

[1]http://homepages.inf.ed.ac.uk/lzhang10/maxent_toolkit.html

and north", the output functional chunk sequence are : '[P 运送树木 (freight)] 的 [H 货车、拖拉机 (trucks and tractors)]，[P 南来北往 (going south and north)]'.

The evaluation measure is defined as follows:

$$\text{Accuracy} = \frac{\text{Correctly classified Symbols}}{\text{Total Non-End Symbols}} \quad (a)$$

The performance of each feature is evaluated and ranked as Table 3 shows.

When selecting the proper position area of $Chunk_n$ and $Words_n/POS_n$, the areas change from [0, 0] to [-5, 5] and the performance curves are shown in Figure 2 and Figure 3.

Then the feature in Table 3 is added one by one into classifier and the feature will be moved when it causes performance degradation. Table 4 presents the accuracy changes on 20% development data set.

Form above experimental figures and tables we can get several conclusions:

Figure 2 and Figure 3 display the performance changes under different window sizes (from [0, 0] to [-5, 5]). Then the abscissas of their highest points are chosen as best window sizes. We can find that when the window size is large enough, the performance change will be inconspicuous, which means the information far away from current punctuation has less help in judging whether it is free or not.

Table 3 gives the contribution of each single feature in identifying Non-End Symbols. Comparing with the baseline system proposed in section 3.1, each feature could achieve obvious increase. Therefore our attempt that building a classifier to identify Free Symbols from Non-End Symbols is feasible.

The results in Table 4 show that with features added into classifier the performance raises except for the fifth one (*Left preposition*). Therefore our final feature set will include nine features without the '*Left preposition*'.

At the same time, the top four features are all extended ones and they can achieve 81.83% accuracy while the basic features could only increase the performance less than 1% (0.95% g). This phenomenon indicates that the syntactic information can reflect the structural characteristics of Chinese clauses much better. Therefore we hypothesize that we can use extended features only to build the classifier.

Feature	Accuracy
$Chunk_n$ ($n \in [-4, 4]$)	80.07
Chunk sequence	76.51
Predicate number	75.40
Location	69.57
Left preposition	69.40
$Words_n/POS_n$ ($n \in [-4, 3]$)	68.77
Left verb	68.77
Current POS	66.81
Adjacent Non-End Symbols	66.33
Adjacent brackets	66.19

Table 3. Accuracy and rank of each feature

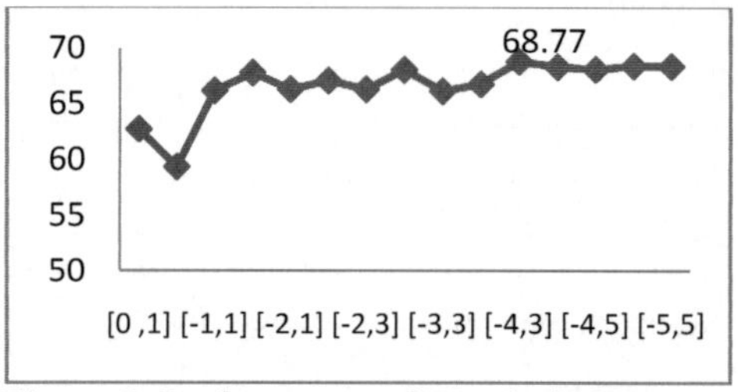

Figure 2. Performance of $Words_n/POS_n$

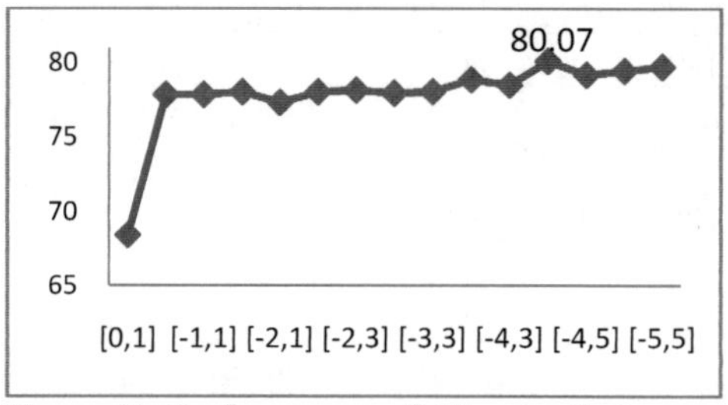

Figure 3. Performance of $Chunk_n$ feature under different context windows

Feature	Accuracy
$Chunk_n$ ($n \in [-4, 4]$)	80.07
(+)Chunk sequence	80.43
(+)Predicates number	80.87
(+)Location	81.83
(+)Left preposition	**81.67**
(+)$Words_n/POS_n$ ($n \in [-4, 3]$)	81.93
(+)Left verb	82.04
(+)Current POS	82.12
(+)Adjacent Non-End Symbols	82.43
(+)Adjacent bracket	82.78

Table 4. Accuracy with adding features on development data set.

4.2 Evaluating System Performance

With the feature set selected in section 4.1, the EDC identification system can be built. The total 14,248 sentences are included to train the classifier for classifying the Non-End Symbol and all test material is used for evaluating the performance of clause recognition.

We consider different modes to evaluate the clause recognition system. One is only using the extended features provided by automatic syntactic parser to validate our guess that the syntactic features are so effective that they will achieve satisfying result without other accessional features (mode_1). The second mode is adding basic word features along with syntactic ones to get the best performance that our current system can obtain (mode_2). Since the chunk features used in this classifier are from the automatic analyses. To clear the influence caused by automatic parsing, we use the lowest level correct chunks to provide syntactic features in the third method. The entirely correct chunks are provided by CIPS-ParsEval-2009 FC bank (Zhou and Li, 2009). As EDC is defined as the description of a high level event, we guess that the highest level chunks might provide more effective information. For example, for the same input sentence "运送树木的货车、拖拉机，南来北往/ the freight trucks and tractors going south and north", its high level chunk sequence will be '[S 运送树木的货车、拖拉机 (freight trucks and tractors)]，[P 南来北往 (going south and north)]'.Then model_4 will use the golden-standard high level chunk features extracted from relevant TCT (Zhou et al., 1997) to clear the upper bound of system performance.

The evaluation measure is defined as follows, and we only use the F-score.

$$\text{Recall} = \frac{\text{Correctly recognized clauses}}{\text{Total correct clauses}} \quad (b)$$

$$\text{Precision} = \frac{\text{Correctly recognized clauses}}{\text{Total recognized clauses}} \quad (c)$$

$$\text{F}-\text{score} = \frac{2\times\text{Precision}\times\text{Recall}}{\text{Precision}+\text{Recall}} \quad (d)$$

Recognition performances of the four modes are shown in Table 5.

In order to deal with some special conditions that our classifier cannot treat well to improve the performance of whole system, a simple rule-based post processing phase is designed which aims at rectifying wrong recognized sentence-level adverbial and independent composition, that is:

When there are only two EDCs are recognized in a sentence and one of which is an adverbial or independent composition, we simply assume that these two EDCs should be merged into a single big EDC.

To estimate the benefit of post-processing, we compare the performances before/after adding post-processing. The contrasts are shown in Table 6.

	mode1	mode2	mode3	mode4
Classifier Accuracy	79.64	80.60	83.46	93.34
System F-score	77.71	78.77	81.29	89.57
Model Size	181 KB	2.2 MB	/	/
Training Time	3.7s	12.6s	/	/

Table 5. Performances on four models

	mode1	mode2	mode3	mode4
F-score (Before)	77.71	78.77	81.29	89.57
F-score (After)	79.43 ⇧ 1.72	81.32 ⇧2.55	84.04 ⇧2.75	90.65 ⇧1.08

Table 6. The Performance changes caused by post-processing

The first line of Table 5 is the accuracy of Non-End Symbol classifier and the second one shows the F-score of whole EDC recognition system. From the two lines we can get this conclusion that the performance of whole system will increase along with the advancement of classifier. We also find that the system performance under automatic lowest level chunk feature does not drop too much comparing with the one under gold-standard chunks (less than 3%), which means existing syntactic parser is good enough to provide the low level chunk features. However, the recognition F-score will increase to nearly 91% when standard high level chunk features are used, which proves that the relationship between high level functional chunks and our defined EDCs are much closer that they are more efficient in recognition. Therefore we can try to build a good high level chunk parser in future. Results of mode_1 and mode_2 show that comparing with the classifier that uses all features, using only syntactic features can save nearly three times of training time and occupy only 1/10 storage space without losing too much reorganization performance. It tells us that when time and storage space is limited we can just use syntactic features.

Table 6 presents the impact of our post-processing. We can find that the processing is effective though it is simple. This result also reflects that current classifier has difficulties to distinguish whether an adverbial or independent composition is at sentence-level or clause-level.

5 Discussions

5.1 EDC Error Types

Because different EDC recognition errors (too long or too short) might cause different problems, we define three error types according to the boundary differences between the recognized EDCs and the gold-standard ones.

(1) '1: N' error: The boundary of a recognized EDC is wider than the gold-standard one.

(2) 'N: 1' error: The boundary of a gold-standard EDC is wider than the recognized one.

(3) 'N: M' error: Several recognized EDCs and the gold-standard ones are crossed on their boundaries.

We do some statistical analysis on all 1584 wrongly recognized EDCs and Table 7 displays the distributional ratios of each error type.

Error type	1:N	N:1	N:M
Ratio (%)	59.2	38.9	1.9

Table 7. Distribution of different EDC recognition errors

5.2 Error Analysis

(1) 1:N Error

When this error happens, it will have no terrible effect on the final whole parse tree if the relations between this wrong recognized EDC and other EDCs remain the same. Like the example sentence in Figure 1, if the second and the third EDCs are wrong recognized as a single one, it will become a little troublesome to parse this EDC as its length is longer than it should be but the tree it builds with other two EDCs will not change. However, if the wrong EDC causes relationship changes, the parse errors might happen on the complete tree. In our system 1: N errors are mainly the following three types:

I. Several sentence-level adverbials are combined.

II. Adjacent EDCs are recognized as a subject or object that they are regarded as a single EDC.

III. Several adverbials at different levels are merged to be one adverbial incorrectly.

For the following sentence:

- [D 四十六亿年来]，[D 在地球表面形成过程中]，[E1 在陆地上，气候呈规律性变化] [E2 在中纬度表现最明显]，[E1 生物由海洋发展到陆地]。
- [D For 4.6 billion years], [D in the process of the formation of the earth's surface], [E1 the climate change regularly on land], [E2 the phenomenon presents clearly in the mid-latitude regions], [E1 organisms develop from ocean to land].

If the first two adverbials are recognized as a single one, error I happens. Then error II occurs when E1 and E2 are merged into one EDC. If the adverbial "在陆地上/on land" of E1 is wrongly recognized as sentence-level and is merged to its adjacent adverbial "在地球表面形成过程中/in the process of the formation of the earth's surface", the third error appears.

The previous two error conditions may not affect the final parser tree and could be regarded as 'tolerable' error. The third situation will change the relationships within EDCs that might affect following parser.

(2) N:1 Error

N: 1 error mainly includes three sub-types.

I. Complex coordinate structure/adverbial clause/attributive clause is wrong separated.

II. Complex subject/object clause is divided.

Conditions II is the reflections of sub-type II in 1: N error. Therefore it is 'tolerable' error. The first errors are caused by complex sentence-like component, like in Figure 1, when the comma in the second EDC is classified as End-Symbol, the error occurs. To solve this problem, one proper method is to consider some features of the relationship between two adjacent possible EDCs. Another way is trying to implement high level chunk parser that can provide sentence-level features instead of current bottom functional chunks.

(3) N:M Error

The proportion of this error is less than 2% that we will not pay much attention to it now.

6 Related works

There have already been some systems for clause identification. Abney (1990) used a clause filter in his CASS parser. The filter could recognize basic clauses and repair difficult cases. Leffa (1998) implemented an algorithm for finding clauses in English and Portuguese texts. He wrote a set of clause identification rules and applied them to a small corpus and achieved a good performance with recall rates above 90%. Orasan (1990) used a hybrid method for clause splitting in the Susanne corpus and obtained F-score of about 85% for this particular task. In the CoNLL-2001 shared task (Erik F et al., 2001), six systems had participated to identify English clauses. They used various machine learning techniques and connectionist methods. On all three parts of the shared task, the boosted decision tree system of Carreras and Marquez (2001) performed best. It obtained an F-score of 78.63.

However, as English and Chinese clauses have different characteristics, the researches on English sometimes ignore punctuation, especially the comma, or they just use a comma as one feature to detect the segmentation without fully using the information of punctuations.

In Chinese, Jin (2004) gave an analysis for the complete usages of the comma. Li (2005) tried to use punctuations to divide long sentence into suitable units to reduce the time consumption in parsing long Chinese sentences. Their processing based on simply rules. Yu (2007) proved that using clause recognition to divide a sentence into independent parts and parse them separately could achieve extremely significant increase on dependency accuracy compared with the deterministic parser which parsed a sentence in sequence. The CIPS-ParsEval-2009 (Zhou and Li, 2009) put forward a task to identify the Chinese EDC and six systems participated. Based on the idea of "HNC" (1998), Wei (2009) used a semantic knowledge corpus to identify EDCs and achieved the performance of F-score 80.84 (open track). Zhou (2009) formulated the task as a sequence labeling problem and applied the structured SVMs model. Their performance was 78.15. Wang (2009) also regarded the task as a sequence labeling problem and considered the CRFs to resolve this problem and got an F-score of 69.08. Chen and Zhou (2009) presented a classification method that identified the boundaries of EDCs using maximum entropy classifier, and the system obtained an F-score of 79.98.

Based on our previous work, some new features are introduced and the performance of each feature is evaluated, our identification system achieved an F-score of 81.32. At the same time, the comparison between two different chunk levels show that high level chunk features are much more powerful that we can devote ourselves to building a good high level parser in future to increase the performance farther.

7 Conclusions

In this paper, we compare the different characteristics between Chinese language and English, and define a new Chinese clause called "Event Descriptive Clause (EDC)". Then on the basis of this definition, we propose an effective method for Chinese EDC identification.

Our work focus on the commas which are usually useful in Chinese clause recognition but always ignored by researchers, and tries different types of features through experiments to clear their different effects in identifying EDC boundaries from commas. At the same time, our statistical model is combined with useful rules to deal with the recognition task better. Finally our automatic EDC recognition system achieved 81.32 of F-score, which is higher than other systems based on the same data set.

Meanwhile, error analyses show that the current identification system has some problems. Therefore we propose several possible methods, expecting to solve these problems and improve the recognition ability of EDC recognition system in future.

Acknowledgements

This work was supported by National Natural Science Foundation of China (No. 60573185, 60873173), National High Technology Research and Development Projects 863 (No. 2007AA01Z173) and Tsinghua-Intel Joint Research Project.

References

Abney Steven, "Rapid Incremental Parsing with Repair". In "Proceedings of the 8th New OED Conference: Electronic Text Research", University of Waterloo, Ontario, 1990.

Carreras, X. and Marquez, L. "Boosting Trees for Clause Splitting". In "Proceedings of CoNLL-2001", Toulouse, France, pp 73-75, 2001.

Chen Liou, Zhou Qiang. "Recognition of Event Descriptive Clause". In "Proceedings of the 1st CIPS-ParsEval", Tsinghua University, Beijing, pp.65-72. 2009.

Ejerhed Eva I., "Finding Clauses in Unrestricted Text by Finitary and Stochastic Methods," In "Proceedings of ANLP '88", pp.219-227, 1998.

Erik F. Tjong Lim Sang and Déjean H. "Introduction to the CoNLL-2001 Shared Task: Clause Identification [A]". In Proc. of CoNLL-2001 [C], Toulouse, France, p53-57, 2001.

Huang Zengyang. "Theory of Hierarchical Network of Concepts". Tsinghua University Press, Beijing, 1998.

Jin Meixun, Mi-Yong Kim, Dongil Kim and Jong-Hyeok Lee. "Segmentation of Chinese Long Sentences Using Commas". Proc. SIGHAN, Barcelona, Spain, pp. 1-8, 2004.

Leffa, Vilson J. "Clause processing in complex sentences, In "Proceedings of LREC'98", Granada, Espanha, 1998.

Li Xing and Chengqing Zong. "A Hierarchical Parsing Approach with Punctuation Processing for Long Complex Chinese Sentences." In Companion Volume to the Proceedings of Conference including Posters/Demos and Tutorial Abstracts, IJCNLP2005, Jeju Island, Korea, pp.9-14, 2005.

Orasan Constantin. "A hybrid method for clause splitting in unrestricted English texts". In "Proceedings of ACIDCA'2000", Monastir, Tunisia, 2000.

Wei Xiangfeng, "Labeling Functional Chunk and Event Sentence Based on the Analysis of Sentence Category". In "Proceedings of the 1st CIPS-ParsEval", Tsinghua University, Beijing, pp.57-64, 2009.

Wang Xi, Wang Jinyong, Liu Chunyang, Wang Qi, and Fu Chunyuan. "CRF-based Chinese Chunking and Event Recognition". In "Proceedings of the 1st CIPS-ParsEval", Tsinghua University, Beijing, pp.53-56. 2009.

Yu Hang. "Automatic Analysis of Chinese Chunks", Graduation thesis of computer science, Tsinghua University，2007.

Yu Kun, Sadao Kurohashi and Hao Liu. "A Three-Step Deterministic Parser for Chinese Dependency Parsing". In "Proceedings of the Human Language Technologies 2007 (HLT2007-NAACL2007)", Rochester, pp.201-204, 2007.

Zhou Junsheng, Yabing Zhang, Xinyu Dai, Jiajun Chen. "Chinese Event Descriptive Clause Splitting with Structured SVMs". In "Proceedings of the 1st CIPS-ParsEval", Tsinghua University, Beijing, pp.73-80, 2009.

Zhou Qiang, Yumei Li. "The Testing Report of CIPS-ParsEval-2009 Workshop". In "Proceedings of the 1st CIPS-ParsEval", Tsinghua University, Beijing, 2009.

Zhou Qiang. "Annotation Scheme for Chinese Treebank". Journal of Chinese Information Processing, pp 18-21, 2004.

Zhou Qiang, Yume Li. "The Design of Chinese Chunk Parsing Task"， The Tenth Chinese National Conference on Computational Linguistics (CNCCL-2009)，Tsinghua University Press, Beijing, pp.130-135, 2009

Zhou Qiang, Wei Zhang, Shiwen Yu, "Chinese Treebank Construction", Journal of Chinese Information Processing, pp42-51, 1997.

Bigram HMM with Context Distribution Clustering for Unsupervised Chinese Part-of-Speech tagging

Lidan Zhang
Department of Computer Science
the University of Hong Kong
Hong Kong
lzhang@cs.hku.hk

Kwok-Ping Chan
Department of Computer Science
the University of Hong Kong
Hong Kong
kpchan@cs.hku.hk

Abstract

This paper presents an unsupervised Chinese Part-of-Speech (POS) tagging model based on the first-order HMM. Unlike the conventional HMM, the number of hidden states is not fixed and will be increased to fit the training data. In favor of sparse distribution, the Dirichlet priors are introduced with variational inference method. To reduce the emission variables, words are represented by their contexts and clustered based on the distributional similarities between contexts. Experiment results show the output state sequence of HMM are highly correlated to the latent annotations of gold POS tags, in context of clustering similarity measures. The other experiments on a real application, unsupervised dependency parsing, reveal that the output sequence can replace the manually annotated tags without loss of accuracies.

1 Introduction

Recently latent variable model has shown great potential in recovering the underlying structures. For example, the task of POS tagging is to recover the appropriate sequence structure given the input word sequence (Goldwater and Griffiths, 2007). One of the most popular example of latent models is Hidden Markov Model (HMM), which has been extensively studied for many years (Rabiner, 1989). The key problem of HMM is how to find an optimal hidden state number and the topology appropriately.

In most cases, the topology of HMM is predefined by exploiting the domain or empirical knowledge. This topology will be fixed during the whole process. Therefore how to select the optimal topology for a certain application or a set of training data is still a problem, because many researches show that varying the size of the state space greatly affects the performance of HMM. Generally there are two ways to adjust the state number: top-down and bottom-up methods. In the bottom-up methods (Brand, 1999), the state number is initialized with a relatively large number. During the training, the states are merged or trimmed and ended with a small set of states. On the other hand, the top-down methods (Siddiqi et al., 2007) start from a small state set and split one or some states until no further improvement can be obtained. The bottom-up approaches require huge computational cost in deciding the states to be merged, which makes it impractical for applications with large state space. In this paper, we focus on the latter approaches.

Another problem in HMM is that EM algorithm might yield local maximum value. Johnson (2007) points out that training HMM with EM gives poor results because it leads to a fairly flat distribution of hidden states when the empirical distribution is highly skewed. A multinomial prior, which favors sparse distribution, is a good choice for natural language tasks. In this paper, we proposed a new procedure for inferring the HMM topology and estimating its parameters simultaneously. Gibbs sampling has been used in infinite HMM (iHMM) (Beal et al., 2001; Fox et al., 2008; Van Gael et al., 2008) for inference. Unfortunately Gibbs sampling is slow and difficult to be converged. In this paper, we proposed the variational Bayesian inference for the adaptive HMM model with Dirichlet prior. It involves a modification to the Baum-Welch algorithm. In each iteration, we replaced only one hidden state with two new states until convergence.

To reduce the number of observation variables, the words are pre-clustered and represented by the exemplar within the same cluster. It is a one-to-many clustering, because the same word play different roles under different contexts. We evaluate the similarity between the distribution of contexts, with the assumption that the context distribution implies syntactic pattern of the given word (Zelling, 1968; Weeds and Weir, 2003). With this clustering, more contextual information can be considered without increasing the model complexity. A relatively simple model is important for unsupervised task in terms of computational burden and data sparseness. This is the reason why we do not increase the order of HMM(Kaji and Kitsuregawa, 2008; Headden et al., 2008).

With unsupervised algorithms, there are two aspects to be evaluated (Van Gael et al., 2009). Fist one is how good the outcome clusters are. We compare the HMM results with the manually POS tags and report the similarity measures based on information theory. On the other hand, we test how good the outputs act as an intermediate results. In many natural language tasks, the inputs are word class, not the actual lexical item, for reason of sparsity. In this paper, we choose the unsupervised dependency parsing as the application to investigate whether our clusters can replace the manual labeled tags or not.

The paper is organized as below: in section 2, we describe the definition of HMM and its variance inference. We present our dynamic HMM in section 3. To overcome the context limitation in the first-order HMM, we present our distributional similarity clustering in section 4. In section 5, we reported the results of the mentioned experiments while section 6 concludes the paper.

2 Terminology

The task of POS tagging is to assign a syntactic category sequence to the input words. Let $\mathcal{S}$ be defined as the set of all possible hidden states, which are expected to be highly correlated to POS tags. Σ represents the set of all words. Therefore the task is to find a sequence of tag sequence $S = s_1...s_n \in \mathcal{S}$ given a sequence of words (i.e. a sentence, $W = w_1...w_n \in \Sigma$). The optimal tags is to maximize the conditional probability $p(S|W)$, which is equal to:

$$\begin{aligned}\max_S p(S|W) &= \max_S p(S)p(W|S)\\ &= \max_S p(W,S)\end{aligned} \tag{1}$$

In this paper,we consider the first-order HMM, where the POS tags are regarded as hidden states and words as observed variables. According to the Markov assumption, the best sequence of tags S for a given sequence of words W is done by maximizing (with $s_0 = 0$) the joint probability:

$$p(W,S) = \prod_{i=1}^{n} p(s_i|s_{i-1})p(w_i|s_i) \tag{2}$$

where w_0 is the special boundary marker of sentences.

2.1 Variational Inference for HMM

Let the HMM be modeled with parameter $\theta = (A, B, \pi)$, where $A = \{a_{ij}\} = \{P(s_t = j|s_{t-1} = i)\}$ is the transition matrix governing the dynamic of the HMM. $B = \{b_t(i)\} = \{P(w_t = i|s_t\})$ is the state emission matrix and $\pi = \{\pi_i\} = \{P(s_1 = i)\}$ assigns the initial probabilities to all hidden states. In favor of sparse distributions, a natural choice is to encode Dirichlet prior into parameters $p(\theta)$. In particular, we have:

$$\begin{aligned}p(A) &= \prod_{i=1}^{N} Dir(\{a_{i1},...,a_{iN}\}\,|u^{(A)})\\ p(B) &= \prod_{i=1}^{N} Dir(\{b_{i1},...,b_{iN}\}\,|u^{(B)})\\ p(\pi) &= Dir(\{\pi_1,...,\pi_N\}\,|u^{(\pi)})\end{aligned} \tag{3}$$

where the Dirichlet distribution of order N with hyperparameter vector u is defined as:

$$Dir(x|u) = \frac{\Gamma(\sum_{i=1}^{N} u_i)}{\prod_{i=1}^{N} \Gamma(u_i)} \prod_{i=1}^{N} x_i^{u_i - 1}. \quad (4)$$

In this paper, we consider the symmetric Dirichlet distribution with a fixed length, i.e. $u = [\sum_{i=1}^{N} u_i/N, ..., \sum_{i=1}^{N} u_i/N]$.

In the Bayesian framework, the model parameters are also regarded as hidden variables. The marginal likelihood can be calculated by summing up all hidden variables. According to the Jensen's inequality, the lower bound of marginal likelihood is defined as:

$$\begin{aligned} \ln p(W) &= \ln \int \sum_S p(\theta)p(W, S|\theta)d\theta \\ &\geq \int \sum_S q(\theta, S) \ln \frac{p(W, S, \theta)}{q(\theta, S)} d\theta \quad (5) \\ &= \mathcal{F} \end{aligned}$$

Generally, Variational Bayesian Inference aims to find a tractable distribution $q(\theta, s)$ that maximizes the lower bound $\mathcal{F}$. To make inference flexible, the posterior distribution can be assumed to be factorized according to the mean-field assumption. We have:

$$p(W, S, \theta) \approx q(S, \theta) = q_\theta(\theta)q_S(S) \quad (6)$$

Then an extension of EM algorithm (called Baum-Welch algorithm) can be used to alternately optimize the q_S and q_θ. The EM process is described as follows:

- **E Step**: Forward-Backward algorithm to find the optimal state sequence $S^{(t+1)} = \arg\max p(S^{(t)}|W, \theta^{(t)})$
- **M Step**: The parameters $\theta^{(t+1)}$ are re-estimated given the optimal state $S^{(t+1)}$

The E and M steps are repeated until a convergence criteria is satisfied. Beal (2003) proved that only need to do minor modifications in M step (in 1) is needed, when Dirichlet prior is introduced.

3 Adaptive Hidden Markov Model

As aforementioned, the key problem of HMM is how to initialize the number of hidden states and select the topology of HMM. In this paper, we use the top-down scheme: starting from a small number of states, only one state is chosen in each step and splitted into two new states. This binary split scheme is described in Figure 1.

Algorithm 1 Outline of our adpative HMM

Initialization: Initialize: $t = 0$, $N^{(t)}$
repeat
  Optimization: Find the optimal parameters for current N^t
  Candidate Generation: Split states and generate candidate HMMs
  Candidate Selection: Select the optimal HMM from the candidates, whose hidden state number is N^{t+1}
until No further improvement can be achieved after splitting

In the following, we will discuss the details of each step one by one.

3.1 Candidate Generation

Let $N^{(t)}$ represent the number of hidden states at timestep t. The problem is how to choose the states for splitting. A straightforward way is to select all states and generate $N^{(t)} + 1$ candidate HMMs, including the original un-splitted one. Obviously the exhaustive search is inefficient especially for large state space. To make the algorithm more efficient, some constraints must be set to narrow the search space.

Intuitively entropy implies uncertainty. So hidden states with large conditional entropies are desirable to be splitted. We can define the conditional entropy of the state sequences given observation W as:

$$H(S|W) = -\sum_S [P(S|W) \log P(S|W)] \quad (8)$$

Our assumption is the state to be splitted must be the states sequence with the highest conditional entropy value. This entropy can be recursively calculated with complexity $O(N^2T)$ (Hernando et al., 2005). Here N is the number of

$$A^{(t+1)} = \{a_{ij}^{(t+1)}\} = \exp[\psi(\omega_{ij}^{(A)}) - \psi(\sum_{j=1}^{N} \omega_{ij}^{(A)})] \;; \quad \omega_{ij}^{(A)} = u_j^{(A)} + \mathbb{E}_{q(s)}[n_{ij}]$$

$$B^{(t+1)} = \{b_{ik}^{(t+1)}\} = \exp[\psi(\omega_{ik}^{(B)}) - \psi(\sum_{k=1}^{T} \omega_{ik}^{(B)})] \;; \quad \omega_{ik}^{(B)} = u_k^{(B)} + \mathbb{E}_{q(s)}[n'_{ik}] \tag{7}$$

$$\pi^{(t+1)} = \{\pi_i^{(t+1)}\} = \exp[\psi(\omega_i^{(\pi)}) - \psi(\sum_{i=1}^{N} \omega_j^{(\pi)})]; \quad \omega_i^{(\pi)} = u_i^{(\pi)} + \mathbb{E}_{q(s)}[n''_i]$$

Figure 1: Parameters update equations in M-step. Here $\mathbb{E}$ is the expectation with respect to the model parameters. And n_{ij} is the expected number of transition from state s_i to state s_j; n'_{ik} is the expected number of times word w_k occurs with state s_i; n''_i is the occurrence of $s_0 = i$

states and T is the length of sequence. Using this entropy constraint, the size of candidate state set is always smaller than the minimal value between N and T.

3.2 Candidate Selection

Given the above candidate set, the parameters of each HMM are to be updated. Note that we just update the parameters related to the split state, whilst keep the others fixed. Suppose the i-th hidden state is replaced by two new states. First the transition matrix is enlarged from $N^{(t)} \times N^{(t)}$ dimension to $(N^{(t)} + 1) \times (N^{(t)} + 1)$ dimension, by inserting one column and row after the i-th column and row. In the process of update, we only change the items in the two (i and $i + 1$) rows and columns. The other elements irrelevant to the split state are not involved in the update procedure. Similarly EM algorithm is used to find the optimal parameters. Note that most of the calculations can be skipped by making use of the forward and backward probability matrix achieved in the previous step. Therefore the convergence is fast.

Given the candidate selection, we can use a modified Baum-Welch algorithm to find optimal states and parameters. Here we use the algorithm in (Siddiqi et al., 2007) with some modifications for the Dirichlet prior. In particular, in E step, we follow their partial Forward-Background algorithm to calculate $\mathbb{E}[n_{ij}]$ and $\mathbb{E}[n'_{ik}]$, if s_i or s_j is candidate state to be splitted. Then in M-step, only rows and columns related to the candidate state are updated according to equation (7). The detailed description is given as appendix.

Finally it is natural to use variational bound of marginal likelihood in equation (5) for model scoring and convergence criterion.

4 Distributional Clustering

To reduce the number of observation variables, the words are clustered before HMM training. Intuitively, the words share the similar contexts have similar syntactic property. The categories of many words are varied in different contexts. In other words, the cluster of a given word is heavily dependent on the context it appears. For example, 发现 can be a noun (meaning: discovery) if it acts as an object, or a verb (meaning: to discover) if it is followed with a noun. Furthermore the introduction of context can overcome the limited context in the first-order HMM.

The underlying hypothesis of clustering based on distributional similarity is that the words occurring in similar contexts behave as similar syntactic roles. In this work, the context of a word is a trigram consist of the word immediately preceding the target and the word immediately following it. The similarity between two words is measured by Pointwise Mutual Information (PMI) between the context pair in which they appear:

$$PMI(w_i, w_j) = \log \frac{P(c_i, c_j)}{P(c_i)P(c_j)} \tag{9}$$

where c_i denotes the context of w_i. $P(c_i, c_j)$ is the co-occurrence probability of c_i and c_j, and

$P(c_i) = \sum_j P(c_i, c_j)$ is the occurrence probability of c_i. In our experiments, the cutoff context count is set to 10, which means the frequency less than the threshold is labeled as the unknown context.

The above distributional similarity can be used as a distance measure. Hence any clustering algorithm can be adopted. In this paper, we use the affinity propagation algorithm (Frey and Dueck, 2007). Its parameter 'dampfact' is set to 0.9, and the other parameters are set as default. After running the clustering algorithm, the contexts are clustered into 1869 clusterings. It is noted that one word might be classified into several clusters , if its contexts are clustered into several clusters.

5 Experiments

As aforementioned, the outputs of our HMM model are evaluated in two ways, clustering metric and parsing performance. The data used in all experiments are the Chinese data set in CoNLL-2007 shared task. The number of tokens in training, development and test sets are 609,060, 49,620 and 73,153 respectively. We use all training data set for training the model, whose maximum length is 242.

The hyper parameters of Dirichlet priors are initialized in a homogeneous way. The initial hidden state is set to 40 in all experiments. After several iterations, the hidden states number converged to 247, which is much larger than the size of the manually defined POS tags. Our expectation is the refinement variables can reveal the deep granularity of the POS tags.

5.1 Clustering Evaluation

In this paper, we use information theoretic based metrics to quantify the information shared by two clusters. The most common information-based clustering metric is the variational of Information (VI)(Meilă, 2007). Given the clustering result C_r and the gold clustering C_g, VI sums up the conditional entropy of one cluster distribution given the other one:

$$\begin{aligned} \mathrm{VI}(C_r, C_g) &= H(C_r) + H(C_g) - 2I(C_r, C_g) \\ &= H(C_r|C_g) + H(C_g|C_r) \end{aligned} \quad (10)$$

where $H(C_r)$ is the entropy associated with the clustering C_r, and mutual information $I(C_r, C_g)$ quantifies the mutual dependence between two clusterings, or say the shared information between two variables. It is easy to see that VI$\in [0, \log(N)]$, where N is the number of data points. However, the standard VI is not normalized, which favors clusterings with a small number of clusters. It can be normalized by dividing by $\log(N)$, because the number of training instances are fixed. However the normalized VI score is misleadingly large, if the N is very large which is the case in our task. In this paper only un-normalized VI scores are reported to show the score ranking.

To standardize the measures to have fixed bounds, (Strehl and Ghosh, 2003) defined the normalized Mutual Information (NMI) as:

$$NMI(C_r, C_g) = \frac{I(C_r, C_g)}{\sqrt{H(C_r)H(C_g)}} \quad (11)$$

NMI takes its lower bound of 0 if no information is shared by two clusters and the upper bound of 1 if two clusterings are identical. The NMI however, still has problems, whose variation is sensitive to the choice of the number of clusters.

Rosenberg and Hirschberg (2007) proposed V-measure to combine two desirable properties of clustering: homogeneity (h) and completeness (c) as follows:

$$\begin{aligned} h &= 1 - H(C_g|C_r)/H(C_g) \\ c &= 1 - H(C_r|C_g)/H(C_r) \\ V &= 2hc/(h + c) \end{aligned} \quad (12)$$

Generally homogeneity and completeness runs in opposite way, whose harmonic mean (i.e. V-measure) is a comprise score, just like F-score for the precision and recall.

Let us first examine the contextual word clustering performance. The VI score between distributional word categories and gold standard is 2.39. The NMI and V-measure score are 0.53 and 0.48, respectively.

The clustering performance of the HMM outputs are reported in Figure 2. The best VI score achieved was 3.9524, while V-measure was 62.09% and NMI reached 0.8051. Previous

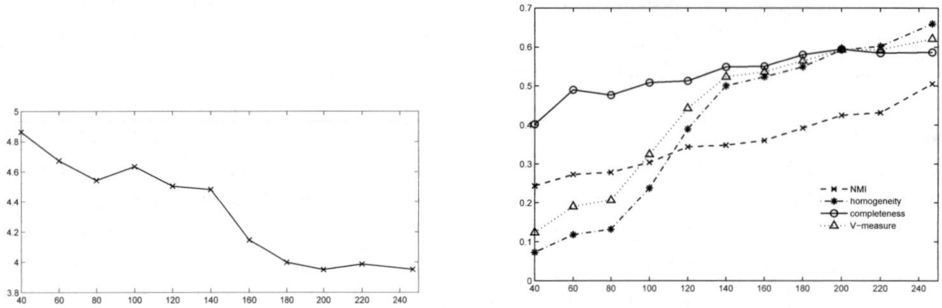

(a) VI score

(b) normalized scores

Figure 2: Clustering evaluation metrics against number of hidden states

work of Chinese tagging focuses on the tagging accuracies, e.g. Wang (Wang and Schuurmans,) and Huang et al. (Huang et al., 2007). To our knowledge, this is the first work to report the distributional clustering similarity measures based on informatics view for Chinese . Similar works can be found on English of WSJ corpus (Van Gael et al., 2009). Their best results of VI, V-measure, achieved with Pitman-Yor prior, were 3.73 and 59%. We believe the Chinese results are not good as English correspondences because of the rich unknown words in Chinese (Tseng et al., 2005).

5.2 Dependency Parsing Evaluation

The next experiment is to test the goodness of the outcome states of our model in the context of real tasks. In this work, we consider unsupervised dependency parsing for a fully unsupervised system. The dependency parsing is to extract the dependency graph whose nodes are the words of the given sentence. The dependency graph is a directed acyclic graph in which every edge links from a head word to its dependent. Because we work on unsupervised methods in this paper, we choose a simple generative head-outward model (Dependency Model with Valence, DMV) (Klein and Manning, 2004; Headden III et al., 2009) for parsing. The data through the experiment is restricted to the sentences up to length 10 (excluding punctuation).

Because the main purpose is to test the HMM output rather than to improve the parsing performance, we select the original DMV model without extensions or modifications. Starting from the root, DMV generates the head, and then each head recursively generates its left and right dependents. In each direction, the possible dependents are repeatedly chosen until a STOP marker is seen. DMV use inside-outside algorithm for re-estimation. We choose the “harmonic” initializer proposed in (Klein and Manning, 2004) for initialization. The valence information is the simplest binary value indicating the adjacency. For different HMM candidates with varied hidden state number, we directly use the outputs as the input of the DMV and trained a set of models. Performing test on these individual models, we report the directed dependency accuracies (the fraction of words assigned the correct parent) in Figure 3.

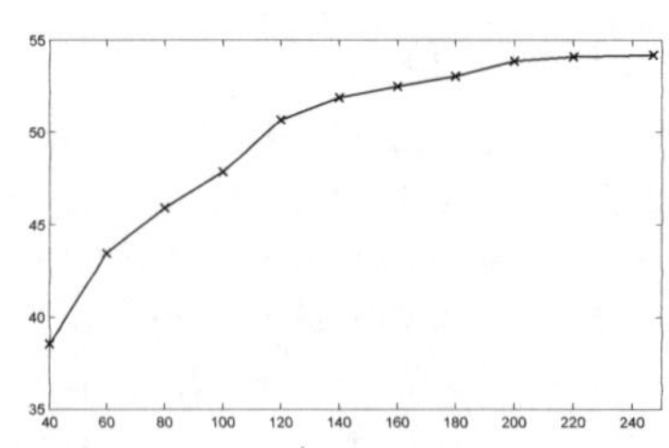

Figure 3: Directed accuracies for different hidden states

It is noted that the accuracy monotonically

increases when the number of states increases. The most drastic increase happened when state changes from 40 to 120. The accuracy increased from 38.56% to 50.60%. If the state number is larger than 180, the increase is not obvious. The final best accuracy is 54.20%, which improve the standard DMV model by 5.6%. Therefore we can see that the introduction of more annotations can help the parsing results. However, the improvement is limited and stable when the number of state number is large. To further improve the parsing performance, one might turn to the extension of DMV model, e.g. introducing more knowledge (prior or lexical information) or more sophistical smoothing techniques. However, the development of parser is not the focus of this paper.

6 Conclusion and Future Work

This paper works on the unsupervised Chinese POS tagging based on the first-order HMM. Our contributions are: 1). The number of hidden states can be adjusted to fit the data. 2). For inference, we use the variational inference, which is faster and is guaranteed theoretically to convergence. 3). To overcome the context limitation in HMM, the words are clustered based on distributional similarities. It is a 1-to-many clustering, which means one word might be classified into different clusters under different contexts. Finally, experiments show the hidden states are correlated to the latent annotations of the standard POS tags.

The future work includes to improve the performance by incorporating a small amount of supervision. The typical supervision used before is dictionary extracted from a large corpus like Chinese Gigaword. Another interesting idea is to select some exemplars (Haghighi and Klein, 2006).

References

Beal, Matthew J., Zoubin Ghahramani, and Carl Edward Rasmussen. 2001. The infinite hidden markov model. In *NIPS*, pages 577–584.

Beal, M. J. 2003. Variational algorithms for approximate bayesian inference. *Phd Thesis. Gatsby Computational Neuroscience Unit, University College London.*

Brand, Matthew. 1999. An entropic estimator for structure discovery. In *Proceedings of the 1998 conference on Advances in neural information processing systems II*, pages 723–729, Cambridge, MA, USA. MIT Press.

Fox, Emily B., Erik B. Sudderth, Michael I. Jordan, and Alan S. Willsky. 2008. An hdp-hmm for systems with state persistence. In *ICML '08: Proceedings of the 25th international conference on Machine learning*.

Frey, Brendan J. and Delbert Dueck. 2007. Clustering by passing messages between data points. *Science*, 315:972–976.

Goldwater, Sharon and Tom Griffiths. 2007. A fully bayesian approach to unsupervised part-of-speech tagging. In *Proceedings of the 45th Annual Meeting of the Association of Computational Linguistics*, pages 744–751, Prague, Czech Republic, June. Association for Computational Linguistics.

Haghighi, Aria and Dan Klein. 2006. Prototype-driven learning for sequence models. In *Proceedings of the main conference on Human Language Technology Conference of the North American Chapter of the Association of Computational Linguistics*, pages 320–327.

Headden, III, William P., David McClosky, and Eugene Charniak. 2008. Evaluating unsupervised part-of-speech tagging for grammar induction. In *COLING '08: Proceedings of the 22nd International Conference on Computational Linguistics*, pages 329–336, Morristown, NJ, USA. Association for Computational Linguistics.

Headden III, William P., Mark Johnson, and David McClosky. 2009. Improving unsupervised dependency parsing with richer contexts and smoothing. In *Proceedings of Human Language Technologies: The 2009 Annual Conference of the North American Chapter of the Association for Computational Linguistics*, pages 101–109, Boulder, Colorado, June. Association for Computational Linguistics.

Hernando, D., V. Crespi, and G. Cybenko. 2005. Efficient computation of the hidden markov model entropy for a given observation sequence. volume 51, pages 2681–2685.

Huang, Zhongqiang, Mary Harper, and Wen Wang. 2007. Mandarin part-of-speech tagging and discriminative reranking. In *Proceedings of the 2007 Joint Conference on Empirical Methods in Natural Language Processing and Computational Natural Language Learning (EMNLP-CoNLL)*, pages

1093–1102, Prague, Czech Republic, June. Association for Computational Linguistics.

Johnson, Mark. 2007. Why doesn't EM find good HMM POS-taggers? In *Proceedings of the 2007 Joint Conference on Empirical Methods in Natural Language Processing and Computational Natural Language Learning (EMNLP-CoNLL)*, pages 296–305, Prague, Czech Republic, June. Association for Computational Linguistics.

Kaji, Nobuhiro and Masaru Kitsuregawa. 2008. Using hidden markov random fields to combine distributional and pattern-based word clustering. In *COLING '08: Proceedings of the 22nd International Conference on Computational Linguistics*, pages 401–408, Morristown, NJ, USA. Association for Computational Linguistics.

Klein, Dan and Christopher Manning. 2004. Corpus-based induction of syntactic structure: Models of dependency and constituency. In *Proceedings of the 42nd Meeting of the Association for Computational Linguistics (ACL'04), Main Volume*, pages 478–485, Barcelona, Spain, July.

Meilă, Marina. 2007. Comparing clusterings—an information based distance. volume 98, pages 873–895.

Rabiner, Lawrence R. 1989. A tutorial on hidden markov models and selected applications in speech recognition. In *Proceedings of the IEEE*, pages 257–286.

Rosenberg, Andrew and Julia Hirschberg. 2007. V-measure: A conditional entropy-based external cluster evaluation measure. In *Proceedings of the 2007 Joint Conference on Empirical Methods in Natural Language Processing and Computational Natural Language Learning (EMNLP-CoNLL)*, pages 410–420.

Siddiqi, Sajid, Geoffrey Gordon, and Andrew Moore. 2007. Fast state discovery for hmm model selection and learning. In *Proceedings of the Eleventh International Conference on Artificial Intelligence and Statistics (AI-STATS)*.

Strehl, Alexander and Joydeep Ghosh. 2003. Cluster ensembles — a knowledge reuse framework for combining multiple partitions. *Journal of Machine Learning Research*, 3:583–617.

Tseng, Huihsin, Daniel Jurafsky, and Christopher Manning. 2005. Morphological features help pos tagging of unknown words across language varieties. pages 32–39.

Van Gael, Jurgen, Yunus Saatci, Yee Whye Teh, and Zoubin Ghahramani. 2008. Beam sampling for the infinite hidden markov model. In *ICML '08: Proceedings of the 25th international conference on Machine learning*.

Van Gael, Jurgen, Andreas Vlachos, and Zoubin Ghahramani. 2009. The infinite HMM for unsupervised PoS tagging. In *Proceedings of the 2009 Conference on Empirical Methods in Natural Language Processing*, pages 678–687, Singapore, August. Association for Computational Linguistics.

Wang, Qin Iris and Dale Schuurmans. Improved estimation for unsupervised part-of-speech tagging. page 2005, Wuhan, China.

Weeds, Julie and David Weir. 2003. A general framework for distributional similarity. In *Proceedings of the 2003 conference on Empirical methods in natural language processing*, pages 81–88, Morristown, NJ, USA. Association for Computational Linguistics.

Zelling, Harris. 1968. *Mathematical sturcture of language*. NewYork:Wiley.

APPENDIX

Pseudo-code of the extended Baum-Welch Algorithm in our dynamic HMM

Input: Time step t:
State Candidate: $k \rightarrow (k^{(1)}, k^{(2)})$;
Sate Number: N^t;
Model Parameter: $\theta^{(t)} = (A^{(t)}, B^{(t)}, \pi^{(t)})$;
Initialize
$u^{(l)}[k^{(1)}, k^{(2)}] \leftarrow [\frac{u^{(l)}[k]}{2}, \frac{u^{(l)}[k]}{2}], l \in \{A, B, \pi\}$
$\pi_{k^{(1)}} \leftarrow \frac{1}{2}\pi_k; \pi_{k^{(2)}} \leftarrow \frac{1}{2}\pi_k$
$a_{\bar{k}k^{(i)}} \leftarrow \frac{1}{2}a_{\bar{k}k^{(i)}}; a_{k^{(i)}\bar{k}} \leftarrow a_{k^{(i)}\bar{k}}$;
$a_{k^{(i)}k^{(j)}} \leftarrow \frac{1}{2}a_{k^{(i)}k^{(j)}}$, here $i, j \in 1, 2, \bar{k} \neq k$
repeat
E step:
update forward: $\alpha_t(k^{(1)})$ and $\alpha_t(k^{(2)})$
backward: $\beta_t(k^{(1)})$ and $\beta_t(k^{(2)})$
update $\xi_t(i, j)$ and $\gamma_t(i)$; if $i, j \in \{k^{(1)}, k^{(2)}\}$
update $\mathbb{E}[n_{ij}] = \sum_t \xi_t(i, j) / \sum_t \gamma_t(i)$
$\mathbb{E}[n_{ik}] = \sum_{t, w_t = k} \gamma_t(j) / \sum_t \gamma_t(j)$
M step:
update $\theta^{(t+1)}$ using equation (7)
until $(\triangle\mathcal{F} < \varepsilon)$
Output: $\theta^{(t+1)}, \mathcal{F}$

Mining Large-scale Parallel Corpora from Multilingual Patents: An English-Chinese example and its application to SMT

Bin Lu[†], **Benjamin K. Tsou**[†§], **Tao Jiang**[$], **Oi Yee Kwong**[†], **and Jingbo Zhu**[£]

[†]Department of Chinese, Translation & Linguistics, City University of Hong Kong

[§]Research Centre on Linguistics and Language Information Sciences, Hong Kong Institute of Education

[$]ChiLin Star Corp., Southern Software Park, Zhuhai, China

[£]Natural Language Processing Lab, Northeastern University, Shenyang, China

{lubin2010, rlbtsou, jiangtaoster}@gmail.com, rlolivia@cityu.edu.hk, zhujingbo@mail.neu.edu.cn

Abstract

In this paper, we demonstrate how to mine large-scale parallel corpora with multilingual patents, which have not been thoroughly explored before. We show how a large-scale English-Chinese parallel corpus containing over 14 million sentence pairs with only 1-5% wrong can be mined from a large amount of English-Chinese bilingual patents. To our knowledge, this is the largest single parallel corpus in terms of sentence pairs. Moreover, we estimate the potential for mining multilingual parallel corpora involving English, Chinese, Japanese, Korean, German, etc., which would to some extent reduce the parallel data acquisition bottleneck in multilingual information processing.

1 Introduction

Multilingual data are critical resources for building many applications, such as machine translation (MT) and cross-lingual information retrieval. Many parallel corpora have been built, such as the Canadian Hansards (Gale and Church, 1991), the Europarl corpus (Koehn, 2005), the Arabic-English and English-Chinese parallel corpora used in the NIST Open MT Evaluation.

However, few parallel corpora exist for many language pairs, such as Chinese-Japanese, Japanese-Korean, Chinese- French or Japanese-German. Even for language pairs with several parallel corpora, such as Chinese-English and Arabic-English, the size of parallel corpora is still a major limitation for SMT systems to achieve higher performance.

In this paper, we present a way which could, to some extent, reduce the parallel data acquisition bottleneck in multilingual language processing. Based on multilingual patents, we show how an enlarged English-Chinese parallel corpus containing over 14 million high-quality sentence pairs can be mined from a large number of comparable patents harvested from the Web. To our knowledge, this is the largest single parallel corpus in terms of parallel sentences. Some SMT experiments are also reported. Moreover, we investigate the potential to get large-scale parallel corpora for languages beyond the Canadian Hansards, Europarl and UN news used in NIST MT Evaluation by estimating the quantity of multilingual patents involving English, Chinese, Japanese, Korean, German, etc.

Related work is introduced in Section 2. Patents, PCT patents, multilingual patents are described in Section 3. Then an English-Chinese parallel corpus, its mining process and application to SMT are introduced in Section 4, followed by the quantity estimation of multilingual patents involving other language pairs in Section 5. We discuss the results in Section 6, and conclude in Section 7.

2 Related Work

Parallel sentences could be extracted from parallel documents or comparable corpora. Different approaches have been proposed to align sentences in parallel documents consisting of the same content in different languages based on the following information: a) the sentence length in bilingual sentences (Brown et al. 1991; Gale and Church, 1991); b) lexical information in bilingual dictionaries (Ma, 2006); c) statistical translation model (Chen, 1993), or the composite of more than one approach (Simard and Plamondon, 1998; Moore, 2002).

To overcome the lack of parallel documents, comparable corpora are also used to mine parallel sentences, which raises further challenges since the bilingual contents are not strictly parallel. For instance, Zhao and Vogel (2002) investigated the mining of parallel sentences for Web bilingual news. Munteanu and Marcu (2005) presented a method for discovering parallel sentences in large Chinese, Arabic, and English comparable, non-parallel corpora based on a maximum entropy classifier. Cao et al., (2007) and Lin et al., (2008) proposed two different methods utilizing the parenthesis pattern to extract term translations from bilingual web pages. Jiang et al. (2009) presented an adaptive pattern-based method which produced Chinese-English bilingual sentences and terms with over 80% accuracy.

Only a few papers were found on the related work in the patent domain. Higuchi et al. (2001) used the titles and abstracts of 32,000 Japanese-English bilingual patents to extract bilingual terms. Utiyama and Isahara (2007) mined about 2 million parallel sentences by using two parts in the *description* section of Japanese-English comparable patents. Lu et al. (2009) derived about 160K parallel sentences from Chinese-English comparable patents by aligning sentences and filtering alignments with the combination of different quality measures. Another closely related work is the English-Chinese parallel corpus (Lu et al., 2010), which is largely extended by this work, in which both the number of patents and that of parallel sentences are augmented by about 100%, and more SMT experiments are given. Moreover, we show the potential for mining parallel corpora from multilingual patents involving other languages.

For statistical machine translation (SMT), tremendous strides have been made in two decades, including Brown et al. (1993), Och and Ney (2004) and Chiang (2007). For the MT evaluation, NIST (Fujii et al., 2008; 2010) has been organizing open evaluations for years, and the performance of the participants has been improved rapidly.

3 Patents and Multilingual Patents

A patent is a legal document representing "*an official document granting the exclusive right to make, use, and sell an invention for a limited period*" (Collins English Dictionary[1]). A patent application consists of different sections, and we focus on the text, i.e. only *title, abstract, claims and description.*

3.1 PCT Patents

Since the invention in a patent is only protected in the filing countries, a patent applicant who wishes to protect his invention outside the original country should file patents in other countries, which may involve other languages.

The Patent Cooperation Treaty (PCT) system offers inventors and industry an advantageous route for obtaining patent protection internationally. By filing one *"international"* patent application under the PCT via the World Intellectually Property Organization (WIPO), protection of an invention can be sought simultaneously (i.e. the priority date) in each of a large number of countries.

The number of PCT international applications

[1] Retrieved March 2010, from http://www.collinslanguage.com/

filed is more than 1.7 million [2]. A PCT international application may be filed in any language accepted by the relevant receiving office, but must be published in one of the official publication languages (Arabic, Chinese, English, French, German, Japanese, Korean, Russian and Spanish). Other highly used languages for filing include Italian, Dutch, Finnish, Swedish, etc. Table 1 [3] shows the number of PCT applications for the most used languages of filing and publication.

	Lang. of Filing	Share (%)	Lang. of Publication	Share (%)
English	895K	52.1	943K	54.9
Japanese	198K	11.5	196K	11.4
German	185K	10.8	184K	10.7
French	55K	3.2	55K	3.2
Korean	24K	1.4	3K[4]	0.2
Chinese	24K	1.4	24K	1.4
Other	336K	19.6	313K	18.2
Total	1.72M	100	1.72M	100

Table 1. PCT Application Numbers for Languages of Publication and Filing

From Table 1, we can observe that English, Japanese and German are the top 3 languages in terms of PCT applications, and English accounts for over 50% of applications in terms of language of both publication and filing.

3.2 Multilingual Patents

A PCT application does not necessarily mean a multilingual patent. An applicant who has decided to proceed further with his PCT international application must fulfill the requirements for entry into the PCT national phase at the patent offices of countries where he seeks protection. For example, a Chinese company may first file a Chinese patent in China patent office and then file its international application also in Chinese under the PCT. Later on, it may have the patent translated into English and file it in USA patent office, which means the patent becomes bilingual. If the applicant continues to file it in Japan with Japanese, it would be trilingual. Even more, it would be quadrilingual or involve more languages when it is filed in other countries with more languages.

Such multilingual patents are considered comparable (or noisy parallel) because they are not parallel in the strict sense but still closely related in terms of information conveyed (Higuchi et al., 2001; Lu et al., 2009).

4 A Large English-Chinese Parallel Corpus Mined from Bilingual Patents

In this section, we introduce the English-Chinese bilingual patents harvested from the Web and the method to mine parallel sentences from them. SMT experiments on the final parallel corpus are also described.

4.1 Harvesting English-Chinese Bilingual Patents

The official patent office in China is the State Intellectual Property Office (SIPO). In early 2009, by searching on its website, we found about 200K Chinese patents previously filed as PCT applications in English and crawled their *bibliographical data, titles, abstracts* and *the major claim* from the Web, and then *other claims* and *descriptions* were also added. Since some contents are in the image format, the images were OCRed and the texts recognized were manually verified.

All PCT patent applications are filed through WIPO. With the Chinese patents mentioned above, the corresponding English patents were searched from the website of WIPO by the PCT publication numbers to obtain relevant sections of the English PCT applications, including *bibliographical data, title, abstract, claims* and *description.* About 80% (160K) out of the Chinese patents found their corresponding English ones. Some contents of the English patents were OCRed by WIPO.

[2] Retrieved Apr., 2010 from http://www.wipo.int/pctdb/en/. The data below involving PCT patents comes from the website of WIPO.

[3] The data in this and other tables in the following sections involving PCT patents comes from the website of WIPO.

[4] Korean just became one of the official publication languages for the PCT system since 2009, and thus the number of PCT patents with Korean as language of publication is small.

We automatically split the patents into individual sections according to the respective tags inside the patents, and segmented each section sentences according to punctuations. The statistics of each section for Chinese and English patents are shown in Table 2.

Sections	Chinese		English	
	#Char	#Sent	#Word	#Sent
Title	2.7M	157K	1.6M	157K
Abstract	33M	596K	20M	784K
Claim	367M	6.8M	217M	7.4M
Desc.	2,467M	48.8M	1,353M	54.0M
Total	2,870M	56.2M	1,591M	62.3M

Table 2. Statistics of Comparable Patents

4.2 Mining Parallel Sentences from Bilingual Patents

The sentences in each section of Chinese patents were aligned with those in the corresponding section of the corresponding English patents to find parallel sentences after the Chinese sentences were segmented into words.

Since the comparable patents are not strictly parallel, the individual alignment methods mentioned in Section 2 would be not effective: 1) the length-based method is not accurate since it does not consider content similarity; 2) the bilingual dictionary-based method cannot deal with new technical terms in the patents; 3) the translation model-based method would need training data to get a translation model. Thus, in this study we combine these three methods to mine high-quality parallel sentences from comparable patents.

We first use a bilingual dictionary to preliminarily align the sentences in each section of the comparable patents. The dictionary-based similarity score P_d of a sentence pair is computed based on a bilingual dictionary as follows (Utiyama and Isahara, 2003):

$$p_d(S_c, S_e) = \frac{\sum_{w_c \in S_c} \sum_{w_e \in S_e} \frac{\gamma(w_c, w_e)}{\deg(w_c)\deg(w_e)}}{(l_e + l_c)/2}$$

where w_c and w_e are respectively the word types in Chinese sentence S_c and English sentence S_e; l_c and l_e respectively denote the lengths of S_c and S_e in terms of the number of words; and $\gamma(w_c, w_e)$ = 1 if w_c and w_e is a translation pair in the bilingual dictionary or are the same string, otherwise 0; and

$$\deg(w_c) = \sum_{w_e \in S_e} \gamma(w_c, w_e)$$

$$\deg(w_e) = \sum_{w_e \in S_c} \gamma(w_c, w_e).$$

For the bilingual dictionary, we combine three ones: namely, LDC_CE_DIC2.0 [5] constructed by LDC, bilingual terms in HowNet and the bilingual lexicon in Champollion (Ma, 2006).

We then remove sentence pairs using length filtering and ratio filtering: 1) for length filtering, if a sentence pair has more than 100 words in the English sentence or more than 333 characters in the Chinese one, it is removed; 2) for length ratio filtering, we discard the sentence pairs with Chinese-English length ratio outside the range of 0.8 to 1.8. The parameters here are set empirically.

We further filter the parallel sentence candidates by learning an IBM Model-1 on the remaining aligned sentences and compute the translation similarity score P_t of sentence pairs by combining the translation probability value of both directions (i.e. Chinese->English and English->Chinese) based on the trained IBM-1 model (Moore, 2002; Chen, 2003; Lu et al, 2009). It is computed as follows:

$$p_t(S_c, S_e) = \frac{log(P(S_e \mid S_c)) + log(P(S_c \mid S_e))}{l_c + l_e}$$

where $P(S_e \mid S_c)$ denotes the probability that a translator will produce S_e in English when presented with S_c in Chinese, and vice versa for $P(S_c \mid S_e)$. Sentence pairs with

[5] http://projects.ldc.upenn.edu/Chinese/LDC_ch.htm

similarity score P_t lower than a predefined threshold are filtered out as wrong aligned sentences.

Table 3 shows the sentence numbers and the percentages of sentences kept in each step above with respect to all sentence pairs. In the first row of Table 3, *1.DICT* denotes the first step of using the bilingual dictionary to align sentences; *2. FL* denotes the length and ratio filtering; *3. TM* refers to the third and final step of using translation models to filter sentence pairs.

	1. DICT	2.FL	3. TM (final)
Abstr.	503K	352K (70%)	166K (33%)
Claims	6.0M	4.3M (72.1%)	2.0M (33.4%)
Desc.	38.6M	26.8M (69.4%)	12.1M (31.3%)
Total[6]	45.1M	31.5M (69.8%)	14.3M (31.7%)

Table 3. Numbers of Sentence Pairs

Both the 31.5M parallel sentences after the second step *FL* and the final 14.3M after the third step *TM* are manually evaluated by randomly sampling 100 sentence pairs for each section. The evaluation metric follows the one in Lu et al. (2009), which classifies each sentence pair into *Correct, Partially Correct* or *Wrong*. The results of manual evaluation are shown in Table 4.

	Section	Correct	Partially Correct	Wrong
2. FL	Abstr.	85%	7%	8%
	Claims	83%	10%	7%
	Desc.	69%	15%	15%
3. TM (final)	Abstr.	97%	2%	1%
	Claims	92%	3%	5%
	Desc.	89%	8%	3%

Table 4. Manual Evaluation of the Corpus

From Table 4, we can see that: 1) In the final corpus, the percentages of *correct* parallel sentences are quite high, and the wrong percentages are no higher than 5%; 2) Without the final step of TM, the accuracies of 31.5M sentence pairs are between 69%-85%, and the percentages of wrong pairs are between 7%-15%; 3) The abstract section shows the highest correct percentage, while the description section shows the lowest.

Thus, we could conclude that the mined 14M parallel sentences are of high quality with only 1%-5% wrong pairs, and our combination of bilingual dictionaries and translation models for mining parallel sentences are quite effective.

4.3 Chinese-English Statistical Machine Translation

A Chinese-English SMT system is setup using Moses (Koehn, 2007). We train models based on different numbers of parallel sentences mined above. The test set contains 548 sentence pairs which are randomly selected and different from the training data. The sizes of the training data and BLEU scores for the models are shown in Table 5.

System	BLEU (%)	#Sentence Pairs for training
Model-A	17.94	300K
Model-B	19.96	750K
Model-C	20.09	1.5M
Model-D	20.98	3M
Model-E	22.60	6M

Table 5. SMT Experimental Results

From Table 5, we can see that the BLEU scores are improving steadily when the training data increases. When the training data is enlarged by 20 times from 300K to 6M, the BLEU score increases to 22.60 from 17.94, which is quite a significant improvement. We show the translations of one Chinese sample sentence in Table 6 below.

CN Sent.	电机 主轴 伸入 压缩机 壳体 内 的 工作 腔 中 ，
Ref.	the main shaft of the electric motor extends into the working cavity of the compressor shell ,
Model-A	the motor main shaft into the compressor the chamber

[6] Here the total number does not include the number of titles, which are directly treated as parallel.

Model-B	motor shaft into the compressor housing . the working chamber
Model-C	motor shaft into the compressor housing . the working chamber
Model-D	motor spindle extends into the compressor housing . the working chamber
Model-E	motor spindle extends into the working chamber of the compressor housing ,

Table 6. Translations of One Chinese Sentence

From Table 6, we can see the translations given by Model-A to Model-C are lack of the main verb, the one given by Model-D has an ordering problem for the head noun and the modifier, and the one given by Model-E seems better than the others and its content is already quite similar to the reference despite the lexical difference.

5 Multilingual Corpora for More Languages

In this section, we describe the potential of building large-scale parallel corpora for more languages, especially Asian languages by using the 1.7 million PCT patent applications and their national correspondents. By using PCT applications as the pivot, we can build multilingual parallel corpora from multilingual patents, which would greatly enlarge parallel data we could obtain.

The patent applications filed in one country should be in the official language(s) of the country, e.g. the applications filed in China should be in Chinese, those in Japan be in Japanese, and so on. In Table 7, the second column shows the total numbers of patent applications in different countries which were previously filed as PCT ones; and the third column shows the total numbers of applications in different countries, which were previously filed as PCT ones with English as language of publication.

National Phase Country[7]	ALL	English as Lang. of Publication
Japan	424K	269K
China	307K	188K
Germany	32K	10K
R. Korea	236K	134K
China & Japan	189K	130K
China & R. Korea	154K	91K
Japan & R. Korea	158K	103K
China & Japan & R. Korea	106K	73K

Table 7. Estimated Numbers of Multilingual Patents

The number of the Chinese-English bilingual patents (CE) in Table 7 is about 188K, which is consistent with the number of 160K found in Section 4.1 since the latter contains only the applications up to early 2009. Based on Table 7, we estimate below the rough sizes of bilingual corpora, trilingual corpora, and even quadrilingual corpora for different languages.

1) Bilingual Corpora with English as one language

Compared to CE (188K), the Japanese-English bilingual corpus (269K) could be 50% larger in terms of bilingual patents, the Korean-English one (134K) could be about 30% smaller, and the German-English one (10K) would be much smaller.

2) Bilingual Corpora for Asian Languages

The Japanese-Chinese bilingual corpus (189K) could be comparable to CE (188K) in terms of bilingual applications, the Chinese-Korean one (154K) could be about 20% smaller, and the Japanese-Korean one (158K) is quite similar to the Chinese-Korean one.

3) Trilingual Corpora

In addition to bilingual corpora, we can also build trilingual corpora from trilingual patents. It is quite interesting to note that the trilingual corpora could be quite large even compared to the bilingual corpora.

The trilingual corpora for Chinese, Japanese and English (130K) could be only 30% smaller than CE in terms of patents. The trilingual corpus

[7] For the national phase of the PCT System, the statistics are based on data supplied to WIPO by national and regional patent Offices, received at WIPO often 6 months or more after the end of the year concerned, i.e. the numbers are not up-to-date .

for Chinese, Korean and English (91K) and that for Japanese, Korean and English (103K) are also quite large. The number of the trilingual patents for the Asian languages of Chinese, Japanese and Korean (106K) is about 54% of that of CE.

4) Quadrilingual Corpora

The number of the quadrilingual patents for Chinese, Japanese, Korean and English (73K) is about 38% of that of CE. From these figures, we could say that a large proportion of the PCT applications published in English later have been filed in all the three Asian countries: China, Japan, and R. Korea.

6 Discussion

The websites from which the Chinese and English patents were downloaded were quite slow to access, and were occasionally down during access. To avoid too much workload for the websites, the downloading speed had been limited. Some large patents would cost much time for the websites to respond and had be specifically handled. It took considerable efforts to obtain these comparable patents.

In addition our English-Chinese corpus mined in this study is at least one order of magnitude larger, we give some other differences between ours and those introduced in Section 2 (Higuchi et al., 2001; Utiyama and Isahara, 2007; Lu et al, 2009)

1) Their bilingual patents were identified by the priority information in the US patents, and could not be easily extended to language pairs without English; while our method using PCT applications as the pivot could be easily extended to other language pairs as illustrated in Section 5.

2) The translation process is different: their patents were filed in USA Patent Office in English by translating from Japanese or Chinese, while our patents were first filed in English as a PCT application, and later translated into Chinese. The different translation processes may have different characteristics.

Since the PCT and multilingual patent applications increase rapidly in recent years as discussed in Section 3, we could expect more multilingual patents to enlarge the large-scale parallel corpora with the new applications and keep them up-to-date with new technical terms. On the other hand, patents are usually translated by patent agents or professionals, we could expect high quality translations from multilingual patents. We have been planning to build trilingual and quadrilingual corpora from multilingual patents.

One possible limitation of patent corpora is that the sentences are all from technical domains and written in formal style, and thus it is interesting to know if the parallel sentences could improve the performance of SMT systems on NIST MT evaluation corpus containing news sentences and web sentences.

7 Conclusion

In this paper, we show how a large high-quality English-Chinese parallel corpus can be mined from a large amount of comparable patents harvested from the Web, which is the largest single parallel corpus in terms of the number of parallel sentences. Some sampled parallel sentences are available at http://www.livac.org/smt/parpat.html, and more parallel sentences would be publicly available to the research community.

With 1.7 million PCT patent applications and their corresponding national ones, there are considerable potentials of constructing large-scale high-quality parallel corpora for languages. We give an estimation on the sizes of multilingual parallel corpora which could be obtained from multilingual patents involving English, Chinese, Japanese, Korean, German, etc., which would to some extent reduce the parallel data acquisition bottleneck in multilingual information processing.

Acknowledgements

We wish to thank Mr. Long Jiang from Microsoft Research Asia and anonymous reviewers for their valuable comments.

References

Brown, Peter F., Jennifer C. Lai, and Robert L. Mercer. 1991. Aligning sentences in parallel corpora. In *Proceedings of ACL*. pp.169-176.

Brown, Peter F., Stephen A. Della Pietra, Vincent J. Della Pietra, and Robert L. Mercer. 1993. Mathematics of statistical machine translation: Parameter estimation. *Computational Linguistics*, *19*(2), 263-311.

Cao, Guihong, Jianfeng Gao and Jianyun Nie. 2007. A System to Mine Large-scale Bilingual Dictionaries from Monolingual Web Pages. In *Proceedings of MT Summit*. pp. 57-64.

Chen, Stanley F. 1993. Aligning sentences in bilingual corpora using lexical information. In *Proceedings of ACL*. pp. 9-16.

Chiang, David. 2007. Hierarchical phrase-based translation. *Computational Linguistics,* 33(2), 201–228.

Fujii, Atsushi, Masao Utiyama, Mikio Yamamoto, and Takehito Utsuro. 2008. Overview of the patent translation task at the NTCIR-7 workshop. In *Proceedings of the NTCIR-7 Workshop*. pp. 389-400. Tokyo, Japan.

Fujii, Atsushi, Masao Utiyama, Mikio Yamamoto, Takehito Utsuro, Terumasa Ehara, Hiroshi Echizen-ya and Sayori Shimohata. 2010. Overview of the patent translation task at the NTCIR-8 workshop. In *Proceedings of the NTCIR-8 Workshop*. Tokyo, Japan.

Gale, William A., and Kenneth W. Church. 1991. A program for aligning sentences in bilingual corpora. In *Proceedings of ACL*. pp.79-85.

Higuchi, Shigeto, Masatoshi Fukui, Atsushi Fujii, and Tetsuya Ishikawa. PRIME: A System for Multi-lingual Patent Retrieval. In *Proceedings of MT Summit VIII*, pp.163-167, 2001.

Koehn, Philipp. 2005. Europarl: A parallel corpus for statistical machine translation. In *Proceedings of MT Summit X*.

Koehn, Philipp, Hieu Hoang, Alexandra Birch, Chris Callison-Burch, et al. 2007. Moses: Open source toolkit for statistical machine translation. In *Proceedings of ACL Demo Session*. pp. 177-180.

Lin, Dekang, Shaojun Zhao, Benjamin V. Durme and Marius Pasca. 2008. Mining Parenthetical Translations from the Web by Word Alignment. In *Proceedings of ACL-08*. pp. 994-1002.

Jiang, Long, Shiquan Yang, Ming Zhou, Xiaohua Liu, and Qingsheng Zhu. 2009. Mining Bilingual Data from the Web with Adaptively Learnt Patterns. In *Proceedings of ACL-IJCNLP*. pp. 870-878.

Lu, Bin, Benjamin K. Tsou, Jingbo Zhu, Tao Jiang, and Olivia Y. Kwong. 2009. The Construction of an English-Chinese Patent Parallel Corpus. *MT Summit XII 3rd Workshop on Patent Translation*.

Lu, Bin, Tao Jiang, Kapo Chow and Benjamin K. Tsou. 2010. Building a Large English-Chinese Parallel Corpus from Comparable Patents and its Experimental Application to SMT. *LREC Workshop on Building and Using Comparable Corpora*. Malta. May, 2010.

Ma, Xiaoyi. 2006. Champollion: A Robust Parallel Text Sentence Aligner. In *Proceedings of the 5th International Conference on Language Resources and Evaluation (LREC)*. Genova, Italy.

Moore, Robert C. 2002. Fast and Accurate Sentence Alignment of Bilingual Corpora. In *Proceedings of AMTA*. pp.135-144.

Munteanu, Dragos S., and Daniel Marcu. 2005. Improving Machine Translation Performance by Exploiting Non-parallel Corpora. *Computational Linguistics*, *31*(4), 477–504.

Och, Franz J., and Hermann Ney. 2004. The Alignment Template Approach to Machine Translation. *Computational Linguistics*, *30*(4), 417-449.

Simard, Michel, and Pierre Plamondon. 1998. Bilingual Sentence Alignment: Balancing Robustness and Accuracy. *Machine Translation*, *13*(1), 59-80.

Utiyama, Masao, and Hitoshi Isahara. 2007. A Japanese-English patent parallel corpus. In *Proceeding of MT Summit XI*. pp. 475–482.

Zhao, Bing, and Stephen Vogel. 2002. Adaptive Parallel Sentences Mining from Web Bilingual News Collection. In *Proceedings of Second IEEE International Conference on Data Mining (ICDM'02)*.

Studies on Automatic Recognition of Common Chinese Adverb's Usages Based on Statistical Methods

Hongying Zan
College of Information Engineering, Zhengzhou University
iehyzan@zzu.edu.cn

Junhui Zhang
College of Information Engineering, Zhengzhou University
zhangj.zzu@gmail.com

Xuefeng Zhu
Key Laboratory of Computational Linguistics(Peking University) of China Ministry Education
yusw@pku.edu.cn

Shiwen Yu
Key Laboratory of Computational Linguistics(Peking University) of China Ministry Education
yusw@pku.edu.cn

Abstract

The study on Automatic Recognizing usages of Modern Chinese Adverbs is one of the important parts of the NLP-oriented research of Chinese Functional words Knowledge Base. To solve the problems of the existing rule-based method of adverbs' usages recognition based on the previous work, this paper has studied automatically recognizing common Chinese adverbs' usages using statistical methods. Three statistical models, viz. CRF, ME, and SVM, are used to label several common Chinese adverbs' usages on the segmentation and part-of-speech tagged corpus of People's Daily(Jan 1998). The experiment results show that statistical-based method is effective in automatically recognizing of several common adverbs' usages and has good application prospects.

1 Introduction

Chinese vocabulary can be divided into functional words and notional words. In the field of Natural Language Processing(NLP), many studies on text computing or word meaning understanding are focused on the notional words, rarely involving functional words. Especially in some common NLP application fields, such as text summarization, text classification, information retrieval, and so on, the researchers mainly take notional words as features, and list some functional word as stop words without considering their influence on text meaning. This will impact the deep analysis of text semantic, especailly for chinese, and become the bottleneck of machine understanding on text content, and impede further improving the performance of application systems. Due to Chinese lacking morphological changes(Li X., 2005), Chinese functional words undertake the grammatical functions and grammatical meanings, and in other language these functions are mainly undertaken by morphological changes. So, functional words play an more important role in Chinese semantic understanding and grammatical analysis. The study on functional words of modern Chinese semantic in Chinese text processing and understanding has great significance.

Yu(Yu S., 2004), Liu(Liu, Y., 2004), et al, have defined the generalized functional words as adverbs, conjunctions, prepositions, modal particles, auxiliary, and localizer words. From the statistic, the number of modern Chinese adverbs is about 1000 with the broad definition standard. Compared with other fuctional words, the adverbs number is much larger. The function and usages of modern Chinese adverbs vary widely from each other, especially some common adverbs. Therefore for modern Chinese text understanding, adverbs are the important text features which can not be neglected. For the modern Chinese adverbs, only using the segmentation and part-of-speech tagging information for Chinese text automatic processing and understanding is not enough. So, particular study on the usage of adverbs in texts comprehensive is indispensable, and the automatic identification of adverbs' usage in some extend is of great significance.

2 Related Researches

The work of automatically recognizing usages of adverbs of modern Chinese is part of the NLP-oriented research of Modern Chinese Functional Words Knowledge Base. Yu et al. proposed the idea of building the “Trinity” knowledge-base of generalized functional words(Yu, S., 2004), and defined the generalized functional words as adverbs, conjunctions, prepositions, modal particles, auxiliary, and localizer words(Yu, S., 2004)(Liu, Y., 2004). Zan et al. described adverb’s usages using formal rules(Zan, H., 2007a), and initially built the machine-oriented modern Chinese adverb dictionary and the usage rule base(Zan, H., 2007b),. Hao et al. imported the dictionary and rule base(Hao, L., 2007). Based on the previous work, Liu et al. realized an automatically rule-based recognizing system and got precision at 74.89%(Liu, R., 2008).

The rule-based method has the advantage of simple, intuitive, strong pertinence, etc, but it also has the shortcomings of lower coverage, and it is difficult to be further optimized or generalized. For example, there are some adverbs which different usages are difficult to describe using formal rules, such as:

（1）想睡觉尽管睡，反正是星期天。

[(1)It is Sunday, you can sleep in at will.]

（2）她们俩听报告时尽管说话，报告的内容根本没听见。

[(2)They were always talking while listensing report, so they catched nothing of the report content.]

In the adverb usage dictionary, the adverb “jinguan/尽管” has two meanings: <d_jin3guan3_1> and <d_jin3guan3_2>. The meaning of “jinguan/尽管” in sentence (1) is belong to <d_jin3guan3_1>, it means the action or behavior can be without any limitations; the meaning of “jinguan/尽管” in sentence (2) is belong to <d_jin3guan3_2>, it means the action or behavior is continuously. This two meanings are very easy to distinguish manually, but they are hard to identify automatically. The two meanings’ discrimination cannot accurately describe using formal rules.

Moreover, the rule-based method also exists some other problem, for example, some adverbs’ usages require modifying verb phrase, or clauses, or used in imperative, and so on. These problems need deep syntactic even semantic knowledge to solve. But this is lack in the segmentation and part-of-speech tagging corpus. So, the rule-based method will be unable to identify the adverbs’ usages in such situations.

To solve the problems of the existing rule-based method of adverbs’ usages recognition, based on the foundation of the previous work, this article considers using statistical method to recognize adverbs’ usages automatically. This method can be continuously optimized according to actual training data and language model, it will avoid the limitations of rule-based method.

3 Studies on Automatic Recognition of Adverbs’ Usages Based on Statistical methods

In NLP, the research can be divided into three questions: point, sequence, and structure(Vapnik V., 1998). For the Chinese adverbs’ usages recognition task, it can be taken as a point question which classify the context of adverbs, and also can be taken as a sequence question which recognize the adverb sequence in the sentence. So, we choose three statistical models: Conditional Random Fields(CRF), Maximum Entropy(ME), and Support Vector Machine(SVM), which have good performance and used widely in the field of machine learning. CRF and ME model can be used in sequence tagging, and SVM is a better statistical models in categories.

3.1 Statistical models

CRF is advanced by J. Lafferty(Lafferty J., 2001). It is one of the undirected graph models. Given input sequence corresponding conditional probability of label sequence, this model‘s training target is to find the maximum of conditional probability. It has been widely used in the field of NLP, such as Chinese Word Segmentation(Miao X., 2007), Named Entity Recognition(Chen W., 2006)(Shi S., 2006)(Guo J., 2007)(Zhang J., 2006), Syntactic Analysis(Fei Sha, 2003), and so on.

ME has been widely used for classification problem. The basic idea of ME is to dig the potential constraint conditions in the known event sets, and then choose a model which must satisfy the known constraint conditions, while possibly let the unknown event uniform distribution. In the NLP applications, the language model based ME does not dependent on domain knowledge, and is independent of the specific task. It has been use in many key fields of NLP, and has achieved good results in Named Entity Recognition(Wang J., 2005), POS tagging(Zhang L., 2008), Chunking Analysis（Li S., 2003）, Text Emotional Tendencies Classification(Liu, K. 2008).

SVM is a statiscal machine learning method and has good performance in classification(Vapnik V., 1998). In NLP, SVM is widely used in Phrases recognition(Li, G., 2005), Word Sense Disambiguation(Yu, K., 2005)(Lu, Z., 2006), Text classification, and so on. SVM has good generalization ability, and can well classify the data in the training sample limited circumstances. To the usage recognition of adverbs, the available data is limited, so using SVM may be good.

CRF, ME and SVM are the outstanding statistical models in machine learning. CRF can well consider the mutual influence between usage marks, and overcomes the problem of marker offset. This is good for some rare usage recognition of adverb. The language model built by ME method is independent to specific tasks, and domain knowledge. ME can effectively use context information, and comprehensively evaluate the various characteristics. SVM has good generalization ability, and can well classify the data in the training sample limited circumstances. The advantages of these models are beneficial to recognize adverbs' usages correctly.

In this paper, we use CRF++[1], the ME toolkit maxent[2] of Zhang Le, and LibSVM[3] toolkit as the automatic tagging tool in our experiments.

3.2 Feature Selection of Models

Linguists Firth once said "You shall know a word by the company it keeps"(Firth, 1957). This refers to the mean of a word can only be judged and identified from the words associated with it. To the adverbs' usage recognition, it also needs to get the word's usage knowledge from the contexts. Through analyzing some examples, we found that words and part of speech in the contexts are useful to identify adverbs' usages. Therefore, in our experiment, to CRF and ME model, we select 3 template features as table 1. The value of n can take 2, 3, 4, 5, 6, and 7.

Table 1 Feature Template

ID	Meanings
T1	words, within the destined context window *n*
T2	the part of speech, within the destined context window *n*
T3	the words + part of speech + the combination of both, within the destined context window *n*

In the SVM experiment, the feature is numeric characteristics. To the adverb in the sentence, through selecting the window size of the context, and then calculating the mutual information(MI) of the features in the window and the adverb, the result of MI as feature vector. The MI between word *w* and word *u* can be calculated as follows,

$$I = \log \frac{p_1 * p_2}{p} \qquad (1)$$

Where:

p1: the frequency of *u* in the corpus

p2: the frequency of t in the corpus

p: the co-occurrence frequency of *w* and *u*

4 Experiments and Results Analysis

4.1 Experimental Corpus

The experimental data is the segmentation and part-of-speech tagged corpus of People's Daily(Jan 1998). First, we use the rule-based method(Liu, R., 2008) to tag the adverbs' usages in the experimental data. Then, we manually check the tagging results and get he standard corpus for experiment data. Observing the experiment data, the usage distribution of many adverbs' is very imbalance. Some adverbs have hardly appeared, and some usages of some adverbs have hardly appeared. If we choose this kind of adverbs for statistical experiment, it will bring great effect to the experiment results. Therefore, after analyzing the corpus, we consider to

---

[1] CRF++: Yet Another Toolkit[CP/OL]. http://www.chasen.org/~taku/software/CRF++

[2] http://homepages.inf.ed.ac.uk/s0450736/maxent_toolkit.html

[3] http://www.csie.ntu.edu.tw/~cjlin/libsvm

choose seven common Chinese adverbs which usage distribution is somewhat balanced in the corpus as the object of statistical learning.

4.2 Performance Evaluation

In the experiment, we use the precision(P) as the evaluation measure of the experimental results. To the word *W* and its usage *i*, we define P as followed:

$$P = \frac{\text{the correct tag number of usage } i}{\text{the tag number of usage } i} \quad (2)$$

4.3 Analysis of Experimental Results

In order to verify the performance of models, to every adverb, we use 4 fold cross-validation experiments. The results are the average results of cross-validation.

Experiment 1: Performance comparison experiment of Statistical methods and rule method

Aiming at the different statistical models, by selecting different feature, we did 3 groups experimental separately. For CRF and ME, we select T1 while n=2. To SVM we take MI as feature while the window size is 2. Results are shown in Table 2.

Table 2 The experiment result of rule-based method and the statistic-based method

Method / Adverb	Rule-based	CRF	ME	SVM
bian/便	0.409	0.459	0.453	0.876
fenbie/分别	0.506	0.673	0.679	0.905
Jiu/就	0.339	0.776	0.608	0.59
tebie/特别	0.697	0.783	0.652	0.932
yi/已	0.511	0.91	0.71	0.974
shifen/十分	0.712	0.95	0.865	0.993
xianhou/先后	0.963	0.575	0.59	0.846
average precision	**0.55**	**0.729**	**0.66**	**0.885**

From Table 2 we can see that the statistic-based results are better than the rule-based results on the whole. The average precision has been raised from 55% to 88.5%. It can clearly be seen that the statistical method has better adaptability and good application prospect in automatic identification of modern Chinese adverbs' usages.

At the same time, we can see that the statistical result of adverb "xianhou/先后" is obviously lower than the rule-based method. This is because the different usage of it can be easily distinguished from its rule, so the precision of rule-based method is higher than statistic-based method. To these words, we consider to use the method that combines the statistics-based and rules-based method.

Experiment 2: Statistical experiment under different feature template

By choosing different feature templates, this experiment to analyze the influence of different feature to the statistical method. Figure 1 is the average results of 6 adverbs(removing adverb "xian hou/先后") using three models. The abscissa 1-6 is the feature in the template T1 while n take 2, 3, 4, 5, 6, 7 separately. Figure 2 is the average results of these adverbs using CRF and ME with template T1, T2, and T3(see Table 1). The abscissa 1-3, 4-6, 7-9 ,10-12, 13-15, 16-18, is T1, T2, T3 while n take 2, 3 ,4 ,5, 6, 7.

From Figure 1 and Figure 2, we can see that the precision of statistical results have not great changes by choosing different context window. In general it can be achieved the best result within the window size (-4, +4) of the context. So, in the current scale of corpus, big window size may be not better when recognizing usages of adverbs, and it may bring more noise for recognizing with the increase of window size. But observing experimental results of specific words, we found that it's not all of the words exist this phenomenon. Figure 3 and Figure 4 is the result of adverb "jiu/就" and "bian/便" using three models with T1(n=2,…,7).

From Figure 3 and Figure 4, we can see that to different adverbs, the results of three models are not same, and even have big difference. To adverb "jiu/就", CRF is the best, SVM is the worst. To adverb "bian/便", SVM is the best, and the difference between CRF and ME is not very large. (Ma Z., 2004) also pointed out that every adverb needs to be synthetically analyzed and researched.

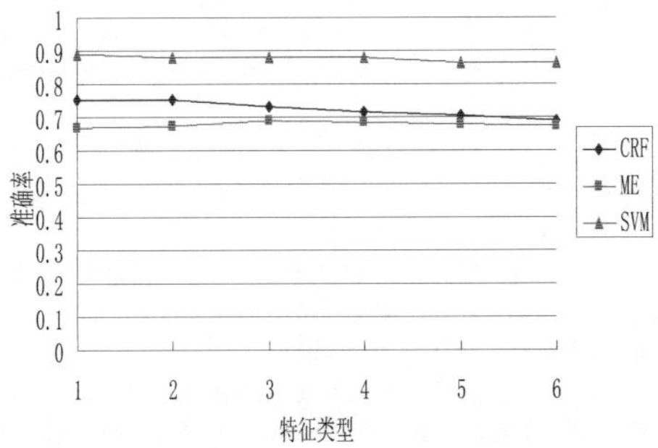

Figure 1 Average result of three models with T1(n=2,…,7)

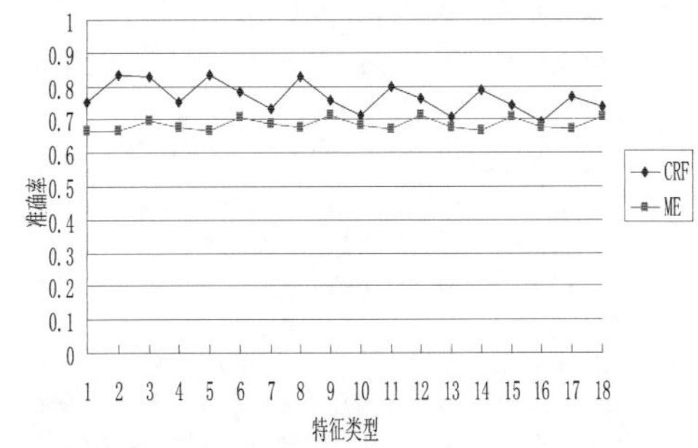

Figure 2 Average result of CRF and ME with T1, T2, T3(n=2,..,7)

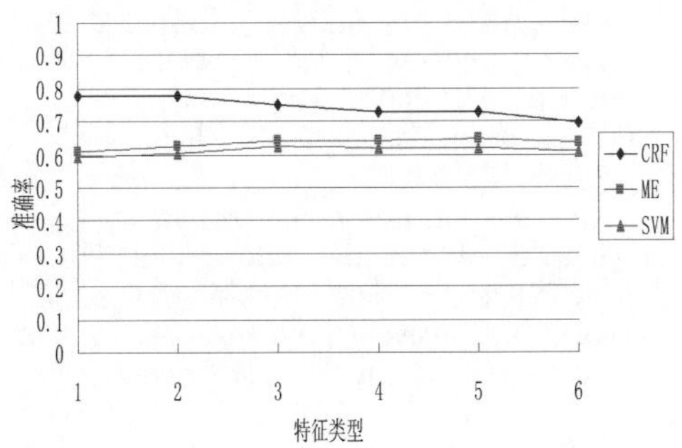

Figure 3 Adverb Result of adverb "jiu/就" using three models with T1(n=2,…7)

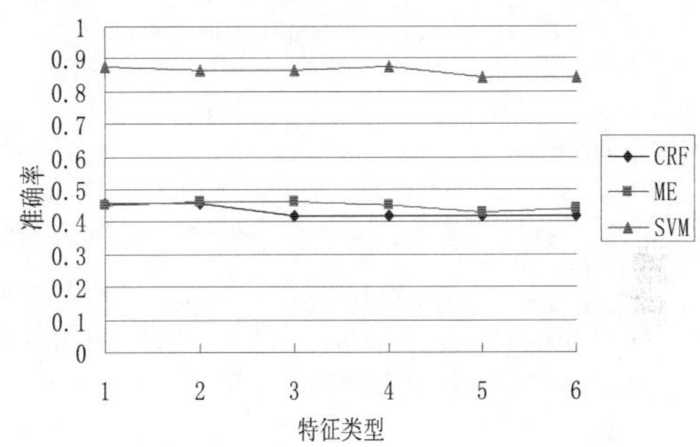

Figure 4 Adverb Result of adverb "bian/便" using three models with T1(n=2,…7)

So, to different adverb, we may be select different statistical model based on its own characteristics. For some common Chinese adverb, it's very important to study and contrast case-by-case.

5 Conclusions

The article makes a preliminary study on automatically recognizing common adverbs' usages. From the experimental results wen can see, compared with the rule-based method, statistic-based method has obvious advantages.

This article is a continuation of the work of Functional Word Knowledge Base. Furthermore, we will study the method that combines the rule-based method and the statistic-based method to automatically recognizing adverbs' usages, and further enhance the recognition precision. We hope our study can help the Chinese lexical semantic analysis, and make a good base to the Chinese text machine understanding and the application of natural language processing.

Acknowledgement

The work in this paper was supported by the China National Natural Science Foundation (No. 60970083), the Open Project Program of the Key Laboratory of Computational Linguistics(Peking University)(KLCL 1004) of China Ministry Education, and the Outstanding Young Talents Technology Innovation Foundation of Henan Province(No. 104100510026).

References

Chen Wenliang, Zhang Yujie, Hitoshi Isahara. *Chinese named entity recognition with conditional random fields.* In 5th SIGHAN Workshop on Chinese Language Processing, Australia, 2006.

Fei Sha , Fernando Pereira. *Shallow parsing with conditional random fields.* In: the proceedings of Human Language Technology/North American chapter of the Association for Computational Linguistics annual meeting, 2003: 213-220.

Firth J R., *A Synopsis of L inguistic Theory 1930 - 1955* In Studies on L inguistic Analysis. L ondon: B lackwell 1957 : 101-126

Guo Jiaqing, *Studies on the Chinese Named Entity Recognition based on conditional random fields.* Doctoral dissertation of the Shenyang Aviation Industry Colledge, China. 2007.

Hao, Liping, Zan, Hongying, Zhang, Kunli, *Research on Chinese Adverb Usage for Machine Recognition.* In : Proceedings of the 7th International Conference on Chinese Computing (ICCC2007): 122-125

Lafferty, J., McCallum, A., Pereira F,. *Conditional random fields: probabilistic models for segmenting and labeling sequence data.* In the Proceedings of International Conference on Machine Learning, 2001: 282-289.

Li, Xiaoqi, et al. *The teaching materials on the modern Chinese funciotnal word.* Peking University press, Beijing, China, 2005. (in Chinese)

Li, Guozheng, Wang, Meng, *Introduction on the Support Vector Machine*. The electronic Industry Press. Beijing, China, 2005.

LI, Sujian, Liu, Qun, Yang Zhifeng, *Chunk Parsing with Maximum Entropy Principle*, Chinese Journal of Computers, 2003(12), 1722-1727.

Liu, Kang; Zhao, Jun, *Sentence Sentiment Analysis Based on Cascaded CRFs Model*, Journal of Chinese Information Processing, 2008(1), 123-128.

Liu, Rui,. et al. *The Automatic Recognition Research on Contemporary Chinese Language*, Computer Science, 2008(8A): 172-174. (in Chinese)

Liu, Yun, *The construcion of Chinese funtional words konwledge base*. Peking University. Postdoctoral reports of Peking University. 2004.

Lu, Zhimao, Liu, ting, *Survey of the statitical word sense disambiguation study*. Jounal of Electroniics, 2006.2

Ma,.Zhen, *Study Methodology of the Modern Chinese Function Words*. Commercial Press.2004.(in Chinese)

Miao Xuelei. *A Random Conditional Fields Based Method to Chinese Word Sense Disambiguation Research.* Shenyang Institute of Aeronautical Engineering. 2007.

Shi Shumin, Wang Zhiqiang, Zhou Lang, *Chinese Named Entity Recognition based on conditional random fields.* In the Proceedings of the 3rd students computational linguistics conference . 2006.(In Chinese)

Vapnik V., *Statistical Learning Theory*. Wiley-Interscience ublication. John Wiley&Sons, Inc,1998

Wang, Jiangwei, *Chinese named entity recognition Based on Maximum Entropy*, Doctoral dissertation of Nanjing University of Science and Technology, 2005.

Yu, Kun, Guan, Gang, Zhou, Ming. *Resume information extraction with cascaded hybrid model.* Proceedings of the 43rd Annual Meeting on Association for Computational Linguistics. Ann Arbor, Michigan. 2005 : 499-506

Yu, Shiwen, et al. Knowledge-base of Generalized Functional Words of Contemporary Chinese[J]. Journal of Chinese Language and Computing, 13(1): 89-98. 2004.

Zan, Hongying, Zhang Kunli, Chai,Yumei Yu, Shiwen. *The Formal Description of Modern Chinese adverbs' usages.* In Proceedings of the 9th Chinese Lexical Semantics Workshop(CLSW-2007), 52-56. 2007. (in Chinese)

Zan, Hongying, Zhang, Kunli, Chai,Yumei, Yu, Shiwen. *Studies on the Functional Word Knowledge Base of Contemporary Chinese.* Journal of Chinese Information Processing,2007(5): 107-111. (in Chinese)

Zhang Jian, *Studies on the English Named Entity Recognition based on conditional random fields*. Doctoral dissertation of the Harbin Industry University, China. 2006.

Zhang, Lei, *Study of Chinese POS Tagging Based on Maximum Entropy*, Doctoral dissertation of Dalian University of Technology, 2008.

Automatic Identification of Predicate Heads in Chinese Sentences

Xiaona Ren[a] **Qiaoli Zhou**[a] **Chunyu Kit**[b] **Dongfeng Cai**[a]
Knowledge Engineering Research Center[a]
Shenyang Aerospace University
Department of Chinese, Translation and Linguistics[b]
City University of Hong Kong
rxn_nlp@163.com ctckit@cityu.edu.hk

Abstract

We propose an effective approach to automatically identify predicate heads in Chinese sentences based on statistical pre-processing and rule-based post-processing. In the preprocessing stage, the maximal noun phrases in a sentence are recognized and replaced by "NP" labels to simplify the sentence structure. Then a CRF model is trained to recognize the predicate heads of this simplified sentence. In the post-processing stage, a rule base is built according to the grammatical features of predicate heads. It is then utilized to correct the preliminary recognition results. Experimental results show that our approach is feasible and effective, and its accuracy achieves 89.14% on Tsinghua Chinese Treebank.

1 Introduction

It is an important issue to identify predicates in syntactic analysis. In general, a predicate is considered the head of a sentence. In Chinese, it usually organizes two parts into a well-formed sentence, one with a subject and its adjunct, and the other with an object and/or complement (Luo *et al.*, 1994). Accurate identification of predicate head is thus critical in determining the syntactic structure of a sentence. Moreover, a predicate head splitting a long sentence into two shorter parts can alleviate the complexity of syntactic analysis to a certain degree. This is particularly useful when long dependency relations are involved. Without doubt, this is also a difficult task in Chinese dependency parsing (Cheng *et al.*, 2005).

Predicate head identification also plays an important role in facilitating various tasks of natural language processing. For example, it enhances shallow parsing (Sun *et al.*, 2000) and head-driven parsing (Collins, 1999), and also improves the precision of sentence similarity computation (Sui *et al.*, 1998a). There is reason to expect it to be more widely applicable to other tasks, e.g. machine translation, information extraction, and question answering.

In this paper, we propose an effective approach to automatically recognize predicate heads of Chinese sentences based on a preprocessing step for maximal noun phrases [1](MNPs). MNPs usually appear in the location of subject and object in a sentence. The proper identification of them is thus expected to assist the analysis of sentence structure and/or improve the accuracy of predicate head recognition.

In the next section, we will first review some related works and discuss their limitations, followed by a detailed description of the task of recognizing predicate heads in Section 3. Section 4 illustrates our proposed approach and Section 5 presents experiments and results. Finally we conclude the paper in Section 6.

2 Related Works

There exist various approaches to identify predicate heads in Chinese sentences. Luo and Zheng (1994) and Tan (2000) presented two rule-based methods based on contextual features and part of speeches. A statistical approach was presented in Sui and Yu (1998b), which utilizes a decision tree model. Gong *et al.* (2003) presented their hybrid method combining both rules and statistics. These traditional approaches only make use of the static and dynamic grammatical features of the quasi-predicates to identify the predicate heads. On this basis, Li and Meng (2005) proposed a method to further utilize syntactic relations between the subject and the predicate in a sentence. Besides the above monolingual proposals, Sui and Yu (1998a) discussed a bilingual strategy to recognize predicate heads in Chinese

[1] Maximal noun phrase is the noun phrase which is not contained by any other noun phrases.

sentences with reference to those in their counterpart English sentences.

Nevertheless, these methods have their own limitations. The rule-based methods require effective linguistic rules to be formulated by linguists according to their own experience. Certainly, this is impossible to cover all linguistic situations concerned, due to the complexity of language and the limitations of human observation. In practice, we also should not underestimate the complexity of feature application, the computing power demanded and the difficulties in handing irregular sentence patterns. For instance, a sentence without subject may lead to an incorrect recognition of predicate head. For corpus-based approaches, they rely on language data in huge size but the available data may not be adequate. Those bilingual methods may first encounter the difficulty of determining correct sentence alignment in the case that the parallel data consist of much free translation.

Our method proposed here focuses on a simple but effective means to help identify predicate heads, i.e., MNP pre-processing. At present, there has some substantial progress in automatic recognition of MNP. Zhou *et al.* (2000) proposed an efficient algorithm for identifying Chinese MNPs by using their structure combination, achieving an 85% precision and an 82% recall. Dai *et al.* (2008) presented another method based on statistics and rules, reaching a 90% F-score on HIT Chinese Treebank. Jian *et al.* (2009) employed both left-right and right-left sequential labeling and developed a novel "fork position" based probabilistic algorithm to fuse bidirectional results, obtaining an 86% F-score on the Penn Chinese Treebank. Based on these previous works, we have developed an approach that first identifies the MNPs in a sentence, which are then used in determining the predicate heads in the next stage.

3 Task Description

The challenge of accurate identification of predicate heads is to resolve the problem of quasi-predicate heads in a sentence. On the one hand, the typical POSs of predicate heads in Chinese sentences are verbs, adjectives and descriptive words[2]. Each of them may have multiple instances in a sentence. On the other hand, while a simple sentence has only one predicate head, a complex sentence may have multiple ones. The latter constitutes 8.25% in our corpus. Thus, the real difficulty lies in how to recognize the true predicate head of a sentence among so many possibilities.

Take a simple sentence as example:

这/rN 种/qN 有/v 特大/a 翅膀/n 的/uJDE 大/a 鸟/n 没有/v 足够/aD 的/uJDE 支撑/v 力/n 和/cC 前进/v 力/n 。/wE

The quasi-predicate heads (verbs and adjectives) include 有/v, 特大/a, 大/a, 没有/v, 支撑/v, and 前进/v. However, there are two MNPs in this sentence, namely, "这/rN 种/qN 有/v 特大/a 翅膀/n 的/uJDE 大/a 鸟/n" and "足够/aD 的/uJDE 支撑/v 力/n 和/cC 前进/v 力/n". These two MNPs cover most quasi-predicate heads in the sentence, except 没有/v, the true predicate head that we want.

An MNP is a complete semantic unit, and its internal structure may include different kinds of constituents (Jian *et al.*, 2009). Therefore, the fundamental structure of a sentence can be made clear after recognizing its MNPs. This can help filter out those wrong quasi-predicates for a better shortlist of good candidates for the true predicate head in a sentence.

In practice, the identification of predicate head begins with recognizing MNPs in the same sentence. It turns the above example sentence into:

[这/rN 种/qN 有/v 特大/a 翅膀/n 的/uJDE 大/a 鸟/n] 没有/v [足够/aD 的/uJDE 支撑/v 力/n 和/cC 前进/v 力/n] 。/wE

These MNPs are then replaced with the conventional label "NP" for noun phrase, resulting in a simplified sentence structure as follows.

NP/NP 没有/v NP/NP 。/wE

This basic sentence structure can largely alleviates the complexity of the original sentence and narrows down the selection scope of quasi-predicates for the true head. In this particular example, the only verb left in the sentence after MNP recognition is the true predicate head.

4 Predicate Head Identification

This section describes the process of identifying predicate heads in sentences. As illustrated in Figure 1 below, it can be divided into three steps:

Step 1: recognize the MNPs in a sentence and replace the MNPs with "NP" label to simplify the sentence structure.

Step 2: recognize the predicate heads in the resulted simplified structure.

[2] We only focus on Verbs and adjectives in this work.

Step 3: post-process the preliminary results to correct the wrong predicate heads according to heuristics in a rule base.

4.1 MNP Recognition

The MNP recognition is performed via a trained CRF model on unlabeled data. We adopt the method in Dai *et al.* (2008), with modified templates for the different corpus. Each feature is composed of the words and POS tags surrounding the current word i, as well as different combination of them. The context window of template is set to size 3. Table 1 shows the feature template we use.

Type	Features	
Unigram	$Word_i$	Pos_i
Bigram	$Word_i/Pos_i$	
Surrounding	$Word_{i-1}/Word_i$	Pos_{i-1}/Pos_i
	$Word_i/Word_{i+1}$	Pos_i/Pos_{i+1}
	$Word_{i-2}/Pos_{i-2}$	Pos_{i-2}/Pos_{i-1}
	$Pos_{i-2}/Pos_{i-1}/Pos_i$	Pos_{i-3}/Pos_{i-2}
	$Pos_{i-1}/Pos_i/Pos_{i+1}$	$Word_{i+3}/Pos_{i+3}$
	$Pos_{i+1}/Pos_{i+2}/Pos_{i+3}$	$Word_{i+2}/Word_{i+3}$

Table 1: Feature Template

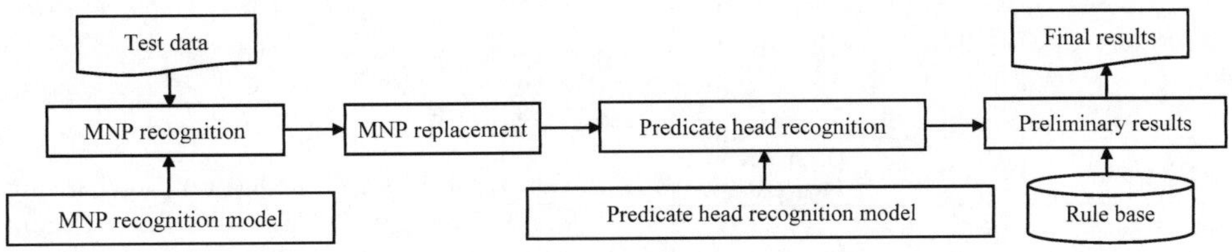

Figure 1: Flow Chart of Predicate Head Identification

The main effective factors for MNPs recognition are the lengths of MNPs and the complexity of sentence in question. We analyze the length distribution of MNPs in TCT[3] corpus, finding that their average length is 6.24 words and the longest length is 119 words. Table 2 presents this distribution in detail.

Length of MNP	Occurrences	Percentage (%)
len<5	3260	48.82
5≤len<10	2348	35.17
len≥10	1069	16.01

Table 2: Length Distribution of MNPs in TCT Corpus

The MNPs longer than 5 words cover 50% of total occurrences, indicating the relatively high complexity of sentences. We trained a CRF model using this data set, which achieves an F-score of 83.7% on MNP recognition.

4.2 Predicate Head Identification

After the MNPs in a sentence are recognized, they are replaced by "NP" label to rebuild a simplified sentence structure. It largely reduces the difficulty in identifying predicate heads from this simplified structure.

We evaluate our models by their precision in the test set, which is formulated as

$$Precision = \frac{right\_sentences}{Sum\_sentences} * 100\% \quad (1)$$

The *right_sentences* refer to the number of sentences whose predicate heads are successfully identified, and the *sum_sentences* to the total number of sentences in the test set. We count a sentence as *right_sentence* if and only if *all* its predicate heads are successfully identified, including those with multiple predicate heads.

For each predicate head, we need an appropriate feature representation *f (i, j)*. We test the model performance with different context window sizes of template. The results are shown in Table 3 as follows.

Template	Context window size	Precision (%)
Temp1	2	79.27
Temp2	3	82.59
Temp3	4	81.37

Table 3: Precisions of Predicate Heads Recognition under Different Context Window Sizes

It shows that the window size of 3 words gives the highest precision (82.59%). Therefore we apply this window size, together with other features in our CRF model, including words, POSs, phrase tags and their combinations. There are 24 template types in total.

4.3 Post-processing

The post-processing stage is intended to correct errors in the preliminary identification results of

[3] Tsinghua Chinese Treebank ver1.0.

predicate heads, by applying linguistic rules formulated heuristically. We test each rule to see if it improves the recognition accuracy, so as to retrieve a validated rule base. The labeling of predicate heads follows the standard of TCT and a wrong labeling is treated as an error.

There are three main types of error, according to our observation. The first is that no predicate head is identified. The second is that the whole sentence is recognized as an MNP, such that no predicate head is recognized. The third is that the predicate head is incorrectly identified, such as "是" in the expression "认为…是…", where the correct answer is "认为" according to the TCT standard.

Error types	Percentage	Improved percentage
No predicate head	17.50%	2.44%
a sentence as an MNP	10.63%	1.11%
"认为…是…"	8.75%	0.56%
Others	63.12%	2.77%

Table 4: Types of Error

Table 4 lists different types of error, together with their percentage in all sentences whose predicate heads have been mistakenly identified, and the improvement in percentage after the post-processing. To correct these errors, a number of rules for post-processing are formulated. The main rules are the followings:

- If no predicate head is recognized in a sentence, we label the first verb as the predicate head.

Error sample：自/p [1 8 4 0/m 年/qT 鸦片战争/nR] 后/f ，/wP [中国/nS 逐步/d 沦为/v 半殖民地/b 半封建/b 社会/n] 。/wE

Corrected：自/p [1 8 4 0/m 年/qT 鸦片战争/nR] 后/f ，/wP [中国/nS 逐步/d **沦为/v** 半殖民地/b 半封建/b 社会/n] 。/wE

- If the whole sentence is recognized as an MNP, such that no predicate head is identified, we label the first verb as the predicate head.

Error sample：[针灸/n 包括/v 针/n 和/cC 灸/n 两/m 部分/n] 。/wE

Corrected：[针灸/n **包括/v** 针/n 和/cC 灸/n 两/m 部分/n] 。/wE

- For expression "认为…是…", we label "认为" as the predicate head.

Error sample：[另/rB 一/m 种/qN 观点/n] 认为/v 档案学/n 是/vC [兼/d 有/v 社会科学/n 和/cC 自然科学/n 性质/n 的/uJDE 综合性/b 科学/n] 。/wE

Corrected：[另/rB 一/m 种/qN 观点/n] **认为/v** 档案学/n 是/vC [兼/d 有/v 社会科学/n 和/cC 自然科学/n 性质/n 的/uJDE 综合性/b 科学/n] 。/wE

There are also other rules in the rule base besides the above ones. For example, if the first word of a sentences is "如" or "诸如", it is labeled as the predicate head.

5 Experiments

5.1 Data Sets

Our experiments are carried out on the Tsinghua Chinese Treebank (TCT). Every constituent of a sentence in TCT is labeled by human expert. We randomly extract 5000 sentences from TCT and remove those sentences that do not have predicate head. Finally, our data set contains 4613 sentences, in which 3711 sentences are randomly chosen as training data and 902 sentences as testing data. The average length of these sentences in training set is 20 words.

The number of quasi-predicate heads in a sentence is a critical factor to determine the performance of predicate head recognition. Reducing the number of quasi-predicate heads can improve the recognition precision. Table 5 shows the percentage of quasi-predicate heads in training data before and after MNP replacement.

Number of quasi-predicates	Percentage before MNP replacement(%)	Percentage after MNP replacement(%)
1	12.50	49.69
2	19.62	27.22
3	20.37	12.37
>3	47.51	10.72

Table 5: The Percentage of Quasi-predicate Heads Before and After MNP Replacement

From Table 5, we can see that almost half sentences contain more than three quasi-predicate heads. Only 12.5% of sentences have only one quasi-predicate head before MNP replacement. However, after MNPs are replaced with the "NP" label, only 10.72% contain more than three quasi-predicate heads and nearly 50% contain only one quasi-predicate head. We have evidence that MNP pre-processing can reduce the number of quasi-predicate heads and lower the complexity of sentence structures.

5.2 Results and Discussion

For comparison purpose, we developed four different models for predicate head recognition. Models 1 and 2 are CRF models, the former recognizing predicate heads directly and the later recognizing MNPs at the same time. Model 3 recognizes predicate heads based on MNP pre-processing. Model 4 is based on model 3, including the post-processing stage. Table 6 shows the recognition performance of each model using the best context window size.

Model	Context window size	Number of correct sentences	Precision(%)
model 1	4	680	75.39
model 2	4	687	76.16
model 3	3	745	82.59
model 4	3	804	**89.14**

Table 6: Performance of Different Models

Comparing these models, we can see that the additional feature in model 2 leads to 1% improvement in precision over model 1. Moreover, the MNP pre-processing in model 3 results in a large increase in accuracy, compared to model 1. It indicates that the MNP pre-processing does improve the precision of recognition. Compared with model 3, model 4 achieves a precision even 6.55% higher, indicating that the post-processing is also an effective step for recognition.

As shown, the performance is affected by the effect of MNP recognition. There are three kinds of relation between the predicate heads and the types of MNP recognition error:

Relation 1: The whole sentence is recognized as an MNP.

Relation 2: The boundaries of an MNP are incorrectly recognized and the MNP does not contain the predicate head.

Relation 3: The boundaries of an MNP are incorrectly recognized and the MNP contains the predicate head. Table 7 shows the distribution of these three relations in the recognition errors.

Relation	Number of sentences	Percentage(%)
Relation 1	17	5.47
Relation 2	281	90.35
Relation 3	13	4.18

Table 7: Distribution of the Three Relations in Recognition Errors

In our approach, the errors of relation 1 and relation 3 can be solved by the post-processing, as presented in Section 4.3. Relation 2 holds the largest proportion among the three. But the error rate of predicate head recognition only reaches 31.67% in this case. That is to say, although the MNP boundaries are incorrectly recognized, the accuracy of predicate head recognition can still reach 68.33%.

Chen (2007) proposed a probabilistic model (model 5) for recognizing predicate heads in Chinese sentences. The probabilities of quasi-predicates are estimated by maximum likelihood estimation. A discounted model is used to smooth parameters. We compare his model with our model 3 using different contextual features on TCT corpus. Table 8 shows the comparison results.

The highest precision of model 3 is 82.59% when the context window size is set to 3. For model 5, it is 70.62% at a context window size of 4. Experimental results show that the precision of our method is about 12% higher than Chen's.

Context window size	Model	Precision (%)
2	model 5	69.18
	model 3	79.27
3	model 5	70.18
	model 3	**82.59**
4	model 5	**70.62**
	model 3	81.37

Table 8: Comparison between model 3 and Chen's model

Beside Chen's method, the Stanford Parser can also recognize the predicate heads in simple Chinese sentences. The root node of dependency tree is the predicate head. For a comparison, we randomly extract two hundred simple sentences in our test data to compare it with the outputs of our model 3. We also train a model of predicate head recognition (model 6), which assumes that all MNPs are successfully identified. The comparison is shown in Table 9. We can see that the precision of model 6 is 8.35% higher than model 3. This means that our method still has a certain room for further improvement.

Stanford Parser	model 3	model6
78.17%	83.15%	91.5%

Table 9: Comparison between model 3 and Stanford Parser

5.3 Error Analysis

As shown above, the post-processing can correct most errors in the recognition of predicate heads. But we also observe some errors that cannot be corrected this way. For example,

地理学/n以/p 描述性/n 记载/v [地理/n 知识/n] 为主/v 。/wE

The predicate head here is "为主", but usually "记载" is recognized as the predicate head. This is because "记载" can be used either as a verb or a noun. There are many verbs of this kind in Chinese, such as "主张" and "应用". Mistakes caused by the flexibility of Chinese verb and the ambiguity of sentence structure appear to deserve more of our effort. Meanwhile, there are also some other unusual cases that cannot be properly solved with statistical methods.

6 Conclusion

Identification of predicate heads is important to syntactic parsing. In this paper, we have presented a novel method that combines both statistical and rule-based approaches to identify predicate heads based on MNP pre-processing and rule-based post-processing. We have had a series of experiments to show that this method achieves a significant improvement over some state-of-the-art approaches. Furthermore, it also provides a simple structure of sentence that can be utilized for parsing.

In the future, we will study how semantic information can be applied to further improve the precision of MNP recognition and predicate head identification. It is also very interesting to explore how this approach can facilitate parsing, including shallow parsing.

Acknowledgments

We would like to thank the anonymous reviewers for their helpful comments and suggestions. We also thank Billy Wong of City University of Hong Kong for his much-appreciated input during the writing process.

References

Zhiqun Chen. 2007. Study on recognizing predicate of Chinese sentences. *Computer Engineering and Applications,* 43(17): 176-178.

Yuchang Cheng, Asahara Masayuki, and Matsumoto Yuji. 2005. Chinese deterministic dependency analyzer: examining effects of global features and root node finder. *In Proceedings of the Fourth SIGHAN Wordshop on Chinese Language Processing,* pp. 17-24.

Cui Dai, Qiaoli Zhou, and Dongfeng Cai. 2008. Automatic recognition of Chinese maximal-length noun phrase based on statistics and rules. *Journal of Chinese Information Processing,* 22(6): 110-115.

Xiaojin Gong, Zhensheng Luo, and Weihua Luo. 2003. Recognizing the predicate head of Chinese sentences. *Journal of Chinese Information Processing,* 17(2): 7-13.

Ping Jian, and Chengqing Zong. 2009. A new approach to identifying Chinese maximal-length phrase using bidirectional labeling. *CAAI Transactions on Intelligent Systems,* 4(5): 406-413.

Guochen Li, and Jing Meng. 2005. A method of identifying the predicate head based on the correpondence between the subject and the predicate. *Journal of Chinese Information Processing,* 19(1): 1-7.

Zhensheng Luo, and Bixia Zheng. 1994. An approach to the automatic analysis and frequency statistics of Chinese sentence patterns. *Journal of Chinese Information Processing,* 8(2): 1-9.

Zhifang Sui, and Shiwen Yu. 1998a. The research on recognizing the predicate head of a Chinese simple sentence in EBMT. *Journal of Chinese Information Processing,* 12(4): 39-46.

Zhifang Sui, and Shiwen Yu. 1998b. The acquisition and application of the knowledge for recognizing the predicate head of a Chinese simple sentence. *Journal of Peking University (Science Edition),* 34(2-3): 221-229.

Honglin Sun, and Shiwen Yu. 2000. Shallow parsing: an overview. *Contemporary Linguistics,* 2(2): 74-83.

Hui Tan. 2000. Center predicate recognization for scientific article. *Journal of WuHan University (Natural Science Edition),* 46(3): 1-3.

Qiang Zhou, Maosong Sun, and Changning Huang. 2000. Automatically identify Chinese maximal noun phrase. *Journal of Software,* 11(2): 195-201.

Michael Collins. 1999. *Head-driven statistical models for natural language parsing.* Ph. D. Thesis, University of Pennsylvania.

Selecting Optimal Feature Template Subset for CRFs

Xingjun Xu[1] and **Guanglu Sun**[2] and **Yi Guan**[1] and
Xishuang Dong[1] and **Sheng Li**[1]
1: School of Computer Science and Technology,
Harbin Institute of Technology,
150001, Harbin, China
2: School of Computer Science and Technology,
Harbin University of Science and Technology
150080, Harbin, China
xxjroom@163.com; guanglu.sun@gmail.com
guanyi@hit.edu.cn; dongxishuang@gmail.com
lisheng@hit.edu.cn

Abstract

Conditional Random Fields (CRFs) are the state-of-the-art models for sequential labeling problems. A critical step is to select optimal feature template subset before employing CRFs, which is a tedious task. To improve the efficiency of this step, we propose a new method that adopts the maximum entropy (ME) model and maximum entropy Markov models (MEMMs) instead of CRFs considering the homology between ME, MEMMs, and CRFs. Moreover, empirical studies on the efficiency and effectiveness of the method are conducted in the field of Chinese text chunking, whose performance is ranked the first place in task two of CIPS-ParsEval-2009.

1 Introduction

Conditional Random Fields (CRFs) are the state-of-the-art models for sequential labeling problem. In natural language processing, two aspects of CRFs have been investigated sufficiently: one is to apply it to new tasks, such as named entity recognition (McCallum and Li, 2003; Li and McCallum, 2003; Settles, 2004), part-of-speech tagging (Lafferty et al., 2001), shallow parsing (Sha and Pereira, 2003), and language modeling (Roark et al., 2004); the other is to exploit new training methods for CRFs, such as improved iterative scaling (Lafferty et al., 2001), L-BFGS (McCallum, 2003) and gradient tree boosting (Dietterich et al., 2004).

One of the critical steps is to select optimal feature subset before employing CRFs. McCallum (2003) suggested an efficient method of feature induction by iteratively increasing conditional log-likelihood for discrete features. However, since there are millions of features and feature selection is an NP problem, this is intractable when searching optimal feature subset. Therefore, it is necessary that selects feature at feature template level, which reduces input scale from millions of features to tens or hundreds of candidate templates.

In this paper, we propose a new method that adopts ME and MEMMs instead of CRFs to improve the efficiency of selecting optimal feature template subset considering the homology between ME, MEMMs, and CRFs, which reduces the training time from hours to minutes without loss of performance.

The rest of this paper is organized as follows. Section 2 presents an overview of previous work for feature template selection. We propose our optimal method for feature template selection in Section 3. Section 4 presents our experiments and results. Finally, we end this paper with some concluding remarks.

2 Related Work

Feature selection can be carried out from two levels: feature level (feature selection, or FS), or feature template level (feature template selection, or FTS). FS has been sufficiently investigated and share most concepts with FTS. For example, the target of FS is to select a subset from original feature set, whose optimality is measured by an evaluation criterion (Liu and Yu, 2005). Similarly, the target of FTS is to select a subset from original feature template set. To achieve optimal feature subset, two problems in original set must be eliminated: irrelevance and redundancy (Yu and Liu, 2004). The only difference between FS and FTS is that the number of elements in feature template set is much less than that in feature set.

Liu and Yu (2005) classified FS models into three categories: the filter model, the wrapper model, and the hybrid model. The filter model (Hall 2000; Liu and Setiono, 1996; Yu and Liu, 2004) relies on general characteristics of the data to evaluate and select feature subsets without any machine learning model. The wrapper model (Dy and Brodley, 2000; Kim et al., 2000; Kohavi and John, 1997) requires one predetermined machine learning model and uses its performance as the evaluation criterion. The hybrid model (Das, 2001) attempts to take advantage of the two models by exploiting their different evaluation criteria in different search stages.

There are two reasons to employ the wrapper model to accomplish FTS: (1) The wrapper model tends to achieve better effectiveness than that of the filter model with respect of a more direct evaluation criterion; (2) The computational cost is tractable because it can reduce the number of subsets sharply by heuristic algorithm according to the human knowledge. And our method belongs to this type.

Lafferty (2001) noticed the homology between MEMMs and CRFs, and chose optimal MEMMs parameter vector as a starting point for training the corresponding CRFs. And the training process of CRFs converges faster than that with all zero parameter vectors.

On the other hand, the general framework that processes sequential labeling with CRFs has also been investigated well, which can be described as follows:

1. Converting the new problem to sequential labeling problem;
2. Selecting optimal feature template subset for CRFs;
3. Parameter estimation for CRFs;
4. Inference for new data.

In the field of English text chunking (Sha and Pereira, 2003), the step 1, 3, and 4 have been studied sufficiently, whereas the step 2, how to select optimal feature template subset efficiently, will be the main topic of this paper.

3 Feature Template Selection

3.1 The Wrapper Model for FTS

The framework of FTS based on the wrapper model for CRFs can be described as:

1. Generating the new feature template subset;
2. Training a CRFs model;
3. Updating optimal feature template subset if the new subset is better;
4. Repeating step 1, 2, 3 until there are no new feature template subsets.

Let N denote the number of feature templates, the number of non-empty feature template subsets will be (2^N-1). And the wrapper model is unable to deal with such case without heuristic methods, which contains:

1. Atomic feature templates are firstly added to feature template subset, which is carried out by: Given the position i, the current word W_i and the current part-of-speech P_i are firstly added to current feature template subset, and then W_{i-1} and P_{i-1}, or W_{i+1} and P_{i+1}, and so on, until the effectiveness is of no improvement. Taking the Chinese text chunking as example, optimal atomic feature template subset is $\{W_{i-3}\sim W_{i+3}, P_{i-3}\sim P_{i+3}\}$;

2. Adding combined feature templates properly to feature template set will be helpful to improve the performance, however, too many combined feature templates will result in severe data sparseness problem. Therefore, we present three restrictions for combined feature templates: (1) A combined feature template that contains more than three atomic templates are not allowable; (2) If a combined feature template contains three atomic feature template, it can only contain at most one atomic word template; (3) In a combined template, at most one word is allowable between the two most adjacent atomic templates; For example, the combined feature templates, such as $\{P_{i-1}, P_i, P_{i+1}, P_{i+2}\}$, $\{W_i, W_{i+1}, P_i\}$, and $\{P_{i-1}, P_{i+2}\}$, are not allowable, whereas the combined templates, such as $\{P_i, P_{i+1}, P_{i+2}\}$, $\{P_{i-1}, W_i, P_{i+1}\}$, and $\{P_{i-1}, P_{i+1}\}$, are allowable.

3. After atomic templates have been added, $\{W_{i-1}, W_i\}$, or $\{W_i, W_{i+1}\}$, or $\{P_{i-1}, P_i\}$, or $\{P_i, P_{i+1}\}$ are firstly added to feature template subset. The template window is moved forward, and then backward. Such process will repeat with expanding template window, until the effectiveness is of no improvement.

Tens or hundreds of training processes are still needed even if the heuristic method is introduced. People usually employ CRFs model to estimate the effectiveness of template subset However, this is more tedious than that we use ME or MEMMs instead. The idea behind this lie in three aspects: first, in one iteration, the Forward-Backward Algorithm adopted in CRFs training is time-consuming; second, CRFs need more iterations than that of ME or MEMMs to converge because of larger parameter space; third, ME, MEMMs, and CRFs, are of the same type (log-linear models) and based on the same principle, as will be discussed in detail as follows.

3.2 Homology of ME, MEMMs and CRFs

ME, MEMMs, and CRFs are all based on the Principle of Maximum Entropy (Jaynes, 1957). The mathematical expression for ME model is as formula (1):

$$P(y \mid x) = \frac{1}{Z(x)} \exp\left(\sum_{i=1}^{m} \lambda_i f_i(x, y)\right) \qquad (1)$$

, and Z(x) is the normalization factor.

MEMMs can be considered as a sequential extension to the ME model. In MEMMs, the HMM transition and observation functions are replaced by a single function $P(Y_i|Y_{i-1}, X_i)$. There are three kinds of implementations of MEMMs (McCallum et al., 2000) in which we realized the second type for its abundant expressiveness. In implementation two, which is denoted as MEMMs_2 in this paper, a distributed representation for the previous state Y_{i-1} is taken as a collection of features with weights set by maximum entropy, just as we have done for the observations X_i. However, label bias problem (Lafferty et al., 2001) exists in MEMMs, since it makes a local normalization of random field models. CRFs overcome the label bias problem by global normalization.

Considering the homology between CRFs and MEMMs_2 (or ME), it is reasonable to suppose that a useful template for MEMMs_2 (or ME) is also useful for CRFs, and vice versa. And this is a necessary condition to replace CRFs with ME or MEMMs for FTS.

3.3 A New Framework for FTS

Besides the homology of these models, the other necessary condition to replace CRFs with ME or MEMMs for FTS is that all kinds of feature templates in CRFs can also be expressed by ME or MEMMs. There are two kinds of feature templates for CRFs: one is related to Y_{i-1}, which is denoted as $g(Y_{i-1}, Y_i, X_i)$; the other is not related to Y_{i-1}, which is denoted as $f(Y_i, X_i)$. Both of them can be expressed by MEMMs_2. If there is only the second kind of feature templates in the subset, it can also be expressed by ME. For example, the feature function $f(Y_i, P_i)$ in CRFs can be expressed by feature template $\{P_i\}$ in MEMMs_2 or ME; and $g(Y_{i-1}, Y_i, P_i)$ can be expressed by feature template $\{Y_{i-1}, P_i\}$ in MEMM_2.

Therefore, MEMMs_2 or ME can be employed to replace CRFs as machine learning model for improving the efficiency of FTS.

Then the new framework for FTS will be:

1. Generating the new feature template subset;
2. Training an MEMMs_2 or ME model;
3. Updating optimal feature template subset if the new subset is better;
4. Repeating step 1, 2, 3 until there are no new feature template subsets.

The wrapper model evaluates the effectiveness of feature template subset by evaluating the model on testing data. However, there is a serious efficiency problem when decoding a sequence by MEMMs_2. Given N as the length of a sentence, C as the number of candidate labels, the time complexity based on MEMMs_2 is $O(NC^2)$ when decoding by viterbi algorithm. Considering the C different Y_{i-1} for every word in a sentence, we need compute $P(Y_i|Y_{i-1}, X_i)$ (N.C) times for MEMMs_2.

Reducing the average number of candidate label C can help to improve the decoding efficiency. And in most cases, the Y_{i-1} in $P(Y_i|Y_{i-1}, X_i)$ is not necessary (Koeling, 2000; Osbome, 2000). Therefore, to reduce the average number of candidate labels C, it is reasonable to use an ME model to filter the candidate label. Given a threshold T ($0 \le T \le 1$), the candidate label filtering algorithm is as follows:

1. CP = 0;
2. While CP <= T
   a) Add the most probable candidate label Y' to viterbi algorithm;
   b) Delete Y' from the candidate label set;
   c) CP = P(Y'|X_i) + CP.

If the probability of the most probable candidate label has surpassed T, other labels are discarded. Otherwise, more labels need be added to viterbi algorithm.

4 Evaluation and Result

4.1 Evaluation

We evaluate the effectiveness and efficiency of the new framework by the data set in the task two of

CIPS-ParsEval-2009 (Zhou and Li, 2010). The effectiveness is supported by high F-1 measure in the task two of CIPS-ParsEval-2009 (see Figure 1), which shows that optimal feature template subset driven by ME or MEMMs is also optimal for CRFs. The efficiency is shown by significant decline in training time (see Figure 3), where the baseline is CRFs, and comparative methods are ME or MEMMs.

We design six subsets of feature template set and six experiments to show the effectiveness and efficiency of the new framework. As shown in Table 1 and Table 2, the 1~3 experiments shows the influence of the feature templates, which are unrelated to Y_{i-1}, for both ME and CRFs. And the 4~6 experiments show the influence of the feature templates, which are related to Y_{i-1}, for both MEMMs_2 and CRFs. In table 1, six template subsets can be divided into two sets by relevance of previous label: 1, 2, 3 and 4, 5, 6. Moreover, the first set can be divided into 1, 2, and 3 by distances between features with headwords; the second set can be divided into 4, 5 and 6 by relevance of observed value. In order to ensure the objectivity of comparative experiments, candidate label filtering algorithm is not adopted.

Task2			
Rank	No.	boundary+type	boundary+type+relation
1	01	93.20	92.10
2	15	92.85	91.76
3	12	92.36	
4	10_a	92.11	90.94
5	10_b	92.11	90.94
6	17	91.98	89.85
7	10_c	91.76	90.63
8	10_d	91.75	90.67
9	14	91.29	90.13
10	00	90.39	88.88

Figure 1: the result in the task two of CIPS-ParsEval-2009

1	W_i, W_{i-1}, W_{i-2}, W_{i+1}, W_{i+2}, P_i, P_{i-1}, P_{i-2}, P_{i+1}, P_{i+2}, $W_{i-1}\_W_i$, $W_i\_W_{i+1}$, $W_{i-1}\_W_{i+1}$, $P_{i-1}\_P_i$, $P_{i-2}\_P_{i-1}$, $P_i\_P_{i+1}$, $P_{i-1}\_P_{i+1}$, $P_{i-1}\_P_i\_P_{i+1}$, $P_{i-2}\_P_{i-1}\_P_i$, $P_i\_P_{i+1}\_P_{i+2}$, $W_i\_P_{i+1}$, $W_i\_P_{i+2}$, $P_i\_W_{i-1}$, $W_{i-2}\_P_{i-1}\_P_i$, $P_i\_W_{i+1}\_P_{i+1}$, $P_{i-1}\_W_i\_P_i$, $P_i\_W_{i+1}$
2	W_{i-3}, W_{i+3}, P_{i-3}, P_{i+3}, $W_{i-3}\_W_{i-2}$, $W_{i+2}\_W_{i+3}$, $P_{i-3}\_P_{i-2}$, $P_{i+2}\_P_{i+3}$
3	W_{i-4}, W_{i+4}, P_{i-4}, P_{i+4}, $W_{i-4}\_W_{i-3}$, $W_{i+3}\_W_{i+4}$, $P_{i-4}\_P_{i-3}$, $P_{i+3}\_P_{i+4}$
4	Y_{i-1}
5	$Y_{i-1}\_P_i\_P_{i+1}$, $Y_{i-1}\_P_i$, $Y_{i-1}\_P_{i-1}\_P_i$
6	$Y_{i-1}\_P_{i-4}$, $Y_{i-1}\_P_{i+4}$

Table 1: six subsets of feature template set

id	Model	FT subset
1	ME vs. CRFs	1
2	ME vs. CRFs	1, 2
3	ME vs. CRFs	1, 2, 3
4	MEMMs vs. CRFs	1, 2, 4
5	MEMMs vs. CRFs	1, 2, 4, 5
6	MEMMs vs. CRFs	1, 2, 4, 5, 6

Table 2: six experiments

4.2 Empirical Results

The F-measure curve is shown in Figure 2. For the same and optimal feature template subset, the F-1 measure of CRFs is superior to that of ME because of global normalization; and it is superior to that of MEMMs since it overcomes the label bias.

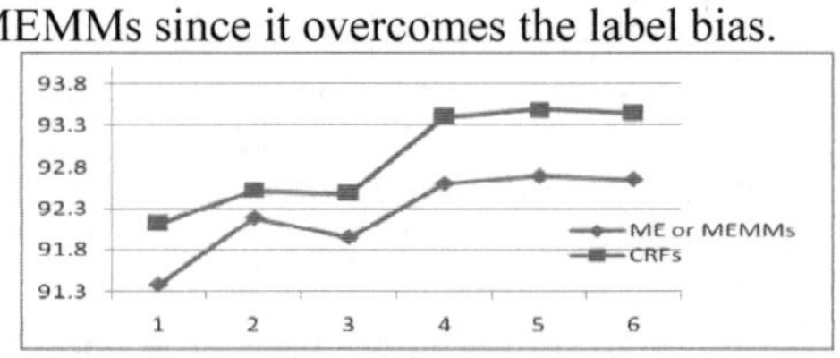

Figure 2: the F-measure curve

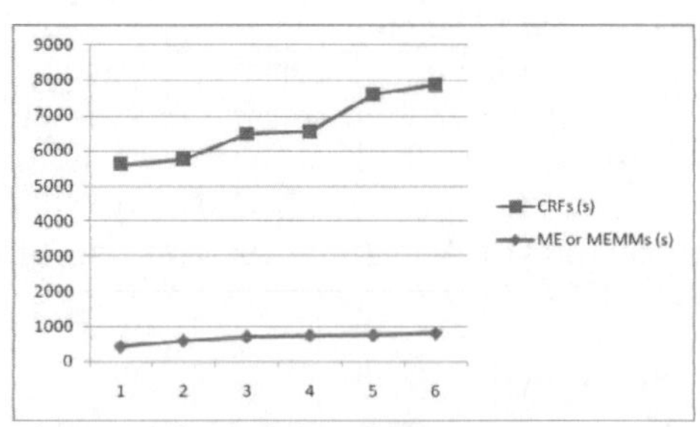

Figure 3: the training time curve

The significant decline in training time of the new framework is shown in Figure 3, while the testing time curve in Figure 4 and the total time curve in Figure 5. The testing time of ME is more than that of CRFs because of local normalization; and the testing time of MEMMs_2 is much more than that of CRFs because of N.C times of $P(Y_i|Y_{i-1}, X_i)$ computation.

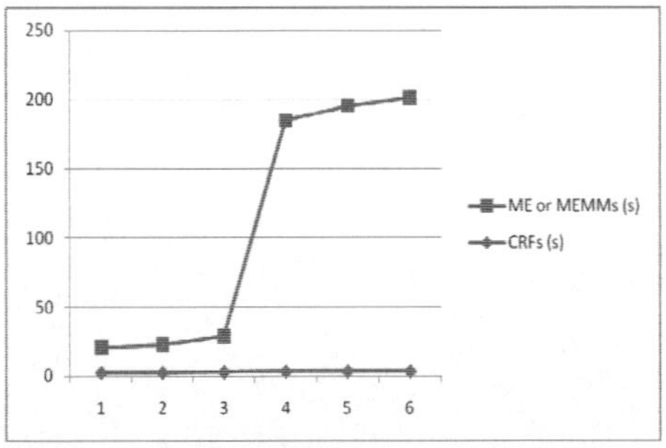

Figure 4: the testing time curve

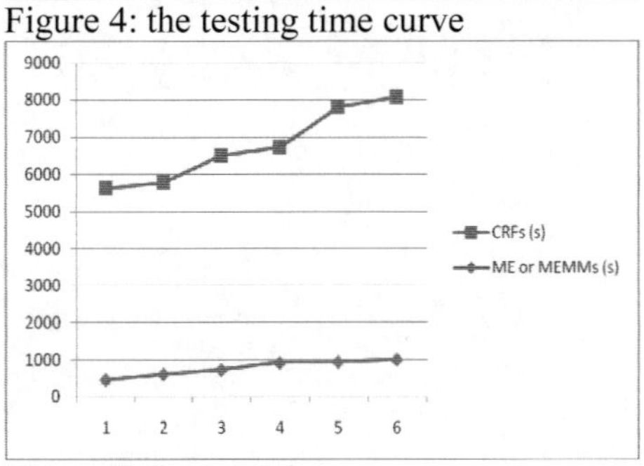

Figure 5: the total time curve

All results of ME and MEMMs in figures are represented by the same line because performances of these two models are the same when features are only related to observed values.

5 Conclusions

In this paper, we propose a new optimal feature template selection method for CRFs, which is carried out by replacing the CRFs with MEMM_2 (ME) as the machine learning model to address the efficiency problem according to the homology of these models. Heuristic method and candidate label filtering algorithm, which can improve the efficiency of FTS further, are also introduced. The effectiveness and efficiency of the new method is confirmed by the experiments on Chinese text chunking.

Two problems deserve further study: one is to prove the homology of ME, MEMMs, and CRFs theoretically; the other is to expand the method to other fields.

For any statistical machine learning model, feature selection or feature template selection is a computation-intensive step. This work can be adequately reduced by means of analyzing the homology between models and using the model with less computation amount. Our research proves to be a successful attempt.

References

Das Sanmay. 2001. Filters, wrappers and a boosting-based hybrid for feature selection. In Proceedings of the Eighteenth International Conference on Machine Learning, pages 74–81.

Dietterich Thomas G., Adam Ashenfelter, Yaroslav Bulatov. 2004. Training Conditional Random Fields via Gradient Tree Boosting. In Proc. of the 21th International Conference on Machine Learning (ICML).

Dy Jennifer G., and Carla E. Brodley. 2000. Feature subset selection and order identification for unsupervised learning. In Proceedings of the Seventeenth International Conference on Machine Learning, pages 247–254.

Hall Mark A.. 2000. Correlation-based feature selection for discrete and numeric class machine learning. In Proceedings of the Seventeenth International Conference on Machine Learning, pages 359–366.

Jaynes, Edwin T.. 1957. Information Theory and Statistical Mechanics. Physical Review 106(1957), May. No.4, pp. 620-630.

Kim YongSeog, W. Nick Street and Filippo Menczer. 2000. Feature Selection in Unsupervised Learning via Evolutionary Search. In Proceedings of the Sixth ACM SIGKDD International Conference on Knowledge Discovery and Data Mining, pages 365–369.

Koeling Rob. 2000. Chunking with Maximum Entropy Models. In Proceeding of CoNLL-2000 and LLL-2000, Lisbon, Portugal, 2000, pp. 139-141.

Kohavi Ron, and George H. John. 1997. Wrappers for feature subset selection. Artificial Intelligence, 97(1-2):273–324.

Lafferty John, Andrew McCallum, and Fernando Pereira. 2001. Conditional Random Fields: Probabilistic Models for Segmenting and Labeling Sequence Data. Proceedings of the Eighteenth International Conference on Machine Learning.

Li Wei, and Andrew McCallum. 2003. Rapid Development of Hindi Named Entity Recognition using Conditional Random Fields and Feature Induction. ACM Transactions on Asian Language Information Processing (TALIP).

Liu Huan, and Lei Yu. 2005. Toward Integrating Feature Selection Algorithms for Classification and Clustering. IEEE Transactions on knowledge and Data Engineering, v.17 n.4, p.491-502.

Liu Huan, and Rudy Setiono. 1996. A probabilistic approach to feature selection - a filter solution. In Proceedings of the Thirteenth International Conference on Machine Learning, pages 319–327.

McCallum Andrew. 2003. Efficiently Inducing Features of Conditional Random Fields. In Proceedings of the Nineteenth Conference on Uncertainty in Artificial Intelligence.

McCallum Andrew, DAyne Freitag, Fernando Pereira. 2000. Maximum Entropy Markov Models for Information Extraction and Segmentation. In Proceedings of ICML'2000, Stanford, CA, USA, 2000, pp. 591-598.

McCallum Andrew, and Wei Li. 2003. Early Results for Named Entity Recognition with Conditional Random Fields, Feature Induction and Web-Enhanced Lexicons. In Proceedings of The Seventh Conference on Natural Language Learning (CoNLL-2003), Edmonton, Canada.

Osbome Miles. 2000. Shallow Parsing as Part-of-speech Tagging. In Proceeding of CoNLL-2000 and LLL-2000, Lisbon, Portugal, 2000,pp. 145-147.

Roark Brian, Murat Saraclar, Michael Collins, and Mark Johnson. 2004. Discriminative language modeling with conditional random fields and the perceptron algorithm. Proceedings of the 42nd Annual Meeting of the Association for Computational Linguistics.

Settles Burr. 2004. Biomedical Named Entity Recognition Using Conditional Random Fields and Rich Feature Sets. COLING 2004 International Joint Workshop on Natural Language Processing in Biomedicine and its Applications (NLPBA).

Sha Fei, and Fernando Pereira. 2003. Shallow Parsing with Conditional Random Fields. Proceedings of the 2003 conference of the North American Chapter of the Association for Computational Linguistics on Human Language Technology, Edmonton, Canada.

Yu Lei, and Huan Liu. 2004. Feature selection for high-dimensional data: a fast correlation-based filter solution. In Proceedings of the twentieth International Conference on Machine Learning, pages 856–863.

Zhou Qiang, and Yumei Li. 2010. Chinese Chunk Parsing Evaluation Tasks. Journal of Chinese Information Processing.

A Statistical NLP Approach for Feature and Sentiment Identification from Chinese Reviews

Zhen Hai[1] **Kuiyu Chang**[1] **Qinbao Song**[2] **Jung-jae Kim**[1]

[1]School of Computer Engineering, Nanyang Technological University, Singapore 639798
{haiz0001, askychang, jungjae.kim}@ntu.edu.sg

[2]Department of Computer Science and Technology, Xi'an Jiaotong University, Xi'an 710049, China
qbsong@mail.xjtu.edu.cn

Abstract

Existing methods for extracting features from Chinese reviews only use simplistic syntactic knowledge, while those for identifying sentiments rely heavily on a semantic dictionary. In this paper, we present a systematic technique for identifying features and sentiments, using both syntactic and statistical analysis. We firstly identify candidate features using a proposed set of common syntactic rules. We then prune irrelevant candidates with topical relevance scores below a cut-off point. We also propose an association analysis method based on likelihood ratio test to infer the polarity of opinion word. The sentiment of a feature is finally adjusted by analyzing the negative modifiers in the local context of the opinion word. Experimental results show that our system performs significantly better than a well-known opinion mining system.

1 Introduction

There were 420 million Internet users in China by the end of June 2010. As a result, online social media in China has accumulated massive amount of valuable peer reviews on almost anything. Mining this pool of Chinese reviews to detect features (e.g. "手机" mobile phone) and identify the corresponding sentiment (e.g. positive, negative) has recently become a hot research area. However, the vast majority of previous work on feature detection only uses simplistic syntactic natural language processing (NLP) approaches, while those on sentiment identification depend heavily on a semantic dictionary. Syntactic approaches are often prone to errors due to the informal nature of online reviews. Dictionary-based approaches are more robust than syntactic approaches, but must be constantly updated with new terms and expressions, which are constantly evolving in online reviews.

To overcome these limitations, we propose a statistical NLP approach for Chinese feature and sentiment identification. The technique is in fact the core of our Chinese review mining system, called Idea Miner or iMiner. Figure 1 shows the architectural overview of iMiner, which comprises five modules, of which Module Ⅲ (Opinion Feature Detection) and Ⅳ (Contextual Sentiment Identification) are the main focus of this paper.

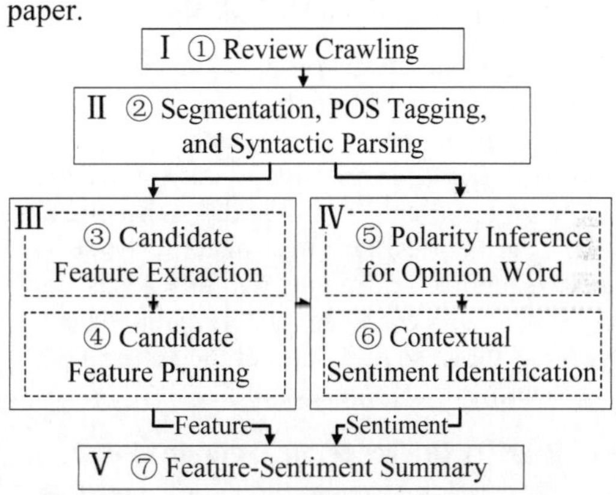

Figure 1: Overview of the iMiner system.

2 Related Work

Qiu *et al.* (2007) used syntactic analysis to identify features[1] in Chinese sentences, which is similar to the methods proposed by Zhuang *et al.* (2006) and Xia *et al.* (2007). However, syntactic analysis alone tends to extract many invalid features due to the colloquial nature of online reviews, which are often abruptly concise or

[1] A feature refers to the subject of an opinion.

grammatically incorrect. To address the issue, our approach employs an additional step to prune candidates with low topical relevance, which is a statistical measure of how frequently a term appears in one review and across different reviews.

Pang *et al.* (2002) examined the effectiveness of using supervised learning methods to identify document level sentiments. But the technique requires a large amount of training data, and must be re-trained whenever it is applied to a new domain. Furthermore, it does not perform well at the sentence level. Zhou *et al.* (2008) and Qiu *et al.* (2008) proposed dictionary-based approaches to infer contextual sentiments from Chinese sentences. However, it is difficult to maintain an up-to-date dictionary, as new expressions emerge frequently online. In contrast, to identify the sentiment expressed in a review region[2], our method first infers the polarity of an opinion word by using statistical association analysis, and subsequently analyzes the local context of the opinion word. Our method is domain independent and uses only a small set of 80 polarized words instead of a huge dictionary.

2.1 Topic Detection and Tracking

The task of Topic Detection and Tracking is to find and follow new events in a stream of news stories. Fukumoto and Suzuki (2000) proposed a domain dependence criterion to discriminate a topic from an event, and find all subsequent similar news stories. Our idea of topical relevance is related but different; we only focus on the relevance of a candidate feature with respect to a review topic, so as to extract the features on which sentiments are expressed.

2.2 Polarity Inference for Opinion Word

Turney (2002) used point-wise mutual information (PMI) to predict the polarity of an opinion word *O*, which is calculated as MI_1-MI_2, where MI_1 is the mutual information between word *O* and positive word "excellent", and MI_2 denotes the mutual information between *O* and negative word "poor". Instead of PMI, our method uses the likelihood ratio test (LRT) to compute the semantic association between an opinion word and each seed word, since LRT leads to better results in practice. Finally, the polarity is calculated as the weighted sum of the polarity values of all seed words, where the weights are determined by the semantic association.

2.3 Feature-Sentiment Pair Identification

Turney (2002) proposed an unsupervised learning algorithm to identify the overall sentiments of reviews. However, his method does not detect features to associate with the sentiments. Shi and Chang (2006) proposed to build a huge Chinese semantic lexicon to extract both features and sentiments. Other lexicon-based work for identifying feature-sentiment pair was proposed by Yi *et al.* (2003) and Xia *et al.* (2007). We propose a new statistical NLP approach to identify feature-sentiment pairs, which uses not only syntactic analysis but also data-centric statistical analysis. Most importantly, our approach requires no semantic lexicon to be maintained.

3 Feature Detection

Module III in iMiner aims to detect opinion features, which are subjects of reviews, such as the product itself like "手机" (mobile phone) or specific attributes like "屏幕" (screen).

Example 1: "我喜欢这款手机的颜色" (I like the color of this mobile phone).

In example 1, the noun "颜色" (color) indicates a feature. Some features are expressed implicitly in review sentences, as shown below.

Example 2: "太贵了，我买不起" (Too expensive, I cannot afford it).

In example 2, the noun "价格" (price) is the opinion feature of this sentence, but it does not occur explicitly. In this paper, we do not deal with implicit features, but instead focus on the extraction of explicit features only.

3.1 Candidate Feature Extraction

According to our observation, features are generally expressed as nouns and occur in certain patterns in Chinese reviews. Typically, a noun acting as the object or subject of a verb is a potential feature. In addition, when a clause contains only a noun phrase without any verbs, the headword of the noun phrase is also a candidate. Due to the colloquial nature of online reviews, it is complicated and nearly impossible to collect all possible syntactic roles of features. Thus, we

[2] A review region is a sentence or clause which contains one and only feature.

Table 1: Dependence relations and syntactic rules for candidate feature extraction.

Relation	Rule	Interpretation	Example (3-5)
VOB	$(N, VOB) \Rightarrow (N, C)$	If term is noun (N) and depends on another component with relation VOB, extract as candidate (C).	"我喜欢这款**手机**" (I like the **mobile phone**). The noun "手机" relies on the word "喜欢" with relation VOB, thus, "手机" is extracted as candidate.
SBV	$(N, SBV) \Rightarrow (N, C)$	If term is noun (N) and depends on another component with relation SBV, extract as candidate (C).	"**屏幕**太小了" (The **screen** is too small). The noun "屏幕" depends on the word "小" with relation SBV, thus "屏幕" is extracted as candidate.
HED	$(N, HED) \Rightarrow (N, C)$	If term is noun (N) and governs another component with relation HED, extract as candidate (C).	"漂亮的**外观**" (beautiful **exterior**). The noun "外观" governs the word "漂亮" with relation HED, thus, "外观" is extracted as candidate.

only use the aforementioned three primary patterns to extract an initial set of candidates.

Dependence Grammar (Tesniere, 1959) explores asymmetric governor-dependent relationship between words, which are then combined into the dependency structure of sentences. The three dependency relations SBV, VOB, and HED correspond to the three aforementioned patterns. For each relation, we define a rule with additional restrictions for candidate feature extraction, as shown in Table 1.

Candidate features are extracted in the following manner: for each word, we first determine if it is a noun; if so, we apply the VOB, SBV, and HED rules sequentially. A noun matching any of the rules is extracted as a candidate feature.

3.2 Candidate Feature Pruning

Due to the informal nature of online reviews, a large number of irrelevant candidates are extracted by the three syntactic rules. Thus, we need to further prune them by using additional techniques.

Intuitively, candidates that are found in many reviews should be more representative compared to candidates that occur in only a few reviews. This characteristic of candidates can be captured by the topical relevance (TR) score. TR can be used to measure how strongly a candidate feature is relevant to a review topic. The TR of a candidate is described by two indicators, i.e., dispersion and deviation. Dispersion indicates how frequently a candidate occurs across different reviews, while deviation denotes how many times a candidate appears in one review. The topical relevance score (TRS) is calculated by combining both dispersion and deviation. Candidate features with high TRS are supposed to be highly relevant, while those with TRS lower than a specified threshold are rejected.

Formally, let the i-th candidate feature be denoted by T_i, and the j-th review document[3] by D_j. The weight of feature T_i in document D_j is denoted by W_{ij}, which could be computed based on $TF.IDF$ (Luhn, 1957) shown in formula (1):

$$W_{ij} = \begin{cases} (1+\log TF_{ij}) * \log \dfrac{N}{DF_i} & if\ TF_{ij} > 0 \\ 0 & otherwise \end{cases} \quad (1)$$

TF_{ij} denotes the term frequency of T_i in D_j, and DF_i denotes the document frequency of T_i; N indicates the number of documents in the corpus. We compute the standard deviation S_i:

$$S_i = \sqrt{\frac{\sum_{j=1}^{N}(W_{ij} - \overline{W}_i)^2}{N-1}} \quad (2)$$

where the average weight of T_i across all documents is calculated as follows:

$$\overline{W}_i = \frac{1}{N}\sum_{j=1}^{N} W_{ij}\ .$$

The dispersion $Disp_i$ of T_i is then calculated:

$$Disp_i = \frac{\overline{W}_i}{S_i} \quad (3)$$

The deviation $Devi_{ij}$ of T_i in D_j is computed:

[3] A review document refers to a forum review, which tends to be shorter than full length editorial articles.

$$Devi_{ij} = W_{ij} - \overline{W_j'} \quad (4)$$

The average scalar weight of all candidate features in D_j is calculated as follows:

$$\overline{W_j'} = \frac{1}{M}\sum_{i=1}^{M} W_{ij}$$

where M is the vocabulary size of D_j.

We can obtain the topical relevance score TRS_{ij} of T_i in D_j finally as follows:

$$TRS_{ij} = Disp_i * Devi_{ij} \quad (5)$$

By combining the dispersion and deviation, the quantity TRS_{ij} thus captures the topical relevance strength of T_i with respect to the topic of document D_j.

All candidates of a document are then sorted in descending order of TRS, and those with TRS above a pre-specified threshold are extracted as opinion features. In fact, we can extract candidates at the document, paragraph, or sentence resolution. In practice, we observe no significant performance differences at the various resolutions.

3.3 Experimental Evaluation

We collected 2,986 real-life review documents about mobile phones from major online Chinese forums. Each document corresponds to a forum topic, where each paragraph in a document matches a thread under the topic. Of these, we manually annotated the features and sentiment orientations expressed in 219 randomly selected documents, which include 600 review sentences.

To evaluate the performance of our approach, we first conducted an experiment for extracting candidate features. We then performed three other experiments for pruning the candidates at the document, paragraph, and sentence levels, respectively. For each experiment, we tried several different thresholds, i.e., percentage of TRS mean (TRSM) of all candidates. The average F-measure (F), precision (P), and recall (R) of the results at the three levels are shown in Figure 2. The highest F-measure results of feature detection with and without pruning are shown in Table 2 for easy comparison.

Table 2: Feature detection results.

Feature Detection	P (%)	R (%)	F (%)
No Pruning	71.61	90.69	80.03
Pruning (33% TRSM)	81.56	85.22	83.35

As line 2 of Table 2 shows, feature detection without pruning achieves 90.69% recall, which shows that the proposed syntactic rules have excellent coverage. However, its precision is not so promising, achieving only 71.61%, which means that many irrelevant candidates are also extracted by our rules. Thus, relying on syntactic analysis alone is not good enough, and we need to take one more step to prune the candidate features.

As line 3 of Table 2 shows, after pruning the candidate set, precision improved remarkably by 10% to 81.56%, while recall dropped slightly to 85.22%. For online review mining, precision is much more important than recall, because users' confidence in iMiner rely heavily on the accuracy of the results they see (precision), and not on what they don't see (recall).

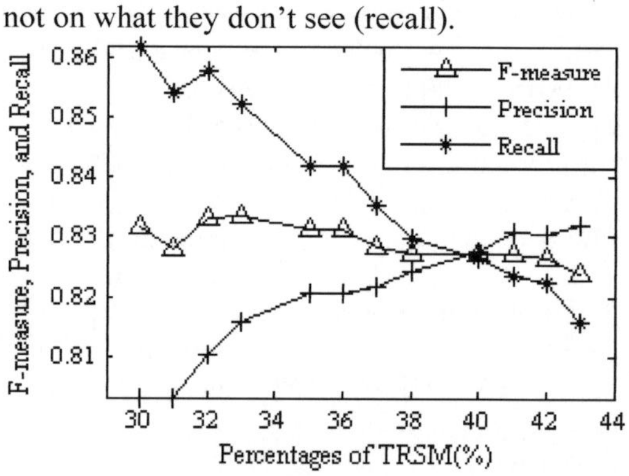

Figure 2: iMiner feature pruning results.

Figure 2 plots the results of pruning at various TRSM thresholds. The best F-measure of 83.35% was achieved with a 33% TRSM. If we increase the threshold to 43%, the precision increases to 83.19%, while the recall drops to 81.57%. By exploring the distribution of a candidate in corpus, its topical relevance with respect to the review topic can be measured statistically, which allows the noisy candidates to be pruned effectively. From the results in Figure 2, our idea of topical relevance is shown to be highly effective in detecting features.

Table 3: Characteristics of FBS and iMiner.

Aspects	FBS	iMiner
Candidates	Nouns from POS tagger	Nouns from synthetic analysis
Pruning	Association Mining	Topical Relevance
Opinion word	Adjectives	Adjectives, verbs
Polarity inference	Dictionary based	LRT association based
Sentiment Resolution	Sentence	Sentence, clause
Negation	Single	Single, double

We compared our results with that of the association mining-based method in Feature-based Summarization (FBS) (Hu and Liu, 2004) on the same dataset. Table 3 summarizes the differences between FBS and iMiner, parts of which are elaborated in Section 4. The results of FBS with various support thresholds are shown in Figure 3. The support corresponds to the percentage of total number of review sentences. FBS attained the highest F-measure of 76.35% at a support of 0.4% with 79.6% precision and 73.36% recall. As the support increases, the precision also increases from 62.99% to 86.92%, while the recall decreases from 91.61% to 61.86%. Comparing the best results of the two systems, iMiner beats FBS by 7% in F-Measure, 1.96% in precision, and 11.86% in recall.

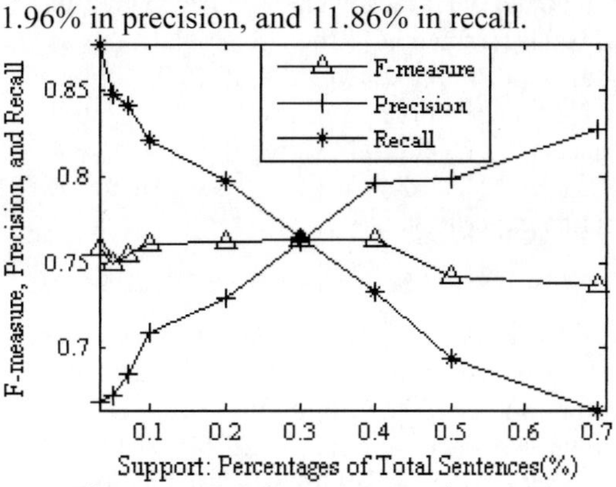

Figure 3: FBS feature extraction results.

We find that FBS suffers from the following limitations: (1) FBS extracted an additional 14.11% noisy candidate features due to the lack of syntactic analysis, which requires more extensive pruning; and (2) FBS only considers sentence frequency in computing the support to identify frequent candidate features, ignoring the candidate frequency within the sentence.

3.4 Feature Extraction Error Analysis

We categorize our feature extraction errors into 4 main types, FE1 to FE4, as follows.

FE1: When more than one candidate exists in a review region, our algorithm may pick the wrong features due to misplaced priorities. Note that we assume only one (dominant) feature per region in both our algorithm and the labeled dataset. A total of 43% errors were due to picking the wrong dominant candidate.

Example 6: "声音太小，让人听不清楚" (The sound is too weak, people cannot listen clearly).

In example 6, both "声音" and "人" are extracted as features. However, the noun "人" is an incorrect feature detected by our algorithm.

FE2: The proposed set of common syntactic rules is not comprehensive, missing out 23% of true features.

Example 7: "对于这个机子我很讨厌" (I am sick about this phone).

In example 7, the noun "机子" is a missed feature. This is in fact a POB dependence relation, which is outside the scope of our three rules.

FE3: About 22% errors are due to irrelevant features possessing high TR scores, and therefore which are not pruned subsequently.

Example 8: "我好喜欢的哦没有钱买" (I like it very much, but I have no money to buy it).

In example 8, the noun "钱" is incorrectly confirmed as a feature due to its high TR score.

FE4: About 9% errors are due to incorrect POS tags.

Example 9: "听电话时它老卡" (Consistent interruption during phone calls).

In example 9, the verb "卡" is extracted incorrectly as a feature, since it is incorrectly tagged as a noun. The remaining 3% of the errors are due to the system incorrectly extracting features from sentences that contain no opinions.

4 Contextual Sentiment Identification

The main task of module Ⅳ in iMiner is to identify the contextual sentiment of a feature. A two-step approach is proposed: (1) The polarity of an opinion word within a review region is inferred via association analysis based on the likelihood ratio test; and (2) the sentiment is validated against the contextual information of the opinion word in the region and finalized.

4.1 Polarity Inference for Opinion Word

To infer polarity, an opinion word is first identified in a review region, as described in Figure 4. Note that we consider not only adjectives but also verbs as opinion words. We then measure the association between the opinion word and each seed word. We calculate the polarity value of the opinion word as the association weighted sum of polarities of all seed words.

Example 10: "这款机子价格很便宜" (The price of this mobile phone is very cheap).

Example 10 contains an adjective "便宜" (cheap) that governs the feature "价格" (price); thus "便宜" is extracted as an opinion word.

1. feature T_i and word W_j in the same region
2.   if (W_j = adjective and depends on T_i)
3.   extract W_j as opinion word;
4.   else if (W_j = adjective and governs T_i)
5.   extract W_j as opinion word;
6.   else if (W_j = verb and governs T_i)
7.   extract W_j as opinion word;

Figure 4: Extracting Opinion Word

A set of polarized words were collected from corpus as seed words, including 35 positive words, 36 negative words, and 9 neutral words. Each seed word is assigned a polarity weight from -10 to 10. For example, "漂亮" (lovely) has a score of 10, "普通" (common) has a score of 0, and "差劲" (lousy) has a score of -10.

To measure the semantic association A_{ij} between an opinion word O_i and each seed word S_j, we propose a formula based on the likelihood ratio test (Dunning, 1993), as follows:

$$A_{ij} = 2[\log L(p_1, k_1, n_1) + \log L(p_2, k_2, n_2) - \log L(p, k_1, n_1) - \log L(p, k_2, n_2)] \quad (6)$$

where

$$L(p,k,n) = p^k (1-p)^{n-k};$$

$$p = \frac{k_1 + k_2}{n_1 + n_2},\ p_1 = \frac{k_1}{n_1},\ p_2 = \frac{k_2}{n_2};$$

$$n_1 = k_1 + k_3,\ n_2 = k_2 + k_4.$$

The variable $k_1(O, S)$ in Table 4 refers to the count of documents containing both opinion word O and seed word S, $k_2(O, \bar{S})$ indicates the number of documents containing O but not S, $k_3(\bar{O}, S)$ counts the number of documents containing S but not O, while $k_4(\bar{O}, \bar{S})$ tallies the count of documents containing neither O nor S.

Table 4: Document counts.

	S	$\bar{S}$
O	$k_1(O, S)$	$k_2(O, \bar{S})$
$\bar{O}$	$k_3(\bar{O}, S)$	$k_4(\bar{O}, \bar{S})$

The higher the quantity A_{ij}, the stronger the semantic association is between the opinion word and the seed word.

The polarity value OV_i of the opinion word O_i is computed as the association weighted average of all seed word polarity values:

$$OV_i = \sum_{j=1}^{L} \frac{A_{ij}}{A_i} * SV_j \quad (7)$$

The sum A_i of all association strength is calculated as follows:

$$A_i = \sum_{j=1}^{L} A_{ij};$$

where A_{ij} denotes the association between O_i and S_j, SV_j indicates the polarity value of S_j, and L is the size of the seed word list.

After performing association analysis, we then classify the polarity value OV_i using an upper bound $V+$ and lower bound $V-$, such that if V_i is larger than $V+$, then the polarity is inferred as positive; conversely if V_i is smaller than $V-$, then the polarity is inferred as negative; otherwise, it is neutral. Here, the $V+$ and $V-$ boundaries refer to thresholds that can be determined experimentally.

4.2 Contextual Sentiment Identification

Apart from inferring the polarity of opinion words, we also examine additional contextual information around the opinion words. In fact, the final sentiment is determined by combining the polarity with the contextual information. In this work, we focus on negative modifiers, as shown in the examples below.

Example 11: "我不喜欢这款手机" (I do not like this mobile phone).

In example 11, the polarity of the opinion word "喜欢" (like) is inferred as positive, but the review region expresses a negative orientation to the feature "手机", because a negation word "不" (not) modifies "喜欢". Thus, it is important to locate negative modifiers.

Example 12: "手机屏幕不是不漂亮" (The screen of this mobile phone is not unlovely).

In example 12, the polarity of opinion word "漂亮" (lovely) is inferred as positive. By examining its direct modifier, i.e., "不" (un-), we identify the sentiment of "不漂亮" (unlovely) as negative. However, the final sentiment about the feature "屏幕" (screen) is actually positive due to the earlier negation "不是" (not), which modifies the latter "不漂亮" (unlovely). This is what we call a double negation sentence, which is not uncommon in reviews. Therefore, it is necessary to take two additional steps to capture the double negation as follows.

Figure 5 shows the main steps of identifying contextual sentiment. For an opinion word O_i in the review region, we first determine if there exists an adverb modifying it. If so, we extract the adverb as the direct modifier. If the modifier has a negative meaning, then we reverse the prior polarity of O_i. Similarly, we can take one additional step to locate the double negation modifier and finally identify the contextual sentiment orientation.

```
for each opinion word O_i
  if (a word W_j = adverb and depends on O_i)
    extract W_j as direct modifier;
    if (word W_j = negation word)
      reverse the prior polarity of O_i;
    if (word W_k = adverb and relies on W_j)
      extract W_k as indirect modifier;
      if (word W_k = negation word)
        reverse the current polarity of O_i;
output the current polarity of O_i;
```

Figure 5: Identifying the Contextual Sentiment

4.3 Experimental Evaluation

Since features are detected prior to the sentiments, there is a possibility for an erroneous feature (i.e., a false positive feature) to be associated with a sentiment. We thus conducted two different experiments. In the first case, we enumerate all extracted feature-sentiment pairs, including the wrong features. In the second scenario, we enumerate the feature-sentiment pairs only for those correctly extracted features. For each experiment, we further evaluated the result with (C) and without (N.C.) contextual information.

We select the best case of feature detection and then run our sentiment identification algorithm on the review dataset described in section 3.3; the polarity thresholds *V-* and *V+* are set to 0.45 and 0.5, respectively.

Table 5: Results for all features.

Systems		P (%)	R (%)	F (%)
iMiner	N.C.	57.07	58.21	57.63
	C.	**70.3**	**71.72**	**71**
FBS		49.70	45.80	47.67

Table 5 shows the results for all detected features (correct and incorrect). As shown in line 2, our method achieved an F-measure of 57.63% without considering contextual information, while precision and recall are 57% and 58.21%, respectively. Adding contextual information, as line 3 shows, boosts the F-measure to 71%, a remarkable 13.37% improvement.

Table 6 shows the results for just the correctly extracted features. As shown in line 2, in the case of not considering contextual information, our method achieved an F-measure of 63.17%, while precision and recall were 69.05% and 58.21%, respectively. By considering contextual information, line 3 shows that the F-measure improved to 77.82% which is 14.65% better, with precision and recall at 85.06% and 71.72%, respectively. The above results show that local contextual analysis of double and single negation can significantly improve the accuracy of sentiment orientation identification.

Table 6: Results for correctly detected features.

Systems		P (%)	R (%)	F (%)
iMiner	N.C.	69.05	58.21	63.17
	C.	**85.06**	**71.72**	**77.82**
FBS		62.45	45.80	52.84

By examining the results shown in line 3 (in bold) of both Tables 5 and 6, the F-measure on correctly identified features increases from 71% to 77.82%, while the precision increases drastically from 70.3% to 85.06%. The results show that our two-step approach of identifying sentiment orientation is reasonable and effective and that a great many of sentiments can be identified correctly for related features, especially for those correctly detected one. However, in practice there is no way to tell the correctly identified features from the incorrect ones, thus Table 5 is a more realistic gauge of our approach..

Lastly, we compared our approach to sentiment identification with FBS (see Table 3). The best results are used, as shown in the last rows of Table 5 and 6. When considering all features extracted, the F-measure of FBS is only 47.67%, which is 23.33% lower than that of iMiner, where both precision and recall are 49.70% and 45.80%, respectively. Considering only the correctly detected features, iMiner widens its lead over FBS to 25% in terms of F-measure.

There are several explanations for the poor results of FBS: (1) The inferior results of feature detection affect the subsequent task of sentiment identification; and (2) the polarity inference depends heavily on a semantic dictionary WordNet. In our experiments for FBS, we used an extended version of the "同义词词林" Thesaurus containing 77,492 words, and a sentiment lexicon with 8,856 words that is part of mini (free) HowNet, and lastly our seed word list containing 80 words.

4.4 Sentiment Identification Error Analysis

We classify our sentiment identification errors into 5 main types, SE1 to SE5, as follows.

SE1: Sentiment identification relies heavily on feature extraction, which means that if features are detected wrongly, it is impossible for the sentiment identified to be correct. About 49% of false sentiments are due to incorrectly extracted features.

Even for the correctly extracted features, there are still several errors as listed below.

SE2: Incorrectly identified opinion words can lead to mistakes in inferring sentiments, accounting for 14% of the errors.

SE3: Errors in detecting contextual information about opinion words led to 12% of the wrong sentiment identification results.

SE4: Both the quality and quantity of seed words influence sentiment identification.

SE5: The threshold choices for V+ and V- directly impact the polarity inference of opinion words, affecting the sentiment identification.

SE4 and SE5 errors account for the remaining 25% of the erroneous sentiment results.

5 Conclusion

The main contribution of this paper is the proposed systematic technique of identifying both features and sentiments for Chinese reviews. Our proposed approach compares very favorably against the well-known FBS system on a small-scale dataset. Our feature detection is 7% better than FBS in terms of F-measure, with significantly higher recall. Meanwhile, our approach of identifying contextual sentiment achieved around 23% better F-measure than FBS.

We plan to further explore effective methods to deal with the various feature and sentiment errors. In addition, we plan to explore the extraction of implicit features, since a significant number of reviews express opinion via implicit features. Lastly, we plan to test out these improvements on a large-scale dataset.

Acknowledgement

We thank Harbin Institute of Technology's Center for Information Retrieval in providing their Language Technology Platform (LTP) software. This research was supported in part by Singapore Ministry of Education's Academic Research Fund Tier 1 grant RG 30/09.

References

Dunning, T. E. 1993. Accurate methods for the statistics of surprise and coincidence. Computational Linguistics 19(1).

Fukumoto, Fumiyo, and Yoshimi Suzuki. 2000. Event Tracking based on Domain Dependence, SIGIR.

Hu, Minqing, and Bing Liu. 2004. Mining and summarizing customer reviews, SIGKDD, Seattle, WA, USA.

Luhn, Hans Peter. 1957. A statistical approach tomechanized encoding and searching of literary information. IBM Journal of Research and Development 1 (4):309-17.

Pang, Bo, Lillian Lee, and Shivakumar Vaithyanathan. 2002. Thumbs up? Sentiment Classification using Machine Learning Techniques, EMNLP.

Qiu, Guang, Kangmiao Liu, Jiajun Bu, Chun Chen, and Zhiming Kang. 2007. Extracting opinion topics for Chinese opinions using dependence grammar, ADKDD, California, USA.

Qiu, Guang, Can Wang, Jiajun Bu, Kangmiao Liu, and Chun Chen. 2008. Incorporate the Syntactic Knowledge in Opinion Mining in User-generated Content, WWW, Beijing, China.

Shi, Bin, and Kuiyu Chang. 2006. Mining Chinese Reviews, ICDM Data Mining on Design and Marketing Workshop.

Tesniere, L. 1959. Elements de Syntaxe Structurale: Librairie C. Klincksieck, Paris.

Turney, Peter D. 2002. Thumbs Up or Thumbs Down? Semantic Orientation Applied to Unsupervised Classification of Reviews, ACL, Philadelphia.

Xia, Yunqing, Ruifeng Xu, Kam-Fai Wong, and Fang Zheng. 2007. The Unified Collocation Framework for Opinion Mining. International Conference on Machine Learning and Cybernetics.

Yi, Jeonghee, Tetsuya Nasukawa, Razvan Bunescu, and Wayne Niblack. 2003. Sentiment Analyzer: Extracting Sentiments about a Given Topic using Natural Language Processing Techniques, ICDM.

Zhou, Chao, Guang Qiu, Kangmiao Liu, Jiajun Bu, Mingcheng Qu, and Chun Chen. 2008. SOPING : a Chinese customer review mining system, SIGIR, Singapore.

Zhuang, Li, Feng Jing, and Xiaoyan Zhu. 2006. Movie Review Mining and Summarization, CIKM.

Exploring Deep Belief Network for Chinese Relation Extraction

Yu Chen[1], Wenjie Li[2], Yan Liu[2], Dequan Zheng[1], Tiejun Zhao[1]
[1]School of Computer Science and Technology, Harbin Institute of Technology, China
{chenyu, dqzheng, tjzhao}@mtlab.hit.edu.cn
[2]Department of Computing, The Hong Kong Polytechnic University, Hong Kong
{cswjli, csyliu}@comp.polyu.edu.hk

Abstract

Relation extraction is a fundamental task in information extraction that identifies the semantic relationships between two entities in the text. In this paper, a novel model based on Deep Belief Network (DBN) is first presented to detect and classify the relations among Chinese entities. The experiments conducted on the Automatic Content Extraction (ACE) 2004 dataset demonstrate that the proposed approach is effective in handling high dimensional feature space including character N-grams, entity types and the position information. It outperforms the state-of-the-art learning models such as SVM or BP neutral network.

1 Introduction

Information Extraction (IE) is to automatically pull out the structured information required by the users from a large volume of plain text. It normally includes three sequential tasks, i.e., entity extraction, relation extraction and event extraction. In this paper, we limit our focus on relation extraction.

In early time, pattern-based approaches were the main focus of most research studies in relation extraction. Although pattern-based approaches achieved reasonably good results, they have some obvious flaws. It requires expensive handcraft work to assemble patterns and not all relations can be identified by a set of reliable patterns (Willy Yap, 2009). Also, once the interest of task is transferred to a different domain or a different language, patterns have to be revised or even rewritten. That is to say, the discovered patterns are heavily dependent on the task in a specific domain or on a particular corpus.

Naturally, a vast amount of work was spent on feature-based machine learning approaches in later years. In this camp, relation extraction is typically cast as a classification problem, where the most important issue is to train a model to scale and measure the similarity of features reflecting relation instances. The entity semantic information expressing relation was often formulated as the lexical and syntactic features, which are identical to a certain linear vector in high dimensions. Many learning models are capable of self-training and classifying these vectors according to similarity, such as Support Vector Machine (SVM) and Neural Network (NN).

Recently, kernel-based approaches have been developing rapidly. These approaches involved kernels of structure representations, like parse tree or dependency tree, in similarity calculation. In fact, feature-based approaches can be viewed as the special and simplified kinds of kernel-based approaches. They used dot-product as the kernel function and did not range over the intricate structure information (Ji, et al. 2009).

Relation extraction in Chinese received quite limited attention as compared to English and other western languages. The main reason is the unique characteristic of Chinese, such as more flexible grammar, lack of boundary information and morphological variations etc (Sun and Dong, 2009). Especially, the existing Chinese syntactic analysis tools at current stage are not yet reliable to capture the valuable structured information. It is urgent to develop approaches that are in particular suitable for Chinese relation extraction.

In this paper, we explore the use of Deep Belief Network (DBN), a new feature-based machine learning model for Chinese relation extraction. It is a neural network model developed under the deep learning architecture that is claimed by Hinton (2006) to be able to automatically learn a deep hierarchy of features with increasing levels of abstraction for the complex problems like natural language processing (NLP). It avoids assembling patterns that express the semantic relation information and meanwhile it succeeds to produce accurate model that is not confined to the parsing results.

The rest of this paper is structured in the following manner. Section 2 reviews the previous work on relation extraction. Section 3 presents task definition, briefly introduces the DBN model and the feature construction. Section 4 provides the experimental results. Finally, Section 5 concludes the paper.

2 Related Work

Over the past decades, relation extraction had come to a significant progress from simple pattern-based approaches to adapted self-training machine learning approaches.

Brin (1998) used Dual Iterative Pattern Relation Expansion, a bootstrapping-based system, to find the largest common substrings as patterns. It had the ability of searching patterns automatically and was good for large quantity of uniform contexts. Chen (2006) proposed graph algorithm called label propagation, which transferred the pattern similarity to probability of propagating the label information from any vertex to its nearby vertices. The label matrix indicated the relation type.

Feature-based approaches utilized the linear vector of carefully chosen lexical and syntactic features derived from different levels of text analysis and ranging from part-of-speech (POS) tagging to full parsing and dependency parsing (Zhang 2009). Jing and Zhai (2007) defined a unified graphic representation of features that served as a general framework in order to systematically explore the information at diverse levels in three subspaces and finally estimated the effectiveness of these features. They reported that the basic unit feature was generally sufficient to achieve state-of-art performance. Meanwhile, over-inclusion complex features were harmful.

Kernel-based approaches utilize kernel functions on structures between two entities, such as sequences and trees, to measure the similarity between two relation instances. Zelenok (2003) applied parsing tree kernel function to distinguish whether there was an existing relationship between two entities. However, they limited their task on Person-affiliation and organization-location.

The previous work mainly concentrated on relation extraction in English. Relatively, less attention was drawn on Chinese relation extraction. However, its importance is being gradually recognized. For instance, Zhang et al. (2008) combined position information, entity type and context features in a feature-based approach and Che (2005) introduced the edit distance kernel over the original Chinese string representation.

DBN is a new feature-based approach for NLP tasks. According to the work by Hinton (2006), DBN consisted of several layers including multiple Restricted Boltzmann Machine (RBM) layers and a Back Propagation (BP) layer. It was reported to perform very well in many classification problems (Ackley, 1985), which is from the origin of its ability to scale gracefully and be computationally tractable when applied to high dimensional feature vectors. Furthermore, to against the combinations of feature were intricate, it detected invariant representations from local translations of the input by deep architecture.

3 Deep Belief Network for Chinese Relation Extraction

3.1 Task Definition

Relation extraction, promoted by the Automatic Content Extraction (ACE) program, is a task of finding predefined semantic relations between pairs of entities from the texts. According to the ACE program, an entity is an object or a set of objects in the world while a relation is an explicitly or implicitly stated relationship between entities. The task can be formalized as:

$$(e_1, e_2, s) \rightarrow r \qquad (1)$$

where e_1 and e_2 are the two entities in a sentence s under concern and r is the relation between them. We call the triple (e_1, e_2, s) the relation candidate. According to the ACE 2004 guideline [1], five relation types are defined. They are:

Role: it represents an affiliation between a Person entity and an Organization, Facility, or GPE (a Geo-political entity) entities.

Part: it represents the part-whole relationship between Organization, Facility and GPE entities.

At: it represents that a Person, Organization, GPE, or Facility entity is location at a Location entities.

Near: it represents the fact that a Person, Organization, GPE or Facility entity is near (but not necessarily "At") a Location or GPE entities.

Social: it represents personal and professional affiliations between Person entities.

3.2 Deep Belief Networks (DBN)

DBN often consists of several layers, including multiple RBM layers and a BP layer. As illustrated in Figure 1, each RBM layer learns its parameters independently and unsupervisedly. RBM makes the parameters optimal for the relevant RBM layer and detect complicated features, but not optimal for the whole model. There is a supervised BP layer on top of the model which fine-tunes the whole model in the learning process and generates the output in the inference process. RBM keeps information as more as possible when it transfers vectors to next layer. It makes networks to avoid local optimum. RBM is also adopted to ensure the efficiency of the DBN model.

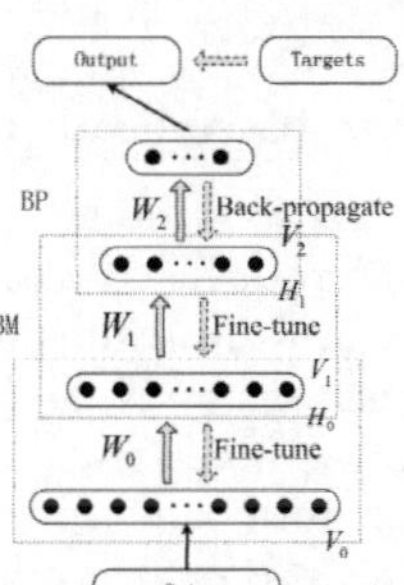

Fig. 1. The structure of a DBN.

[1] available at http://www.nist.gov/speech/tests/ace/.

Deep architecture of DBN represents many functions compactly. It is expressible by integrating different levels of simple functions (Y. Bengio and Y. LeCun). Upper layers are supposed to represent more "abstract" concepts that explain the input data whereas lower layers extract "low-level features" from the data. In addition, none of the RBM guarantees that all the information conveyed to the output is accurate or important enough. The learned information produced by preceding RBM layer will be continuously refined through the next RBM layer to weaken the wrong or insignificant information in the input. Multiple layers filter valuable features. The units in the final layer share more information from the data. This increases the representation power of the whole model. The final feature vectors used for classification consist of sophisticated features which reflect the structured information, promote better classification performance than direct original feature vector.

3.3 Restricted Boltzmann Machine (RBM)

In this section, we will introduce RBM, which is the core component of DBN. RBM is Boltzmann Machine with no connection within the same layer. An RBM is constructed with one visible layer and one hidden layer. Each visible unit in the visible layer V is an observed variable v_i while each hidden unit in the hidden layer H is a hidden variable h_j. Its joint distribution is

$$p(v,h) \propto \exp(-E(v,h)) = e^{h^T W v + b^T x + c^T h} \quad (2)$$

In RBM, $(v,h) \in \{0,1\}^2$ and $\theta = (W,b,c)$ are the parameters that need to be estimated, W is the weight tying visible layer and hidden layer. b is the bias of units v and c is the bias of units h.

To learn RBM, the optimum parameters are obtained by maximizing the joint distribution $p(v,h)$ on the training data (Hinton, 1999). A traditional way is to find the gradient between the initial parameters and the expected parameters. By modifying the previous parameters with the gradient, the expected parameters can gradually approximate the target parameters as

$$W^{(\tau+1)} = W^{(\tau)} + \eta \frac{\partial \log P(v^0)}{\partial W}\bigg|_{W^\tau} \quad (3)$$

where η is a parameter controlling the leaning rate. It determines the speed of W converging to the target.

Traditionally, the Monte Carlo Markov chain (MCMC) is used to calculate this kind of gradient.

$$\frac{\partial \log p(v,h)}{\partial w} = \langle h^0 v^0 \rangle - \langle h^\infty v^\infty \rangle \quad (4)$$

where $\log p(v,h)$ is the log probability of the data. $\langle h^0 v^0 \rangle$ denotes the multiplication of the average over the data states and its relevant sample in hidden unit. $\langle h^\infty v^\infty \rangle$ denotes the multiplication of the average over the model states in visible units and its relevant sample in hidden units.

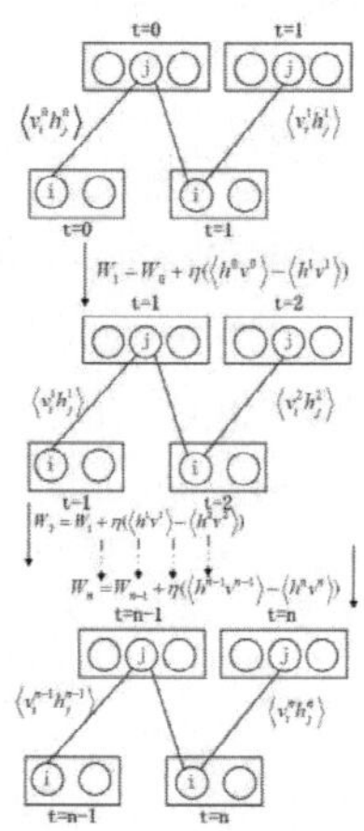

Fig. 2. Learning RBM with CD-based gradient estimation

However, MCMC requires estimating an exponential number of terms. Therefore, it typically takes a long time to converge to $\langle h^\infty v^\infty \rangle$. Hinton (2002) introduced an alternative algorithm, i.e., the contrastive divergence (CD) algorithm, as a substitution. It is reported that CD can train the model much more efficiently than MCMC. To estimate the distribution $p(x)$, CD considers a series of distributions $\{ p_n(x) \}$ which indicate the distributions in n steps. It approximates the gap of two different Kullback-Leiler divergences as

$$CD_n = KL(p_0 \| p_\infty) - KL(p_n \| p_\infty) \quad (5)$$

Maximizing the log probability of the data is exactly the same as minimizing the Kullback–Leibler divergence between the distribution of the data p_0 and the equilibrium distribution p_∞ defined by the model.

In our experiments, we set n to be 1. It means that in each step of gradient calculation, the estimate of the gradient is used to adjust the weight of RBM as Equation 6.

$$\frac{\partial \log p(v,h)}{\partial W} = \langle h^0 v^0 \rangle - \langle h^1 v^1 \rangle \quad (6)$$

Figure 2 below illustrates the process of learning RBM with CD-based gradient estimation.

3.4 Back-Propagation (BP)

The RBM layers provide an unsupervised analysis on the structures of data set. They automatically detect sophisticated feature vectors. The last layer in DBN is the BP layer. It takes the output from the last RBM layer and applies it in the final supervised learning process. In DBN, not only is the supervised BP layer used to generate the final categories, but it is also used to fine-tune the whole network. Specifically speaking, when the BP layer is changed during its iterating process, the changes are passed to the other RBM layers in a top-to-bottom sequence.

3.5 The Feature Set

DBN is able to detect high level hidden features from lexical, syntactic and/or position characteristic. As mentioned in related work, over-inclusion complex features are harmful. We therefore involve only three kinds of low level features in this study. They are described below.

3.5.1 Character-based Features

Since Chinese text is written without word boundaries, the word-level features are limited by the efficiency of word segmentation results. In the paper presented by H. Jing (2003) and some others, they observed that pure character-based models can even outperform word-based models. Li et al.'s (2008) work relying on character-based features also achieved significant performance in relation extraction. We denote the character dictionary as $D=\{d_1, d_2, \ldots, d_N\}$. In our experiment, N is 1500. To an e, it's character-based feature vector is $V(e)=\{ v_1, v_2, \ldots, v_N \}$. Each unit v_i can be valued as Equation 8.

$$v_i = \begin{cases} 1 & d_i \in e \\ 0 & d_i \notin e \end{cases} \quad (7)$$

3.5.2 Entity Type Features

According to the ACE 2004 guideline, there are five entity types in total, including Person, Organization, GPE, Location, and Facility. We recognize and classify the relation between the recognized entities. The entities in ACE 2004 corpus were labeled with these five types. Type features are distinctive for classification. For example, the entities of Location cannot appear in the Role relation.

3.5.3 Relative Position Features

We define three types of position features which depict the relative structures between the two entities, including Nested, Adjacent and Separated. For each relation candidate triple (e_1, e_2, s), let e.start and e.end denote the starting and end positions of e in a document. Table 1 summarizes the conditions for each type, where $i, j \subset \{1,2\}$ and $i \neq j$.

Type	Condition
Nested	$(e_i.\text{start}, e_i.\text{end}) \supset (e_j.\text{start}, e_j.\text{end})$
Adjacent	$e_i.\text{end}=e_j.\text{start}-1$
Separated	$(e_i.\text{start}<e_j.\text{start})\&(e_i.\text{end}+1<e_j.\text{start})$

Table 1. The internal postion structure features between two named entities

We combine the character-based features of two entities, their type information and position information as the feature vector of relation candidate.

3.6 Order of Entity Pair

A relation is basically an order pair. For example, "Bank of China in Hong Kong" conveys the ACE-style relation "At" between two entities "Bank of China (Organization)" and "Hong Kong (Location)". We can say that Bank of China can be found in Hong Kong, but not vice verse. The identified relation is said to be correct only when both its type and the order of the entity pair are correct. We don't explicitly incorporate such order restriction as an individual feature but use the specified rules to sort the two entities in a relation once the relation type is recognized. As for those symmetric relation types, the order needs not to be concerned. Either order is considered correct in the ACE standard. As for those asymmetric relation types, we simply select the first (in adjacent and separated structure) or outer (in nested structures) as the first entity. In most cases, this treatment leads to the correct order. We also make use of entity types to verify (and rectify if necessary) this default order. For example, considering "At" is a relation between a Person, Organization, GPE, or Facility entity and a Location entity, the Location entity must be placed after the Person, Organization, GPE, or Facility entity in a relation.

4 Experiments and Evaluations

4.1 Experiment Setup

The experiments are conducted on the ACE 2004 Chinese relation extraction dataset, which consists of 221 documents selected from broadcast news and newswire reports. There are 2620 relation instances and 11800 pairs of entities have no relationship in the dataset. The size of the feature space is 3017.

We examine the proposed DBN model using 4-fold cross-validation. The performance is measured by precision, recall, and F-measure.

$$F\text{-measure}=\frac{2*\text{Precision}*\text{Recall}}{\text{Precision}+\text{Recall}} \quad (8)$$

In the following experiments, we plan to test the effectiveness of the DBN model in three ways:

Detection Only: For each relation candidate, we only recognize whether there is a certain relationship between the two entities, no matter what type of relation they hold.

Detection and Classification in Sequence: For each relation candidate, when it is detected to be an instance of relation, it proceeds to detect the type of the relation the two entities hold.

Detection and Classification in Combination: We define N+1 relation label, N for relation types defined by ACE and one for NULL indicating there is no relationship between the two entities. In this way, the processes of detection and classification are combined.

We will compare DBN with a well-known Support Vector Machine model (labeled as SVM in the tables) and a traditional BP neutral network model (labeled as NN (BP only)). Among them, SVM has been successfully applied in many classification applications. We use the LibSVM toolkit[2] to implement the SVM model.

4.2 Evaluation on Detection Only

We first evaluate relation detection, where only two output classes are concerned, i.e. NULL (which means no relation recognized) and RELATION. The parameters used in DBN, SVM and NN (BP only) are tuned experimentally and the results with the best parameter settings are presented in Table 2. In each of our experiments, we test many parameters of SVM and chose the best set of that to show below.

Regarding the structure of DBN, we experiment with different combinations of unit numbers in the RBM layers. Finally we choose DBN with three RBM layers and one BP layer. And the numbers of units in each RBM layer are 2400, 1800 and 1200 respectively, which is the best size of each layer in our experiment. Our empirical results showed that the numbers of units in adjoining layers should not decrease the dimension of feature vector too much when casting the vector transformation. NN has the same structure as DBN. As for SVM, we choose the linear kernel with the penalty parameter C=0.3, which is the best penalty coefficient, and set the other parameters as default after comparing different kernels and parameter values.

Model	Precision	Recall	F-measure
DBN	67.8%	70.58%	69.16%
SVM	73.06%	52.42%	61.04%
NN (BP only)	51.51%	61.77%	56.18%

Table 2. Performances of DBN, SVM and NN models for detection only

As showed in Table 2, with their best parameter settings, DBN performs much better than both SVM and NN (BP only) in terms of F-measure. It tells that DBN is quite good in this binary classification task. Since RBM is a fast approach to approximate global optimum of networks, its advantage over NN (BP only) is clearly demonstrated in their results.

4.3 Evaluation on Detection and Classification in Sequence

In the next experiment, we go one step further. If a relation is detected, we classified it into one of the 5 pre-defined relation types. For relation type classification, DBN and NN (BP only) have the same structures as they are in the first experiment. We adopt SVM linear kernel again and set C to 0.09 and other parameters as default. The overall performance of detection and classification of three models are illustrated in Table 3 below. DBN again is more effective than SVM and NN.

Model	Precision	Recall	F-measure
DBN	63.67%	59%	61.25%
SVM	67.78%	47.43%	55.81%
NN	61%	45.62%	52.2%

Table 3. Performances of DBN and other classification models for detection and classification in sequence

4.4 Evaluation on Detection and Classification in Combination

In the third experiment, we unify relation detection and relation type classification into one classification task. All the candidates are directly classified into one of the 6 classes, including 5 relation types and a NULL class. Parameter settings of the three models in this experiment are identical to those in the second experiment, except that C in SVM is set to 0.1.

Model	Precision	Recall	F-measure
DBN	65.8%	59.15%	62.3%
SVM	75.25%	44.07%	55.59%
NN (BP only)	63.2%	45.7%	53.05%

Table 4. Performances of DBN, SVM and NN models for detection and classification in combination

As demonstrated, DBN outperforms both SVM and NN (BP only) in all these three experiments consistently. In this regard, the

[2] http://www.csie.ntu.edu.tw/~cjlin/libsvm/

advantages of DBN over the other two models are apparent. RBM approximates expected parameters rapidly and the deep DBN architecture yields stronger representativeness of complicated, efficient features.

Comparing the results of the second and the third experiments, SVM perform better (although not quite significantly) when detection and classification are in sequence than in combination. This finding is consistent with our previous work (to be added later). It can possibly be that preceding detection helps to deal with the severe unbalance problem, i.e. there are much more relation candidates that don't hold pre-defined relations. However, DBN obtaining the opposite result cause by that the amount of examples we have is not sufficient for DBN to self-train itself well for type classification. We will further exam this issue in our feature work.

4.5 Evaluation on DBN Structure

Next, we compare the performance of DBN with different structures by changing the number of RBM layers. All the candidates are directly classified into 6 types in this experiment.

DBN	Precision	Recall	F-measure
3 RBMs + BP	65.8%	59.15%	62.3%
2 RBMs + BP	65.22%	57.1%	60.09%
1 RBM + BP	64.35%	55.5%	59.6%

Table 5. Performance RBM with different layers

The results provided in Table 5 show that the performance can be improved when more RBM layers are incorporated. Multiple RBM layers enhance representation power. Since it was reported by Hinton (2006) that three RBM layer is enough to detect the complex features and more RBM layer are of less help, we do not try to go beyond the three layers in this experiment. Note that the improvement is more obvious from two layers to three layers than from one layer to two layers.

4.6 Error Analysis

Finally, we provide the test results for individual relation types in Table 6. We can see that the proposed model performs better on "Role" and "Part" relations. When taking a closer look at their relation instance distributions, the instances of these two types comprise over 63% percents of all the relation instances in the dataset. Clearly their better results benefit from the amount of training data. It further implies that if we have more training data, we should be able to train a more powerful DBN. The same characteristic is also observed in Table 7 which shows the distributions of the identified relations against the gold standard. However, the sizes of "At" relation instances and "Role' relation instances are similar, its result is much worse. We believe it is from the origin of that the position feature is not distinctive for "At" relation, as shown in Table 8. "Near" and "Social" are two symmetric relation types. Ideally, they should have better results. But due to quite small number of training examples, you can see that they are actually the types with the worst F-measure.

Type	Precision	Recall	F-measure
Role	65.19%	69.2%	67.14%
Part	67.86%	71.43%	69.59%
At	51.15%	60%	55.22%
Near	15.38%	33.33%	20.05%
Social	25%	35.71%	29.41%

Table 6. Performance of DBN for each relation type

Standard \ Identified	R	P	A	N	S	Null
Role (R)	191	1	5	0	0	96
Part (P)	1	95	**12**	0	0	32
At (A)	4	8	111	2	1	91
Near (N)	0	1	0	2	0	10
Social (S)	1	0	0	0	5	14

Table 7. Distribution of the identified relations

Type	Adjacent	Separated	Nested
Role	7	63	223
Part	1	17	122
At	21	98	98
Near	0	8	5
Social	10	10	10

Table 8. Statistic of position feature

The main mistakes observed in Table 7 are wrongly classifying a "Part" relation as a "At" relations. We further inspect these 12 mistakes and find that it is indeed difficult to distinct the two types for the given entity pairs. Here is a typical example: entity 1: 美国民主党 (the Democratic Party of the United States, defined as an organization entity), entity 2: 美国 (the United States, defined as a GPE entity). Therefore, the major problem we have to face is how to effectively recall more relations. Given the limited training resources, it is needed to well explore the appropriate external knowledge or the Web resources.

5 Conclusions

In this paper we present our recent work on applying a novel machine learning model, namely Deep Belief Network, to Chinese relation extraction. DBN is demonstrated to be effective for Chinese relation extraction because of its strong representativeness. We conduct a series of experiments to prove the benefits of DBN. Experimental results clearly show the strength of DBN which obtains better performance than other existing models such as SVM and the traditional BP neutral network. In the future, we will explore if it is possible to incorporate the appropriate external knowledge in order to recall more relation instances, given the limited training resource.

References

Ackley D., Hinton G. and Sejnowski T. 1985. A learning algorithm for Boltzmann machines, *Cognitive Science*, 9.

Brin Sergey. 1998. Extracting patterns and relations from world wide web, *In Proceedings of WebDB Workshop at 6th International Conference on Extending Database Technology (WebDB'98)*, 172-183.

Che W.X. Improved-Edit-Distance Kernel for Chinese Relation Extraction, *In Dale, R.,Wong, K.-F., Su, J., Kwong, O.Y. (eds.) IJCNLP 2005.LNCS(LNAI)*. vol. 2651.

H. Jing, R. Florian, X. Luo, T. Zhang, A. Ittycheriah. 2003. How to get a Chinese name (entity): Segmentation and combination issues. *In proceedings of EMNLP*. 200-207.

Hinton, G.. 1999. Products of experts. In Proceedings of the Ninth International. *Conference on Artificial Neural Networks (ICANN)*. Vol. 1, 1–6.

Hinton, G. E. 2002. Training products of experts by minimizing contrastive divergence, *Neural Computation, 14*(8), 1711–1800.

Hinton G. E., Osindero S. and Teh Y. 2006. A fast learning algorithm for deep belief nets, *Neural Computation*, 18. 1527–1554.

Ji Zhang, You Ouyang, Wenjie Li and Yuexian Hou. 2009. A Novel Composite Kernel Approach to Chinese Entity Relation Extraction. *in Proceedings of the 22nd International Conference on the Computer Processing of Oriental Languages*, Hong Kong, pp240-251.

Ji Zhang, You Ouyang, Wenjie Li, and Yuexian Hou. 2009. *Proceedings of the 22nd International Conference on Computer Processing of Oriental Languages*. 236-247.

Jiang J. and Zhai C. 2007. A Systematic Exploration of the Feature Space for Relation Extraction, *In Proceedings of NAACL/HLT*, 113–120.

Jinxiu Chen, Donghong Ji, Chew L., Tan and Zhengyu Niu. 2006. Relation extraction using label propagation based semi-supervised learning, *In Proceedings of ACL'06*, 129–136.

Li W.J., Zhang P., Wei F.R., Hou Y.X. and Lu, Q. 2008. A Novel Feature-based Approach to Chinese Entity Relation Extraction, *In Proceeding of ACL 2008 (Companion Volume)*, 89–92

Sun Xia and Dong Lehong, 2009. Feature-based Approach to Chinese Term Relation Extraction. *International Conference on Signal Processing Systems.*

Willy Yap and Timothy Baldwin. 2009. Experiments on Pattern-based Relation Learning. *Proceeding of the 18th ACM conference on Information and knowledge management*. 1657-1660.

Y. Bengio and Y. LeCun. 2007. Scaling learning algorithms towards ai. *Large-Scale Kernel Machines*. MIT Press.

Zelenko D. Aone C and Richardella A. 2003. Kernel Methods for Relation Extraction, *Journal of Machine Learning Research 2003(2),* 1083–1106.

Zhang P., Li W.J., Wei F.R., Lu Q. and Hou Y.X. 2008. Exploiting the Role of Position Feature in Chinese Relation Extraction, *In Proceedings of the 6th International Conference on Language Resources and Evaluation (LREC).*

Exploring English Lexicon Knowledge for Chinese Sentiment Analysis

Yulan He Harith Alani
Knowledge Media Institute
The Open University
Milton Keynes MK6 6AA, UK
{y.he, h.alani}@open.ac.uk

Deyu Zhou
School of Computer Science and Engineering
Southeast University
Nanjing, China
d.zhou@seu.edu.cn

Abstract

This paper presents a weakly-supervised method for Chinese sentiment analysis by incorporating lexical prior knowledge obtained from English sentiment lexicons through machine translation. A mechanism is introduced to incorporate the prior information about polarity-bearing words obtained from existing sentiment lexicons into latent Dirichlet allocation (LDA) where sentiment labels are considered as topics. Experiments on Chinese product reviews on mobile phones, digital cameras, MP3 players, and monitors demonstrate the feasibility and effectiveness of the proposed approach and show that the weakly supervised LDA model performs as well as supervised classifiers such as Naive Bayes and Support vector Machines with an average of 83% accuracy achieved over a total of 5484 review documents. Moreover, the LDA model is able to extract highly domain-salient polarity words from text.

1 Introduction

Sentiment analysis aims to understand subjective information such as opinions, attitudes, and feelings expressed in text. It has become a hot topic in recent years because of the explosion in availability of people's attitudes and opinions expressed in social media including blogs, discussion forums, tweets, etc. Research in sentiment analysis has mainly focused on the English language. There have been few studies in sentiment analysis in other languages due to the lack of resources, such as subjectivity lexicons consisting of a list of words marked with their respective polarity (positive, negative or neutral) and manually labeled subjectivity corpora with documents labeled with their polarity.

Pilot studies on cross-lingual sentiment analysis utilize machine translation to perform sentiment analysis on the English translation of foreign language text (Banea et al., 2008; Bautin et al., 2008; Wan, 2009). The major problem is that they cannot be generalized well when there is a domain mismatch between the source and target languages. There have also been increasing interests in exploiting bootstrapping-style approaches for weakly-supervised sentiment classification in languages other than English (Zagibalov and Carroll, 2008b; Zagibalov and Carroll, 2008a; Qiu et al., 2009). Other approaches use ensemble techniques by either combining lexicon-based and corpus-based algorithms (Tan et al., 2008) or combining sentiment classification outputs from different experimental settings (Wan, 2008). Nevertheless, all these approaches are either complex or require careful tuning of domain and data specific parameters.

This paper proposes a weakly-supervised approach for Chinese sentiment classification by incorporating language-specific lexical knowledge obtained from available English sentiment lexicons through machine translation. Unlike other cross-lingual sentiment classification methods which often require labeled corpora for training and therefore hinder their applicability for cross-domain sentiment analysis, the proposed approach does not require labeled documents. Moreover, as opposed to existing weakly-supervised sentiment classification approaches which are rather complex, slow, and require careful parameter tuning, the proposed approach is simple and computationally efficient; rendering more suitable for online and real-time sentiment classification from the Web.

Our experimental results on the Chinese reviews of four different product types show that the LDA model performs as well as the supervised classifiers such as Naive Bayes and Support Vector Machines trained from labeled corpora. Although this paper primarily studies sentiment analysis in Chinese, the proposed approach is applicable to any other language so long as a machine translation engine is available between the selected language and English.

The remainder of the paper is organized as follows. Related work on cross-lingual sentiment classification and weakly-supervised sentiment classification in languages other than English are discussed in Section 2. The proposed mechanism of incorporating prior word polarity knowledge into the LDA model is introduced in Section 3. The experimental setup and results of sentiment classification on the Chinese reviews of four different products are presented in Section 4 and 5 respectively. Finally, Section 6 concludes the paper.

2 Related Work

Pilot studies on cross-lingual sentiment analysis rely on English corpora for subjectivity classification in other languages. For example, Mihalcea et al. (2007) make use of a bilingual lexicon and a manually translated parallel text to generate the resources to build subjectivity classifiers based on Support Vector Machines (SVMs) and Naive Bayes (NB) in a new language; Banea et al. (2008) use machine translation to produce a corpus in a new language and train SVMs and NB for subjectivity classification in the new language. Bautin et al. (2008) also utilize machine translation to perform sentiment analysis on the English translation of a foreign language text.

More recently, Wan (2009) proposed a co-training approach to tackle the problem of cross-lingual sentiment classification by leveraging an available English corpus for Chinese sentiment classification. Similar to the approach proposed in (Banea et al., 2008), Wan's method also uses machine translation to produced a labeled Chinese review corpus from the available labeled English review data. However, in order to alleviate the language gap problem that the underlying distributions between the source and target language are different, Wan builds two SVM classifiers, one based on English features and the other based on Chinese features, and uses a bootstrapping method based on co-training to iteratively improve classifiers until convergence.

The major problem of the aforementioned cross-lingual sentiment analysis algorithms is that they all utilize supervised learning to train sentiment classifiers from annotated English corpora (or the translated target language corpora generated by machine translation). As such, they cannot be generalized well when there is a domain mismatch between the source and target language. For example, For example, the word 'compact' might express positive polarity when used to describe a digital camera, but it could have negative orientation if it is used to describe a hotel room. Thus, classifiers trained on one domain often fail to produce satisfactory results when shifting to another domain.

Recent efforts have also been made for weakly-supervised sentiment classification in Chinese. Zagibalov and Carroll (2008b) starts with a one-word sentiment seed vocabulary and use iterative retraining to gradually enlarge the seed vocabulary by adding more sentiment-bearing lexical items based on their relative frequency in both the positive and negative parts of the current training data. Sentiment direction of a document is then determined by the sum of sentiment scores of all the sentiment-bearing lexical items found in the document. The problem with this approach is that there is no principal way to set the optimal number of iterations. They then suggested an iteration control method in (Zagibalov and Carroll, 2008a) where iterative training stops when there is no change to the classification of any document over the previous two iterations. However, this does not necessarily correlate to the best classification accuracy.

Similar to (Zagibalov and Carroll, 2008b), Qiu et al. (2009) also uses a lexicon-based iterative process as the first phase to iteratively enlarge an initial sentiment dictionary. But instead of using a one-word seed dictionary as in (Zagibalov and Carroll, 2008b), they started with a much larger HowNet Chinese sentiment dictionary[1] as the initial lexicon. Documents classified by the first phase are taken as the training set to train the SVMs which are subsequently used to revise the results produced by the first phase.

Other researchers investigated ensemble techniques for weakly-supervised sentiment classification. Tan et al. (2008) proposed a combination of lexicon-based and corpus-based approaches that first labels some examples from a give domain using a sentiment lexicon and then trains a supervised classifier based on the labeled ones from the first stage. Wan (2008) combined sentiment scores calculated from Chinese product reviews using the Chinese HowNet sentiment dictionary and from the English translation of Chinese reviews using the English MPQA subjectivity lexicon[2]. Various weighting strategies were explored to combine sentiment classification outputs from different experimental settings in order to improve classification accuracy.

Nevertheless, all these weakly-supervised sentiment classification approaches are rather complex and require either iterative training or careful tuning of domain and data specific parameters, and hence unsuitable for online and real-time sentiment analysis in practical applications.

3 Incorporating Prior Word Polarity Knowledge into LDA

Unlike existing approaches, we view sentiment classification as a generative problem that when an author writes a review document, he/she first decides on the overall sentiment or polarity (positive, negative, or neutral) of a document, then for each sentiment, decides on the words to be used. We use LDA to model a mixture of only three topics or sentiment labels, i.e. positive, negative and neutral.

Assuming that we have a total number of S sentiment labels; a corpus with a collection of D documents is denoted by $C = \{d_1, d_2, ..., d_D\}$; each document in the corpus is a sequence of N_d words denoted by $d = (w_1, w_2, ..., w_{N_d})$, and each word in the document is an item from a vocabulary index with V distinct terms denoted by $\{1, 2, ..., V\}$. The generative process is as follows:

- Choose distributions $\varphi \sim Dir(\beta)$.
- For each document $d \in [1, D]$, choose distributions $\pi_d \sim Dir(\gamma)$.
- For each of the N_d word position w_t, choose a sentiment label $l_t \sim Multinomial(\pi_d)$, and then choose a word $w_t \sim Multinomial(\varphi_{l_t})$.

The joint probability of words and sentiment label assignment in LDA can be factored into two terms:

$$P(\mathbf{w}, \mathbf{l}) = P(\mathbf{w}|\mathbf{l})P(\mathbf{l}|d). \qquad (1)$$

Letting the superscript $-t$ denote a quantity that excludes data from the tth position, the conditional posterior for l_t by marginalizing out the random variables φ and π is

$$P(l_t = k|\mathbf{w}, \mathbf{l^{-t}}, \beta, \gamma) \propto \frac{N_{w_t,k}^{-t} + \beta}{N_k^{-t} + V\beta} \times \frac{N_{k,d}^{-t} + \gamma_k}{N_d^{-t} + \sum_k \gamma_k}, \qquad (2)$$

where $N_{w_t,k}$ is the number of times word w_t has associated with sentiment label k; N_k is the the number of times words in the corpus assigned to sentiment label k; $N_{k,d}$ is the number of times sentiment label k has been assigned to some word tokens in document d; N_d is the total number of words in the document collection.

Each words in documents can either bear positive polarity ($l_t = 1$), or negative polarity ($l_t = 2$), or is neutral ($l_t = 0$). We now show how to incorporate polarized words in sentiment lexicons as prior information in the Gibbs sampling process. Let

$$Q_{t,k} = \frac{N_{w_t,k}^{-t} + \beta}{N_k^{-t} + V\beta} \times \frac{N_{k,d}^{-t} + \gamma_k}{N_d^{-t} + \sum_k \gamma_k} \qquad (3)$$

[1] http://www.keenage.com/download/sentiment.rar

[2] http://www.cs.pitt.edu/mpqa/

We can then modify the Gibbs sampling equation as follows:

$$P(l_t = k|\mathbf{w}, \mathbf{l}^{-\mathbf{t}}, \beta, \gamma) \propto \begin{cases} \mathbb{I}(k = S(w_t)) \times Q_{t,k} & \text{if } S(w_t) \text{ is defined} \\ Q_{t,k} & \text{otherwise} \end{cases} \quad (4)$$

where the function $S(w_t)$ returns the prior sentiment label of w_t in a sentiment lexicon and it is defined if word w_t is found in the sentiment lexicon. $\mathbb{I}(k = S(w_t))$ is an indicator function that takes on value 1 if $k = S(w_t)$ and 0 otherwise.

Equation 4 in fact applies a hard constraint that when a word is found in a sentiment lexicon, its sampled sentiment label is restricted to be the same as its prior sentiment label defined in the lexicon. This constraint can be relaxed by introducing a parameter to control the strength of the constraint such that when word w_t is found in the sentiment lexicon, Equation 4 becomes

$$P(l_t = k|\mathbf{w}, \mathbf{l}^{-\mathbf{t}}, \beta, \gamma) \propto (1 - \lambda) \times Q_{t,k} + \lambda \times \mathbb{I}(k = S(w_t)) \times Q_{t,k} \quad (5)$$

where $0 \leq \lambda \leq 1$. When $\lambda = 1$, the hard constraint will be applied; when $\lambda = 0$, Equation 5 is reduced to the original unconstrained Gibbs sampling as defined in Equation 2.

While sentiment prior information is incorporated by modifying conditional probabilities used in Gibbs sampling here, it is also possible to explore other mechanisms to define expectation or posterior constraints, for example, using the generalized expectation criteria (McCallum et al., 2007) to express preferences on expectations of sentiment labels of those lexicon words. We leave the exploitation of other mechanisms of incorporating prior knowledge into model training as future work.

The document sentiment is classified based on $P(\mathbf{l}|d)$, the probability of sentiment label given document, which can be directly obtained from the document-sentiment distribution. We define that a document d is classified as positive if $P(\mathbf{l_{pos}}|d) > P(\mathbf{l_{neg}}|d)$, and vice versa.

Table 2: Data statistics of the four Chinese product reviews corpora.

	No. of Reviews		*Vocab*
Corpus	*positive*	*Negative*	*Size*
Mobile	1159	1158	8945
DigiCam	853	852	5716
MP3	390	389	4324
Monitor	341	342	4712

4 Experimental Setup

We conducted experiments on the four corpora[3] which were derived from product reviews harvested from the website IT168[4] with each corresponding to different types of product reviews including mobile phones, digital cameras, MP3 players, and monitors. All the reviews were tagged by their authors as either positive or negative overall. The statistics of the four corpora are shown in Table 2.

We explored three widely used English sentiment lexicons in our experiments, namely the MPQA subjectivity lexicon, the appraisal lexicon[5], and the SentiWordNet[6] (Esuli and Sebastiani, 2006). For all these lexicons, we only extracted words bearing positive or negative polarities and discarded words bearing neutral polarity. For SentiWordNet, as it consists of words marked with positive and negative orientation scores ranging from 0 to 1, we extracted a subset of 8,780 opinionated words, by selecting those whose orientation strength is above a threshold of 0.6.

We used Google translator toolkit[7] to translate these three English lexicons into Chinese. After translation, duplicate entries, words that failed to translate, and words with contradictory polarities were removed. For comparison, we also tested a Chinese sentiment lexicon, NTU Sentiment Dictionary (NTUSD)[8] (Ku and Chen, 2007) which

[3] http://www.informatics.sussex.ac.uk/users/tz21/dataZH.tar.gz
[4] http://product.it168.com
[5] http://lingcog.iit.edu/arc/appraisal_lexicon_2007b.tar.gz
[6] http://sentiwordnet.isti.cnr.it/
[7] http://translate.google.com
[8] http://nlg18.csie.ntu.edu.tw:

Table 1: Matched polarity words statistics (positive/negative).

Lexicon	*Chinese*				*English*			
	Mobile	DigiCam	MP3	Monitors	Mobile	DigiCam	MP3	Monitors
(a)MPQA	261/253	183/174	162/135	169/147	293/331	220/241	201/153	210/174
(b)Appraisal	279/165	206/127	180/104	198/105	392/271	330/206	304/153	324/157
(c)SentiWN	304/365	222/276	202/213	222/236	394/497	306/397	276/310	313/331
(d)NTUSD	338/319	263/242	239/167	277/241	–			
(a)+(c)	425/465	307/337	274/268	296/289	516/607	400/468	356/345	396/381
(a)+(b)+(c)	495/481	364/353	312/280	344/302	624/634	496/482	447/356	494/389
(a)+(c)+(d)	586/608	429/452	382/336	421/410	–			

was automatically generated by enlarging an initial manually created seed vocabulary by consulting two thesauri, tong2yi4ci2ci2lin2 and the Academia Sinica Bilingual Ontological WordNet 3.

Chinese word segmentation was performed on the four corpora using the conditional random fields based Chinese Word Segmenter[9]. The total numbers of matched polarity words in each corpus using different lexicon are shown in Table 1 with the left half showing the statistics against the Chinese lexicons (the original English lexicons have been translated into Chinese) and the right half listing the statistics against the English lexicons. We did not translate the Chinese lexicon NTUSD into English since we focused on Chinese sentiment classification here. It can be easily seen from the table that in general the matched positive words outnumbered the matched negative words using any single lexicon except SentiWordNet. But the combination of the lexicons results in more matched polarity words and thus gives more balanced number of positive and negative words. We also observed the increasing number of the matched polarity words on the translated English corpora compared to their original Chinese corpora. However, as will be discussed in Section 5.2 that the increasing number of the matched polarity words does not necessarily lead to the improvement of the sentiment classification accuracy.

We modified GibbsLDA++ package[10] for the model implementation and only used hard constraints as defined in Equation 4 in our experiments. The word prior polarity information was also utilized during the initialization stage that if a word can be found in a sentiment lexicon, the word token is assigned with its corresponding sentiment label. Otherwise, a sentiment label is randomly sampled for the word. Symmetric Dirichlet prior β was used for sentiment-word distribution and was set to 0.01, while asymmetric Dirichlet prior γ was used for document-sentiment distribution and was set to 0.01 for positive and neutral sentiment labels, and 0.05 for negative sentiment label.

5 Experimental Results

This section presents the experimental results obtained under two different settings: LDA model with translated English lexicons tested on the original Chinese product review corpora; and LDA model with original English lexicons tested on the translated product review corpora.

5.1 Results with Different Sentiment Lexicons

Table 3 gives the classification accuracy results using the LDA model with prior sentiment label information provided by different sentiment lexicons. Since we did not use any labeled information, the accuracies were averaged over 5 runs and on the whole corpora. For comparison purposes, we have also implemented a baseline model which simply assigns a score +1 and -1 to any matched positive and negative word respectively based on a sentiment lexicon. A review document is then classified as either positive or negative according to the aggregated sentiment scores. The baseline results were shown in brackets in Table 3 .

`8080/opinion/pub1.html`

[9]`http://nlp.stanford.edu/software/stanford-chinese-segmenter-2008-05-21.tar.gz`

[10]`http://gibbslda.sourceforge.net/`

Table 3: Sentiment classification accuracy (%) by LDA, numbers in brackets are baseline results.

Lexicon	*Mobile*	*DigiCam*	*MP3*	*Monitors*	*Average*
(a)MPQA	82.00 (63.53)	80.93 (67.59)	78.31 (68.42)	81.41 (64.86)	80.66 (66.10)
(b)Appraisal	71.95 (56.28)	80.46 (60.54)	77.28 (61.36)	80.67 (57.98)	77.59 (59.04)
(c)SentiWN	81.10 (62.45)	78.52 (57.13)	79.08 (64.57)	75.55 (55.34)	78.56 (59.87)
(d)NTUSD	82.61 (71.21)	78.70 (68.23)	78.69 (75.87)	84.63 (74.96)	81.16 (72.57)
(a)+(c)	81.18 (65.95)	78.70 (65.18)	83.83 (67.52)	80.53 (62.08)	81.06 (65.18)
(a)+(b)+(c)	81.48 (62.84)	80.22 (65.88)	80.23 (65.60)	78.62 (61.35)	80.14 (63.92)
(a)+(c)+(d)	82.48 (69.96)	84.33 (69.58)	83.70 (71.12)	82.72 (65.59)	83.31 (69.06)
Naive Bayes	86.52	82.27	82.64	86.21	84.41
SVMs	84.49	82.04	79.43	83.87	82.46

It can be observed from Table 3 that the LDA model performs significantly better than the baseline model. The improvement ranges between 9% and 19% and this roughly corresponds to how much the model learned from the data. We can thus speculate that LDA is indeed able to learn the sentiment-word distributions from data.

Translated English sentiment lexicons perform comparably with the Chinese sentiment lexicon NTUSD. As for the individual lexicon, using MPQA subjectivity lexicon gives the best result among all the English lexicons on all the corpora except the MP3 corpus where MPQA performs slightly worse than SentiWordNet. The combination of MPQA and SentiWordNet performs significantly better than other lexicons on the MP3 corpus, with almost 5% improvement compared to the second best result. We also notice that the combination of all the three English lexicons does not lead to the improvement of classification accuracy which implies that the quality of a sentiment lexicon is indeed important to sentiment classification. The above results suggest that in the absence of any Chinese sentiment lexicon, MPQA subjectivity lexicon appears to be the best candidate to be used to provide sentiment prior information to the LDA model for Chinese sentiment classification.

We also conducted experiments by including the Chinese sentiment lexicon NTUSD and found that the combination of MPQA, SentiWordNet, and NTUSD gives the best overall classification accuracy with 83.31% achieved. For comparison purposes, we list the 10-fold cross validation results obtained using the supervised classifiers, Naive Bayes and SVMs, trained on the labeled corpora as previously reported in (Zagibalov and Carroll, 2008a). It can be observed that using only English lexicons (the combination of MPQA and SentiWordNet), we obtain better results than both NB and SVMs on the MP3 corpus. With an additional inclusion of NTUSD, LDA outperforms NB and SVMs on both DigiCam and MP3. Furthermore, LDA gives a better overall accuracy when compared to SVMs. Thus, we may conclude that the unsupervised LDA model performs as well as the supervised classifiers such as NB and SVMs on the Chinese product review corpora.

5.2 Results with Translated Corpora

We ran a second set of experiments on the translated Chinese product review corpora using the original English sentiment lexicons. Both the translated corpora and the sentiment lexicons have gone through stopword removal and stemming in order to reduce the vocabulary size and thereby alleviate data sparseness problem. It can be observed from Figure 1 that in general sentiment classification on the original Chinese corpora using the translated English sentiment lexicons gives better results than classifying on the translated review corpora using the original English lexicons on both the Mobile and Digicam corpora. However, reversed results are observed on the Monitor corpus that classifying on the translated review corpus using the English sentiment lexicons outperforms classifying on the

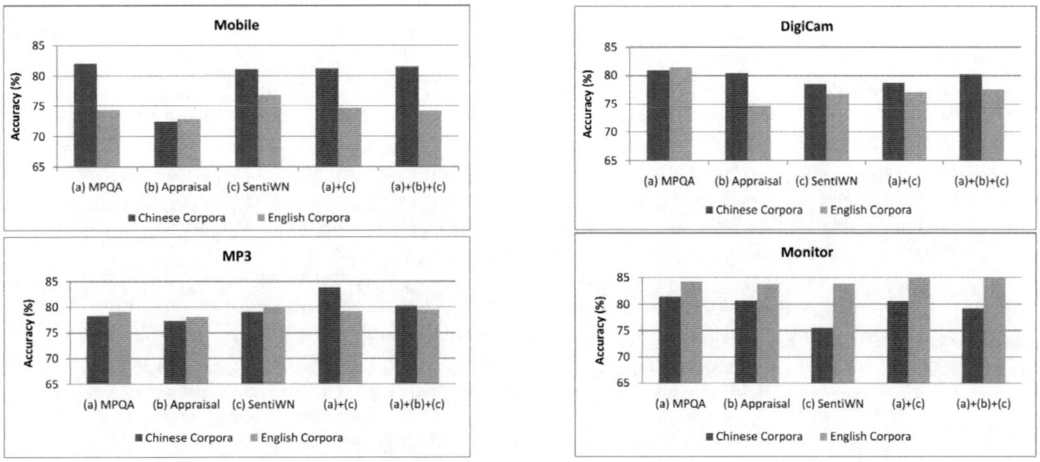

Figure 1: Comparison of the performance on the Chinese corpora and their translated corpora in English.

original Chinese review corpus using the translated sentiment lexicons. In particular, the combination of the MPQA subjectivity lexicon and SentiWordNet gives the best result of 84% on the Monitor corpus. As for the MP3 corpus, classifying on the original Chinese reviews or on the translated reviews does not differ much except that a better result is obtained on the Chinese corpus when using the combination of the MPQA subjectivity lexicon and SentiWordNet. The above results can be partially explained by the ambiguities and changes of meanings introduced in the translation. The Mobile and DigiCam corpora are relatively larger than the MP3 and Monitors corpora and we therefore expect more ambiguities being introduced which might result in the change of document polarities.

5.3 Extracted Polarity-Bearing Words

LDA is able to extract polarity-bearing words. Table 4 lists some of the polarity words identified by the LDA model which are not found in the original sentiment lexicons. We can see that LDA is indeed able to recognize domain-specific positive or negative words, for example, 蓝牙 (bluetooth) for mobile phones, 小巧 (compact) for digital cameras, 金属 (metallic) for MP3, 纯平 (flat screen) and 变形 (deformation) for monitors.

The iterative approach proposed in (Zagibalov and Carroll, 2008a) can also automatically acquire polarity words from data. However, it appears that only positive words were identified by their approach. Our proposed LDA model can extract both positive and negative words and most of them are highly domain-salient as can be seen from Table 4.

6 Conclusions

This paper has proposed a mechanism to incorporate prior information about polarity words from English sentiment lexicons into LDA model learning for weakly-supervised Chinese sentiment classification. Experimental results of sentiment classification on Chinese product reviews show that in the absence of a language-specific sentiment lexicon, the translated English lexicons can still produce satisfactory results with the sentiment classification accuracy of 81% achieved averaging over four different types of product reviews. With the incorporation of the Chinese sentiment lexicon NTUSD, the classification accuracy is further improved to 83%. Compared to the existing approaches to cross-lingual sentiment classification which either rely on labeled corpora for classifier learning or iterative training for performance gains, the proposed approach is simple and readily to

Table 4: Extracted example polarity words by LDA.

Corpus	*Positive*	*Negative*
Mobile	优点 (advantage), 大 (large), 好用 (easy to use), 快 (fast), 舒服 (comfortable), 蓝牙 (bluetooth), 新 (new), 容易 (easy)	坏 (bad), 差 (poor), 慢 (slow), 没 (no;not), 难 (difficult;hard), 少 (less), 只是 (but), 修 (repair)
DigiCam	优点 (advantage), 小巧 (compact), 强 (strong;strength), 长焦 (telephoto), 动态 (dynamic), 全 (comprehensive), 专业 (professional), 上手 (get started)	后悔 (regret), 坏 (bad), 差 (poor), 慢 (slow), 暗 (dark), 贵 (expensive), 难 (difficult;hard), 耗电 (consume much electricity), 塑料 (plastic), 修 (repair)
MP3	小巧 (compact), 快 (fast), 强 (strong;strength), 更 (even), 质感 (textual), 全 (comprehensive), 金属 (metallic), 十分 (very)	不 (no;not), 差 (poor), 坏 (bad), 有点 (rather), 根本 (simply), 次 (substandard), 死机 (crash), 没 (no), 但是 (but)
Monitors	容易 (easy), 新 (new), 纯平 (flat screen), 舒服 (comfortable), 显亮 (looks bright), 锐利 (sharp), 亮 (bright), 自动 (automatic)	变形 (deformation), 偏色 (color cast bad), 坏 (bad), 差 (poor), 没 (no;not), 漏光 (leakage of light), 黑屏 (black screen), 退 (refund;return), 暗 (dark), 抖动 (jitter)

be used for online and real-time sentiment classification from the Web.

One issue relating to the proposed approach is that it still depends on the quality of machine translation and the performance of sentiment classification is thus affected by the language gap between the source and target language. A possible way to alleviate this problem is to construct a language-specific sentiment lexicon automatically from data and use it as the prior information source to be incorporated into the LDA model learning.

References

Banea, C., R. Mihalcea, J. Wiebe, and S. Hassan. 2008. Multilingual subjectivity analysis using machine translation. In *Proceedings of the EMNLP*, pages 127–135.

Bautin, M., L. Vijayarenu, and S. Skiena. 2008. International sentiment analysis for news and blogs. In *Proceedings of the International Conference on Weblogs and Social Media (ICWSM)*.

Esuli, A. and F. Sebastiani. 2006. SentiWordNet: A publicly available lexical resource for opinion mining. In *Proceedings of LREC*, volume 6.

Ku, L.W. and H.H. Chen. 2007. Mining opinions from the Web: Beyond relevance retrieval. *Journal of the American Society for Information Science and Technology*, 58(12):1838–1850.

McCallum, A., G. Mann, and G. Druck. 2007. Generalized expectation criteria. Technical Report 2007-60, University of Massachusetts Amherst.

Mihalcea, R., C. Banea, and J. Wiebe. 2007. Learning multilingual subjective language via cross-lingual projections. In *Proceedings of the ACL*, pages 976–983.

Qiu, L., W. Zhang, C. Hu, and K. Zhao. 2009. Selc: a self-supervised model for sentiment classification. In *Proceeding of the CIKM*, pages 929–936.

Tan, S., Y. Wang, and X. Cheng. 2008. Combining learn-based and lexicon-based techniques for sentiment detection without using labeled examples. In *Proceedings of the SIGIR*, pages 743–744.

Tseng, H., P. Chang, G. Andrew, D. Jurafsky, and C. Manning. 2005. A conditional random field word segmenter. In *Fourth SIGHAN Workshop on Chinese Language Processing*, volume 37.

Wan, X. 2008. Using bilingual knowledge and ensemble techniques for unsupervised Chinese sentiment analysis. In *Proceedings of the EMNLP*, pages 553–561.

Wan, X. 2009. Co-training for cross-lingual sentiment classification. In *Proceedings of the ACL*, pages 235–243.

Zagibalov, T. and J. Carroll. 2008a. Automatic seed word selection for unsupervised sentiment classification of Chinese text. In *Proceedings of the COLING*, pages 1073–1080.

Zagibalov, T. and J. Carroll. 2008b. Unsupervised classification of sentiment and objectivity in chinese text. In *Proceedings of the IJCNLP*, pages 304–311.

Exploiting Social Q&A Collection in Answering Complex Questions

Youzheng Wu **Hisashi Kawai**
Spoken Language Communication Group, MASTAR Project
National Institute of Information and Communications Technology
2-2-2 Hikaridai, Keihanna Science City, Kyoto 619-0288, Japan
{youzheng.wu, hisashi.kawai}@nict.go.jp

Abstract

This paper investigates techniques to automatically construct training data from social Q&A collections such as Yahoo! Answer to support a machine learning-based complex QA system[1]. We extract cue expressions for each type of question from collected training data and build question-type-specific classifiers to improve complex QA system. Experiments on 10 types of complex Chinese questions verify that it is effective to mine knowledge from social Q&A collections for answering complex questions, for instance, the F_3 improvement of our system over the baseline and translation-based model reaches 7.9% and 5.1%, respectively.

1 Introduction

Research on the topic of QA systems has mainly concentrated on answering factoid, definitional, reason and opinion questions. Among the approaches proposed to answer these questions, machine learning techniques have been found more effective in constructing QA components from scratch. Yet these supervised techniques require a certain scale of (question, answer), short for Q&A, pairs as training data. For example, (Echihabi et al., 2003) and (Sasaki, 2005) constructed 90,000 English Q&A pairs and 2,000 Japanese Q&A pairs, respectively for their factoid QA systems. (Cui et al., 2004) constructed 76 term-definition pairs for their definitional QA systems. (Stoyanov et al., 2005) required a known subjective vocabulary for their opinion QA. (Higashinaka and Isozaki, 2008) used 4,849 positive and 521,177 negative examples in their reason QA system. Among complex QA systems, many other types of questions have not been well studied, apart from reason and definitional questions. Appendix A lists 10 types of complex Chinese questions and their examples we discussed in this paper.

According to the related studies on QA, supervised machine-learning technique may be effective for answering these questions. To employ the supervised approach, we need to reconstruct training Q&A pairs for each type of question, though this is an extremely expensive and labor-intensive task. To deal with the acquisition problem of training Q&A pairs, we investigate techniques to automatically construct training data by utilizing social Q&A collections crawled from the Web, which contains millions of user-generated Q&A pairs. Many studies (Surdeanu et al., 2008) (Duan et al., 2008) have been done on retrieving similar Q&A pairs from social QA websites as answers to test questions. Our study, however, regards social Q&A websites as a knowledge repository and aims to mine knowledge from them for synthesizing answers to questions from multiple documents. There is very little literature on this aspect. Our work can be seen as a kind of query-based summarization (Dang, 2006) (Harabagiu et al., 2006) (Erkan and Radev, 2004), and can also be employed to answer questions that have not been answered in social Q&A websites.

[1]Complex questions cannot be answered by simply extracting named entities. In this paper complex questions do not include definitional questions.

This paper mainly focuses on the following three steps: (1) automatically constructing question - type-specific training Q&A pairs from the social Q&A collection; (2) extracting cue expressions for each type of question from the collected training data, and (3) building question-type-specific classifiers to filer out noise sentences before using a state-of-the-art IR formula to select answers.

We evaluate our system on 10 types of Chinese questions by using the Pourpre evaluation tool (Lin and Demner-Fushman, 2006). The experimental results show the effectiveness of our system, for instance, the F_3/NR improvement of our system over the baseline and translation-based model reaches 7.9%/11.1%, and 5.1%/5.6%, respectively.

2 Social Q&A Collection

Recently launched social QA websites such as Yahoo! Answer[2] and Baidu Zhidao[3] provide an interactive platform for users to post questions and answers. After questions are answered by users, the best answer can be chosen by the asker or nominated by the community. The number of Q&A pairs on such sites has risen dramatically. These pairs could collectively form a source of training data that is required in supervised machine-learning-based QA systems.

In this paper we aim to explore such user-generated Q&A collections to automatically collect Q&A training data. However, social collections have two salient characteristics: textual mismatch between questions and answers (i.e., question words are not necessarily used in answers); and user-generated spam or flippant answers, which are unfavorable factors in our study. Thus, we only crawl questions and their best answers to form Q&A pairs, wherein the best answers are longer than the empirical threshold. Finally, 60.0 million Q&A pairs were crawled from Chinese social QA websites. These pairs will be used as the source of training data required in our study.

[2] `http://answers.yahoo.com/`
[3] `http://zhidao.baidu.com/`

3 Our Complex QA System

The typical complex QA system architecture is a cascade of three modules. The Question Analyzer analyzes test questions and identifies answer types of questions. The Document Retriever & Answer Candidate Extractor retrieves documents related to questions from the given collection (*Xinhua* and *Lianhe Zaobao* newspapers from 1998-2001 were used in this study) for consideration, and segments the documents into sentences as answer candidates. The Answer Extraction module applies state-of-the-art IR formulas (e.g., KL-divergence language model) to directly estimate similarities between sentences (1,024 sentences were used in our case) and questions, and selects the most similar sentences as the final answers. Given three answer candidates, s_1 = "*Solutions to global warming range from changing a light bulb to engineering giant reflectors in space ...*", s_2 = "*Global warming will bring bigger storms and hurricanes that will hold more water ...*", and s_3 = "*nuclear power is the relatively low emission of carbon dioxide (CO_2), one of the major causes of global warming,*" to the question of "What are the hazards of global warming?", however, it is hard for this architecture to select the correct answer, s_2, because the three candidates contain the same question words "global warming".

According to our observation, answers to a type of question usually contain some type-of-question dependent cue expressions ("will bring" in this case). This paper argues that the above QA system can be improved by using such question-type-specific cue expressions. For each test question, we perform the following three steps. (1) Collecting question-type-specific Q&A pairs from the social Q&A collection which question types are same as the test question to form positive training data. Similarly, negative Q&A pairs are also collected which question types are different from the test question. (2) Extracting and weighting question-type-specific cue expressions from the collected Q&A pairs. (3) Building a question-type-specific classifier by employing the cue expressions and the collected Q&A pairs, which removes noise sentences from answer candidates before using the Answer Extraction module.

3.1 Collecting Q&A Pairs

We first introduce the notion of the *answer type informer* of the question as follows. In a question, a short subsequence of tokens (typically 1-3 words) that are adequate for question classification is considered an answer-type informer, e.g., "hazard" in the question of "What are the hazards of global warming?" This paper makes the following assumption: type of complex question is determined by its answer type informer. For example, the question of "What are the hazards of global warming?" belongs to hazard-type question, because its answer type informer is "hazard". Therefore, the task of recognizing question-types is shifted to identifying *answer type informer* of question.

In this paper, we regard answer-type informer recognition as a sequence tagging problem and adopt conditional random fields (CRFs) because many work has shown that CRFs have a consistent advantage in sequence tagging. We manually label 3,262 questions with answer-type informers to train a CRF, which classifies each question word into a set of tags $O = \{I_B, I_I, I_O\}$: I_B for a word that begins an informer, I_I for a word that occurs in the middle of an informer, and I_O for a word that is outside of an informer. In the following feature templates used in the CRF model, w_n and t_n, refer to word and PoS, respectively; n refers to the relative position from the current word n=0. The feature templates include the following four types: unigrams of w_n and t_n, where n=$-2, -1, 0, 1, 2$; bigrams of $w_n w_{n+1}$ and $t_n t_{n+1}$, where n=$-1, 0$; trigrams of $w_n w_{n+1} w_{n+2}$ and $t_n t_{n+1} t_{n+2}$, where n=$-2, -1, 0$; and bigrams of $O_n O_{n+1}$, where n=$-1, 0$.

The trained CRF model is then employed to recognize answer-type informers from questions of social Q&A pairs. Finally, we recognized 103 answer-type informers in which frequencies are larger than 10,000. Moreover, the numbers of answer type informers for which frequencies are larger than 100, 1,000, and 5,000 are 2,714, 807, and 194, respectively.

Based on answer-type informers of questions recognized, we can collect training data for each type of question as follows: (1) Q&A pairs are grouped together in cases in which the answer-type informers X of their questions are the same, and (2) Q&A pairs clustered by informers X are regarded as the positive training data of X-type questions. For instance, 10,362 Q&A pairs grouped via informer X (="hazard") are regarded as positive training data of answering hazard-type questions. Table 1 lists some questions, which, together with their best answers, are employed as the training data of the corresponding type of questions. For each type of question, we also randomly select some Q&A pairs that do not contain informers in questions as negative training data. Preprocessing of the training data, including word segmentation, PoS tagging, and named entity (NE) tagging (Wu et al., 2005), is conducted. We also replace each NE with its tag type.

Qtype	Questions of Q&A pairs
Hazard-type	What are the **hazards** of the trojan.psw.misc.kah virus? What are the **hazards** of RMB appreciation on China's economy? **Hazards** of smoke What are the **hazards** of contact lenses? What are the **hazards** of waste accumulation?
Casualty-type	What were the **casualties** on either side from the U.S.-Iraq war? What were the **casualties** of the Sino-French War? What were the **casualties** of the Sichuan earthquake in 2008? What were the **casualties** of highway accidents over the years? What were the **casualties** of the Ryukyu Islands tsunami?
Reason-type	What are the main **reasons** of China's water shortage? What are the **reasons** of asthma? What are the **reasons** of blurred photos? What are the **reasons** of air pollution? The **reasons** for the soaring prices!

Table 1: Questions (translated from Chinese) of social Q&A pairs (words in bold denote answer-type informers of questions). These questions and their best answers are regarded as positive training data for hazard-type question.

3.2 Cue Expressions

We extract lexical and PoS-based n-grams as cue expressions from the collected training data. To reduce the dimensionality of the cue expression space, we first select the top 3,000 lexical unigrams using the formula: $score_w = tf_w \times log(idf_w)$, where $tf(w)$ denotes the frequency of word w, and $idf(w)$ represents the inverted document frequency of w that indicates its global importance. Table 2 shows some of the learned unigrams. The top 300 unigrams are then used as seeds to learn lexical bigrams and trigrams iteratively. Only lexical bigrams and trigrams that contain seed unigrams with frequencies larger than the thresholds are retained as lexical features. Moreover, we extract PoS-based unigrams and bigrams as cue expressions.

Further, we assign each extracted feature s_i a weight calculated using the equation $weight_{s_i} = c_1^{s_i}/(c_1^{s_i} + c_2^{s_i})$, where, $c_1^{s_i}$ and $c_2^{s_i}$ denote its frequencies in positive and negative training Q&A pairs, respectively.

Qtype	Top Unigrams
Hazard-type	危害/hazard 导致/lead to 造成/cause 引起/give rise to 产生/bring about 影响/influence 损害/damage
Casualty-type	伤亡/casualty 死亡/death 受伤/hurt 失踪/missing 遇难/wrecked 阵亡/die in battle 负伤/wounded

Table 2: Top unigrams learned from hazard-type and casualty-type Q&A pairs

3.3 Classifiers

As mentioned above, we use the extracted cue expressions and the collected Q&A pairs to build question-type-specific classifiers, which is used to remove noise sentences from answer candidates. For classifiers, we employ multivariate classification SVMs (Thorsten Joachims, 2005) that can directly optimize a large class of performance measures like F_1-Score, prec@k (precision of a classifier that predicts exactly k = 100 examples to be positive) and error-rate (percentage of errors in predictions). Instead of learning a univariate rule that predicts the label of a single example in conventional SVMs (Vapnik, 1998), multivariate SVMs formulate the learning problem as a multivariate prediction of all examples in the data set. Considering hypotheses $\overline{h}$ that map a tuple $\overline{\mathbf{x}}$ of n feature vectors $\overline{\mathbf{x}} = (\mathbf{x_1}, ..., \mathbf{x_n})$ to a tuple $\overline{y}$ of n labels $\overline{y} = (y_1, ..., y_n)$, multivariate SVMs learn a classifier

$$\overline{h}_{\mathbf{w}}(\overline{\mathbf{x}}) = argmax_{\overline{y}' \in \overline{Y}} \{\mathbf{w}^T \Psi(\overline{x}, \overline{y}')\} \quad (1)$$

by solving the following optimization problem.

$$min_{\mathbf{w}, \xi \geq 0} \quad \frac{1}{2}\|\mathbf{w}\|^2 + C\xi \quad (2)$$

$$s.t.: \quad \forall \overline{y}' \in \overline{Y} \backslash \overline{y} : \mathbf{w}^T[\Psi(\overline{x}, \overline{y}) - \Psi(\overline{x}, \overline{y}')] \geq \Delta(\overline{y}', \overline{y}) - \xi \quad (3)$$

where, $\mathbf{w}$ is a parameter vector, Ψ is a function that returns a feature vector describing the match between $(\mathbf{x_1}, ..., \mathbf{x_n})$ and $(y_1', ..., y_n')$, Δ denotes types of multivariate loss functions, and ξ is a slack variable.

4 Experiments

The NTCIR 2008 test data set (Mitamura et al., 2008) contains 30 complex questions[4] we discussed here. However, a small number of test questions are included for some question types, e.g.; it contains only 1 hazard-type, 1 scale-type, and 3 significance-type questions. To form a more complete test set, we create another 65 test questions[5]. Therefore, the test data used in this paper includes 95 complex questions.

For each test question we also provide a list of weighted nuggets, which are used as the gold standard answers for evaluation. The evaluation is conducted by employing Pourpre v1.0c (Lin and Demner-Fushman, 2006), which uses the standard scoring methodology for TREC other questions (Voorhees, 2003), i.e., answer nugget recall NR, nugget precision NP, and a combination score F_3 of NR and NP. For better understanding, we evaluate the systems when outputting the top N sentences as answers.

[4]Because definitional, biography, and relationship questions in the NTCIR 2008 test set are not discussed here.

[5]The approach of creating test data is same as that in the NTCIR 2008.

	F_3 (%)			NR (%)			NP (%)		
	$N=1$	$N=5$	$N=10$	$N=1$	$N=5$	$N=10$	$N=1$	$N=5$	$N=10$
Baseline	9.82	18.18	21.95	9.44	19.85	27.64	34.35	25.32	18.96
TransM	9.76	20.47	24.76	9.44	19.85	33.10	31.96	21.73	13.57
Ours$_{lin}$	10.92	22.61	25.74	10.49	25.95	34.70	34.98	23.40	15.11
Ours$_{errorrate}$	12.37	23.10	27.74	12.05	26.98	37.03	33.22	26.48	18.67
Ours$_{pre@k}$	8.96	22.85	29.85	8.72	25.67	38.78	26.28	28.82	20.45

Table 3: Overall performance for the test data

4.1 Overall Results

Table 3 summarizes the evaluation results for several N values. The baseline refers to the conventional method introduced in Section 3, which does not employ question-type-specific classifiers before the Answer Extraction. The baseline can be expressed by the formula:

$$sim(q,s) = \frac{\langle V_q \cdot V_s \rangle}{\|V_q\| \times \|V_s\|} \quad (4)$$

where, V_q and V_s are the vectors of the question and candidate answer. The TransM denotes a translation model for QA (Xue, et al., 2008) (Bernhard et al., 2009), which uses Q&A pairs as the parallel corpus, with questions to the "source" language and answers corresponding to the "target" language. This model can be expressed by:

$$P(q|S) = \prod_{w \in q}((1-\gamma)P_{mx}(w|S) + \gamma P_{ml}(w|C))$$
$$P_{mx}(w|S) = (1-\zeta)P_{ml}(w|S) + \zeta \sum_{t \in S} P(w|t)P_{ml}(t|S) \quad (5)$$

where, q is the question, S the sentence, $P(w|t)$ the probability of translating a sentence term t to the question term w, which is obtained by using the GIZA++ toolkit (Och and Ney, 2003). We use six million Q&A pairs to train IBM model 1 for obtaining word-to-word probability $P(w|t)$. Ours$_{errorrate}$ and Ours$_{pre@k}$ denote our models that are based on classifiers optimizing performance measure error-rate and prec@k, respectively. Ours$_{lin}$, a linear interpolation model, that combines scores of classifiers and the baseline, which is similar to (Mori et al., 2008) and can be expressed by the equation:

$$sim(q,s)' = sim(q,s) + \alpha \times \phi(s) \quad (6)$$

where, $\phi(s)$ is the score calculated by classifiers (Thorsten Joachims, 2005) and α denotes the weight of the score.

This experiment shows that: (1) Question-type-specific classifiers can greatly outperform the baseline; for example, the F_3 improvements of Ours$_{errorrate}$ and Ours$_{pre@k}$ over the baseline in terms of N=10 are 5.8% and 7.9%, respectively. (2) Ours$_{errorrate}$ is better than Ours$_{pre@k}$ when $N < 10$. The average numbers of sentences retained in Ours$_{errorrate}$ and Ours$_{pre@k}$ are 130, and 217, respectively. That means the precision of the classifier optimizing errorrate is superior to the classifier optimizing prec@k, while the recall is relatively inferior. (3) Ours$_{lin}$ is worse than Ours$_{errorrate}$ and Ours$_{pre@k}$, which indicates that using question-type-specific classifiers by classification is better than using it by interpolation like (Mori et al., 2008). (4) Our models also outperform TransM, e.g.; the F_3 improvement is 5.1% when N is set to 10. TransM exploits the social Q&A collection without consideration of question types, while our models select and exploit the social Q&A pairs of the same question types. Thereby, this experiment also indicates that it is better to exploit social Q&A pairs by type of question. The performance ranking of these models when N=10 is: Ours$_{prec@k}$ > Ours$_{errorrate}$ > Ours$_{lin}$ > TransM > Baseline.

4.2 Impact of Features

In order to evaluate the contributions of individual features to our models, this experiment is conducted by gradually adding them. Table 4 summarizes the performance of $\text{Our}_{prec@k}$ on different set of features, L and P represent lexical and PoS-based features, respectively. This table demonstrates that all the lexical and PoS features can positively impact $\text{Our}_{prec@k}$, especially, the contribution of the PoS-based features is largest.

Features	F_3	NR	NP
Lunigram	23.44	31.23	17.32
+Lbigram +Ltrigram	25.34	33.15	18.87
+Punigram	28.24	36.27	20.18
+Pbigram	29.85	38.78	20.45

Table 4: Impact of features on $\text{Our}_{prec@k}$.

4.3 Improvement

As discussed in Section 2, the writing style of social Q&A collections slightly differs from that of our complex QA system, which is an unfavorable circumstance in utilizing social Q&A collections. For better understanding we randomly select 100 Q&A training pairs of each type of question acquired in Section 3, and manually classify each Q&A pair into NON-NOISE and NOISE[6] categories. Figure 1 reports the percentage of NON-NOISE. This figure indicates that 71% of the training pairs of the scale-type questions are noises, which may lead to a small improvement.

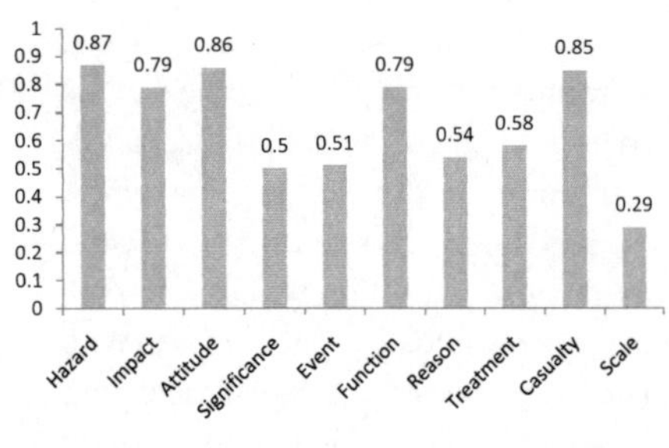

Figure 1: Percentage of NON-NOISE pairs by type of questions.

To further improve the performance, we employ k-fold cross validation to remove noises from the collected training data in Section 3.1. Specifically, the collected training data are first divided into k (= 5) sets. Secondly, k-1 sets are used to train classifiers that are applied to classify the Q&A pairs in the remaining set. Finally, part of the Q&A pairs classified as negative pairs are removed[7]. According to Figure 1, we remove 20% of the training data from the negative pairs for the hazard-type, impact-type, and function-type questions, and 40% of the training data for significance-type, event-type, and reason-type questions. Because the sizes of the training pairs of the other four types of questions are small, we do not use this approach on them. Table 5 shows the results of $\text{Ours}_{pre@k}$ on the above six types of questions. The numbers in brackets indicate absolute improvements over the system based on the data without removing noises. N is the number of answer sentences to a question. The experiment shows that the performance is generally improved by removing noise in the training Q&A pairs using k-fold cross-validation.

	F_3 (%)	NR (%)	NP (%)
$N = 1$	$9.6_{+2.1}$	$9.3_{+2.0}$	$30.8_{+7.4}$
$N = 5$	$21.6_{+0.7}$	$24.9_{+1.2}$	$26.0_{-1.3}$
$N = 10$	$28.6_{+0.9}$	$37.9_{+1.7}$	$19.2_{-0.2}$

Table 5: Performance of $\text{Ours}_{pre@k}$ after removing noises in the training Q&A pairs.

4.4 Subjective evaluation

Pourpre v1.0c evaluation is based on n-gram overlap between the automatically produced answers and the human generated reference answers. Thus, it is not able to measure conceptual equivalent. In subjective evaluation, the answer sentences returned by systems are labeled by a native Chinese assessor. Figure 2 shows the distribution of the ranks of the first correct answers for all questions. This figure demonstrates that the $\text{Ours}_{pre@k}$ answers 57 questions which

[6]NOISE means that the Q&A pair is not useful in our study.

[7]We do not remove all negative Q&A pairs to ensure the coverage of training data because the classifiers have relatively lower recall, as mentioned in Section 3.3.

first answers are ranked in top 3, which is larger than that of the baseline, i.e., 49. Moreover, the $\text{Ours}_{pre@k}$ contains only 11.5% of questions which answers are ranked after top 10, while this number of the baseline is 20.7%.

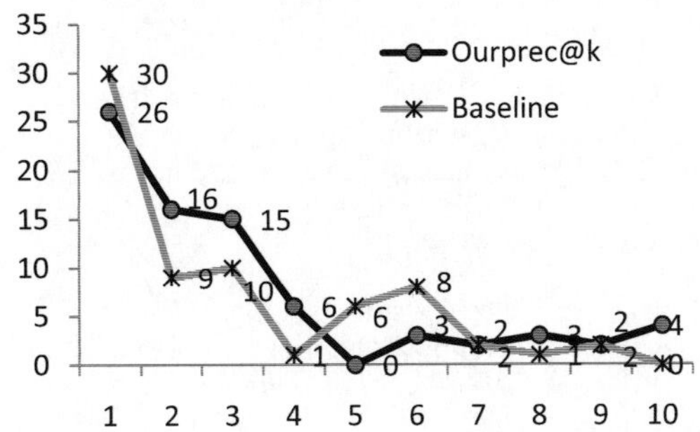

Figure 2: Distribution of the ranks of first answers.

5 Related Work

Recently, some pioneering studies on the social Q&A collection have been conducted. Among them, much of the research aims to retrieve answers to queried questions from the social Q&A collection. For example, (Surdeanu et al., 2008) proposed an answer ranking engine for non-factoid questions by incorporating textual features into a machine learning approach. (Duan et al., 2008) proposed searching questions semantically equivalent or close to the queried question for a question recommendation system. (Agichtein et al., 2008) investigated techniques of finding high-quality content in the social Q&A collection, and indicated that 94% of answers to questions with high quality have high quality. (Xue, et al., 2008) proposed a retrieval model that combines a translation-based language model for the question part with a query likelihood approach for the answer part.

Another category of study regards the social Q&A collection as a kind of knowledge repository and aims to mine knowledge from it for generating answers to questions. To the best of our knowledge, there is very limited work reported on this aspect. This paper is similar to (Mori et al., 2008), but different from it as follows. (1) (Mori et al., 2008) collects training data for each test question using 7-grams for which centers are interrogatives, while this paper collects training data for each type of question using answer type informers. (2) About the knowledge learned, we extract lexical/class-based, PoS-based unigrams, bigrams, and trigrams. (Mori et al., 2008) only extracts lexical bigrams. (3) They incorporated knowledge learned by interpolating with the baseline. However, we utilize the learned knowledge to train a binary classifier, which can remove noise sentences before answer selection.

6 Conclusion

This paper investigated a technique for mining knowledge from social Q&A websites for improving a sentence-based complex QA system. More specifically, it explored a social Q&A collection to automatically construct training data, and created question-type-specific classifier for each type of question to filter out noise sentences before answer selection.

The experiments on 10 types of complex Chinese questions show that the proposed approach is effective; e.g., the improvement in F_3 reaches 7.9%. In the future, we will endeavor to reduce NOISE pairs in the training data, and to extract type-of-question dependent features. Future research tasks also include adapting the QA system to a topic-based summarization system, which, for example, summarizes accidents according to "casualty", "reason", and summarizes events according to "reason", "measure," "impact", etc.

Appendix A. Examples of 10 Types of Questions.

References

Abdessamad Echihabi and Daniel Marcu. 2003. A Noisy-Channel Approach to Question Answering. In *Proc. of ACL 2003*, Japan.

Delphine Bernhard and Iryna Gurevych. 2009. Combining Lexical Semantic Resources with Question & Answer Archives for Translation-based Answer Finding. In *Proc. of ACL-IJCNLP 2009*, Singapore, pp728-736.

Ellen M. Voorhees. 2003 Overview of the TREC 2003 Question Answering Track. In *Proc. of TREC 2003*, pp54-68, USA.

Qtype	Examples
危 害/Hazard-type	全球气候变暖的**危害**是什么？What are the **hazards** of global warming?
作用/Function-type	联合国的**作用**是什么？What are the **functions** of the United Nations?
影 响/Impact-type	列举911事件对美国的**影响**。List the **impact** of the 911 attacks on the United States.
意义/Significance-type	列举中国加入WTO的**意义**。List the **significance** of China's accession to the WTO.
态 度/Attitude-type	列举各国对巴以冲突的**态度**。List the **attitudes** of other countries toward the Israeli-Palestinian conflict.
措施/Measure-type	日本在节能减排方面采取了哪些**措施**？What **measures** have been taken for energy-saving and emissions-reduction in Japan?
原 因/Reason-type	全球气候变暖的**原因**是什么？What are the **reasons** for global warming?
伤亡/Casualty-type	列举洛克比空难的**伤亡**。List the **casualties** of the Lockerbie Air Disaster.
事 件/Event-type	列举北爱尔兰和平和平谈判**事件**。List the **events** in the Northern Ireland peace process.
规 模/Scale-type	介绍一下昆明世界园艺博览会的**规模**。Give information about the **scale** of the Kunming World Horticulture Exposition.

Eugene Agichtein, Carlos Castillo, Debora Donato. 2008 Finding High-Quality Content in Social Media. In *Proc. of WSDM 2008*, California, USA.

Franz J. Och and Hermann Ney. 2003. A systematic Comparison of Various Statistical Alignment Models. In *Computational Linguistics*, 29(1):19-51.

Gunes Erkan and Dragomir Radev. 2004. LexRank: Graph-based Lexical Centrality as Salience in Text. In *Journal of Artificial Intelligence Research*,22:457-479.

Hang Cui, Min Yen Kan, and Tat Seng Chua. 2004. Unsupervised Learning of Soft Patterns for Definition Question Answering. In *Proc. of WWW 2004*.

Hoa Trang Dang. 2006. Overview of DUC 2006. In *Proc. of TREC 2006*.

Huizhong Duan, Yunbo Cao, Chin Yew Lin, and Yong Yu. 2008. Searching Questions by Identifying Question Topic and Question Focus. In *Proc. of ACL 2008*, Canada, pp 156-164.

Jimmy Lin and Dina Demner-Fushman. 2006. Will Pyramids Built of Nuggets Topple Over. In *Proc. of HLT/NAACL2006*, pp 383-390.

Mihai Surdeanu, Massimiliano Ciaramita, and Hugo Zaragoza. 2008. Learning to Rank Answers on Large Online QA Collections. In *Proc. of ACL 2008*, Ohio, USA, pp 719-727.

Ryuichiro Higashinaka and Hideki Isozaki. 2008. Corpus-based Question Answering for why-Questions. In *Proc. of IJCNLP 2008*, pp 418-425.

Tatsunori Mori, Takuya Okubo, and Madoka Ishioroshi. 2008. A QA system that can answer any class of Japanese non-factoid questions and its application to CCLQA EN-JA task. In *Proc. of NTCIR2008*, Tokyo, pp 41-48.

Sanda Harabagiu, Finley Lacatusu, Andrew Hickl. 2006. Answering Complex Questions with Random Walk Models. In *Proc. of the 29th SIGIR*, pp 220-227, ACM.

Ves Stoyanov, Claire Cardie, and Janyce Wiebe. 2005. Multi-Perspective Question Answering Using the OpQA Corpus. In *Proc. of HLT/EMNLP 2005*, Canada, pp 923-930.

Teruko Mitamura, Eric Nyberg, Hideki Shima, Tsuneaki Kato, Tatsunori Mori, Chin-Yew Lin, Ruihua Song, Chuan-Jie Lin, Tetsuya Sakai, Donghong Ji and Noriko Kando. 2008. Overview of the NTCIR-7 ACLIA Tasks: Advanced Cross-Lingual Information Access. In *Proc. of NTCIR 2008*.

Thorsten Joachims. 2005. A Support Vector Method for Multivariate Performance Measures. In *Proc. of ICML2005*, pp 383-390.

Vladimir Vapnik 1998. Statistical learning theory. John Wiley.

Xiaobing Xue, Jiwoon Jeon, W.Bruce Croft. 2008. Retrieval Models for Question and Answer Archives. In *Proc. of SIGIR 2008*, pp 475-482.

Yutaka Sasaki. 2005. Question Answering as Question-biased Term Extraction: A New Approach toward Multilingual QA. In *Proc. of ACL 2005*, pp 215-222.

Youzheng Wu, Jun Zhao, Bo Xu, and Hao Yu. 2005. Chinese Named Entity Recognition Model based on Multiple Features. In *Proc. of HLT/EMNLP 2005*, Canada, pp 427-434.

Yuanjie Liu, Shasha Li, Yunbo Cao, Chin-Yew Lin, Dingyi Han, Yong Yu. 2008. Understanding and Summarizing Answers in Community-Based Question Answering Services. In *Proc. of COLING 2008*, Manchester, pp 497-504.

Treebank of Chinese Bible Translations

Andi Wu
GrapeCity Inc.
andi.wu@grapecity.com

Abstract

This paper reports on a treebanking project where eight different modern Chinese translations of the Bible are syntactically analyzed. The trees are created through dynamic treebanking which uses a parser to produce the trees. The trees have been going through manual checking, but corrections are made not by editing the tree files but by re-generating the trees with an updated grammar and dictionary. The accuracy of the treebank is high due to the fact that the grammar and dictionary are optimized for this specific domain. The tree structures essentially follow the guidelines of the Penn Chinese Treebank. The total number of characters covered by the treebank is 7,872,420 characters. The data has been used in Bible translation and Bible search. It should also prove useful in the computational study of the Chinese language in general.

1 Introduction

Since the publication of the Chinese Union Version (CUV 和合本) in 1919, the Bible has been re-translated into Chinese again and again in the last 91 years. The translations were done in different time periods and thus reflect the changes in the Chinese language in the last century. They also represent different styles of Chinese writing, ranging over narration, exposition and poetry. Due to the diversity of the translators' backgrounds, some versions follow the language standards of mainland China, while other have more Taiwan or Hong Kong flavor. But they have one thing in common: they were all done very professionally, with great care put into every sentence. Therefore the sentences are usually well-formed. All this makes the Chinese translations of the Bible a high-quality and well-balanced corpus of the Chinese language.

To study the linguistic features of this text corpus, we have been analyzing its syntactic structures with a Chinese parser in the last few years. The result is a grammar that covers all the syntactic structures in this domain and a dictionary that contains all the words in this text corpus. A lot of effort has also been put into tree-pruning and tree selection so that the bad trees can be filtered out. Therefore we are able to parse most of the sentences in this corpus correctly and produce a complete treebank of all the Chinese translations.

The value of such a treebank in the study and search of the Bible is obvious. But it should also be a valuable resource for computational linguistic research outside the Bible domain. After all, it is a good representation of the syntactic structures of Chinese.

2 The Data Set

The text corpus for the treebank includes eight different versions of Chinese translations of the Bible, both the Old Testament and the New Testament. They are listed below in chronological order with their Chinese names, abbreviations, and years of publication:

- Chinese Union Version (和合本 CUV 1919)
- Lv Zhenzhong Version (吕振中译本 LZZ 1946)
- Sigao Bible (思高圣经 SGB 1968)
- Today's Chinese Version (现代中文译本 TCV 1979)
- Recovery Version (恢复本 RCV 1987)
- New Chinese Version (新译本 NCV 1992)
- Easy-to-Read Version (普通话译本 ERV 2005)
- Chinese Standard Bible (中文标准译本 CSB 2008)

All these versions are in vernacular Chinese (白话文) rather than classical Chinese (文言文), with CUV representing "early vernacular" (早期白话文) and the later versions representing contemporary Chinese. The texts are all in simplified Chinese. Those translations which were published in traditional Chinese were converted to simplified Chinese. For a linguistic comparison of those different versions, see Wu *et al* (2009).

In terms of literary genre, more than 50% of the Bible is narration, about 15% poetry, 10% exposition, and the rest a mixture of narrative, prosaic and poetic writing. The average number of characters in a single version is close to one million and the total number of characters of these eight versions is 7,672,420.

Each book in the Bible consists of a number of chapters which in turn consist of a number of verses. A verse often corresponds to a sentence, but it may be composed of more than one sentence. On the other hand, some sentences may span multiple verses. To avoid the controversy in sentence segmentation, we preserved the verse structure, with one tree for each verse. The issues involved in this decision will be discussed later.

3 Linguistic Issues

In designing the tree structures, we essentially followed the Penn Chinese Treebank (PCTB) Guidelines (Xia 2000, Xue & Xia 2000) in segmentation, part-of-speech tagging and bracketing. The tag set conforms to this standard completely while the segmentation and bracketing have some exceptions.

In segmentation, we provide word-internal structures in cases where there can be variations in the granularity of segmentation. For example, a verb-complement structure such as 吃饱 is represented as

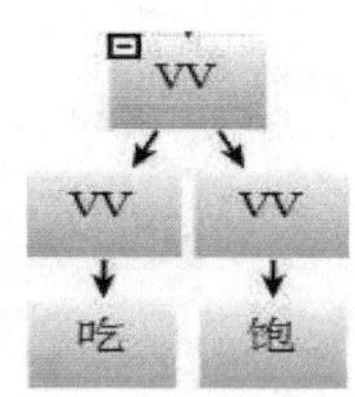

so that it can be treated either as a single word or as two individual words according to the user's needs. A noun-suffix structure such as 以色列人 is represented as

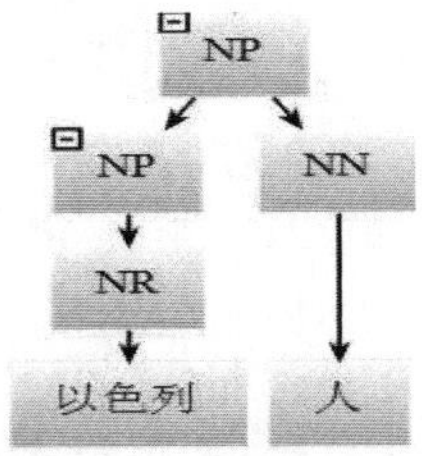

to accommodate the need of segmenting it into either a single word or two separate words. Likewise, a compound word like 天地 is represented as

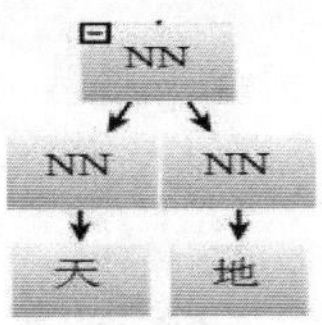

to account for the fact that it can also be analyzed as two words. This practice is applied to all the morphologically derived words discussed in Wu (2003), which include all linguistic units that function as single words syntactically but lexically contains two or more words. The nodes for such units all have (1) an attribute that specifies the word type (e.g. Noun-Suffix, Verb-Result, etc.) and (2) the sub-units that make up the whole word. The user can use the word type and the layered structures to take different cuts of the trees to get the segmentation they desire.

In bracketing, we follow the guidelines of Penn Chinese treebank, but we simplified the sentence structure by omitting the CP and IP nodes. Instead, we use VP for any verbal unit, whether it is a complete sentence or not. Here is an example where the tree is basically a projection of the verb, with all other elements being the arguments or adjuncts of the VP:

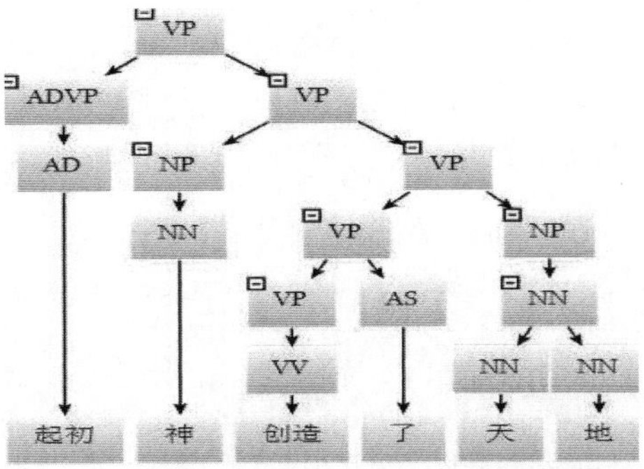

There are two reasons for doing this. First of all, we choose not to represent movement relationships with traces and empty categories which are not theory-neutral. They add complexities to automatic parsing, making it slower and more prone to errors. Secondly, as we mentioned earlier, the linguistic units we parse are verses which are not always a sentence with an IP and a CP. Therefore we have to remain flexible and be able to handle multiple sentences, partial sentences, or any fragments of a sentence. The use of VP as the maximal project enables us to be consistent across different chunks. Here is a verse with two sentences:

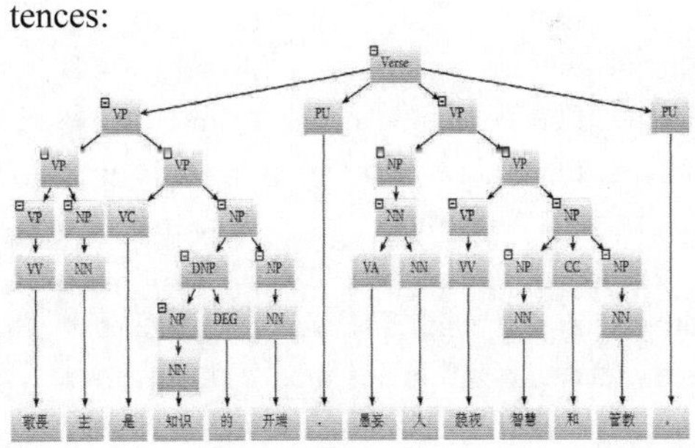

Notice that both sentences are analyzed as VPs and the punctuation marks are left out on their own. Here is a verse with a partial sentence:

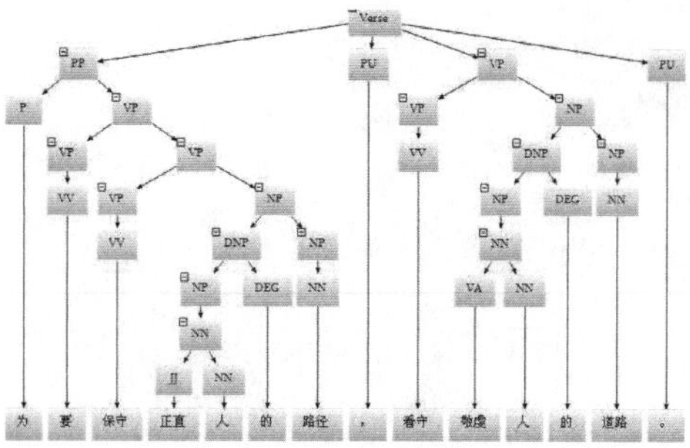

This verse contains a PP and a VP. Since it is not always possible to get a complete sentence within a verse, we aim at "maximal parses" instead of complete parses, doing as much as we can be sure of and leaving the rest for future processing. To avoid the clause-level ambiguities as to how a clause is related to another, we also choose to leave the clausal relations unspecified. Therefore, we can say that the biggest linguistic units in our trees are clauses rather than sentences. In cases where verses consist of noun phrases or prepositional phrases, the top units we get can be NPs or PPs. In short, the structures are very flexible and partial analysis is accepted where complete analysis is not available.

While the syntactic structure in this treebank is underspecified compared to the Penn Chinese Treebank, the lexical information contained in the trees are considerably richer. The trees are coded in XML where each node is a complex attribute-value matrix. The trees we have seen above are visualizations of the XML in a tree viewer where we can also view the attributes of each node in a tooltip, as shown below:

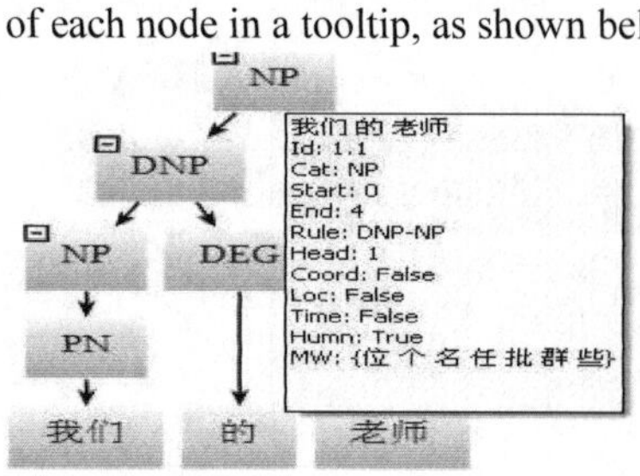

Here, the attributes tell us among other things that (1) this node is formed by the rule "DNP-NP", (2) the head of this phrase is its second child (position is 0-based), (3) there is no coordination in this phrase, (4) this is not a location phrase, (5) this is not a time phrase, (6) the NP is a human being, and (7) the head noun can take any of those measure words (量词): 位，个，名，任，批，群 and 些. There are many other attributes and a filter is applied to determine which attributes will show up when the XML is generated.

4 Computational Issues

As we have mentioned above, the trees are generated automatically by a Chinese parser. It is well-known that the state-of–the-art natural language parsers are not yet able to produce syntactic analysis that is 100% correct. As a result, the automatically generated trees contain errors and manual checking is necessary. The question is what we should do when errors are found.

The approach adopted by most treebanking projects is manual correction which involves editing the tree files. Once the trees have been modified by hand, the treebank becomes static. Any improvement or update on the treebank will require manual work from then on and automatic parsing is out of the picture. This has several disadvantages. First of all, it is very labor-intensive and not everyone can afford to do it. Secondly, the corrections are usually token-based rather than type-based, which requires repetitions of the same correction and opens doors to inconsistency. Finally, this approach is not feasible with trees with complex feature structures where manual editing is difficult if not impossible.

To avoid these problems, we adopted the approach of dynamic treebanking (Oepen *et al* 2002) where corrections/updates are not made in the tree files but in the grammar and dictionary that is used to generate the trees. Instead of fixing the trees themselves, we improve the tree-generator and make it produce the correct trees. Every error found the trees can be traced back to some problem in the grammar rules, dictionary entries, or the tree selection process. Once a "bug" is resolved, all problems of the same kind will be resolved throughout the whole treebank. In this approach, we never have to maintain a static set of trees. We can generate the trees at any time with any kind of customization based on users' requirement.

Dynamic treebanking requires a high-accuracy syntactic parser which is not easy to build. A Chinese parser has the additional challenge of word segmentation and name entity recognition. These problems become more manageable once the texts to be parsed are narrowed down to a specific domain, in our case the domain of Biblical texts.

The dictionary used by our parser is based on the Grammatical Knowledge Base of Contemporary Chinese (GKBCC) licensed from Beijing University. It is a wide-coverage, feature-rich dictionary containing more than 80,000 words. On top of that, we added all the words in the eight translations, including all the proper names, which are not in the GKBCC. The total vocabulary is about 110,000 words. Since we follow the PCTB guidelines in our syntactic analysis, the grammatical categories of GKBCC were converted to the PCTB POS tags.

With all the words in the dictionary, which eliminates the OOV problem, the only problem left in word segmentation is the resolution of combinational ambiguities and overlapping ambiguities. We resolve these ambiguities in the parsing process rather than use a separate word segmenter, because most wrong segmentations can be ruled out in the course of syntactic analysis (Wu and Jiang 1998).

Our grammar is in the HPSG framework. In addition to feature-rich lexical projections, it also bases its grammatical decisions on the words in the preceding and following contexts. Multiple trees are generated and sorted according to structural properties. The treebank contains the best parse of each verse by default, but it can also provide the top *N* trees. The grammar is not intended to be domain-specific. Almost all the rules there apply to other domains as well. But the grammar is "domain-complete" in the sense that all the grammatical phenomena that occur in this domain are covered.

The developers of the treebank only look at the top tree of each verse. If it is found to be incorrect, they can fix it by (1) refining the conditions of the grammar rules, (2) correcting or adding attribute values in the lexicon, or (3) fine-tuning tree ranking and tree selection. For phrases which occur frequently in the text or phrases which are hard to analyze, we store their correct analysis in a database so that they can be looked up just like a dictionary entry. These "pre-generated" chunks are guaranteed to have the correct analysis and they greatly reduce the complexity of sentence analysis.

The same grammar and dictionary are used to parse the eight different versions. The development work is mainly based on CSB. Therefore the trees of the CSB text have higher accuracy than those of other versions. However, due to the fact that all the eight versions are translations of the same source text, they share a large number of common phrases. As our daily regression tests show, most fixes made in CSB also benefit the analysis of other versions.

5 Evaluation

Due to the optimization of the grammar and dictionary for the Bible domain, the accuracy of this Chinese parser is much higher than any other general-purpose Chinese parsers when the texts to be parsed are Chinese Bible texts. Therefore the accuracy of the trees is higher than any other automatically generated trees. Unfortunately, there is not an existing treebank of Chinese Bible translations that can be used as a gold standard for automatic evaluation. We can only examine the quality through manual inspection. However, there does exist a segmented text of the CUV translation.[1] Using this text as the gold standard is ideal because the development data for our system is CSB rather than CUV or other versions.

As we have mentioned above, the segmentation from the trees can be customized by taking different cuts in cases where word-internal structures are available. In order to make our segmentation match the existing CUV segmentation as closely as possible, we studied the CUV segments and made a decision for each type of words. For example, in a verb-complement construction where both the verb and the directional/resultative complement are single characters, the construction will be treated as a single word.

We evaluated the segmentation of our CUV trees with the scoring script used in the first international Chinese segmentation bakeoff (Sproat & Emerson 2003). Here are the results:

Recall:	99.844%
Precision:	99.826%
F-Score:	99.845%

We don't show the OOV numbers as they are not relevant here, because all the words have been exhaustively listed in our dictionary.

Of a total of 31151 verses in the Bible, 30568 verses (98.13%) do not contain a single error (whole verses segmented correctly).
Of course, segmentation accuracy does not imply parsing accuracy, though wrong segmentation necessarily implies a wrong parse. Since we do not have a separate word segmenter and segmentation is an output of the parsing process, the high segmentation accuracy does serve as a reflection of the quality of the trees. There would be many more segmentation errors if the trees had many errors.

6 Use of the Treebank

The treebank has been used in the area of Bible translation and Bible search. In Bible translation, the trees are aligned to the trees of the original Hebrew and Greek texts[2]. By examining the correspondences between the Chinese trees and the Hebrew/Greek trees, one is able to measure how faithful each translation is to the original. In Bible search, the trees makes it possible to use more intelligent queries based not only on words but on syntactic relations between words as well.

An obvious use of the treebank is to train a statistical parser. Though the domain speci-

[1] The segmented CUV text was provided by Asia Bible Society.

[2] The Hebrew and Greek trees were also provided by Asia Bible Society.

ficity of the treebank makes it less likely to build from it a good lexicalized statistical parser that can be used in the general domain, we can still extract a lot of non-lexical syntactic information from it. It can fill many of the gaps in the parsers that are built from other treebanks which consist mainly of news articles.

A special feature of this treebank is that it is built from a number of parallel texts -- different Chinese translations of the same verses. By aligning the parallel trees (ideally through the original Hebrew and Greek trees as pivots), we can acquire a knowledge base of Chinese synonyms and paraphrases. Presumably, the different Chinese subtrees corresponding to the same Hebrew/Greek subtree are supposed to convey the same meaning. The words and phrases covered by those subtrees therefore represent Chinese expressions that are synonymous. A knowledge base of this kind can be a valuable addition to the lexical study of Chinese.

7 Summary

We presented a Chinese treebank of parallel Bible translations. The treebank is built through dynamic treebanking where the trees are automatically generated by a Chinese parser optimized for parsing Biblical texts. The trees can serve as a useful resource for different language projects.

References

Sproat, Richard and Thomas Emerson. 2003. The First International Chinese Segmentation Bakeoff. In *Proceedings of the Second SIGHAN Workshop on Chinese Language Processing*, July 11-12, Sapporo, Japan.

Wu, Andi, J. and Z. Jiang, 1998. Word segmentation in sentence analysis, in Proceedings of 1998 International Conference on Chinese Information Processing, pp. 46--51. 169--180, Beijing, China.

Wu, Andi. 2003. Customizable Segmentation of Morphological Derived Words in Chinese. In *International Journal of Computational Linguistics and Chinese Language Processing*, 8(1):1-27.

Wu, And, Arron Ma, Dong Wang. 2009. Fidelity and Readablity – a quanatative comparison of Chinese translations of the New Testament. Proceedings of the Conference on "Interpretation of Biblical Texts in Chinese Contexts", Sichuan Univeristy, December 2009.

Xia, Fei. 2000. *Segmentation Guidelines for the Penn Chinese Treebank (3.0).* Technical Report, University of Pennsylvania.

Xia, Fei. 2000. *The Part-Of-Speech Tagging Guidelines for the Penn Chinese Treebank (3.0).* Technical Report, University of Pennsylvania.

Xue, Nianwen and Fei Xia. 2000. *The Bracketing Guidelines for the Penn Chinese Treebank (3.0).* Technical Report, University of Pennsylvania.

Oepen, Stephan, Dan Flickinger, Kristina Toutanova, Christoper D. Manning. 2002. LinGO Redwoods: A Rich and Dynamic Treebank for HPSG In *Proceedings of The First Workshop on Treebanks and Linguistic Theories (TLT2002)*, Sozopol, Bulgaria.

Using Topic Sentiment Sentences to Recognize Sentiment Polarity in Chinese Reviews

Jiang Yang
School of Literature
Communication University of China
yangjiang@cuc.edu.cn

Min Hou
Broadcast Media Language Branch
Communication University of China
houminxx@263.net

Abstract

An approach to recognizing sentiment polarity in Chinese reviews based on topic sentiment sentences is presented. Considering the features of Chinese reviews, we firstly identify the topic of a review using an n-gram matching approach. To extract candidate topic sentiment sentences, we compute the semantic similarity between a given sentence and the ascertained topic and meanwhile determine whether the sentence is subjective. A certain number of these sentences are then selected as representatives according to their semantic similarity value with relation to the topic. The average value of the representative topic sentiment sentences is calculated and taken as the sentiment polarity of a review. Experiment results show that the proposed method is feasible and can achieve relatively high precision.

1 Introduction

Sentiment analysis, also known as "opinion mining", is the problem of analyzing the sentiment, opinion or any other subjectivity of written texts. With its potential applications to opinion search engine, public opinion analysis, product promotion, etc., sentiment analysis has been receiving increasing interest in recent years.

What sentiment analysis processes are texts with subjectivity which mainly describe the writers' (or on behalf of a group or an organization) private thoughts, attitudes or opinions on phenomena, persons, affairs and so on. Although various kinds of writings such as narration and exposition are possible to contain subjectivity, argumentation is the focus of sentiment analysis on which researchers put much strength at present. As a kind of argumentation and a typical and common subjective text, a review comments on some specific phenomenon, person or affair. Reviews, especially news reviews, have a certain degree of influence on public opinion in virtue of mass media. Domain-specific reviews like automobile, hotel, movie reviews have potential commercial value respectively. Therefore, recognizing sentiment polarity (SP thereafter) in reviews becomes necessary and practical.

Language is a hierarchical symbol system, which allows sentiment analysis to be conducted on different language levels. In general, most current studies concerning sentiment analysis are about determining the SP of words, phrases or sentences. Only a fraction of them addressed discourse level sentiment analysis. This paper, aiming at recognizing the overall SP of Chinese reviews, proposes a topic-sentiment-sentence based approach to carry out a discourse level sentiment analysis.

The remainder of this paper is organized as follows. Related works are presented in section 2. Section 3 is problem analysis and method description. Section 4 describes topic identification and topic sentiment sentence extraction. Section 5 is about recognizing SP in Chinese reviews using the extracted topic sentiment sentences. Section 6 is the experiment results and section 7 is the conclusion.

2 Related Works

The SP determination can be generally conducted on three language levels: the word level, the sentence level and the discourse level. The two main popular approaches, especially in real-world applications, have been based on machine learning techniques and based on semantic analysis techniques. Research aiming at recognizing the overall SP of discourse is represented by Turney (2002), Pang et al. (2002) and Yi et al. (2003). Turney proposed an unsupervised learning algorithm to classify the sentiment orientation of reviews. The mutual information difference between the given word or phrase and the words "poor" and "excellent" was calculated respectively to measure its semantic orientation; then the average semantic orientation of all the words in a given text was regarded as the overall semantic orientation. Pang et al. employed such classification models as Naïve Bayesian model, Maximum Entropy model and Support Vector Machine model to classify the semantic orientation of movie reviews, in which the features of models selected included unigrams, bigrams, parts of speech, word position, feature frequency and feature presence. Yi et al. firstly analyzed the grammatical structure of sentences using NLP techniques. The semantic orientation of a sentence then is determined by referring to a sentiment lexicon and a sentiment pattern database. They applied the approach to classifying the overall SP of document.

Other related works are concerning the sentiment analysis of sentences and words which underlie recognizing the overall SP of a whole text. Wiebe et al. (2000, 2004) proved that the subjectivity of a sentence could be judged according to the adjectives in it. Kim & Hovy (2004) and Weibe & Riloff (2005) explored the classification of subjective and objective sentences. Yu et al. (2003) put forward an approach to extract opinionated sentences in order to serve an automatic question answering system. The extracted sentences were classified and the SP of each was determined. Hu & Liu (2004) took advantage of WordNet to obtain sentiment words and their orientations. The polarity of a sentence thus is judged according to the dominant semantic orientation of sentiment words.

For Chinese, Wang et al. (2005) proposed a hybrid approach to recognize the semantic orientations of sentences in reviews based on heuristic rules and Bayesian classification technique. Wang et al. (2007) applied a Multi-redundant-labeled CRFs method on sentence sentiment analysis. Experiments showed it solved ordinal regression problems effectively and obtained global optimal result over multiple cascaded subtasks. Meng et al. (2008) designed a recognition system of text valence based on key word template in which they proposed template matching arithmetic and text valence value arithmetic for the calculation of the valence of Chinese texts. Zheng et al. (2009) conducted a research on sentiment analysis to Chinese traveler reviews by SVM algorithm.

3 Problem Analysis and Method Description

3.1 Discourse Structure of Chinese Texts

The overall SP of a Chinese text is the sum of the SP of all its component parts. However, the importance of each component part in a given text varies. This is because no matter which writing style a text belongs to, it has a particular discourse structure which determines the importance of the component parts.

Discourse structure is the organization and constitution law of language units (greater than sentence) within a discourse. It formally indicates the hierarchy of discourse contents, semantically guarantees the integrity of discourse contents and logically reflects the coherence of discourse contents. In a word, discourse structure is the unity of discourse form, discourse meaning and discourse logic. A discourse consists of several semantic parts. The central meaning of a discourse is the aggregation of the central meaning of its semantic parts in a certain logic way. A semantic part is the set of paragraphs. It may be composed of as small as only a paragraph or as large as even a whole chapter. The basis for partitioning semantic parts depends on the writing styles, i.e., narration, description, argumentation and exposition. For argumentation, a typical argumentation may be divided into 4 parts as introduction, viewpoint presentation, demonstration and conclusion. Recognizing semantic parts has great significance in understanding the central idea of a text.

3.2 Features of Chinese Reviews

Chinese reviews are a kind of argumentation. According to what is reviewed, they can be categorized into finance reviews (e.g., stock review), literature reviews (e.g., book review), product reviews (e.g., automobile review), current affairs reviews (e.g., news review), etc. Generally speaking, Chinese reviews bear the following features.

Firstly, the topic of a Chinese review is explicit. A Chinese review always comments on some specific phenomenon, person or affair. The object it deals with is very explicit.

Secondly, a Chinese review has generally only one topic. Thus, in a Chinese review, the reviewer always explicitly expresses his/her opinion towards the topic. The sentiment of the discussed topic is rather explicit. Some Chinese reviews may discuss subtopics and corresponding opinions on each subtopic may be shown. But it will not change or influence the reviewer's basic sentiment on the topic.

Thirdly, the topic of a Chinese review is closely related to its title. Chinese Reviews often use concise expressions in titles to show clearly the topics or the themes. Therefore, the topic of a review can generally be found in its title.

Fourthly, Chinese reviews have fixed expression patterns. A typical Chinese review consists of 4 semantic parts as is mentioned above. The reviewer's sentiment expressions towards the topic generally appears in the "viewpoint presentation" and "conclusion" part.

To prove the correctness of our knowledge of Chinese reviews, we conducted a survey on 560 Chinese reviews which were collected from newspapers and the Internet. The manually examined results, which are showed as follows, verify the above mentioned 4 features of Chinese reviews.

Table 1 A Survey on Features of Chinese Reviews

Features		Percent
Explicit Topic		100
One Topic		100
Title Reflects Topic		99.64
Discourse Structure	I-D-C[1]	40.17
	I-V-D-C	33.9
	I-V-D	18.75
	others	7.18

[1] "I" stands for introduction, "D" for demonstration, "C" for conclusion and "V" for viewpoint presentation.

3.3 Topic Sentiment Sentence

According to the above analysis, the SP of a Chinese review is manifested by a certain expression pattern through several semantic parts, and its overall SP is generally expressed in the "viewpoint presentation" and "conclusion" part. Thus a straightforward idea to obtain the SP of a Chinese review is to: (1) partition the review into several semantic parts; (2) distinguish the viewpoint presentation part and the conclusion part; (3) analyze only the sentiment of the viewpoint presentation part and the conclusion part and take the result as the overall SP of the review. Intuitively, this seemingly simple method can achieve very good result.

However, to perform an automatic discourse structure analysis itself is actually a hard task and will lose precision during the processing; to distinguish different semantic parts by means of language cues without a discourse structure analysis can only solve some instead of all problems. Therefore, we introduce the concept of topic sentiment sentence.

A topic sentiment sentence is defined as a sentence bearing both the topic concept and sentiment towards that topic. The topic sentiment sentences in a Chinese review are the intersection of the topic sentences and sentiment sentences in it. Topic sentiment sentences are representative for sentiment analysis because, firstly, they are homogeneous in topic. And more importantly, the sentiment bearing in these sentences refer to the same topic. This makes sentiment in each sentence computable. Earlier works like Turney (2002) or Pang et al (2002) don't take into account the topic and the sentiment relating to that topic together as a whole, thus makes the result less reliable in that the sentiment words and phrases processed are not homogeneous in topic. Secondly, the degree of semantic similarity between topic sentiment sentences and the topic of the review reflects a potential relatedness between the topic sentiment sentences and their corresponding semantic parts. The more a topic sentiment sentence is similar in meaning to the topic, the more likely it appears in the viewpoint presentation part or conclusion part. This is just the reason we avoid an analysis of discourse structure of a review. We also try to avoid an automatic partition of semantic parts of a review since the topic sentiment sentences themselves potentially point out the corresponding semantic parts they belong to. Thirdly, the distribution of the topic sentiment sentences, including density and extensity, reflects more or less the writer's intensity of attitude toward what is being discussed and can help with detailed sentiment analysis.

To summarize, with topic sentiment sentences, we can compute the SP of a Chinese review in a more simple and effective way without an automatic discourse structure analysis. Moreover, we can obtain a "shallow" structure since topic sentiment sentences potentially reflect the discourse structure of Chinese reviews.

3.4 Method

We thus propose a new method to recognize the sentiment polarity of Chinese reviews using topic sentiment sentences. It is described as follows. (1) Identify the topic of a review using an n-gram matching approach. (2) Extract candidate topic sentiment sentences, compute the semantic similarity between a given sentence and the ascertained topic and meanwhile determine whether the sentence is subjective. (3) A certain number of these sentences are selected as representatives according to their semantic similarity value with relation to the topic. The average value of the representative topic sentiment sentences is calculated and taken as the sentiment polarity of a review.

Experiment results show that the proposed method is feasible and can achieve relatively high precision.

4 Topic Identification and Topic Sentiment Sentence Extraction

4.1 Topic Identification of Chinese Reviews

The topic of a Chinese review is presented as a set of strings $T=\{Wn_1, Wn_2, \ldots, Wn_i\}$, in which Wn_i refers to a word or several continuous words and n indicates the number of words in a Wn_i. The evaluation of whether any candidate Wn_i belongs to T depends on its position and frequency. Wn_i's position reflects its distribution degree $D(Wn_i)$: the more extensive Wn_i distributes in a review, the more likely it relates to the topic. Wn_i's frequency reflects its importance degree $I(Wn_i)$: the more times Wn_i appears in a review, the more likely it relates to the topic. Thus the degree of Wn_i belongs to T is defined as membership degree $C(Wn_i)$ and is measured by the formula:

$$C(Wn_i)= \alpha \cdot D(Wn_i) + \beta \cdot I(Wn_i) \quad (1)$$

In (1), $D(Wn_i)$ is determined by the number of paragraphs in which $D(Wn_i)$ appears and the total number of paragraphs of a text, $I(Wn_i)$ is the binary logarithm of the frequency of Wn_i in a text, α and β are the weighted coefficients to adjust the weights of $D(Wn_i)$ and $I(Wn_i)$.

In order to quickly obtain T, an n-gram matching based approach is applied according to the following algorithm.

(1) Strings separated by punctuations in the title and the main text are segmented and then stored respectively in queue T_q and B_q.

(2) For n=1 to m ($1 \leqslant m \leqslant$ the maximum length of T_q), take out a Wn_i from T_q successively and search it in B_q. If there is a Wn_i in B_q, then insert it into the index table $G=\{Wn_i$, position, frequency$\}$. When n=1, which means there is only one word in Wn_i, Wn_i should be a content word.

(3) Calculate the value of $C(Wn_i)$ for every Wn_i and add Wn_i to T if its $C(Wn_i)$ is greater than the threshold L_c. In this paper, we choose α=0.25, β=1, and L_c=0.8 according to our experience and experiment results.

4.2 The Extraction of Topic Sentiment Sentences

Topic sentiment sentences are essential in the analysis of the SP of reviews. Sentiment analysis based on topic sentiment sentences excludes unrelated sentiment and makes "homogeneous" sentiment computable. Topic sentiment sentences are extracted by 2 steps.

(1) Extract topic sentences from a review. Given a definite T, to extract topic sentences is actually the computing of semantic similarity of candidate sentences and the topic T. Factors that influence the similarity degree are the amount of identical words and strings, the length of identical words and strings, the position of a candidate sentence, semantic similarity of non-identical words.

The amount of identical words and strings. The more identical words or strings a candidate sentence has with T, the more likely they are similar in topic.

The length of identical words and strings. The longer an identical string (counted by word) shared by a candidate sentence and T, the more likely they are similar in topic.

The position of a candidate sentence. We hold that sentences in a paragraph are not in the same importance. As is the general common knowledge, the beginning and ending sentence in a paragraph are often more important than other sentences and thus receive more weights.

We use HowNet, a Chinese ontology, to compute the semantic similarity and assign each candidate sentence a value of similarity. If the similarity value of a sentence is greater than the threshold Ls, it is taken as a topic sentence.

(2) Extract sentiment sentences from topic sentences. We use a precompiled sentiment lexicon to roughly judge whether a sentence expresses sentiment or not.

Through the above procedures, the topic sentiment sentences in a Chinese review, each with a value indicating the distance in similarity with the topic, are extracted and arranged into order by value. We call them the set of candidate topic sentiment sentences.

5 Recognizing the Sentiment Polarity Based on Topic Sentiment Sentences

Based on section 3.3, in Chinese reviews, the higher similarity degree a topic sentiment sentence gets, the more likely it is a key sentence expressing the writers' basic sentiment orientation. But meanwhile, to avoid excessively relying on too few candidate topic sentiment sentences, more sentences are required to be analyzed to assure precision. Therefore, the number of sentences selected from the set of candidate topic sentiment sentences for final sentiment analysis is quite a question worth careful consideration.

Different Chinese reviews have different numbers of topic sentiment sentences. How many topic sentiment sentences a review has is determined by various factors. We find out, after an investigation of 560 Chinese reviews, that generally a Chinese review has not more than 7 topic sentiment sentences and the average number of that is about 4. Besides, long reviews tend to have rather more topic sentiment sentence. Thus we define that for any review the number of topic sentiment sentences which are needed to be analyzed as:

$$N(tss)=4\pm\gamma \qquad (2)$$

γ in the above formula is an adjustable parameter which is determined by the ratio of the length of the analyzing review and the average length of a set of reference reviews.

N(tss) topic sentiment sentences with most weights are drawn from the set of candidate topic sentiment sentences and then are computed by a sentence-level sentiment analyzer. The average score of them is taken as O(r), i.e. the overall SP of a review.

$$O(r)=\frac{1}{N(tss)}\sum_{i=1}^{N(tss)}SP(tss_i) \qquad (3)$$

We use a semantic approach in the sentence-level sentiment analyzer. For each sentence, a Chinese dependency parser is used to distinguish the dependency relations between language units, especially the probable relations between the topic words and the sentiment expressions, and the relations between the sentiment expressions and their modifiers. Making use of the syntactic information, the sentiment of a sentence is determined mainly by the sentiment expressions in it according to a precompiled sentiment lexicon. Meanwhile, the following factors are considered.

Negatives. Negatives inverse the sentiment of a sentence.

Connectors. Some connectors strengthen the original sentiment while others inverse the original sentiment.

Intensifiers. Intensifiers make the original sentiment more forcefully.

Discourse makers. In linguistics, a discourse marker is a word or phrase that is relatively syntax-independent and does not change the meaning of the sentence. However, discourse marker itself has certain semantic orientation: some of them are positive, some are negative and others are neutral. Thus discourse marker help recognize the SP in a sentence.

Punctuations. We pay special attention to question mark and exclamatory mark, especially when there is a negative in a question sentence.

6 Experiments and Results

6.1 Data

The data used in the experiment are Chinese current affairs reviews. They are originally collected from the website http://opinion.people.com.cn/ and then cleansed and stored as text. 400 texts are randomly selected from the reviews set. 3 annotators are trained and then instructed to annotate the topic sentiment sentences and judge the SP the 400 reviews individually. The following table shows the general information of the annotation result.

Table 2 General Information of the Annotation Results

Annotator	Pos. texts	Neg. texts	Other texts
1	87	302	11
2	93	298	9
3	88	288	14

Finally we get 370 texts (86 positive and 284 negative) totally agreed by the 3 annotators. We use them as the test reviews.

6.2 Resources

In order to perform an SP analysis, the following resources are required to use.

Sentiment Lexicon. We manually build up the sentiment lexicon. The words and phrases in the lexicon are mainly from three dictionaries: Positive Word Dictionary, Negative Word Dictionary and A Student's Positive and Negative Word Dictionary. We also get some words from HowNet Sentiment Dictionary and NTUSD. For each word or phrase, we give its part of speech, positive value and negative value. The positive and negative values of words and phrases are manually assigned by annotators according to human intuition.

Other lexicons. We collect as many negatives, connectors, intensifiers and discourse markers as we can and make them into different lexicons.

HowNet. As a Chinese ontology, HowNet is used to compute the semantic similarity of words.

LTP. LTP (Language Technology Platform developed by HIT) is a package of tools to process Chinese text, with a Chinese dependency parser in it. We use the dependency parser to perform a syntactic analysis of sentences.

CUCSeg. CUCSeg is a Chinese pos tagger. We use it to segment Chinese words.

6.3 Results of the Extraction of Topic Sentiment Sentences Experiment

The extraction of topic sentiment sentences is a vital task in this research. Annotators judge in the test reviews which sentences are topic sentiment sentences firstly and method described in 4.2 is applied and the result of which is evaluated. We adopt the commonly used precision, recall and F-measure to measure the result. It shows as follows.

Table 3 Result of the Extraction of topic Sentiment Sentences

Threshold	Precision	Recall	F_1
L_s=0.64	89.9	82.3	86.1
L_s=0.55	86.1	90.6	88.3
L_s=0.37	77.8	98.4	88.1

The above result shows we get a rather high precision and recall when L_s=0.55.

6.4 Results of Recognizing the SP of Chinese Reviews Experiment

We use precision to measure the result. Comparison is made among Turney's method (2002), Pang's SVM method (2002) and our method.

Table 4 Result of the SP of Chinese reviews

Method	Precision
Turney's	74.39
Pang's SVM	82.9
Ours	86.8

Compared to reports in earlier works, our approach achieves a relatively high precision.

We reexamine the 49 texts which are judged wrong, together with the 4 extracted representative topic sentiment sentences of each text. Error analysis shows that about 35% of errors are made by the topic identification step, about 49% of errors are made by the sentence-level sentiment analysis, about 4% of errors are made due to the faultiness of the sentiment lexicon. And the causes of other errors are to be explored.

7 Conclusion

We have presented a topic sentiment sentence-based approach to explore the overall sentiment polarity of Chinese reviews. Considering the features of Chinese reviews, we identify the topic of a review using an n-gram approach. To extract topic sentiment sentences, we compute the semantic similarity of a candidate sentence and the ascertained topic and meanwhile determine whether the sentence is subjective. A certain number of these sentences are selected as representatives according to their semantic similarity value with relation to the topic. The average value of the representative topic sentiment sentences is calculated and taken as the sentiment polarity of a review.

Error analysis indicates that to enhance the identification of topic, to build up a better sentence-level sentiment analyzer and to compile a better sentiment lexicon will help improve the final result.

Acknowledgements

We thank Prof. Ting Liu at Harbin Institute of Technology for sharing the LTP package and Mr. Zhendong Dong for sharing the HowNet. We highly appreciate that Hanbing Zhao, Nan Li and Yifu Xue have done a lot of heavy and tedious annotation work for this research.

References

Hu, M. and Liu, Bing. 2004. Mining and summarizing customer reviews. In Proceedings of the 10th ACM SIGKDD.168- 177.

Kim, S., Hovy E. 2004. Determining the Sentiment of Opinions. In Proceedings of COLING-04: the 20th International Conference on Computational Linguistics.

Lun-Wei Ku and Hsin-Hsi Chen 2007. Mining Opinions from the Web: Beyond Relevance Retrieval. Journal of American Society for Information Science and Technology, Special Issue on Mining Web Resources for Enhancing Information Retrieval, 58(12): 1838-1850.

Meng, F., L. Cai, B. Chen, and P. Wu. 2008. Research on the recognition of text valence. Journal of Chinese Computer Systems, 28(2007): 1-4.

Pang Bo, Lillian Lee, and Shivakumar Vaithyanathan. 2002. Thumbs up? Sentiment classification using machine learning techniques. In Proceedings of EMNLP, pages 79-86.

Turney, P. 2002. Thumbs Up or Thumbs Down? Semantic Orientation Applied to Unsupervised Classification of Reviews. In Proceedings of the 40th Annual Meeting of the Association for Computational Linguistics. 417-424.

Wang, Gen and Jun Zhao. 2007. Sentence Sentiment Analysis Based on Multi-redundant-labeled CRFs. Journal of Chinese Information Processing, 21(5): 51-56.

Wang, C., Lu, J., Zhang, G. 2005. A semantic classification approach for online Product reviews. In Proceedings of the 2005 IEEE/WIC/ACM International Conference on web intelligence (WI'5).

Wang, G. and Zhao, J. 2007. Sentence Sentiment Analysis Based on Multi-redundant-labeled CRFs. Journal of Chinese Information Processing. 5, 51-56.

Wang,C. J. Lu and G. Zhang. 2005. A semantic classification approach for online product reviews, In Proceedings of the 2005 IEEE/WIC/ACM International Conference on Web Intelligence. 276-279.

Wiebe J. 2000. Learning subjective adjectives from corpora. In Proceeding of the 17th National Conference on Artificial intelligence. Menlo Park, Calif. AAAI Press, 735-740.

Wiebe J., Riloff E.2005. Creating Subjective and Objective Sentence Classifiers from Unannotated Text. In: Proceedings of CICLING.

Wiebe J., Wilson T., BrueeR., Bell M. and Martin M.2004. Learning subjective language, Computational Linguistics, 30(3):277-308.

Yi J., Nasukawa T., Bunescu R., Niblack W.2003.Sentiment analyzer: Extracting sentiments about a given topic using natural language processing techniques. In Proceeding of the Third IEEE International Conference on Data Mining.

Yu, H. and Hatzivassiloglou Vasileios.2003. Towards answering opinion questions. In Proceeding of EMNLP. 2003.

Zheng, W. and Q. Ye. 2005. Sentiment classification of Chinese traveler reviews by support vector machine algorithm. In The Third International Symposium on Intelligent Information Technology Application, 335-338.

The Method of Improving the Specific Language Focused Crawler

Shan-Bin Chan
Graduate School of Fundamental Science and Engineering
Waseda University
chrisjan@yama.info.waseda.ac.jp

Hayato Yamana
Graduate School of Fundamental Science and Engineering
Waseda University
yamana@yama.info.waseda.ac.jp

Abstract

In recent years, more and more CJK (Chinese, Japanese, and Korean) web pages appear in the Internet. The information in the CJK web page also becomes more and more important. Web crawler is a kind of tool to retrieve web pages. Previous researches focused on English web crawlers and the web crawler is always optimized for English web pages. We found that the performance of the web crawler is worse in retrieving CJK web pages. We tried to enhance the performance of the CJK crawler by analyzing the web link structure, anchor text, and host name on the hyperlink and changing the crawling algorithm. We distinguish the top-level domain name and the language of the anchor text on hyperlinks. The method that distinguishes the language of the anchor text on hyperlinks is not used on CJK language specific crawler by other researches. Control experiment is used in this research. According to the experimental results, when the target crawling language is Japanese, the 87% of the crawled web pages are Japanese web pages and improves the efficiency about 0.24% compares to the baseline results. When the target crawling language is Chinese, the 88% of the crawled web pages are Chinese web pages and improves the efficiency about 0.07% compares to the baseline results. When the target crawling language is Korean, the 71% of the crawled web pages are Korean web pages and improves the efficiency about 10% compares to the baseline results.

1 Introduction

The growth of web pages in the internet becomes rapidly in recent years. How to efficiently collect web pages and how to gather more language or topic relative web pages become important. Focused crawling is a kind of method that collects topic specific web pages. (Chakrabarti et al., 1999) Intelligent crawling that can self-learning and predicating makes the focus crawling more efficient. (Chara et al., 2001) Mining for patterns and relations over text, structures, and links is an interesting research. (Neel et al., 2001) In the past few years, the researches are focused on the topic specific focused crawling and optimized the performance of focus crawler for crawling English web pages. Web pages are not only described in English but also in other languages. Our research will be emphasized on the study of language specific focused crawler and how to optimize the crawler for specific language (For example: Chinese, Japanese, and Korean).

Huge amounts of hyperlinks on the CJK web pages link to English web pages. But the hyperlinks on the English web pages almost don't link to the CJK web pages. If we deeply crawl the web pages from CJK seed sets, finally we will gather many English web pages. In this kind of situation, the efficiency of the CJK focus crawler is very worse.

Our research method is that the first we extract the domain name from the hyperlink URL and then determine the top-level domain. For example, if we try to focus crawl the Japanese web pages and the top-level domain in the hyperlink URLs is .jp, this focus crawler will queue these URLs for the next crawling. If the top-level domain in the hyperlink URLs is not .jp, we will distinguish the language of the anchor text of the hyperlink. If the language of the anchor text is Japanese, we also queue these URLs for the next crawling. Otherwise, we drop the URLs.

This research uses the Nutch as the crawler and uses the Hadoop as the storage. Because of the web pages is enormous, Hadoop is a very efficient tool that can store and process vast amounts of data. We choose the URLs on the DMOZ as the seeds set and extract the URLs by the top-level domain name .cn, .tw, .jp, .kr, .com, .net. After extracting the URLs, we sort these URLs by language (Chinese, Japanese, and Korean). We use these sorted URLs as the seeds set for crawling by Nutch.

The experiment method in our research is control experiment. We divided our experiment to two groups. One is control group and the other one is experimental group. The crawling methods of the control group use the default crawling algorithm in Nutch. The crawling methods of the experimental group use the modified crawling rules provided by us. After crawling by both control group and experimental group, we compare the crawled web pages between baseline results and experimental results. Finally, the results show that we can improve the crawling efficiency by using our modified method.

2 Related Researches

2.1 Web data collection of specific topic

The research of focus crawler is applied in the medical information science. (Thanh et al., 2005) Their research mentions that there are relationships between the hyperlink URLs and the 50 words before and after hyperlinks with the contents in the crawling target pages. And they also mention that if the URL filters are applied in the breadth-first crawling, The crawled results will be better then without URL filters.

2.2 Collection methods of specific language web pages

Tamura (2006) introduces the research of specific language web pages focus crawler. Their research is focused on the collection of Thai language web pages. When crawling, the link selection methods of their research are descript as below:

1. When the authors collect web page j on web server i, they distinguish the language of web page j.
2. If the language of the web page j is Thai, Nr(i) increases 1. (Nr(i) is Thai language web page counts of web server i)
3. Na(i) increases 1. (Na(i) is collected page counts of web server i)
4. Extract the hyperlinks in the web page j.
5. Drop the hyperlink that top-level domain is not Thai.
6. Drop the hyperlink that has been crawled.
7. If the language of web page j is Thai, queue the remained hyperlinks to high priority.
8. If the language of web page j is not Thai, queue the remained hyperlinks to low priority.

The research data set is collected from famous portal web pages in Thailand from July to August in 2004. They download 18,344,217 HTML pages from 574,111 servers, and use this data set for simulating their selective collection method. The estimation methods are as below:

- Server-based filtering, aggressive: No limits when the crawler chooses the new web server.
- Server-based filtering, conservative: Only Thai servers when the crawler chooses the new web server.
- Directory-based filtering, conservative: Only Thai directory when the crawler chooses the directory on the server.
- Hard focused: Drop all the hyperlinks when the web page is not Thai language.
- Soft focused: If the web page is Thai language, queue the hyperlinks with high priority. If the web page is no Thai language, queue the hyperlinks with low priority.
- BFS: Breath-first search.
- Perfect: First, the crawler uses the breath-first search. When the crawler

found a hyperlink, which is Thai, web page, the crawler start to follow this Thai hyperlink and crawl the web pages from this URL.

The result of the estimation method "Perfect" is obvious. While crawling, when the total amount of crawled web pages increase, the cumulative Thai web page ratio increase smoothly from 92% to 99%.

2.3 Seeds set generation method for web crawler

HITS algorithm is used to generate crawler seeds set. (Shervin et al., 2003) Their research considered that it's better to crawl the most important web pages on the resource limited internet. They use the collected web pages to draw a web graph and perform the HITS algorithm to generate seeds set for crawler.

2.4 Focus crawling for dark web forums

Dark web forum is a kind of forum that the contents are associated with cybercrime, hate, and extremism. Fu (2010) developed a focus crawler for crawling dark web forums by using language-independent features, including URL tokens, anchor text, and level features. They also use forum software-specific traversal strategies and wrappers to support incremental crawling. Their system maintains up-to-date collections of 109 forums in multiple languages. Their focus crawler gathers contents from three regions, which are U.S. domestic supremacist, Middle Eastern extremist, and Latin groups. Their human-assisted accessibility mechanism can access identified forums with a success rate of over 90%.

2.5 The differences between previous studies

The previous researches almost focus on the English web page crawlers or the topic specific crawlers. There are few researches about the CJK language specific focus crawlers. The method that judges the top-level domain name of the URLs on hyperlinks has been studied on crawling Thai web pages. And the crawling method of judgment the language of an anchor text on the hyperlink has not studied by other researchers. We consider that if we combine the top-level domain name judgment method and anchor text language distinguish method, we will enhance the efficiency more on crawling CJK web pages. So, we use this combined method to enhance the performance of CJK language specific focus crawler.

3 Methods

The probability is very high that hyperlinks on the CJK web pages link to English web pages. And the probability is very low that hyperlinks on the English web pages link to CJK web pages. If we crawl the web pages deeply from CJK seed sets, finally we will gather huge amounts of English web pages.

We implement the control experiment to resolve the problems that mentioned above. We split our research to 5 steps and show the process in the Figure 1.

Before crawling, a seeds set is very important for the crawler. DMOZ (http://www.dmoz.org) is the biggest web directory service in the world. We use the URLs in the DMOZ as the seeds set. Our URLs extraction method shows as follow.

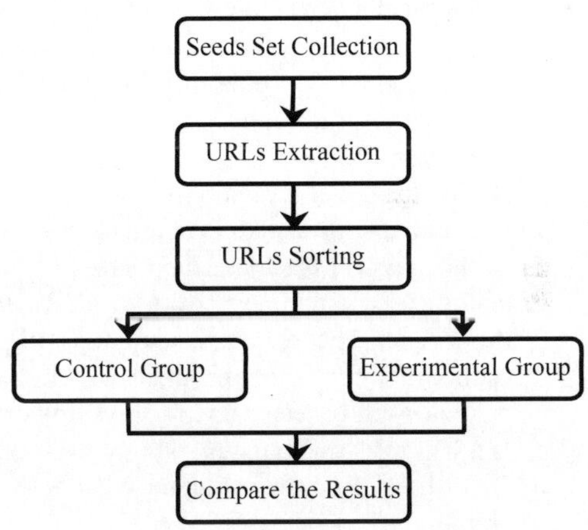

Figure 1. Research Process

- Download the XML formatted web directory data from DMOZ homepage on October 26th 2009.
- Extract URLs form XML formatted web directory data.
- Sort the URLs by top-level domain. (.cn, .tw, .jp, .kr, .com, .net, etc...)

- Choose the .cn, .tw, .jp, .kr, .com, .net top-level domains for language distinguish.
- Use the Perl Lingua::LanguageGuesser which produced by Nakagawa Laboratory of Tokyo University to distinguish the language (Chinese, Japanese, and Korean) of each web pages in the sorted URLs. Perl Lingua::LanguageGuesser is a language distinguisher that is based on N-Gram text categorization. (William et al., 1994)
- Use these sorted seeds sets and perform crawling by using Nutch.

We implement our research by separating into two groups, control group and experimental group. The control group follows the default crawling rules supported by Nutch. And we change the crawling rules in experimental group by importing a URLs queuing replacement plug-in into Nutch. We will explain the modified URLs queuing rules by using the Chinese web pages collection procedures.

- If the top-level domain in the URL is .cn, store this URL to the queue. The reason is that it is high probability that the web page with .cn domain name is a Chinese web page.
- If the top-level domain in the URL is not .cn, distinguish the language of the anchor text on the hyperlink. Then, if the anchor text is Chinese, store the URL to the queue. The reason is that it is high probability that the web page which hyperlink with Chinese anchor text links to is a Chinese a web page.
- Drop the URLs from queue when other situations.

At the final stage, calculates the percentage of each language and compares the results between baseline results and experimental results.

4 Results

URLs extracted from DMOZ that with .com domain is 1,964,053, .net domain is 182,595, .jp domain is 130,125, .cn domain is 14,769, .tw domain is 10,259, .kr domain is 4,910. Figure 2 shows the percentage of each domain.

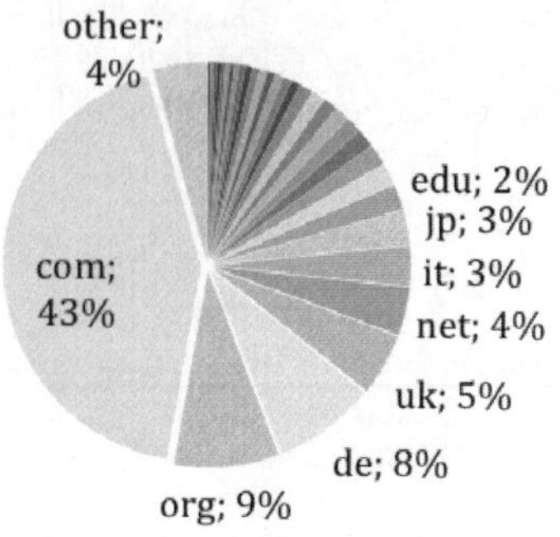

Figure 2. Distribution of DMOZ top-level domains

CJK web page counts in each top-level domain (.com and .net, .cn, .tw, .jp, .kr) are shown in Table 1. We extract 43,216 Chinese URLs, 175,666 Japanese URLs, and 5,252 Korean URLs. We randomly pick 1,000 URLs for each language from these CJK URLs and start to crawl by using these URLs as seeds sets.

We write two functions into URLs queuing replacement plug-in on Nutch. One is html text language distinguisher, and the other one is web page counter. We use the same language distinguisher that supported by Nakagawa Laboratory of Tokyo University with seeds set extraction stage.

Domain	CN	JP	KR
com&net	24,851	56,256	1,975
cn	11,937	40	1
tw	6,220	573	16
jp	147	118,729	14
kr	61	68	3,246
Total	43,216	175,666	5,252

Table 1. CJK web page counts from each top-level domain

Figure 3 shows the crawling process of this research. The original Nutch crawl process is that crawl the web pages from seeds set, parse the html text, extract the URLs from hyperlinks, store the URLs to the queue, and implement the breadth-first crawling. In order to recording the language of URLs, after parsing the html text, we add a Nutch plug-in to judges the language of the html text. Then write the URL of this web page to a language specific file (Chinese, Japanese, Korean, Other) for counting. And then extract all the hyperlinks and store the URLs to the queue. Control group implements the process described above.

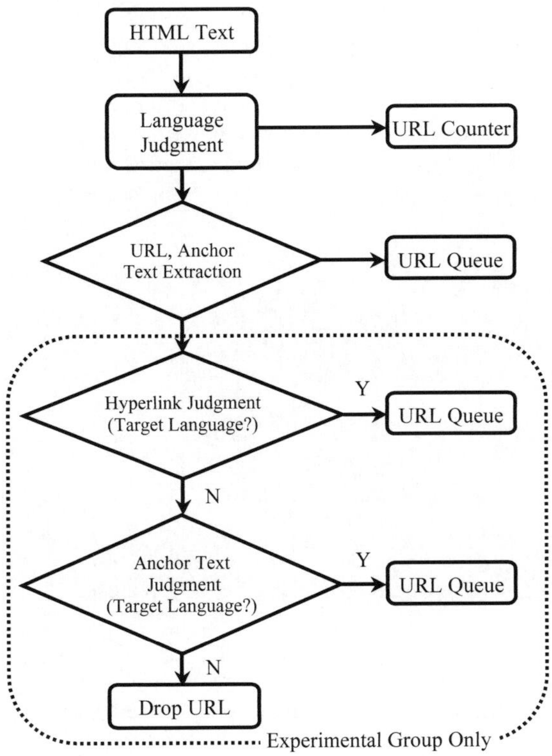

Figure 3. Crawling process

Experimental group also implements the process of control group. After the control group process, we add top-level domain judgment on hyperlinks. When we are focusing on crawling Chinese web pages, and if the top-level domain on hyperlinks is .cn, we store the URL of this hyperlink to the queue. If the top-level domain on hyperlinks is not .cn, we check the anchor text of the hyperlink. If the language of the anchor is Chinese, we also store the URL of this hyperlink to the queue. Otherwise, drop the URLs from queue. We don't prioritize the URLs in queue in this research. In order to not crawling the web pages that are not Chinese, we decide to drop these URLs that may not be Chinese web pages.

We pick a Chinese web page as the crawling example for experimental group. The crawler chooses a URL "http://www.bsc.org.cn/" in the sorted DOMZ seed sets. First, we parse the HTML text of this URL and extract the hyperlinks and anchor text from HTML text. We get a part of the hyperlink and anchor text shown in Table 2.

Anchor text	Hyperlinks
中国科学技术协会	http://www.cast.org.cn
中国科学院生物物理研究所	http://www.ibp.ac.cn
IUPAB	http://www.iupab.org
Asian Biophysics Association	http://www.aba-bp.com
美国生物物理学会	http://www.biophysics.org
Protein and Cell	http://www.protein-cell.org
…	…

Table 2. A part of anchor text and hyperlinks extracted from "http://www.bsc.org.cn/"

Second, according to the URL queuing rules mentioned above, we show a part of matched hyperlinks and anchor text shown in Table 3.

Anchor text	Hyperlinks	Matched	Page lang
中国科学技术协会	http://www.cast.org.cn	Yes	CHS
中国科学院生物物理研究所	http://www.ibp.ac.cn	Yes	CHS
IUPAB	http://www.iupab.org	No	ENG
Asian Biophysics Association	http://www.aba-bp.com	No	ENG
美国生物物理学会	http://www.biophysics.org	No	ENG
Protein and Cell	http://www.protein-cell.org	No	ENG

Table 3. A part of matched hyperlinks by using experimental group queuing rules from "http://www.bsc.org.cn/"

Finally, we use these matched hyperlinks as the URLs for next crawling loop.

The web page crawled results of control group and experimental group from Feb. 5th to Feb. 12th 2010 show in Table 4. Because of the longer processing time of language distinguish in experimental group, the total crawl results of experimental results are fewer then baseline results.

	Chinese	Japanese	Korean	Other	Total
KR-C·	12,523	1,926	80,049	36,273	130,771
KR-E	1,757	380	11,328	2,386	15,851
JP-C	6,555	66,235	108	2,838	75,736
JP-E	1,179	11,890	24	465	13,558
CN-C	112,924	2,468	1.052	11,321	127,765
CN-E	10,078	202	99	1,015	11,394

Table 4. The crawled web pages for each language

When the crawling target language is Korean, the language percentage of gathered web pages in baseline results shows as Figure 4. Total 130,771 web pages are crawled and 61.21% are Korean web pages.

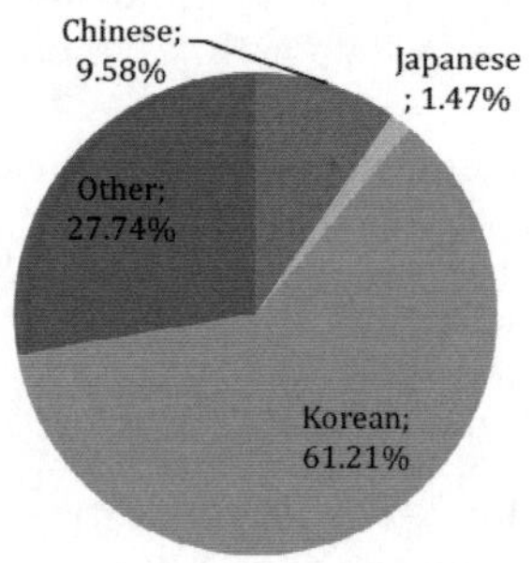

Figure 4. Language distribution of Korean baseline results

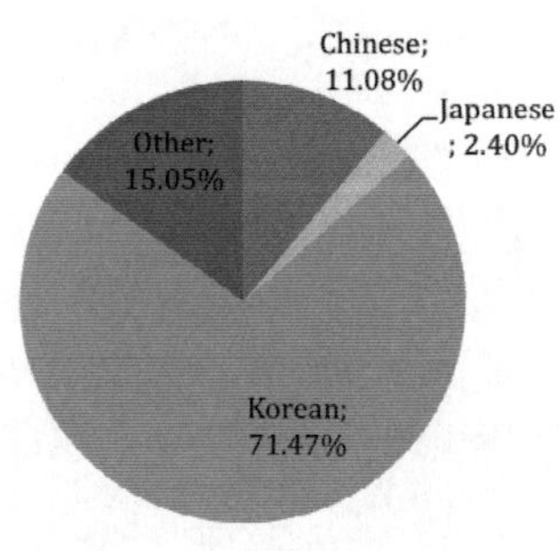

Figure 5. Language distribution of Korean experimental results

When the crawling target language is Korean, the language percentage of gathered web pages in experimental results shows as Figure 5. Total 15,851 web pages are crawled and 71.47% are Korean web pages.

According to the crawled results in Figure 4 and Figure 5, our methods can improve about 10% efficiency in crawling Korean web pages.

When the crawling target language is Japanese, the language percentage of gathered web pages in baseline results shows as Figure 6. Total 75,736 web pages are crawled and 87.46% are Japanese web pages.

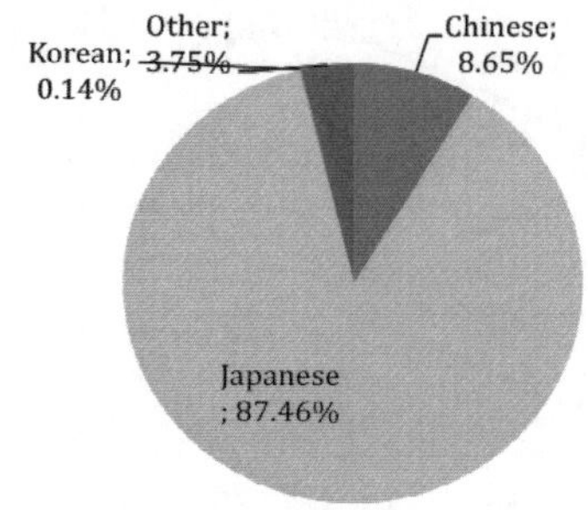

Figure 6. Language distribution of Japanese baseline results

When the crawling target language is Japanese, the language percentage of gathered web pages in experimental results shows as Figure 7. Total 13,558 web pages are crawled and 87.70% are Japanese web pages.

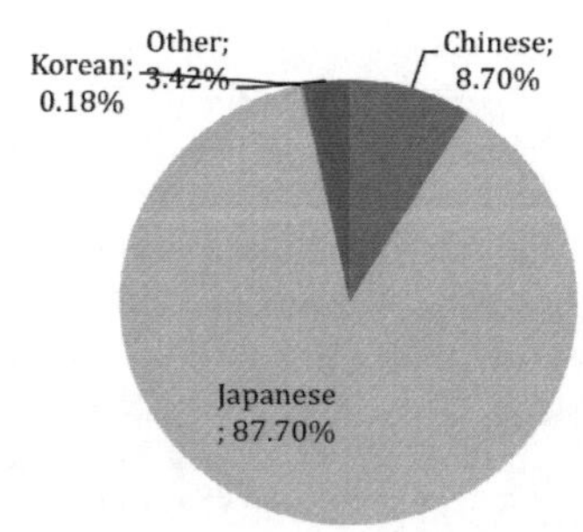

Figure 7. Language distribution of Japanese experimental results

According to the crawled results in Figure 6 and Figure 7, our methods can improve about 0.24% efficiency in crawling Japanese web pages.

· KR(Korean)、JP(Japanese)、CN(Chinese)、C(Baseline Results)、E(Experimental Results)

When the crawling target language is Chinese, the language percentage of gathered web pages in baseline results shows as Figure 8. Total 127,765 web pages are crawled and 88.38% are Japanese web pages.

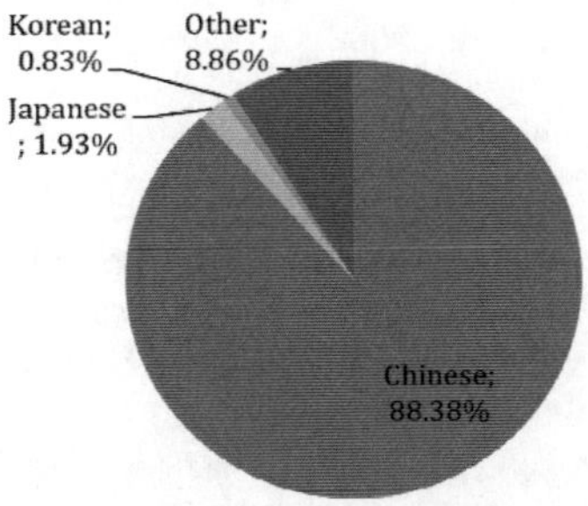

Figure 8. Language distribution of Chinese baseline results

When the crawling target language is Chinese, the language percentage of gathered web pages in experimental results shows as Figure 9. Total 11,394 web pages are crawled and 88.45% are Japanese web pages.

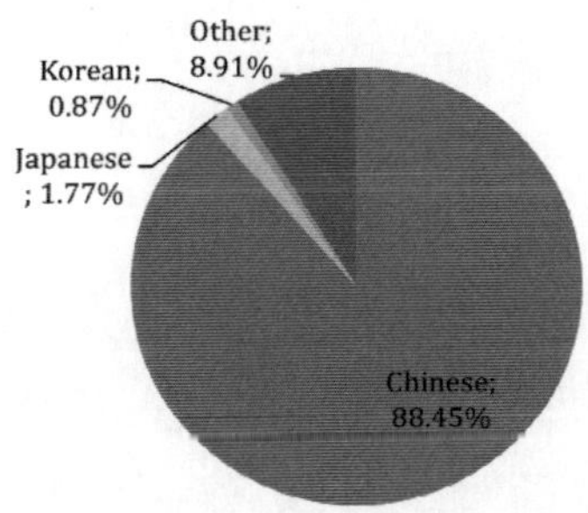

Figure 9. Language distribution of Chinese experimental results

According to the crawled results in Figure 8 and Figure 9, our methods can improve about 0.07% efficiency in crawling Chinese web pages.

The experimental results show that the efficiency improvement of Korean crawling is very obvious. The efficiency improvement of Chinese and Japanese are lower then 1%, actually the improvement is unobvious. We picked some URLs from crawling log to analyze why the improvement of Korean language specific crawler is obvious. We found that many Korean web pages content multi-language links on the main page, such as English, Chinese, Japanese, etc.... It is high probability that the hyperlinks on the Korean web pages link to web pages which are other languages. The languages of anchor text on Chinese or Japanese web pages are always Chinese or Japanese. So following our modified crawling rules, the crawled Korean web pages increase conspicuously and the crawled Chinese or Japanese web pages increase unobvious.

5 Conclusions

The purpose of this research is to enlarge the crawling amounts of language specific crawler. We propose language judgment on anchor text method to enhance the efficiency of the focus crawler. And combine the method which is distinguish the top-level domain name of URLs on hyperlinks to implement a control experiment in this research.

This research also proposes language specific focus crawler by importing a plug-in into Nutch and crawling the web pages with a modified algorithm. This method can easily program, install, and implement modified crawling rules by using plug-in on Nutch.

According to the comparison of control group and experimental group, the efficiency improvement is obvious on Korean focus crawler. And the efficiency improvement is unobvious on Chinese and Japanese focus crawler. It is because many hyperlinks on the Korean web pages link to web pages that are other languages. So that the improvement of Korean web pages crawling is obvious.

Perl language guesser is implemented by using JAVA external call. If we can use the JAVA language guesser, the crawling speed will be improved.

The append function of Hadoop is defective. Only new file can be appended, data can't append to existing file in Hadoop. In order to counting the crawled URLs, immediately append the URLs list to a log file in Hadoop is impossible. So Perl script called by JAVA external call is used to replace the flawed append function in Hadoop. But this kind of method occurs a lot of "Out of memory" and "IOExpection" errors in JAVA. These errors slow down the gather speed of web pages. If the append function in Hadoop is flawless, the collection speed of web pages will be boosted.

According to the crawled results in experimental group, the percentage of crawled Chinese web pages by Chinese focus crawler is 88%. The percentage of crawled Japanese web pages by Japanese focus crawler is 87%. The percentage of crawled Korean web pages by Korean focus crawler is 71%. We will increase the efficiency of language specific crawler more in the future work.

This research uses DMOZ as the seed sets. We extract CJK URLs from DMOZ data. Actually, the percentage of CJK URLs in DMOZ data is very low. We will try to use the famous CJK portal web sites as the seed sets in the future work.

Acknowledgements

This research is supported by Waseda University Global COE Program "International Research and Education Center for Ambient SoC" and JST Program "Multimedia Web Analysis Framework towards Development of Social Analysis Software."

References

Charu C. Aggarwal, Fatima Al-Garawi, and Philip S. Yu. 2001. *Intelligent Crawling on the World Wide Web with Arbitrary Predicates*, WWW conference.

DMOZ: The Open Directory Project is the largest, most comprehensive human-edited directory of the Web. http://www.dmoz.org

Hadoop: A reliable, scalable, and distributed computing system. http://hadoop.apache.org

HITS: Hyperlink-Induced Topic Search. http://en.wikipedia.org/wiki/HITS_algorithm

Lingua::LanguageGuesser. http://gensen.dl.itc.u-tokyo.ac.jp/LanguageGuesser/LanguageGuesser_ja.html

Neel Sundaresan, and Jeonghee Yi. 2001. *Mining the Web for Relations*, Computer Networks, Volume 33, Issue 1-6: 699-711.

Nutch: A JAVA based open source web crawler developed by Apache Software Foundation. http://nutch.apache.org

Shervin Daneshpajouh, Mojtaba Mohammadi Nasiri, and Mohammad Ghodsi. 2003. *A Fast Community Based Algorithm For Generating Web Crawler Seeds Set.*

Soumen Chakrabarti, Martin van den Berg, and Byron Dom. 1999. *Focused Crawling: A New Approach to Topic Specific Resource Discovery*, WWW Conference.

Tamura Takayuki, Somboonviwat Kulwadee, and Kitsuregawa Masaru. 2006. *A Method for Language Specific Web Crawling and Its Evaluation*, The IEICE transactions on information and systems, J89-D(2):199-209.

Thanh Tin Tang, David Hawking, Nick Craswell, and Kathy Griffiths. 2005. *Focused Crawling for both Topical Relevance and Quality of Medical Information*, CIKM.

Tianjun Fu, Ahmed Abbasi, and Hsinchun Chen. 2010. *A Focused Crawler for Dark Web Forums*, Journal of The American Society for Information Science and Technology, 61(6):1213-1231

William B. Cavnar and John M. Trenkle. 1994. *N-gram-based text categorization*, In Symposium On Document Analysis and Information Retrieval:161–176.

Active Learning Based Corpus Annotation

Hongyan Song[1] and Tianfang Yao[2]
Shanghai Jiao Tong University
Department of Computer Science and Engineering
Shanghai, China 200240
[1]songhongyan@sjtu.org
[2]yao-tf@cs.sjtu.edu.cn

Abstract

Opinion Mining aims to automatically acquire useful opinioned information and knowledge in subjective texts. Research of Chinese Opinioned Mining requires the support of annotated corpus for Chinese opinioned-subjective texts. To facilitate the work of corpus annotators, this paper implements an active learning based annotation tool for Chinese opinioned elements which can identify topic, sentiment, and opinion holder in a sentence automatically.

1 Introduction

Opinion Mining is a novel and important research topic, aiming to automatically acquire useful opinioned information and knowledge in subjective texts (Liu et al, 2008). This technique has wide and many real world applications, such as e-commerce, business intelligence, information monitoring, public opinion poll, e-learning, newspaper and publication compilation, and business management. For instance, a typical opinion mining system produces statistical results from online product reviews, which can be used by potential customers when deciding which model to choose, by manufacturers to find out the possible areas of improvement, and by dealers for sales plan evaluation (Yao et al, 2008).

According to Kim and Hovy (2004), an opinion is composed of four parts, namely, topic, holder, sentiment, and claim, in which the holder expresses the claim including positive or negative sentiment towards the topic. For example, in the sentence *I like this car*, *I* is the holder, *like* is the positive sentiment, *car* is the topic, and the whole sentence is the claim.

Research on Chinese opinion mining technology requires the support of annotated corpus for Chinese opinioned-subjective text. Since the corpus includes deep level information related to word segmentation, part-of-speech, syntax, semantics, opinioned elements, and some other information, the finished annotation is very complicated. Hence, it is necessary to develop an automatic tool to facilitate the work of annotators so that the efficiency and accuracy of annotation can be improved.

When developing the automatic annotation tool, we find it is most difficult for the tool to annotate opinioned elements automatically. Because unlike other elements such as part-of-speech, and dependency relationship that needed to be annotated in the corpus, there is no available tool that can identify opinioned elements automatically. Special classifiers should be constructed to solve this problem.

In traditional supervised learning tasks, training process consumes all the available annotated training instances, so a classifier with high classification accuracy might be constructed. When training a classifier for opinioned elements, it is very expensive and time-consuming to get annotated instances. On the other hand, unannotated instances are abundant in this case, because all the texts in the corpus can be regarded as unannotated instances before being annotated. This scenario is very appropriate for active learning application. An active learning algorithm picks up the instances which will improve the performance of the classifier to the largest extent into the training set, and often produce classifier with higher accuracy using less training instances.

Active learning algorithm is featured with smaller training set size, less influence from unbalanced training data and better classification performance comparing to classical learning algorithm. This paper experimentally demonstrates the validity of active learning algorithm when used for opinioned elements identification and proposes a computational method for overall system performance evaluation which consists of F-measure, training time, and number of training instances.

2 Related Work

Common active learning algorithms can be divided into two classes, membership query and selective sampling (Dagan and Engelson, 1995). For membership query, algorithm constructs learning instances by itself according to the knowledge learnt, and submits the instances for human processing (Angluin, 1988) (Sammut and Banerji, 1986) (Shapiro, 1982). Although this method has proved high learning efficiency (Dagan and Engelson, 1995), it can be applied in fewer scenarios. Since constructing meaningful training instance without the knowledge of target concept is rather difficult. As to selective sampling, algorithm picks up training instances which can improve the performance of the classifier to the largest extent from a large variety of available instances. Algorithm in this class can be further divided into stream-based algorithm and pool-based algorithm according to how instances are saved (Long *et al*, 2008). For stream-based algorithm (Engelson and Dagon, 1999) (Freund *et al*, 1997), unannotated instances are submitted to the system successively. All the instances not selected by the algorithms will be discarded. As to pool-based algorithm (Muslea *et al*, 2006) (McCallum and Nigam, 1998) (Lewis and Gail, 1994), the algorithm choose the most appropriate training instances from all the available instances. Instance not selected might have chance to be picked up in the next round. Though its computational complexity is higher, selective sampling is widely used as an active learning method for no prior knowledge of the target concept is required.

Although much research has been made in the field, we found no case which deals with multi-classification problem in active learning. Besides, there is no available method to evaluate the performance of active learning in information extraction.

3 Active Learning Based Corpus Annotation

3.1 System Structure

The pool-based active learning algorithm is composed of two main parts: a learning engine and a selecting engine (Figure 1). The learning engine uses instances in the training set to improve the performance of the classifier. The selecting engine picks up unannotated instances according to preset rules, submits these instances for human annotation, and incorporates these instances into the training set after the annotation is completed. The learning engine and the selecting engine work in turns. The performance of the classifier tends to improve with the increasing of the training set size. When the preset condition is met, the training process will finish.

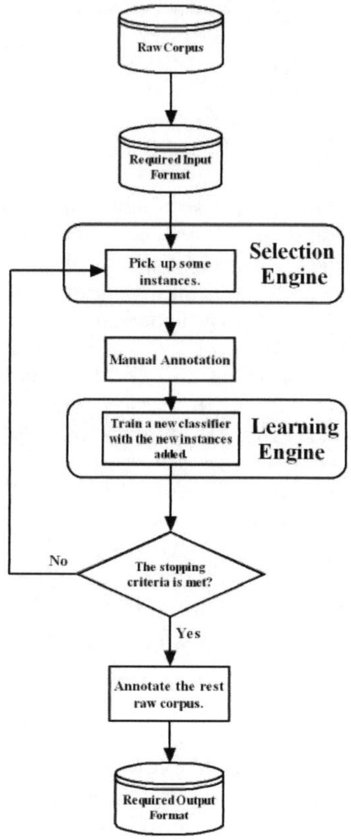

Figure 1 System Workflow

For our active learning based annotation tool, the workflow is as follows.

1. Convert raw texts into the format which the algorithm can deal with.
2. Selecting engine picks up instances which are expected to improve the performance of the classifier to the largest extent.
3. Annotate these instances manually.
4. Learning engine incorporate these annotated instances into the training set, and use the new training set to train the classifier.
5. Find out whether the performance of the classifier satisfies the preset standard. If not, go to step 2.
6. Use the classifier to identify the opinioned element in the unannotated dataset.
7. Convert the result into the required format.

3.2 Learning Engine

The learning engine maintains the classifier by iteratively training classifiers with new training sets. The classifier adopted determines the up limit of the system performance. We use Support Vector Machine (SVM) (Vapnik, 1995) (Boser *et al*, 1992) (Chang and Lin, 1992) as the classifier for our system for its high generalization performance even with feature vectors of high dimension and its ability to manage kernel functions that map input data to higher dimensional space without increasing computational complexity.

3.3 Selecting Engine

In our system, selecting engine picks up instances for human annotation, and puts the annotated instance into the training set. The strategy adopted when selecting training instance is critical to the overall performance of the active learning algorithm. A good strategy will more likely to produce a classifier with high accuracy from less training instances.

The strategy we adopted here is to choose the instances which the classifier is most unsure about which class they belong to. For a linear bi-classification SVM, these instances are the ones closest to the separating hyper plane. That means, the selecting engine will choose training instances according to their geometric distances to the hyper plane. The instance with least distance will be selected as the next instance to be added into the training set while the other instances will be saved for future reference.

The computational complexity of getting the distance between an instance and the hyper plane is low. However, this method can not be applied to SVM with non-linear kernel for geometric distances are meaningless in these cases. We use radial basis function, which is non-linear, as the kernel function in our system for it outperforms linear kernel in the experiment. Hence, we must find another method to pick up training instances.

Non-linear SVM decides the class an instance belongs to according to its decision function value.

$$y(\vec{x}) = \sum_{\vec{x}_s \in S} \alpha_s y_s K(\vec{x} \cdot \vec{x}_s) + b \qquad (1)$$

The instance will be classified into one certain class if $y(\vec{x}) > 0$, or the other class if $y(\vec{x}) < 0$. However, it will be difficult to classify the instance according to SVM theory if $y(\vec{x}) = 0$. Hence, we may deduce that SVM is most unsure when classifying an instance with least absolute decision function value.

We define the Predict Value (PV) as the value based on which selecting engine picks up training instances.

For bi-classification SVM, we have PV equals to the absolute decision function value, namely,

$$\text{PV}(\vec{x}) = \left| y(\vec{x}) \right| \qquad (2)$$

Instances with the minimum PV will be selected into the training set before other instances.

For example, if we want to identify all the topics in the sentence,

I like this car very much, but the price is a little bit too high.
我很喜欢这款车，但是价钱高了点！

The PV of each instance in the sentences are listed in Table 1. They are calculated from the decision function of the SVM gained from the last round of iteration.

Instances	PV
我 I	0.260306643320642
很 very	0.553855024703612
喜欢 like	0.427269428974918
这 this	0.031682276068012
款 type	0.366598504697780
车 car	0.095961213527654
，	0.178633448748979
但是 but	0.092571306234562
价钱 price	0.052164989563922
高 high	0.539913276317129
了 (auxiliary word)	0.458036102580422
点 a little bit	0.439936293288062
！	0.375263535139242

Table 1 Example of 2-Classification SVM Predict Value

Suppose all the instances in this sentence have not been added into the training set. *This* (0.0316), *price* (0.0521), and *but* (0.0925) will be selected into the training set successively for they have the minimal PVs.

For multi-classification SVM, it will be more complicated to find the training instances. Because common multi-classification SVM is implemented by voting process (Hsu and Lin, 2002), there are $\frac{1}{2}t\cdot(t-1)$ decision function values in t-classification SVM.

In our system, we need to classify instances into 4 classes, namely, *topic*, *holder*, *sentiment* and *other*. So a 4-classification SVM is adopted. Suppose for an instance, we get 6 Decision Function Values from 6 bi-classification SVMs as in Table 2.

No.	Classification	Decision Function Value	Result
1	Class 0 Vs Class 1	1.00032792289507	0
2	Class 0 Vs Class 2	0.999999993721249	0
3	Class 0 Vs Class 3	1.00032792289507	0
4	Class 1 Vs Class 2	0.106393804825973	1
5	Class 1 Vs Class 3	-5.20417042793042E-18	3
6	Class 2 Vs Class 3	-0.106393804825973	3

Table 2 Example of 4-Classification SVM Decision Process

For each bi-classification SVM, the class instance belongs to is determined by whether the decision function value is greater than or less than zero. The instance in Table 2 belongs to Class 0 since there 3 votes out of 6 votes for Class 0. When deciding which class an instance belongs to, only the decision function values from bi-classification SVMs with correct votes will work on the certainty of the final result. Hence, we define Predict Value for multi-classification SVMs as the arithmetic mean value of the absolute decision function value of every bi-classification SVM with correct vote,

$$\mathrm{PV}(\vec{x})=\frac{1}{k}\sum_{t=1,t\in\{\text{bi-classification SVMs with correct votes}\}}^{k}\left|y_t(\vec{x})\right| \quad (3)$$

For the instance in Table2, the value is calculated from the decision function values from bi-classification SVMs numbered 1, 2, and 3.

3.4 Experiments

To prove the validity of active learning algorithm and find out the relations between the performance of the classifiers and the way the classifiers are trained, we carried out batches of experiments.

In most information extraction tasks, a word and its context are considered a learning sample, and encoded as feature vectors. In our experiments, context data includes the part-of-speech tag, dependency relation, word semantic meaning, and word disambiguation information of the word being classified, its neighboring words and its parent word in dependency grammar. Part-of-speech tag and dependency relation are common features for Chinese Natural Language Processing (NLP) tasks[1]. We get word semantic meaning from HowNet, which is an online common-sense knowledge base unveiling inter-conceptual relations and inter-attribute relations of concepts as connoting in lexicons of the Chinese and their English equivalents (Zhendong Dong and Qiang Dong, 1999). Given an occurrence of a word in natural language text, word sense disambiguation is the process of identifying which sense of the word is intended if the word has a number of distinct senses. According to Song and Yao (2009), this information may help in Chinese NLP tasks such as topic identification.

Lack of explicit boundary between training instances and testing instances is a great difference between common machine learning algorithm and learning algorithm designed for corpus annotation. For common machine learning algorithm such as human face recognition, the quantity of training instances is limited while the testing instances could be infinite. It is unnecessary and impossible to annotate all the testing instances. However, when annotating a corpus, all the texts need to be annotated are decided beforehand. Although tools automated part of the annotation process, the results still need to be reviewed for several times to ensure the quality of annotation. That means in an annotation scenario, all the data to be processed are available during the training stage.

The raw texts used in our experiments are taken from forums of chinacars.com. These texts include explicit subjective opinion and informal network language, which are necessary for opinion mining research. Most of them are comments composed of one or more sentences on certain type of vehicle. The detailed opinion elements distributions are showed in table 3.

We use all the texts as testing data set and a subset of it as a training data set. First of all, we pick up 10 instances for each class, and train a simple classification model with them. Then, the baseline system picks up k instances in sequence and adds them into the training data set to train a new classification model iteratively until the training data set is as large as the testing data set,

[1] We use Language Technology Platform (LTP), developed by Center for Information Retrieval, Harbin Institute of Technology, for part-of-speech tagging, dependency relationship analysis and word sense disambiguation in our experiment.

while the active learning system picks up instances according to the strategy in Chapter 3.3.

Type	No. of Instances
Topic	638
Sentiment	769
Holder	46
Other	1500
Total	2953

Table 3 Detailed Information of the Data Set

We use three bi-classification model to test the performance of the active learning system on topic, sentiment, and holder identification separately and a four-classification model to identify the three opinion elements simultaneously. The results of the experiments are illustrated in Figure 2, 3, 4, and 5 respectively. Table 4, 5, and 6 provide the detailed F-measure trends while different numbers of instances are added into the training data set in each rounds. For each experiment, we try to compare the performances when we add different number of instances into the training data set in each round of iteration.

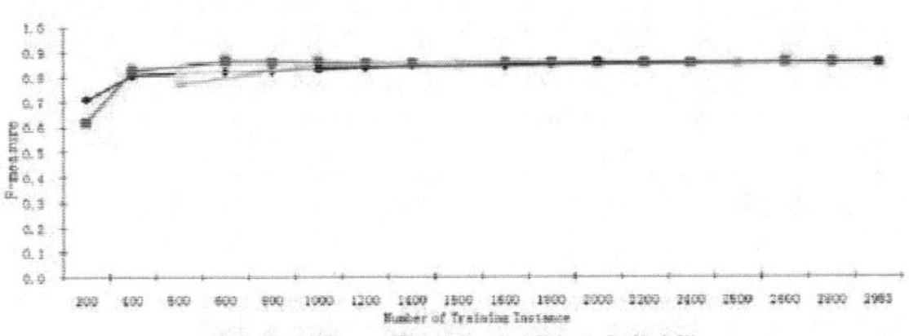

Figure 2 Topic Identification

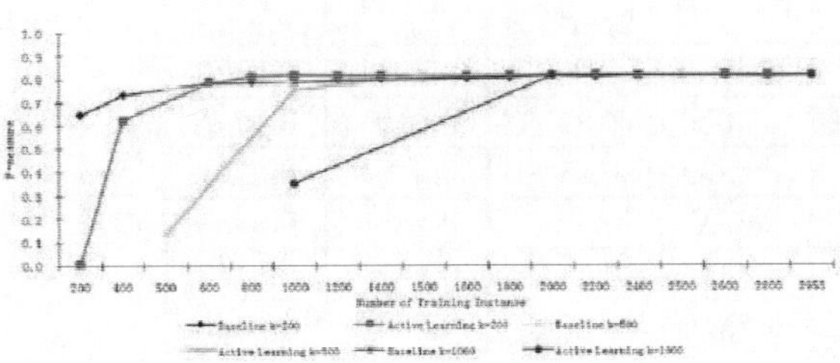

Figure 3 Sentiment Identification

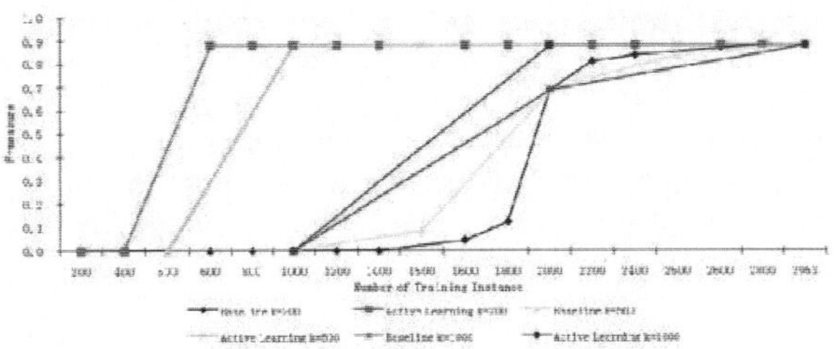

Figure 4 Holder Identification

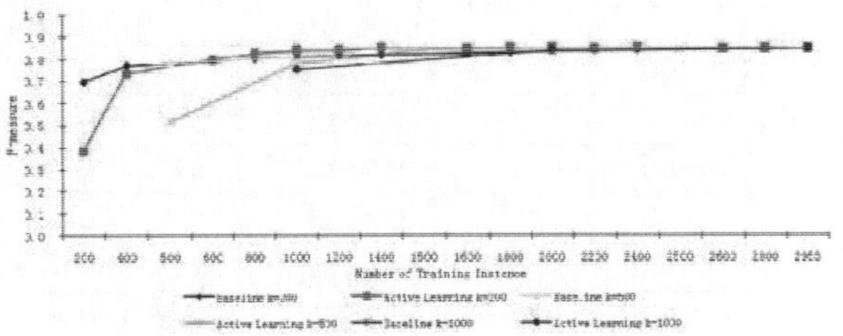

Figure 5 All Opinion Elements Identification

As are illustrated in the figures, the active learning system can always achieve better or at least no worse performance than baseline system. For example, when adding 200 instances in each round for topic identification task (Figure2 and Table 4), the active learning system reaches its peak value in F-measure (0.8644) with only 600 training instances. This F-measure value is even higher than the value the baseline system get (0.8604) after taking all the 2953 training instances.

The active learning system outperforms the baseline system greatly especially when dealing with unbalanced data set (Figure 4 and Table 4). In opinion holder identification task, the baseline system can not find any holder until 1600 training instances are taken while the active learning system reaches its peak F-measure value (0.8810) with only 600 training instances. That means when using active learning algorithm, it is possible for us to save some time for optimizing the parameters when dealing with unbalanced data.

The number of instances added to the training data set in each round (*k*) influences the performance of the active learning algorithm in a large extent. When a smaller value is assigned to k, the active learning system will tend to achieve better F-measure (Table 4) with less training instances comparing to the baseline system. Advantages of the active learning system will be diminished by the increase in k (Table 6).

4 Evaluation of Active Learning Algorithm

For active learning algorithm based on membership query, its training process will probably take longer time by the time the optimum classier is found, since the training process consists of several rounds of iteration. At the beginning of the iteration, the classification speed of the model is much faster due to less training instances are used and the model is simple. With more and more training instances are added into the training data set, the model will become more complex and more time will be needed for classifica-

No. of Instances	Topic		Sentiment		Holder		All Three Elements	
	Baseline	Active Learning	Baseline	Active Learning	Baseline	Active Learning	Baseline	Active Learning
200	0.7118	0.6221	0.6481	0.0103	0.0000	0.0000	0.6968	0.3874
400	0.8072	0.8287	0.7344	0.6239	0.0000	0.0000	0.7691	0.7336
600	0.8237	**0.8644**	0.7845	0.7860	0.0000	**0.8810**	0.7907	0.7979
800	0.8250	0.8625	0.7876	0.8133	0.0000	0.8810	0.8020	0.8240
1000	0.8386	0.8613	0.7878	**0.8189**	0.0000	0.8810	0.8101	0.8378
1200	0.8389	0.8588	0.7992	0.8153	0.0000	0.8810	0.8128	0.8377
1400	0.8489	0.8588	0.8011	0.8141	0.0000	0.8810	0.8178	0.8471
1600	0.8450	0.8581	0.8033	0.8150	0.0426	0.8810	0.8211	0.8468
1800	0.8521	0.8581	0.8059	0.8183	0.1224	0.8810	0.8271	0.8479
2000	0.8528	0.8585	0.8169	0.8197	0.6857	0.8810	0.8348	**0.8481**
2200	0.8560	0.8583	0.8109	**0.8200**	0.8101	0.8810	0.8372	0.8468
2400	0.8592	0.8592	0.8186	0.8195	0.8395	0.8810	0.8404	0.8474
2600	0.8620	0.8610	0.8165	0.8205	0.8675	0.8810	0.8440	0.8463
2800	0.8578	0.8610	0.8138	0.8177	0.8810	0.8810	0.8464	0.8443
2953	**0.8604**	0.8604	**0.8183**	0.8183	**0.8810**	0.8810	**0.8446**	0.8446

Table 4 F-measure Trends when *k*=200

No. of Instances	Topic		Sentiment		Holder		All Three Elements	
	Baseline	Active Learning	Baseline	Active Learning	Baseline	Active Learning	Baseline	Active Learning
500	0.8198	0.7730	0.7616	0.1369	0.0000	0.0000	0.7831	0.5173
1000	0.8386	0.8508	0.7878	0.7566	0.0000	**0.8837**	0.8101	0.7776
1500	0.8468	0.8592	0.8039	0.8175	0.0833	0.8810	0.8194	0.8398
2000	0.8528	**0.8610**	0.8169	**0.8183**	0.6857	0.8810	0.8348	**0.8484**
2500	0.8626	0.8583	0.8168	0.8205	0.8395	0.8810	0.8427	0.8463
2953	**0.8604**	0.8604	**0.8183**	0.8183	**0.8810**	0.8810	**0.8446**	0.8446

Table 5 F-measure Trends when *k*=500

No. of Instances	Topic		Sentiment		Holder		All Three Elements	
	Baseline	Active Learning	Baseline	Active Learning	Baseline	Active Learning	Baseline	Active Learning
1000	0.8386	0.8335	0.7878	0.3514	0.0000	0.0000	0.8101	0.7534
2000	0.8528	0.8581	0.8169	0.8170	0.6857	**0.8810**	0.8348	0.8376
2953	**0.8604**	**0.8604**	**0.8183**	**0.8183**	**0.8810**	0.8810	**0.8446**	**0.8446**

Table 6 F-measure Trends when *k*=1000

tion. On account of the features of active learning algorithm, we believe it is necessary to find a way to balance the performance of the classifier and the time it take in training process for a thorough evaluation of the algorithm.

We define the measurement for time as:

$$T = \frac{k}{C} \tag{4}$$

where C is the number of all the possible training instances available, k is the number of training instances added into the training data set in each round of iteration. T is the approximate value of the inverse ratio of the time it takes for training process. T will have a greater value if the training process takes less time. Its range is (0, 1] just similar to F-measure.

We define the measurement for the training instances used as:

$$K = (1 - \frac{n}{C}) \tag{5}$$

where n is the number of the training instances actually used. K will have a greater value if less training instances are used in the training process. The range of K is [0, 1).

To judge the overall performance of an active learning algorithm, we consider the F-measure (F) of the classifier, the time it takes during the training process, and the training instances used. We define the Active Learning Performance (*ALP*) as the harmonic mean of the three aspects:

$$ALP = \frac{1}{\frac{\alpha}{K} + \frac{\beta}{F} + \frac{\gamma}{T}} = \frac{F \cdot k \cdot (C-n)}{\alpha \cdot F \cdot C \cdot k + \beta \cdot k(C-n) + \gamma \cdot F \cdot C(C-n)} \tag{6}$$

where $\alpha+\beta+\gamma=1$, and $\alpha, \beta, \gamma \in [0,1]$. They are the weights for the three measurements. The greater the value of a certain weight is, the more important the measurement is in the overall performance. The greater the value of the *ALP* is, the better the performance of the active learning algorithm. For instance, when training a classifier for sentiment identification using active learning algorithm, we get a classifier with F-measure of 0.8189 using 1000 training instances and a classifier with F-measure of 0.8200 using 2200 training instances (Table 4). Suppose $\alpha=\beta=\gamma=\frac{1}{3}$, we calculate the value of *ALP* for the two cases according to equation (6) and get 0.1714 and 0.1507 as results respectively. That means a people with no preference among F-measure, the number of training instances adopted and the time used during training process will choose to get a classifier with less training instances, less training time and less F-measure value.

5 Conclusion

This paper experimentally demonstrates the validity of active learning algorithm when used for opinioned elements identification and proposed a computational method for overall system performance evaluation which consists of F-measure, training time, and number of training instances. According to our tests, active learning algorithm outperforms the base line system in most of the cases especially when fewer instances are added into the training data set in each round of iteration. However, the method could extent the training time in a large scale. To balance the pros and cons of active learning algorithm, it might be helpful to adjust the number of training instances added in each round dynamically in the training process. For instance, add less training instances at the beginning of the training process to ensure a high peak value of F-measure could be achieved and add more training instances later so that time spent on training process could be reduced.

Acknowledgments

The author of this paper would like to thank Information Retrieval Lab, Harbin Institute of Technology for providing the tool (LTP) used in experiments. This research was supported by National Natural Science Foundation of China Grant No.60773087.

References

Andrew K. McCallum, Kamal Nigam. 1998. Employing EM in Pool-based Active Learning for Text Classification. In Proceedings of *the 15th International Conference on Machine Learning.*

Bernhard E. Boser, Isabelle M. Guyon, and Vladimir N. Vapnik. 1992. A Training Algorithm for Optimal Margin Classifiers. In Proceedings of *the Fifth*

Annual Workshop on Computational Learning Theory.

Chih-Chung Chang and Chih-Jen Lin. 2001. LIBSVM: a library for support vector machines. Software available at http://www.csie.ntu.edu.tw/~cjlin/ libsvm

Chih-Wei Hsu and Chih-Jen Lin. 2002. A Comparison of Methods for Multi-class Support Vector Machines. *IEEE Transactions on Neural Networks.*

Claude Sammut and Ranan B. Banerji. 1986. Learning Concepts by Asking Questions. *Machine Learning: An Artificial Intelligence Approach,* 1986, 2: 167-191

Dana Angluin. 1988. Queries and Concept Learning. *Machine Learning*, 1988, 2(4): 319-342

David D. Lewis, William A. Gail. 1994. A Sequential Algorithm for Training Text Classifiers. In Proceedings of *the 17th Annual International ACM SIGIR Conference on Research and Development in Information Retrieval.*

Ehud Y. Shapiro. 1982. *Algorithmic Program Debugging*. M.I.T. Press.

Ido Dagan, Sean P. Engelson. 1995. Committee-Based Sampling for Training Probabilistic Classifiers. In Proceedings of *the International Conference on Machine Learning.*

Ion Muslea, Steven Minton, Craig A. Knoblock. 2006. Active Learning with Multiple Views. *Journal of Artificial Intelligence Research*, 2006, 27(1): 203-233.

Quansheng Liu, Tianfang Yao, Gaohui Huang, Jun Liu, Hongyan Song. 2008. A Survey of Opinion Mining for Texts. *Journal of Chinese Information Processing*. 2008, 22(6):63-68.

Jun Long, Jianping Yin, En Zhu, and Wentao Zhao. A Survey of Active Learning. 2008. *Journal of Computer Research and Development*, 2008, 45(z1): 300-304.

Shlomo A. Engelson, Ido Dagon. 1999. Committee-based Sample Selection for Probabilistic Classifiers. *Journal of Artificial Intelligence Research*, 1999, 11: 335-360.

Hongyan Song, Jun Liu, Tianfang Yao, Quansheng Liu, Gaohui Huang. 2009. Construction of an Annotated Corpus for Chinese Opinioned-Subjective Texts. *Journal of Chinese Information Processing*, 2009, 23(2): 123-128.

Hongyan Song and Tianfang Yao. 2009. Improving Chinese Topic Extraction Using Word Sense Disambiguation Information. In Proceedings of *the 4th International Conference on Innovative Computing, Information and Control.*

Soo-Min Kim and Eduard Hovy. 2004. Determining the Sentiment of Opinions. In Proceedings of *the Conference on Computational Linguistics*: 1367-1373.

Tianfang Yao, Xiwen Cheng, Feiyu Xu, Hans Uszkoreit, and Rui Wang. 2008. A Survey of Opinion Mining for Texts. *Journal of Chinese Information Processing*, 2008, 22(3): 71-80.

Vladimir N. Vapnik. 1995. The Nature of Statistical Learning Theory. Springer.

Yoav Freund, H.Sebastian Seung, Eli Shamir, Naftali Tishby. 1997. Selective Sampling Using the Query by Committee Algorithm. *Machine Learning*, 28(2-3): 133-168

Zhendong Dong and Qiang Dong. 1999. HowNet. http://www.keenage.com

Improving Chinese Word Segmentation by Adopting Self-Organized Maps of Character N-gram

Chongyang Zhang
iFLYTEK Research
cyzhang@iflytek.com

Zhigang Chen
iFLYTEK Research
zgchen@iflytek.com

Guoping Hu
iFLYTEK Research
gphu@iflytek.com

Abstract

Character-based tagging method has achieved great success in Chinese Word Segmentation (CWS). This paper proposes a new approach to improve the CWS tagging accuracy by combining Self-Organizing Map (SOM) with structured support vector machine (SVM) for utilization of enormous unlabeled text corpus. First, character N-grams are clustered and mapped into a low-dimensional space by adopting SOM algorithm. Two different maps are built based on the N-gram's preceding and succeeding context respectively. Then new features are extracted from these maps and integrated into the structured SVM methods for CWS. Experimental results on Bakeoff-2005 database show that SOM-based features can contribute more than 7% relative error reduction, and the structured SVM method for CWS proposed in this paper also outperforms traditional conditional random field (CRF) method.

1 Introduction

It is well known that there is no space or any other separators to indicate the word boundary in Chinese. But word is the basic unit for most of Chinese natural language process tasks, such as Machine Translation, Information Extraction, Text Categorization and so on. As a result, Chinese word segmentation (CWS) becomes one of the most fundamental technologies in Chinese natural language process.

In the last decade, many statistics-based methods for automatic CWS have been proposed with development of machine learning and statistical method (Huang and Zhao, 2007). Especially, the character-based tagging method which was proposed by Nianwen Xue (2003) achieves great success in the second International Chinese word segmentation Bakeoff in 2005 (Low et al., 2005). The character-based tagging method formulates the CWS problem as a task of predicting a tag for each character in the sentence, i.e. every character is considered as one of four different types in 4-tag set: B (begin of word), M (middle of word), E (end of word), and S (single-character word).

Most of these works train tagging models only on limited labeled training sets, without using any unsupervised learning outcomes from innumerous unlabeled text. But in recent years, researchers begin to exploit the value of enormous unlabeled corpus for CWS. Some statistics information on co-occurrence of sub-sequences in the whole text has been extracted from unlabeled data and been employed as input features for tagging model training (Zhao and Kit , 2007).

Word clustering is a common method to utilize unlabeled corpus in language processing research to enhance the generalization ability, such as part-of-speech clustering and semantic clustering (Lee et al., 1999 and B Wang and H Wang 2006). Character-based tagging method usually employs N-gram features, where an N-gram is an N-character segment of a string. We believe that there are also semantic or grammatical relationships between most of N-grams and these relationships will be useful in CWS. Intuitively, assuming the training data contains the bigram "色/列"(The last two characters of the word "Israel" in Chinese), not contain the bigram "耳/其"(The last two characters of the word "Turkey" in Chinese), if we could cluster the two bigrams together according to unlabeled corpus and employ it as a feature for supervised training of tagging model, maybe we will know that there should be a word boundary after "耳/其" though we only find the existence of word boundary after "色/列" in the training data. So we investigate how to apply clustering method onto unlabeled data for the purpose of improving CWS accuracy in this paper.

This paper proposes a novel method of using unlabeled data for CWS, which employs Self-Organizing Map (SOM) (Kohonen 1982) to organize Chinese character N-grams on a two-dimensional array, named as "N-gram cluster map" (NGCM), in which the character N-grams similar in grammatical structure and semantic meaning are organized in the same or adjacent position. Two different arrays are built based on the N-gram's preceding context and succeeding context respectively because sometimes N-gram is just a part of Chinese word and does not share similar preceding and succeeding context in the same time. Then NGCM-based features are extracted and applied to tagging model of CWS. Two tagging models are investigated, which are structured support vector machine (SVM) (Tsochantaridis et al., 2005) model and Confidential Random Fields (CRF) (Lafferty et al., 2001). The experimental results show that NGCM is really helpful to CWS. In addition, we find that the structured SVM achieves better performance than CRF.

The rest of this paper is organized as follows: Section 2 presents self-organizing map and the idea of N-gram cluster maps. Section 3 describes structured SVM and how to use the NGCMs based features in CWS. Section 4 shows experimental results on Bakeoff-2005 database and Section 5 gives our conclusion.

2 N-gram cluster maps

Supervised learning method for CWS needs enough pre-labeled corpus with word boundary information for training. The final CWS performance relies heavily on the quality of the training data. The training data is limited and cannot cover completely the linguistic phenomenon. But unlabeled corpus can be obtained easily from internet. One intuitive method is to extract information from unsupervised learning results from enormous unlabeled data to enhance supervised learning.

2.1 Self-Organizing Map

The Self-Organizing Map (SOM) (Kohonen 1982), sometimes called Kohonen map, was developed by Teuvo Kohonen in the early 1980s. Different from other clustering method, SOM is a type of artificial neural network on the basis of competitive learning to visualize higher dimensional data in a low-dimensional space (usually 1D or 2D) while preserving the topological properties of the input space. Figure 1 displays a 2D SOM.

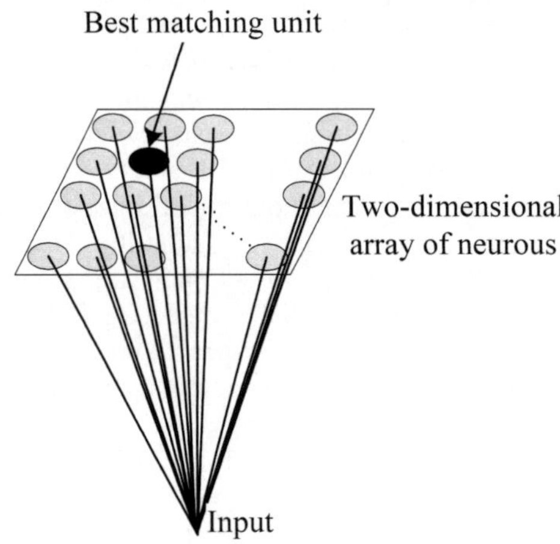

Figure 1: SOM model

In SOM, the input is a lot of data samples, and each sample is represented as a vector $x_i, i = 1,2,...,M$, where M is the number of the input vectors. SOM will cluster all these samples into L neurons, and each neuron is associated with a weight vector $w_i, i = 1,2,...,L$, where L is the total number of the neurons. w_j is of the same dimensions as the input data vectors x_i. The learning algorithm of SOM is as follows:

1. Randomize every neuron's weight vector w_i ;
2. Randomly select an input vector x_t ;

3. Find the winning neuron j, whose associate weight vector w_j has the minimal distance to x_t;
4. Update the weight vector of all the neurons according to the following formula:

   $w_i \leftarrow w_i + \eta\phi(i,j)(x_t - w_i)$

   Where η is the learning-rate and $\phi(i,j)$ is the neighborhood function. A simple choice defines $\phi(i,j)=1$ for all neuron i in a neighborhood of radius r of neuron j and $\phi(i,j)=0$ for all other neurons. η and $\phi(i,j)$ usually varied dynamically during learning for best results;
5. Continue step 2 until maximum number of iterations has been reached or no noticeable changes are observed.

2.2 SOM-based N-gram cluster maps

Self-organizing semantic maps (Ritter and Kohonen 1989, 1990) are SOMs that have been organized according to word similarities, measured by the similarity of the short contexts of the words. Our algorithm of building N-gram cluster maps is similar to self-organizing semantic maps. Because sometimes N-gram is just part of Chinese word and do not share similar preceding and succeeding context in the same time, so we build two different maps according to the preceding context and the succeeding context of N-gram individually. In the end we build two NGCMs: NGCMP (NGCM according to preceding context) and NGCMS (NGCM according to succeeding context).

In this paper we only consider bigram cluster maps. So our purpose is to acquire a 2GCMP and a 2GCMS. The large-scale unlabeled corpus we used for training NGCMs is about 3.5G in size. It was obtained easily from websites like Sohu, Netease, Sina and People Daily. When the cut-off threshold is set to 5, we got about 9K different characters and 380K different bigrams by counting the corpus. For each bigram, a 9K-dimensional sparse vector can be derived from the preceding character of the bigram. Therefore a collection of 380K vector samples are generated, which is denoted as P. Another vector collection S which considers succeeding character was obtained using the same method.

Our implementation used SOM-PAK package Version 1.0 (Kohonen et al., 1996). We set the topology type to rectangular and the map size to 15×15. In the training process, we used P and S as input data respectively. After the training we acquired a 2GCMP and a 2GCMS, meanwhile each bigram was mapped to one neuron. Because the number of neurons is much smaller than the number of bigrams, each neuron in the map was labeled with multiple bigrams. The 2GCMP and 2GCMS are shown in Figure 2 and Figure 3 respectively. The comment boxes in the figures show some samples of bigrams mapped in the same neuron.

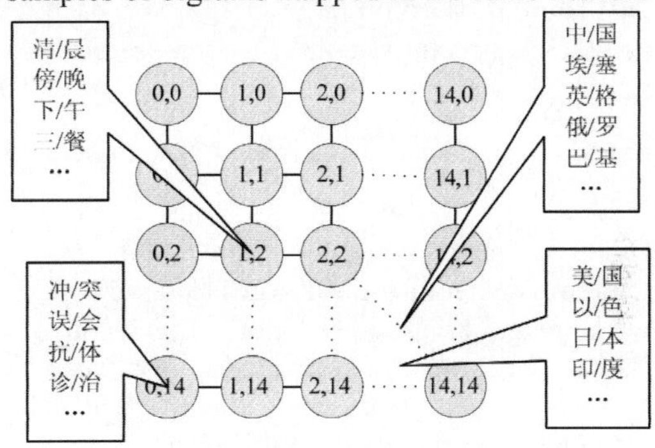

Figure 2: 2GCMP

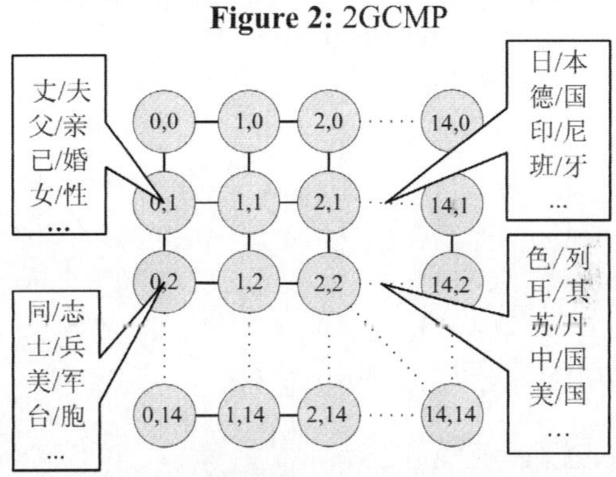

Figure 3: 2GCMS

After checking the results, we find that most of the meaningless bigrams that contain characters from more than one word, such as the bigram "京天" in "...北京天坛...", are organized into the same neurons in the map, and most of the first or last bigrams of the country names are organized into a few adjacent neurons, such as "色/列", "耳/其", "中/国" and "美/国"in 2GCMS, "巴/基", "埃/塞", "英/格", "俄/罗", and "中/国" in 2GCMP. We also tried to use the preceding and the succeeding context together in NGCM training just like the method used in the self-organizing semantic maps. We found that the bigrams of "巴/基", "埃/塞" and "俄/罗" will never be assigned to the same neuron again, which indicates that we need to build two NGCMs according to preceding and succeeding context separately.

3 Integrate NGCM into Structured SVM for CWS

3.1 Structured support vector machine

The structured support vector machine can learn to predict structured y, such as trees sequences or sets, from x based on large-margin approach. We employ a structured SVM that can predict a sequence of labels $y=(y^1,...,y^T)$ for a given observation sequence $x=(x^1,...,x^T)$, where $y^t \in \Sigma$, Σ is the label set for y.

There are two types of features in the structured SVM: transition features (interactions between neighboring labels along the chain), emission features (interactions between attributes of the observation vectors and a specific label).we can represent the input-output pairs via joint feature map (JFM)

$$\psi(x,y)=\begin{pmatrix} \sum_{t=1}^{T}\phi(x^t)\otimes\Lambda^c(y^t) \\ \eta\sum_{t=1}^{T-1}\Lambda^c(y^t)\otimes\Lambda^c(y^{t+1}) \end{pmatrix}$$

where

$\Lambda^c(y)\equiv(\delta(y_1,y),\delta(y_2,y),...,\delta(y_K,y))'$

$\in\{0,1\}^K$, $y\in\{y_1,y_2,...,y_K\}=\Sigma$

Kronecker delta δ ,$\delta_{i,j}=\begin{cases}1,i=j\\0,i\neq j\end{cases}$

$\phi(x)$ denotes an arbitrary feature representation of the inputs. The sign "$\otimes$" expresses tensor product defined as $\otimes$: $R^d\times R^k\rightarrow R^{dk}$, $[a\otimes b]_{i+(j-1)d}=[a]_i[b]_j$. T is the length of an observation sequence. $\eta\geq 0$ is a scaling factor which balances the two types of contributions.

Note that both transition features and emission features can be extended by including higher-order interdependencies of labels (e.g. $\Lambda^c(y^t)\otimes\Lambda^c(y^{t+1})\otimes\Lambda^c(y^{t+2})$),by including input features from a window centered at the current position (e.g. replacing $\phi(x^t)$ with $\phi(x^{t-r},...,x^t,...x^{t+r})$)or by combining higher-order output features with input features (e.g. $\sum_t\phi(x^t)\otimes\Lambda^c(y^t)\otimes\Lambda^c(y^{t+1})$)

The w-parametrized discriminant function $F: X\times Y\rightarrow R$ interpreted as measuring the compatibility of x and y is defined as:

$$F(x,y;w)=\langle w,\psi(x,y)\rangle$$

So we can maximize this function over the response variable to make a prediction

$$f(x)=\arg\max_{y\in Y} F(x,y,w)$$

Training the parameters can be formulated as the following optimization problem.

$$\min_{w,\xi}\frac{1}{2}\langle w,w\rangle+\frac{C}{n}\sum_{i=1}^{n}\xi_i$$

$$s.t.\forall i,\forall y\in Y:$$

$$\langle w,\psi_i(x_i,y_i)-\psi_i(x_i,y)\rangle\geq\Delta(y_i,y)-\xi_i$$

where n is the number of the training samples, ξ_i is a slack variable , $C\geq 0$ is a constant controlling the tradeoff between training error minimization and margin maximization, $\Delta(y^1,y)$ is the loss function ,usually the number of misclassified tags in the sentence.

3.2 Features set for tagging model

For a training sample denoted as $x=(x^1,...,x^T)$ and $y=(y^1,...,y^T)$. We chose first-order interdependencies of labels to be transition features, and dependencies between labels and N-grams (n=1, 2, 3) at current position in observed input sequence to be emission features.

So our JFM is the concatenation of the follow vectors

$$\sum_{t=1}^{T-1}\Lambda^c(y^t)\otimes\Lambda^c(y^{t+1}),$$

$$\sum_{t=1}^{T}\phi(x^{t+m})\otimes\Lambda^c(y^t), m\in\{-1,0,1\}$$

$$\sum_{t=1}^{T}\phi(x^{t+m},x^{t+m+1})\otimes\Lambda^c(y^t), m\in\{-2,-1,0,1\}$$

$$\sum_{t=1}^{T}\phi(x^{t+m-1},x^{t+m},x^{t+m+1})\otimes\Lambda^c(y^t), m\in\{-1,0,1\}$$

Figure 4 shows the transition features and the

emission features of N-grams (n=1, 2) at y_3. The emission features of 3-grams are not shown here because of the large number of the interactions.

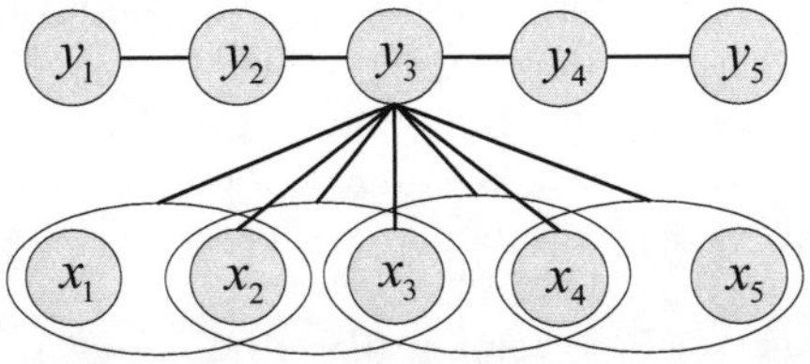

Figure 4: the transition features and the emission features at y_3 for structured SVM

3.3 Using NGCM in CWS

Two methods can be used for extracting the features from NGCMs to expend features definition in section 3.2.

One method is to treat NGCM just as a clustering tool and do not take into account the similarity between adjacent neurons. So a new feature with L dimensions can be generated, where L is the number of the neurons or classes. Only one value of the L dimension equals to 1 and others equal to 0. We call it NGCM *clustering* feature.

Another way of using the NGCM is to adopt the position of the neurons which current N-gram mapped in the NGCM as a new feature. So every feature has D dimensions (D equals to the dimension of the NGCM, every dimension is corresponding to the coordinate value in the NGCM). In this way, N-gram which is originally represented as a high dimensional vector based on its context is mapped into a very low-dimensional space. We call it NGCM *mapping* feature.

In this paper, we only consider the NGCM clustering or mapping features related to the current label y_i. We also extract features from the quantization error of current N-gram because the result of the NGCM is very noisy. Then our previous JFM in section 3.2 is concatenated with the following features:

$$\sum_{t=1}^{T} \varphi^{2\text{GCMS}}(x^{t+m}, x^{t+m+1}) \otimes \Lambda^c(y^t), m \in \{-2,-1\}$$

$$\sum_{t=1}^{T} \varphi^{2\text{GCMP}}(x^{t+m}, x^{t+m+1}) \otimes \Lambda^c(y^t), m \in \{0,1\}$$

$$\sum_{t=1}^{T} \eta^{2\text{GCMS}}(x^{t+m}, x^{t+m+1}) \otimes \Lambda^c(y^t), m \in \{-2,-1\}$$

$$\sum_{t=1}^{T} \eta^{2\text{GCMP}}(x^{t+m} x^{t+m+1}) \otimes \Lambda^c(y^t), m \in \{0,1\}$$

where $\varphi^{2\text{GCMS}}(x)$ denotes the NGCM feature from 2GCMS, $\varphi^{2\text{GCMP}}(x)$ denotes the NGCM feature from 2GCMP. $\eta^{\text{NGCM}}(x)$ denotes the quantization error of current N-gram x on its NGCM.

In 15×15 size NGCM, when we use the NGCM clustering feature $\varphi^{2\text{GCMS}}(x)$ and $\varphi^{2\text{GCMP}}(x) \in \{0,1\}^{15\times15}$. When we use the NGCM mapping feature $\varphi^{2\text{GCMS}}(x)$ and $\varphi^{2\text{GCMP}}(x) \in \{0,1,...,14\}^2$. Notice that the dimension of the NGCM clustering feature is much higher than the NGCM mapping feature.

As an example, the process of import features from NGCMs at y_3 is presented in Figure 5.

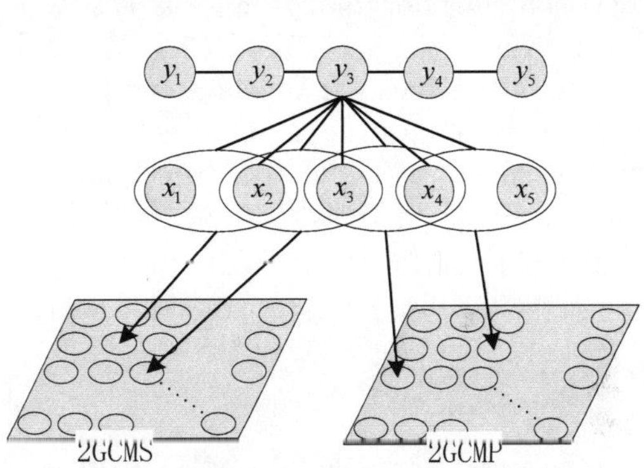

Figure 5: Using 2GCMS and 2GCMP as input to structured SVM

4 Applications and Experiments

4.1 Corpus

We use the data adopted by the second International Chinese Word Segmentation Bakeoff (Bakeoff-2005). The corpus size information is listed in Table 1.

Corpus	As	CityU	MSRA	PKU
Training(M)	5.45	1.46	2.37	1.1
Test(K)	122	41	107	104

Table 1: Corpus size of Bakeoff-2005 in number of words

4.2 Text Preprocessing

Text is usually mixed up with numerical or alphabetic characters in Chinese natural language, such as "我在 office 上班到晚上 9 点". These numerical or alphabetic characters are barely segmented in CWS. Hence, we treat these symbols as a whole "character" according to the following two preprocessing steps. First replace one alphabetic character to four continuous alphabetic characters with E1 to E4 respectively, five or more alphabetic characters with E5. Then replace one numerical number to four numerical numbers with N1 to N4 and five or more numerical numbers with N5. After text preprocessing, the above examples will be "我在 E5 上班到晚上 N1 点".

4.3 Character-based tagging method for CWS

Previous works show that 6-tag set achieved a better CWS performance (Zhao et al., 2006). Thus, we opt for this tag set. This 6-tag set adds 'B2' and 'B3' to 4-tag set which stand for the type of the second and the third character in a Chinese word respectively. For example, the tag sequence for the sentence "上海世博会/将/持续/半年(Shanghai World Expo / will / last / six months)" will be "B B2 B3 M E S B E B E".

4.4 Experiments

The F-measure is employed for evaluation, which is defined as follows:

$$\text{Precision: } P = \frac{\text{num of correctly segmented words}}{\text{num of the system output words}}$$

$$\text{Recall: } R = \frac{\text{num of correctly segmented words}}{\text{num of total words in test data}}$$

$$\text{F-measure: } F = \frac{2 \times P \times R}{P + R}$$

To compare with other discriminative learning methods we first developed a baseline system using conditional random field (CRF) without using NGCM feature and then we developed another CRF system: CFCRF (using NGCM clustering features). In the end we developed three structured SVM CWS systems: SVM (without using NGCM features), CFSVM (using NGCM clustering features), and MFSVM (using NGCM mapping features). The features for the baseline CRF system are the same with the SVM system. The features for CFCRF are the same with CFSVM. The result of the CRF system using NGCM mapping features cannot be given here, because it is difficult to support continuous-value features for CRF method which is based on the Maximum Entropy Model.

We use CRF++ version 0.5 (Kudu, 2009) to build our CRF models. The cut-off threshold is set to 2(using the features that occurs no less than 2 times in the given training data) and the hyper-parameter is set to 4.5. We use svm^{hmm} version 3.1 to build our structured SVM models. The cut-off threshold is set to 2. The precision parameter is set to 0.1. The tradeoff between training error minimization and margin maximization is set to 1000.

The comparisons between CRF, CFCRF, SVM, CFSVM and MFSVM are shown in Table 2.

Corpus		As	CityU	MSRA	PKU
CRF baseline	P	0.945	0.943	0.971	0.953
	R	0.955	0.942	0.970	0.946
	F	0.950	0.942	0.971	0.950
CFCRF	P	0.948	0.956	0.973	0.959
	R	0.959	0.961	0.972	0.952
	F	0.953	0.958	0.973	0.955
SVM	P	0.949	0.957	0.972	0.953
	R	0.959	0.959	0.972	0.946
	F	0.954	0.958	0.972	0.950
CFSVM	P	0.952	0.959	0.974	0.958
	R	0.960	0.964	0.974	0.952
	F	**0.956**	**0.961**	**0.974**	**0.955**
MFSVM	P	0.950	0.957	0.974	0.958
	R	0.961	0.963	0.974	0.951
	F	**0.956**	0.960	**0.974**	0.954

Table 2: The results of our systems

4.5 Discussion

From Table 2, we can see that:

1) The NGCM feature is useful for CWS. The feature achieves 13.9% relative error reduction on CRF method and 7.2% relative error reduction on structured SVM method;
2) CFSVM and MFSVM achieve similar performance, differ from the expectation of MFSVM should be better than CFSVM. We think that this is because the size of 2GCMs is too small. Due to the limitation of our

computer and time we only get two 15×15 size 2GCMs, similarity between adjacent neurons on the two small 2GCMs is very week, NGCM cluster feature performs as good as NGCM mapping feature on CWS. But due to the dimensions of the NGCM cluster feature is much larger than the NGCM mapping feature, the training time of the CFSVM is much longer than the MFSVM;

3) It is obvious that structured SVM performs better than CRF, demonstrating the benefit of large margin approach.

5 Conclusion

This paper proposes an approach to improve CWS tagging accuracy by combining SOM with structured SVM. We use SOM to organize Chinese character N-grams on a two-dimensional array, so that the N-grams similar in grammatical structure and semantic meaning are organized in the same or adjacent position. Two different maps are built based on the N-gram's preceding and succeeding context respectively. Then new features are extracted from these maps and integrated into the structured SVM methods for CWS. Experimental results on Bakeoff-2005 database show that SOM-based features can contribute more than 7% relative error reduction, and the structured SVM method for CWS, to our knowledge, first proposed in this paper also outperforms traditional CRF method.

In future work, we will try to organizing all the N-grams on a much larger array, so that every neuron will be labeled by a single N-gram. Our ultimate objective is to reduce the dimension of input features for supervised CWS learning , such as structured SVM , by replacing N-gram features with two-dimensional NGCM mapping features in most of Chinese natural language process tasks.

References

B.Wang, H.Wang 2006.*A Comparative Study on Chinese Word Clustering. Computer Processing of Oriental Languages.* Beyond the Orient: The Research Challenges Ahead, pages 157-164

Chang-Ning Huang and Hai Zhao. 2007. *Chinese word segmentation: A decade review.* Journal of Chinese Information Processing, 21(3):8–20.

Chung-Hong Lee & Hsin-Chang Yang.1999, *A Web Text Mining Approach Based on Self-Organizing Map*, ACM-library

G.Bakir, T.Hofmann, B.Scholkopf, A.Smola, B. Taskar, and S. V. N. Vishwanathan, editors. 2007 *Predicting Structured Data.* MIT Press, Cambridge, Massachusetts.

Hai Zhao, Chang-Ning Huang, Mu Li, and Bao-Liang Lu. 2006. *Effective tag set selection inChinese word segmentation via conditional random field modeling.* In Proceedings of PACLIC-20, pages 87–94. Wuhan, China.

Hai Zhao, Chang-Ning Huang, and Mu Li. 2006.*An improved Chinese word segmentation system with conditional random field.* In SIGHAN-5, pages 162–165, Sydney, Australia, July 22-23.

Hai Zhao and Chunyu Kit. 2007. *Incorporating global information into supervised learning for Chinese word segmentation.* In PACLING-2007, pages 66–74, Melbourne,Australia, September 19-21.

H.Ritter, and T.Kohonen, 1989. *Self-organizing semantic maps.* Biological Cybernetics, vol. 61, no. 4, pp. 241-254.

I.Tsochantaridis,T.Joachims,T.Hofmann,and Y.Altun. 2005. *Large Margin Methods for Structured and Interdependent Output Variables*, Journal of Machine Learning Research (JMLR), 6(Sep):1453-1484.

Jin Kiat Low, Hwee Tou Ng, and Wenyuan Guo.2005. *A maximum entropy approach to Chinese word segmentation.* In Proceedings of the Fourth SIGHAN Workshop on Chinese Language Processing, pages 161–164. Jeju Island,Korea.

J.Lafferty,A.McCallum, F.Pereira. 2001. *Conditional random fields: Probabilistic models for segmenting and labeling sequence data.* In Proceedings of the International Conference on Machine Learning (ICML). San Francisco: Morgan Kaufmann Publishers, 282−289.

Nianwen Xue and Susan P. Converse., 2002, *Combining Classifiers for Chinese Word Segmentation*, In Proceedings of First SIGHAN Workshop on Chinese Language Processing.

Nianwen Xue. 2003. *Chinese word segmentation as character tagging.* Computational Linguistics and Chinese Language Processing, 8(1):29–48.

R.Sproat and T.Emerson. 2003.*The first international Chinese word segmentation bakeoff.* In The Second SIGHAN Workshop on Chinese

Language Processing, pages 133–143.Sapporo, Japan.

S.Haykin, 1994. Neural Networks: *A Comprehensive Foundation*. NewYork: MacMillan.

T.Joachims, T.Finley, Chun-Nam Yu. 2009, *Cutting-Plane Training of Structural SVMs*, Machine Learning Journal,77(1):27-59.

T.Joachims. 2008 . svm^{hmm} *Sequence Tagging with Structural Support Vector Machines*, http://www.cs.cornell.edu/People/tj/svm_light/svm_hmm.html

T.Honkela, 1997. *Self-Organizing Maps in Natural Language Processing. PhD thesis, Helsinki University of Technology*, Department of Computer Science and Engineering, Laboratory of Computer and Information Science.

T.Kohonen. *1982.Self-organized formation of topologically correct feature maps*. Biological Cybernetics, 43, pp. 59-69.

T.Kohonen., J.Hynninen, J.Kangas, J.Laaksonen, 1996 ,*SOM_PAK: The Self-Organizing Map Program Package*,Technical Report A31, Helsinki University of Technology , http://www.cis.hut.fi/nnrc/nnrc-programs.html

T.Kudu.2009. CRF++: *Yet another CRF toolkit*.:http://crfpp.sourceforge.net/.

Y.Altun, I.Tsochantaridis, T.Hofmann. 2003. *Hidden Markov Support Vector Machines*. In Proceedings of International Conference on Machine Learning (ICML).

CMDMC: A Diachronic Digital Museum of Chinese Mandarin

Hou Min[1], **Zou Yu**[1], **Teng Yonglin**[1], **He Wei**[1]
Wang Yan[1,2], **Liu Jun**[1,2], and **Wu Jiyuan**[1,2]
[1]Broadcast Media Language Branch, National Language Resources Monitoring and Research Center at Communication University of China
[2]School of Literature, Communication University of China
Beijing 100024, China
{houmin, zouiy, tengyonglin, hewei}@cuc.edu.cn, forget1812@sina.com, {aaa_0119, wjy__00}@163.com

Abstract

Modern Chinese Mandarin has gone through near a hundred years, it is very important to store its representative sample in digital form permanently. In this paper, we propose a Chinese Mandarin Digital Multi-modal Corpus (CMDMC), which is a digital speech museum with diachronic, opened, cross-media and sharable features. It has over 3460 hours video and audio files with metadata tagging. The materials, which were generated by the authoritative speakers (e.g. announcers at TV or radio station) with normality, are required samples if we can get them. Based on this resource, we also intend to analyze the syntactic correlations of prosodic phrase in broadcasting news speech, and compare the phonetic and prosodic features in movie dialogues among several same-name movies in different historical eras.

1 Introduction

Modern Chinese Mandarin has gone through near a hundred years. As language changes as society develops, Mandarin must be periodically marked with the different features of different historical eras. It is very important to design and construct a Chinese Mandarin Digital Multi-modal Corpus (CMDMC), and store its representative sample in digital form permanently.

It's international trend to establish large-scale natural language corpus, and many countries pay more attention to research and preserve their national language. For instance, the Linguistic Data Consortium (LDC) is an open consortium of universities, companies and government research laboratories. It creates, collects and distributes speech and text databases, lexicons, and other resources for research and development purposes[1]. Since its foundation, the LDC has delivered data to 197 member institutions and 458 non-member institutions. Moreover, European Language Resources Association (ELRA)[2] is the driving force to make available the language resources for language engineering and to evaluate language engineering technologies. In order to achieve this goal, ELRA is active in identification, distribution, collection, validation, standardization, improvement, in promoting the production of language resources, in supporting the infrastructure to perform evaluation campaigns and in developing a scientific field of language resources and evaluation. In this paper, we intend to establish the CMDMC with the goal of showing the history of the development of Chinese Mandarin, and representation the real character in different historical eras.

The paper is organized as follows: Section 2 describes the resources and data processing of our CMDMC. The experiment and evaluation is designed and carried out in section 3. Section 4 is dedicated to analyze the syntactic correlations of prosodic phrase in broadcast news speech on CNR (China National Radio), and compare the

[1] The Linguistic Data Consortium (LDC), http://www.ldc.upenn.edu.

[2] European Language Resources Association (ELRA), http://www.elra.info/.

phonetic and prosodic features in movie dialogues. Finally, some conclusions and outlines of our future work are given in section 5.

2 General Description of CMDMC

In order to show the history of the development of Chinese Mandarin, and representation the real character in different historical periods, the CMDMC, which is a dynamic miniature model (or speech museum) with diachronic, opened, cross-media and sharable features, is designed and constructed by Broadcast Media Language Branch of National Language Resources Monitor & Research Center at Communication University of China.

In China, announcers in Radio & TV stations, as well as movie or stage actors, are the authority of the national language standardization. Therefore, the speech in radio, television and movie can be taken as the paradigm and representative of Mandarin. They can reflect the phonetic situation of that era. All of these are the source of the sample data for CMDMC.

2.1 Description of Resources

In order to fully demonstrate the development of Chinese Mandarin by the past 100 years, we try to collect all the video or audio materials in different periods. Therefore, a state-of-the-art classification is defined based on the corpora that we got.

Language styles: According to characteristic speaking styles of different media, there are three categories was defined, such as broadcast media language, movie or drama dialogue, and the dialogue in folk art (e.g. *xiangsheng, pingshu* etc.) and so on. To sum up, the three speaking styles accounted for about 64.9%, 27.2% and 7.9% of total corpora, respectively.

Mediums: The materials can be divided into audio, video, text and image/picture. The audio or video files are the main materials in our corpus, and the aligned texts are transcribed based on the audio or video. The documents of image are subsidiary corpora.

Historical eras: Based on the characteristics of social and language changes, we also define six historical stages of Chinese Mandarin: 1) Before1949 (or 1919-1949), it is a theoretical stage for corpora collection. In fact, the earliest speech materials, which we can collect, is released in 1932; 2) 1949-1965; 3) 1966-1977; 4) 1978-1989; 5) 1990-1999; 6) 2000 to today. Table 1 shows the distribution of detailed data in different eras.

Eras	Broadcast media (hours)	Movie /drama (hours)	Folk art (hours)	Percent of total (%)
1932-49		39.3		1.1
1949-65	5.2	191.4	20	6.2
1966-77	17.5	93.0		3.2
1978-89	52.4	145.9	75.5	7.9
1990-99	43.5	137.5	11.5	5.6
2000--	2131.5	337.0	167.1	76.0
Total	2250.1	944.1	274.1	

Table 1: The distribution of video and audio materials in different eras.

2.2 Data Processing

The data processing includes metadata tagging, text transcription and aligning, phonetic and prosodic annotation, POS and syntactic tagging and so on.

As for labeling prosodic phrase boundaries, we strictly dependent on the prosodic criteria and perception by using the wave files and their transcriptions, which use many prosodic features such as F0 contour, energy contour etc. At the same time, some spoken phenomena are considered.

3 Experiment and Evaluation

Firstly, in order to investigate the correlations between prosody and syntax, about 13 hours speech materials were selected to segment and label, including break index, stress index and summary of emotional tendentiousness etc. Before the real annotation, six transcribers have been trained in accordance with the prosodic labeling conventions, until a high consistency of prosodic annotation can be carried out.

According to above experiment and annotation, the number of occurrences of the various boundaries was calculated in table 2.

Secondly, we also designed a perception experiment to determine phonetic diversification for elimination as much as possible the subjectivity which could be caused by the different personal intuition of language. Ten people attended the perception experiment of this study: 3 men and 7 women. The average age is 25 years. Nearly all of them were graduates majoring in linguistics. During the experiment, the participants were asked to discriminate 12 paragraphs of random materials and judge the naturalness, pitch, and speech rate of the sentences produced in each paragraph. These 12 paragraphs consisted of 4 from 21 paragraphs of the 1995 version, 4 from 21 paragraphs of the 1975 version and 4 from modern materials.

Boundaries			
Types	Index	Marker	Frequency
PW	1	/1, /1+	55237
PP	2	/2	28867
C-PP	2	/2*	5976
IP	3	/3	7147
IG	4	/4	2781
MEC	5	/5	1770

Table 2: Distribution of all boundaries. The PW, PP, C-PP, IP, IG and MEC are the abbreviation of prosodic word, normal prosodic phrase, complex prosodic phrase, intonational phrase, intonational group and meaning expression cluster respectively.

In the perceptive procedure, we disordered all these materials for experiment, and three choices were given to these ten people: 1) natural, in conformity with the standard of modern Mandarin; 2) fairly natural, close to the standard of modern Mandarin; 3) unnatural, a little stagy. Every paragraph was released twice with an interval of 10 seconds. After one hour of continuous work, a 10-minute break was given.

Only the results with at least a 90% agreement rate were considered for analysis.

4 Related Works

Based on this resource, we intend to analyze the syntactic correlations of prosodic phrase in broadcasting news speech on CNR, and compare the phonetic and prosodic features in movie dialogues among several same-name movies in different historical eras.

4.1 Correlation between Syntax & Prosody

In English, there is a strong correlation between prosodic phrase boundaries and syntactic phrase boundaries (Price *et al.* 1991). That is to say, prosodic phrase boundaries can play an important role in understanding utterance as punctuation marks do in written language. An investigation propose that boundary strength according to the measure, which the boundary strength is applied to syntactic structures and the phrase structure is viewed as an immediate constituency tree exclusively, corresponds much more closely to empirical prosodic boundary strength than does syntactic boundary strength according to a standard measure (Abney, 1992). In Greek, some study indicated that prosodic phrasing has a 95% identification rate, and a major effect on final tonal boundaries (Botinis *et al.* 2004).

In Chinese, some researchers also proposed a statistical model to predict prosodic words from lexical words. In their model, both length of the word and the tagging from POS are two essential features to predict prosodic words, and the results showed approximately 90% of prediction for prosodic words (Chen *at el.* 2004).

What the correlation between syntax and prosody is in Chinese broadcasting news speech? In order to investigate the syntactic correlations of prosodic phrase in real read speech on radio, we chose the representative speech materials from *Xinwen he Baozhi Zhaiyao* (*News and Newspapers Summary*) from CMDMC, which is a very famous broadcast news program of CNR.

This news program contains more syntactic, semantic and prosodic information, speaking styles and high quality voice in real context. Therefore, 908 programs, which contain 454 hours speech data from January 2006 to June 2008, were selected for pre-processing. After the pre-processing step, we selected two female's 13 hours speech materials (one female announcer's material forms the main data, and another one's is supplemented for comparable data) as a core database, which segmentation, transcription and prosodic annotation (including break index, stress index and summary of emotional tendentiousness etc) was made by six transcribers.

According to the characteristic of broadcasting news speech, a new prosodic hierarchical structure (Zou *et al.* 2009) and two different types of prosodic phrase (i.e. the normal prosodic phrase and the complex prosodic phrase) boundaries were defined and used in our data labeling.

Categories	Location	Top pitch value			Bottom pitch value		
		N	SD	Mean	N	SD	Mean
PW	Left	3478	3.917	16.1	3253	4.761	8.5
	Right	3701	4.894	14.7	3165	5.457	9.9
PP	Left	1741	3.891	14.7	1718	4.302	6.2
	Right	627	3.481	16.5	492	5.077	9.3
C-PP	Left	314	4.085	13.5	317	4.135	4.8
	Right	361	3.616	17.9	285	5.092	10.0
IP	Left	536	4.817	12.9	456	5.575	3.9
	Right	531	3.019	18.8	473	3.720	13.8
IG	Left	211	4.363	11.4	203	6.055	4.7
	Right	229	2.377	19.4	185	2.927	15.0
MEC	Left	104	4.238	8.1	95	4.937	2.6
	Right	22	2.178	18.7	12	2.893	16.2

Table 3: The distribution of pitch on different boundaries. The phonetic acoustic data of each syllable was extracted by Praat script, and the foundational frequency was normalized by semitones, the normalization formula is $ST=12*log(F_0/F_{ref})/log2$ (the female's reference frequency is 100Hz). (*"top" is the mean of the highest pitch value at the first tone and the fourth tone; "bottom" is the mean of the lowest pitch value at the third tone and the fourth tone; "N" refers the number of samples; "SD" is the abbreviation of standard deviation*)

In the further step, we selected 100 minutes speech materials from core annotated data, and investigated its features of pitch and duration at boundary (Zou *et al.* 2010). The detailed data are shown in table 3 and 4 respectively.

Boundaries				
Types	**Marker**	**N**	**Mean**	**SD**
PW	/1 or/1+	118	65.2	61.714
PP	/2	659	97.6	84.140
C-PP	/2*	193	108.7	82.483
IP	/3	877	343.2	138.906
IG	/4	375	699.2	254.287
MEC	/5	31	771.0	208.580

Table 4: The mean of silent pause duration at boundaries.

There are two ways of representation to pitch feature at prosodic boundary: Firstly, the pitch contour is un-continuity; secondly, the pitch resetting of the declination contour (de Pijper *et al* 1994). According to Table 3, we can find that there is a few resetting of bottom pitch value at PW boundary, that is to say, the bottom of the PW boundary right is 1.4 semitones higher than that of its left. At other boundaries, the bottom pitch values at right side are much higher than that at left side, for instance, there is 3.1, 5.2, 9.9, 11.3 and 13.6 semitones resetting from PP to MEC boundary successively. Especially, at the IP boundary its resetting has about two times than that of C-PP boundary. This shows that there are very obvious prosodic feature at various boundaries in broadcasting news speech.

Generally, we know that 90ms is the floor of threshold for perceiving the silent pause. From Table 4, the mean of silent pause duration from long to short followed by MEC > IG > IP > C-PP > PP > PW. Except there is no perceived silent pause at PW boundary, the other boundaries have obvious silent pause that can be perceived. The length of silent pause at PP and C-PP are 97.6ms and 108.7ms respectively, and the length at IP has over three times longer than that at C-PP. According to this, we propose that the PP and C-PP lie in the same position at the prosodic hierarchical structure, and the C-PP is a special prosodic phrase.

From our core data we got 6728 C-PPs. According to the C-PP that contains the number of PW, we divided them into four categories, such as three-PW, four-PW, five-PW and six-PW. The distribution of them is shown in Table 5.

After preliminary analysis we found that the C-PP, which contains three PWs, has a simple syntactic structure although it is absolute majority in the number, and that is compose of four PWs should be done for correlations of prosody and syntax. There are about 6 types of prosodic structure if the C-PP contains four PWs. The detail data of this type C-PP followed in table 6.

From the data, we know that the fourth type, which is *(A+B) +(C+D)*, is the most, and that is composed by *(A+B) +C+D* is the least in all of the six types. Although there are just six types of prosodic structure that can be found, there are more than 985 syntactic categories in this 1835 C-PPs. There are 23 types which occur more than 10 times, and most of them occur only one time. To some extent, it can explain that the syntactic structure is more complex than the prosodic one.

An example of prosodic and syntactic structures in the utterance, which is *ou1 yang2 yu3 hang2 yi4 zhi1 shou3 jin3 jin0 bao4 zhu4 lou2 ti1 de0 lan2 gan1* (Ouyang Yuhang held fast to the staircase railing with one hand), is given in figure 1. The left side of figure is the prosodic structure, and the syntactic one lies at the right side.

In figure 1, there is a little difference of *jin3 jin0 bao4 zhu4 lou2 ti1 de0 lan2 gan1* (紧紧抱住楼梯的栏杆) between its prosodic structure "*A+(B+C+D)*" and its syntactic structure "[VP [VP *jin3jin0*/adv *bao4zhu4*/v] [NP [AP *lou2ti1*/n *de0*/u] [NP *lan2gan1*/n]]]", but the differences between its prosodic and syntactic structure are obvious because the *jin3 jin0* is stressed in speech for semantic expression.

Categories	Example	Num.
Three-PW	开展/1+ 互利/1 合作/2*	4433
Four-PW	第九次/1+ 全国/1 代表/1 大会/2*	1835
Five-PW	国际/1 市场/2 原油/1 期货/1 价格/2*	414
Six-PW	遭/1+ 不明/1 身份/2 武装/1 人员/2 袭击/2*	46
Total		6728

Table 5: The distribution of four kinds of C-PP

Types	Example	Num.	Percent (%)
A+(B+C)+D	与/1+ 不利/1 因素/2 并存/2*	441	24.03
A+(B+C+D)	分获/1+ 一/1 二/1 三等奖/2*	495	26.98
A+B+(C+D)	国家/1+ 著名/1+ 一级/1 演员/2*	97	5.29
(A+B)+(C+D)	将/1 上涨/2 一成/1 左右/2*	529	28.83
(A+B+C)+D	中国/1 民间/1 国宝/2 称号/2*	259	14.11
(A+B)+C+D	受/1 美股/2 大跌/2 拖累/2*	14	0.76
Total		1835	100

Table 6: The distribution of prosodic type in C-PP of four-PW

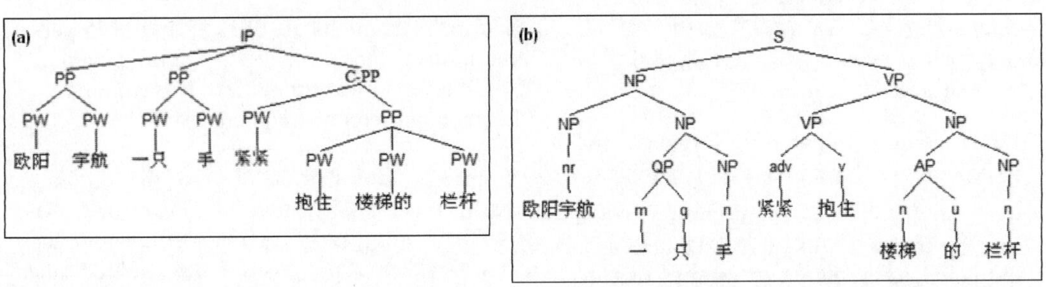

Figure 1: An example of (a) prosodic structure vs. (b) syntactic structure in an utterance: *ou1 yang2 yu3 hang2 yi4 zhi1 shou3 jin3 jin0 bao4 zhu4 lou2 ti1 de0 lan2 gan1* (Ouyang Yuhang held fast to the staircase railing with one hand).

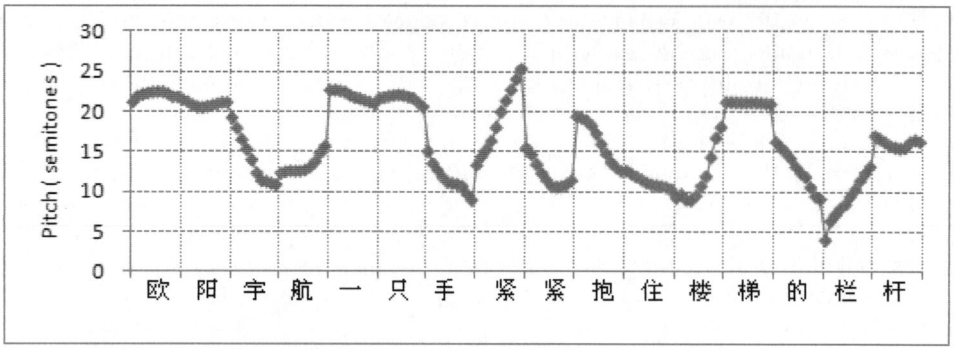

Figure 2: The pitch contour of the same utterance.

Figure 2 shows the pitch contour of the same utterance. In this utterance, there is a nesting structure at *jin3 jin0 bao4 zhu4 lou2 ti1 de0 lan2 gan1* (held fast to the staircase railing) based on the length of perceived silent pause. Furthermore, the pitch declination trend within the C-PP is obvious despite small resetting between *zhu4* and *lou2*. So we suggest that there is a stable prosodic pattern within a C-PP in broadcasting news speech.

Conversely, what is the correlation between the prosody and syntax? From above analysis, we know that the conjunction and particle, such as 的(*de0*), 等(*deng3*),和(*he2*), 但(*dan4*) and so on, more likely attached to the end of left structure or the beginning of right one and form a prosodic word. If it has just four lexical words including the conjunction or particle they form a prosodic word by itself. That is to say, it has very great flexibility in prosodic structures for conjunctions and particles, such as "占(*zhan4*)/1+ 全国(*quan2guo2*)/1 湿地(*shi1di4*)/1 面积的(*mian4ji1 de0*)/2* (*occupy/1+ country-wide/1everglade/1 acreage/2**)", "和(*he2*)/1 社会 (*she4hui4*)/2 救助 (*jiu4zhu4*)/1 制度 (*zhi4du4*)/2* (*and/1 social/2 assistance/1 system/2**)" and so on.

4.2 Diachronic Comparative Phonetic and Prosodic Analysis in Movie Dialogues

Which diachronic phonetic changes happened in Mandarin by the past 100 years? We also analyze and compare the phonetic features of Chinese Mandarin among several same-name movies in different historical eras from CMDMC (Wang *et al.* 2010). In order to minimize the divergence of the variables and maximize the reliability of conclusions, we chose two pairs of same-name movies screened in different historical periods. These movies are: *Pingyuan Youjidui* (*The Plains Guerrillas*) shot in 1955 and 1975, *Dujiang Zhencha Ji* (*Reconnaissance across the Yangtze River*) shot in 1954 and 1974 respectively.

Pitch Feature: In the analysis of pitch, we put aside the stresses and the neutral tone syllables, and make the statistical investigations on the top pitch value and the bottom pitch value of the syllables.

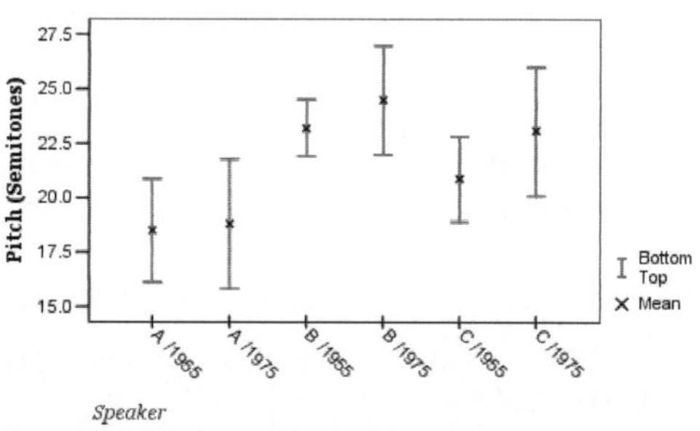

Figure 3: The pitch data of 1955 and 1975 version in *the Plains Guerrillas*. The fundamental frequency also was normalized by semitones; the male's reference frequency is 50Hz.

Figure 3 shows that the mean of the top pitch value in the 1950s' materials is lower than that of 1970s'. In the 1955 version, the leading character, Speaker A, possesses a mean value of the top pitch value which is 20.9 semitones. This value is lower than that of 1975s' by a difference of 0.9 semitones. The negative character, Speaker B, has a mean value of the top pitch value which is 24.5 semitones in the 1955 version. The value in the 1975 version is 27 semitones, with a difference of 2.5 semitones left, also showing that the value in the 1975 version is comparatively high. Comparing the data of the bottom pitch value in the 1955 version with that in the 1975 version, we know that these data seem closer than the top pitch value, but still the higher ones belong to the 1975 version. That the bottom pitch value is higher tells us that the whole pitch register is raised.

Furthermore, we can easily see from Figure 3 that the pitch range of the same character in the 1975 version is wider. Speaker A of the 1955 version has a pitch range of 4.8 semitones. In contrast, the same character in the 1975 version has a pitch range of 6 semitones. Speaker C of the 1955 version has 4 semitones pitch range, but in the 1975 version, he has 5.9 semitones pitch range. The gap between them is 1.9 semitones. Through this comparison, we find that the pitch range in the 1975 version is wider than that in the 1955 version in the whole.

To some extent, the speaking, both the top pitch value and the bottom pitch value in the 1975 version are higher. This proves that, on the whole, the pitch of the 1970s' materials is higher and more unnatural than that of 50s' because of the effect by the Cultural Revolution era. And this also proves the feeling of the participants in the perceptional experiment at section 3 about the 1970s' materials, that is, the 1970s' Mandarin has a loud and sonorous voice; the characters pronounce harder; the general pitch is higher.

Duration feature: In the respect of duration, we also compared and analyzed the presenters' speech on TV in 2005[3] with the materials extracted from the movie dialogues the 1955 and the 1975. Table 7 is the relevant data.

According to table 7, there is a little difference of the durations mean among them (following four tones), especially it's very closely between the 1975 and the 2005, and those of the 1975 version are a few longer than those of the 1955 version. But, except the first tone (Sig. =.077), the differences of the duration means between the others, which is in the 1955, the 1975 and the 2005, are significant (Sig. =.000, .000, .002<.05 respectively).

		mean	SD	N
Movie:1955	T1	153.6	69.5	243
	T2	136.8	58.1	242
	T3	132.8	58.7	321
	T4	133.5	52.0	539
Movie:1975	T1	177.8	72.1	258
	T2	155.5	52.0	263
	T3	152.5	57.6	289
	T4	156.7	59.9	505
TV: 2005	T1	163.1	65.7	1471
	T2	156.0	66.5	1743
	T3	156.8	67.6	1054
	T4	145.9	62.3	2652

Table 7: The duration mean of four tones in movie dialogues (1955 and 1975) vs. that of presenters' spoken language on TV in 2005(ms).

Demonstrations of the four-syllable prosodic words: The comparative pitch contour of two four-syllable prosodic words, which are "*bu2 yao4 lu4 mian4*" (don't appear) and "*gan4 shen2 me0 de0*" (What are you doing?), are shown in Figure 4 and 5, respectively.

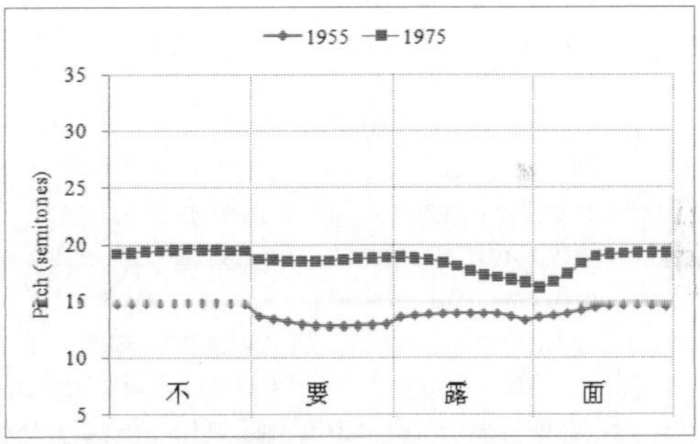

Figure 4: The pitch contour of "*bu2 yao4 lu4 mian4*" (don't appear)

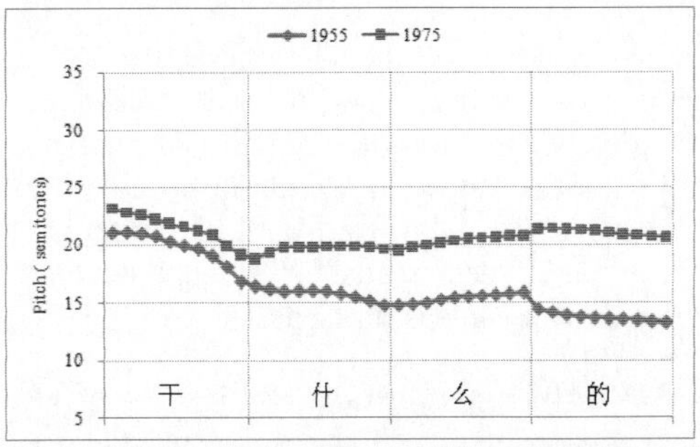

Figure 5: The pitch contour of "*gan4 shen2 me0 de0*" (What are you doing?)

[3] In this work, we just chose the male's speech data from Zou (2007).

By observing the above two figures, we find that the pitch contour of the 1975 and that of the 1955 are almost identical except the latter is always lower than the former. This may explain that although the Mandarin has gone through a hundred years, the pitch pattern is relatively stable.

5 Conclusions and Future Work

This paper proposes to design a Chinese Mandarin Digital Multi-modal Corpus (CMDMC). Through this corpus, the historical trace of Mandarin development can be followed; the fresh and alive data and material resources can be drawn up for the modern researchers and successors. We also intend to analyze the syntactic correlations of prosodic phrase in broadcasting news speech, and compare the phonetic and prosodic features in movie dialogues among several same-name movies in different historical eras. The contributions are as follows.

Firstly, the syntactic structure is more complex than the prosodic structure, some conjunction and particle, such as *de0, deng3, he2, dan4* and so on, more likely attached to the end of left structure or the beginning of right one and form a prosodic word, if the number of lexical words mismatch the prosodic words. Otherwise, they have almost similar structure.

Secondly, the speech of 1970s in last century is greatly influenced by the special era. People usually use exaggerated voice, pronounce hard and raise the pitch unnaturally, giving others a taste of lecturing and ordering. In contrast, the speech of Mandarin in 1950s is more natural and close to the daily life pronunciation and intonation. Even so, the pitch patterns have no big changes, and this may explain that the pitch patterns are comparatively stable in Chinese Mandarin.

Future research will include treatment of correlation between syntax and prosody within IP or IG, ideally comparing the diachronic phonetic or prosodic changes in Mandarin by the past 100 years. Additionally, we would like to tackle the problem of data management, update and periodical increasing as time passes.

6 Acknowledgements

This work was supported by the Department of Science and Technology at Ministry of Education (No. 107118), and "211" Key Projects of Communication University of China (No. 21103010105, 21103010106). We would like to thank the anonymous reviewers for their insightful comments.

References

Abney, S. 1992. Prosodic Structure, Performance Structure and Phrase Structure. *Proceedings of 5th Darpa Workshop on Speech & Natural Language.*

Botinis, A., Ganetsou, S., Griva, M., and Bizani, H. 2004. Prosodic Phrasing and Syntactic Structure in Greek. *Proceedings of FONETIK 2004*, Dept. of Linguistics, Stockholm University.

Chen, Keh-jiann, Tseng, Chiu-yu, Peng, Hua-jiu and Chen, Chi-ching. 2004. Predicting Prosodic Words from Lexical Words -- A First Step towards Predicting Prosody from Text . *Proceedings of the 4th International Symposium on Chinese Spoken Language Processing (ISCSLP 2004).* Hong Kong, 173-176.

de Pijper, J. R., and Sanderman, A. A. 1994. On the Perceptual Strength of Prosodic Boundaries and its Relation to Suprasegmental Cues. *Journal of the Acoustical Society of America*, 96(4), 2037-2047.

Price, P., Ostendorf, M., Shattuck-Hufnagel, S., and Fong, C. 1991. The Use of Prosody in Syntactic Disambiguation. *Journal of the Acoustic Society of American*, 90, 2956-2970.

Wang Yan, Liu Jun, Kan Minggang, Hou Min, Zou Yu. 2010. Phonetic Diachronic Diversification in Mandarin: A Case of the Same Movie's Dialogue in 1950s and 1970s. *Proc. of YWCL 2010*, Wuhan, Hubei, Oct 10-13. (Accepted)

Zou Yu. 2007. *A Formal Study on Prosody of Presenter's Spoken Language Based on Broadcast Speech Corpus*. PhD thesis, Communication University of China.

Zou Yu, He Wei, Zhang Yuqiang, Hou Min and Zhu Weibin. 2009. A Special Prosodic Phrasing in Broadcasting News Programs. *Computational Sciences and Optimization: Theory, Simulation and Experiment (Vol. 2)*, Sanya, Hainan, China, 24-26 April, 406-408.

Zou Yu, Wu Jiyuan, He Wei, Hou Min, Teng Yonglin. 2010. Syntactic Correlations of Prosodic Phrase in Broadcasting News Speech. *The 6th IEEE International Conference on Natural Language Processing and Knowledge Engineering (NLP-KE 2010)*, Beijing, China, Aug. 21-23.

Kazakh Segmentation System of Inflectional Affixes

Gulila.Altenbek
1.Information Science and Engineering Colleges
Xinjiang University,
Xinjiang Lab. of Multilanguage Information Technology ,
830046，P.R. China.
2. Harbin Institute of Technology, Harbin
gla@xju.edu.cn

WANG Xiao-long
Institute of Computer Science and Technology,
Harbin Institute of Technology, Harbin,
150001, P.R. China.
wangxl@insun.hit.edu.cn

Abstract

This paper focuses on the automatic segmentation of inflectional affixes of the Kazakh Language (KL) on the basis of studying the corpus of KL. Kazakh is an agglutinative language with word structures formed by productive affixation of derivational and inflectional suffixes to stems. Based on the analysis of the configuration of inflectional affixes, it firstly constructs the Finite-State Automation and the segmentation of inflectional affixes. Secondly it targets at specially constructing the Finite-State Automations of nouns and verbs, which are the most changeable and complex part of speech of KL. And thirdly it adopts the methods of Bidirectional Omni-Word Segmentation and lexical analysis to achieve the goal of stemming and fine segmentation of inflectional affixes of KL. And finally it gives an additional account of studying the segmentation of ambiguous inflectional affixes. The paper intends to improve the accuracy and the quickness of stemming the inflectional affixes of KL.

1 Introduction

Lexical or morphemic analysis is to turn the character string of natural language into "the word string". During the process, at first it takes "the word" out,, and then conducts the morphological analysis of the internal components of "the word", and finally it ends up with the tagging. Many language processing tasks, including parsing, semantic analysis, information retrieval, and machine translation usually require a morphological analysis of the language beforehand.

As we know, Kazakh Language belongs to Turkish Language group of Altaic Language Family, whose unique language features decide that we should focus on its Inflectional Morphology is inflectionally changed. Kazakh language is written right-to-left in the Arabic alphabet with some modifications.

This paper attaches importance to analyzing the nouns and the verbs, which have great difficulties in affixes segmentation. And this paper will definitely contribute to the further study of lexical analysis of KL.

2 Related works

There have been some related studies, such as, Martin Porter has proposed "English Stemming Processor" (1980), which is most widely used; The Longest-March put forward by Kut is a type of word Segmentation algorithm based on the Turkish Lexicon(1995).Beihang University has finished its CDWS Chinese Word Segmentation System (nan-yuan.Liang, 1987); Tsinghua University has also completed its SEG Chinese Word Segmentation System(Da-yang Shen et al.,1997); and <The Grammatical Knowledge-base of Contemporary Chinese> edited by Peking University was also published(Shi-Wen,Yu, 2003).

And the study of lexical analysis of minority languages has also achieved a lot in China, Some researches(A.Gulila and A.M i j i t, 2004, K.Aykiz et al.,2006, YuSufu, 2005) have been done in the lexical analysis of Uighur Language conducted Xinjiang; the Automatic Segmentation System of Mongolian language conducted by Inner Mongolia University (U.Nasun, 1997) ; And the lexical analysis of kazakh Language conducted by our project is in progress (A.Gulila and A.Dawel,2007) and so on.

There have been several main approaches or algorithms to segment inflectional affixes, including maximum matching algorithm based on mechanic matching of character strings, rules-based algorithm, statistics-based algorithm, and the combination of both rules-based and statistics-based algorithms.

3 Kazakh Morphology

3.1 Kazakh Morphology

Kazakh is an agglutinative language with word structures formed by affixes to grammatically or meaningfully change the words.Kazakh morphology is an affixal system consisting mainly of suffixes and a few prefixes. According to linguistic theory, the word of the text consists of the root or the stem and the affix.(Milat etc. 2003, ding-jin Zhang. 2004).

• *Word root* is the core of the whole word structure, which is the essential morpheme to convey the basic content of its meaning.

• *Word stem* is a new word generated by adding various affixes to the root, which is also called a derivative word. It expresses the complete and full meaning.

• *Affixes* are divided into inflectional affixes and derivational affixes. The study of derivational affixes focuses on the derivational words, which can be formed by adding prefixes or suffixes or prefixes plus suffixes. Meanwhile the meanings of the derivational words will be changed. While the study of inflectional affixes pays attention to the Inflectional Morphology, which shows grammatical changes between words but does not change word meanings.

3.2 The Analysis of Inflectional Affixes

We focus on most general morphological rules which are common rules related to morpheme segmentation. The inflectional affixes in Kazakhh language are divided into the following four types:

1) *Plural:* KL has six various affixes to express the plural form of words, which usually are directly linked to the general nouns, pronouns and numerals.

2) *Personal pronoun possessive*: KL has six various affixes to express the possessive forms of personal pronouns.

3) *Case*: KL has seven various affixes to express the different cases. So KL has seven cases. Case endings are applied only to the last element of a noun phrase, which are closely linked to the following verbs.

4) *Predicative Person*: The first, second and third personal pronouns are usually followed by the words with additive predicative personal elements.

The above-mentioned four types of inflectional affixes can be used separately or linked together. Suffixes in Kazakh are complex, especially when a stem is linked with many suffixes. There are some rules we can follow to add affixes to word roots. See Figure 1: (Right-to-Left)

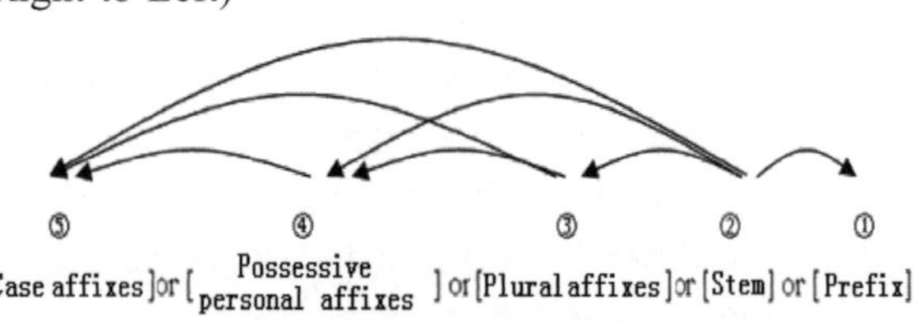

Figure 1. Rules to guide the connections of inflectional affixes

3.3 The Finite-state Automaton model of inflectional affixes of KL

Finite-State Automata (FSA) can be used to describe the possible word forms of a language. We have already applied the model of FSA into the lexical analysis of KL. The following figure shows a FSA model of inflectional changes of a noun. See Figure 2:

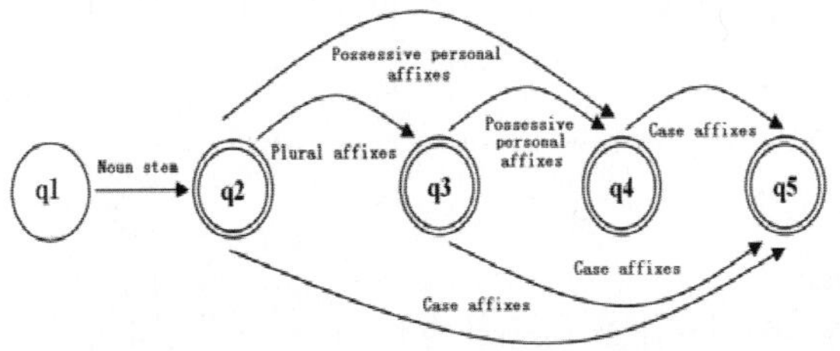

Figure 2. The FSA model of inflectional changes of a noun.

4 The Finite-state Transducer (FST) of Kazakh Words

As a typical agglutinative language, Kazakh words are formed by adding various suffix to word roots. But the Kazakh language itself does not have prefixes with exception of some borrowed or loaned prefixes from foreign words. And there are some rules guiding the usage and connection of various suffixes. Thus we can apply FST to establish a model for Kazakh words. The process of establishing a FST model can be divided into the following steps(E.Gülşen & A.Eşref. 2004):

Step 1: Establish a Right-to-Left FSM.

Step 2: Tag affixes

Step 3: Reverse the Right-to-Left FSM, and get a Non-deterministic Finite-state Automaton (NFA)

Step 4: Convert the NFA to a Deterministic Finite-state Automaton (DFA) and establish a Left-to-Right FSM.

The Kazakh words that can be added affixes to themselves are the followings: nouns, numerals, adjectives, pronouns, verbs, adverbs and so on. Among them, nouns and verbs are the most difficult parts of speech to be segmented. Take these two parts of speech as examples:

4.1 Inflectional Affixes of Nouns

Step 1: Establish a Right-to-Left FSM .

The four types of inflectional affixes can be added to stems under the guidance of some rules which also decide the FSM. We can apply the FSM to segment stens and we can analyze the FSM from right to left. See Figure 3:

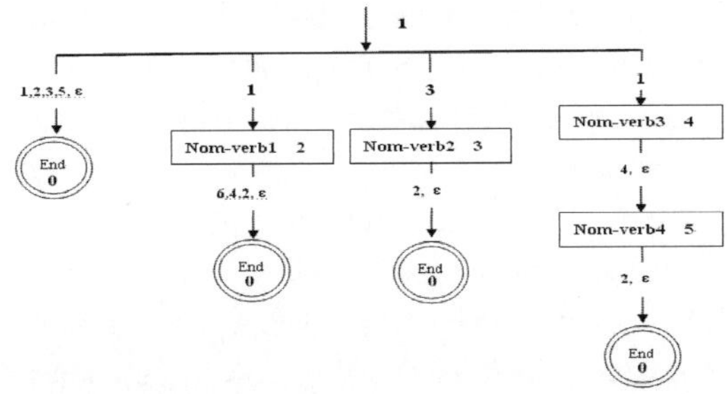

Figure 3. Right-to-Left FSM of inflectional affixes.

Step 2: Tag affixes

How to tag depends on the types of inflectional affixes, in which each type is given a value as its expressing value. Those affixes will be stored in the database as well as those expressing values. See Table 1

Table 1. Types and Expressing Values of Inflectional Affixes of Nouns.

inflectional affixes Type	value	Inflectional affixes type	value
Plural	1	Personal pronoun possessive: plural	4
Case	2	predicative person: singular	5
Personal pronoun possessive: singular	3	predicative person: plural	6

Step 3: Reverse the Right-to-Left FSM to form a Left-to-Right FSM

Reverse the Right-to-Left FSM, and form a Non-deterministic Finite-state Automaton (NFA) (See Figure 4). The number in each circle of Figure 4 represents the state value consistent with the state value of Figure 3. The types and expressing values are also marked above the lines in Figure 4.

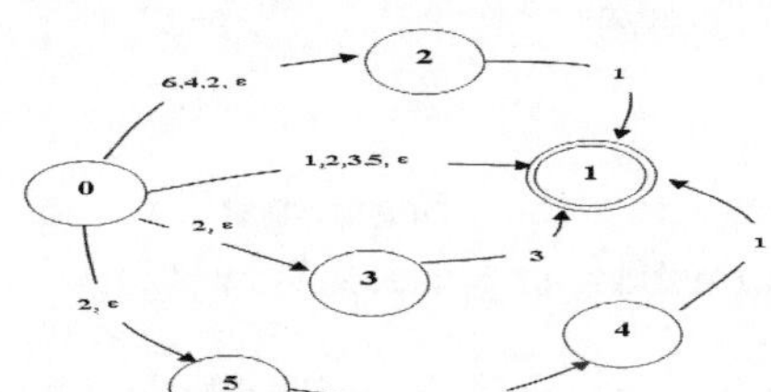

Figure 4. Left-to-Right NFA of inflectional affixes.

Step 4: Convert NFA to DFA

The multi-switches and "ε" switches of an expressing value of NFA makes the realization of NFA on computer very complex. Therefore, we should convert the NFA to be a DFA with the purpose of making each inputted expressing value facing one switch and making "ε" switch nonexistent. We adopt "subset construction algorithm"[A.V.Aho et al. ,1986] to conduct the operation. We make each state of the new DFA correspondent to a subset of the NFA. As Table 2 shows, the start state (A)of DFA contains one element "0" and the start state of NFA. We know that all other states can be achieved from the state "0" through "ε" switches. Thus, the start state of DFA could be A={0，1，2，3，4，5}. The numbers in the brackets represent inputted expressing values or types of affixes. The next state of DFA should be started with A and "1，2，3，4，5"can be separately inputted as expressing values. The FAS can thus be established.

Table 2. The Conversion from NFA to DFA of Inflectional Affixes.

E-closure({0})={0,1,2,3,4,5}*A E-closure(A,1)={1} *B	E-closure(C,1)={1} B
E-closure(A,2)={1,2,3} *C E-closure(A,4)={2,4} *D	E-closure(D,1)={1} B
E-closure(A,6)={2} *E	E-closure(E,1)={1} B

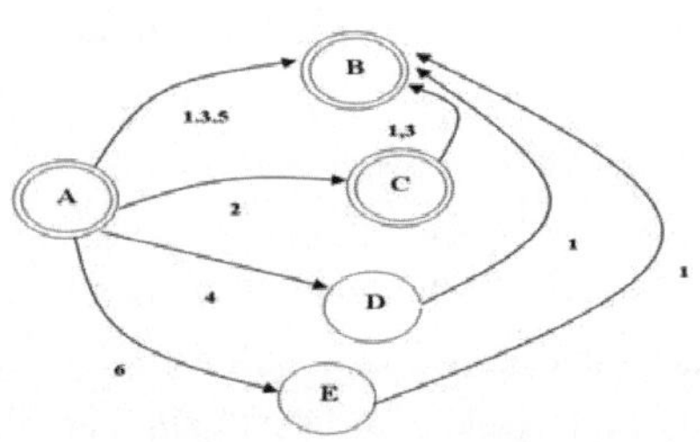

Figure 5. FSM of Inflectional Affixes of Nouns.
inflectional affixes of verbs.

5 Approaches to the Segmentation of Inflectional Affixes of Kazakh Words

Some mathematical frameworks or modeling methodologies can be used for morphology learning and word segmentation: maximum likelihood (ML) modeling, probabilistic maximum a posteriori (MAP) models, finite state automata (FSA), etc.

The algorithms suitable for the segmentation of inflectional affixes of Kazakh words include the followings: Bidirectional Maximum Matching and Omni-word Segmentation.

5.1 Bidirectional Matching Algorithm

Forward and backward algorithm is applied for the segmentation of a given word is examined for the words whose surface forms change after concatenation. The basic idea of this approach is to conduct the segmentation of inflectional affixes from left side of a character string to its right side and vice versa. But during the process, the critical issue is to determine the border between stens and inflectional affixes. Under many situations, vague borders between stens and inflectional affixes cause the inaccurate stemming. Thus, this algorithm can solve this problem.

5.2 Omni-word Segmentation Algorithm

The basic idea of this algorithm is to find all the segmentation forms of character strings waited for the segmentation starting from position "i". For Kazakh text, we should find all the segmentation forms of a word. We just leave the issue of ambiguity for later discussion.

5.3 The Combination of Bidirectional Omni-word Segmentation Algorithm and The Lexical Analysis

1) The segmentation of inflectional affixes is conducted from the left side of a Kazakh word and then matched with the table of inflectional affixes. In general the inflectional affixes are formed by short character strings. Therefore some inflectional affixes maybe become sub-strings of other inflectional affixes. It is very possible that there are many successful matches of inflectional affixes, that is to say, there will be various segmentations of inflectional affixes of a word, But only one of them is accurate. So we need to classify the inflectional affixes and enact the rules to guide their connection order. According to those rules we just search one type of inflectional affixes and adopt Maximum matching algorithm to avoid the problem of many segmentations of an affix. When conducting the segmentation of inflectional affixes

and the stem extraction, we call the far right side of segmentation border "candidate border" .

2) The extract stems is conducted from the right side of a Kazakh word and then matched with the lexicon in order to find the candidate border of the sten. The ability to form new words for some affixes is very strong, so many stems which are added to various derivational affixes become new stems of other words. So the situation is the same with the segmentation of inflectional affixes. We should conduct Omni-word Segmentation and list all the possible segmentation forms of affixes.

We should deal with some special problems when conducting segmentation of inflectional affixes. Borders of stens will be changed somewhat when some inflectional affixes are added to the stens. Changes would occur like vowel deletion and lenition reduction. Sometimes it is impossible to find the complete match in the lexicon. Under such situation, we should apply orthographic rule of Kazakh language to deal with it.

6 The Analysis of the Ambiguity of Inflectional Affixes

6.1 Rule-based analysis of Ambiguity

To prevent over-segmentation and secure the semantic identity of a word, stem and suffix boundary is chosen as the primary target of segmentation.

Suppose the right border of inflectional affix is indicated as S1 while the left border of sten as S2. The ambiguity probably occurred in the segmentation is listed below as well as its solution.

1) S1=S2 (Under various situations, it is possible that S1 is S2): Under this situation we should segment the longest sten.

2) S1 ≠S2 (Under this situation, we also consider the following two cases see Figure 8)

Case 1:

(1) The sub-string on the right side of S1 will be regarded as the candidate stem. And then we should apply orthographic rule to make a choice of the candidate stem and the sub-string on the left side of S1.

(2) If some variants of the words do exist, a new sten is formed; otherwise, go to Step 5.

(3) We should search the new sten in the lexicon

(4) If we succeed to find the new sten in the lexicon, please tag the stem and the inflectional affix (the left sub-string of S1)

(5) End

Case 2:We should apply probability statistics to solve the problem.

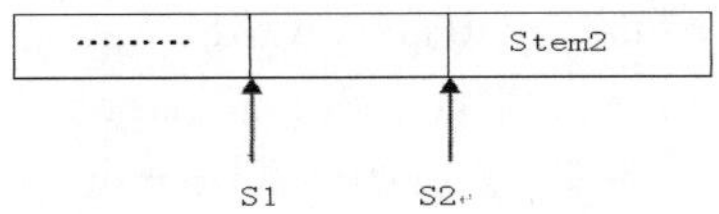

Figure 6(a). Case 1: (S1 ≠S2).

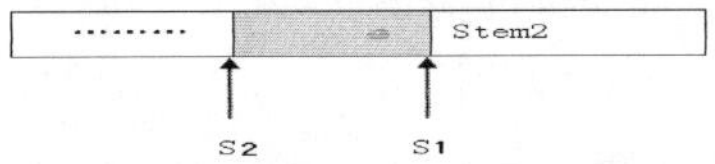

Figure 6(b). Case 2: (S1 ≠S2).

3) Non-matched stems but with matched inflectional affixes

We adopt the same solution to deal with this situation. That is to say, we at first should apply orthographic rule to make a choice of the sub-string on the left side of S1 and the sub-string on the right side of S1.And we also try to find the existence of lenition reduction. If we could not find the new sten in the lexicon, we should change to apply probability statistics to analyze.

4) Non-matched stens with non-matched inflectional affixes

We should search the inflectional affixes from the left side of the word to be segmented. If we could not find the match in the lexicon, we should judge the suffix and the sub-string on the right side by use of orthographic rule. And then we continue to search the candidate stem in the lexicon. If the match does exist, we tag the word as a sten; otherwise we tag it as an unregistered word.

5) Non-matched inflectional affixes with matched stems.

We consider the sub-string on the left side of the stem as the candidate derivational affix and search the match in the table of derivational affixes. If the match could be found in the table and its type is the same with the stem , we should tag the word as a stem; otherwise we tag it as an unregistered word.

6.2 The ambiguity analysis based on Bayesian classification

The principle of Semantic Bayesian classifier is to consider the information of surrounding words of ambiguous words in a large context. Each practical word contains potentially useful information to imply the possible semantics of the ambiguous words. This Classifier is not a features selection but a combination of all features. The ambiguous words of the corpus should be semantically tagged in advance.Table 3 lists some symbols presented by this paper.

Table 3. Symbols Agreement.

Symbol	Meaning
W	An ambiguous word
s1,…,sk,…,sK	ALL the different segmentations of W
c1,…,ci,…,cI	the context in which W is in the corpus
v1,…,vj,…,vJ	the context features of the Disambiguation

When selecting the types, the Bayesian classifier using Bayesian decision-making rules could be used; those rules can minimize the error probability (R. O.Duda, P. E. Hart. ,1973).

According to simple Bayesian assumption, we have revised the decision making rules, as follows:

Simple Bayesian decision-making rules.

$$\text{Decide } S' \text{ if } S' = \text{argmax}_{sk}[\log P(s_k) + \textstyle\sum_{vj \text{ in } c} \log P(v_j|s_k)] \quad (1)$$

P (v_j | s_k) and P (s_k) in the formula can be calculated using the maximum likelihood estimates from the tagging of training in Corpus:

$$\begin{aligned} s' &= \arg_{s_k} \max P(s_k/c) \\ &= \arg_{s_k} \max \frac{P(c/s_k)}{P(c)} P(s_k) \\ &= \arg_{s_k} \max P(c/s_k) P(s_k) \\ &= \arg_{s_k} \max[\log P(c/s_k) + \log P(s_k)] \end{aligned}$$

$$P(v_j \mid s_k) = \frac{C(v_j, s_k)}{\sum_t C(v_t, s_k)}$$

$$P(s_k) = \frac{C(s_k)}{C(w)} \quad (2)$$

C(vj,sk) in the formula is the number to show how many times sk is to be segmented by vj in the context of training materials; C (sk) is the number to show how many times that sk occur in the training corpus; and C (w) is the total number to show how many times the unambiguous words occur.

```
comment: Training
for all stemmings of w do
        for all words vj in the vocabulary do
                P(vj | sk) = C(vj,sk) / Σt C(vt,sk)
        end
end
for all stemmings sk of w do
                P(sk) = C(sk) / C(w)
end
 comment:Disambiguation
 for all stemmings sk of w do
        score(sk)=logP(sk)
        for all words vj in the context window c do
            score(sk)=score(sk) + log P(vj| sk)
        end
 end
 choose s'=argmax sk score(sk)
```

Figure 7. Bayes Disambiguation.

7 The Design of the System

In the process of segmenting affixes in Kazakh language, the main task is to segment the prefixes, stems, and inflectional affixes. For this purpose, About 60,000 stems and 438 tables of affixes are collected as the basis of segmentation. The stem list consists of almost all the common stems except from the domain specific words and rarely used words. The realization of the whole system experiences the following steps:

1) Take a Kazakh word from a text.

2) Establish a FSM of a noun or a verb. If possible, directly give the result of segmentation and return to step 1;otherwise turn to the next step.

3) Adopt the combination of Bidirectional Omni-word Segmentation Algorithm and the Lexical Analysis to analyze for the words to be segmented. If possibly segmented, directly give the result of the segmentation and return to step 1; otherwise adopt Bayesian Classification by use of the parameters from the training corpus to select the correct segmentation of ambiguous words.

4) The result of tagging the segmentation of affixes .

The corpus contains 150，992 words, among which 51% is used as training corpus while the rest as test corpus. The accuracy rates generated from the testes conducted for this paper include Precision 1 and Precision 2. We can define two evaluation functions, as follows:

Definition 1:The accuracy rate of inflectional affixes segmentation of words.

$$precision1 = \frac{\text{numbers of correct extracted stems}}{\text{total words}} \times 100\% \quad (3)$$

Definition 2: The accuracy rate of inflectional affixes segmentation of ambiguous words

$$precision2 = \frac{\text{numbers of correct extracted ambiguous words}}{\text{total number of ambiguous words}} \times 100\% \quad (4)$$

8 Experimental results

8.1 The comparison of the segmentation speeds

Table 5 shows the comparison of the segmentation speeds, in which we compare the system adopting FSM to the system not adopting FSM. We have tested 10，000 words and the result of the comparison is quite obvious, which indicates the high segmentation speed of the system adopting FSM.

Table 4. The comparison of Two segmentation speeds.

Type of segmentation	The number of tested words	Total time used for segmentation (Ms)	average velocity (Ms/words)
not adopting FSM	100,00	24，422	2.4422
adopting FSM	100,00	19，408	1.9408

8.2 The Analysis of the result of inflectional affixes segmentation

This paper adopts the combination of bidirectional omni-segmentation and rule-based segmentation to segment inflectional affixes and extract stems.

Table 5. The contrast of affix segmentations by use of different algorithms.

Algorithms	Precision1 (%)
Omni-word Segmentation	78.1
Maximum matching	74.2
Combination of bidirectional omni-segmentation and lexical analysis	84.0

The tests show that the final one improves the accuracy rate of affix segmentation and realizes the segmentation of inflectional affixes.

8.3 The Analysis of segmentation of ambiguous words

This paper puts forward that we should firstly adopt rule-based approach or algorithm to the segmentation of ambiguous words, if without any result, we should adopt Bayesian Classification to the segmentation of ambiguous words. In the test corpora, among 74,026 words 922 words are ambiguous words. So at first we should adopt rule-based algorithm to deal with those ambiguous words, in which 600 ambiguous words can be correctly dealt with; and then we should adopt Bayesian Classification Algorithm to further improve the accuracy rate of the segmentation of ambiguous words. As a result, the accuracy rate of the segmentation of ambiguous words can be reached to 84.38%. Table 7 shows the analysis of the segmentation of ambiguous words.

Table 6. The analysis of the segmentation of ambiguous words.

Algorithm to deal with ambiguous words	Total number of ambiguous words of test corpora	Number of correctly segmented ambiguous words	Precision2 (%)
Rule-based segmentation of ambiguous words	922	532	57.70%
Bayesian classification	390	246	63.07%

9 Conclusion and Future Study

This paper firstly analyzes the morphemic structure in the corpus of Kazakh Language, and especially studies stem extraction and affix segmentation. It establishes the FSM of inflectional affixes and then conducts the segmentation of inflectional affixes. The process starts with the analysis of FSM of the words to be segmented. If successfully achieved, the result would be considered as the result of segmentation. Otherwise, the algorithm of combining the bidirectional omni-word segmentation and ruled based segmentation should be adopted to segment the inflectional affixes, which better solves the problem of segmenting inflectional affixes. At last the paper presents that we should apply the method of statistics to disambiguate the segmentation of inflectional affixes of ambiguous words. Compared to other approaches, this approach improves the accuracy rate and the segmentation speed of segmenting inflectional affixes.

But there exist other problems presented in this paper, such as unregistered words. We should continue to make efforts to improve the accuracy rate of the segmentation of inflectional affixes through further enlarging the vocabulary of the dictionary and adopting the method of statistics. And we should be well-trained in obtaining parameters of segmentation models of Kazakh Language, making the language model close to the reality language itself.

Acknowledgment

This work is funded by the Natural Science Foundation of China(NSFC)(No.60763005), And the Project of China Ministry of Education (No.MZ115-92).

References

A.Kut, A. Aplkoçak, E.Özkarahan. 1995.Bilgi bulma sistemleri için otomatic turkçe dizinleme yöntemi. In Bilişim Bildirileri, Dokuz Eylül University, İzmir, Turkey.

A.V.Aho,R.Sethi&J.D.Ullman. 1986. Compilers: principles,techniques,tools[R].Reading,MA:Addison Wesley.

A.Gulila ,A.M i j i t.2004 .Reseach on Uighur Word Segmentation, Journal of Chinese information processing ,l . 18(6):61-65.

A.Gulila, A.Dawel.2007.Study on the Rule-based Kazakh Word Lemmatization, 11TH Symposium national language and information Proceedings ,Xishuangbanna, 109-114.

E.Gülşen , A.Eşref. 2004. An affix stripping morphological analyzer for Turkish, Proceedings of the International Conference on Artificial Intelligence and Application,Austria,299-304.

K.Aykiz,K.Kaysar,I.Turgun,2006.Morphological Analysis of Uighur Noun for Natural Language Information Processing,Journal of Chinese information processing，20(3)：43-48.

Liang nan-yuan. 1987.The Mordern Printed Chinese Distinguishing Word System, Journal of Chinese information processing,l . 1 (2)：44-52.

M.F.Porter. 1980.An algorithm for suffix stripping", Program ,14(3)：130−137.

Milat etc. 2003.Contemporary Kazakh language, Xinjiang People's Publishing House.

R. O.Duda, P. E. Hart. 1973. Pattern Classification and Scene Analysis,John Wiley and Sons, New York,10-43.

Shen Da-yang,Huang Chang-ning,Sun Moa-song, 1997. The approaches of Information integration and bestpath seaching inCWASS, Journal of Chinese information processing, l . 11 (2）：34-47.

U.Nasun, 1997 .The automatic segmentation system of Mongolian roots, stems, word, Journal of Inner Mongolia University ,NO2：53-57.

YuShi-Wen,2003.TheGrammatical Knowledge-base of Contemporary Chinese-A Complete Specification, Tsinghua University Press.

Zhang ding-jin. 2004.Modern Kazakh language practicality grammar，The central University for Nationalities Publishing House.

Yusup Abaidula ， Rezwangul, Abdiryim Sali. 2005.The Research and Development of Computer Aided Contemporary Uighur Language Tagging System. Journal of Chinese Language and Computing.

Space Characters in Chinese Semi-structured Texts

Rongzhou Shen
School of Informatics
University of Edinburgh
rshen@inf.ed.ac.uk

Claire Grover
School of Informatics
University of Edinburgh
grover@inf.ed.ac.uk

Ewan Klein
School of Informatics
University of Edinburgh
ewan@inf.ed.ac.uk

Abstract

Space characters can have an important role in disambiguating text. However, few, if any, Chinese information extraction systems make full use of space characters. However, it seems that treatment of space characters is necessary, especially in cases of extracting information from semi-structured documents. This investigation aims to address the importance of space characters in Chinese information extraction by parsing some semi-structured documents with two similar grammars - one with treatment for space characters, the other ignoring it. This paper also introduces two post processing filters to further improve treatment of space characters. Results show that the grammar that takes account of spaces clearly out-performs the one that ignores them, and so concludes that space characters can play a useful role in information extraction.

1 Introduction

It is well known that a snippet of text in Chinese (or some other oriental languages) consists of a span of continuous characters without delimiting white spaces to identify words. Therefore, most parsing systems do not make full use of space characters when parsing. Furthermore, even though Latin-based languages such as English have delimiting white spaces between words, most systems treat them as no more than delimiting characters. Therefore, space characters are usually stripped out of the text before processing.

However, this is intuitively wrong. (Rus and Summers, 1994) stated that *"the non-textual content of documents complement the textual content and should play an equal role"*. This paper shows that space character plays an equal role as the textual content, where it can be used not only to construct a certain layout, but also to signal a certain syntactic structure. Some researchers have been seen to make use of space characters, but they mainly use spaces to create or recognise certain special layouts. For example, (Rus and Summers, 1994) used white spaces to reformat documents into somewhat structured styles; (Ng et al., 1999) and (Hurst and Nasukawa, 2000) used spaces to recognise tables in free text. Wrapper generation is more related to our research since it uses layout to extract structured content from documents (Irmak and Suel, 2006; Chen et al., 2003). However, wrapper generation is too high level, this paper is aimed at exploring the effects of space characters at a lower level.

In this paper, we focus on semi-structured documents (in our case, real-world Chinese Curricula Vitae), since these types of documents tend to contain more space layout information. This paper is intended to address the importance of space characters not only in layout extraction, but also in information extraction. To do so, Daxtra Technologies' grammar formalism and their additional elements for basic space character treatment is introduced [1]. Then an improved treatment plan is given for further disambiguation. Finally, we perform evaluation of the tools on a set of real-world CVs and give proposals for future work.

2 Space Characters

A space character, when considered as punctuation, is a blank area devoid of content, serving to separate words, letters, numbers and other punctuation. (Jones, 1994) found broadly three types of punctuation marks: delimiting, separating and disambiguating. Similarly, space characters have three different functionalities: delimiting, structuring and disambiguating.

Space characters are natural delimiters in some languages. In English and many other Latin-based languages for example, spaces are used for separating words and certain punctuation marks (e.g. period and colon). However, in formal Chinese typesetting, spaces are not used to delimit words or characters. Hence the need for automatic word segmentation systems (Zhang et al., 2003). The current segmentation systems mainly focus on resolving ambiguities and detecting new words in segmenting text with *no* spaces (Gao et al., 2005). However, ambiguities can be caused not only by characters themselves, but also the spaces and layout around them. The paper will later demonstrate this in terms of recognising entities, but the same should apply to segmentation.

Therefore, Chinese documents can have white spaces, it is up to the author of the document to decide when to use spaces, which makes dealing with people's spacing habits one of the reasons to include treatment of space characters in linguistic systems.

Structuring refers to space characters being used for layout purposes. For example, spaces and tabs can be used to create tables, putting spaces in front of a piece of text means to start a new paragraph etc. In some cases, such structuring space characters represent a relation between the elements that the spaces are delimiting. For the following example, each line contains a label and a value separated using spaces to create a table.

姓名(Name)	李某某
年龄(Age)	25岁
Email	li25@gmail.com
籍贯(Place of Birth)	上海

Disambiguating spaces occur where an unintentional ambiguity could result if the spaces were not there. Two types of ambiguities are usually caused by ignoring the effect of white space:

Overlapping Ambiguity, where a set of tokens can either be appended to the previous set of tokens to form an entity, or precede the next set of tokens to form a different entity. For example, in a Chinese CV's job history section, the following two situations could occur:

1999年10月1	日本公司会计
1999.10.1	A Japanese Company Accountant
1999年10月1日	本公司会计
1999.10.1	Accountant in this company

In the above example, two spans of text use exactly the same set of characters, but since the space is not in the same place, they have different meanings. Thus ignoring white space in this case could result in an overlapping ambiguity.

Combinatorial Ambiguity, where two sets of tokens can either be joined to form a single entity, or be separated to form two different entities. For example, "经理␣助理" could mean Manager Assistant when joined together, or since there are spaces in between the two words "经理" and "助理", they could also mean Manager and Assistant.

[1] Daxtra Technologies provides software for resume/CV parsing and extraction for candidate acquisition: http://www.daxtra.com

3 Basic Space Character Treatment

Daxtra Technologies' parsing system is a grammar formalism used to develop grammatical rules for recognising Named Entities and Relations. The system is based on context free grammar, but includes additional elements for integrating linguistic information (e.g. grammar and lexicon) and layout information (e.g. space characters) to parse structured and unstructured text. Along with parsing the text, the parser also labels the matched text with XML tags.

A typical Daxtra grammar rule looks like the following:

```
: person =
     person-firstname
   + person-lastname !ATTACHED_L
: person =
     person-firstname
   + person-midname !ATTACHED_L
   + person-lastname !ATTACHED_L
```

As the above example illustrates, a rule begins with a colon and the rule's name. For example, consider the following two person names:

Rongzhou Shen
Andrew Peter Baker

assuming that "Rongzhou Shen" matches the first rule and "Andrew Peter Baker" matches the second rule, then both will be surrouned by `<person>` XML tags.

Contents following the equal sign are a combination of other defined grammar rule names or lexicon names to build up the body of the `person` rules. Thus, for the first `person` rule to match a piece of text, the sub contents of the text must match `person-firstname` and `person-lastname` in the order given. Any other contents between a right hand side rule name and its XML tag replacement (i.e. the square bracketed contents) are attributes attached to the rule. These attributes include layout information.

For describing layout information, the Daxtra grammar formalism offers three types of space grammar rule: `ATTACHED` (`ATTACHED_L`, `ATTACHED_R`), `TABULATION` (`TABULATION_L`, `TABULATION_M`, `TABULATION_R`) and `LINEBREAK` (`LINEBREAK_L`, `LINEBREAK_M`, `LINEBREAK_R`).

`ATTACHED` This attribute checks the matching contents of the attached rule for surrounding spaces. Accordingly, `ATTACHED_L` detects spaces on the left of the matching contents, and `ATTACHED_R` detects spaces on the right of the matching contents.

`TABULATION` Similar to `ATTACHED`, this checks for tabulation characters in the matching contents. `TABULATION_L`, `TABULATION_M` and `TABULATION_R` checks for tabulations before, inside or after the matching text respectively. A tabulation is either a tab character or a span of more than three continuous white spaces.

`LINEBREAK` As the name suggests, this attribute checks for line breaks in the matching text. `LINEBREAK_L`, `LINEBREAK_M` and `LINEBREAK_R` checks for line breaks before, inside or after the matching text respectively.

4 Improved Algorithm

Although the Daxtra grammar formalism offers a full range of space layout descriptors, questions still arise. Consider the job history examples in Table 1. The first one would parse correctly with some simple grammar such as the following (assuming that we have all the needed lexicons):

```
: history = date-range !ATTACHED_R
          + company !ATTACHED_R
          + occupation !ATTACHED_R
          + occupation
```

However, the same rule would become ambiguous for the second example, where there is a space

Original	1999 - 2000	3CR Health Beauty International Ltd.	助理经理␣助理会计
Translation	1999 - 2000	3CR Health Beauty International Ltd.	Assis. Manager␣Assis. Accountant
Original	1995 - 1997	EMaiMai.com Hong Kong Ltd.	经理␣助理␣␣会计
Translation	1995 - 1997	EMaiMai.com Hong Kong Ltd.	Manager␣Assistant␣␣Accountant

Table 1: An example job history section in a CV file

between "经理" (Manager) and "助理" (Assistant). In such a case, two matches are found, as shown in Table 2.

We may notice that the word "助理" (Assistant) is closer to the word "经理" (Manager) than the word "会计" (Accountant), hence the correct entities being "经理助理" (Manager Assistant) and "会计" (Accountant). If on the other hand, there were more spaces between "经理" (Manager) and "助理" (Assistant) than "助理" (Assistant) and "会计" (Accountant), we may infer that the entities would be "经理" (Manager) and "助理会计" (Assistant Accountant).

Therefore, more control is needed for incorporating space layout information. For example, the problem in Table 2 can be resolved by comparing the number of spaces between the words. To do so, we replaced the spaces with XML tags with an attribute indicating the number of spaces replaced. For example, a span of four spaces will become: `<w spaces='4' />`. Based on such a transformation, we came up with the following post-processing filters for resolving ambiguities and other errors caused by space characters:

Filter *least-space* For different matches of the same rule, always choose the match that has the least number of spaces *inside* the entities.

For example, consider the two cases in Table 3. They both have exactly the same set of characters, but are in fact two different combinations, as indicated by the translations in the table.

Assuming that a simple rule like the following is used to match both the job histories:

```
: history   = date !ATTACHED_R
            + company
            + occupation
```

Then for (1) in Table 3, the two possible matches are shown in Table 4.

Therefore, the first match yields a total of one space inside the entities (between "年" and "冬"), while the second match yields three spaces (between "冬" and "宝洁公司"). Thus the first match is chosen.

Similarly for (2) in Table 3, there are two possible matches (see Table 5), in which the first has four spaces inside the entities and the second has two spaces, so the system chooses the second match.

Filter *equal-space* For a parsing with only one possible match, check whether the entity contains an unequal number of spaces between characters.

For example, "中国会计准则␣␣上市公司" (Chinese Accountant Regulations␣␣Listed Company) can be recognised by the system as a `company` entity, but it is in fact not. Thus in this case, the filter *equal-space* will reject it - there are no spaces between the first six characters, but two spaces appear after them, so the two spaces are not considered as part of an entity.

5 Evaluation

The evaluation data is a set of entities extracted from 314 real world CVs. The original CVs were all MS Word files, then converted to plain text using

Original	1995 - 1997	EMaiMai.com Hong Kong Ltd.	经理␣助理	会计
Translation	1995 - 1997	EMaiMai.com Hong Kong Ltd.	Manager Assistant	Accountant
Match 1	1995 - 1997	EMaiMai.com Hong Kong Ltd.	经理	助理会计
Translation	1995 - 1997	EMaiMai.com Hong Kong Ltd.	Manager	Assistant Accountant
Match 2	1995 - 1997	EMaiMai.com Hong Kong Ltd.	经理助理	会计
Translation	1995 - 1997	EMaiMai.com Hong Kong Ltd.	Manager Assistant	Accountant

Table 2: The second example's two matching variants

Original (1)	2002年␣冬␣␣␣宝洁公司全球会计和财务
Translated	2002␣Winter␣␣␣P&G Global Accountant and Finance
Original (2)	2002年␣␣␣冬␣宝␣洁␣公司全球会计和财务
Translated	2002␣␣␣Dong␣Bao␣Jie␣Company Global Accountant and Finance

Table 3: Examples showing two different combinations using the same set of characters. (Note: "DongBaoJie" and "Winter P&G" have the same characters in Chinese.

Match 1	2002年␣冬	␣␣␣	宝洁公司	全球会计和财务
Translation	2002␣Winter	␣␣␣	P&G Company	Global Accountant and Finance
Match 2	2002年	␣	冬␣␣␣宝洁公司	全球会计和财务
Translation	2002	␣	Dong␣␣␣BaoJie Company	Global Accountant and Finance

Table 4: Two possible matches of (1) in Table 3

Match 1	2002年␣␣␣冬	␣	宝␣洁公司	全球会计和财务
Translation	2002␣␣␣Winter	␣	P␣&G Company	Global Accountant and Finance
Match 2	2002年	␣␣␣	冬␣宝␣洁公司	全球会计和财务
Translation	2002	␣␣␣	Dong␣Bao␣Jie Company	Global Accountant and Finance

Table 5: Two possible matches of (2) in Table 3

wvWare [2]. The converted files were all encoded using UTF-8. To demonstrate generality of the rules and filters, the selected CVs included differents kinds of layout, among which plain paragraphs, tables and lists are the most common. Table 6 shows the types of entities extracted.

To evaluate the effect of the different treatments of space characters, four sets of data were prepared, Table 7 shows the list of data.

For annotating the gold set, we performed named entity recognition using the latest grammar rules, then hand corrected the mistakes to produce a gold data set. For evaluation method, we used the standard Precision/Recall/F-score measures. To compute the standard measures, the XML output from the original parsed texts are converted to a CoNLL style format. For the example in Table 8, the converted CoNLL format looks like Figure 1.

5.1 The Results

A total of 24,434 entities were annotated in the gold set, Table 9 shows the distribution of the entity types among the whole set of entities.

After running each version of the grammar (i.e. Baseline, Version 1, Version 2) on the whole set of

[2] wvWare is an opensource project for accessing and converting MS Word files: http://wvware.sourceforge.net/

	Number of correctly labeled characters	Number of gold annotated characters	Number of system annotated characters	Precision (%)	Recall (%)	F1 (%)
Baseline	272901	302491	321059	85.00	90.22	87.53
Version 1	285736	302491	305339	93.58	94.46	94.02
Version 2	287365	302491	303948	94.54	95.00	94.77

Table 10: Results of each version computed against the gold data set

Entity Type	**Examples**
date	1990年10月1日, 1990.10.01
date-range	1998/10/1 - 1999/10/1
company	中信实业银行上海分行(Zhongxin Industrial Bank Shanghai Branch)
occupation	会计(Accountant), 经理助理(Manager Assistant)
person	沈容舟(Shen Rongzhou)
educational	爱丁堡大学(University of Edinburgh), 国防科大(University of National Defenses)
degree	学士(Bachelor), 硕士学位(Masters Degree)
subject	物理(Physics), 物理化学(Physical Chemistry)

Table 6: Types of named entities extracted from CVs.

Data name	**Description**
Gold	Human annotated data
Baseline	Daxtra grammar without space attributes
Version 1	Daxtra grammar with space attributes
Version 2	Daxtra grammar with space attributes and **least-space** filter and **equal-space** filter.

Table 7: The four sets of data prepared

Text	冬␣宝␣洁公司␣全球会计和财务
Translation	Dong␣Bao␣Jie Company␣Global Accountant and Finance
Rule	: history = company + occupation

Table 8: A sample text and its matching rule

```
冬  B-company
#space  I-company
宝  I-company
#space  I-company
洁  I-company
公  I-company
司  I-company
#space  O
全  B-occupation
球  I-occupation
会  I-occupation
计  I-occupation
和  I-occupation
财  I-occupation
务  I-occupation
```

Figure 1: The converted CoNLL style format for Table 8

CVs and converting the XML output into CoNLL format, there were a total of four sets of result files (including Gold annotated data set) and 1256 result files in total (one result file per CV). We then performed pair-wise comparisons of the result files from each version with the result files in the gold data set. Table 10 shows the final results.

As can be seen from Table 10, Version 1 is a great improvement over the Baseline in that both F1 score and precision increased by over 6%, while recall rose by 4.24%. This strongly indicates that the importance of space layout information is not to be

Entity Type	Total Number
date	10006
date-range	166
company	5456
occupation	3993
person	783
educational	1686
degree	1039
subject	1305
Total	24434

Table 9: Distribution of entity types in the CVs

neglected in named entity recognition tasks. A much lower number of system annotated characters for Version 1 shows that the layout information is disambiguating multiple matches, thus rejecting many predictions.

Although not as significant, Version 2 has still gained an improvement on performance over Version 1 by 0.75% in F1 score. A lower number of predicted annotations and a higher number of correctly predicted annotations both indicate more ambiguities have been resolved as a result.

Further investigations into the errors made by the Baseline showed that most ambiguities were overlapping ambiguities (over 90%). A possible reason for the smaller number of combinatorial ambiguities could be that people tend to be careful in writing their CVs, and tend to disambiguate entities by themselves. For example, instead of writing "经理 助理", separating the two words using a space, people will use punctuation marks to divide them. Furthermore, the case where people put spaces between each character wasn't so often seen: there were 16 CVs in total where such a case was found. Thus filter *equal-space* did not disambiguate many.

Further dividing the results down into smaller parts, we found that most of the ambiguities in the Baseline came from *company*, *educational*, *occupation* and *subject* names. This has two main causes: (1) These entities' grammar contain many generative rules, so ambiguities can not be avoided; (2) The context around these entities contain the most layout information (e.g. job history, educational history). Date and date-range entities were not affected so much by the layout information since they are straightforward to recognise. However, there was one case where the Baseline predicted a date wrongly:

> 1995年1月1日～1997年1月1　　日本公司樱花银行上海分行
> 1995.1.1 - 1997.1.1　　Japan Sakura Bank Shanghai Branch

The Baseline version predicted "1997年1月1日" as a single entity of type *date*. This is obviously a human typing error, where the author missed out "日" on the end of the date. This error was later fixed by Version 1.

From to the above discussion, we may know that *least-space* is mainly targeted at resolving overlapping ambiguities (which account for more than 90% of the ambiguities found), thus making it the more significant filter of the two.

Although Version 1 and Version 2 both had improvements over the Baseline, many errors still occur and they are categorized as follows:

- Rejections caused by filter *equal-space* were in fact real entities, uneven spaces in the entities were mostly human typing error;
- Choices made by filter *least-space* were occasionally wrong. This happens most often when two matches have a very small difference in the number of spaces inside entities;
- Grammars either overgenerate (cause plain tokens to be predicted as entities) or undergenerate (cause entities to be not detected);
- Lack of lexicon.

6 Conclusion

This paper has attempted to address the importance of space characters in Chinese linguistic parsing or information extraction in semi-structured documents. Essentially, space characters can contribute to the syntactic structure of texts and should not be only treated as delimiters or be stripped out of the document. This is especially true for semi-structured documents such as CVs.

As our results indicate, integrating simple layout information with linguistic grammars can greatly improve the performance of information extraction. A further improvement can be achieved using the two filters introduced in the fourth section.

Although Daxtra's grammar formalism is chosen as the tool for information extraction, since it already includes treatment of space characters, other tools are also available to carry out the same job. For example, Edinburgh University Language Technology Group's LT-TTT2 (Grover and Tobin, 2006) [3].

Our paper focuses mainly on Chinese CVs, but space layout information can be used widely in other languages and documents. In English for example, although words are separated by a single space, spaces are not always used as delimiters (e.g. constructing tables, columns), thus providing the need for integrating space layout. In terms of document types, plain paragraph based text (e.g. articles, blogs etc.) may not be affected too much by space characters, but integrating space layout information in parsing these documents should not decrease performance either. Furthermore, semi-structured documents may not be just limited to CVs: people's online portfolios, advertisements etc. all have space layout information attached. Therefore, much investigation still needs to be done on the effect of space characters in different types of documents.

References

Chen, Liangyou, Hasan M. Jamil, and Nan Wang. 2003. Automatic wrapper generation for semi-structured biological data based on table structure identification. *Database and Expert Systems Applications, International Workshop on*, 0:55.

Gao, Jiangfeng, Mu Li, Andi Wu, and Chang-Ning Huang. 2005. Chinese Word Segmentation and Named Entity Recognition: A Pragmatic Approach. *Computational Linguistics*, 31(4):531 – 574.

Grover, Claire and Richard Tobin. 2006. Rule-based chunking and reusability. In *Proceedings of the Fifth International Conference on Language Resources and Evaluation (LREC 2006)*, Genoa, Italy.

Hurst, Matthew and Tetsuya Nasukawa. 2000. Layout and Language: Integrating Spatial and Linguistic Knowledge for Layout Understanding Tasks. In *Proceedings of COLING*, pages 334 – 340.

Irmak, Utku and Torsten Suel. 2006. Interactive Wrapper Generation with Minimal User Effort. In *Proceedings of the 15th International Conference on World Wide Web*, pages 553 – 563.

Jones, Bernard. 1994. Exploring The Role of Punctuation in Parsing Natural Text. In *Proceedings of 15th Conference on Computational Linguistics*, pages 421 – 425.

Ng, Hwee Tou, Chung Yong Lim, and Jessica Li Teng Koo. 1999. Learning to Recognize Tables in Free Text. In *Proceedings of the 37th annual meeting of the Association for Computational Linguistics on Computational Linguistics*, pages 443 – 450.

Rus, Daniela and Kristen Summers. 1994. Using White Space for Automated Document Structuring. Technical Report TR94-1452, Cornell University, Department of Computer Science, July.

Zhang, Hua-Ping, Hong-Kui Yu, De-Yi Xiong, and Qun Liu. 2003. HMM-based Chinese Lexical Analyzer ICTCLAS. In *Proceedings of the Second SIGHAN Workshop on Chinese Language Processing*, pages 184 – 187.

[3]http://www.ltg.ed.ac.uk/software/lt-ttt2

The CIPS-SIGHAN CLP 2010 Chinese Word Segmentation Bakeoff

Hongmei Zhao and Qun Liu
Key Laboratory of Intelligent Information Processing,
Institute of Computing Technology, Chinese Academy of Sciences
{zhaohongmei,liuqun}@ict.ac.cn

Abstract

The CIPS-SIGHAN CLP 2010 Chinese Word Segmentation Bakeoff was held in the summer of 2010 to evaluate the current state of the art in word segmentation. It focused on the cross-domain performance of Chinese word segmentation algorithms. Eighteen groups submitted 128 results over two tracks (open training and closed training), four domains (literature, computer science, medicine and finance) and two subtasks (simplified Chinese and traditional Chinese). We found that compared with the previous Chinese word segmentation bakeoffs, the performance of cross-domain Chinese word segmentation is not much lower, and the out-of-vocabulary recall is improved.

1 Introduction

Chinese is written without inter-word spaces, so finding word-boundaries is an essential first step in many natural language processing tasks ranging from part of speech tagging to parsing, reference resolution and machine translation.

SIGHAN, the Special Interest Group for Chinese Language Processing of the Association for Computational Linguistics, successfully conducted four prior word segmentation bakeoffs, in 2003 (Sproat and Emerson, 2003), 2005 (Emerson, 2005), 2006 (Levow, 2006) and 2007 (Jin and Chen, 2007), and the bakeoff 2007 was jointly organized with the Chinese Information Processing Society of China (CIPS). These evaluations established benchmarks for word segmentation with which researchers evaluate their segmentation system.

After years of intensive researches, Chinese word segmentation has achieved a quite high precision, though the out-of-vocabulary problem is still a continuing challenge. However, the performance of segmentation is not so satisfying for out-of-domain text.

The CIPS-SIGHAN CLP 2010 Chinese Word Segmentation Bakeoff continues the ongoing series of the SIGHAN Chinese Word Segmentation Bakeoff. It was organized by Institute of Computing Technology, Chinese Academy of Sciences (abbreviated as ICT below). It focused on the cross-domain performance of Chinese word segmentation algorithms. And the bakeoff results will be reported in conjunction with the First CIPS-SIGHAN joint conference on Chinese Language Processing, Beijing, China.

2 Details of the Evaluation

2.1 Corpora

There are two kinds of corpora in the evaluation, with one using the simplified Chinese characters and another using the traditional Chinese characters. For the simplified Chinese corpora, the test corpora, reference corpora, and the unlabeled training corpora were provided by ICT, and the labeled training corpus (1 month data of The People's Daily in 1998) was provided by Peking University. For the traditional Chinese corpora, all the training, test and reference corpora were provided by the Hongkong City University.

There are four domains in this evaluation. Before the releasing of the test data, two of them (literature and computer science, we abbreviate "computer science" to "computer" below) are known to the participants (we provided the corresponding unlabeled training

corpora			Characters	Tokens	Word Types	TTR	OOV Rate
Simplified Chinese	Test	Literature	50,637	35,736	6,364	0.18	0.069
		Computer	53,382	35,319	4,150	0.12	0.152
		Medicine	50,969	31,490	5,076	0.16	0.11
		Finance	53,253	33,028	4,918	0.15	0.087
	Training	Labeled	1,820,456	1,109,947	55,303	0.05	
		Unlabeled-L	100,352				
		Unlabeled-C	103,764				
Traditional Chinese	Test	Literature	54,357	36,378	8,141	0.22	0.094
		Computer	67,321	43,499	6,197	0.14	0.094
		Medicine	68,090	43,458	6,510	0.15	0.075
		Finance	74,461	47,144	6,652	0.14	0.068
	Training	Labeled	1,863,298	1,146,988	63,588	0.06	
		Unlabeled-L	105,653				
		Unlabeled-C	109,303				

Table1. Overall corpus statistics

Site ID	Site Name	Contact	Simplified Chinese	Traditional Chinese
S1	College of Computer and Information Engineering, Anyang Normal University, Henan province, China	Jiangde Yu	◆◇	◆◇
S2	Institute of Intelligent Information Processing, Beijing Information Science & Technology University	Wenjie Su	◆	
S3	Beijing Institute of Technology	Huaping Zhang	◇	
S4	Center for Language Information Processing Institute, Beijing Language and Culture University	Zhiyong Luo	◇	
S5	Beijing University of Posts and Telecommunications	Caixia Yuan	◆◇	
S6	Dalian University of Technology	Huiwei Zhou	◆◇	
S7	Fudan University	Xipeng Qiu	◆	◆
S8	Shenzhen Graduate School Harbin Institute of Technology	Jianping Shen	◇	◇
S9	Language Technologies Institute, Carnegie Mellon University	Qin Gao	◆◇	
S10	National Central University, Taiwan	Yu-Chieh Wu	◆	◆
S11	Natural Language Processing Lab, Northeastern University, China	Huizhen Wang	◆	
S12	National Laboratory of Pattern Recognition, Institute of Automation, Chinese Academy of Science	Kun Wang	◆	
S13	Institute of Computer Science and Technology, Peking University	Liang Zong	◆	
S14	Institute of Computational Linguistics, Peking University	Mairgup	◆	
S15	Queensland University of Technology	Eric Tang	◆◇	◆◇
S16	Institute of Information Science, Academia Sinica, Taiwan	Cheng-Lung Sung	◆	◆
S17	Natural Language Processing Lab, Suzhou University	Junhui Li	◆	
S18	Anhui Speech and language Technology Engineering Research Center	Zhigang Chen	◆◇	

Table 2. Participating groups (◆=closed track, ◇=open track, there are four domains on every track)

corpora for each during the training phrase), and another two domains (medicine and finance) are unknown to the participants (without any in-domain training corpora). All corpora are UTF-8 encoded. Details on each corpus are provided in Table 1. We introduce a type-token ratio (TTR) to indicate the vocabulary diversity in each corpus.

During the process of building the reference corpora for the simplified Chinese word segmentation subtask, we manually check the automatically segmented results of the test data against the standard provided in "The Specification for the Basic Processing of Contemporary Chinese Corpus from Peking University". In this process, we refer to the labeled training data frequently with a view to keep the annotation consistency between these two kinds of corpora. Furthermore, we made a comparison test which compared the segmentation of the same character strings present in both corpora automatically, and corrected the inconsistent cases. However, in the labeled training corpus, there are minor incorrect segmentation cases against the standard from Peking University, such as "赢家" (yin2 jia1, with the meaning of "the winner", this word should be regarded as a word according to the above-mentioned standard), and there are also a few interior inconsistent cases in this corpus, such as "患有" and "患 有" (huan4 you3, with the meaning of "suffer from"). Whenever the segmentation of the reference corpora was different from the above-mentioned incorrect or inconsistent segmentation in the training corpus, we followed the standard from Peking University. All the evaluation corpora can be accessible from the Chinese Linguistic Data Consortium at: http://www.chineseldc.org.

2.2 Rules and Procedures

This bakeoff followed a strict set of guidelines and a rigid timetable. The detailed instructions for the bakeoff can be found at http://www.cipsc.org.cn/clp2010/cfpa.htm. The training material of simplified Chinese word segmentation was available starting April 1, the training material of traditional Chinese word segmentation was available April 23, testing material was available June 9, and the results had to be returned to the organizer by email by June 11 no later than 18:00 Beijing time.

The participating groups ("sites") of CIPS-SIGHAN CLP 2010 Bakeoff registered by email. There are two subtasks in this evaluation: word segmentation for simplified Chinese text and word segmentation for traditional Chinese text. The participating sites were required to declare which subtask they would participate in. The open and closed tracks were defined as follows:

- For the closed training evaluation, participants can only use data provided by the organizer to train their systems. Specifically, the following data resources and software tools are not permitted to be used in the training:
  1. Unspecified corpus;
  2. Unspecified dictionary, word list or character list: include the dictionaries of named entity, character lists for specific type of Chinese named entities, idiom dictionaries, semantic lexicons, etc.;
  3. Human-encoded rule bases;
  4. Unspecified software tools, include word segmenters, part-of-speech taggers, or parsers which are trained using unspecified data resources.

  The character type information to distinguish the following four character types can be used in training: Chinese characters, English letters, digits and punctuations.
- In the Open training evaluation, participants can use any language resources, including the training data provided by the organizer.

Participants were asked to submit their data using specific naming conventions, and from the result file name we can see in which track the result was run, as well as other necessary information. Of course, the results on both tracks are welcomed.

Scoring was done automatically using a combination of Perl and shell scripts. The scripts (Sproat and Emerson, 2003, 2005) used for scoring can be downloaded from http://www.sighan.org/bakeoff2005/. The bakeoff organizer provided an on-line scoring system to all the participants who had submitted their bakeoff results for their follow-up experiments.

2.3 Participating sites

Eighteen sites submitted results and a technical report. Mainland China had the greatest number with 14, followed by Taiwan (2), the United States (1) and Australia (1). A summary of participating groups and the tracks for which they submitted results can be found in Table 2 on the preceding page. There are more sites who had registered for the bakeoff. However, several of them withdrew due to technical difficulties or other problems. Altogether 128 runs were submitted for scoring.

3 Results

3.1 Baseline and topline experiments

Following previous bakeoffs, to provide a basis for comparison, we computed baseline and topline scores for each of the corpora. When computing a baseline, we compiled a dictionary of all the words in the labeled training corpus, and then we used this dictionary with a simple left-to-right maximal match algorithm to segment the test corpus. The results of this experiment are shown in Table 3. We expect systems to do at least as well as the baseline. The topline employed the same procedure, but instead used the dictionary of all the words in the test corpus. These results are presented in Table 4. We expect systems to generally underperform this topline, because no one could exactly know the set of words that occur in the test corpus.

In these and subsequent tables, we list the word count for the test corpus, test recall (R), test precision (P), balanced F score (where F = 2PR/(P+R)), the out-of-vocabulary (OOV) rate on the test corpus, the recall on OOV words (Roov), and the recall on in-vocabulary words (Riv).

3.2 Raw scores

All the results are presented in Tables 5-20. Column headings are as above, except for "Cr" and "Cp" for which see Section 3.3. All tables are sorted by F score.

3.3 Statistical significance of the results

Following previous bakeoffs, let us assume that the recall rates represent the probability p that a word will be successfully identified, and let us further assume the binomial distribution is appropriate for this experiment. Given the Central Limit Theorem for Bernouli trials — e.g. (Grinstead and Snell, 1997), then the 95% confidence interval is given as $\pm 2\sqrt{p(1-p)/n}$, where n is the number of trials (words). The recall-based confidences ($\pm 2\sqrt{p(1-p)/n}$) are given as "Cr" in Tables 5-20. Similarly, we can assume the precision rates represent the probability that a character string that has been identified as a word is really a word. And the precision-based confidences are given as "Cp" in the tables. They can be interpreted as follows: To decide whether two systems are significantly different (at the 95% confidential level), one just has to compute whether their confidence intervals overlap. If at least one of the "Cr" and "Cp" are different, we can treat these two systems as significantly different (at the 95% confidential level). Using this criterion all systems in this bakeoff are significantly different from each other.

4 Discussion

4.1 Comparison between open and closed tracks

In this bakeoff, there are 8 systems that ran on both closed and open tracks, which result in 32 pairs of scores for F measure and OOV recall respectively. Table 21 shows the results of these systems. We can see that their scores of F measures on open track don't have advantage over their counterparts on the closed track: only 14 scores (in 32 scores) on open track are higher than their counterparts on the closed track. This is different from the previous bakeoffs. But for OOV recall, the case is different. There are 23 scores (in 32 scores) on open track are higher than their counterparts on the closed track.

4.2 Improved OOV recall over the prior bakeoffs

From all the results, we can see that the widest variation among systems lies in the OOV recall rate. And dealing with unknown words is still the most difficult problem of Chinese word segmentation.

However, while comparing the top OOV recall rates of this bakeoff with those of the prior four bakeoffs, we found the OOV recall rates of this bakeoff achieved an obvious improvement. Table 22 shows the comparisons. We managed to find four pairs of test corpora with similar OOV rates for comparisons. In the comparisons, most top OOV recall rates of bakeoff 2010 are much higher than their counterparts of prior bakeoffs. An exception comes from the open track of medicine domain for traditional CWS subtask, and because only 3 systems submitted results, this comparison seems less meaningful.

4.3 Performance under different domains

We listed the top performance by F measure on every track, domain and subtask on Table 23.

Generally we think that cross-domain word segmentation will lead to a lower performance than in-domain word segmentation. In this bakeoff, it seems that the best performance of cross-domain word segmentation is at almost the same level of that of the prior bakeoffs. We know that the performance of different test set is incomparable. However, the performance in the out-of-domain text is somewhat surprising to us. We guess one reason may be the usage of domain adaptive technology, another reason may be the new technologies used by the participants. We hope to see the exact reasons in the technological reports of participants in the coming conference.

We provided unlabeled data to two domains. However, we did not see significant difference on the performance of closed test between these domains and other domains. Some participants pointed out that it is because the size of the unlabeled data is rather small.

And we found that among four domains, the performance (by the value of F measure and OOV recall, with scores in bold in the table) on finance is always the best or very close to the best. Perhaps this is because the OOV rate on finance test corpus is rather low.

Corpus		Word Count	R	P	F	OOV	R_{oov}	R_{iv}
Simplifed Chinese	L	35736	0.917	0.862	0.889	0.069	0.156	0.973
	C	35319	0.856	0.632	0.727	0.152	0.163	0.98
	M	31490	0.886	0.774	0.826	0.11	0.123	0.981
	F	33028	0.914	0.803	0.855	0.087	0.233	0.979
Traditional Chinese	L	36378	0.863	0.788	0.824	0.094	0.041	0.948
	C	43499	0.873	0.701	0.778	0.094	0.01	0.963
	M	43458	0.886	0.81	0.846	0.075	0.027	0.955
	F	47144	0.888	0.826	0.855	0.068	0.006	0.952

Table 3. Baseline scores: Results for maximum match with training vocabulary (L=literature, C=computer, M=medicine, F=finance)

Corpus		Word Count	R	P	F	OOV	R_{oov}	R_{iv}
Simplifed Chinese	L	35736	0.986	0.99	0.988	0.069	0.996	0.985
	C	35319	0.991	0.993	0.992	0.152	0.99	0.991
	M	31490	0.989	0.991	0.99	0.11	0.98	0.99
	F	33028	0.994	0.995	0.994	0.087	0.995	0.994
Traditional Chinese	L	36378	0.981	0.988	0.985	0.094	0.998	0.979
	C	43499	0.988	0.991	0.99	0.094	0.996	0.987
	M	43458	0.984	0.989	0.986	0.075	0.992	0.983
	F	47144	0.981	0.986	0.984	0.068	0.997	0.98

Table 4. Topline scores: Results for maximum match with testing vocabulary (L=literature, C=computer, M=medicine, F=finance)

Site ID	Word Count	R	C_r	P	C_p	F	OOV	R_{oov}	R_{iv}
S5	35736	0.945	±0.00241	0.946	±0.00239	0.946	0.069	0.816	0.954
S6	35736	0.94	±0.00251	0.942	±0.00247	0.941	0.069	0.649	0.961
S12	35736	0.937	±0.00257	0.937	±0.00257	0.937	0.069	0.652	0.958
S10	35736	0.936	±0.00259	0.932	±0.00266	0.934	0.069	0.564	0.964
S11	35736	0.931	±0.00268	0.936	±0.00259	0.934	0.069	0.648	0.952
S18	35736	0.932	±0.00266	0.935	±0.00261	0.933	0.069	0.654	0.953
S14	35736	0.925	±0.00279	0.931	±0.00268	0.928	0.069	0.667	0.944
S9	35736	0.92	±0.00287	0.925	±0.00279	0.923	0.069	0.625	0.942
S7	35736	0.915	±0.00295	0.925	±0.00279	0.92	0.069	0.577	0.94
S13	35736	0.916	±0.00293	0.922	±0.00284	0.919	0.069	0.613	0.939
S16	35736	0.917	±0.00292	0.921	±0.00285	0.919	0.069	0.699	0.933
S1	35736	0.908	±0.00306	0.918	±0.00290	0.913	0.069	0.556	0.935
S17	35736	0.909	±0.00304	0.903	±0.00313	0.906	0.069	0.707	0.924
S15	35736	0.907	±0.00307	0.862	±0.00365	*0.884*	0.069	0.206	0.959
S2	35736	0.695	±0.00487	0.744	±0.00462	*0.719*	0.069	0.381	0.719

Table 5. Simplified Chinese: Literature -- Closed (italics indicate performance below baseline)

Site ID	Word Count	R	Cr	P	Cp	F	OOV	R_{oov}	R_{iv}
S6	35736	0.958	±0.00212	0.953	±0.00224	0.955	0.069	0.655	0.981
S3	35736	0.965	±0.00194	0.94	±0.00251	0.952	0.069	0.814	0.976
S18	35736	0.942	±0.00247	0.943	±0.00245	0.942	0.069	0.702	0.959
S9	35736	0.939	±0.00253	0.943	±0.00245	0.941	0.069	0.699	0.957
S1	35736	0.908	±0.00306	0.916	±0.00293	0.912	0.069	0.535	0.936
S5	35736	0.893	±0.00327	0.918	±0.00290	0.905	0.069	0.803	0.899
S4	35736	0.897	±0.00322	0.907	±0.00307	0.902	0.069	0.688	0.913
S15	35736	0.869	±0.00357	0.873	±0.00352	0.871	0.069	0.657	0.885
S8	35736	0.836	±0.00392	0.841	±0.00387	0.838	0.069	0.609	0.853

Table 6. Simplified Chinese: Literature --Open (italics indicate performance below baseline)

Site ID	Word Count	R	C_r	P	C_p	F	OOV	R_{oov}	R_{iv}
S6	35319	0.953	±0.00225	0.95	±0.00232	0.951	0.152	0.827	0.975
S11	35319	0.948	±0.00236	0.945	±0.00243	0.947	0.152	0.853	0.965
S12	35319	0.941	±0.00251	0.94	±0.00253	0.94	0.152	0.757	0.974
S9	35319	0.938	±0.00257	0.936	±0.00260	0.937	0.152	0.805	0.962
S13	35319	0.939	±0.00255	0.934	±0.00264	0.937	0.152	0.81	0.962
S18	35319	0.935	±0.00262	0.934	±0.00264	0.935	0.152	0.792	0.961
S5	35319	0.946	±0.00241	0.914	±0.00298	0.93	0.152	0.808	0.971
S14	35319	0.941	±0.00251	0.916	±0.00295	0.928	0.152	0.796	0.967
S7	35319	0.934	±0.00264	0.919	±0.00290	0.926	0.152	0.739	0.969
S10	35319	0.915	±0.00297	0.915	±0.00297	0.915	0.152	0.594	0.972
S17	35319	0.921	±0.00287	0.9	±0.00319	0.91	0.152	0.748	0.952
S1	35319	0.89	±0.00333	0.908	±0.00308	0.899	0.152	0.592	0.943
S15	35319	0.876	±0.00351	0.844	±0.00386	0.86	0.152	0.457	0.951
S16	35319	0.876	±0.00351	0.799	±0.00426	0.836	0.152	0.456	0.952
S2	35319	0.713	±0.00481	0.641	±0.00511	*0.675*	0.152	0.257	0.795

Table 7. Simplified Chinese: Computer -- Closed (italics indicate performance below baseline)

Site ID	Word Count	R	Cr	P	Cp	F	OOV	R_{oov}	R_{iv}
S9	35319	0.95	±0.00232	0.95	±0.00232	0.95	0.152	0.82	0.973
S18	35319	0.948	±0.00236	0.946	±0.00241	0.947	0.152	0.812	0.973
S6	35319	0.948	±0.00236	0.929	±0.00273	0.939	0.152	0.735	0.986
S3	35319	0.951	±0.00230	0.926	±0.00279	0.938	0.152	0.775	0.982
S8	35319	0.951	±0.00230	0.915	±0.00297	0.932	0.152	0.77	0.983
S5	35319	0.918	±0.00292	0.896	±0.00325	0.907	0.152	0.771	0.945
S1	35319	0.893	±0.00329	0.908	±0.00308	0.9	0.152	0.607	0.944
S4	35319	0.892	±0.00330	0.88	±0.00346	0.886	0.152	0.791	0.91
S15	35319	0.859	±0.00370	0.878	±0.00348	0.868	0.152	0.668	0.893

Table 8. Simplified Chinese: Computer -- Open (italics indicate performance below baseline)

Site ID	Word Count	R	C_r	P	C_p	F	OOV	R_{oov}	R_{iv}
S6	31490	0.942	±0.00263	0.936	±0.00276	0.939	0.11	0.75	0.965
S18	31490	0.937	±0.00274	0.934	±0.00280	0.936	0.11	0.761	0.959
S5	31490	0.94	±0.00268	0.928	±0.00291	0.934	0.11	0.761	0.962
S7	31490	0.927	±0.00293	0.924	±0.00299	0.925	0.11	0.714	0.953
S10	31490	0.933	±0.00282	0.915	±0.00314	0.924	0.11	0.642	0.969
S11	31490	0.924	±0.00299	0.922	±0.00302	0.923	0.11	0.756	0.944
S12	31490	0.93	±0.00288	0.917	±0.00311	0.923	0.11	0.674	0.961
S14	31490	0.928	±0.00291	0.918	±0.00309	0.923	0.11	0.73	0.953
S9	31490	0.923	±0.00300	0.917	±0.00311	0.92	0.11	0.729	0.947
S13	31490	0.917	±0.00311	0.911	±0.00321	0.914	0.11	0.699	0.944
S1	31490	0.902	±0.00335	0.907	±0.00327	0.904	0.11	0.633	0.935
S16	31490	0.9	±0.00338	0.896	±0.00344	0.898	0.11	0.596	0.937
S17	31490	0.894	±0.00347	0.873	±0.00375	0.884	0.11	0.647	0.925
S15	31490	0.885	±0.00360	0.804	±0.00447	0.842	0.11	0.218	0.967
S2	31490	0.735	±0.00497	0.74	±0.00494	*0.738*	0.11	0.378	0.779

Table 9. Simplified Chinese: Medicine -- Closed (italics indicate performance below baseline)

Site ID	Word Count	R	Cr	P	Cp	F	OOV	R_{oov}	R_{iv}
S9	31490	0.94	±0.00268	0.936	±0.00276	0.938	0.11	0.768	0.962
S18	31490	0.941	±0.00266	0.935	±0.00278	0.938	0.11	0.787	0.96
S6	31490	0.951	±0.00243	0.92	±0.00306	0.935	0.11	0.67	0.986
S3	31490	0.953	±0.00239	0.913	±0.00318	0.933	0.11	0.704	0.984
S5	31490	0.917	±0.00311	0.907	±0.00327	0.912	0.11	0.704	0.943
S4	31490	0.91	±0.00323	0.901	±0.00337	0.906	0.11	0.725	0.933
S1	31490	0.904	±0.00332	0.906	±0.00329	0.905	0.11	0.635	0.937
S15	31490	0.865	±0.00385	0.846	±0.00407	0.855	0.11	0.559	0.903
S8	31490	0.839	±0.00414	0.832	±0.00421	*0.836*	0.11	0.618	0.866

Table 10. Simplified Chinese: Medicine -- Open (italics indicate performance below baseline)

Site ID	Word Count	R	C_r	P	C_p	F	OOV	R_{oov}	R_{iv}
S6	33028	0.959	±0.00218	0.96	±0.00216	0.959	0.087	0.827	0.972
S12	33028	0.957	±0.00223	0.956	±0.00226	0.957	0.087	0.813	0.971
S9	33028	0.956	±0.00226	0.955	±0.00228	0.956	0.087	0.857	0.965
S11	33028	0.953	±0.00233	0.956	±0.00226	0.955	0.087	0.871	0.961
S18	33028	0.955	±0.00228	0.956	±0.00226	0.955	0.087	0.848	0.965
S5	33028	0.956	±0.00226	0.952	±0.00235	0.954	0.087	0.849	0.966
S10	33028	0.945	±0.00251	0.941	±0.00259	0.943	0.087	0.666	0.972
S7	33028	0.94	±0.00261	0.942	±0.00257	0.941	0.087	0.719	0.961
S13	33028	0.943	±0.00255	0.94	±0.00261	0.941	0.087	0.773	0.959
S14	33028	0.948	±0.00244	0.928	±0.00284	0.937	0.087	0.761	0.965
S1	33028	0.925	±0.00290	0.938	±0.00265	0.931	0.087	0.664	0.95
S17	33028	0.935	±0.00271	0.915	±0.00307	0.925	0.087	0.736	0.954
S16	33028	0.91	±0.00315	0.906	±0.00321	0.908	0.087	0.562	0.943
S15	33028	0.904	±0.00324	0.865	±0.00376	0.884	0.087	0.321	0.96
S2	33028	0.736	±0.00485	0.752	±0.00475	*0.744*	0.087	0.23	0.784

Table 11. Simplified Chinese: Finance -- Closed (italics indicate performance below baseline)

Site ID	Word Count	R	Cr	P	Cp	F	OOV	R_{oov}	R_{iv}
S9	33028	0.96	±0.00216	0.96	±0.00216	0.96	0.087	0.847	0.971
S6	33028	0.964	±0.00205	0.95	±0.00240	0.957	0.087	0.763	0.983
S18	33028	0.948	±0.00244	0.955	±0.00228	0.951	0.087	0.853	0.957
S3	33028	0.963	±0.00208	0.938	±0.00265	0.95	0.087	0.758	0.982
S1	33028	0.925	±0.00290	0.937	±0.00267	0.931	0.087	0.669	0.95
S5	33028	0.928	±0.00284	0.934	±0.00273	0.931	0.087	0.808	0.939
S8	33028	0.893	±0.00340	0.896	±0.00336	0.894	0.087	0.796	0.902
S4	33028	0.885	±0.00351	0.893	±0.00340	0.889	0.087	0.757	0.897
S15	33028	0.853	±0.00390	0.85	±0.00393	*0.851*	0.087	0.438	0.893

Table 12. Simplified Chinese: Finance -- Open (italics indicate performance below baseline)

Site ID	Word Count	R	C_r	P	C_p	F	OOV	R_{oov}	R_{iv}
S10	36378	0.942	±0.00245	0.942	±0.00245	0.942	0.094	0.788	0.958
S1	36378	0.888	±0.00331	0.905	±0.00307	0.896	0.094	0.728	0.904
S7	36378	0.869	±0.00354	0.91	±0.00300	0.889	0.094	0.698	0.887
S16	36378	0.871	±0.00351	0.891	±0.00327	0.881	0.094	0.67	0.891
S15	36378	0.864	±0.00359	0.789	±0.00428	0.825	0.094	0.105	0.943

Table 13. Traditional Chinese: Literature -- Closed (italics indicate performance below baseline)

Site ID	Word Count	R	C_r	P	C_p	F	OOV	R_{oov}	R_{iv}
S1	36378	0.905	±0.00307	0.9	±0.00315	0.902	0.094	0.775	0.918
S8	36378	0.868	±0.00355	0.802	±0.00418	0.834	0.094	0.503	0.905
S15	36378	0.804	±0.00416	0.722	±0.00470	*0.761*	0.094	0.234	0.863

Table 14. Traditional Chinese: Literature -- Open (italics indicate performance below baseline)

Site ID	Word Count	R	C_r	P	C_p	F	OOV	R_{oov}	R_{iv}
S10	43499	0.948	±0.00213	0.957	±0.00195	0.952	0.094	0.666	0.977
S7	43499	0.933	±0.00240	0.949	±0.00211	0.941	0.094	0.791	0.948
S1	43499	0.908	±0.00277	0.931	±0.00243	0.919	0.094	0.684	0.931
S16	43499	0.913	±0.00270	0.917	±0.00265	0.915	0.094	0.663	0.939
S15	43499	0.868	±0.00325	0.85	±0.00342	0.859	0.094	0.316	0.926

Table 15. Traditional Chinese: Computer -- Closed (italics indicate performance below baseline)

Site ID	Word Count	R	C_r	P	C_p	F	OOV	R_{oov}	R_{iv}
S1	43499	0.911	±0.00273	0.924	±0.00254	0.918	0.094	0.698	0.933
S8	43499	0.875	±0.00317	0.829	±0.00361	0.851	0.094	0.594	0.904
S15	43499	0.789	±0.00391	0.736	±0.00423	*0.761*	0.094	0.35	0.834

Table 16. Traditional Chinese: Computer -- Open (italics indicate performance below baseline)

Site ID	Word Count	R	C_r	P	C_p	F	OOV	R_{oov}	R_{iv}
S10	43458	0.953	±0.00203	0.957	±0.00195	0.955	0.075	0.798	0.966
S7	43458	0.908	±0.00277	0.932	±0.00242	0.92	0.075	0.771	0.919
S1	43458	0.905	±0.00281	0.924	±0.00254	0.914	0.075	0.725	0.919
S16	43458	0.9	±0.00288	0.915	±0.00268	0.908	0.075	0.668	0.919
S15	43458	0.871	±0.00322	0.815	±0.00373	0.842	0.075	0.115	0.932

Table 17. Traditional Chinese: Medicine -- Closed (italics indicate performance below baseline)

Site ID	Word Count	R	C_r	P	C_p	F	OOV	R_{oov}	R_{iv}
S1	43458	0.903	±0.00284	0.903	±0.00284	0.903	0.075	0.729	0.917
S8	43458	0.879	±0.00313	0.814	±0.00373	0.846	0.075	0.48	0.912
S15	43458	0.811	±0.00376	0.74	±0.00421	*0.774*	0.075	0.254	0.856

Table 18. Traditional Chinese: Medicine -- Open (italics indicate performance below baseline)

Site ID	Word Count	R	C_r	P	C_p	F	OOV	R_{oov}	R_{iv}
S10	47144	0.964	±0.00172	0.962	±0.00176	0.963	0.068	0.812	0.975
S7	47144	0.925	±0.00243	0.939	±0.00220	0.932	0.068	0.793	0.935
S16	47144	0.922	±0.00247	0.929	±0.00237	0.925	0.068	0.732	0.935
S1	47144	0.891	±0.00287	0.912	±0.00261	0.901	0.068	0.676	0.907
S15	47144	0.875	±0.00305	0.834	±0.00343	*0.854*	0.068	0.169	0.926

Table 19. Traditional Chinese: Finance -- Closed (italics indicate performance below baseline)

Site ID	Word Count	R	C_r	P	C_p	F	OOV	R_{oov}	R_{iv}
S1	47144	0.903	±0.00273	0.916	±0.00256	0.91	0.068	0.721	0.916
S8	47144	0.832	±0.00344	0.76	±0.00393	*0.794*	0.068	0.356	0.866
S15	47144	0.811	±0.00361	0.753	±0.00397	*0.781*	0.068	0.235	0.853

Table 20. Traditional Chinese: Finance -- Open (italics indicate performance below baseline)

Subtask	Site ID	Track	Literature		Computer		Medicine		Finance	
			F	R_{oov}	F	R_{oov}	F	R_{oov}	F	R_{oov}
Simplified Chinese	S1	◆	0.913	0.556	0.899	0.592	0.904	0.633	0.931	0.664
		◇	0.912	0.535	0.9	0.607	0.905	0.635	0.931	0.669
	S5	◆	0.946	0.816	0.93	0.808	0.934	0.761	0.954	0.849
		◇	0.905	0.803	0.907	0.771	0.912	0.704	0.931	0.808
	S6	◆	0.941	0.649	0.951	0.827	0.939	0.75	0.959	0.827
		◇	0.955	0.655	0.939	0.735	0.935	0.67	0.957	0.763
	S9	◆	0.923	0.625	0.937	0.805	0.92	0.729	0.956	0.857
		◇	0.941	0.699	0.95	0.82	0.938	0.768	0.96	0.847
	S15	◆	0.884	0.206	0.86	0.457	0.842	0.218	0.884	0.321
		◇	0.871	0.657	0.868	0.668	0.855	0.559	0.851	0.438
	S18	◆	0.933	0.654	0.935	0.792	0.936	0.761	0.955	0.848
		◇	0.942	0.702	0.947	0.812	0.938	0.787	0.951	0.853
Traditional Chinese	S1	◆	0.896	0.728	0.919	0.684	0.914	0.725	0.901	0.676
		◇	0.902	0.775	0.918	0.698	0.903	0.729	0.91	0.721
	S15	◆	0.825	0.105	0.859	0.316	0.842	0.115	0.854	0.169
		◇	0.761	0.234	0.761	0.35	0.774	0.254	0.781	0.235

Table 21. Comparison: closed track vs. open track (◆=closed track, ◇=open track)

bakeoff	corpus	characters	OOV rate	word count	closed track		open track	
					R_{oov}	F	R_{oov}	F
2007	CKIP	traditional Chinese	0.074	90678	0.740	0.947	0.780	0.956
2010	medicine		0.075	43458	0.798	0.955	0.729	0.903
2006	UPUC	simplified Chinese	0.088	155K	0.707	0.933	0.768	0.944
2010	finance		0.087	33028	0.871	0.955	0.853	0.951
2005	CityU	traditional Chinese	0.074	41K	0.736	0.941	0.806	0.962
2010	medicine		0.075	43458	0.798	0.955	0.729	0.903
2003	PK	simplified Chinese	0.069	17K	0.763	0.940	0.799	0.959
2010	literature		0.069	35736	0.816	0.946	0.814	0.952

Table 22. Comparisons of top OOV recall rates of different bakeoffs on the test corpora with similar OOV rates (2003, 2005, 2006 and 2007 represent the SIGHAN bakeoff 2003, 2005, 2006 and 2007 respectively, and 2010 represents the CIPS-SIGHAN CLP 2010 bakeoff)

			Closed Track						Open Track					
		OOV	ID	R	P	F	R_{oov}	R_{iv}	ID	R	P	F	R_{oov}	R_{iv}
S	L	0.069	S5	0.945	0.946	0.946	0.816	0.954	S6	0.958	0.953	0.955	0.655	0.981
	C	0.152	S6	0.953	0.95	0.951	0.827	0.975	S9	0.95	0.95	0.95	0.82	0.973
	M	0.11	S6	0.942	0.936	0.939	0.75	0.965	S9	0.94	0.936	0.938	0.768	0.962
									S18	0.941	0.935	0.938	0.787	0.96
	F	0.087	S6	0.959	0.96	**0.959**	**0.827**	0.972	S9	0.96	0.96	**0.96**	**0.847**	0.971
T	L	0.094	S10	0.942	0.942	0.942	0.788	0.958	S1	0.905	0.9	0.902	**0.775**	0.918
	C	0.094	S10	0.948	0.957	0.952	0.666	0.977	S1	0.911	0.924	0.918	0.698	0.933
	M	0.075	S10	0.953	0.957	0.955	0.798	0.966	S1	0.903	0.903	0.903	0.729	0.917
	F	0.068	S10	0.964	0.962	**0.963**	**0.812**	0.975	S1	0.903	0.916	**0.91**	**0.721**	0.916

Table 23. Top performance on every subtask, domain, and track (S=simplified Chinese test, T=traditional Chinese test, L=literature, C=computer, M=medicine, F=finance)

5 Conclusions & Future Directions

The CIPS-SIGHAN CLP 2010 Chinese Word Segmentation Bakeoff successfully brought together a collection of 18 strong research groups to assess the progress of this fundamental research in Chinese language processing.

There is clearly no single best system. And the participating sites S1, S10, S9, S6, S5 and S18 have all achieved respectable scores on different track runs of this bakeoff. An improvement on the OOV recall over the prior bakeoffs has been observed.

It is the first time to apply word segmentation bakeoff on four domains. It's also the first time to use unlabeled training corpora in the bakeoff to test the unsupervised or semi-supervised learning ability of the segmentation system. Unsupervised or Semi-supervised learning needs to incorporate large amounts of unlabeled data. We design the evaluation with two unknown domains without any in-domain training corpora, compared with two known domains each with an in-domain unlabeled training corpus. Although no significant difference has been found, it's still worth it. The size of our unlabeled training corpora was too small in this bakeoff, and we hope to improve this in next evaluation.

The word segmentation is a necessary pre-processing phase for the downstream processing tasks. In future evaluations, we hope to see the integration of word segmentation task with a higher level task such as machine translation, with a view to exactly evaluate the impact of improvements in word segmentation on broader downstream applications.

Acknowledgement

This work is supported by the National Natural Science Foundation of China (Grant No. 90920004). We gratefully acknowledge the generous assistance of the organizations listed below who provided the data and the Chinese word segmentation standard for this bakeoff; without their support, it could not have taken place:

- City University of Hong Kong
- Institute for Computational Linguistics, Beijing University, Beijing, China

We thank Le Sun for his organization of the First CIPS-SIGHAN Joint Conference on Chinese Language Processing of which this bakeoff is part. We thank Lili Zhao for her segmentation-inconsistency-checking program and other preparation works for this bakeoff, and thank Guanghui Luo and Siyang Cao for the online scoring system they set up and maintained. We thank Yajuan Lü for her helpful suggestions on this paper. Finally we thank all the participants for their interest and hard work in making this bakeoff a success.

References

Charles Grinstead and J. Laurie Snell. 1997. *Introduction to Probability.* American Mathematical Society, Providence, RI.

Gina-Anne Levow. 2006. *The third international Chinese language processing bakeoff: Word segmentation and named entity recognition.* In Proceedings of the Fifth SIGHAN Workshop on Chinese Language Processing, pages 108–117, Sydney, Australia, July. Association for Computational Linguistics.

Guangjin Jin and Xiao Chen. 2007. *The Fourth International Chinese Language Processing Bakeoff: Chinese Word Segmentation, Named Entity Recognition and Chinese POS Tagging.* In the Sixth SIGHAN Workshop on Chinese Language Processing, pages 69-81, Hyderabad, India.

Richard Sproat and Thomas Emerson. 2003. *The first international Chinese word segmentation bakeoff. In The Second SIGHAN Workshop on Chinese Language Processing,* pages 133–143, Sapporo, Japan.

Thomas Emerson. 2005. *The second international Chinese word segmentation bakeoff.* In Proceedings of the Fourth SIGHAN Workshop on Chinese Language Processing, pages 123–133, Jeju Island, Korea.

A Multi-layer Chinese Word Segmentation System Optimized for Out-of-domain Tasks

Qin Gao
Language Technologies Institute
Carnegie Mellon University
qing@cs.cmu.edu

Stephan Vogel
Language Technologies Institute
Carnegie Mellon University
stephan.vogel@cs.cmu.edu

Abstract

State-of-the-art Chinese word segmentation systems have achieved high performance when training data and testing data are from the same domain. However, they suffer from the generalizability problem when applied on test data from different domains. We introduce a multi-layer Chinese word segmentation system which can integrate the outputs from multiple heterogeneous segmentation systems. By training a second layer of large margin classifier on top of the outputs from several Conditional Random Fields classifiers, it can utilize a small amount of in-domain training data to improve the performance. Experimental results show consistent improvement on F1 scores and OOV recall rates by applying the approach.

1 Introduction

The Chinese word segmentation problem has been intensively investigated in the past two decades. From lexicon-based methods such as Bi-Directed Maximum Match (BDMM) (Chen et al., 2005) to statistical models such as Hidden Markove Model (HMM) (Zhang et al., 2003), a broad spectrum of approaches have been experimented. By casting the problem as a character labeling task, sequence labeling models such as Conditional Random Fields can be applied on the problem (Xue and Shen, 2003). State-of-the-art CRF-based systems have achieved good performance. However, like many machine learning problems, generalizability is crucial for a domain-independent segmentation system. Because the training data usually come from limited domains, when the domain of test data is different from the training data, the results are still not satisfactory.

A straight-forward solution is to obtain more labeled data in the domain we want to test. However this is not easily achievable because the amount of data needed to train a segmentation system are large. In this paper, we focus on improving the system performance by using a relatively small amount of manually labeled in-domain data together with larger out-of-domain corpus[1]. The effect of mingling the small in-domain data into large out-of-domain data may be neglectable due to the difference in data size. Hence, we try to explore an alternative way that put a second layer of classifier on top of the segmentation systems built on out-of-domain corpus (we will call them sub-systems). The classifier should be able to utilize the information from the sub-systems and optimize the performance with a small amount of in-domain data.

The basic idea of our method is to integrate a number of different sub-systems *whose performance varies on the new domain*. Figure 1 demonstrates the system architecture. There are two layers in the system. In the lower layer, the out-of-domain corpora are used, together with other resources to produce heterogeneous sub-systems. In the second layer the outputs of the sub-systems in the first layer are treated as input to the classifier. We train the classifier with small in-domain data. All the sub-systems should have

[1]From this point, we use the term *out-of-domain corpus* to refer to the general and large training data that are not related to the test domain, and the term *in-domain corpus* to refer to small amount of data that comes from the *same* domain of the test data

reasonable performance on all domains, but their performance on different domains may vary. The job of the second layer is to find the best decision boundary on the target domain, in presence of all the decisions made by the sub-systems.

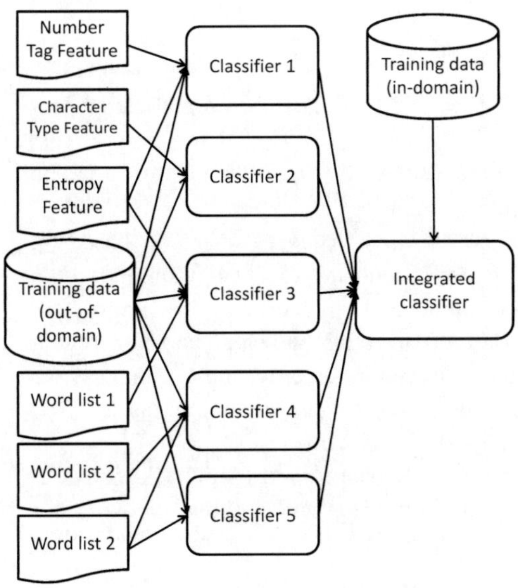

Figure 1: The architecture of the system, the first layer (sub-systems) is trained on general out-of-domain corpus and various resources, while the second layer of the classifier is trained on in-domain corpus.

Conditional Random Fields (CRF) (Lafferty et al., 2001) has been applied on Chinese word segmentation and achieved high performance. However, because of its conditional nature the small amount of in-domain corpus will not significantly change the distributions of the model parameters trained on out-of-domain corpus, it is more suitable to be used in the sub-systems than in the second-layer classifier. Large margin models such as Support Vector Machine (SVM) (Vapnik, 1995) can be trained on small corpus and generalize well. Therefore we chose to use CRF in building sub-systems and SVM in building the second-layer. We built multiple CRF-based Chinese word segmentation systems using different features, and then use the marginal probability of each tag of all the systems as features in SVM. The SVM is then trained on small in-domain corpus, results in a decision hyperplane that minimizes the loss in the small training data. To integrate the dependencies of output tags, we use SVM-HMM (Altun et al., 2003) to capture the interactions between tags and features. By applying SVM-HMM we can bias our decision towards most informative CRF-based system w.r.t. the target domain. Our methodology is similar to (Cohen and Carvalho, 2005), who applied a cross-validation-like method to train sequential stacking models, while we directly use small amount of in-domain data to train the second-layer classifiers.

The paper is organized as follows, first we will discuss the CRF-based sub-systems we used in section 2, and then the SVM-based system combination method in section 3. Finally, in section 4 the experimental results are presented.

2 CRF-based sub-systems

In this section we describe the sub-systems we used in system. All of the sub-systems are based on CRF with different features. The tag set we use is the 6-tag (B1, B2, B3, M, E, S) set proposed by Zhao et al (2006). All of the sub-systems use the same tag set, however as we will see later, the second-layer classifier in our system does not require the sub-systems to have a common tag set. Also, all of the sub-systems include a common set of character features proposed in (Zhao and Kit, 2008). The offsets and concatenations of the six n-gram features (the feature template) are: $C_{-1}, C_0, C_1, C_{-1}C_0, C_0C_1, C_{-1}C_1$. In the remaining part of the section we will introduce other features that we employed in different sub-systems.

2.1 Character type features

By simply classify the characters into four types: Punctuation (P), Digits (D), Roman Letters (L) and Chinese characters (C), we can assign character type tags to every character. The idea is straight-forward. We denote the feature as CTF.

Similar to character feature, we also use different offsets and concatenations for character type features. The feature template is identical to character feature, i.e. CTF_{-1}, CTF_0, CTF_1, $CTF_{-1}CTF_0$, CTF_0CTF_1, $CTF_{-1}CTF_1$ are used as features in CRF training.

2.2 Number tag feature

Numbers take a large portion of the OOV words, which can easily be detected by regular expressions or Finite State Automata. However there are often ambiguities on the boundary of numbers. Therefore, instead of using detected numbers as final answers, we use them as features. The number detector we developed finds the longest substrings in a sentence that are:

- Chinese Numbers (N)
- Chinese Ordinals (O)
- Chinese Dates (D)

For each character of the detected numbers/ordinal/date, we assign a tag that reflects the position of the character in the detected number/ordinal/date. We adopt the four-tag set (B, M, E, S). The position tags are appended to end of the number/ordinal/date tags to form the number tag feature of that character. I.e. there are totally 13 possible values for the number tag feature, as listed in Table 1.[2]

	Number	Ordinal	Date	Other
Begin	NB	OB	DB	
Middle	NM	OM	DM	XX
End	NE	OE	DE	
Single	NS	*OS**	*DS**	

Table 1: The feature values used in the number tag feature, note that OS and DS are never observed because there is no single character ordinal/date by our definition.

Similar to character feature and character type feature, the feature template mention before is also applied on the number tag feature. We denote the number tag features as NF.

2.3 Conditional Entropy Feature

We define the *Forward Conditional Entropy* of a character C by the entropy of all the characters that follow C in a given corpus, and the *Backward Conditional Entropy* as the entropy of all the characters that precede C in a given corpus. The conditional entropy can be computed easily from a character bigram list generated from the corpus. Assume we have a bigram list $B = \{B_1, B_2, \cdots, B_N\}$, where every bigram entry $B_k = \{c_{i_k}, c_{j_k}, n_k\}$ is a triplet of the two consecutive characters c_{i_k} and c_{j_k} and the count of the bigram in the corpus, n_k. The Forward Conditional Entropy of the character C is defined by:

$$H_f(C) := \sum_{c_{i_k}=C} \frac{n_k}{Z} \log \frac{n_k}{Z}$$

where $Z = \sum_{c_{i_k}=C} n_k$ is the normalization factor.

And the Backward Conditional Entropy can be computed similarly.

We assign labels to every character based on the conditional entropy of it. If the conditional entropy value is less than 1.0, we assign feature value 0 to the character, and for region $[1.0, 2.0)$, we assign feature value 1. Similarly we define the region-to-value mappings as follows: $[2.0, 3.5) \rightarrow 2$, $[3.5, 5.0) \rightarrow 4$, $[5.0, 7.0) \rightarrow 5$, $[7.0, +\infty) \rightarrow 6$. The forward and backward conditional entropy forms two features. We will refer to these features as EF.

2.4 Lexical Features

Lexical features are the most important features to make sub-systems output different results on different domains. We adopt the definition of the features partially from (Shi and Wang, 2007). In our system we use only the $L_{begin}(C_0)$ and $L_{end}(C_0)$ features, omitting the $L_{mid}C_0$ feature. The two features represent the maximum length of words found in the lexicon that contain the current character as the first or last character, correspondingly. For feature values equal or greater than 6, we group them into one value.

Although we can find a number of Chinese lexicons available, they may or may not be generated according to the same standard as the training data. Concatenating them into one may bring in noise and undermine the performance. Therefore, every lexicon will generate its own lexical features.

3 SVM-based System Combination

Generalization is a fundamental problem of Chinese word segmentation. Since the training data may come from different domains than the test data, the vocabulary and the distribution can also

[2] Two of the tags, OS and DS are never observed.

be different. Ideally, if we can have labeled data from the same domain, we can train segmenters specific to the domain. However obtaining sufficient amount of labeled data in the target domain is time-consuming and expensive. In the mean time, if we only label a small amount of data in the target domain and put them into the training data, the effect may be too small because the size of out-of-domain data can overwhelm the in-domain data.

In this paper we propose a different way of utilizing small amount of in-domain corpus. We put a second-layer classifier on top of the CRF-based sub-systems, the output of CRF-based sub-systems are treated as features in an SVM-HMM (Altun et al., 2003) classifier. We can train the SVM-HMM classifier on a small amount of in-domain data. The training procedure can be viewed as finding the optimal decision boundary that minimize the hinge loss on the in-domain data. Because the number of features for SVM-HMM is significantly smaller than CRF, we can train the model with as few as several hundred sentences.

Similar to CRF, the SVM-HMM classifier still treats the Chinese word segmentation problem as character tagging. However, because of the limitation of training data size, we try to minimize the number of classes. We chose to adopt the two-tag set, i.e. class 1 indicates the character is the end of a word and class 2 means otherwise. Also, due to limited amount of training data, we do not use any character features, instead, the features comes directly from the output of sub-systems. The SVM-HMM can use any real value features, which enables integration of a wide range of segmenters. In this paper we use only the CRF-based segmenters, and the features are the marginal probabilities (Sutton and McCallum, 2006) of all the tags in the tag set for each character. As an example, for a CRF-based sub-system that outputs six tags, it will output six features for each character for the SVM-HMM classifier, corresponding to the marginal probability of the character given the CRF model. The marginal probabilities for the same tag (e.g. B1, S, etc) come from different CRF-based sub-systems are treated as distinct features.

	Features	Lexicons
S1	CF, CTF	None
S2	CF, NF	ADSO, CTB6
S3	CF, CTF, NF	ADSO
S4	CF, CTF, NF, EF	ADSO, CTB6
S5	CF, EF	None
S6	CF, NF	None
S7	CF, CTF	ADSO
S8	CF, CTF	CTB6

Table 2: The configurations of CRF-based subsystems. S1 to S4 are used in the final submission of the Bake-off, S5 through S8 are also presented to show the effects of individual features.

When we encounter data from a new domain, we first use one of the CRF-based sub-system to segment a portion of the data, and manually correct obvious segmentation errors. The manually labeled data are then processed by all the CRF-based sub-systems, so as to obtain features of every character. After that, we train the SVM-HMM model using these features.

During decoding, the Chinese input will also be processed by all of the CRF-based sub-systems, and the outputs will be fed into the SVM-HMM classifier. The final decisions of word boundaries are based solely on the classified labels of SVM-HMM model.

For the Bake-off system, we labeled two hundred sentences in each of the unsegmented training set (A and B). Since only one submission is allowed, the SVM-HMM model of the final system was trained on the concatenation of the two training sets, i.e. four hundred sentences.

The CRF-based sub-systems are trained using CRF++ toolkit (Kudo, 2003), and the SVM-HMM trained by the SVM^{struct} toolkit (Joachims et al., 2009).

4 Experiments

To evaluate the effectiveness of the proposed system combination method, we performed two experiments. First, we evaluate the system combination method on provided training data in the way that is similar to cross-validation. Second, we experimented with training the SVM-HMM model with the manually labeled data come from cor-

	Micro-Average				Macro-Average			
	P	R	F1	OOV-R	P	R	F1	OOV-R
S1	0.962	0.960	0.961	0.722	0.962	0.960	0.960	0.720
S2	0.965	0.966	0.966	0.725	0.965	0.966	0.966	0.723
S3	0.966	0.967	0.967	0.731	0.966	0.967	0.967	0.729
S4	0.968	0.969	0.968	0.731	0.967	0.969	**0.969**	0.729
S5	0.962	0.960	0.961	0.720	0.962	0.960	0.960	0.718
S6	0.963	0.961	0.962	0.730	0.963	0.961	0.961	0.729
S7	0.966	0.967	0.966	0.723	0.966	0.967	0.967	0.720
S8	0.963	0.960	0.962	0.727	0.963	0.960	0.960	0.726
CB	0.969	0.969	**0.969**	**0.741**	0.969	0.969	**0.969**	**0.739**

Table 3: The performance of individual sub-systems and combined system. The Micro-Average results come from concatenating all the outputs of the ten-fold systems and then compute the scores, and the Macro-Average results are calculated by first compute the scores in every of the ten-fold systems and then average the scores.

	Set A				Set B			
	P	R	F1	OOV-R	P	R	F1	OOV-R
S1	0.925	0.920	0.923	0.625	0.936	0.938	0.937	0.805
S2	0.934	0.934	0.934	0.641	0.941	0.930	0.935	0.751
S3	0.940	0.937	0.938	0.677	0.938	0.926	0.932	0.752
S4	0.942	0.940	0.941	0.688	0.944	0.929	0.936	0.776
CB1	0.943	0.941	0.942	0.688	0.948	0.936	0.942	0.794
CB2	0.941	0.940	0.941	0.692	0.939	0.949	0.944	**0.821**
CB3	0.943	0.939	**0.941**	**0.699**	0.950	0.950	**0.950**	0.820

Table 4: The performance of individual systems and system combination on Bake-off test data, CB1, CB2, and CB3 are system combination trained on labeled data from domain A, B, and the concatenation of the data from both domains.

responding domains, and tested the resulting systems on the Bake-off test data.

For experiment 1, We divide the training set into 11 segments, segment 0 through 9 contains 1733 sentences, and segment 10 has 1724 sentence. We perform 10-fold cross-validation on segment 0 to 9. Every time we pick one segment from segment 0 to 9 as test set and the remaining 9 segments are used to train CRF-based subsystems. Segment 10 is used as the training set for SVM-HMM model. The sub-systems we used is listed in Table 2.

In Table 3 we provide the micro-level and macro-level average of performance the ten-fold evaluation, including both the combined system and all the individual sub-systems. Because the system combination uses more data than its sub-systems (segment 10), in order to have a fair comparison, when evaluating individual subsystems, segment 10 is appended to the training data of CRF model. Therefore, the individual subsystems and system combination have exactly the same set of training data.

As we can see in the results in Table 3, the system combination method (Row CB) has improvement over the best sub-system (S4) on both F1 and OOV recall rate, and the OOV recall rate improved by 1%. We should notice that in this experiment we actually did not deal with any data from different domains, the advantage of the proposed method is therefore not prominent.

We continue to present the experiment results of the second experiment. In the experiment we labeled 200 sentences from each of the unlabeled bake-off training set A and B, and trained the SVM-HMM model on the labeled data. We compare the performance of the four sub-systems and the performance of the system combination method trained on: 1) 200 sentences from A, 2) 200 sentences from B, and 3) the concatenation of the 400 sentences from both A and B. We show the scores on the bake-off test set A and B in Table 4.

As we can see from the results in Table 4, the system combination method outperforms all the individual systems, and the best performance is observed when using both of the labeled data from domain A and B, which indicates the potential of further improvement by increasing the amount of in-domain training data. Also, the individual sub-systems with the best performance on the two domains are different. System 1 performs well on Set B but not on Set A, so does System 4, which tops on Set A but not as good as System 1 on Set B. The system combination results appear to be much more stable on the two domains, which is a preferable characteristic if the segmentation system needs to deal with data from various domains.

5 Conclusion

In this paper we discussed a system combination method based on SVM-HMM for the Chinese word segmentation problem. The method can utilize small amount of training data in target domains to improve the performance over individual sub-systems trained on data from different domains. Experimental results show that the method is effective in improving the performance with a small amount of in-domain training data.

Future work includes adding more heterogeneous sub-systems other than CRF-based ones into the system and investigate the effects on the performance. Automatic domain adaptation for Chinese word segmentation can also be an outcome of the method, which may be an interesting research topic in the future.

References

Altun, Yasemin, Ioannis Tsochantaridis, and Thomas Hofmann. 2003. Hidden markov support vector machines. In *Proceedings of International Conference on Machine Learning (ICML)*.

Chen, Yaodong, Ting Wang, and Huowang Chen. 2005. Using directed graph based bdmm algorithm for chinese word segmentation. pages 214–217.

Cohen, William W. and Vitor Carvalho. 2005. Stacked sequential learning. In *Proceedings of the International Joint Conference on Artificial Intelligence (IJ-CAI)*.

Joachims, Thorsten, Thomas Finley, and Chun-Nam John Yu. 2009. Cutting-plane training of structural svms. *Machine Learning*, 77(1):27–59.

Kudo, Taku. 2003. CRF++: Yet another crf toolkit. Web page: http://crfpp.sourceforge.net/.

Lafferty, John, Andrew McCallum, and Fernando Pereira. 2001. Conditional random fields: Probabilistic models for segmenting and labeling sequence data. In *Proceedings of International Conference on Machine Learning (ICML)*.

Shi, Yanxin and Mengqiu Wang. 2007. A dual-layer crfs based joint decoding method for cascaded segmentation and labeling tasks. In *Proceedings of the International Joint Conference on Artificial Intelligence (IJ-CAI)*.

Sutton, Charles and Andrew McCallum, 2006. *Introduction to Statistical Relational Learning*, chapter An Introduction to Conditional Random Fields for Relational Learning. MIT Press.

Vapnik, Vladimir N. 1995. *The Nature of Statistical Learning Theory*. Springer.

Xue, Nianwen and Libin Shen. 2003. Chinese word segmentation as lmr tagging. In *Proceedings of the second SIGHAN workshop on Chinese language processing*, pages 176–179.

Zhang, Huaping, Qun Liu, Xueqi Cheng, Hao Zhang, and Hongkui Yu. 2003. Chinese lexical analysis using hierarchical hidden markov model. In *Proceedings of the second SIGHAN workshop on Chinese language processing*, pages 63–70.

Zhao, Hai and Chunyu Kit. 2008. Unsupervised segmentation helps supervised learning of character tagging for word segmentation and named entity recognition. In *The Sixth SIGHAN Workshop on Chinese Language Processing (SIGHAN-6)*, pages 106–111.

Zhao, Hai, Chang-Ning Huang, Mu Li, and Bao-Liang Lu. 2006. Effective tag set selection in chinese word segmentation via conditional random field modeling. In *Proceedings of the 20th Pacific Asia Conference on Language, Information and Computation (PACLIC-20)*, pages 87–94.

HMM Revises Low Marginal Probability by CRF for Chinese Word Segmentation*

Degen Huang, Deqin Tong, Yanyan Luo
Department of Computer Science and Engineering
Dalian University of Technology
huangdg@dlut.edu.cn, {tongdeqin, ziyanluoyu}@gmail.com

Abstract

This paper presents a Chinese word segmentation system for CIPS-SIGHAN 2010 Chinese language processing task. Firstly, based on Conditional Random Field (CRF) model, with local features and global features, the character-based tagging model is designed. Secondly, Hidden Markov Models (HMM) is used to revise the substrings with low marginal probability by CRF. Finally, confidence measure is used to regenerate the result and simple rules to deal with the strings within letters and numbers. As is well known that character-based approach has outstanding capability of discovering out-of-vocabulary (OOV) word, but external information of word lost. HMM makes use of word information to increase in-vocabulary (IV) recall. We participate in the simplified Chinese word segmentation both closed and open test on all four corpora, which belong to different domains. Our system achieves better performance.

1 Introduction

Chinese Word Segmentation (CWS) has witnessed a prominent progress in the first four SIGHAN Bakeoffs. Since Xue (2003) used character-based tagging, this method has attracted more and more attention. Some previous work (Peng et al., 2004; Tseng et al., 2005; Low et al., 2005) illustrated the effectiveness of using characters as tagging units, while literatures (Zhang et al., 2006; Zhao and Kit, 2007a; Zhang and Clark, 2007) focus on employing lexical words or subwords as tagging units. Because the word-based models can capture the word-level contextual information and IV knowledge. Besides, many strategies are proposed to balance the IV and OOV performance (Wang et al., 2008).

CRF has been widely used in sequence labeling tasks and has a good performance (Lafferty et al., 2001). Zhao and Kit (2007b; 2008) attempt to integrate global information with local information to further improve CRF-based tagging method of CWS, which provides a solid foundation for strengthening CRF learning with unsupervised learning outcomes.

In order to increase the accuracy of tagging using CRF, we adopt the strategy, which is: if the marginal probability of characters is lower than a threshold, the modified component based on HMM will be trigged; combining the confidence measure the results will be regenerated.

2 Our word segmentation system

In this section, we describe our system in more details. Three modules are included in our system: a basic character-based CRF tagger, HMM which revises the substrings with low marginal probability and confidence measure which combines them to regenerate the result. In addition, we also use some rules to deal with the strings within letters and numbers.

2.1 Character-based CRF tagger

Tag Set A 6-tag set is adopted in our system. It includes six tags: B, B2, B3, M, E and S. Here, Tag B and E stand for the first and the last position in a multi-character word, respectively. S stands for a single-character word. B2 and B3 stand for the second and the third position in a

* The work described in this paper is supported by Microsoft Research Asia Funded Project.

multi-character word. M stands for the fourth or more rear position in a multi-character word with more than four characters. The 6-tag set is proved to work more effectively than other tag sets in improving the segmentation performance of CRFs by Zhao et al. (2006).

Feature templates In our system, six n-gram templates, namely, C_{-1}, C_0, C_1, $C_{-1}C_0$, C_0C_1, $C_{-1}C_1$ are selected as features, where C stands for a character and the subscripts -1, 0 and 1 stand for the previous, current and next character, respectively. Furthermore, another one is character type feature template $T_{-1}T_0T_1$. We use four classes of character sets which are predefined as: class N represents numbers, class L represents non-Chinese letters, class P represents punctuation labels and class C represents Chinese characters.

Except for the character feature, we also employ global word feature templates. The basic idea of using global word information for CWS is to inform the supervised learner how likely it is that the subsequence can be a word candidate. The accessor variety (AV) (Feng et al., 2005) is opted as global word feature, which is integrated into CRF successfully in literatures (Zhao and Kit, 2007b; Zhao and Kit, 2008). The AV value of a substring s is defined as:

$$AV(s) = \min\{L_{av}(s), R_{av}(s)\} \quad (1)$$

Where the left and right AV values $L_{av}(s)$ and $R_{av}(s)$ are defined, respectively, as the number of its distinct predecessors and the number of its distinct successors.

Multiple feature templates are used to represent word candidates of various lengths identified by the AV criterion. Meanwhile, in order to alleviate the sparse data problem, we follow the feature function definition for a word candidate s with a score $AV(s)$ in Zhao and Kit (2008), namely:

$$f_n(s) = t,\ 2^t \leq AV(s) < 2^{t+1} \quad (2)$$

In order to improve the efficiency, all candidates longer than five characters are given up. The AV features of word candidates can't directly be utilized to direct CRF learning before being transferred to the information of characters. So we only choose the one with the greatest AV score to activate the above feature function for that character.

In the open test, we only add another feature of 'FRE', the basic idea of which is if a string matches a word in an existing dictionary, it may be a clue that the string is likely a true word. Then more word boundary information can be obtained, which may be helpful for CRF learning on CWS. The dictionary we used is downloaded from the Internet[①] and consists of 108,750 words with length of one to four characters. We get FRE features similar to the AV features.

2.2 HMM revises substrings with low marginal probability

The MP (short for marginal probability) of each character labeled with one of the six tags can be got separately through the basic CRF tagger. Here, B replaces 'B' and 'S' , and I represents other tags ('B_2', 'B_3', 'M', 'E'). So each character has corresponding new MP as defined in formula (3) and (4).

$$P_B = \frac{(P_S + P_B)}{\sum P_t} \quad (3)$$

$$P_I = \frac{(P_{B_2} + P_{B_3} + P_M + P_E)}{\sum P_t} \quad (4)$$

Where $t \in \{S, B, B_2, B_3, M, E\}$ and P_t can be calculated by using forward-backward algorithm and more details are in Lafferty et al. (2001).

A low confident word refers to a word with word boundary ambiguity which can be reflected by the MP of the first character of a word. That is, it's a low confident word if the MP of the first character of the word is lower than a threshold β (it's an empirical value and can be obtained by experiments). After getting the new MP, all these low confident candidate words are recombined with their direct predecessors until the occurrence of a word that the MP of its first character is above the threshold β, and then a new substring is generated for post processing.

Then, we use class-based HMM to re-segment the substrings mentioned above. Given a word

---

[①] http://ccl.pku.edu.cn/doubtfire/Course/Chinese%20Information%20Processing/Source_Code/Chapter_8/Lexicon_full.zip

w_i, a word class c_i is the word itself. Let W be the word sequence, let C be its class sequence, and let $W^{\#}$ be the segmentation result with the maximum likelihood. Then, a class-based HMM model (Liu, 2004) can be got.

$$\begin{aligned} W^{\#} &= \arg\max_{W} P(W) \\ &= \arg\max_{W} P(W \mid C)P(C) \\ &= \arg\max_{w_1 w_2 \ldots w_m} \prod_{i=1}^{m} p'(w_i \mid c_i)P(c_i \mid c_{i-1}) \\ &= \arg\max_{w_1 w_2 \ldots w_m} \prod_{i=1}^{m} P(c_i \mid c_{i-1}) \qquad (5) \end{aligned}$$

Where $P(c_i \mid c_{i-1})$ indicates the transitive probability from one class to another and it can be obtained from training corpora.

The word boundary of results from HMM is also represented by tag 'B' and 'I' which meaning are the same as mentioned in above.

2.3 Confidence measure and post processing for final result

There are two segmentation results for substrings with low MP candidates after reprocessing using HMM. Analyzing experiments data, we find wrong tags labeled by CRF are mainly: OOV words in test data, IV words and incorrect words recognized by CRF. Rectifying the tags with lower MP simply may produce an even worse performance in some case. For example, some OOV words are recognized correctly by CRF but with low MP. So, we can't accept the revised results completely. A confidence measure approach is used to resolve this problem. Its calculation is defined as:

$$P_C = P_{C_o} + \lambda(1 - P_{C_o}) \qquad (6)$$

P_{C_o} is the MP of the character as 'I', λ is the premium coefficient. Based on the new value, a threshold t was used, if the value was lower than t, the original tag 'I' will be rejected and changed into the tag 'B' which is labeled by HMM.

At last, we use a simple rule to post-process the result directed at the strings that containing letters, numbers and punctuations. If the punctuation (not all punctuations) is half-width and the string before or after are composed of letters and numbers, combine all into a string as a whole. For an example, '.', '/', ':', '%' and '\' are usually recognized as split tokens. So, it needs handling additionally.

3 Experiments results and analysis

We evaluate our system on the corpora given by CIPS-SIGHAN 2010. There are four test corpora which belong to different domains. The details are showed in table 1.

Domain	Testing Data	OOV rate
A	149K	0.069
B	165K	0.152
C	151K	0.110
D	157K	0.087

Table 1. Test corpora details

A, B, C and D represent literature, computer science, medical science and finance, respectively.

3.1 Closed test

The rule for the closed test in Bakeoff is that no additional information beyond training corpora is allowed. Following the rule, the closed test is designed to compare our system with other CWS systems. Five metrics of SIGHAN Bakeoff are used to evaluate the segmentation results: F-score (F), recall (R), precision (P), the recall on IV words (R_{IV}) and the recall on OOV words (Roov). The closed test results are presented in table 2.

Domain	R	P	F	R_{oov}	$R^{②}_{IV}$
A	0.932	0.936	0.934	0.662	0.952
	0.940	0.942	0.941	0.649	0.961
B	0.950	0.948	0.949	0.831	0.971
	0.953	0.950	0.951	0.827	0.975
C	0.934	0.932	0.933	0.751	0.957
	0.942	0.936	0.939	0.750	0.965
D	0.955	0.957	0.956	0.837	0.966
	0.959	0.960	0.959	0.827	0.972

Table 2. Evaluation closed results on all data sets

② In order to analyze our results, we got value of R_{IV} from the organizers because it can't be obtained from the scoring system on http://nlp.ict.ac.cn/demo/CIPS-SIGHAN2010/#.

In each domain, the first line shows the results of our basic CRF segmenter and the second one shows the final results dealt with HMM through confidence measure, which make it clear that using the confidence measure can improve the overall F-score by increasing value of R and P.

Domain	ID	R	P	F	R_{oov}	R_{IV}
A	5	0.945	0.946	0.946	0.816	0.954
	our	0.940	0.942	0.941	0.649	0.961
	12	0.937	0.937	0.937	0.652	0.958
B	our	0.953	0.950	0.951	0.827	0.975
	11	0.948	0.945	0.947	0.853	0.965
	12	0.941	0.940	0.940	0.757	0.974
C	our	0.942	0.936	0.939	0.750	0.965
	18	0.937	0.934	0.936	0.761	0.959
	5	0.940	0.928	0.934	0.761	0.962
D	our	0.959	0.960	0.959	0.827	0.972
	12	0.957	0.956	0.957	0.813	0.971
	9	0.956	0.955	0.956	0.857	0.965

Table 3. Comparison our closed results with the top three in all test sets

Next, we compare it with other top three systems. From the table 3 we can see that our system achieves better performance on closed test. In contrast, the values of R_{IV} of our method are superior to others', which contributes to the model we use. Whether the features of AV for character-based CRF tagger or HMM revising, they all make good use of word information of training corpora.

3.2 Open test

In the open test, the only additional source we use is the dictionary mentioned above. We get one first and two third best. Our result is showed in table 4. Compared with closed test, the value of R_{IV} is increased in all test corpora. But we only get the higher value of F in domain of literature. The reasons will be analyzed as follows:

In the open test, the OOV words are split into pieces because our model may be more dependent on the dictionary information. Consequently, we get higher value of R but lower P. The training corpora are the same as closed test, but it is different that FRE features are added. The additional features enhance the original information of IV words, so the value of R_{IV} is improved to some extent. However, they have side effects for OOV segmentation. We will continue to solve this problem in the future work.

Domain	R	P	F	R_{oov}	R_{IV}
A	0.956	0.947	0.952	0.636	0.980
	0.958	0.953	0.955	0.655	0.981
B	0.943	0.921	0.932	0.716	0.985
	0.948	0.929	0.939	0.735	0.986
C	0.947	0.915	0.931	0.659	0.983
	0.951	0.92	0.935	0.67	0.986
D	0.962	0.948	0.955	0.760	0.981
	0.964	0.95	0.957	0.763	0.983

Table 4. Evaluation open results on all test sets

4 Conclusions and future work

In this paper, a detailed description on a Chinese segmentation system is presented. Based on intermediate results from a CRF tagger, which employs local features and global features, we use class-based HMM to revise the substrings with low marginal probabilities. Then, a confidence measure is introduced to combine the two results. Finally, we post process the strings within letters, numbers and punctuations using simple rules. The results above show that our system achieves the state-of-the-art performance.

The MP plays the important role in our method and HMM revises some errors identified by CRF. Besides, the word features are proved to be informative cues in obtaining high quality MP. Therefore, our future work will focus on how to make CRF generate more reliable MP of characters, including exploring other word information or more unsupervised segmentation information.

References

Feng Haodi, Kang Chen, Chuyu Kit, Xiaotie Deng. 2005. *Unsupervised segmentation of Chinese corpus using accessor variety*, In: Natural Language Processing IJCNLP, pages 694-703, Sanya, China.

Lafferty John, Andrew McCallum and Fernando Pereira. 2001. *Conditional Random Fields: probabilistic models for segmenting and labeling sequence data*, In: Proceedings of ICML-18, pages 282-289, Williams College, USA.

Liu Qun, Huaping Zhang, Hongkui Yu and Xueqi Chen. 2004. *Chinese lexical analysis using cascaded Hidden Markov Model*, Journal of computer research and development 41(8): 1421-1429.

Low Kiat Jin, Hwee Tou Ng and Wenyuan Guo. 2005. *A Maximum Entropy Approach to Chinese Word Segmentation.* In: Proceedings of the Fourth SIGHAN Workshop on Chinese Language Processing, pages 161-164, Jeju Island, Korea.

Peng Fuchun, Fangfang Feng and Andrew McCallum. 2004. *Chinese segmentation and new word detection using Conditional Random Fields*, In: COLING 2004, pages 562-568, Geneva, Switzerland.

Tseng Huihsin, Pichuan Chang et al. 2005. *A Conditional Random Field Word Segmenter for SIGHAN Bakeoff 2005.* In: Proceedings of the Fourth SIGHAN Workshop on Chinese Language Processing, pages 168-171, Jeju Island, Korea.

Wang Zhenxing, Changning Huang and Jingbo Zhu. 2008. *Which perform better on in-vocabulary word segmentation: based on word or character?* In: Processing of the Sixth SIGHAN Workshop on Chinese Language Processing, pages 61-68, Hyderabad, India.

Xue Nianwen. 2003. *Chinese word segmentation as character tagging*, Computational Linguistics and Chinese Language Processing 8(1): 29-48.

Zhang Yue and Stephen Clark. 2007. *Chinese Segmentation with a Word-Based Perceptron Algorithm.* In: Proceedings of the 45th Annual Meeting of the Association for Computational Linguistics, pages 840-847, Prague, Czech Republic.

Zhang Ruiqiang, Genichiro Kikui and Eiichiro Sumita. 2006. *Subword-based tagging by Conditional Random Fields for Chinese word segmentation*, In: Proceedings of the Human Language Technology Conference of the NAACL, pages 193-196, New York, USA.

Zhao Hai, Changning Huang, Mu Li and Baoliang Lu. 2006. *Effective tag set selection in Chinese word segmentation via Conditional Random Field modeling*, In: PACLIC-20, pages 87-94, Wuhan, China.

Zhao Hai and Chunyu Kit. 2007a. *Effective subsequence based tagging for Chinese word segmentation*, Journal of Chinese Information Processing 21(5): 8-13.

Zhao Hai and Chunyu Kit. 2007b. *Incorporating global information into supervised learning for Chinese word segmentation*, In: PACLING-2007, pages 66-74, Melbourne, Australia.

Zhao Hai and Chunyu Kit. 2008. *Unsupervised segmentation helps supervised learning of character tagging for word segmentation and named entity recognition*, In: Proceedings of the Six SIGHAN Workshop on Chinese Language Processing, pages 106-111, Hyderabad, India.

A Chinese Word Segmentation System Based on Structured Support Vector Machine Utilization of Unlabeled Text Corpus

Chongyang Zhang
Anhui Province Engineering Laboratory of Speech and Language, University of Science and Technology of China
cyzhang9@mail.ustc.edu.cn

Zhigang Chen
Anhui Province Engineering Laboratory of Speech and Language, University of Science and Technology of China
Chenzhigang@ustc.edu

Guoping Hu
Anhui Province Engineering Laboratory of Speech and Language, University of Science and Technology of China
Applecore@ustc.edu

Abstract

Character-based tagging method has achieved great success in Chinese Word Segmentation (CWS). This paper proposes a new approach to improve the CWS tagging accuracy by structured support vector machine (SVM) utilization of unlabeled text corpus. First, character N-grams in unlabeled text corpus are mapped into low-dimensional space by adopting SOM algorithm. Then new features extracted from these maps and another kind of feature based on entropy for each N-gram are integrated into the structured SVM methods for CWS. We took part in two tracks of the Word Segmentation for Simplified Chinese Text in bakeoff-2010: Closed track and Open track. The test corpora cover four domains: Literature, Computer Science, Medicine and Finance. Our system achieved good performance, especially in the open track on the domain of medicine, our system got the highest score among 18 systems.

1 Introduction

In the last decade, many statistics-based methods for automatic Chinese word segmentation (CWS) have been proposed with development of machine learning and statistical method (Huang and Zhao, 2007). Especially, character-based tagging method which was proposed by Nianwen Xue (2003) achieves great success in the second International Chinese word segmentation Bakeoff in 2005 (Low et al., 2005). The character-based tagging method formulates the CWS problem as a task of predicting a tag for each character in the sentence, i.e. every character is considered as one of four different types in 4-tag set: B (begin of word), M (middle of word), E (end of word), and S (single-character word).

Most of these works train tagging models only on limited labeled training sets, without using any unsupervised learning outcomes from unlabeled text. But in recent years, researchers begin to exploit the value of enormous unlabeled corpus for CWS, such as some statistics information on co-occurrence of sub-sequences in the whole text has been extracted from unlabeled data and been employed as input features for tagging model training (Zhao and Kit , 2007).

Word clustering is a common method to utilize unlabeled corpus in language processing research to enhance the generalization ability, such as part-of-speech clustering and semantic clustering (Lee et al., 1999 and B Wang and H Wang 2006). Character-based tagging method usually employs N-gram features, where an N-gram is an N-character segment of a string. We believe that there are also semantic or grammatical relationships between most of N-grams and these relationships will be useful in CWS. Intuitively, assuming the training data contains the bigram "色/列"(The last two characters of the word "Israel" in Chinese), not contain the bigram "耳/其"(The last two characters of the word "Turkey" in Chinese), if we could cluster the two bigrams together according to unlabeled corpus and employ it as a feature for supervised training of tagging model, then maybe we will know that there should be a word boundary after "耳/其" though we only find the existence of word boundary after "色/列" in the training data. So we investigate how to apply clustering method onto unlabeled data for the purpose of improving CWS accuracy in this paper.

This paper proposes a novel method of using unlabeled data for CWS, which employs Self-Organizing Map (SOM) (Kohonen 1982) to organize Chinese character N-grams on a two-dimensional array, named as "N-gram cluster map" (NGCM), in which the character N-grams similar in grammatical structure and semantic meaning are organized in the same or adjacent position. Two different arrays are built based the N-gram's preceding context and succeeding context respectively because normally N-gram is just part of Chinese word and doesn't share similar preceding and succeeding context in the same time. Then NGCM-based features are extracted and applied to tagging model of CWS. Another kind of feature based on entropy for each N-gram is also introduced for improving the performance of CWS.

The rest of this paper is organized as follows: Section 2 describes our system; Section 3 describes structured SVM and the features which are obtained from labeled corpus and also unlabeled corpus; Section 4 shows experimental results on Bakeoff-2010 and Section 5 gives our conclusion.

2 System description

2.1 Open track:

The architecture of our system for open track is shown in Figure 1. For improving the cross-domain performance, we train and test with dictionary-based word segmentation outputs. On large-scale unlabeled corpus we use Self-Organizing Map (SOM) (Kohonen 1982) to organize Chinese character N-grams on a two-dimensional array, named as "N-gram cluster map" (NGCM), in which the character N-grams similar in grammatical structure and semantic meaning are organized in the same or adjacent position. Then new features are extracted from these maps and integrated into the structured SVM methods for CWS.

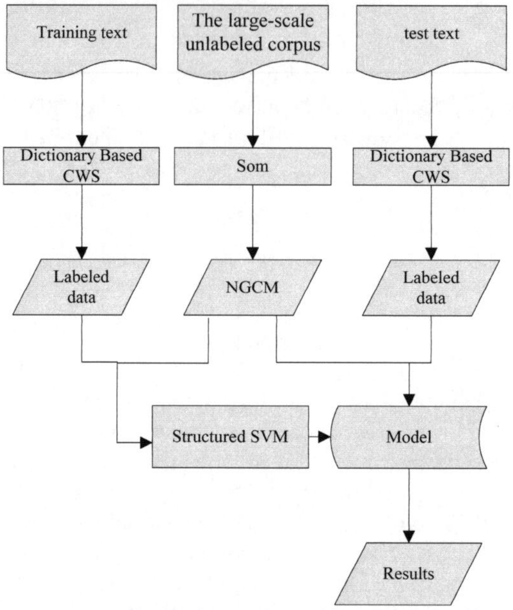

Figure 1: Open track system

2.2 Closed track:

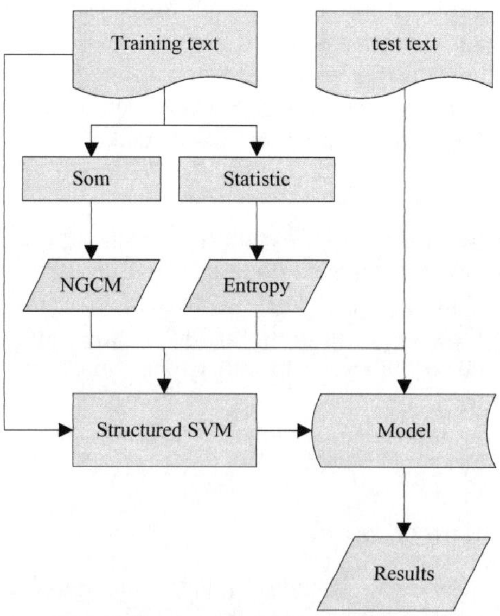

Figure 2: closed track system

Because the large-scale unlabeled corpus is forbidden to be used on closed track. We trained the SOM only on the data provided by organizers. To make up for the deficiency of the sparse data on SOM, we add entropy-based features (ETF) for every N-gram to structured SVM model. The architecture of our system for close track is shown in Figure 2.

3 Learning algorithm

3.1 Structured support vector machine

The structured support vector machine can learn to predict structured y, such as trees sequences or sets, from x based on large-margin approach. We employ a structured SVM that can predict a sequence of labels $y=(y^1,...,y^T)$ for a given observation sequences $x=(x^1,...,x^T)$, where $y^t \in \Sigma$,Σ is the label set for y.

There are two types of features in the structured SVM: transition features (interactions between neighboring labels along the chain), emission features (interactions between attributes of the observation vectors and a specific label).we can represent the input-output pairs via joint feature map (JFM)

$$\psi(x,y)=\begin{pmatrix} \sum_{t=1}^{T}\phi(x^t)\otimes\Lambda^c(y^t) \\ \eta\sum_{t=1}^{T-1}\Lambda^c(y^t)\otimes\Lambda^c(y^{t+1}) \end{pmatrix}$$

where

$\Lambda^c(y)\equiv(\delta(y_1,y),\delta(y_2,y),...,\delta(y_K,y))'$

$\in\{0,1\}^K,\ y\in\{y_1,y_2,...,y_K\}=\Sigma$

Kronecker delta δ ,$\delta_{i,j}=\begin{cases}1,i=j\\0,i\neq j\end{cases}$

$\phi(x)$ denotes an arbitrary feature representation of the inputs. The sign "$\otimes$" expresses tensor product defined as $\otimes$: $R^d\times R^k \rightarrow R^{dk}$, $[a\otimes b]_{i+(j-1)d}=[a]_i[b]_j$. T is the length of an observation sequence. $\eta\geq 0$ is a scaling factor which balances the two types of contributions.

Note that both transition features and emission features can be extended by including higher-order interdependencies of labels (e.g. $\Lambda^c(y^t)\otimes\Lambda^c(y^{t+1})\otimes\Lambda^c(y^{t+2})$),by including input features from a window centered at the current position (e.g. replacing $\phi(x^t)$ with $\phi(x^{t-r},...,x^t,...x^{t+r})$)or by combining higher-order output features with input features (e.g. $\sum_t\phi(x^t)\otimes\Lambda^c(y^t)\otimes\Lambda^c(y^{t+1})$)

The w-parametrized discriminant function $F:X\times Y\rightarrow R$ interpreted as measuring the compatibility of x and y is defined as:

$$F(x,y;w)=\langle w,\psi(x,y)\rangle$$

So we can maximize this function over the response variable to make a prediction

$$f(x)=\arg\max_{y\in Y}F(x,y,w)$$

Training the parameters can be formulated as the following optimization problem.

$$\min_{w,\xi}\frac{1}{2}\langle w,w\rangle+\frac{C}{n}\sum_{i=1}^{n}\xi_i$$

$$s.t.\forall i,\forall y\in Y:$$

$$\langle w,\psi_i(x_i,y_i)-\psi_i(x_i,y)\rangle\geq\Delta(y_i,y)-\xi_i$$

where n is the number of the training set, ξ_i is a slack variable , $C\geq 0$ is a constant controlling the tradeoff between training error minimization and margin maximization, $\Delta(y^1,y)$ is the loss function ,usually the number of misclassified tags in the sentence.

3.2 Features set for tagging model

For a training sample denoted as $x=(x^1,...,x^T)$ and $y=(y^1,...,y^T)$. We chose first-order interdependencies of labels to be transition features, and dependencies between labels and N-grams (n=1, 2, 3, 4) at current position in observed input sequence to be emission features.

So our JFM is the concatenation of the follow vectors

$$\sum_{t=1}^{T-1}\Lambda^c(y^t)\otimes\Lambda^c(y^{t+1})$$

$$\sum_{t=1}^{T}\phi(x^{t+m})\otimes\Lambda^c(y^t),m\in\{-1,0,1\}$$

$$\sum_{t=1}^{T}\phi(x^{t+m}x^{t+m+1})\otimes\Lambda^c(y^t),m\in\{-2,-1,0,1\}$$

$$\sum_{t=1}^{T}\phi(x^{t+m-1}x^{t+m}x^{t+m+1})\otimes\Lambda^c(y^t),$$

$$m\in\{-2,-1,0,1,2\}$$

$$\sum_{t=1}^{T}\phi(x^{t+m-1}x^{t+m}x^{t+m+1}x^{t+m+2})\otimes\Lambda^{c}(y^{t}),$$
$$m\in\{-3,-2,-1,0,1,2\}$$

Figure 3 shows the transition features and the emission features of N-grams (n=1, 2) at y_3. The emission features of 3-grams and 4-grams are not shown here because of the large number of the dependencies.

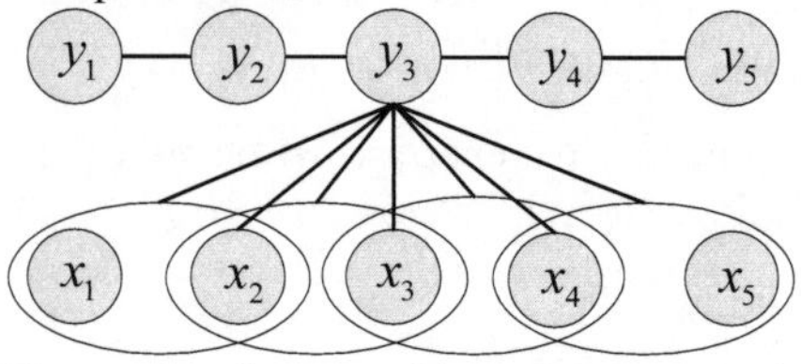

Figure 3: the transition features and the emission features at y_3 for structured SVM

3.3 SOM-based N-gram cluster maps and the NGCM *mapping* feature

The Self-Organizing Map (SOM) (Kohonen 1982), sometimes called Kohonen map, was developed by Teuvo Kohonen in the early 1980s.

Self-organizing semantic maps (Ritter and Kohonen 1989, 1990) are SOMs that have been organized according to word similarities, measured by the similarity of the short contexts of the words. Our algorithm of building N-gram cluster maps is similar to self-organizing semantic maps. Because normally N-gram is just part of Chinese word and do not share similar preceding and succeeding context in the same time, so we build two different maps according to the preceding context and the succeeding context of N-gram individually. In the end we build two NGCMs: NGCMP (NGCM according to preceding context) and NGCMS (NGCM according to succeeding context).

Due to the limitation of our computer and time we only get two 15×15 size 2GCMs for open track system from large-scale unlabeled corpus which was obtained easily from websites like Sohu, Netease, Sina and People Daily.

The 2GCMP and 2GCMS we got for the open track task are shown in Figure 4 and Figure 5 respectively.

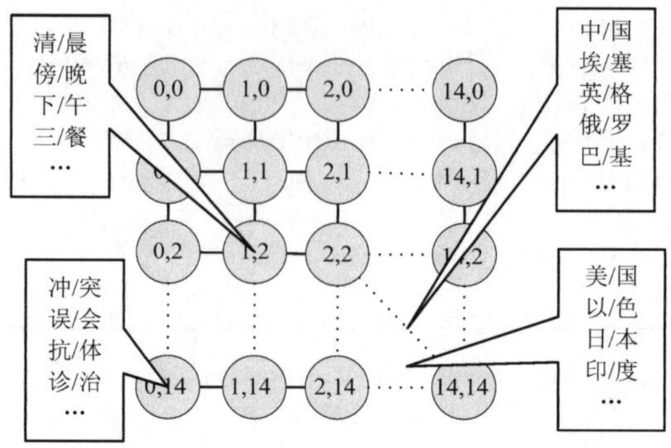

Figure 4: 2GCMP

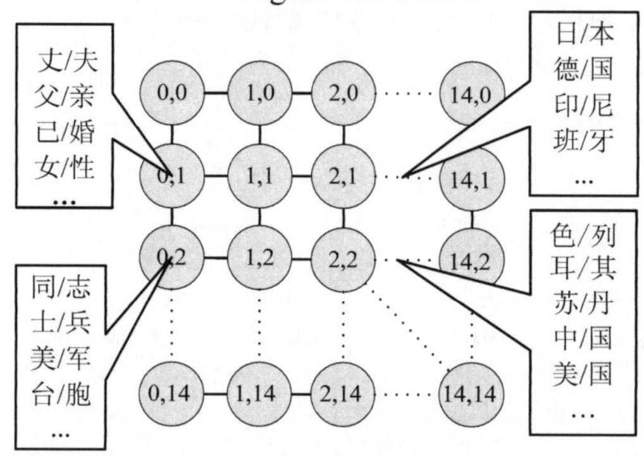

Figure 5: 2GCMS

After checking the results, we find that the 2GCMS have following characters:1) most of the meaningless bigrams that contain characters from more than one word, such as the bigram "京天" in "...北京天坛..." , are organized into the same neurons in the map, 2) most of the first or last bigrams of the country names are organized into a few adjacent neurons, such as "色/列", "耳/其", "中/国" and "美/国"in 2GCMS , "巴/基", "埃/塞", "英/格", "俄/罗" , and "中/国" in 2GCMP.

Two 20×1 size 2GCMs are trained for the closed track system only on the data provided by organizers. The results are not as good as the results of the 15×15 size 2GCMs because of the less training data. The second character described above is no longer apparent as well as the 15×15 size 2GCMs, but it still kept the first character.

Then we adopt the position of the neurons which current N-gram mapped in the NGCM as a new feature. So every feature has D dimensions (D equals to the dimension of the NGCM, every dimension is corresponding to the coordinate value in the NGCM). In this way, N-gram which is originally represented as a high dimensional vector based on its context is mapped into a very low-dimensional space. We call it NGCM mapping feature. So our previous JFM in section 3.2 is concatenated with the following features:

$$\sum_{t=1}^{T} \varphi^{\text{2GCMS}}(x^{t+m}x^{t+m+1}) \otimes \Lambda^c(y^t), m \in \{-2,-1\}$$

$$\sum_{t=1}^{T} \varphi^{\text{2GCMP}}(x^{t+m}x^{t+m+1}) \otimes \Lambda^c(y^t), m \in \{0,1\}$$

$$\sum_{t=1}^{T} \eta^{\text{2GCMS}}(x^{t+m}x^{t+m+1}) \otimes \Lambda^c(y^t), m \in \{-2,-1\}$$

$$\sum_{t=1}^{T} \eta^{\text{2GCMP}}(x^{t+m}x^{t+m+1}) \otimes \Lambda^c(y^t), m \in \{0,1\}$$

where $\varphi^{\text{2GCMS}}(x)$ and $\varphi^{\text{2GCMP}}(x)$ $\in \{0,1,...,14\}^2$ denote the NGCM mapping feature from 2GCMS and 2GCMP respectively. $\eta^{\text{NGCM}}(x)$ denotes the quantization error of current N-gram x on its NGCM.

As an example, the process of import features from NGCMs at y_3 is presented in Figure 6.

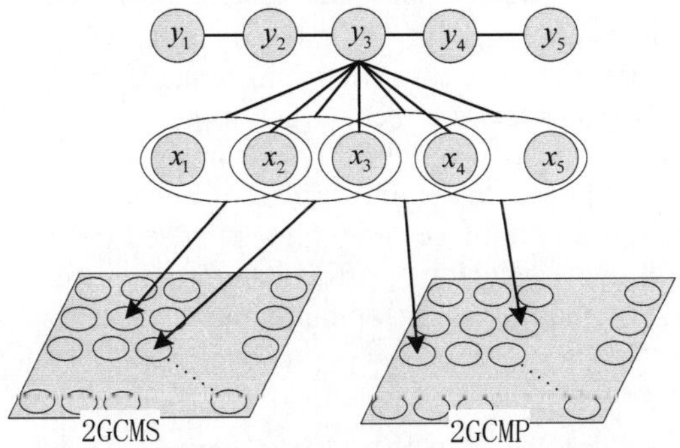

Figure 6: Using 2GCMS and 2GCMP as input to structured SVM

3.4 Entropy-based features

On closed track, the entropy of the preceding and succeeding characters conditional on the N-gram and also the self-information of the N-gram are used as features for the structured SVM methods. Then our previous JFM in section 3.2 is concatenated with the following features:

$$\sum_{t=1}^{T} H(P \mid N = x^{Ngram}) \otimes \Lambda^c(y^t),$$

$$x^{Ngram} \in \{x^{t+1}x^{t+2}, x^{t+1}x^{t+2}x^{t+3}, x^{t+1}x^{t+2}x^{t+3}x^{t+4}\}$$

$$\sum_{t=1}^{T} H(S \mid N = x^{Ngram}) \otimes \Lambda^c(y^t),$$

$$x^{Ngram} \in \{x^{t-2}x^{t-1}, x^{t-3}x^{t-2}x^{t-1}, x^{t-4}x^{t-3}x^{t-2}x^{t-1}\}$$

$$\sum_{t=1}^{T} I(N = x^{Ngram}) \otimes \Lambda^c(y^t)$$

$x^{Ngram} \in$ all the ngrams used in section 3.2

Where P and S denote the set of the preceding and succeeding characters respectively. The entropy: $H(X \mid N = x^{Ngram}) = -\sum_{X \in x^t} p(x^t \mid x^{Ngram}) \log p(x^t \mid x^{Ngram})$

The self-information of the N-gram $N = x^{Ngram}$: $I(x^{Ngram}) = -\log p(x^{Ngram})$

4 Applications and Experiments

4.1 Text Preprocessing

Text is usually mixed up with numerical or alphabetic characters in Chinese natural language, such as "我在 office 上班到晚上 9 点". These numerical or alphabetic characters are barely segmented in CWS. Hence, we treat these symbols as a whole "character" according to the following two preprocessing steps. First replace one alphabetic character to four continuous alphabetic characters with E1 to E4 respectively, five or more alphabetic characters with E5. Then replace one numerical number to four numerical numbers with N1 to N4 and five or more numerical numbers with N5. After text preprocessing, the above examples will be "我在 E5 上班到晚上 N1 点".

4.2 Character-based tagging method for CWS

Previous works show that 6-tag set achieved a better CWS performance (Zhao et al., 2006). Thus, we opt for this tag set. This 6-tag set adds 'B2' and 'B3' to 4-tag set which stand for the type of the second and the third character in a Chinese word respectively. For example, the tag sequence for the sentence "上海世博会/将/持续/半

年(Shanghai World Expo / will / last / six months)" will be "B B2 B3 M E S B E B E".

4.3 Results in the bakeoff-2010

We use svm^{hmm} version 3.1 to build our structured SVM models. The cut-off threshold is set to 2. The precision parameter is set to 0.1. The tradeoff between training error minimization and margin maximization is set to 1000.

We took part in two tracks of the Word Segmentation for Simplified Chinese Text in bakeoff-2010: c (Closed track), o (Open track). The test corpora cover four domains: A (Literature), B (Computer Science), C (Medicine), D (Finance).

Precision(P),Recall(R),F-measure(F),Out-Of-Vocabulary Word Recall(OOV RR) and In-Vocabulary Word Recall(IV RR) are adopted to measure the performance of word segmentation system.

Table 1 shows the results of our system on the word segmentation task for simplified Chinese text in bakeoff-2010. Table 2 shows the comparision between our system results and best results in bakeoff-2010.

		R	P	F1	OOV RR	IV RR
A	c	0.932	0.935	0.933	0.654	0.953
	o	0.942	0.943	0.942	0.702	0.959
B	c	0.935	0.934	0.935	0.792	0.961
	o	0.948	0.946	0.947	0.812	0.973
C	c	0.937	0.934	0.936	0.761	0.959
	o	0.941	0.935	0.938	0.787	0.96
D	c	0.955	0.956	0.955	0.848	0.965
	o	0.948	0.955	0.951	0.853	0.957

Table 1: The results of our systems

		F1(Bakeoff-2010)	F1(Our system)
A	c	0.946	0.933
	o	0.955	0.942
B	c	0.951	0.935
	o	0.95	0.947
C	c	0.939	0.936
	o	0.938	0.938
D	c	0.959	0.955
	o	0.96	0.951

Tabel 2: The comparision between our system results and best results in bakeoff-2010

It is obvious that our systems are stable and reliable even in the domain of medicine when the F-measure of the best results was decreased. Our open track system performs better than closed track system, demonstrating the benefit of the dictionary-based word segmentation outputs and the NGCMs which are training on large-scale unlabeled corpus.

5 Conclusion

This paper proposes a new approach to improve the CWS tagging accuracy by structured support vector machine (SVM) utilization of unlabeled text corpus. We use SOM to organize Chinese character N-grams on a two-dimensional array, so that the N-grams similar in grammatical structure and semantic meaning are organized in the same or adjacent position. Then new features extracted from these maps and another kind of feature based on entropy for each N-gram are integrated into the structured SVM methods for CWS. Our system achieved good performance, especially in the open track on the domain of medicine, our system got the highest score among 18 systems.

In future work, we will try to organizing all the N-grams on a much larger array, so that every neuron will be labeled by a single N-gram. The ultimate objective is to reduce the dimension of input features for supervised CWS learning by replacing N-gram features with two-dimensional NGCM mapping features.

References

B.Wang, H.Wang 2006.A Comparative Study on Chinese Word Clustering. *Computer Processing of Oriental Languages.* Beyond the Orient: The Research Challenges Ahead, pages 157-164

Chang-Ning Huang and Hai Zhao. 2007. Chinese word segmentation: A decade review. Journal of Chinese Information Processing, 21(3):8–20.

Chung-Hong Lee & Hsin-Chang Yang.1999, *A Web Text Mining Approach Based on Self-Organizing Map*, ACM-library

G.Bakir, T.Hofmann, B.Scholkopf, A.Smola, B. Taskar, and S. V. N. Vishwanathan, editors. 2007 *Predicting Structured Data.* MIT Press, Cambridge, Massachusetts.

Hai Zhao, Chang-Ning Huang, Mu Li, and Bao-Liang Lu. 2006. *Effective tag set selection inChinese word segmentation via conditional random field modeling.* In Proceedings of PACLIC-20, pages 87–94. Wuhan, China.

Hai Zhao, Chang-Ning Huang, and Mu Li. 2006.*An improved Chinese word segmentation system with conditional random field.* In SIGHAN-5, pages 162–165, Sydney, Australia, July 22-23.

Hai Zhao and Chunyu Kit. 2007. *Incorporating global information into supervised learning for Chinese word segmentation.* In PACLING-2007, pages 66–74, Melbourne,Australia, September 19-21.

H.Ritter, and T.Kohonen, 1989. *Self-organizing semantic maps*. Biological Cybernetics, vol. 61, no. 4, pp. 241-254.

I.Tsochantaridis,T.Joachims,T.Hofmann,and Y.Altun. 2005. *Large Margin Methods for Structured and Interdependent Output Variables*, Journal of Machine Learning Research (JMLR), 6(Sep):1453-1484.

Jin Kiat Low, Hwee Tou Ng, and Wenyuan Guo.2005. *A maximum entropy approach to Chinese word segmentation.* In Proceedings of the Fourth SIGHAN Workshop on Chinese Language Processing, pages 161–164. Jeju Island,Korea.

J.Lafferty,A.McCallum, F.Pereira. 2001. *Conditional random fields: Probabilistic models for segmenting and labeling sequence data.* In Proceedings of the International Conference on Machine Learning (ICML). San Francisco: Morgan Kaufmann Publishers, 282–289.

Nianwen Xue and Susan P. Converse., 2002, *Combining Classifiers for Chinese Word Segmentation*, In Proceedings of First SIGHAN Workshop on Chinese Language Processing.

Nianwen Xue. 2003. *Chinese word segmentation as character tagging*. Computational Linguistics and Chinese Language Processing, 8(1):29–48.

R.Sproat and T.Emerson. 2003.*The first international Chinese word segmentation bakeoff.* In The Second SIGHAN Workshop on Chinese Language Processing, pages 133–143.Sapporo, Japan.

S.Haykin, 1994. Neural Networks: *A Comprehensive Foundation*. NewYork: MacMillan.

T.Joachims, T.Finley, Chun-Nam Yu. 2009, *Cutting-Plane Training of Structural SVMs*, Machine Learning Journal,77(1):27-59.

T.Joachims. 2008 . svm^{hmm} *Sequence Tagging with Structural Support Vector Machines*, http://www.cs.cornell.edu/People/tj/svm_light/svm_hmm.html

T.Honkela, 1997. *Self-Organizing Maps in Natural Language Processing. PhD thesis, Helsinki University of Technology*, Department of Computer Science and Engineering, Laboratory of Computer and Information Science.

T.Kohonen. 1982.*Self-organized formation of topologically correct feature maps*. Biological Cybernetics, 43, pp. 59-69.

T.Kohonen., J.Hynninen, J.Kangas, J.Laaksonen, 1996 ,*SOM_PAK: The Self-Organizing Map Program Package*,Technical Report A31, Helsinki University of Technology , http://www.cis.hut.fi/nnrc/nnrc-programs.html

Y.Altun, I.Tsochantaridis, T.Hofmann. 2003. *Hidden Markov Support Vector Machines.* In Proceedings of International Conference on Machine Learning (ICML).

Chinese Word Segmentation with Conditional Support Vector Inspired Markov Models

Yu-Chieh Wu
[1]Dep. of Computer Science and Information Engineering;
National Central University
[2]Finance Department
Ming Chuan University
Taipei, Taiwan
bcbb@db.csie.ncu.edu.tw

Jie-Chi Yang
Graduate Institute of Network Learning
National Central University
Taoyuan, Taiwan
yang@cl.ncu.edu.tw

Yue-Shi Lee
Dep. of Computer Science and Information Engineering
Ming Chuan University
Taoyuan, Taiwan
leeys@mcu.edu.tw

Abstract

In this paper, we present the proposed method of participating SIGHAN-2010 Chinese word segmentation bake-off. In this year, our focus aims to quick train and test the given data. Unlike the most structural learning algorithms, such as conditional random fields, we design an in-house development conditional support vector Markov model (CMM) framework. The method is very quick to train and also show better performance in accuracy than CRF. To give a fair comparison, we compare our method to CRF with three additional tasks, namely, CoNLL-2000 chunking, SIGHAN-3 Chinese word segmentation. The results were encourage and indicated that the proposed CMM produces better not only accuracy but also training time efficiency. The official results in SIGHAN-2010 also demonstrates that our method perform very well in traditional Chinese with fine-tuned features set.

1 Introduction

Since 2006 Chinese word segmentation bakeoff in SIGHAN-3 (Levow, 2006), this is the third time to join the competition (Wu et al., 2006, 2007). In this year, we join the SIGHAN bakeoff task in both traditional and simplified Chinese closed word segmentation. Unlike most western languages, there is no explicit space between words. The goal of word segmentation is to identify words given the sentence. This technique provides important features for downstream purposes. Examples include Chinese part-of-speech (POS) tagging (Wu et al., 2007), Chinese word dependency parsing (Wu et al., 2007, 2008).

With the rapid growth of structural learning algorithms, such as conditional random fields (CRFs) (Lafferty et al., 2001) and maximum-margin Markov models (M^3N) (Taskar et al., 2003) have received a great attention and become a prominent learning algorithm to many sequential labeling tasks. Examples include part-of-speech (POS) tagging (Shen et al., 2007) and syntactic phrase chunking (Suzuki et al., 2007). The Chinese word segmentation can also be treated as a character-based tagging task in (Xue and Converse, 2002). One feature of sequential labeling is that it aims at finding non-recursive chunk fragments in a given sentence. Among these approaches, CRF has been wildly used in recent SIGHAN bakeoff tasks (Jin and Chen, 2008; Levow, 2006).

Although these approaches do not suffer from so-called label-bias problems (Lafferty et al., 2001), one limitation is that they are inefficient to train with large-scale, especially large category data. On the other hand, non-structural learning approaches (e.g. maximum entropy models) which learn local predictors usually cost much better training time performance than structural learning algorithms. These methods condition on local context features and incorporate fix-length history information. Although higher order feature (longer history) maybe useful to some tasks, the exponential scaled inference time is also intractable in practice.

Support vector machines (SVMs) which is one of the state-of-the-art supervised learning algorithms have been widely employed as local classifiers to many sequential labeling tasks (Taku and Matsumoto, 2001; Wu et al., 2006, 2008). Specially, the training time of linear kernel SVM with either L_1-norm (Joachims, 2006; Keerthi et al., 2008) or L_2-norm (Keerthi and DeCoste, 2005; Hsieh et al., 2008) can now be obtained in linear time. Even local classifier-based approaches have the drawbacks of label-bias problems, training nonstructural linear SVM is scalable to large-scale data. By means of so-called one-versus-all multiclass SVM training, it is also scalable to large-category data.

In this paper, we present our Chinese word segmentation based on the proposed conditional support vector Markov models for sequential labeling tasks, especially Chinese word segmentation. Unlike structural learning algorithms, our method can be simply trained without considering the entire structures and hence the training time scales linearly with the number of training examples. In this framework, to alleviate the ease of label-bias problems, the state transition probability is ignored. Instead, we merely utilize the property of label relationships between chunks (Wu et al., 2008). To demonstrate our method, we compare to several well-known structural learning algorithms, like CRF (Kudo et al., 2004), and SVM-HMM (Joachims et al., 2009) on two well-known data, namely, CoNLL-2000 syntactic chunking, SIGHAN-3 Chinese word segmentation tasks. By following this, we apply the model to the Chinese word segmentation tasks of SIGHAN-2010 this year. The empirical results showed that our method is not only fast but also achieving more superior accuracy than structural learning methods. In traditional Chinese, our method also achieves the state-of-the-art performance in accuracy with fined-tune features.

2 Conditional support vector Markov models

Traditional conditional Markov models (CMM) is to assign the tag sequence which maximizes the observation sequence.

$$P(s_1, s_2, ..., s_n \mid o_1, o_2, ..., o_n)$$

Where s_i is the tag of word i. For the first order left-to-right CMM, the chain rule decomposes the probabilistic function as:

$$P(s_1, s_2, ..., s_n \mid o_1, o_2, ..., o_n) = \prod_{i=1}^{n} P(s_i \mid s_{i-1}, o_i) \quad (1)$$

Therefore, we can employ a local classifier to predict $P(s_i \mid s_{i-1}, o_i)$ and the optimal tag sequence can be efficiently searched by using conventional Viterbi algorithm.

The graphic illustration of the K-th order left-to-right CMM is shown in Figure 1. The chain probability decompositions of the other K-th order CMM in Figure 1 are:

$$P(s,o) = \prod_{i=1}^{n} P(s_i \mid o_i) \quad (2)$$

$$P(s,o) = \prod_{i=2}^{n} P(s_i \mid o_i, s_{i-1}) \quad (3)$$

$$P(s,o) = \prod_{i=3}^{n} P(s_i \mid o_i, s_{i-1}, s_{i-2}) \quad (4)$$

$$P(s,o) = \prod_{i=3}^{n} P(s_i \mid o_i, s_{i-1}, \hat{s}_{i-1}) \quad (5)$$

Equations (2), (3), and (4) are merely standard zero, first and second order decompositions, while equation (5) is the proposed greedy second order CMM decomposition which will be discussed in next section.

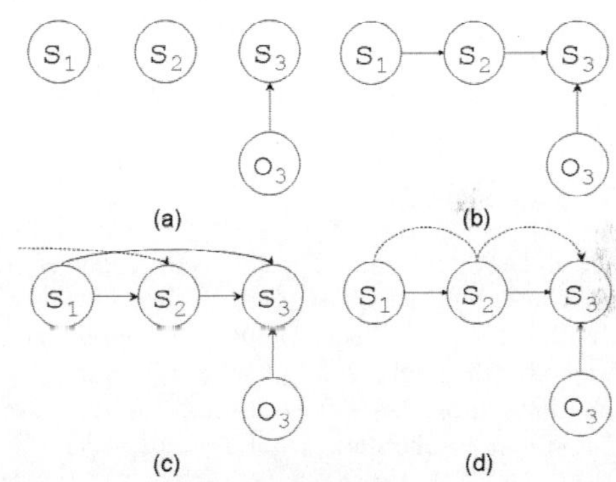

Figure 1: K-th order conditional Markov models: (a) the standard 0(zero) order CMM, (b) first order CMM, (c) second order CMM, and (d) the proposed second order CMM

The above decompositions merge the transition and emission probability with single function. McCallum et al. (2000) further combined the locally trained maximum entropy with the infered transition score. However, our conditional support vector Markov models make different chain probability. We replace the original transition probability with transition validity score, i.e.

$$P(s,o) = \prod_{i=2}^{n} \widetilde{P}(s_i \mid s_{i-1}) P(s_i \mid o_i) \quad (6)$$

$$P(s,o)=\prod_{i=3}^{n}\hat{P}(s_i\mid s_{i-1})P(s_i\mid o_i,s_{i-1},\hat{s}_{i-1}) \quad (7)$$

The transition validity score is merely a Boolean flag which indicates the relationships between two neighbor labels. Equation (6) and (7) are zero-order and *our second order* chain probabilities. We will introduce the proposed inference algorithm and how to obtain the transition validity score automatically without concerning the change of chunk representation.

2.1 Tag transitions

In this paper, we do not explicitly adopt the state transitions for our CMM. Instead, a chunk-relation pair is used. Nevertheless, one important property to sequential chunk labeling is that there is only one phrase type in a chunk. For example, if the previous word is tagged as begin of noun phrase (B-NP), the current word must not be end of the other phrase (E-VP, E-PP, etc). Therefore, we only model relationships between chunk tags to generate valid phrase structure.

Wu et al. (2007, 2008) presented an automatic chunk pair relation construction algorithm which can handle so-called IOB1/IOB2/IOE1/IOE2 (Kudo and Matsumoto, 2001) chunk representation structures with either left-to-right or right-to-left directions. Here, we extend this idea and generalize to fit to more chunk tags. That is we can model the S-tag, B2, B3 tags with dividing the leading tags into two categories. For details can refer the literatures.

3 Empirical Results

Three large-scale and large-category dataset is used to evaluate the proposed method, namely, CoNLL-2000 syntactic chunking (Tjong Kim Sang and Buchholz, 2000), Chinese POS tagging, and three of SIGHAN-3 word segmentation tasks. Table 1 shows the statistics of those datasets.

Feature type	CoNLL-2000	SIGHAN-3
Unigram	w_{-2}~w_{+2}	w_{-2}~w_{+2}
Bigram	$(w_{-2},w_{-1}),(w_{-1},w_0),$ $(w_0,w_{+1}),$ $(w_{+1},w_{+2}),(w_{+1},w_{-1})$	$(w_{-2},w_{-1}),(w_{-1},w_0),$ $(w_0,w_{+1}),$ $(w_{+1},w_{+2}),(w_{+1},w_{-1})$
POS	p_{-2}~p_{+2}	
POS bigram	$(p_{-2},p_{-1}),(p_{-1},p_0),$ $(p_0,p_{+1}),(p_{+1},p_{+2}),$ (p_{+1},p_{-1})	
POS trigram	$(p_{-2},p_{-1},p_0),$ $(p_{-1},p_0,p_{+1}),(p_{-3},p_{-2},p_{-1}),$ $(p_0,p_{+1},p_{+2}),$ (p_{+1},p_{+2},p_{+3})	
(Word+POS) bigram	$(w_{-1},p_0),(w_{-2},p_{-1})$ $(w_0,p_{+1}),$ (w_{+1},p_{+2})	
Other features	2~4 suffix letters 2~4 prefix letters Orthographic feature (Wu et al., 2008)	AV feature of 2~6 grams (Zhou and Kit, 2007)

Figure 2: Feature templates used in experiments

CoNLL-2000 chunking task is a well-known and widely evaluated in many literatures (Suzuki et al., 2007; Ando and Zhang, 2005; Kudo and Matsumoto, 2001; Wu et al., 2008; Daumé III and Marcu, 2005). The training data was derived from Treebank WSJ section 15-18 while section 20 was used for testing. The goal is to find the non-recursive phrase structures in a sentence, such as noun phrase (NP), verb phrase (VP), etc. There are 11 phrase types in this dataset. We follow the previous best settings for SVMs (Kudo and Matsumoto, 2001; Wu et al., 2008). The IOE2 is used to represent the phrase structure and tagged the data with backward direction.

The training and testing data of the Chinese POS tagging is mainly derived from the Academic Sinica's balanced corpus (version 3.0). Seventy-five percent out of the data is used for training while the remaining 25% is used for testing. However, the task of the Chinese POS tagging is very different from classical English POS tagging in that there is no word boundary information in Chinese text. To achieve this, Ng and Low (2004) gave a successful study on Chinese POS tagging. Just as English phrase chunking, the IOB-tags can be used to represent the Chinese word and its part-of-speech tag. For example, the tag B-ADJ means the first character of a Chinese word which POS tag is ADJ (adjective). n this task, we simply use the IOB2 to represent the chunk structure. In this way, the tagger needs to recognize the chunk tag by considering 118 (59*2) categories at once.

As discussed in (Zhou and Kit, 2007), using more complex chunk representation bring better segmentation accuracy in several Chinese word segmentation benchmarks. It is very useful in particular to represent long Chinese word (in particular proper nouns). By following this line, we apply the six tags B, BI, I, IE, E, and S to represent the Chinese word. BI and IE are the *interior after begin* and *interior before end* of a chunk. B/I/E/S tags indicate the begin/interior/end/single of a chunk. Figure 2 lists the used feature set in both experiments.

3.1 Settings

We included the Liblinear with square loss (Hsieh et al., 2008) into our conditional Markov models as classification algorithms. In basic, the SVM was designed for binary classification problems. To port to multiclass problems, we adopted the well-known one-versus-all (OVA) method. One good property of OVA is that parameter estimation process can be trained indivi-

Table 2: SIGHAN-3 word segmentation results

SIGHAN-3	UPUC			MSRA			CityU		
Method	$F_{(\beta)}$	Training Time	Testing Time	$F_{(\beta)}$	Training Time	Testing Time	$F_{(\beta)}$	Training Time	Testing Time
Our method	93.86	0.06 hr	15.15 s	96.22	0.45 hr	15.41 s	97.26	0.26 hr	25.32 s
CRF	93.76	1.17 hr	23.48 s	96.11	3.63 hr	17.06 s	97.29	4.34 hr	31.29 s
SVM-HMM	Out-of-memory			Out-of-memory			Out-of-memory		
Best approach (Zhou and Kit, 2007)	94.28	N/A	N/A	96.34	N/A	N/A	97.43	N/A	N/A
Second best approach	93.30	N/A	N/A	96.30	N/A	N/A	97.20	N/A	N/A

Table 3: Official evaluation results of the traditional and simplified Chinese word segmentation tasks

Task	Literature					Computer				
	Recall	Precision	F1	OOV-RR	IV-RR	Recall	Precision	F1	OOV-RR	IV-RR
Traditional	0.942	0.942	0.942	0.788	0.958	0.948	0.957	0.952	0.666	0.977
Simplified	0.936	0.932	0.934	0.564	0.964	0.915	0.915	0.915	0.594	0.972
Task	Medicine					Finance				
	Recall	Precision	F1	OOV-RR	IV-RR	Recall	Precision	F1	OOV-RR	IV-RR
Traditional	0.953	0.957	0.955	0.798	0.966	0.964	0.962	0.963	0.812	0.975
Simplified	0.933	0.915	0.924	0.642	0.969	0.945	0.941	0.943	0.666	0.972

dually. This is in particularly useful to the tasks which involve training large number of features and categories (Wu et al., 2008). To obtain the probability output from SVM, we employ the sigmoid function with fixed parameter A=-2 and B=0 as (Platt, 1999).

3.2 Comparison to structural learning

The overall experimental results are summarized in Table 1. Column "All" denotes as the $F_{(\beta)}$ score of all chunk types, while "NP" is the $F_{(\beta)}$ score of the noun phrase only. The final two columns list the entire training and testing times.

As shown in Table 1, it is surprising that the proposed CMM outperforms the other structural learning methods, CRF and SVM-HMM. In terms of training time, our method shows substantial faster than CRF. However, in terms of testing time, our method is worse than CRF. The main reason is that we do not optimize the code and implementation. We trust this can be further improved.

Table 1: Syntactic chunking results of the proposed CMM and the selected structural learning methods.

Method	All	NP	Training Time	Testing Time
Our method	94.51	94.95	0.15 hr	13.72 s
CRF	93.67	93.93	0.88 hr	6.20 s
SVM-HMM	93.90	94.20	0.20 hr	13.60 s

Table 2 shows the experimental results of the SIGHAN-3 bake-off tasks. We ran and conducted the experiments with UPUC, MSRA, and CityU datasets. The final two rows in Table 5 list the top 1 and 2 scores of published papers.

Here, the SVM-HMM still suffer from the scalability problems. Similar to the findings in the Chinese POS tagging task, the zero-order CMM achieved the optimal accuracy among first-order, full second order and the proposed inference algorithms. The training time is still very efficient for most CMMs. In comparison to CRF, our method did clearly perform better accuracy (excepted for the CityU) and require much less training time. For example, for the CityU dataset, our 0-order CMM took less than 15 minutes to train, while the CRF takes 4.34 hours in training.

However, we observe that our CMM yielded better testing time speed than CRF in this task. We further exploit the trained SVM models and found that the produced weights were not as dense as CRF which produces many nonzero weights per category. In addition, we observed that our implementation worked very efficient in the small category tasks.

For the three datasets, our method produced very competitive results as previous best approach which also made use of CRF as classifiers.

Although we use the same techniques to derive global features (assessor variety (AV) feature with 2~6 grams) from both training and testing data, our CMMs and the conducted CRF could not perform as well as (Zhou and Kit, 2007). In our experiments, both CRF and CMMs received the same training set. Hence the CRF and our CMMs is comparable in this experiment.

3.3 Official Results in SIGHAN-2010

To apply CMM to SIGHAN-2010, we design the following strategy. First the classifier parameters, feature set should be improved. To achieve this, 1/4 of the training data was used as development set, while the remaining 3/4 training data was used to train the classifier. Second, we combine multi-classifier to enhance the accuracy. The CRF and our CMM with basic feature set were trained to predict the initial labels of the testing data. Then the predicted labels were included as features to train the final-stage classifier. The final classifier is still our CMM. Third, the post-processing method (Low et al., 2005) is employed to enhance the unknown word segmentation.

Table 4 lists the empirical results of the development set. By validate with development data, we found that C=1.25 and use the E-BIES representation method (Wu et al., 2008) yields better accuracy than B-BIES (Zhou and Kit, 2007). Meanwhile, CRF seems to be suitable for B-BIES representation method.

The classifier parameters were fixed and then we try to search the optimal feature set via the incremental add-and-check method. That is, we use the initial feature set as basis and add one feature type from the pool and verify the goodness of the feature with the development data. Figure 3 figures out the used features of each pass.

In this year, the process was completely run-through for the traditional Chinese task. Unfortunately we have insufficient time to apply the same technique to Simplified Chinese task. Table 3 lists the official results in the SIGHAN 2010 Chinese word segmentation bake-off.

Table 4: Empirical results of the development set of single CRF and our CMM

Development dataset	Traditional Chinese		Simplified Chinese	
	B-BIES	E-BIES	B-BIES	E-BIES
Our method	97.40	97.42	97.34	97.37
CRF	97.07	97.10	97.07	96.96

4 Conclusion

In this paper, we investigate the issues of sequential chunk labeling and present the conditional support vector Markov models for this purpose. The experiments were conducted with two well-known datasets, includes CoNLL-2000 text chunking and SIGHAN-3 Chinese word segmentation. The experimental results showed that our method scales very well while achieving surprising good accuracy than structural learning methods. On the SIGHAN-3 task, the proposed method outperformed CRF, while substantially reduced the training time. We also apply such method to the SIGHAN-2010 traditional Chinese segmentation with fined tuned feature set. The result was also encouraged. Our approach obtains the best accuracy in this task. In terms of Simplified Chinese, we achieve mid-rank place due to the very limited time-constraint. In the future, we plan to completely adopt this method to the Simplified Chinese word segmentation with the elaborated feature selection metrics and the same post-processing method.

The full online demonstration of the proposed conditional support vector Markov models can be found at the web site[1].

Feature Name	Pass1: CRF/CMM	Pass2: CMM
Character	w_{-2}~w_{+2}	Feature set of Pass1
Character N-gram	(w_{-2},w_{-1}),(w_{-1},w_0), (w_0,w_{+1}),(w_{+1},w_{+2}),(w_{+1},w_{-1})	
Special Character flags (Low et al., 2005)	w_{-2}~w_{+2}	
Others	[2]AV feature and its 2-gram combinations	[2]AV feature and its 2-gram and 3-gram combinations
Future flags[1]	*N/A*	t_{+1}, t_{+2}, t_{+3},(t_0,t_{+2}),(t_{+1},t_{+2}),(w_0,t_{+1}),(w_0,t_{+2})

[1]Future flags: the predicted tags of previous classifier

Figure 3: Feature templates used in experiments

References

Rie K. Ando, and Tong Zhang. 2005. A high-performance semi-supervised learning method for text chunking, In *Proc. of ACL*, pp. 1-9.

Bernhard E. Boser, Isabelle M. Guyon, Vladimir N. Vapnik. 1992. A training algorithm for optimal margin classifiers, In *Proc. of COLT*, pp. 144-152.

Andrew McCallum, Dayne Freitag, and Fernando C. N. Pereira. 2000. Maximum entropy Markov models for information extraction and segmentation, In *Proc. of ICML*, pp. 591.598.

Hal Daumé III and Daniel Marcu. 2005. Learning as search optimization: approximate large margin methods for structured prediction, In *Proc. of ICML*, pp. 169-176.

Guangjin Jin and Xiao Chen. 2008. The Fourth International Chinese Language Proces sing Bakeoff: Chinese Word Segmentation Named Entity Recognition and Chinese POS Tagging. In *Proc. of the SIGHAN Workshop on Chinese Language Processing*, pp. 69-81.

[1] http://140.115.112.118/bcbb/Chunking.htm

Thorsten Joachims. 2006. Training linear SVMs in linear time, In *Proc. of KDD*, pp. 217-226.

Thorsten Joachims, Thomas Finley, and Chun-Nam Yu. 2009. Cutting-Plane Training of Structural SVMs, Machine Learning Journal, to appear.

Sathiya Keerthi and Dennis DeCoste. 2005. A modified finite Newton method for fast solution of large scale linear SVMs, JMLR, 6: 341-361.

Taku Kudo and Yuji Matsumoto. 2001. Chunking with support vector machines. In *Proc. of NAACL*, pp. 192-199.

Taku Kudo, Kaoru Yamamoto, and Yuji Matsumoto. 2004. Applying conditional random fields to Japanese morphological analysis, In *Proc. of EMNLP*, pp. 230-237.

John Lafferty, Andrew McCallum, and Fernando Pereira. 2001. Conditional random fields: probabilistic models for segmenting and labeling sequence data, In *Proc. of ICML*, pp. 282-289.

Gina-Anne Levow. 2006. The third international Chinese language processing bakeoff: Word segmentation and named entity recognition. In *Proc. of the SIGHAN Workshop on Chinese Language Processing*, pp. 108–117.

Jin Kiat Low, Hwee Tou Ng, and Wenyuan Guo. 2005. A maximum entropy approach to Chinese word segmentation. In *Proc. of the SIGHAN Workshop on Chinese Language Processing*, pp. 161-164.

Hwee Tou Ng and Jin Kiat Low. 2004. Chinese part-of-speech tagging. one-at-a-time or all-at-once? word-based or character-based? In *Proc. of EMNLP*, pp. 277-284.

John Platt. 1999. Probabilistic outputs for support vector machines and comparisons to regularized likelihood methods, In Advances in Large Margin Classifiers.

Jun Suzuki, Akinori Fujino, and Hideki Isozaki. 2007. Semi-supervised structural output learning based on a hybrid generative and discriminative approach, In *Proc. of EMNLP-CoNLL*, pp. 791-800.

Jun Suzuki and Hideki Isozaki. 2008. Semi-Supervised Sequential Labeling and Segmentation using Giga-word Scale Unlabeled Data. In *Proc. of ACL*, pp. 665-673.

Ben Taskar, Carlos Guestrin, and Daphne Koller. 2003. Max-margin Markov networks, In *Proc. of NIPS*.

Eric F. Tjong Kim Sang, and Sabine Buchholz. 2000. Introduction to the CoNLL-2000 shared task: chunking. In *Proc. of CoNLL*, pp. 127-132.

Yu-Chieh Wu, Jie-Chi Yang, Yue-Shi Lee, and Show-Jane Yen. 2006. Efficient and robust phrase chunking using support vector machines, In *Asia Information Retrieval Symposium (AIRS)*, pp. 350-361.

Yu-Chieh Wu, Jie-Chi Yang, and Yue-Shi Lee. 2008. Description of the NCU Chinese Word Segmentation and Part-of-Speech Tagging for SIGHAN Bakeoff 2008, In *Proc. of the SIGHAN Workshop on Chinese Language Processing*, pp. 161-166, 2008.

Yu-Chieh Wu, Yue-Shi Lee, and Jie-Chi Yang. Robust and efficient multiclass SVM models for phrase pattern recognition, Pattern recognition, 41(9): 2874-2889, 2008.

Yu-Chieh Wu, Jie-Chi Yang, and Qian Xiang Lin. 2006. Description of the NCU Chinese word segmentation and named entity recognition System for SIGHAN Bakeoff 2006, In *Proc. of the SIGHAN Workshop on Chinese Language Processing*, pp. 209-212.

Yu-Chieh Wu, Yue-Shi Lee, and Jie-Chi Yang. 2008. Robust and efficient Chinese word dependency analysis with linear kernel support vector machines, In *Proc. of the COLING*, pp. 135-138.

Yu-Chieh Wu, Jie-Chi Yang, and Yue-Shi Lee. 2007. Multilingual deterministic dependency parsing framework using modified finite Newton method Support Vector Machines. In *Proc. of the EMNLP/CoNLL*, pp.1175-1181.

Tong Zhang, Fred Damerau, and David Johnson. 2002. Text chunking based on a generalization Winnow, JMLR, 2: 615-637.

Hai Zhao and Chunyu Kit. 2007. Incorporating global information into supervised learning for Chinese word segmentation, In *Proc. of PACLIC*, pp.66-74.

A Boundary-Oriented Chinese Segmentation Method Using N-Gram Mutual Information

Ling-Xiang Tang[1], **Shlomo Geva**[1], **Andrew Trotman**[2], **Yue Xu**[1]

[1]Faculty of Science and Technology
Queensland University of Technology
Brisbane, Australia
{l4.tang,s.geva,yue.xu}@qut.edu.au

[2]Department of Computer Science
University of Otago
Dunedin, New Zealand
andrew@cs.otago.ac.nz

Abstract

This paper describes our participation in the Chinese word segmentation task of CIPS-SIGHAN 2010. We implemented an n-gram mutual information (NGMI) based segmentation algorithm with the mixed-up features from unsupervised, supervised and dictionary-based segmentation methods. This algorithm is also combined with a simple strategy for out-of-vocabulary (OOV) word recognition. The evaluation for both open and closed training shows encouraging results of our system. The results for OOV word recognition in closed training evaluation were however found unsatisfactory.

1 Introduction

Chinese segmentation has been an interesting research topic for decades. Lots of delicate methods are used for providing good Chinese segmentation. In general, on the basis of the required human effort, Chinese word segmentation approaches can be classified into two categories: supervised and unsupervised.

Particularly, supervised segmentation methods can achieve a very high precision on the targeted knowledge domain with the help of training corpus—the manually segmented text collection. On the other hand, unsupervised methods are suitable for more general Chinese segmentation where there is no or limited training data available. The resulting segmentation accuracy with unsupervised methods may not be very satisfying, but the human effort for creating the training data set is not absolutely required.

In the Chinese word segmentation task of CIPS-SIGHAN 2010, the focus is on the performance of Chinese segmentation on cross-domain text. There are in total two types of evaluations: closed and open. We participated in both closed and open training evaluation tasks and both simplified and traditional Chinse segmentation subtasks. For the closed training evaluation, the provided resource for system training is limited and using external resources such as trained segmentation software, corpus, dictionaries, lexicons, etc are forbidden; especially, human-encoded rules specified in the segmentation algorithm are not allowed.

For the bakeoff of this year, we implemented a boundary-oriented NGMI-based algorithm with the mixed-up features from supervised, unsupervised and dictionary-based methods for the segmentation of cross-domain text. In order to detect words not in the training corpus, we also used a simple strategy for out-of-vocabulary word recognition.

2 A Boundary-Oriented Segmentation Method

2.1 N-Gram Mutual Information

It is a challenge to segment text that is out-of-domain for supervised methods which are good at the segmentation for the text that has been seen segmented before. On the other hand, unsupervised segmentation methods could help to discover words even if they are not in vocabularies. To conquer the goal of segmenting text that is out-of-domain and to take advantage of the training corpus, we use n-gram mutual information (NGMI)(Tang et al., 2009) — an unsupervised boundary-oriented segmentation method and make it trainable for cross-domain text segmentation.

As an unsupervised segmentation approach, NGMI is derived from the character-based mutual information(Sproat & Shih, 1990), but unlike its ancestor it can additionally recognise words longer than two characters. Generally, mutual information is used to measure the association strength of two adjoining entities (characters or words) in a given corpus. The stronger association, the more likely it is that they should be together. The association score MI for the adjacent two entities (x and y) is calculated as:

$$MI(x,y) = \log \frac{\frac{freq(xy)}{N}}{\frac{freq(x)}{N}\,\frac{freq(x)}{N}} \approx \log \frac{p(xy)}{p(x)p(y)} \quad (1)$$

where *freq(x)* is the frequency of entity *x* occurring in the given corpus; *freq(xy)* is the frequency of entity *xy* (*x* followed by *y*) occurring in the corpus; *N* is the size of entities in the given corpus; *p(x)* is an estimate of the probability of entity *x* occurring in corpus, calculated as *freq(x)/N*.

NGMI separates words by choosing the most probable boundaries in the unsegmented text with the help of a frequency table of n-gram string patterns. Such a frequency table can be built from any selected text.

The main concept of NGMI is to find the boundaries between words by combining contextual information rather than looking for just words. Any place between two Chinese characters could be a possible boundary. To find the most rightful ones, boundary confidence (BC) is introduced to measure the confidence of having words separated correctly. In other words, BC measures the association level of the left and right characters around each possible boundary to decide whether the boundary should be actually placed.

For any input string, suppose that we have:

$$s = c_1c_2c_3 \ldots c_ic_{i+1} \ldots c_{n-2}c_{n-1}c_n \quad (2)$$

The *boundary confidence* of a possible boundary (|) is defined as:

$$BC(L|R) = NGMI_{min}(L|R) \quad (3)$$

where L and R are the adjoining left and right segments with up to two characters from each side of the boundary (|) and $L = c_{i-2}c_{i-1}$, $R = c_ic_{i+1}$; and $NGMI_{min}$ is calculated as:

$$\begin{aligned} NGMI_{min}(L|R) = \min\big(&MI(c_{i-1}, c_i), \\ &MI(c_{i-2}c_{i-1}, c_i), \\ &MI(c_{i-1}, c_ic_{i+1}), \\ &MI(c_{i-2}c_{i-1}, c_ic_{i+1})\big) \end{aligned} \quad (4)$$

Basically, $NGMI_{min}$ considers mutual information of k ($k=2$, *or* $k=4$) pairs of segments around the boundary; the one with the lowest value is used as the score of boundary confidence. Those segment pairs used in $NGMI_{min}$ calculation are named adjoining segment pairs (ASPs). Each ASP consists of a pair of adjoining segments.

For the boundary confidence of the boundaries at the beginning or end of an input string, we can retrieve only one character from one side of the boundary. So for these two kinds of boundaries differently we have:

$$\begin{aligned} &NGMI_{min}(c_1|c_2c_3) \\ &= \min\big(MI(c_1, c_2),\ MI(c_1, c_2c_3)\big) \end{aligned} \quad (5)$$

$$\begin{aligned} &NGMI_{min}(c_{n-2}c_{n-1}|c_n) \\ &= min\big(MI(c_{n-1}, c_n),\ MI(c_{n-2}c_{n-1}, c_n)\big) \end{aligned} \quad (6)$$

For any possible boundary the lower confidence score it has, the more likely it is an actual boundary. A threshold then can be set to decide whether a boundary should be placed. So even without a lexicon, it is still probable to segment text with a certain precision which just simply means the suggested words are all out-of-vocabulary. Hence, NGMI can be subsequently used for OOV word recognition.

2.2 Supervised NGMI

The idea of making NGMI trainable is to turn the segmented text into a word based frequency table. It is a table that records only words, adjoining word pairs and their frequencies. For example, given a piece of training text – "A B C E B C A B" (where A, B, C and E are n-gram Chinese words), its frequency table should look like the following:

A|B	2
B|C	2
C|E	1
C|A	1
A	2
B	3
C	2
E	1

Also, when doing the boundary confidence computation, any substrings (children) of the words (parents) in this table are set to have the same frequency as their parents'.

3 Segmentation System Design

3.1 Frequency Table and Its Alignment

In order to resolve ambiguity and also recognise OOV terms, statistical information of n-gram string patterns in test files should be collected. There are in total two groups of frequency information used in the segmentation. One is from the training data, recording the frequency information of the actual words and the adjoining word pairs; the other is from the unsegmented text, containing frequency information of all possible n-gram patterns.

However, the statistical data collected from the unsegmented test file contains many noise patterns. It is necessary to remove those noise patterns from the table to avoid negative impact on the final BC computation. Therefore, an alignment of the pattern frequencies obtained from the test file is performed to reduce noise.

The frequency alignment is conducted in a few steps. First, build a frequency table of all string patterns for the unsegmented text including those having a frequency of one. Second, the frequency table is sorted by the frequency and the length of the patterns. Longer patterns have a higher ranking than the shorter ones; for patterns of same length the ones having higher frequency are ranked higher than those having lower. Next, starting from the beginning of the table where the longest and the most frequent pattern have the highest ranking, retrieve one record each time and remove from the table all its sub-patterns which have the same frequency as its parent's.

After such a frequency alignment is done, two frequency tables are merged into one and ready for the final boundary confidence calculation.

3.2 Segmentation

In the training and the system testing stages, the segmentation results using boundary confidence alone for word disambiguation were found unsatisfactory. Trying to achieve as high performance as possible, the overall word segmentation for the bakeoff is done by using a hybrid algorithm which is a combination of NGMI for general word segmentation, and the backward maximum match (BMM) method for the final word disambiguation.

Since it is common for a Chinese document containing various types of characters: Chinese, digit, alphabet and characters from other languages, segmentation needs to be considered for two particular forms of Chinese words: 1) words containing non-Chinese characters such as numbers or letters; and 2) words containing purely Chinese characters.

In order to simplify the process of overall segmentation, boundaries are automatically added to the places in which Chinese characters precede non-Chinese characters. Additionally, for words containing numbers or letters, we only search those begin with numbers or letters and end with Chinese character(s) against the given lexicons. If the search fails, the part with all non-Chinese characters remains the same and a boundary is added between the non-Chinese character and the Chinese character.

For example, to segment a sentence "一万多人喜迎１９９８年新春佳节", it consists of there following main steps:

- First, because of …迎 | １ …, only "一万多人喜迎" requires initial segmentation.
- Next, find a matched word "１９９８年" in a given lexicon.

- Last, segment “新春佳节”.

So the critical part of the segmentation algorithm is to segment strings with purely Chinese characters.

By already knowing the actual word information (i.e. a vocabulary from the labelled training data), it can be set in our algorithm that when computing BCs each possible boundary is assigned with a score falling in one of the following four BC categories:

- INSEPARATABLE
- THRESHOLD
- normal boundary confidence score
- ABSOLUTE-BOUNDARY

INSEPARATABLE means the characters around the possible boundary are a part of an actual word; ABSOLUTE-BOUNDARY means the adjoining segments pairs are not seen in any words or string patterns. THRESHOLD is a threshold value that is given to a possible boundary for which only one of ASPs can be found in the word pair table, and its length is greater than two.

After finishing all BC computations for an input string, it then can be broken down into segments separated by the boundaries having a BC score that is lower than or equals to the threshold value. For each segment, it can be checked if it is a word in the vocabulary or if it is an OOV term using an OOV judgement formula that will be discussed in Section 3.3. If a segment is not a word or an OOV term, it means there is an ambiguity in that segment. For example, given a sentence “…送行李…”, the substring “送行李” inside the sentence can be either segmented into “送行 | 李” or “送 | 行李”.

To disambiguate it, a segment is divided into two chunks at the place having the lowest BC score. If one of the chunks is a word or OOV term, this two-chunk breaking-down operation continues on the remaining non-word chunk until both divided chunks are words, or none of them is a word or an OOV term. After this recursive operation is finished, if there are still non-word chunks left they will be further segmented using the BMM method.

The overall segmentation algorithm for an all-Chinese string can be summarised as follows:

1) Compute BC for each possible boundary.
2) Input string becomes segments that are separated by the boundaries having a low BC score (not higher than the threshold).
3) For each remaining non-word segment resulting from step 2, it gets recursively broken down into two chunks at the place having the lowest BC among this segment based on the scores from step 1. This breaking-down-into-two-chunk loop continues on the non-word chunk if the other is a word or an OOV term; otherwise, all the remaining non-word chucks are further segmented using the backward maximum match method.

3.3 OOV Word Recognition

We use a simple strategy for OOV word detection. It is assumed that an n-gram string pattern can be qualified as an OOV word if it repeats frequently within only a short span of text or a few documents. So to recognise OOV words, the statistical data extracted from the unsegmented text needs to contain not only pattern frequency information but also document frequency information. However, the documents in the test data are boundary-less. To obtain document frequencies for string patterns, we separate test files into a set of virtual documents by splitting them according size. The size of the virtual document (VDS) is adjustable.

For a given non-word string pattern *S*, we then can compute its probability of being an OOV term by using:

$$OOV\_P(S) = \frac{tf}{df} \quad (7)$$

where *tf* is the term frequency of the string pattern *S*; *df* is the virtual document frequency of the string pattern. Then *S* is considered an OOV candidate, if it satisfies:

$$OOV_{P(S)} > OOV\_THRES \quad (8)$$

where *OOV_THRES* is an adjustable threshold value used to filter out the patterns with lower probability of being OOV words. However, using this strategy could have side effects on the segmentation performance because not all the suggested OOV words could be correct.

4 Experiments

4.1 Experimental Environment

OS	GNU/Linux 2.6.32.11-99.fc12.x86_64
CPU	Intel(R) Core(TM)2 Duo CPU E6550 @ 2.33GHz
MEM	8G memory
BUILD	DEBUG build without optimisation

Table 1. Software and Hardware Environment.

The information of operating system and hardware used in the experiments is given in Table 1.

4.2 Parameters Settings

Parameter	Value
N	# of words in training corpus
THRESHOLD	log(1/N)
VDS	10,000bytes
OOV_THRES	2.3

Table 2. System settings used in both closed and open training evaluation.

Table 2 shows the parameters used in the system for segmentation and OOV recognition.

4.3 Closed and Open Training

For both closed and open training evaluations, the algorithm and parameters used for segmentation and OOV detection are exactly the same. This is true except for an extra dictionary - cc-cedict (MDBG) being used in the open training evaluation.

4.4 Segmentation Efficiency

SUBTASK	DOMAIN	TIME
simplified (closed)	A	2m19.841s
	B	2m1.405s
	C	1m57.819s
	D	1m54.375s
simplified (open)	A	3m52.726s
	B	3m20.907s
	C	3m10.398s
	D	3m22.866s
traditional (closed)	A	2m33.448s
	B	2m56.056s
	C	3m7.103s
	D	3m14.286s
traditional (open)	A	3m14.595s
	B	3m41.634s
	C	3m53.839s
	D	4m10.099s

Table 3. The execution time of segmentations for four different domains in both simplified and traditional Chinese subtasks.

Table 3 shows the execution time of all tasks for generating the segmentation outputs. The execution time listed in the table includes the time for loading the training frequency table, building the frequency table from the test file, and producing the actual segmentation results.

5 Evaluation

5.1 Segmentation Results

Task	R	P	F1	R_{OOV}	RR_{OOV}	RR_{IV}
Simplified Chinese						
A (c)	0.907	0.862	0.884	0.069	0.206	0.959
A (o)	0.869	0.873	0.871	0.069	0.657	0.885
B (c)	0.876	0.844	0.86	0.152	0.457	0.951
B (o)	0.859	0.878	0.868	0.152	0.668	0.893
C (c)	0.885	0.804	0.842	0.110	0.218	0.967
C (o)	0.865	0.846	0.855	0.110	0.559	0.903
D (c)	0.904	0.865	0.884	0.087	0.321	0.960
D (o)	0.853	0.850	0.851	0.087	0.438	0.893
Traditional Chinese						
Task	**R**	**P**	**F1**	**R_{OOV}**	**RR_{OOV}**	**RR_{IV}**
A (c)	0.864	0.789	0.825	0.094	0.105	0.943
A (o)	0.804	0.722	0.761	0.094	0.234	0.863
B (c)	0.868	0.85	0.859	0.094	0.316	0.926
B (o)	0.789	0.736	0.761	0.094	0.35	0.834
C (c)	0.871	0.815	0.842	0.075	0.115	0.932
C (o)	0.811	0.74	0.774	0.075	0.254	0.856
D (c)	0.875	0.834	0.854	0.068	0.169	0.926
D (o)	0.811	0.753	0.781	0.068	0.235	0.853

Table 4. The segmentation results for four domains in both closed and open training evaluations. (c) – closed; (o) – open; A - Literature; B – Computer; C – Medicine; D – Finance. R_{OOV} is the OOV rate in the test file.

In the Chinese word segmentation task of CIPS-SIGHAN 2010, the system performance is measured by five metrics: recall (R), precision (P), F-measure (F1), recall rate of OOV words (RR_{OOV}), and recall rate of words in vocabulary (RR_{IV}).

The official results of our system for both open and closed training evaluation are given in Table 4. The recall rates, precision values, and F1-scores of all tasks show promising results of our system in the segmentation for cross-domain text. However, the gaps between our scores and the bakeoff bests also suggest that there is still plenty of room for performance improvements in our system.

The OOV recall rates (RRoov) showed in Table 4 demonstrate that the OOV recognition strategy used in our system can achieve a certain level of OOV word discovery in closed training evaluation. The overall result for the OOV word recognition is not very satisfactory if comparing it with the best result from other bakeoff participants. But for the open training evaluation the OOV recall rate picked up significantly, which indicates that the extra dictionary - cc-cedict covers a fair amount of terms for various domains.

5.2 Possible Further Improvements

Due to finishing the implementation of our segmentation system in a short time, we believe that there might be many program bugs which had negative effects on our system and leaded to producing results not as expected. In an analysis of the segmentation outputs, words starting with numbers were found incorrectly segmented because of the different encodings used in the training and test files for digits. Moreover, the disambiguation in breaking down a non-word segment which contains at least an n-gram word could lead to an all-single-character-word segmentation. This should certainly be avoided.

Also, the current OOV word recognition strategy may detect a few good OOV words, but also introduces incorrect segmentation consistently through the whole input text if OOV words are mistakenly identified. If this OOV word recognition used in our system can be further improved, it can help to alleviate the problem of performance deterioration.

For the open training, if language rules can be encoded in both word segmentation and OOV word recognition, it certainly is another beneficial method to improve the overall precision and recall rate.

6 Conclusions

In this paper, we describe a novel hybrid boundary-oriented NGMI-based segmentation method, which combines a simple strategy for OOV word recognition. The evaluation results show reasonable performance of our system in cross-domain text segmentation even with the negative effects from system bugs and the OOV word recognition strategy. It is believed that the segmentation system can be improved by fixing the existing program bugs, and having a better OOV word recognition strategy. Performance can also be further improved by incorporating language or domain specific knowledge into the system.

References

MDBG. *CC-CEDICT download.* from http://www.mdbg.net/chindict/chindict.php?page=cc-cedict

Sproat, Richard, and Chilin Shih. 1990. A statistical method for finding word boundaries in Chinese text. *Computer Processing of Chinese & Oriental Languages, 4*(4): 336-351.

Tang, Ling-Xiang, Shlomo Geva, Yue Xu, and Andrew Trotman. 2009. *Word Segmentation for Chinese Wikipedia Using N-Gram Mutual Information.* Paper presented at the 14th Australasian Document Computing Symposium (ADCS 2009).

Adaptive Chinese Word Segmentation with Online Passive-Aggressive Algorithm

Wenjun Gao
School of Computer Science
Fudan University
Shanghai, China
wjgao616@gmail.com

Xipeng Qiu
School of Computer Science
Fudan University
Shanghai, China
xpqiu@fudan.edu.cn

Xuanjing Huang
School of Computer Science
Fudan University
Shanghai, China
xjhuang@fudan.edu.cn

Abstract

In this paper, we describe our system[1] for CIPS-SIGHAN-2010 bake-off task of Chinese word segmentation, which focused on the cross-domain performance of Chinese word segmentation algorithms. We use the online passive-aggressive algorithm with domain invariant information for cross-domain Chinese word segmentation.

1 Introduction

In recent years, Chinese word segmentation (CWS) has undergone great development (Xue, 2003; Peng et al., 2004). The popular method is to regard word segmentation as a sequence labeling problems. The goal of sequence labeling is to assign labels to all elements of a sequence.

Due to the exponential size of the output space, sequence labeling problems tend to be more challenging than the conventional classification problems. Many algorithms have been proposed and the progress has been encouraging, such as SVM^{struct} (Tsochantaridis et al., 2004), conditional random fields (CRF) (Lafferty et al., 2001), maximum margin Markov networks (M3N) (Taskar et al., 2003) and so on. After years of intensive researches, Chinese word segmentation achieves a quite high precision. However, the performance of segmentation is not so satisfying for out-of-domain text.

There are two domains in domain adaption problem, a source domain and a target domain. When we use the machine learning methods for Chinese word segmentation, we assume that training and test data are drawn from the same distribution. This assumption underlies both theoretical analysis and experimental evaluations of learning algorithms. However, the assumption does not hold for domain adaptation(Ben-David et al., 2007; Blitzer et al., 2006). The challenge is the difference of distribution between the source and target domains.

In this paper, we use online margin maximization algorithm and domain invariant features for domain adaptive CWS. The online learning algorithm is Passive-Aggressive (PA) algorithm(Crammer et al., 2006), which passively accepts a solution whose loss is zero, while it aggressively forces the new prototype vector to stay as close as possible to the one previously learned.

The rest of the paper is organized as follows. Section 2 introduces the related works. Then we describe our algorithm in section 3 and 4. The feature templates are described in section 5. Section 6 gives the experimental analysis. Section 7 concludes the paper.

2 Related Works

There are several approaches to deal with the domain adaption problem.

The first approach is to use semi-supervised learning (Zhu, 2005).

The second approach is to incorporate supervised learning with domain invariant information.

The third approach is to improve the present model with a few labeled domain data.

Altun et al. (2006) investigated structured classification in a semi-supervised setting. They presented a discriminative approach that utilizes the

[1]Available at http://code.google.com/p/fudannlp/

intrinsic geometry of inputs revealed by unlabeled data points and we derive a maximum-margin formulation of semi-supervised learning for structured variables.

Self-training (Zhu, 2005) is also a popular technology. In self-training a classifier is first trained with the small amount of labeled data. The classifier is then used to classify the unlabeled data. Typically the most confident unlabeled points, together with their predicted labels, are added to the training set. The classifier is re-trained and the procedure repeated. Note the classifier uses its own predictions to teach itself. Yarowsky (1995) uses self-training for word sense disambiguation, e.g. deciding whether the word plant means a living organism or a factory in a given context.

Zhao and Kit (2008) integrated unsupervised segmentation and CRF learning for Chinese word segmentation and named entity recognition. They found word accessory variance (Feng et al., 2004) is useful to CWS.

3 Online Passive-Aggressive Algorithm

Sequence labeling, the task of assigning labels $\mathbf{y} = y_1, \dots, y_L$ to an input sequence $\mathbf{x} = x_1, \dots, x_L$.

Give a sample $(\mathbf{x}, \mathbf{y})$, we define the feature is $\Phi(\mathbf{x}, \mathbf{y})$. Thus, we can label $\mathbf{x}$ with a score function,

$$\hat{\mathbf{y}} = \arg\max_{\mathbf{z}} F(\mathbf{w}, \Phi(\mathbf{x}, \mathbf{z})), \quad (1)$$

where $\mathbf{w}$ is the parameter of function $F(\cdot)$.

The score function of our algorithm is linear function.

Given an example $(\mathbf{x}, \mathbf{y})$, $\hat{\mathbf{y}}$ is denoted as the incorrect label with the highest score,

$$\hat{\mathbf{y}} = \arg\max_{\mathbf{z} \neq \mathbf{y}} w^T \Phi(\mathbf{x}, \mathbf{z}). \quad (2)$$

The **margin** $\gamma(\mathbf{w}; (\mathbf{x}, \mathbf{y}))$ is defined as

$$\gamma(\mathbf{w}; (\mathbf{x}, \mathbf{y})) = \mathbf{w}^T \Phi(\mathbf{x}, \mathbf{y}) - \mathbf{w}^T \Phi(\mathbf{x}, \hat{\mathbf{y}}). \quad (3)$$

Thus, we calculate the **hinge loss**.

$$\ell(\mathbf{w}; (\mathbf{x}, \mathbf{y}) = \begin{cases} 0, & \gamma(\mathbf{w}; (\mathbf{x}, \mathbf{y})) > 1 \\ 1 - \gamma(\mathbf{w}; (\mathbf{x}, \mathbf{y})), & \text{otherwise} \end{cases} \quad (4)$$

We use the online PA learning algorithm to learn the weights of features. In round t, we find new weight vector $\mathbf{w}_{t+1}$ by

$$\mathbf{w}_{t+1} = \arg\min_{\mathbf{w} \in \mathbb{R}^n} \frac{1}{2} ||\mathbf{w} - \mathbf{w}_t||^2 + \mathcal{C} \cdot \xi,$$
$$\textbf{s.t. } \ell(\mathbf{w}; (\mathbf{x}_t, \mathbf{y}_t)) <= \xi \textbf{ and } \xi >= 0 \quad (5)$$

where C is a positive parameter which controls the influence of the slack term on the objective function.

The algorithms goal is to achieve a margin at least 1 as often as possible, thus the Hamming loss is also reduced indirectly. On rounds where the algorithm attains a margin less than 1 it suffers an instantaneous loss.

We abbreviate $\ell(\mathbf{w_t}; (x, y))$ to ℓ_t. If $\ell_t = 0$ then w_t itself satisfies the constraint in Eq. (5) and is clearly the optimal solution. We therefore concentrate on the case where $\ell_t > 0$.

First, we define the Lagrangian of the optimization problem in Eq. (5) to be

$$\mathcal{L}(\mathbf{w}, \xi, \alpha, \beta) = \frac{1}{2} ||\mathbf{w} - \mathbf{w}_t||^2 + \mathcal{C} \cdot \xi$$
$$+ \alpha(\ell_t - \xi) - \beta\xi$$
$$\textbf{s.t. } \alpha >= 0, \beta >= 0. \quad (6)$$

where α, β is a Lagrange multiplier.

Setting the partial derivatives of $\mathcal{L}$ with respect to the elements of ξ to zero gives

$$\alpha + \beta = \mathcal{C}. \quad (7)$$

The gradient of $\mathbf{w}$ should be zero,

$$\mathbf{w} - \mathbf{w}_t - \alpha(\Phi(\mathbf{x}, \mathbf{y}) - \Phi(\mathbf{x}, \hat{\mathbf{y}})) = 0, \quad (8)$$

we get

$$\mathbf{w} = \mathbf{w}_t + \alpha(\Phi(\mathbf{x}, \mathbf{y}) - \Phi(\mathbf{x}, \hat{\mathbf{y}})). \quad (9)$$

Substitute Eq. (7) and Eq. (9) to dual objective function Eq. (6), we get

$$\mathcal{L}(\alpha) = -\frac{1}{2} ||\alpha(\Phi(\mathbf{x}, \mathbf{y}) - \Phi(\mathbf{x}, \hat{\mathbf{y}}))||^2$$
$$- \alpha(\mathbf{w_t}^T (\Phi(\mathbf{x}, \mathbf{y}) - \Phi(\mathbf{x}, \hat{\mathbf{y}})) + \alpha \quad (10)$$

Differentiate with α, and set it to zero, we get

$$\alpha||\Phi(\mathbf{x},\mathbf{y}) - \Phi(\mathbf{x},\hat{\mathbf{y}})||^2 + \mathbf{w_t}^T(\Phi(\mathbf{x},\mathbf{y}) - \Phi(\mathbf{x},\hat{\mathbf{y}})) - 1 = 0. \quad (11)$$

So,

$$\bar{\alpha} = \frac{1 - \mathbf{w_t}^T(\Phi(\mathbf{x},\mathbf{y}) - \Phi(\mathbf{x},\hat{\mathbf{y}}))}{||\Phi(\mathbf{x},\mathbf{y}) - \Phi(\mathbf{x},\hat{\mathbf{y}})||^2}. \quad (12)$$

From $\alpha + \beta = \mathcal{C}$, we know that $\alpha < \mathcal{C}$, so

$$\bar{\alpha}^* = \min(\mathcal{C}, \bar{\alpha}). \quad (13)$$

Finally, we get update strategy,

$$\mathbf{w_{t+1}} = \mathbf{w}_t + \bar{\alpha}^*(\Phi(\mathbf{x},\mathbf{y}) - \Phi(\mathbf{x},\hat{\mathbf{y}})). \quad (14)$$

Our final algorithm is shown in Algorithm 1. In order to avoiding overfitting, the averaging technology is employed.

```
input  : training data set:
         (x_n, y_n), n = 1, ..., N, and
         parameters: C, K
output: w
Initialize: cw ← 0,;
for k = 0 ··· K − 1 do
    w_0 ← 0 ;
    for t = 0 ··· T − 1 do
        receive an example (x_t, y_t);
        predict:
        ŷ_t = arg max_{z≠y_t} ⟨w_t, Φ(x_t, z)⟩;
        calculate ℓ(w; (x, y));
        update w_{t+1} with Eq.(14);
    end
    cw = cw + w_T ;
end
w = cw/K ;
```

Algorithm 1: Labelwise Margin Maximization Algorithm

4 Inference

The PA algorithm is used to learn the weights of features in training procedure. In inference procedure, we use Viterbi algorithm to calculate the maximum score label.

Let $\omega(n)$ be the best score of the partial label sequence ending with y_n. The idea of the Viterbi algorithm is to use dynamic programming to compute $\omega(n)$:

$$\omega(n) = \max_{n-1}\left(\omega(n-1) + \mathbf{w}^T\phi(x, y_n, y_{n-1})\right) + \mathbf{w}^t\phi(x, y_n) \quad (15)$$

Using this recursive definition, we can evaluate $\omega(N)$ for all y_N, where N is the input length. This results in the identification of the best label sequence.

The computational cost of the Viterbi algorithm is $O(NL^2)$, where L is the number of labels.

5 Feature Templates

All feature templates used in this paper are shown in Table 1. C represents a Chinese character while the subscript of C indicates its position in the sentence relative to the current character, whose subscript is 0. T represents the character-based tag: "B", "B2", "B3", "M", "E" and "S", which represent the beginning, second, third, middle, end or single character of a word respectively.

The type of character includes: digital, letter, punctuation and other.

We also use the word accessor variance for domain adaption. Word accessor variance (AV) was proposed by (Feng et al., 2004) and was used to evaluate how independently a string is used, and thus how likely it is that the string can be a word. The accessor variety of a string s of more than one character is defined as

$$AV(s) = \min\{L_{av}(s), R_{av}(s)\} \quad (16)$$

$L_{av}(s)$ is called the left accessor variety and is defined as the number of distinct characters (predecessors) except "S" that precede s plus the number of distinct sentences of which s appears at the beginning. Similarly, the right accessor variety $R_{av}(s)$ is defined as the number of distinct characters (successors) except "E" that succeed s plus the number of distinct sentences in which s appears at the end. The characters "S" and "E" are defined as the begin and end of a sentence. The word accessor variance was found effective for CWS with unsegmented text (Zhao and Kit, 2008).

Table 1: Feature templates

$C_i, T_0, (i = -1, 0, 1, 2)$
$C_i, C_{i+1}, T_0, (i = -2, -1, 0, 1)$
$T_{-1,0}$
T_c: Type of Character
AV: word accessor variance

6 CIPS-SIGHAN-2010 Bakeoff

CIPS-SIGHAN-2010 bake-off task of Chinese word segmentation focused on the cross-domain performance of Chinese word segmentation algorithms. There are two subtasks for this evaluation:

(1) Word Segmentation for Simplified Chinese Text;

(2) Word Segmentation for Traditional Chinese Text.

The test corpus of each subtask covers four domains: literature, computer science, medicine and finance.

We participate in closed training evaluation of both subtasks.

Firstly, we calculate the word accessor variance $AV_L(s)$of the continuous string s from labeled corpus. Here, we set the largest length of string s to be 4.

Secondly, we train our model with feature temples and $AV_L(s)$.

Thirdly, when we process the different domain unlabeled corpus, we recalculate the word accessory variance $AV_U(s)$ from the corresponding corpus.

Fourthly, we segment the domain corpus with new word accessory variance $AV_U(s)$ instead of $AV_L(s)$.

The results are shown in Table 2 and 3. The results show our method has a poor performance in OOV (Out-Of-Vocabulary) word.

The running environment is shown in Table 4.

Table 4: Experimental environment

OS	Win 2003
CPU	Intel Xeon 2.0G
Memory	4G

We set the max iterative number is 20. Our running time is shown in Table 5. "s" represents second, "chars" is the number of Chinese character, and "MB" is the megabyte. In practice, we found the system can achieve the same performance after 7 loops. Therefore, we just need less half the time in Table 5 actually.

7 Conclusion

In this paper, we describe our system in CIPS-SIGHAN-2010 bake-off task of Chinese word segmentation. Although our method just achieve a consequence of being average and not outstanding, it has an advantage of faster training than other batch learning algorithm, such as CRF and M3N.

In the future, we wish to improve our method in the following aspects. Firstly, we will investigate more effective domain invariant feature representation. Secondly, we will integrate our algorithm with self-training and other semi-supervised learning methods.

Acknowledgments

This work was (partially) funded by 863 Program (No. 2009AA01A346), 973 Program (No. 2010CB327906), and Shanghai Science and Technology Development Funds (No. 08511500302).

References

Altun, Y., D. McAllester, and M. Belkin. 2006. Maximum margin semi-supervised learning for structured variables. *Advances in neural information processing systems*, 18:33.

Ben-David, S., J. Blitzer, K. Crammer, and F. Pereira. 2007. Analysis of representations for domain adaptation. *Advances in Neural Information Processing Systems*, 19:137.

Blitzer, J., R. McDonald, and F. Pereira. 2006. Domain adaptation with structural correspondence learning. In *Proceedings of the 2006 Conference on Empirical Methods in Natural Language Processing*, pages 120–128. Association for Computational Linguistics.

Crammer, Koby, Ofer Dekel, Joseph Keshet, Shai Shalev-Shwartz, and Yoram Singer. 2006. Online passive-aggressive algorithms. *Journal of Machine Learning Research*, 7:551–585.

Table 2: Evaluation results on simplified corpus

		R	P	F1	OOV RR	IV RR
Literature	Best	0.945	0.946	0.946	0.816	0.954
	Our	0.915	0.925	0.92	0.577	0.94
Computer	Best	0.953	0.95	0.951	0.827	0.975
	Our	0.934	0.919	0.926	0.739	0.969
Medicine	Best	0.942	0.936	0.939	0.75	0.965
	Our	0.927	0.924	0.925	0.714	0.953
Finance	Best	0.959	0.96	0.959	0.827	0.972
	Our	0.94	0.942	0.941	0.719	0.961

Table 3: Evaluation results on traditional corpus

		R	P	F1	OOV RR	IV RR
Literature	Best	0.942	0.942	0.942	0.788	0.958
	Our	0.869	0.91	0.889	0.698	0.887
Computer	Best	0.948	0.957	0.952	0.666	0.977
	Our	0.933	0.949	0.941	0.791	0.948
Medicine	Best	0.953	0.957	0.955	0.798	0.966
	Our	0.908	0.932	0.92	0.771	0.919
Finance	Best	0.964	0.962	0.963	0.812	0.975
	Our	00.925	0.939	0.932	0.793	0.935

Table 5: Execution time of training and test phase.

	Task	A	B	C	D
Training	Simp	817.2s	795.6s	774.0s	792.0s
	Trad	903.6s	889.2s	885.6s	874.8s
Test		20327 chars/s, or 17.97 s/MB			

Feng, H., K. Chen, X. Deng, and W. Zheng. 2004. Accessor variety criteria for chinese word extraction. *Computational Linguistics*, 30(1):75–93.

Lafferty, John D., Andrew McCallum, and Fernando C. N. Pereira. 2001. Conditional random fields: Probabilistic models for segmenting and labeling sequence data. In *ICML '01: Proceedings of the Eighteenth International Conference on Machine Learning*.

Peng, F., F. Feng, and A. McCallum. 2004. Chinese segmentation and new word detection using conditional random fields. *Proceedings of the 20th international conference on Computational Linguistics*.

Taskar, Ben, Carlos Guestrin, and Daphne Koller. 2003. Max-margin markov networks. In *Proceedings of Neural Information Processing Systems*.

Tsochantaridis, I., T. Hofmann, T. Joachims, and Y Altun. 2004. Support vector machine learning for interdependent and structured output spaces. In *Proceedings of the International Conference on Machine Learning(ICML)*.

Xue, N. 2003. Chinese word segmentation as character tagging. *Computational Linguistics and Chinese Language Processing*, 8(1):29–48.

Yarowsky, D. 1995. Unsupervised word sense disambiguation rivaling supervised methods. In *Proceedings of the 33rd annual meeting on Association for Computational Linguistics*, pages 189–196. Association for Computational Linguistics.

Zhao, H. and C. Kit. 2008. Unsupervised segmentation helps supervised learning of character tagging for word segmentation and named entity recognition. In *The Sixth SIGHAN Workshop on Chinese Language Processing*, pages 106–111. Citeseer.

Zhu, Xiaojin. 2005. Semi-supervised learning literature survey. Technical Report 1530, Computer Sciences, University of Wisconsin-Madison. http://www.cs.wisc.edu/~jerryzhu/pub/ssl_survey.pdf.

A Character-Based Joint Model
for CIPS-SIGHAN Word Segmentation Bakeoff 2010

Kun Wang and **Chengqing Zong**
National Laboratory of Pattern Recognition
Institute of Automation, Chinese Academy of Science
{kunwang,cqzong}@nlpr.ia.ac.cn

Keh-Yih Su
Behavior Design Corporation
kysu@bdc.com.tw

Abstract

This paper presents a Chinese Word Segmentation system for the closed track of CIPS-SIGHAN Word Segmentation Bakeoff 2010. This system adopts a character-based joint approach, which combines a character-based generative model and a character-based discriminative model. To further improve the cross-domain performance, we use an additional semi-supervised learning procedure to incorporate the unlabeled corpus. The final performance on the closed track for the simplified-character text shows that our system achieves comparable results with other state-of-the-art systems.

1 Introduction

The character-based tagging approach (Xue, 2003) has become the dominant technique for Chinese word segmentation (CWS) as it can tolerate *out-of-vocabulary* (OOV) words. In the last few years, this method has been widely adopted and further improved in many previous works (Tseng et al., 2005; Zhang et al., 2006; Jiang et al., 2008). Among various character-based tagging approaches, the character-based joint model (Wang et al., 2010) achieves a good balance between *in-vocabulary* (IV) words recognition and OOV words identification.

In this work, we adopt the character-based joint model as our basic system, which combines a character-based discriminative model and a character-based generative model. The generative module holds a robust performance on IV words, while the discriminative module can handle the extra features easily and enhance the OOV words segmentation. However, the performance of out-of-domain text is still not satisfactory as that of in-domain text, while few previous works have paid attention to this problem.

To further improve the performance of the basic system in out-of-domain text, we use a semi-supervised learning procedure to incorporate the unlabeled corpora of Literature (Unlabeled-A) and Computer (Unlabeled-B). The final results show that our system performs well on all four testing-sets and achieves comparable segmentation results with other participants.

2 Our system

2.1 Character-Based Joint Model

The character-based joint model in our system contains two basic components:

- The character-based discriminative model
- The character-based generative model.

The character-based discriminative model (Xue, 2003) is based on a Maximum Entropy (ME) framework (Ratnaparkhi, 1998) and can be formulated as follows:

$$P(t_1^n | c_1^n) \approx \prod_{k=1}^{n} P(t_k | t_{k-1}, c_{k-2}^{k+2}) \quad (1)$$

Where t_k is a member of {***B**egin*, ***M**iddle*, ***E**nd*, ***S**ingle*} (abbreviated as B, M, E and S from now on) to indicate the corresponding position of character c_k in its associated word. For example, the word "北京市 (Beijing City)" will be assigned with the corresponding tags as: "北/B (North) 京/M (Capital) 市/E (City)".

This discriminative module can flexibly incorporate extra features and it is implemented with the ME package[1] given by Zhang Le. All training experiments are done with Gaussian prior 1.0 and 200 iterations.

The character-based generative module is a character-tag-pair-based trigram model (Wang et al., 2009) and can be expressed as below:

$$P([c,t]_1^n) \approx \prod_{i=1}^{n} P([c,t]_i \,|\, [c,t]_{i-2}^{i-1}). \qquad (2)$$

In our experiments, SRI Language Modeling Toolkit[2] (Stolcke, 2002) is used to train the generative trigram model with modified Kneser-Ney smoothing (Chen and Goodman, 1998).

The character-based joint model combines the above discriminative module and the generative module with log-linear interpolation as follows:

$$\begin{aligned} Score(t_k) &= \alpha \times \log(P([c,t]_k \,|\, [c,t]_{k-2}^{k-1})) \\ &\quad + (1-\alpha) \times \log(P(t_k \,|\, t_{k-1}, c_{k-2}^{k+2})) \end{aligned} \qquad (3)$$

Where the parameter α $(0.0 \le \alpha \le 1.0)$ is the weight for the generative model. $Score(t_k)$ will be directly used during searching the best sequence. We set an empirical value ($\alpha = 0.3$) to this model as there is no development-set for various domains.

2.2 Features

In this work, the feature templates adopted in the character-based discriminative model are very simple and are listed below:

$(a)\ C_n (n = -2, -1, 0, 12);$

$(b)\ C_n C_{n+1} (n = -2, -1, 0, 1);$

$(c)\ C_{-1} C_1;$

$(d)\ T(C_{-2})T(C_{-1})T(C_0)T(C_1)T(C_2)$

In the above templates, C_n represents a character and the index n indicates the position. For example, when we consider the third character "奥" in the sequence "北京奥运会", template (a) results in the features as following: C_{-2}=北, C_{-1}=京, C_0=奥, C_1=运, C_2=会, and template (b) generates the features as: $C_{-2}C_{-1}$=北京, $C_{-1}C_0$=京奥, C_0C_1=奥运, C_1C_2=运会, and template (c) gives the feature $C_{-1}C_1$=京运.

Template (d) is the feature of character type. Five types classes are defined: dates ("年", "月", "日", the Chinese character for "year", "month" and "day" respectively) represents class 0; foreign alphabets represent class 1; Arabic and Chinese numbers represent class 2; punctuation represents class 3 and other characters represent class 4. For example, when we consider the character "，" in the sequence "八月，阿Q", the feature $T(C_{-2})T(C_{-1})T(C_0)T(C_1)T(C_2)$ will be set to "20341".

When training the character-based discriminative module, we convert all the binary features into real-value features, and set the real-value of C_0 to be 2.0, the value of $C_{-1}C_0$ and C_0C_1 to be 3.0, and the values of all other features to be 1.0. This method sounds a little strange because it is equal to duplicate some features for the maximum entropy training. However, it effectively improves the performance in our previous works.

2.3 Restrictions in constructing lattice

As the closed track allows the participants to use the character type information, we add some restrictions to our system when constructing the character-tag lattice. When we consider a character in the sequence, the type information of both the previous and the next character would be taken into account. The restrictions are list as follows:

- If the previous, the current and the next characters are all English or numbers, we would fix the current tag to be "M";
- If the previous and the next characters are both English or numbers, while the current character is a connective symbol such as "-", "/", "_", "\" etc., we would also fix the current tag to be "M";
- Otherwise, all four tags {B, E, M, S} would be given to the current character.

It is shown that in the Computer domain these simple restrictions not only greatly reduce the number of words segmented, but also speed up the system.

[1] http://homepages.inf.ed.ac.uk/lzhang10/maxent_toolkit.html

[2] http://www.speech.sri.com/projects/srilm/

Domain	Mark	OOV Rate	R	P	F1	R_{OOV}	R_{IV}
Literature	A	0.069	0.937	0.937	0.937	0.652	0.958
Computer	B	0.152	0.941	0.940	0.940	0.757	0.974
Medicine	C	0.110	0.930	0.917	0.923	0.674	0.961
Finance	D	0.087	0.957	0.956	0.957	0.813	0.971

Table 1: Official segmentation results of our system.

Algorithm 1: Semi-Supervised Learning

Given:

- Labeled training corpus: L
- Unlabeled training corpus: U

Use L to train a segmenter S_0;
Use S_0 to segment the unlabeled corpus U and then get labeled corpus U_0;
for $i = 1$ to K **do**
  Add U_{i-1} to L and get a new corpus L_i;
  Use L_i to train a new segmenter S_i;
  Use S_i to segment the unlabeled corpus U and then get labeled corpus U_i;
  if convergence criterion meets
    break
end for

Output: the last segmenter S_K

2.4 Semi-Supervised Learning

In the last decade, Chinese word segmentation has been improved significantly and gets a high precision rate in performance. However, the performance for out-of-domain text is still unsatisfactory at the present. Also, few works have paid attention to the cross-domain problem in Chinese word segmentation task so far.

Self-training and Co-training are two simple semi-supervised learning methods to incorporate unlabeled corpus (Zhu, 2006). In this work, we use an iterative self-training method to incorporate the unlabeled data. A segmenter is first trained with the labeled corpus. Then this segmenter is used to segment the unlabeled data. Then the predicted data is added to the original training corpus as a new training-set. The segmenter will be re-trained and the procedure repeated. To simplify the task, we fix the weight $\alpha = 0.3$ for the generative module of our joint model in the training iterations. The procedure is shown in Algorithm 1. The iterations will not be ended until the similarity of two segmentation results U_{i-1} and U_i reach a certain level. Here we used F-score to measure the similarity between U_{i-1} and U_i: treat U_{i-1} as the benchmark, U_i as a testing-set. From our observation, this method converges quickly in only 3 or 4 iterations for both Literature and Computer corpora.

3 Experiments and Discussion

3.1 Results

In this CIPS-SIGHAN bakeoff, we only participate the closed track for simplified-character text. There are two kinds of training corpora:

- Labeled corpus from News Domain
- Unlabeled corpora from Literature Domain (Unlabeled-A) and Computer Domain (Unlabeled-B).

Also, the testing corpus covers four domains: Literature (Testing-A), Computer (Testing-B), Medicine (Testing-C) and Finance (Testing-D). As there are only two unlabeled corpora for Domain A and B, we thus adopt different strategies for each testing-set:

- Testing-A: Character-Based Joint Model with semi-supervised learning, training on Labeled corpus and Unlabeled-A;
- Testing-B: Character-Based Joint Model with semi-supervised learning, training on Labeled corpus and Unlabeled-B;
- Testing-C and D: Character-Based Joint Model, training on Labeled corpus;

Table 1 shows that our system achieves F-scores for various testing-sets: 0.937 (A), 0.940 (B), 0.923 (C) and 0.957 (D), which are comparable with other systems. Among those four testing domains, our system performs unsatisfactorily on Testing-C (Medicine) even the OOV rate of this domain is not the highest. There are possible reasons for this result: (1) Semi-supervised learning is not conducted for this domain; (2) the statistical property between News and Medicine are significantly different.

Domain	Model	F1	R_{OOV}
A	J + R + S	0.937	0.652
	J + S	0.937	0.646
	J + R	0.936	0.646
	J	0.936	0.642
B	J + R + S	0.940	0.757
	J + S	0.931	0.721
	J + R	0.938	0.744
	J	0.927	0.699
C	J + R	0.923	0.674
	J	0.923	0.674
D	J + R	0.957	0.813
	J	0.954	0.786

Table 2: Performance of various approaches
J: Baseline, the character-based joint model
R: Adding restrictions in constructing lattice
S: Conduct Semi-Supervised Learning

3.2 Discussion

The aim of restrictions in constructing lattice is to improve the performance of English and numerical expressions, both of which appear frequently in Computer and Finance domain. Therefore, the improvements gained from these restrictions are significantly in these two domains (as shown in Table 2).

Besides, the adopted semi-supervised learning procedure improves the performance in Domain A and B., but the improvement is not significant. Semi-supervised learning aims to incorporate large amounts of unlabeled data. However, the size of unlabeled corpora provided here is too small. The semi-supervised learning procedure is expected to be more effective if a large amount of unlabeled data is available.

4 Conclusion

Our system is based on a character-based joint model, which combines a generative module and a discriminative module. In addition, we applied a semi-supervised learning method to the baseline approach to incorporate the unlabeled corpus. Our system achieves comparable performance with other participants. However, cross-domain performance is still not satisfactory and further study is needed.

Acknowledgement

The research work has been partially funded by the Natural Science Foundation of China under Grant No. 60975053, 90820303 and 60736014, the National Key Technology R&D Program under Grant No. 2006BAH03B02, and also the Hi-Tech Research and Development Program ("863" Program) of China under Grant No. 2006AA010108-4 as well.

References

Stanley F. Chen and Joshua Goodman, 1998. An empirical study of smoothing techniques for language modeling. *Technical Report TR-10-98, Harvard University Center for Research in Computing Technology*.

Wenbin Jiang, Liang Huang, Qun Liu and Yajuan Lu, 2008. A Cascaded Linear Model for Joint Chinese Word Segmentation and Part-of-Speech Tagging. In *Proceedings of ACL*, pages 897-904.

Adwait Ratnaparkhi, 1998. Maximum entropy models for natural language ambiguity resolution. University of Pennsylvania.

Andreas Stolcke, 2002. SRILM-an extensible language modeling toolkit. In *Proceedings of the International Conference on Spoken Language Processing*, pages 311-318.

Huihsin Tseng, Pichuan Chang, Galen Andrew, Daniel Jurafsky and Christopher Manning, 2005. A Conditional Random Field Word Segmenter for Sighan Bakeoff 2005. In *Proceedings of the Fourth SIGHAN Workshop on Chinese Language Processing*, pages 168-171.

Kun Wang, Chengqing Zong and Keh-Yih Su, 2009. Which is more suitable for Chinese word segmentation, the generative model or the discriminative one? In *Proceedings of the 23rd Pacific Asia Conference on Language, Information and Computation (PACLIC23)*, pages 827-834.

Kun Wang, Chengqing Zong and Keh-Yih Su, 2010. A Character-Based Joint Model for Chinese Word Segmentation. To *appear in COLING 2010*.

Nianwen Xue, 2003. Chinese Word Segmentation as Character Tagging. *Computational Linguistics and Chinese Language Processing*, 8 (1). pages 29-48.

Ruiqiang Zhang, Genichiro Kikui and Eiichiro Sumita, 2006. Subword-based Tagging for Confidence-dependent Chinese Word Segmentation. In *Proceedings of the COLING/ACL*, pages 961-968.

Xiaojin Zhu, 2006. Semi-supervised learning literature survey. *Technical Report 1530*, Computer Sciences, University of Wisconsin-Madison.

Incorporating New Words Detection with Chinese Word Segmentation

Hua-Ping ZHANG[1] **Jian GAO**[1] **Qian MO**[2] **He-Yan HUANG**[1]
[1] Beijing Institute of Technology, Beijing, P.R.C 100081
[2] Beijing Technology and Business University, Beijing, P.R.C 100048
Email: kevinzhang@bit.edu.cn

Abstract

With development in Chinese words segmentation, in-vocabulary word segmentation and named entity recognition achieves state-of-art performance. However, new words become bottleneck to Chinese word segmentation. This paper presents the result from Beijing Institute of Technology (BIT) in the Sixth International Chinese Word Segmentation Bakeoff in 2010. Firstly, the author reviewed the problem caused by the new words in Chinese texts, then introduced the algorithm of new words detection. The final section provided the official evaluation result in this bakeoff and gave conclusions.

1 Introduction

With the rapid development of Internet with Chinese language, word segmentation received extensive attention. In-vocabulary word segmentation and named entity recognition have achieved state-of-art performance. Chinese words are actually not well defined, and there is not a commonly accepted segmentation lexicon. It is hard to collect all possible new words, or predict new words occurred in the future. New words is the bottleneck to Chinese word segmentation. The problem became more severe with word segmentation on special domain texts, such as computer, medicine and finance. There are much specialized words which are difficult to be exported to the lexicon. So new words detection is very important, which would have more substantial impact on the performance of word segmentation than ambiguous segmentation.

In this paper，we presented a method of new words detection, and then detailed the process of Chinese word segmentation incorporating new words detection. The last section provided the evaluation and gave our conclusions.

2 Problem with new words

In the process of Chinese word Segmentation, there are many mistakes because of new words. These new words are Out of vocabulary (OOV), so the system couldn't distinguish them from original texts, and then impacted the results of word segmentation.

We gave an example from Text C in medicine domain to explain and detect the new words.

“我们以阿司匹林作为对照药物，证实盐酸沙格雷酯治疗 12 周后，糖尿病合并 PAD 患者的无痛行走距离和能够耐受疼痛的最大行走距离都明显改善，ABI 明显改善，明显优于阿司匹林的疗效。”

The sentence should be segmented as follows：

“我们 以 阿司匹林 作为 对照 药物 ， 证实 盐酸沙格雷酯 治疗 12 周后 ， 糖尿病 合并 PAD 患者 的 无痛 行走 距离 和 能够 耐受 疼痛 的 最 大 行走 距离 都 明显 改善 ， ABI 明显 改善 ， 明显 优于 阿司匹林 的 疗效 。 ”

Here, both “阿司匹林” and “盐酸沙格雷酯” are domain words, or new words beyond general segmentation lexicon. Therefore, new words from domain should be detected and added to segmentation lexicon before word segmentation.

3 Word segmentation with new words detection

3.1 Framework

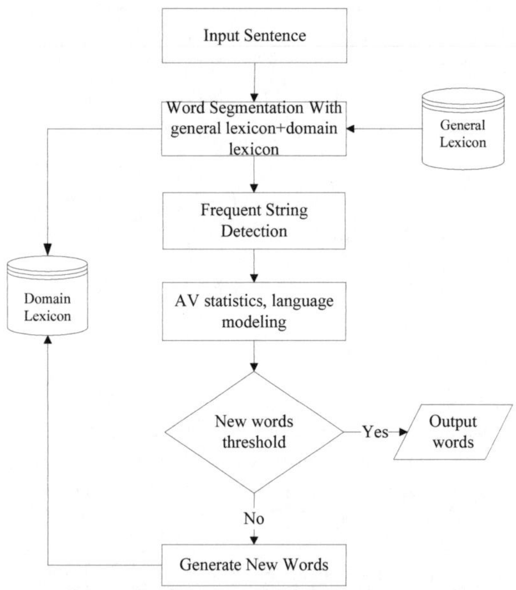

Figure 1: The framework of Chinese word segmentation incorporating with new words detection

As illustrated in Figure 1, Chinese word segmentation with new words detection is a recursive process. The process is given as follows:

1. Making Chinese word segmentation with domain lexicon beyond general lexicon.
2. Frequent string (over twice) finding with postfix tree algorithm, and taking them as new words candidate.
3. Access Variety statistics [Haodi Feng etc. 2004], and language modeling on word formation. [Hemin, 2006]
4. Exporting new words to domain lexicon.
5. Recursively, until no more new word detected.
6. Output final word sequence.

3.2 The process of new words detection

Simple word segmentation is the first step of processing of Chinese language when we deal with a very long Chinese article. The method of word segmentation is based on HHMM, and Zhang and Liu (2003) have given detailed explanation about this.

During the process of word segmentation in the first, the system records the words which occur frequently. We can set a threshold value of words' occurrence frequency. As long as the word occurrence frequency reaches this value, this word could be recorded in the system as frequent string.

With the frequent strings detected, we can do the further analysis. For every frequent string, we check its left and right adjacent one in the original text segmented respectively. Through this step, we find the adjacent words which occur next to some frequent string detected. If the adjacent word also occurs very frequently, or even it occurs at the left or right of the frequent string every time, it's great possibility that the string detected and the adjacent word could merge into one word.

With the detection in above steps, we gain new words from Chinese texts. Then we import these new words into domain lexicon and our lexicon is updated. With the lexicon containing new words, we can do the next cycle recursively and revise continually.

Then, we can see this is a recursive structure. Through the continued process of word segmentation and new words detection, the state of segmentation tends to be steady. The condition of steady state has several kinds such as no more new words detected or the latest result equal to the previous one. At this time, we can break the recursion and output the final result.

This is an example. This sentence is from Text D in finance domain

"雷曼兄弟公司倒闭不到一年，金融市场已经稳定，股市也已回升。" ("The financial market has been stable and the stock has rebounded in less than one year time after Lehman Brother Corporation went bankrupt.")

After word segmentation with original lexicon, this altered sentence is:

"雷/曼/兄弟/公司/倒闭/不/到/一/年/，/金融市场/已经/稳定/，/股市/也/已/回升/。/"

"雷曼兄弟" is a new word as a organization name and it is hard to be collected. Like this kind of word, there are difficulties to add new words to update the lexicon in time. So it is normal to segment this word "雷曼兄弟" into three words.

Through frequent string detection, we gain these three words “雷”, “曼” and “兄弟”. With the adjacent analysis, we find the word “雷” occurs 6 times, “曼” 3 times and “兄弟” 3 times.

The character “雷” occurs 3 times in the detected word “布雷迪” and 3 times at the left of the word “曼”. So we can consider the word “雷曼” as a whole word.

Then we can easily find the words “兄弟” are always at the right of words “雷曼”. So it's necessary to consider “雷曼兄弟” as a whole word.

4 Evaluation

The performance of word segmentation is measured by test precision (P), test recall (R), F score (which is defined as 2PR/(P+R)) and the OOV recall rate.

In this competition, our test corpus involved literature, computer, medicine and Finance, totally 425KB. We take 6 months data of The People's Daily to be the training corpus. From Table 1, we can see the official evaluation result.

	R	P	F1	OOV R	OOV RR	IV RR
A-Literature	0.965	0.94	0.952	0.069	0.814	0.976
B-Computer	0.951	0.926	0.938	0.152	0.775	0.982
C-Medicine	0.953	0.913	0.933	0.11	0.704	0.984
D-Finance	0.963	0.938	0.95	0.087	0.758	0.982

Table 1. Official evaluation result

Our system got high Precision Rate and Recall Rate after testing the texts in four domains, especially Recall Rate is all over 95%. And we also could see that this system detected most new words through several measures of OOV, especially IV RR is all over 97.5%. This proved that the system could be able to get a nice result through processing professional articles in literature, computer, medicine and finance domains, and we believed it also could do well in other domains. This also proved that the method of new words detection with Chinese word segmentation was competitive.

5Conclusion

Through this competition, we've found a lot of problems needed to be solved in Chinese word segmentation and tried our best to improve the system. Finally, we proposed the method of new words detection in Chinese word segmentation. But we still had some shortage during the evaluation and need to improve in the future.

References

Lawrence. R.Rabiner.1989. *A Tutorial on Hidden Markov Models and Selected Applications in Speech Recognition*. Proceedings of IEEE 77(2): pp.257-286.

Hua-Ping Zhang, Qun Liu. *Model of Chinese Words Rough Segmentation Based on N-Shortest-Paths Method*. Journal of Chinese information processing, 2002,16(5):1-7 (in Chinese)

ZHANG Hua-Ping, LIU Qun, Zhang Hao and Cheng Xue-Qi. 2002. *Automatic Recognition of Chinese Unknown Words Recognition*. Proc. of First SigHan attached on COLING 2002

ZHANG Hua-Ping, LIU Qun, YU Hong-Kui, CHENG Xue-Qi, BAI Shuo. *Chinese Named Entity Recognition Using Role Model*. International Journal of Computational Linguistics and Chinese language processing, 2003,Vol. 8 (2)

Mao-yuan Zhang, Zheng-ding Lu, Chun-yan Zou. *A Chinese word segmentation based on language situation in processing ambiguous words*. Information Sciences 162 (2004) 275–285

Gao, Jianfeng, Andi Wu, Mu Li, Chang-Ning Huang,Hongqiao Li, Xinsong Xia, and Haowei Qin. *Adaptive Chinese word segmentation*. ACL2004. July 21-26.

Haodi Feng, Kang Chen, Xiaotie Deng, Weimin Zheng *Accessor Variety Criteria for Chinese Word Extraction*. Computational Linguistics March 2004, Vol. 30, No. 1: 75–93.

Hemin, **Web-Oriented Chinese Meaningful String Mining, M.Sc** Thesis of Graduate University of Chinese Academy of Scienses. 2006

High OOV-Recall Chinese Word Segmenter

Xiaoming Xu, Muhua Zhu, Xiaoxu Fei, and Jingbo Zhu
School of
Information Science and Engineering
Northeastern University
{xuxm, zhumh, feixx}@ics.neu.edu.cn
zhujingbo@mail.neu.edu.cn

Abstract

For the competition of Chinese word segmentation held in the first CIPS-SIGHNA joint conference. We applied a subword-based word segmenter using CRFs and extended the segmenter with OOV words recognized by Accessor Variety. Moreover, we proposed several post-processing rules to improve the performance. Our system achieved promising OOV recall among all the participants.

1 Introduction

Chinese word segmentation is deemed to be a prerequisite for Chinese language processing. The competition in the first CIPS-SIGHAN joint conference put the task of Chinese word segmentation in a more challengeable setting, where training and test data are obtained from different domains. This setting is widely known as *domain adaptation*.

For domain adaptation, either a large-scale unlabeled target domain data or a small size of labeled target domain data is required to adapt a system built on source domain data to the target domain. In this word segmentation competition, unfortunately, only a small size of unlabeled target domain data is available. Thus we focus on handling out-of-vocabulary (OOV) words. For this purpose, our system is based on a combination of subword-based tagging method (Zhang et al., 2006) and accessor variety-based new word recognition method (Feng et al., 2004). In more detail, we adopted and extended subword-based method. Subword list is augmented with new-word list recognized by accessor variety method.

Feature Template	Description
a) $c_n(-2,-1,0,1,2)$	unigram of characters
b) $c_nc_{n+1}(-2,-1,0,1)$	bigram of characters
c) $c_{n-1}c_nc_{n+1}(-1,0,1)$	trigram of characters
d) $P_u(C_0)$	whether punctuation
e) $T(C_{-1})T(C_0)T(C_{+1})$	type of characters

Table 1: Basic Features for CRF-based Segmenter

We participated in the close track of the word segmentation competition, on all the four test datasets, in two of which our system is ranked at the 1st position with respect to the metric of OOV recall.

2 System Description

2.1 Subword-based Tagging with CRFs

The backbone of our system is a character-based segmenter with the application of Conditional Random Fields (CRFs) (Zhao and Kit, 2008). In detail, we apply a six-tag tagging scheme, as in (Zhao et al., 2006). That is , each Chinese character can be assigned to one of the tags in $\{B, B_2, B_3, M, E, S\}$. Refer to (Zhao et al., 2006) for detailed meaning of the tags. Table 1 shows basic feature templates used in our system, where feature templates a, b, d, e are also used in (Zhu et al., 2006) for SVM-based word segmentation.

In order to extend basic CRF-based segmenter, we first collect 2k most frequent words from training data. Hereafter, the list of such words is referred to as *subword list*. Moreover, single-character words [1], if they are not contained in the subword list, are also added. Such proce-

[1]By single-character word, we refer to words that consist solely of a Chinese character.

Feature Template	Description
f) in(str, subword-list)	is str in subword list
g) in(str, confident-word-list)	is str in confident-word list

Table 2: Subword Features for CRF-based Segmenter

dure for constructing a subword list is similar to the one used in (Zhang et al., 2006). To enhance the effect of subwords, we go one step further to build a list, named *confident-word list* here and below, which contains words that are not a portion of other words and are never segmented in the training data. In the competition, 400 most frequent words in the confident-word list are used. With subword list and confident-word list, both training and test data are segmented with forward maximum match method by using the union of subword list and confident-word list. Each segmentation unit (single-character or multi-character unit) in the segmentation results are regarded as "pseudo character" and thus can be represented with the basic features in Table 1 and two additional features as shown in Table 2. See the details of subword-based Chinese word segmentation in (Zhang et al., 2006)

2.2 OOV Recognition with Accessor Variety

Accessor variety (AV) (Feng et al., 2004) is a simple and effective unsupervised method for extraction of new Chinese words. Given a unsegmented text, each substring (candidate word) in the text can be assigned a value according to the following equation:

$$AV(s) = min\{L_{av}(s), R_{av}(s)\} \quad (1)$$

where the left and right AV values, $L_{av}(s)$ and $R_{av}(s)$ are defined to be the number of distinct character types appearing on the left and right, respectively. Candidate words are sorted in the descending order of AV values and most highly ranked ones can be chosen as new words. In practical applications, heuristic filtering rules are generally needed (Feng et al., 2004). We re-implemented the AV method and filtering rules, as in (Feng et al., 2004). Moreover, we filter out candidate words that have AV values less than 3. Unfortunately, candidate word list generated this way still contains many noisy words (substrings that are not words). One possible reason is that unlabeled data (test data) used in the competition is extremely small in size. In order to refine the results derived from the AV method, we make use of the training data to filter the results from two different perspectives.

- Segment test data with the CRF-based segmenter described above. Then we collect (candidate) words that are in the CRF-based segmentation results, but not appear in the training data. Such words are called *CRF-OOV words* hereafter. We retain the intersection of CRF-OOV words and AV-based results as the set of candidate words to be processed by the following step.
- Any candidate word in the intersection of CRF-based and AV-based results will be filtered out if they satisfy one of the following conditions: 1) the candidate word is a part of some word in the training data; 2) the candidate word is formed by connection of consecutive words in the training data; 3) the candidate word contains position words, such as 上 (up), 下 (down), 左 (left), 右 (right), etc.

Moreover, we take all English words in test data as OOV words. A simple heuristic rule is defined for the purpose of English word recognition: an English word is a consecutive sequence of English characters and punctuations between two English characters (including these two characters).

We finally add all the OOV words into subword list and confident-word list.

3 Post-Processing Rules

In the results of subword-based word segmentation with CRFs, we found some errors could be corrected with heuristic rules. For this purpose, we propose following post-processing rules, for handling OOV and in-vocabulary (IV) words, respectively.

3.1 OOV Rules

3.1.1 Annotation-Standard Independent Rules

We assume the phenomena discussed in the following are general across all kinds of annotation standards. Thus corresponding rules can be applied without considering annotation standards of training data.

- A punctuation tends to be a single-character word. If a punctation's previous character and next character are both Chinese characters, i.e. not punctuation, digit, or English character, we always regard the punctuation as a word.

- Consecutive and identical punctuations tend to be joined together as a word. For example, "—" represents a Chinese hyphen which consists of three "-", and "!!!" is used to show emphasizing. Inspired by this observations, we would like to unite consecutive and identical punctuations as a single word.

- When the character " · " appears in the training data, it is generally used as a connections symbol in a foreign person name, such as "圣 · 约翰 (Saint John)". Taking this observation into consideration, we always unite the character " · " and its previous and next segment units into a single word. A similar rule is designed to unite consecutive digits on the sides of the symbol ".", ex. "1.11".

- We notice that four consecutive characters which are in the pattern of *AABB* generally form a single word in Chinese, for example "平平淡淡 (dull)". Taking this observation into account, we always unite consecutive characters in the *AABB* into a single word.

3.1.2 Templates with Generalized Digits

Words containing digits generally belong to a open class, for example, the word "2012年 (AD 2012) " means a date. Thus CRF-based segmenter has difficulties in recognizing such words since they are frequently OOV words. To attack this challenge, we first generalize digits in the training data. In detail, we replaced consecutive digits with "*". For example, the word "2012年" will be transformed into "*年". Second, we collect word templates which consist of three consecutive words on condition that at least one of the words in a template contains the character "*" and that the template appears in the training data more than 4 times. For example, we can get a template like "*月(month) *日(day) 电(publish)". With such templates, we are able to correct errors, say "10月 17日电" into "10月 17日 电".

3.2 IV Rules

We notice that long words have less ambiguity than short words in the sense of being words. For example, characters in "人才济济 (full of talents)" always form a word in the training data, whereas "人才" have two plausible splitting forms, as "人才 (talent)" or "人 (people) 才 (only)". In our system, we collect words that have at least four characters and filter out words which belong to one of following cases: 1) the word is a part of other words; 2) the word consists solely of punctation and/or digit. For example, "唯物主义 (materialism)" and "一百二十 (120)" are discarded, since the former is a substring of the word "唯物主义者 (materialist)" and the latter is a word of digits. Finally we get a list containing about 6k words. If a character sequence in the test data is a member in the list, it is retained as a word in the final segmentation results.

Another group of IV rules concern character sequences that have unique splitting in the training data. For example, "女人们 (women)" is always split as "女人 (woman) 们 (s)". Hereafter, we refer to such character sequences as *unique-split-sequence (USS)*. In our system, we are concerned with UUSs which are composed of less than 5 words. In order to apply UUSs for post-processing, we first collect word sequence of variable length (word number) from training data. In detail, we collect word sequences of two words, three words, and four words. Second, word sequences that have more than one splitting cases in the training data are filtered out. Third, spaces between words are removed to form USSs. For example, the words "女人 (woman) 们 (s)" will form the USS "女人们 ". Finally, we search the test data for each USS. If the searching succeeds, the USS will be replaced with the corresponding word sequence.

4 Evaluation Results

We evaluated our Chinese word segmenter in the close track, in four domain: literature (Lit), com-

Domain	Basic			+OOV			+OOV+IV		
	R_{OV}	R_{IV}	F	R_{OV}	R_{IV}	F	R_{OV}	R_{IV}	F
Lit	.643	.946	.927	.652	.947	.929	.648	.952	.934
Com	.839	.961	.938	.850	.961	.941	.852	.965	.947
Med	.725	.938	.912	.754	.939	.917	.756	.944	.923
Fin	.761	.956	.932	.854	.958	.950	.871	.961	.955

Table 3: Effectiveness of post-processing rules

puter (Com), medicine (Med) and finance (Fin). The results are depicted in Table 4, where R, P and F refer to Recall, Precision, F measure respectively, and R_{OOV} and R_{IV} refer to recall of OOV and IV words respectively. Since OOV words are the obstacle for practical Chinese word segmenters to achieve high accuracy, we have special interest in the metric of OOV recall. We found that our system achieved high OOV recall [2]. Actually, OOV recall of our system in the domains of *computer* and *finance* are both ranked at the 1st position among all the participants. Compared with the systems ranked second in these two domains, our system achieved OOV recall .853 $vs.$ .827 and .871 $vs.$ .857 respectively.

We also examined the effectiveness of post-processing rules, as shown in Table 3, where *Basic* represents the performance achieved before post-processing, *+OOV* represents the results achieved after applying OOV post-processing rules, and *+OOV+IV* denotes the results achieved after using all the post-processing rules, including both OOV and IV rules. As the table shows, designed post-processing rules can improve both IV and OOV recall significantly.

Domain	R	P	F	R_{OOV}	R_{IV}
Lit	.931	.936	.934	.648	.952
Com	.948	.945	.947	.853	.965
Med	.924	.922	.923	.756	.944
Fin	.953	.956	.955	.871	.961

Table 4: Performance of our system in the competition

[2]For the test data from the domain of literature, we actually use combination of our system and forward maximum match, so we will omit the results on this test dataset in our discussion.

5 Conclusions and Future Work

We proposed an approach to refine new words recognized with the accessor variety method, and incorporated such words into a subword-based word segmenter. We found that such method could achieve high OOV recall. Moreover, we designed effective post-processing rules to further enhance the performance of our systems. Our system finally achieved satisfactory results in the competition.

Acknowledgments

This work was supported in part by the National Science Foundation of China (60873091).

References

Feng, Haodi, Kang Chen, Xiaotie Deng, and Weimin zhang. 2004. *Accessor Variety Criteriafor Chinese Word Extraction.* Computational Linguistics 2004, 30(1), pages 75-93.

Zhang, Ruiqiang, Genichiro Kikui, and Eiichiro Sumita. 2006. *Subword-based Tagging by Conditional Random Fileds for Chinese Word Segmentation.* In Proceedings of HLT-NAACL 2006, pages 193-196.

Zhao, Hai, Chang-Ning Huang, and Mu Li. 2006. *Improved Chinese Word Segmentation System with Conditional Random Field.* In Proceedings of SIGHAN-5 2006, pages 162-165.

Zhao, Hai and Chunyu Kit. 2008. *Unsupervised Segmentation Helps Supervised Learning of Character Tagging for Word Segmentation and Named Entity Recognition.* In Proceedings of SIGHAN-6 2008, pages 106-111.

Zhu, Muhua, Yiling Wang, Zhenxing Wang, Huizhen Wang, and Jingbo Zhu. 2006. *Designing Special Post-Processing Rules for SVM-based Chinese Word Segmentation.* In Proceedigns of SIGHAN-5 2006, pages 217-220.

Chinese word segmentation model using bootstrapping

Baobao Chang and Mairgup Mansur
Institute of Computational Linguistics, Peking University
Key Laboratory of Computational Linguistics(Peking University),
Ministry Education, China
chbb@pku.edu.cn, mairgup@yahoo.com.cn

Abstract

We participate in the CIPS-SIGHAN-2010 bake-off task of Chinese word segmentation. Unlike the previous bakeoff series, the purpose of the bakeoff 2010 is to test the cross-domain performance of Chinese segmentation model. This paper summarizes our approach and our bakeoff results. We mainly propose to use χ^2 statistics to increase the OOV recall and use bootstrapping strategy to increase the overall F score. As the results shows, the approach proposed in the paper does help, both of the OOV recall and the overall F score are improved.

1 Introduction

After more than twenty years of intensive researches, considerable progress has been made in improving the performance of Chinese word segmentation. The bakeoff series hosted by the ACL SIGHAN shows that high F scores can be achieved in the closed test tracks, in which only specified training materials can be used in learning segmentation models.

Instead of using lexicon-driven approaches, state-of-art Chinese word segmenter now use character tagging model as Xue(2003) firstly proposed. In character tagging model, no predefined Chinese lexicons are required; a tagging model is learned using manually segmented training texts. The model is then used to assign each character a tag indicating the position of this character within word. Xue's approach has been become the most popular approach to Chinese word segmentation for its high performance and unified way to deal with OOV issues. Most of the segmentation works since then follow this approach. Major improvements in this line of research including: 1) More sophisticated learning models were introduced instead of the maximum entropy model that Xue used, like conditional random fields (CRFs) model which fit the sequence tagging tasks much better than maximum entropy model (Tseng et al.,2005). 2) More tags were introduced, as Zhao et al. (2006) shows 6 tags are superior to 4 tags in achieving high performance. 3) New feature templates were added, such as templates used in representing numbers, dates, letters etc. (Low et al., 2005)

Usually, the performance of segmentation model is evaluated on a test set from the same domain as the training set. Such evaluation does not reveal its ability to deal with domain variation. It is believed that, when test set is from other domains than the domain where training set is from, the learned model normally underperforms substantially.

The CIPS-SIGHAN-2010 bake-off task of Chinese word segmentation is set to focus on the cross-domain performance of Chinese word segmentation model.

We participate in the closed test track for simplified Chinese. Different with the previous bakeoffs, CIPS-SIGHAN-2010 bake-off provides both label corpus and unlabeled corpora. The labeled corpus is composed of texts from newspaper and has about 1.1 million words in total. The two unlabeled corpora cover two domains: literature and computer science, and each domain have about 100K characters in size. The test corpora cover four domains, two of which are literature and computer science, and the other two domains are unknown before releasing.

We build the Chinese word segmenter following the character tagging model. Instead of using CRF model, we use the hidden Markov support vector machines (Altun et al., 2003), which is also a sequence labeling model like CRF. We just show it can also be used to model Chinese segmentation tasks as an alternative other than CRF. To increase the ability of the model to recall OOV words, we propose to use χ^2 statistics and bootstrapping strategy to the overall performance of the model to out-of-domain texts.

2 The hidden Markov support vector machines

The hidden Markov support vector machine (SVM-HMM) is actually a special case of the structural support vector machines proposed by Tsochantaridis et al.(2005) which is a powerful model to structure predication problem. It differs from support vector machine in its ability to model complex structured problems and shares the max-margin training principles with support vector machines. The hidden Markov support vector machine model is inspired by the hidden Markov model and is an instance of structural support vector machine dedicated to solve sequence labeling learning, a problem that CRF model is assumed to solve. In the SVM-HMM model, the sequence labeling problems is modeled by learning a discriminant function F: $X\times Y \rightarrow R$ over the input sequence and the label sequence pairs, thus prediction of label sequence can be derived by maximizing F over all possible label sequences for a specific given input sequence $\mathbf{x}$.

$$f(\mathbf{x};\mathbf{w}) = \arg\max_{\mathbf{y}\in Y} F(\mathbf{x},\mathbf{y};\mathbf{w})$$

In the structural SVMs, F is assumed to be linear in some combined feature representation of the input sequence and the label sequence $\psi(\mathbf{x},\mathbf{y})$, i.e.

$$F(\mathbf{x},\mathbf{y};\mathbf{w}) = \langle \mathbf{w}, \psi(\mathbf{x},\mathbf{y}) \rangle$$

where $\mathbf{w}$ denotes a parameter vector. For the SVM-HMMs, the discriminant function is defined as follows.

$$F(x,y;\mathbf{w}) = \sum_{t=1..T}\sum_{y\in\Sigma} \langle \overline{\mathbf{w}}_y, \mathbf{\Phi}(\mathbf{x}^t) \rangle \delta(y^t, y) + \eta \sum_{t=1..T-1}\sum_{y\in\Sigma}\sum_{y'\in\Sigma} \hat{\mathbf{w}}_{y,y'} \delta(y^t, y)\delta(y^{t+1}, y')$$

Here $\mathbf{w} = (\overline{\mathbf{w}}, \hat{\mathbf{w}})$, $\mathbf{\Phi}(\mathbf{x}^t)$ is the vector of features of the input sequence.

Like SVMs, parameter vector $\mathbf{w}$ is learned with maximum margin principle using training data. To control the complexity of the training problem, cutting plane method is proposed to solve the resulted constrained optimization problem. Thus only small subset of constraints from the full-sized optimization is checked to ensure a sufficiently accurate solution. Roughly speaking, SVM-HMM differs with CRF in its principle of training, both of them could be used to deal with sequence labeling problem like Chinese word segmentation.

3 The tag set and the basic feature templates

As most of other works on segmentation, we use a 4-tag tagset, that is S for character being a single-character-word by itself, B for character beginning a multi-character-word, E for character ending a multi-character-word and M for a character occurring in the middle of a multi-character-word.

We use the following feature template, like most of segmentation works widely used:

(a) C_n (n = -2, -1, 0, 1, 2)
(b) C_nC_{n+1} (n = -2, -1, 0, 1)
(c) $C_{-1}C_{+1}$

Here C refers to character; n refers to the position index relative to the current character. By setting the above feature templates, we actually set a 5-character window to extract features, the current character, 2 characters to its left and 2 characters to its right.

In addition, we also use the following feature templates to extract features representing character type. The closed test track of CIPS-SIGHAN-2010 bake-off allows participants to use four character types, which are Chinese Character, English Letter, digits and punctuations:

(d) T_n (n = -2, -1, 0, 1, 2)
(e) T_nT_{n+1} (n = -2, -1, 0, 1)
(f) $T_{-1}T_{+1}$

Here T refers to character type, its value can be digit, letter, punctuation or Chinese character.

4 The χ^2 statistic features

One of reasons of the performance degradation lies in the model's ability to cope with OOV words while working with the out-of-domain texts. Aiming at preventing the OOV recall from dropping sharply, we propose to use χ^2 statistics as features to the segmentation model.

χ^2 test is one of hypothesis test methods, which can be used to test if two events co-occur just by chance or not. A lower χ^2 score normally means the two co-occurred events are independent; otherwise they are dependent on each other. Hence, χ^2 statistics could also be used to deal with the OOV issue in segmentation models. The idea is very straightforward. If two adjacent characters in the test set have a higher χ^2 score, it is highly likely they form a word or are part of a word even they are not seen in the training set.

We only compute χ^2 score for character bigrams in the training texts and test texts. The χ^2 score of a bigram C_1C_2 can be computed by the following way.

$$\chi^2(C_1,C_2)=\frac{n\times(a\times d-b\times c)^2}{(a+b)\times(a+c)\times(b+d)\times(c+d)}$$

Here,

a refers to all counts of bigram C_1C_2 in the text;

b refers to all counts of bigrams that C_1 occurs but C_2 does not;

c refers to all counts of bigrams that C_1 does not occur but C_2 occurs;

d refers to all counts of bigrams that both C_1 and C_2 do not occur.

n refers to total counts of all bigrams in the text, apparently, $n=a+b+c+d$.

We do the χ^2 statistics computation to the training texts and the test texts respectively. To make the χ^2 statistics from the training texts and test texts comparable, we normalize the χ^2 score by the following formula.

$$\chi^2_{norm}(C_1,C_2)=\left\lfloor\frac{\chi^2(C_1,C_2)-\chi^2_{\min}}{\chi^2_{\max}-\chi^2_{\min}}\times 10\right\rfloor$$

Then we incorporate the normalized χ^2 statistics into the SVM-HMM model by adding two more feature templates as follows:

(g) X_nX_{n+1} (n = -2, -1, 0, 1)
(h) $X_{-1}X_{+1}$

The value of the feature X_nX_{n+1} is the normalized χ^2 score of the bigram C_nC_{n+1}. Note we also compute the normalized χ^2 score to bigram $C_{-1}C_{+1}$.

Because the normalized χ^2 score is one of 11 possible values 0, 1, 2, …, 10, templates (g)-(h) generate 55 features in total.

All features generated from the templates (a)-(f) together with the 55 χ^2 features form the whole feature set. The training texts and test texts are then converted into their feature representations. The feature representation of the training texts is then used to learn the model and the feature representation of the test texts is used for segmentation. By this way, we expect that an OOV word in the test texts might be found by the segmentation model if the bigrams extracted from this word take higher χ^2 scores.

5 the bootstrapping strategy

The addition of the χ^2 features can be also harmful. Even though it could increase the OOV recall, it also leads to drops in IV recall as we found. To keep the IV recall from falling down, we propose to use bootstrapping strategy. Specifically, we choose to use both models with χ2 features and without χ2 features. We train two models firstly, one is χ2-based and another not. Then we do the segmentation to the test text with the two models simultaneously. Two segmentation results can be obtained. One result is produced by the χ2-based model and has a high OOV recall. The other result is produced by the non-χ2-based model and has higher IV recall. Then we do intersection operation to the two results. It is not difficult to understand that the intersection of the two results has both high OOV recall and high IV recall. We then put the intersection results into the training texts to form a new training set. By this new training set, we train again to get two new models, one χ2-based and another not. Then the two new models are used to segment the test texts. Then we do again intersection to the two results and the common parts are again put into the training texts. We

Table-2. The bakeoff results

test set	R	P	F	Riv	Roov
A	0.925	0.931	0.928	0.944	0.667
B	0.941	0.916	0.928	0.967	0.796
C	0.928	0.918	0.923	0.953	0.730
D	0.948	0.928	0.937	0.965	0.761

repeat this process until a plausible result is obtained.

The whole process can be informally described as the following algorithm:

1. let training set T to be the original training set;
2. for I = 0 to K
   1) train a χ^2-based model and a non-χ^2-base model separately using training set T;
   2) use both models to segment test texts;
   3) do intersection to the two segmentation results
   4) put the intersection results into the training set and get the enlarged training set T
3. train the non-χ^2-based model using training set T, and take the output of this model as the final output;
4. end.

6 The evaluation results

The labeled training texts released by the bakeoff are mainly composed of texts from newspaper. A peculiarity of the training data is that all Arabic numbers, Latin letters and punctuations in the data are double-byte codes. As in Chinese texts, there are actually two versions of codes for Arabic numbers, Latin letters and punctuations: one is single-byte codes defined by the western character encoding standard; another is double-byte codes defined by the Chinese character encoding standards. Chinese normally use both versions without distinguishing them strictly.

The four final test sets released by the bakeoff cover four domains, the statistics of the test sets are shown in table-1. (the size is measured in characters)

Table-1. Test sets statistics

test set	domain	size	OOV rate
A	Literature	51K	0.069
B	Computer	64K	0.152
C	Medicines	52K	0.110
D	Finance	56K	0.087

We train all models using SVM-HMMs[1], we set ε to 0.25. This is a parameter to control the accuracy of the solution of the optimization problem. We set C to half of the number of the sentences in the training data. The C parameter is set to trade off the margin size and training error. We also set a cutoff frequency to feature extraction. Only features are seen more than three times in training data are actually used in the models. We set K = 3 and run the algorithm shown in section 5. This gives our final bakeoff results shown in Table-2.

To illustrate whether the χ^2 statistics and bootstrapping strategy help or not, we also show two intermediate results using the online scoring system provided by the bakeoff[2].Table-3 shows the results of the initial non-χ^2-based model using feature template (a)-(f), table-4 shows results of the initial χ^2-based model using feature template (a)-(h).

As we see from the table-1, table-3 and table-4, the approach present in this paper does improve both the overall performance and the OOV recalls in all four domains.

Table-3 Results of initial non-χ^2-based model

test set	R	P	F	Roov
A	0.921	0.924	0.923	0.632
B	0.930	0.904	0.917	0.758
C	0.919	0.906	0.913	0.687
D	0.946	0.924	0.935	0.750

[1]http://www.cs.cornell.edu/People/tj/svm_light/svm_hmm.html

[2] http://nlp.ict.ac.cn/demo/CIPS-SIGHAN2010/#

Table-4 Results of initial χ^2-based model

test set	R	P	F	Roov
A	0.898	0.921	0.910	0.673
B	0.925	0.914	0.920	0.801
C	0.916	0.922	0.919	0.764
D	0.931	0.937	0.934	0.821

We also do a rapid manual check to the final results; one of the main sources of errors lies in the approach failing to recall numbers encoded by one-byte codes digits. For the labeled training corpus provided by the bakeoff almost do not use one-byte codes for digits, and the type feature seems do not help too much. Actually, such numbers can be recalled by simple heuristics using regular expressions. We do a simple number recognition to the test set of domain D. this will increase the F score from 0.937 to 0.957.

7 Conclusions

This paper introduces the approach we used in the CIPS-SIGHAN-2010 bake-off task of Chinese word segmentation. We propose to use χ^2 statistics to increase OOV recall and use bootstrapping strategy to increase the overall performance. As our final results shows, the approach works in increasing both of the OOV recall and overall F-score.

We also show in this paper that hidden Markov support vector machine can be used to model the Chinese word segmentation problem, by which high f-score results can be obtained like CRF model.

Acknowledgements

This work was supported by National Natural Science Foundation of China under Grant No. 60975054 and National Social Science Foundation of China under Grant No. 06BYY048.

We want to thank Professor Duan Huiming and Mr. Han Dongxu for their generous help at the data preprocessing works.

References

Liang, Nanyuan, 1987. ‘‘written Cinese text segmentation system--cdws”. Journal of Chinese Information Processing, Vol.2, NO.2,pp44–52.(in Chinese)

Gao, Jianfeng et al., 2005, Chinese Word Segmentation and Named Entity Recognition: A Pragmatic Approach, Computational Linguistics,Vol.31, No.4, pp531-574.

Huang, Changning et al. 2007, Chinese word segmentation: a decade review. Journal of Chinese Information Processing, Vol.21, NO.3,pp8–19.(in Chinese)

Tseng, Huihsin et al., 2005, A conditional random field word segmenter for SIGHAN 2005, Proceedings of the fourth SIGHAN workshop on Chinese language processing. Jeju Island, Korea. pp168-171

Xue, Nianwen, 2003, Chinese Word Segmentation as Character Tagging, Computational Linguistics and Chinese Language Processing. Vol.8, No.1, pp29-48.

Zhao, Hai et al., 2006, Effective tag set selection in Chinese word segmentation via conditional random field modeling, Proceedings of the 20th Pacific Asia Conference on language, Information and Computation (PACLIC-20), Wuhan, China, pp87-94

Tsochantaridis,Ioannis et al., 2005, Large Margin Methods for Structured and Interdependent Output Variables, Journal of Machine Learning Research (JMLR), No.6, pp1453-1484.

Altun,Yasemin et al.,2003, Hidden Markov Support Vector Machines. Proceedings of the Twentieth International Conference on Machine Learning (ICML-2003), Washington DC, 2003.

Low, Jin Kiat et al.,2005, A Maximum Entropy Approach to Chinese Word Segmentation. Proceedings of the Fourth SIGHAN Workshop on Chinese Language Processing, Jeju Island, Korea,. pp161-164

CRF-based Experiments for Cross-Domain Chinese Word Segmentation at CIPS-SIGHAN-2010

Xiao Qin, Liang Zong, Yuqian Wu, Xiaojun Wan and Jianwu Yang
Institute of Computer Science and Technology
Peking University, China, 100871
{qinxiao,zongliang,wuyuqian,wanxiaojun,yangjianwu}
@cist.pku.edu.cn

Abstract

This paper describes our experiments on the cross-domain Chinese word segmentation task at the first CIPS-SIGHAN Joint Conference on Chinese Language Processing. Our system is based on the Conditional Random Fields (CRFs) model. Considering the particular properties of the out-of-domain data, we propose some novel steps to get some improvements for the special task.

1 Introduction

Chinese word segmentation is one of the most important tasks in the field of Chinese information processing and it is meaningful to intelligent information processing technologies. After a lot of researches, Chinese word segmentation has achieved a high accuracy. Many methods have been presented, among which the CRFs model has attracted more and more attention. Zhao's group used the CRFs model in the task of Chinese word segmentation in Bakeoff-4 and they ranked at the top in all closed tests of word segmentation (Zhao and Kit, 2008). The CRFs model has been widely used because of its excellent performance. However, finding a better segmentation algorithm for the out-of-domain text is the focus of CIP-SIGHAN-2010 bakeoff.

We still consider word segmentation as a sequence labeling problem. What we concern is how to use the unlabeled corpora to enrich the supervised CRFs learning. So we take some strategies to make use of the information of the texts in the unlabeled corpora.

2 System Description

In this section, we will describe our system in details. The system is based on the CRFs model and we propose some novel steps for some improvements. It mainly consists of three steps: preprocessing, CRF-based labeling, and re-labeling.

2.1 Preprocessing

This step mainly includes two operations. First, we should cut the whole text into a series of sentences. We regard '。', '？', '！' and '；' as the symbols of the boundary between sentences. Then we do atomic segmentation to all the sentences. Here Atomic segmentation represents that we should regard the continuous non-Chinese characters as a whole. Take the word 'computer' as an example, we should regard 'computer' as a whole, but not treat it as 8 separate letters of 'c', 'o', 'm', 'p', 'u', 't', 'e', and 'r'.

2.2 CRF-based Labeling

Conditional random field (CRF) is an extension of both Maximum Entropy Model (MEMs) and Hidden Markov Models (HMMs), which was firstly introduced by Lafferty (Lafferty et al., 2001). It is an undirected graphical model trained to maximize the conditional probability of the desired outputs given the corresponding inputs. This model has achieved great successes in word segmentation.

In the CRFs model, the conditional distribution $P(y|x)$ of the labels Y givens observations X directly is defined:

$$P(y/x) = \frac{1}{Z_x}\exp\{\sum_{t=1}^{T}\sum_{k}\lambda_k f_k(y_{t-1}, y_t, x, t)\}$$

y is the label sequence, x is observation sequence, Z_x is a normalization term that makes the probability of all state sequences sum to one; $f_k(y_{t-1}, y_t, t)$ is often a binary-valued feature function and λ_k is the weight of f_k.

In our system, we choose six types of tags according to character position in a word. According to Zhao's work (Zhao et al., 2006a), the 6-tag set enables our system to generate a better CRF model than the 4-tag set. In our experiments, we test both the 6-tag set and the 4-tag set, and the 6-tag set truly has a better result. The 6-tag set is defined as below:

T = {B, B2, B3, M, E, S}

Here B, B2, B3, M, E represent the first, second, third, continuing and end character positions in a multi-character word, and S is the single-character word tag.

We adopt 6 n-gram feature templates as features. Some researches have proved that the combination of 6-tag set and 6 n-gram feature template can achieve a better performance (Zhao et al., 2006a; Zhao et al., 2006b; Zhao and Kit, 2007).

The 6 n-gram feature templates used in our system are C_{-1}, C_0, C_1, $C_{-1}C_0$, C_0C_1, $C_{-1}C_1$. Here C stands for a character and the subscripts -1, 0 and 1 stand for the previous, current and next character, respectively.

Furthermore, we try to take advantage of the types for the characters. For example, in our system D stands for the date, N stands for the number, L stands for the letter, P stands for the punctuation and C stands for the other characters. Introducing these features is beneficial to the CRFs learning.

2.3 Re-labeling step

Since the unlabeled corpora belong to different domains, traditional methods have some limitations. In this section, we propose an additional step to make good use of the unlabelled data for this special task. This step is based on the outputs of the CRFs model in the previous step.

After CRFs learning, we get a training model. With this model, we can label the literature, computer, medicine and finance corpora. According to the outputs of the CRFs model, we choose some labeled sentences with high confidence and add them to the training corpus. Here the selection of high confidence must guarantee that the probability of the sentences selected being correct segmentations is rather high and the number of the sentences selected is not too little or they will make no difference to the generation of the new CRF model. Since the existing training model does not contain the information in the out-of-domain data, we treat the labeled sentences with high confidence as additional training corpus. Then we re-train the CRFs model with the new training data. With the training data extracted from different domains, the training model incorporates more cross-domain information and it can work better in the corresponding cross-domain prediction task.

3 Experiments

3.1 Experiment Setup

There are two sources for the corpora: the training corpora and the test corpus. And in the training corpora, there exist two types of corpus in this task. The labeled corpus is Chinese text which has been segmented into words while the unlabelled corpus covers two domains: literature and computer science. The test corpus contains 4 domains, which are literature, computer science, medicine and finance.

There are four evaluation metrics used in this bake-off task: Precision, Recall, F1 measure (F1 = 2RP/(R+P)) and OOV measure, where R and P are the recall and precision of the segmentation and OOV (Out-Of-Vocabulary Word) is a word which occurs in the reference corpus but does not occur in the labeled training corpus.

Our system uses the CRF++ package Version 0.49 implemented by Taku Kudo[1] from sourceforge.

3.2 Results and Discussions

We test the techniques described in section 2 with the given data. Now we will show the results of each operation.

3.2.1 Preprocessing

As we have mentioned in section 2.1, the first step is to cut the text into a series of sentences.

[1] http://crfpp.sourceforge.net/

Then we should give each character in one sentence a label. Before this step, it is necessary to do atomic segmentation. And we will regard the continuous non-Chinese characters as a whole and give the whole part a single label. This is meaningful to those corpora containing a lot of English words. Due to the diversity of the English words, segmenting the sentences with a lot non-Chinese characters correctly is rather difficult only through CRF learning. We should do atomic segmentation to all training and test corpora. This may achieve a higher accuracy in a certain degree.

The results of word segmentation are reported in Table 1. 'Clouse+/-' indicates whether text clause has been done.

Table 1: Results with clause and without clause

	corpus	Precision	Recall	F
Literature	Clause+	0.922	0.916	0.919
	Clause-	0.921	0.915	0.918
Computer	Clause+	0.934	0.939	0.937
	Clause-	0.934	0.939	0.936
Medicine	Clause+	0.911	0.917	0.914
	Clause-	0.509	0.511	0.510
Finance	Clause+	0.940	0.943	0.941
	Clause-	0.933	0.940	0.937

From Table 1, we can see there is some improvement in different degree and the effect in the medicine corpus is the most obvious. So we can conclude that our preprocessing is useful to the word segmentation.

3.2.2 CRF-based labeling

After preprocessing, we can use CRF++ package to learn and test.

The selection of feature template is also an important factor. For the purpose of comparison, we test two kinds of feature templates in our system. The one is showed in Table 2 and the other one is showed in Table 3.

Table 2: Template 1

Unigram
U00:%x[-1,0]
U01:%x[0,0]
U02:%x[1,0]
U03:%x[-1,0]/%x[0,0]
U04:%x[0,0]/%x[1,0]
U05:%x[-1,0]/%x[1,0]
Bigram
B

Table 3: Template 2

Unigram
U00:%x[-1,0]
U01:%x[0,0]
U02:%x[1,0]
U03:%x[-1,0]/%x[0,0]
U04:%x[0,0]/%x[1,0]
U05:%x[-1,0]/%x[1,0]
U10:%x[-1,1]
U11:%x[0,1]
U12:%x[1,1]
U13:%x[-1,1]/%x[0,1]
U14:%x[0,1]/%x[1,1]
U15:%x[-1,1]/%x[1,1]
Bigram
B

Now we will explain the meanings of the templates. Here is an example. In table 4, we show the format of the input file. The first column represents the word itself and the second represents the feature of the word, where there are five kinds of features: date (D), number (N), letter (L), punctuation (P) and others (C). The meanings of the templates are showed in table 5.

Table 4: the format of the input file for CRF

新	C
年	D
讲	C
话	C
（	P
附	C
图	C
片	C
1	N
张	C
）	P

Table 5: the example of the templates

template	Expanded feature
%x[0,0]	图
%x[0,1]	C
%x[1,0]	片
%x[-1,0]	附
%x[-1,0]/ %x[0,0]	附/图
%x[0,0]/ %x[0,1]	图/C

With two different feature templates, we continue our experiments in the four different domains. The segmentation performances of our system on test corpora using different feature templates are presented in Table 6.

Table 6: Results with different feature templates

	corpus	Precision	Recall	F
Literature	T1	0.917	0.909	0.913
	T2	0.922	0.916	0.919
Computer	T1	0.914	0.902	0.908
	T2	0.934	0.939	0.937
Medicine	T1	0.906	0.905	0.905
	T2	0.911	0.917	0.914
Finance	T1	0.937	0.925	0.931
	T2	0.940	0.943	0.941

Here T1 stands for Template 1 while T2 stands for Template 2.

From the Table 4 we can see the second feature templates make the results of the segmentation improved more significantly.

At the same time we need get the outputs with confidence measure by setting some parameters in CRF test.

3.2.3 Re-labeling

As for the outputs with confidence measure generated by previous step, we should do some special processes. Here we set a particular value as our standard and choose the sentences with confidence above the value. As we know, the test corpora are limited, the higher confidence may cause the corpora meeting our requirements are less. The lower confidence may not guarantee the reliability. So the setting of the confidence value is very significant. In our experiments, we set the parameter at 0.8.

Then we add the sentences whose confidence is above 0.8 to the training corpus. We should re-learn with new corpora, generate the new model and re-test the corpora related with 4 domains. The segmentation performances after relabeling are represented in Table 7.

Table 7: Results with re-labeling and without relabeling

	corpus	Precision	Recall	F
Literature	Re +	0.922	0.916	0.919
	Re -	0.921	0.916	0.918
Computer	Re +	0.934	0.939	0.937
	Re -	0.932	0.934	0.933
Medicine	Re +	0.911	0.917	0.914
	Re -	0.912	0.918	0.915
Finance	Re +	0.940	0.943	0.941
	Re -	0.937	0.941	0.939

Here Re+/- indicates whether the re-labeling step is to be done.

From the results we know, even though the relabeling step makes the results in the medicine corpus a little worse, it has much better effect in the other corpora. Overall, the operation of relabeling is necessary.

3.3 Our results in this bakeoff

In this task, our results are showed in Table 8.

Table 8: our results in this bakeoff

	Precision	Recall	F
Literature	0.922	0.916	0.919
Computer	0.934	0.939	0.937
Medicine	0.911	0.917	0.914
Finance	0.940	0.943	0.941

From Table 6, we can see our system can achieve a high precision, especially in the domains of computer and finance. This proves our methods are fairly effective.

4 Discussion

4.1 Segmentation Features

In our system, we only take advantage of the features of the words. We try to add other features to our experiments such as AV feature (Feng et al., 2004a; Feng et al., 2004b; Hai Zhao et al., 2007) with the expectation of improving the results. But the results are not satisfying. We believe that the feature of words frequency may be an important factor, but how to use it is worth studying. So finding some meaningful and effective features is the crucial point.

4.2 OOV

In our system, we do not process the words out of vocabulary in the special way. The recognition of OOV is still a problem. In a word, there is still much to be done to improve our system. In the present work, we make use of some surface features, and further study should be continued to find more effective features.

5 Conclusion

In this paper, we have briefly described the Chinese word segmentation for out-of-domain texts. The CRFs model is implemented. In order to make the best use of the test corpora, some special strategies are introduced. Further improvement is made with these strategies. However, there is still much to do to achieve more improvement. From the results, we got good experience and knew the weaknesses of our system. These all help to improve the performance of our system in the future.

Acknowledgements

The research described in this paper was supported by NSFC (Grant No. 60875033).

References

Hai Zhao, Changning Huang, and Mu Li. 2006. An improved Chinese Word Segmentation System with Conditional Random Field. *Proceedings of the Fifth SIGHAN Workshop on Chinese Language Processing*, Sydney, Australia.

Hai Zhao and Chunyu Kit. 2007. Incorporating global information into supervised for Chinese word segmentation. In *PACALING-2007*, Melbourne, Australia.

Hai Zhao, Changning Huang, Mu Li and Bao-Liang Lu. 2006b. Effective tag set selection in Chinese word segmentation via conditional random field modeling. In *PACLIC-20*, Wuhan, China.

John Lafferty, Andrew McCallum, and Fernando Pereira. 2001. Conditional random fields: Probabilistic models for segmenting and labeling sequence data. In *Proceeding of ICML 2001*, Morgan Kaufmann, San Francisco, CA

Hai Zhao and Chunyu Kit. 2008. Unsupervised Segmentation Helps Supervised Learning of Character Tagging for Word Segmentation and Named Entity Recognition. *Processing of the Sixth SIGHAN Workshop on Chinese Language Processing*, Hyderabad, India.

Haodi Feng, Kang Chen, Xiaotie Deng, and Weimin Zheng. 2004a. Accessor variety criteria for Chinese word extraction. *Computational Linguistics*.

Haodi Feng, Kang Chen, Chunyu Kit, and Xiaotie Deng. 2004b. Unsupervised segmentation of Chinese corpus using accessor variety. *In First International Joint Conference on Natural Language Processing*. Sanya, Hainan Island, China.

Term Contributed Boundary Tagging by Conditional Random Fields for SIGHAN 2010 Chinese Word Segmentation Bakeoff

Tian-Jian Jiang[†‡] **Shih-Hung Liu**[*‡] **Cheng-Lung Sung**[*‡] **Wen-Lian Hsu**[†‡]

[†]Department of Computer Science, National Tsing-Hua University

[*]Department of Electrical Engineering, National Taiwan University

[‡]Institute of Information Science, Academia Sinica

{tmjiang,journey,clsung,hsu}@iis.sinica.edu.tw

Abstract

This paper presents a Chinese word segmentation system submitted to the closed training evaluations of CIPS-SIGHAN-2010 bakeoff. The system uses a conditional random field model with one simple feature called *term contributed boundaries* (TCB) in addition to the "BI" character-based tagging approach. TCB can be extracted from unlabeled corpora automatically, and segmentation variations of different domains are expected to be reflected implicitly. The experiment result shows that TCB does improve "BI" tagging domain-independently about 1% of the F1 measure score.

1 Introduction

The CIPS-SIGHAN-2010 bakeoff task of Chinese word segmentation is focused on cross-domain texts. The design of data set is challenging particularly. The domain-specific training corpora remain unlabeled, and two of the test corpora keep domains unknown before releasing, therefore it is not easy to apply ordinary machine learning approaches, especially for the closed training evaluations.

2 Methodology

2.1 The "BI" Character-Based Tagging of Conditional Random Field as Baseline

The character-based "OBI" tagging of Conditional Random Field (Lafferty et al., 2001) has been widely used in Chinese word segmentation recently (Xue and Shen, 2003; Peng and McCallum, 2004; Tseng et al., 2005). Under the scheme, each character of a word is labeled as 'B' if it is the first character of a multiple-character word, or 'I' otherwise. If the character is a single-character word itself, "O" will be its label. As Table 1 shows, the lost of performance is about 1% by replacing "O" with "B" for character-based CRF tagging on the dataset of CIPS-SIGHAN-2010 bakeoff task of Chinese word segmentation, thus we choose "BI" as our baseline for simplicity, with this 1% lost bearing in mind. In tables of this paper, SC stands for Simplified Chinese and TC represents for Traditional Chinese. Test corpora of SC and TC are divided into four domains, where suffix A, B, C and D attached, for texts of literature, computer, medicine and finance, respectively.

		R	P	F	OOV
SC-A	OBI	0.906	0.916	0.911	0.539
	BI	0.896	0.907	0.901	0.508
SC-B	OBI	0.868	0.797	0.831	0.410
	BI	0.850	0.763	0.805	0.327
SC-C	OBI	0.897	0.897	0.897	0.590
	BI	0.888	0.886	0.887	0.551
SC-D	OBI	0.900	0.903	0.901	0.472
	BI	0.888	0.891	0.890	0.419
TC-A	OBI	0.873	0.898	0.886	0.727
	BI	0.856	0.884	0.870	0.674
TC-B	OBI	0.906	0.932	0.919	0.578
	BI	0.894	0.920	0.907	0.551
TC-C	OBI	0.902	0.923	0.913	0.722
	BI	0.891	0.914	0.902	0.674
TC-D	OBI	0.924	0.934	0.929	0.765
	BI	0.908	0.922	0.915	0.722

Table 1. OBI vs. BI; where the lost of F > 1%, such as SC-B, is caused by incorrect English segments that will be discussed in the section 4.

2.2 Term Contributed Boundary

The word boundary and the word frequency are the standard notions of frequency in corpus-based natural language processing, but they lack the correct information about the actual boundary and frequency of a phrase's occurrence. The distortion of phrase boundaries and frequencies was first observed in the Vodis Corpus when the bigram "RAIL ENQUIRIES" and trigram "BRITISH RAIL ENQUIRIES" were examined and reported by O'Boyle (1993). Both of them occur 73 times, which is a large number for such a small corpus. "ENQUIRIES" follows "RAIL" with a very high probability when it is preceded by "BRITISH." However, when "RAIL" is preceded by words other than "BRITISH," "ENQUIRIES" does not occur, but words like "TICKET" or "JOURNEY" may. Thus, the bigram "RAIL ENQUIRIES" gives a misleading probability that "RAIL" is followed by "ENQUIRIES" irrespective of what precedes it. This problem happens not only with word-token corpora but also with corpora in which all the compounds are tagged as units since overlapping N-grams still appear, therefore corresponding solutions such as those of Zhang et al. (2006) were proposed.

We uses suffix array algorithm to calculate exact boundaries of phrase and their frequencies (Sung et al., 2008), called *term contributed boundaries* (TCB) and *term contributed frequencies* (TCF), respectively, to analogize similarities and differences with the *term frequencies* (TF). For example, in Vodis Corpus, the original TF of the term "RAIL ENQUIRIES" is 73. However, the actual TCF of "RAIL ENQUIRIES" is 0, since all of the frequency values are contributed by the term "BRITISH RAIL EN QUIRIES". In this case, we can see that 'BRITISH RAIL ENQUIRIES' is really a more frequent term in the corpus, where "RAIL ENQUIRIES" is not. Hence the TCB of "BRITISH RAIL ENQUIRIES" is ready for CRF tagging as "BRITISH/TB RAIL/TB ENQUIRIES/TI," for example.

3 Experiments

Besides submitted results, there are several different experiments that we have done. The configuration is about the trade-off between data sparseness and domain fitness. For the sake of OOV issue, TCBs from all the training and test corpora are included in the configuration of submitted results. For potentially better consistency to different types of text, TCBs from the training corpora and/or test corpora are grouped by corresponding domains of test corpora. Table 2 and Table 3 provide the details, where the baseline is the character-based "BI" tagging, and others are "BI" with additional different TCB configurations: TCB_{all} stands for the submitted results; TCB_{a}, TCB_{b}, TCB_{ta}, TCB_{tb}, TCB_{tc}, TCB_{td} represents TCB extracted from the training corpus A, B, and the test corpus A, B, C, D, respectively. Table 2 indicates that F1 measure scores can be improved by TCB about 1%, domain-independently. Table 3 gives a hint of the major contribution of performance is from TCB of each test corpus.

		R	P	F	OOV
SC-A	BI	0.896	0.907	0.901	0.508
	TCB_{all}	0.917	0.921	0.919	0.699
SC-B	BI	0.850	0.763	0.805	0.327
	TCB_{all}	0.876	0.799	0.836	0.456
SC-C	BI	0.888	0.886	0.887	0.551
	TCB_{all}	0.900	0.896	0.898	0.699
SC-D	BI	0.888	0.891	0.890	0.419
	TCB_{all}	0.910	0.906	0.908	0.562
TC-A	BI	0.856	0.884	0.870	0.674
	TCB_{all}	0.871	0.891	0.881	0.670
TC-B	BI	0.894	0.920	0.907	0.551
	TCB_{all}	0.913	0.917	0.915	0.663
TC-C	BI	0.891	0.914	0.902	0.674
	TCB_{all}	0.900	0.915	0.908	0.668
TC-D	BI	0.908	0.922	0.915	0.722
	TCB_{all}	0.929	0.922	0.925	0.732

Table 2. Baseline vs. Submitted Results

		F	OOV
SC-A	TCB_{ta}	0.918	0.690
	TCB_{a}	0.917	0.679
	$TCB_{ta} + TCB_{a}$	0.917	0.690
	TCB_{all}	0.919	0.699
SC-B	TCB_{tb}	0.832	0.465
	TCB_{b}	0.828	0.453
	$TCB_{tb} + TCB_{b}$	0.830	0.459
	TCB_{all}	0.836	0.456
SC-C	TCB_{tc}	0.897	0.618
	TCB_{all}	0.898	0.699
SC-D	TCB_{td}	0.905	0.557
	TCB_{all}	0.910	0.562

Table 3a. Simplified Chinese Domain-specific TCB vs. TCB_{all}

		F	OOV
TC-A	TCB_{ta}	0.889	0.706
	TCB_{a}	0.888	0.690
	$TCB_{ta} + TCB_{a}$	0.889	0.710
	TCB_{all}	0.881	0.670
TC-B	TCB_{tb}	0.911	0.636
	TCB_{b}	0.921	0.696
	$TCB_{tb} + TCB_{b}$	0.912	0.641
	TCB_{all}	0.915	0.663
TC-C	TCB_{tc}	0.918	0.705
	TCB_{all}	0.908	0.668
TC-D	TCB_{td}	0.927	0.717
	TCB_{all}	0.925	0.732

Table 3b. Traditional Chinese Domain-specific TCB vs. TCB_{all}

4 Error Analysis

The most significant type of error in our results is unintentionally segmented English words. Rather than developing another set of tag for English alphabets, we applies post-processing to fix this problem under the restriction of closed training by using only alphanumeric character information. Table 4 compares F1 measure score of the Simplified Chinese experiment results before and after the post-processing.

		F1 measure score	
		before	after
SC-A	OBI	0.911	0.918
	BI	0.901	0.908
	TCB_{ta}	0.918	0.920
	$TCB_{ta} + TCB_{a}$	0.917	0.920
	TCB_{all}	0.919	0.921
SC-B	OBI	0.831	0.920
	BI	0.805	0.910
	TCB_{tb}	0.832	0.917
	$TCB_{tb} + TCB_{b}$	0.830	0.916
	TCB_{all}	0.836	0.916
SC-C	OBI	0.897	0.904
	BI	0.887	0.896
	TCB_{tc}	0.897	0.901
	TCB_{all}	0.898	0.902
SC-D	OBI	0.901	0.919
	BI	0.890	0.908
	TCB_{td}	0.905	0.915
	TCB_{all}	0.908	0.918

Table 4. F1 measure scores before and after English Problem Fixed

The major difference between gold standards of the Simplified Chinese corpora and the Traditional Chinese corpora is about non-Chinese characters. All of the alphanumeric and the punctuation sequences are separated from Chinese sequences in the Simplified Chinese corpora, but can be part of the Chinese word segments in the Traditional Chinese corpora. For example, a phrase "服用/simvastatin/（/statins 類/的/一/種/）" ('/' represents the word boundary) from the domain C of the test data cannot be either recognized by "BI" and/or TCB tagging approaches, or post-processed. This is the reason why Table 4 does not come along with Traditional Chinese experiment results.

Some errors are due to inconsistencies in the gold standard of non-Chinese character, For example, in the Traditional Chinese corpora, some percentage digits are separated from their percentage signs, meanwhile those percentage signs are connected to parentheses right next to them.

5 Conclusion

This paper introduces a simple CRF feature called term contributed boundaries (TCB) for

Chinese word segmentation. The experiment result shows that it can improve the basic "BI" tagging scheme about 1% of the F1 measure score, domain-independently.

Further tagging scheme for non-Chinese characters are desired for recognizing some sophisticated gold standard of Chinese word segmentation that concatenates alphanumeric characters to Chinese characters.

Acknowledgement

The CRF model used in this paper is developed based on CRF++, http://crfpp.sourceforge.net/

Term Contributed Boundaries used in this paper are extracted by YASA, http://yasa.newzilla.org/

References

John Lafferty, Andrew McCallum, and Fernando Pereira. 2001. Conditional random fields: probabilistic models for segmenting and labeling sequence data. In *Proceedings of International Conference of Machine Learning*, 591–598.

Peter O'Boyle. 1993. A Study of an N-Gram Language Model for Speech Recognition. *PhD thesis*. Queen's University Belfast.

Fuchun Peng and Andrew McCallum. 2004. Chinese segmentation and new word detection using conditional random fields. In *Proceedings of International Conference of Computational linguistics*, 562–568, Geneva, Switzerland.

Cheng-Lung Sung, Hsu-Chun Yen, and Wen-Lian Hsu. 2008. Compute the Term Contributed Frequency. In *Proceedings of the 2008 Eighth International Conference on Intelligent Systems Design and Applications*, 325-328, Washington, D.C., USA.

Huihsin Tseng, Pichuan Chang, Galen Andrew, Daniel Jurafsky, and Christopher Manning. 2005. A conditional random field word segmenter for Sighan bakeoff 2005. In *Proceedings of the Fourth SIGHAN Workshop on Chinese Language Processing*, Jeju, Korea.

Nianwen Xue and Libin Shen. 2003. Chinese word-segmentation as LMR tagging. In *Proceedings of the Second SIGHAN Workshop on Chinese Language Processing*.

Ruiqiang Zhang, Genichiro Kikui, and Eiichiro Sumita. 2006. Subword-based tagging by conditional random fields for Chinese word segmentation. In *Proceedings of the Human Language Technology Conference of the North American Chapter of the Association for Computational Linguistics*, 193-196, New York, USA.

Chinese Word Segmentation based on Mixing Multiple Preprocessor and CRF

Jianping Shen, XuanWang, Hainan Zhao,Wenxiao Zhang
Computer Application Research Center, Shenzhen Graduate School
Harbin Institute of Technology Shenzhen, China, 518055
Email: {jpshen, wangxuan,hnzhao@cs.hitsz.edu.cn} Email: { xiaohit@126.com}

Abstract

This paper describes the Chinese Word Segmenter for our participation in CIPS-SIGHAN-2010 bake-off task of Chinese word segmentation. We formalize the tasks as sequence tagging problems, and implemented them using conditional random fields (CRFs) model. The system contains two modules: multiple preprocessor and basic segmenter. The basic segmenter is designed as a problem of character-based tagging, and using named entity recognition and chunk recognition based on boundary to preprocess. We participated in the open training on Simplified Chinese Text and Traditional Chinese Text, and our system achieved one Rank#5 and four Rank#2 best in all four domain corpus.

1 Introduction

Word is a logical semantic and syntactic unit in natural language (Zhenxing Wang, 2008). Chinese word segmentation is very important for Chinese language processing, which aims to recognize the implicit word boundaries in Chinese text. It is the foundation of most Chinese NLP tasks. In past decades, great success has been achieved in Chinese word segmentation (Nie, et al, 1995; Wang et al, 2000;Zhang, et al, 2002). But there still exist many problems, such as cross-domain performance of Chinese word segmentation algorithms. As the development of the internet, more and more new word has been appearing, Improving the performance of Chinese word segmentation algorithms on OOV (Out-Of-Vocabulary Word, is a word which occurs in the reference corpus but does not occur in the labeled training corpus) is the important research direction. Our system participated in the CIPS-SIGHAN-2010 bake-off task of Chinese word segmentation. And we have done work in dealing with two main sub-tasks: (1) Word Segmentation for Simplified Chinese Text, (2) Word Segmentation for Traditional Chinese Text. Our system formalizes these tasks as consecutive sequence tagging problems, and learns the segmentation using conditional random fields approach. Our system contains two modules, a multiple preprocessor and a basic segmenter. The multiple preprocessor first finds chunks based on boundary dictionary and then uses named entity recognition technology to extract the person, location, organization and special time. The basic segmenter using CRF model is trained to segment the sentence to word which contains one or more characters. The basic segmenter follows the study of Zhenxing Wang, Changning Huang and Jingbo Zhu (2008), but applies more refined features and tags.

The reminder of the paper is organized as follows. In section 2, we briefly describe the task and the details of our system. The experimental results are discussed in section 3. In section 4 we put forward our conclusion.

2 System Description

In this section we describe our system in more detail. The Figure1 is the frame of our system. It contains two modules: multiple preprocessor and basic segmenter.

2.1 Multiple Preprocessor

The preprocessor contain two modules: chunking based on boundary dictionary and NE Reorganization.

2.1.1 Chunking

In one sentence, there are always some characters or words, such as "是", "的","与"," 基于", the character adjacent them can not together with them. We define these characters or words as boundary word. We built a boundary dictionary manual, which contains about 100 words. Once a

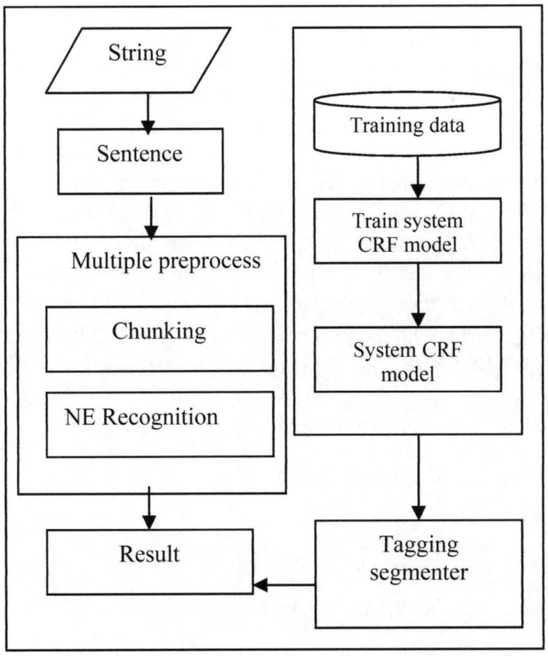

Figure1. Chinese Word Segmenter

sentence input, our system finds boundary words in the sentence first. For example, such as, "欧元区和欧盟成员国的财政部长分别于 15 日和 16 日在布鲁塞尔召开月度例会". In this sentence we can find the boundary word"和" "的" "于" "在" " 分别". Then chunking result is shown below in Figure 2. Using "[ ]" to mark up the chunks.

[欧元区] 和 [欧盟成员国] 的 [财政部长] 分别 于 [15 日] 和 [16 日] 在 [布鲁塞尔] [召开月度例会]

Figure 2. a sentence with chunk in data set

Chunking is very useful to improve the precision of segmentation. Especially when lacking enough training corpus for training CRF model. It can improve the out-of-vocabulary (OOV) word Recall and Precision on cross-domain Chinese word segmentation.

2.1.2 NE Recognition

We will recognize the named entities such as persons, locations organizations. We perform a process of the named entities recognition with forward-backward maximum matching algorithm based on entity dictionary. The dictionary contain location dictionary, person dictionary, family name dictionary, organization dictionary, country dictionary (Jianping Shen and Xuan Wang, 2010). For example, a sentence, "东海证券分析师王万金表示，该结果说明中国南车的价值已被市场所认可". And the processor will find out the location"东海","中国", the family name "王" and person "万金". The NE recognition result is shown below in Figure 3.

[东海]/loc 证券分析师 [王]/fam [万金]/per 表示，该结果说明 [中国]/ [南车]/org 的价值已被市场所认可.

Figure 3.sentence with NE recognition in data set

The location tag with "[ ]/loc", family name tag with "[ ]/fam", person tag with "[ ]/per", organization tag with "[ ]/org".

2.2 Basic Segmenter

We model the segment task as the consecutive sequence labeling problems, such as chunking, and named entity recognition, and train the basic segmenter using conditional random fields approach (Lafferty et al., 2001).

2.2.1 Conditional Random Fields

CRF models are conditional probabilistic sequence and undirected graphical models

CRF models hold two natures. First is the conditional nature, second the exponential nature. The conditional nature of the distribution over label sequence allows CRF models to model real-world data in which the conditional probability of a label sequence can depend on non-independent and interacting features of the observation sequence. The exponential nature of the distribution enables features of different states to be traded off against each other, weighting some states in a sequence as being more important than other states. Following Lafferty et al. and Hanna Wallach, the exponential distribution chosen by John Lafferty et al. is shown as follow:

$$p_\theta(y \mid x) \propto \exp\Big(\sum_{e\in E,k} \lambda_k f_k(e, y|_e, x) + \sum_{v\in V,k} \mu_k g_k(v, y|_v, x)\Big)$$

$$= \exp\Big(\sum_i \sum_k \lambda_k f_k(y_{i-1}, y_i, x)$$

$$+\sum_i \sum_k \mu_k g_k(y_i, x)) \quad (1)$$

Where

$$f_{y',y}(y_u, y_v, x) = \begin{cases} 1 & \text{if } y_u = y' \text{ and } y_v = y \\ 0 & \text{otherwise} \end{cases}$$

And

$$g_{y,x}(y_v, x) = \begin{cases} 1 & \text{if } y_v = y \text{ and } x_v = x \\ 0 & \text{otherwirse} \end{cases}$$

In this situation, the parameters $\lambda_{y',y}$ and $\mu_{y,x}$ corresponding to these features are equivalent to the logarithms of the HMM transition and emission probabilities $p(y'|y)$ and $p(x|y)$. The parameter of the model can be estimated in many ways, such as GIS, IIS, L-BFGS etc.

2.2.2 Segment base on CRF model

When a sentence or chunk (which get from the preprocessor) input, it will be split to the sequences shown in Figure 4.

chunk	sequence
欧盟成员国	欧 盟 成 员 国

Figure 4. Chunk and sequence

Every character in input sentences will be given a label which indicates whether this character is a word boundary. Our basic segmenter is almost the same as the system described in (Zhao et al., 2006) which is learned from training corpus. The CRF model we use is implemented with CRF++ 0.51. The parameters of the CRF segmenter are set as defaults.

Under the CRF tagging scheme, each character in one sentence will be given a label by CRF model to indicate which position this character occupies in a word. In our system, CRF tag set is proposed to distinguish different positions in the multi-character words when the word length is less than 6, namely 6-tag set {B, B2, B3, M, E, O}(Zhenxing Wang ,2008).We defined that B stands for the first and E stands for the last position in a multi-character word. S stands up a single-character word. B2 and B3 stand for the second and the third position in a multi-character word. M stands for the fourth or more rear position in a multi-character word, whose length is larger than four-character. Then we add the entity tag set {B-entity, I-entity, E-entity}. B-entity stands for the first character in a named entity, E-entity stands for the last character in a named entity, and I-entity stands for the other character in a named entity.

We use a greedy forward procedure to select a better feature sets for the segementer according to the evaluation results in the development set. We first start from a basic feature set, and then add each feature outside the basic set and remove each feature inside the basic set one by one to check the effectiveness of each feature by the performance change in the development set. This procedure is repeated until no feature is added or removed or the performance is not improved. The selected features are listed below:

- C_n (n=-2,-1, 0, 1, 2)
- C_nC_{n+1} (n=-1,0)
- $C_{n-1}C_nC_{n+1}$ (n=-1,0,1)
- $C_{n-2}C_{n-1}C_nC_{n+1}$ (n=0,1)

Where C refer to the tag of each character, and C_0 denotes current character and Cn(C-n) denotes the character n positions to the right (left) of current character.

2.2.3 Post-processing

We can obtain the preliminary results through the CRF model-based Segment, but there are some missed or incorrect cases for the digit, English word. For example “the sighan” maybe segment to “th e sig han”, so we will re-segment the “th e sig han” as “the sighan”.

3 Performance and Analysis

In this section we will present our experimental results for these two subtasks. For the Word Segmentation for Simplified Chinese Text subtask, comparing the performance of these four domains, we find that the performance of computer and finance are better than literature and medical. We can find that the OOV RR of literature and medical are lower than the computer and finance. In the test data set, there are many Out-of-vocabulary(OOV), especially the disease. In medical domain, there are many diseases which do not appear in the corpus, and there is the proper name. The segment often can’t recognize disease well, so we add a post-processing procedure, using domain dictionary for medicine, is used to increase the recall measure. The result for medical is shown in Table 2.

domain	R	P	F1	OOV RR	IV RR
literature	0.836	0.841	0.838	0.609	0.853
computer	0.951	0.951	0.932	0.77	0.983
medical	0.839	0.832	0.836	0.796	0.866
finance	0.893	0.896	0.894	0.796	0.902

Table 1: Performance of the four domain Simplified Chinese test data set

R	P	F1	OOV RR	IV RR
0.894	0.882	0.888	0.683	0.901

Table 2: Performance of medical test data set with post-processing using domain dictionary

Word Segmentation for Traditional Chinese Text subtask. We use a Traditional and Simplified Dictionary to translate the named entity dictionary, boundary dictionary from Simplified to Traditional. And then we use our system to segment the traditional test data set. The results are shown in Table 3.

domain	R	P	F1	OOV RR	IV RR
literature	0.868	0.802	0.834	0.503	0.905
computer	0.875	0.829	0.851	0.594	0.904
medical	0.879	0.814	0.846	0.480	0.912
finance	0.832	0.760	0.794	0.356	0.866

Table 3: Performance of four domain Traditional Chinese test data set

4 Conclusion

Through the CIPS-SIGHAN bakeoff, we find our system is effective. And at the same time, we also find some problems of us. Our system still can't performance very good in cross-domain. Especially the Out-of-vocabulary (OOV) recognition. From the experiment we can see that using domain dictionary is a good idea. In the future we will do more work in post-processing. The bakeoff points out the direction for us to improve our system.

References

Huipeng Zhang, Ting Liu, Jinshan Ma, Xiantao Liao,Chinese *Word Segmentation with Multiple Postprocessors in HIT-IRLab, Proceedings of the Fourth SIGHAN Workshop on Chinese Language Processing,* Jeju Island, Republic of Korea October 11-13, 2005

Hai Zhao, Changning Huang et al. 2006. *Effective Tag Set Selection in Chinese Word Segmentation via Conditional Random Field Modeling. In Proceedings of PACLIC-20.* pages 87-94. Wuhan, China, Novemeber.

Zhenxing Wang; Changning Huang; Jingbo Zhu. *The Character-based CRF Segmenter of MSRA&NEU for the 4th Bakeoff. The Sixth SIGHAN Workshop for Chinese Language was be held in conjunction with IJCNLP 2008,* in Hyderabad, India, January 11-12, 2008.

Wei Jiang Jian Zhao Yi Guan Zhiming Xu. *Chinese Word Segmentation based on Mixing Model. Proceedings of the Fourth SIGHAN Workshop on Chinese Language Processing,* Jeju Island, Republic of Korea October 11-13, 2005

Nie, Jian-Yuan, M.-L. Hannan and W.-Y. Jin. 1995.*Unknown word detection and segmentation ofChinese using statistical and heuristic knowledge.Communication of COLIPS*, 5(1&2): 47-57.

Wang, Xiaolong, Fu Guohong, Danial S.Yeung, James N.K.Liu, and Robert Luk. 2000. *Models and algorithms of Chinese word segmentation. In: Proceedings of the International Conference on Artificial Intelligence (IC-AI'2000),* Las Vegas, Nevada, USA, 1279-1284.

Lafferty, J. and McCallum, A. and Pereira, F. *Conditional random fields: Probabilistic models for segmenting and labeling sequence data. MACHINE LEARNING-INTERNATIONAL WORKSHOP THEN CONFERENCE.* 2001, 282-289

Hanna Wallach, *Efficient Training of Conditional Random Fields, In Proceedings of the 6th Annual CLUK Research Colloquium*, 2002.

A domain adaption Word Segmenter

For Sighan Bakeoff 2010

Guo jiang
Institute of Intelligent Information Processing,
Beijing Information Science & Technology University,
Beijing, China, 100192
Guojiang132@gmail.com

Su Wenjie
Institute of Intelligent Information Processing,
Beijing Information Science & Technology University,
Beijing, China, 100192
dev.sunflower@gmail.com

Yangsen Zhang
Institute of Intelligent Information Processing,
Beijing Information Science & Technology University,
Beijing, China, 100192
zhangyangsen@163.com

Abstract

We present a Chinese word segmentation system which ran on the closed track of the simplified Chinese Word Segmentation task of CIPS-SIGHAN-CLP 2010 bakeoffs. Our segmenter was built using a HMM. To fulfill the cross-domain segmentation task, we use semi-supervised machine learning method to get the HMM model. Finally we get the mean result of four domains: P=0.719, R=0.72

1 Introduction

The 2010 Sighan Bakeoff included two types of evaluations:

(1) Closed training: In the closed training evaluation, participants can only use data provided by organizers to train their systems specifically, the following data resources and software tools are not permitted to be used in the training:

1) Unspecified corpus;
2) Unspecified dictionary, word list or character list: include the dictionaries of named entity, character lists for specific type of Chinese named entities, idiom dictionaries, semantic lexicons, etc.
3) Human-encoded rule bases;
4) Unspecified software tools, include word segmenters, part-of-speech taggers, or parsers which are trained using unspecified data resources.

The character type information to distinguish the following four character types can be used in training: Chinese characters, English letters, digits and punctuations.

(2) Open training: In the open training evaluation, participants can use any language resource, including the training data provided by organizers

We prefer character-based Tagging than dictionary based word segmentation in closed training, for we can only use the provide train corpus and scale of the corpus is not large enough. If we select dictionary based method we will encounter the out-of-vocabulary problem. But in character-based Tagging method we can yield a better performance than the dictionary based method for such problem.

2 Algorithm

Ever before 2002 almost all word segment method is based on dictionary. In SIGHAN 2003 bakeoff, a character-based Tagging method was proposed and since then the character-based Tagging method became more and more popular. HMM (Hidden Markov Model) has been used extensively in speech recognition, pos tagging and get good grades. So we chose HMM as our machine learning method to fulfill our task.

We formally define the elements of an HMM, and explain how the model generates an observation sequence.

An HMM is characterized by the following:

1) N, the number of states in the model. we denote the individual states as $s=\{s_1, s\ , \ldots, s\ \}$,and the state at time t as q
2) M, the number of distinct observation symbols per state. we denote the individual symbols as $v=\{v_1, v\ , .., v\ \}$

This work was supported by the national natural science foundation of China (60873013)。Beijing natural science foundation (KZ200811232019); The Open Project Program of the Key Laboratory of Computational Linguistics (Peking University), Ministry of Education;Funding Project for Academic Human Resources Devel-opment in Institutions of Higher Learning Under the Juris-diction of Beijing Municipality (PHR201007131)

3) The state transition probability distribution A= { a_{ij} } where a_{ij} =P [q 1 s_j|q s_i], 1<i,j<N.
4) The observation symbol probability distribution in state j, B={b_j k }, where b_j k P v at t|q s_j
5) The initial state distribution π π_i where π_i P q_1 s_i

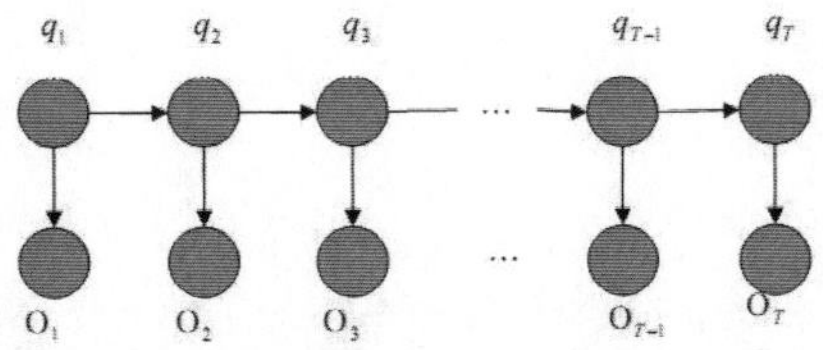

Graph1

For convenience, we use the compact notation A, B, π) to indicate the complete parameter set of the model.

There are three basic problems for HMM, for problem 1 we use forward-backward algorithm, for problem 2 we use Viterbi algorithm, for problem 3 we use Baum-Welch algorithm.

To application HMM to our task we define the HMM five factors as blow:

1) We define the whole labels set as Q={B, M, E, S}, B represents word's begin, M represents word's middle, E represents word's end and S represents single word.
2) We define all Unicode characters as O
3) We define A={a_{ij}}, where a_{ij}=P[prior token=s_i|posterior label =s_j]
4) We define B={ b_j k }, where b_j k =P[current character= v |current label =s_j]
5) We define a sentence as a train sample. So π={sentences start with s, s Q}.

Through the design we transform the character-based tagging problem to HMM problem 2. So we can solve this problem with Viterbi algorithm.

3 Experiment

We use HMM to establish the Word Segment prototype system and make use of the Labeled supplied by the Chinese Academy of Sciences to train the HMM and get the model parameters which will be used for the next iterative scaling. After that, we can get a system based on HMM model. Then, with the help of the gotten system, we process the unlabeled corpus. Once it is finished, we should add the processed corpus to the labeled corpus and get a larger corpus with which we can retrain the HMM. All these steps have been done according four test corpuses: literature, computer, medicine, finance. In the table, R indicates the recall rate, P indicates the precision rate, F1 indicates the macro average, OOV R indicates the out-of-vocabulary (OOV) rate, OOV RR indicates the out-of-vocabulary (OOV) self repair rate, IV RR indicates the out-of-vocabulary (OOV) self repair rate. In order to more easily view data, we have presented the Graph2.

From the table and graph, we can see that the finance corpus has a better result, the computer corpus don't show a good result for the R, P, F1. Generally speaking, this result is a reflection for the difference between the dictionary based Tagging method and character-based Tagging method. After recheck our corpus, we can find that there are more technical terms in the computer corpus than finance corpus. The explanation for the result is that if the system encounter a technical terms, the character-based Tagging method will have a bad performance. In such situation, dictionary based Tagging method may have a better performance. For the OOV R and OOV RR, the system has a not bad performance. Table I and Graph2 show the detailed experimental data.

The results of four test corpus as follow:

Type	R	P	F1	OOV R	OOV RR	IV RR
literature	0.695	0.744	0.719	0.069	0.381	0.719
Computer	0.713	0.641	0.675	0.152	0.257	0.795
medicine	0.735	0.74	0.738	0.11	0.378	0.779
finance	0.736	0.752	0.744	0.087	0.23	0.784

Table1

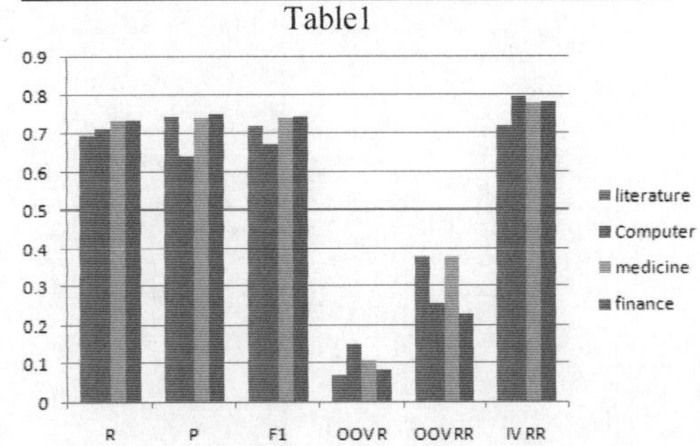

Graph2

4 Conclusion

Our system used a HMM and semi-supervised learning for domain adapting. Our final system achieved a P=0.719, R=0.72. There exist two ways to improve our system performance one is instead our model of CRF, the other is change another way to use the unlabeled data. Because the inherent shortage of HMM we could not get a precise model, and the way we use the unlabeled data can import err to labeled data.

References

Lawrence R. Rabiner. 1989,2. *A Tutorial on Hidden Markov Models and Selected Applications in Speech Recognition.* IEEE, VOL.77,No.2,pp:257-286.

Huang Changning, HaoHai. 2007. *Ten Years of Chinese word segmentation.* Vol. 21, No. 3. *JOURNAL OF CHINESE INFORMATION PROCESSING*

Huihsin Tseng, Pichuan Chang, Galen Andrew, Daniel Jurafsky, Christopher Manning. *A Conditional Random Field Word Segmenter for Sighan Bakeoff 2005.*

Blum A, MITCHELL T. *Combining labeled and unlabeled data with co-training* Proceeding of the 11th Annual conference on Computational Learning Theory.

Holmes, W., Russell, M., 1995b. Speech recognition using a linear dynamic segmental HMM. In: Internat. Conf. on Acoust. Speech Signal Process. 1995, Detroit, MI.

An Double Hidden HMM and an CRF for Segmentation Tasks with Pinyin's Finals

Huixing Jiang **Zhe Dong**
Center for Intelligence Science and Technology
Beijing University of Posts and Telecommunications
Beijing, China
jhx0129@163.com jimmybupt@gmail.com

Abstract

We have participated in the open tracks and closed tracks on four corpora of Chinese word segmentation tasks in CIPS-SIGHAN-2010 Bake-offs. In our experiments, we used the Chinese inner phonology information in all tracks. For open tracks, we proposed a double hidden layers' HMM (DHHMM) in which Chinese inner phonology information was used as one hidden layer and the BIO tags as another hidden layer. N-best results were firstly generated by using DHHMM, then the best one was selected by using a new lexical statistic measure. For close tracks, we used CRF model in which the Chinese inner phonology information was used as features.

1 Introduction

Chinese language has many characteristics not possessed by other languages. One obvious is that the written Chinese text does not have explicit word boundaries like western languages. So word segmentation became very significative for Chinese information processing, and is usually considered as the first step of any further processing. Identifying words has been a basic task for many researchers who have devoted themselves on Chinese text processing.

The biggest characteristic of Chinese language is its trinity of sound, form and meaning (Pan, 2002). Hanyu Pinyin is the form of sound for Chinese text and the Chinese phonology information is explicit expressed by Pinyin which is the inner features of Chinese Characters. And it naturally contributes to the identification of Out-Of-Vacabulary words (OOV).

In our work, Chinese phonology information is used as basic features of Chinese characters in all models. For open tracks, we propose a new double hidden layers HMM in which a new phonology information is built in as a hidden layer, a new lexical association is proposed to deal with the OOV questions and domains' adaptation questions. And for closed tracks, CRF model has been used , combined with Chinese inner phonology information. We used the CRF++ package Version 0.43 by Taku Kudo[1].

In the rest sections of this paper, we firstly introduce the Chinese phonology in Section 2. Then in the Section 3, the models used in our tasks are presented. And the experiments and results are described in Section 4. Finally, we give the conclusions and make prospect on future work.

2 Chinese Phonology

Hanyu Pinyin is the form of sound for Chinese text and the Chinese phonology information is explicit expressed by Pinyin. It is currently the most commonly used romanization system for Standard Mandarin. Hanyu means the Chinese language, and Pinyin means "phonetics", or more literally, "spelling sound" or "spelled sound" (wikipedia, 2010). The system has been employed to teach Mandarin as home language or as second language by China, Malaysia, Singapore et.al. Pinyin has been the most Chinese character's input method for computers and other devices.

[1] http://crfpp.sourceforge.net/

The romanization system was developed by a government committee in the People's Republic of China, and approved by the Chinese government on February 11, 1958. The International Organization for Standardization adopted pinyin as the international standard in 1982, and since then it has been adopted by many other organizations(wikipedia, 2010). In this system, pinyin is composed by initials(pinyin: shengmu), finals(pinyin: yunmu) and tones(pinyin: shengdiao) instead of consonants and vowels used in European language. For example, the Pinyin of "中" is "zhong1" composed by "zh", "ong" and "1". In which "zh" is initial, "ong" is final and "1" is the tone.

Every language has its rhythm and rhyme, so Chinese is no exception. The rhythm system are the driving force from the unconscious habit of language(Edward, 1921). And the Pinyin's finals contribute the Chinese rhythm system, Which is the basic assumption our research based on.

3 Algorithms

Generally the task of segmentation can be viewed as a sequence labeling problem. We first define a tag set as TS = {B, I, E, S}, shown in Table 1.

Table 1: The tag set used in this paper.

Label	Explanation
B	beginning character of a word
I	inner character of a word
E	end character of a word
S	a single character as a word

For the piece "是英国前王妃戴安娜" of the example described in the experiments section, firstly, the TS tags are labeled to it. And its result is "是/S 英/B 国/E 前/S 王/B 妃/E 戴/B 安/I 娜/E". Then the tags are combined sequentially to get the finally result "是_英国_前_王妃_戴安娜".

In this section, A novel HMM solution is presented firstly for open tracks. Then the CRF solution for closed tracks is introduced.

3.1 Double hidden layers' HMM

For a given piece of Chinese sentence, $X = x_1x_2 \ldots x_T$, where $x_i, i = 1, \ldots, T$ is a Chinese character. Suppose that we can give each Chinese character x_i a Pinyin's final y_i. And suppose the label sequence of X is $S = s_1s_2 \ldots s_T$, where $s_i \in TS$ is the tag of x_i. Then what we want to find is an optimal tag sequence S^* which is defined in (1).

$$\begin{aligned} S^* &= \arg\max_S P(S, Y|X) \\ &= \arg\max_S P(X|S, Y)P(S, Y) \end{aligned} \quad (1)$$

The model is described in Fig. 1. For a given piece of Chinese character strings, One hidden layer is label sequence S. Another hidden layer is Pinyin's finals sequence Y. The observation layer is the given piece of Chinese characters X.

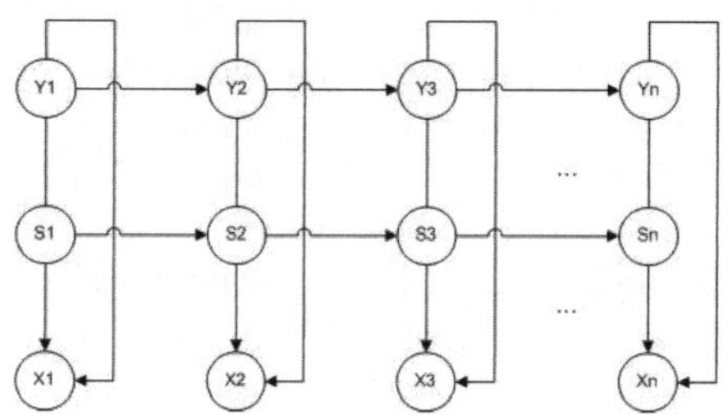

Figure 1: Double Hidden Markov Model

For transition probability, second-order Markov model is used to estimate probability of the double hidden sequences as described in (2).

$$P(S, Y) = \prod_t p(s_t, y_t|s_{t-1}, y_{t-1}) \quad (2)$$

For emission probability, we keep the first-order Markov assumption as shown in (5).

$$P(X|S, Y) = \prod_t p(x_t|s_t, y_t) \quad (3)$$

3.1.1 Nbest results

Based on the work of (Jiang, 2010), a word lattice is also built firstly, then in the second step, the backward A^* algorithm is used to find the top N results instead of using the backward viterbi algorithm to find the top one. The backward A^* search algorithm is described as follow (Wang, 2002; Och, 2001).

3.1.2 Reranking with a new lexical statistic measure

Given two random Chinese characters X and Y and assume that they appears in an aligned region of the corpus. The distribution of the two random Chinese characters could be depicted by a 2 by 2 contingency table shown in Fig. 2(Chang, 2002).

	Y	$\neg Y$
X	a	b
$\neg X$	c	d

Figure 2: A 2 by 2 contingency table

In Fig. 2, a is the counts of X and Y co-occur; b is the counts of the cases that X occurs but Y does not; c is the counts of the cases that X does not occur but Y does; d is the counts of the cases that both X and Y do not occur. The Log-likelihood rate is calculated by (4).

$$\begin{aligned} LLR(x,y) = 2(a \cdot \log \frac{a \cdot N}{(a+b)\cdot(a+c)} \\ + b \cdot \log \frac{b \cdot N}{(a+b)\cdot(b+d)} \\ + c \cdot \log \frac{c \cdot N}{(c+d)\cdot(a+c)} \\ + d \cdot \log \frac{d \cdot N}{(c+d)\cdot(b+d)}) \end{aligned} \quad (4)$$

For the N-best result described in sec. 3.1.1, they can be re-ranked by (5).

$$S^* = \arg\min_S(score_h(S) + \frac{\lambda}{K}\sum_{k=1}^{K} LLR(x_k, y_k)) \quad (5)$$

where $score_h$ is the negative log value of $P(S,Y|X)$. K is the number of breaks in X and x_k is the left Chinese character of the k break and y_k is the right Chinese character of the k break. λ is the regulatory factor(in our experiments $\lambda = 0.45$).

Bigger value of $LLR(x_k, y_k)$ means stronger ability in combining of the two characters x_k and y_k, then they should not be segmented.

3.2 CRF model for closed tracks

Conditional random field, as statistical sequence labeling model, has been used widely in segmentation(Lafferty, 2001; Zhao, 2006). In the closed tracks of the paper, we also use it.

3.2.1 Feature templates

We adopted two main kinds of features: n-gram features and Pinyin's finals features. The n-gram feature set is quite orthodox, they are, namely, C-2, C-1, C0, C1, C2, C-2C-1, C-1C0, C0C1, C1C2. The Pinyin's finals feature set is the same as n-gram feature set. They are described in Table. 2.

Table 2: Feature templates

Templates	Category
C-2, C-1, C0, C1, C2	N-gram: Unigram
C-2C-1, C-1C0, C0C1, C1C2	N-gram: Bigram
P-2, P-1, P0, P1, P2	Phonetic: Unigram
P-2P-1, P-1P0, P0P1, P1P2	Phonetic: Bigram

4 Experiments and Results

4.1 Dataset

We build a basic words dictionary for DHHMM and a Pinyin's finals dictionary for both DHHMM and CRF from The Grammatical Knowledge-base of Contemporary Chinese(Yu, 2001). For the finals dictionary, we give each Chinese character a final extracted from its Pinyin. When it comes to a polyphone, we just combine its all finals simply to one. For example, "中{ong}", "差{a&ai&i}".

The training corpus (5,769 KB) we used is the Labeled Corpus provided by the organizer. We firstly add the Pinyin's finals to each Chinese character of it, then we train the parameters of DHHMM and CRF model on it.

And the test corpus contains four domains: Literature (A), Computer (B), Medicine (C) and Finance(D).

The LLR function's parameters{a, b, c, d} are counted from the current test corpus A, B, C, or D. It's means that for segmenting A, the LLR parameters are counted from A, so the same for segmenting B, C and D.

4.2 Preprocessing

The date, time, numbers and symbols information are easily identified by rules. We propose four regular expressions' processes, in which the regular expressions' processes are handled one after another in order of date, time, numbers and symbols. By now, a rough segmentation can be done. For a character stream, the date, time, numbers and symbols are firstly identified, then the whole stream can be divided by these units to some pieces of character strings which will be segment by the models described in sec. 3. For example, a character stream "2009年的8月31日，是英国前王妃戴安娜12周年忌日。" will be divided to "2009年_的_8月_31日_，_是英国前王妃戴安娜_12_周年忌日_。". Then the pieces "的", "是英国前王妃戴安娜", "周年忌日" will be segmented sequentially by the models described in Section 3.

4.3 Results on DHHMM

We evaluate our system by Precision Rate(6), Recall Rate(7), F1 measure(8) and OOV(Out-Of-Vocabulary) Recall rate(9).

$$P = \frac{C(correct\ words\ in\ segmented\ result)}{C(words\ in\ segmented\ result)} \tag{6}$$

$$R = \frac{C(correct\ words\ in\ segmented\ result)}{C(words\ in\ standard\ result)} \tag{7}$$

$$F1 = \frac{2 * P * R}{P + R} \tag{8}$$

$$OR = \frac{C(correct\ OOV\ in\ segmented\ result)}{C(OOV\ in\ standard\ result)} \tag{9}$$

In (6-9), $C(\cdots)$ is the count of $(\cdots)$.

Table 3 are the results of the DHHMM on open tracks.

In Table 3, $OOVRR$ is the recall rate of OOV, $IVRR$ is the recall rate of IV(In Vocabulary).

4.4 Postprocessing for CRF and Results on It

Since the CRF segmenter will not always return a valid tag sequence that can be translated into segmentation result, some corrections should be made if such error occurs. We devised a dynamic programming routine to tackle this problem: first we compute the valid tag sequence that closest to the output of CRF segmenter (by term closest, we mean least hamming distance), if there is a tie, we choose the one has the least 'S' tags, if the tie still exists, we choose the one that comes lexicographically earlier ($B < I < E < S$, described in Table. 1). Table 4 are the results of the CRF on closed tracks.

Table 3: Results of open tracks using DHHMM: Literature (A), Computer (B), Medicine (C) and Finance(D)

	A	B	C	D
R	0.893	0.918	0.917	0.928
P	0.918	0.896	0.907	0.934
F1	0.905	0.907	0.912	0.931
OOV RR	0.803	0.771	0.704	0.808
IV RR	0.899	0.945	0.943	0.939

Table 4: Results of closed tracks using CRF: Literature (A), Computer (B), Medicine (C) and Finance(D)

	A	B	C	D
R	0.945	0.946	0.94	0.956
P	0.946	0.914	0.928	0.952
F1	0.946	0.93	0.934	0.954
OOV RR	0.816	0.808	0.761	0.849
IV RR	0.954	0.971	0.962	0.966

From the results of Table 3 and Table 4, we can observe that the CRF model outperforms the DHHMM by average 2.72% in F1 measure. In the other hand, from Table 5, we can see that the computation cost in DHHMM is less than half of the time cost and lower one-fifth memory cost than CRF model.

Table 5: The computation cost in DHHMM and CRF

	Time cost(ms)	Memory cost(MB)
DHHMM	34398	16.3
CRF	43415	35

5 Conclusions and Future works

This paper has presented a double hidden lawyers HMM for Chinese word segmentation task in SIGHAN bakeoff 2010. It firstly created N top results and then select the best one from it by a new lexical association.

Chinese phonology (specially by Pinyin's final in text) is very useful inner information of Chinese language, which is the first time used in our models. We have used it in both DHHMM and CRF model.

In future work, there are lots of improvements can be done. Firstly, which polyphone's finals should be used in a given context is a visible question. And the strategy to train the parameter λ described in 3.1.2 can also be improved.

Acknowledgments

This research has been partially supported by the National Science Foundation of China (NO. NSFC90920006). We also thank Caixia Yuan for leading our discuss, Li Sun, Peng Zhang, Yaojing Chen, Zhixu Lin, Gan Lin, Guannan Fang for their useful helps in this work.

References

Wenguo Pan. 2002. *zibenwei yu hanyu yanjiu*:120–141. East China Normal University Press.

Sapir Edward 1921. *Language: An introduction to the study of speech*:230. New York: Harcourt, Brace and company.

wikipedia. 2010. *Pinyin*. http://en.wikipedia.org/wiki /Pinyin#cite_note-6.

Baobao Chang, Pernilla Danielsson, and Wolfgang Teubert. 2002. *Extraction of translation unit from chinese-english parallel corpora*, Proceedings of the first SIGHAN workshop on Chinese language processing:1–5.

Huixing Jiang, Xiaojie Wang, Jilei Tian. 2010. *Second-order HMM for Event Extraction from Short Message*, 15th International Conference on Applications of Natural Language to Information Systems, Cardiff, Wales, UK.

Franz Josef Och, Nicola Ueffing, Hermann Ney. 2001. *An Efficient A* Search Algorithm for Statistical Machine Translation*, Proceedings of the ACL Workshop on Data-Driven methods in Machine Translation 14(Toulouse, France): 1-8.

Ye-Yi Wang, Alex Waibel. 2002. *Decoding Algorithm in Statistical Machine Translation*, Proceedings of the 35th Annual Meeting of the Association for Computational Linguistics and Eighth Conference of the European Chapter of the Association for Computational Linguistics: 366-372.

Yu Shiwen, Zhu Xuefeng, Wang Hui. 2001. *New Progress of the Grammatical Knowledge-base of Contemporary Chinese*, ZHONGWEN XINXI XUEBAO, 2001 Vol. 01.

John Lafferty, A.Mccallum, F.Pereira. 2001. *Conditional Random Field: Probabilitic Models for Segmenting and Labeling Sequence Data.*, Proceedings of the Eighteenth International Conference on Machine Learning: 282–289.

Hai Zhao, Changning Huang, Mu Li. 2006. *An Improved Chinese Word Segmentation System with Conditional Random Field*, Proceedings of the Fifth SIGHAN Workshop on Chinese Language Processing (SIGHAN-5)(Sydney, Australia):162-165.

Combining Character-Based and Subsequence-Based Tagging for Chinese Word Segmentation

Jiangde Yu, Chuan Gu, Wenying Ge
School of Computer and Information Engineering, Anyang Normal University, Anyang 455002, China
jiangde_yu@tom.com, {jkx-20,ligepw}@163.com

Abstract

Chinese word segmentation is the initial step for Chinese information processing. The performance of Chinese word segmentation has been greatly improved by character-based approaches in recent years. This approach treats Chinese word segmentation as a character-word-position-tagging problem. With the help of powerful sequence tagging model, character-based method quickly rose as a mainstream technique in this field. This paper presents our segmentation system for evaluation of CIPS-SIGHAN 2010 in which method combining character-based and subsequence-based tagging is applied and conditional random fields (CRFs) is taken as sequence tagging model. We evaluated our system in closed and open tracks on four corpuses, namely *Literary*, *Computer science*, *Medicine* and *Finance,* and reported our evaluation results.

1 Introduction

In Chinese information processing, word is the minimum unit to be used independently and meaningfully. But, Chinese sentences are written as string of characters without clear delimiters. Therefore, the first step in Chinese information processing is to identify the sequence of words in a sentence, namely Chinese word segmentation. It's the foundation of syntax analysis, semantic analysis and discourse comprehension, and also the important section of machine translation, question answering, information retrieval and information extraction(Jiang Wei, et al., 2007; Liu Qun, et al., 2004).

The research of Chinese word segmentation has been advancing rapidly and has gained many exciting achievements in recent years(Huang Changning, Zhao Hai. 2007; Song Yan, et al., 2009), especially after the First International Chinese Word Segmentation Bakeoff held in 2003. In this field, character-based tagging attracts more eyes and almost all excellent systems in evaluations has adopted this technology thought(Huang Changning, Zhao Hai. 2007; Zhao Hai, Jie Chunyu. 2007). In 2002, Xue presented the first paper about character-based tagging on the 1st international workshop of special interest group on Chinese language processing, SIGHAN. He segmented Chinese words with four character tags: LL, RR, MM and LR, depending on its position within a word using a maximum entropy tagger(Xue N W, Converse S P. 2002). Huang et al. implemented character-based segmentation system with conditional random fields, six word-position tags: B, B2, B3, M, E, S, and TMPT-6 and achieved very excellent results(Huang Changning, Zhao Hai. 2006; Huang Changning, Zhao Hai. 2007). On this base, Zhao hai presented an effective subsequence-based tagging for Chinese word segmentation(Zhao Hai, Jie Chunyu. 2007). All these references considered Chinese segmentation as character or subsequence tagging problem and implemented with statistical language models.

The evaluation for Chinese word segmentation in CIPS-SIGHAN 2010 has two subtasks: word segmentation for simplified Chinese text and for traditional Chinese text. The simplified Chinese corpuses are offered by Institute of Computing Technology(ICT) and Peking University(PKU), and the traditional Chinese corpuses are offered City University of Hong Kong(CityU). The corpuses involved four domains: *literary*, *computer science*, *medicine* and *finance*. Considering plenty of abbreviations, numeric and other non-Chinese strings, our segmentation system adopted a method combining character-based and subsequence-based tagging, and took CRFs as sequence tagging model. CRFs is a kind of conditional probability model for sequence tagging presented by Lafferty et al. in 2001(Lafferty J, et al., 2001). In our experiment, the CRF++0.53 toolkit[1] is used. CRF++ is a simple, customizable, and open source implementation of CRFs for segmenting sequential data. This paper described our system participating CIPS-SIGHAN 2010 and presented our word-position tag set and feature template set and their change in open tracks. Finally, we report the results of our evaluation.

2 Combining character-based and subsequence-based tagging for Chinese word segmentation

In character-based tagging approach to Chinese word segmentation, it tags the word-position of non-Chinese characters, such as punctuation, letter words and numeric, just like what to do with Chinese characters. This method works well when there is a small quantity of these characters. But plenty of these characters will cut down the segmentation performance, especially some abbreviation and programming statement in computer science domain. Considering this, we used a method combining character-based and subsequence-based tagging that is to take an English word or programming statement as a subsequence to tag its word-position. The correct tag for one-character word is S.

2.1 Word-position tag set

In the closed track of traditional Chinese and simplified Chinese, four word-position tag set is used: B (Beginning of word), M(Middle of word), E(End of word) and S(one-character word). The tag set is also used in open tracks of traditional Chinese. And we used six word-position tag set for open tracks of simplified Chinese: B(Beginning of word), B2(2nd character of word), B3(3rd character of word) M(Middle of word), E(End of word) and S(one-character word).

2.2 Feature templates

To define the relationship of some specific language components or information in context and some being forecasted things is the main function of feature template. It is generally considered that feature template is abstracted from a group of context features on same attributes.

In CRF++0.53 toolkit, there are two kind of templates: Unigram template and Bigram template. In word-position tagging Chinese segmentation, available features are rather limited. The main feature needed to take into account is character feature, which includes current character, previous and next character. Jiang, Wang and Guan (2007) abstracted the character features into six templates according different distances from current character. They are Unigram templates. The type and meaning of these templates are presented in table 1. When training with CRFs model, these templates will be extended to thousands of features and every feature has a group of corresponding feature functions. All these functions are very important to CRFs model learning. Seen from table 1, Bigram feature has only one template: $T_{-1}T_0$ which describes the word-position transfer feature of two adjacent characters or subsequences. This feature extends limited features in training. Take four-WORD-POSITION-tag for instance, it can be extended into sixteen features. In our tracks, open or closed one, the seven templates in table 1: C_{-1}, C_0, C_1, $C_{-1}C_0$, C_0C_1, $C_{-1}C_1$, $T_{-1}T_0$ are used.

Table 1 List of feature templates

Type of template	template	Meaning of template
Unigram	C_{-1}	previous character
	C_0	current character
	C_1	next character
	$C_{-1}C_0$	String of current character and previous one
	C_0C_1	String of current character and next one
	$C_{-1}C_1$	String of previous and next character
Bigram	$T_{-1}T_0$	Word-position transfer feature of two adjacent character

[1] Download from this website: http://crfpp.sourceforge.net/

3 Experiments and results

3.1 Data set

Our training and test corpuses are gained from evaluation conference. The training and test corpuses of simplified Chinese are offered by ICT and PKU, while traditional Chinese by CityU. These corpuses involved in four domains: *literary(A)*, *computer science(B)*, *medicine(C)*, *finance(D)*. In addition, we also use the CityU2005 training corpuses which gained from the Bakeoff2005 for open track.

3.2 Evaluation metrics

Five evaluation metrics: precision(*P*), recall(*R*), f-measue(*F1*), out-of-vocabulary words recall rate (*OOV RR*) and In-vocabulary words recall rate (*IV RR*) are used in our evaluation experiments.

3.3 Experiments and results

We adopted combining character-based and subsequence-based tagging for Chinese word segmentation, and conducted closed track experiments on these corpuses. Four word-position tag set(B, M, E, S) and seven templates(C_{-1}, C_0, C_1, $C_{-1}C_0$, C_0C_1, $C_{-1}C_1$, $T_{-1}T_0$) are adopted in closed tracks of simplified and traditional Chinese. Our results of the closed tracks are described in Table 2.

In our open tracks of simplified Chinese, we used six word-position tag set: B, B2, B3, M, E, S and seven templates same with closed tracks. Tag set and templates used in open tracks of traditional Chinese are same with closed tracks, too. In open tracks of traditional Chinese, we trained the combination of CityU2005 and corpus from this conference with CRFs model. The results of open tracks are shown in Table 3.

Talbe 2 Our results of closed tracks

corpuses	domains	*R*	*P*	*F1*	*OOV RR*	*IV RR*
simplified	Literature(A)	0.908	0.918	0.913	0.556	0.935
	Computer science(B)	0.89	0.908	0.899	0.592	0.943
	Medicine(C)	0.902	0.907	0.904	0.633	0.935
	Finance(D)	0.925	0.938	0.931	0.664	0.95
traditional	Literature(A)	0.888	0.905	0.896	0.728	0.904
	Computer(B)	0.908	0.931	0.919	0.684	0.931
	Medicine(C)	0.905	0.924	0.914	0.725	0.919
	Finance(D)	0.891	0.912	0.901	0.676	0.907

Table 3 Our results of open tracks

corpuses	domains	*R*	*P*	*F1*	*OOV RR*	*IV RR*
simplified	Literature(A)	0.908	0.916	0.912	0.535	0.936
	Computer science(B)	0.893	0.908	0.9	0.607	0.944
	Medicine(C)	0.904	0.906	0.905	0.635	0.937
	Finance(D)	0.925	0.937	0.931	0.669	0.95
traditional	Literature(A)	0.905	0.9	0.902	0.775	0.918
	Computer(B)	0.911	0.924	0.918	0.698	0.933
	Medicine(C)	0.903	0.903	0.903	0.729	0.917
	Finance(D)	0.903	0.916	0.91	0.721	0.916

4 Conclusion

As a fundamental task in Chinese information processing, Chinese segmentation gained more eyes in recent years and character-based tagging becomes the main segmentation technology. This paper describes our Chinese word segmentation system for CIPS-SIGHAN 2010. Then we present our word-position tag set and feature templates used in closed tracks and change of these parameters in open tracks. Finally, we report the results of the evaluation.

Acknowledgments

We would like to thank the anonymous reviewers for their helpful comments and suggestions.

References

Huang Changning, Zhao Hai. 2007. *Chinese word segmentation: A decade review. Journal of Chinese Information Processing,* 2007, 21(3):8-19.

Huang Changning, Zhao Hai. 2006. *Character-based tagging: A new method for Chinese word segmentation.* In *Proceedings of Chinese Information Processing Society 25 Annual Conference.* Beijing, China: Tsinghua University Press, 2006:53-63.

Jiang Wei, Wang Xiaolong, Guan Yi. 2007. *Research on Chinese Lexical Analysis System by Fusing Multiple Knowledge Sources. Chinese Journal of Computers*, 2007，30(1):137-145.

Liu Qun, Zhang Huaping, Yu Hongkui. 2004. *Chinese lexical analysis using cascaded hidden Markov model. Journal of Computer Research and Development*, 2004, 41(8):1421-1429.

Lafferty J, Pereira F, McCallum A. 2001. *Conditional random fields: probabilistic models for segmenting and labeling sequence data. In Proceedings of 18th International Conference on Machine Learning*, 2001:282-289.

Song Yan, Cai Dongfeng, Zhang Guiping. 2009. *Approach to Chinese word segmentation based on character-word joint decoding. Journal of Software*, 2009,20(9):2366-2375.

Xue N W, Converse S P. 2002. *Combining classifiers for Chinese word segmentation. In Proceedings of the First SIGHAN Workshop on Chinese Language Processing*. Taipei , Taiwan, China: AS Press, 2002：20-27.

Zhao Hai, Jie Chunyu. 2007. *Effective subsequence-based tagging for Chinese word segmentation. Journal of Chinese Information Processing*, 2007,21(5):8-13.

Chinese Syntactic Parsing Evaluation

Qiang Zhou
Center for Speech and Language Tech.
Research Institute of Information Tech.
Tsinghua University
zq-lxd@tsinghua.edu.cn

Jingbo Zhu
Natural Language Processing Lab.
Northeastern University
zhujingbo@mail.neu.edu.cn

Abstract

The paper introduced the task designing ideas, data preparation methods, evaluation metrics and results of the second Chinese syntactic parsing evaluation (CIPS-Bakeoff-ParsEval-2010) jointed with SIGHAN Bakeoff tasks.

1 Introduction

Syntactic parsing is an important technique in the research area of natural language processing. The evaluation-driven methodology is a good way to spur the its development. Two main parts of the method are a benchmark database and several well-designed evaluation metrics. Its feasibility has been proven in the English language.

After the release of the Penn Treebank (PTB) (Marcus et al., 1993) and the PARSEVAL metrics (Black et al., 1991), some new corpus-based syntactic parsing techniques were explored in the English language. Based on them, many state-of-art English parser were built, including the well-known Collins parser (Collins, 2003), Charniak parser (Charniak and Johnson, 2005) and Berkeley parser (Petrov and Klein, 2007). By automatically transforming the constituent structure trees annotated in PTB to other linguistic formalisms, such as dependency grammar, and combinatory categorical grammar (Hockenmaier and Steedman, 2007), many syntactic parser other than the CFG formalism were also developed. These include Malt Parser (Nivre et al., 2007), MSTParser (McDonald et al., 2005), Stanford Parser (Klein and Manning, 2003) and C&C Parser (Clark and Curran, 2007).

Based on the Penn Chinese Treebank (CTB) (Xue et al., 2002) developed on the similar annotation scheme of PTB, these parsing techniques were also transferred to the Chinese language. (Levy and Manning, 2003) explored the feasibility of applying lexicalized PCFG in Chinese. (Li et al., 2010) proposed a joint syntactic and semantic model for parsing Chinese. But till now, there is not a good Chinese parser whose performance can approach the state-of-art English parser. It is still an open challenge for parsing Chinese sentences due to some special characteristics of the Chinese language. We need to find a suitable benchmark database and evaluation metrics for the Chinese language.

Last year, we organized the first Chinese syntactic parsing evaluation --- CIPS-ParsEval-2009 (Zhou and Zhu, 2009). Five Chinese parsing tasks were designed as follows:

- Task 1: Part-of-speech (POS) tagging;
- Task 2: Base chunk (BC) parsing
- Task 3: Functional chunk (FC) parsing
- Task 4: Event description clause (EDC) recognition
- Task 5: Constituent parsing in EDCs

They cover different levels of Chinese syntactic parsing, including POS tagging (Task 1), shallow parsing (Task 2 & 3), complex sentence splitting (Task 4) and constituent tree parsing (Task 5). The news and academic articles annotated in the Tsinghua Chinese Treebank (TCT ver1.0) were used to build different gold-standard data for them. Some detailed information about CIPS-ParsEval-2009 can be found in (Zhou and Li, 2009).

This evaluation found the following difficult points for Chinese syntactic parsing.

1) There are two difficulties in Chinese POS tagging. One is the nominal verbs. The POS accuracy of them is about 17% lower than the overall accuracy. The other is the unknown

words. The POS accuracy of them is about 40-10% lower than the overall accuracy.

2) The chunks with complex internal structures show poor performance in two chunking tasks. How to recognize them correctly needs more lexical semantic knowledge.

3) The joint recognition of constituent tag and head position show poor performance in the constituent parsing task of EDCs.

Therefore, the second Chinese syntactic parsing evaluation (CIPS-Bakeoff-ParsEval-2010) jointed with SIGHAN Bakeoff tasks was proposed to deal with these problems. Some new designing ideas are as follows:

1) We use the segments sentences as the input of the syntactic parser to test the effects of POS tagging for Chinese parsing.

2) We design a new metric to evaluate performance of event construction recognition in a constituent parser of EDCs.

3) We try to evaluate the performance of event relation recognition in Chinese complex sentence.

In the following sections, we will introduce the task designing ideas, data preparation methods, evaluation metrics and results of the evaluation.

2 Task description

For the syntactic parsing task (Task 2) of the CIPS-Bakeoff-2010, we designed two sub-tasks:

Task 2-1: Parsing the syntactic trees in Chinese event description clauses

Task 2-2: Parsing the syntactic trees in Chinese sentences.

Each subtask is separated as close and open track. In the close track, only the provided training data can be used to build the parsing model. In the open track, other outside language resources can be freely used.

We will give two examples to show the detailed goals of these two sub-tasks:

1) Task 2-1

Input: a Chinese event description clause with correct word segmentation annotations

- 沿途 ， 我们 不时 见到 因 更新 而 伐 倒 的 树木 ， 因 修 路 需 伐倒 的 树木

Ouput: a syntactic parsing tree of the EDC with appropriate constitutent tag, head position and POS tag annotations.

- [dj-2 沿途/s ，/wP [dj-1 我们/rNP [vp-1 不时/d [vp-0 见到/v [np-0-2 [np-2 [vp-1 [pp-1 因/p 更新/v] [vp-1 而/cC 伐倒/v]] 的/uJDE 树木/n] ，/wP [np-2 [vp-1 [pp-1 因/p [vp-0 修/v 路/n]] [vp-1 需/vM 伐倒/v]] 的/uJDE 树木/n]]]]]][1]

2) Task 2-2

Input: a Chinese sentence with correct word segmentation annotations

- 沿途 ， 我们 不时 见到 因 更新 而 伐 倒 的 树木 ， 因 修 路 需 伐倒 的 树 木 ， 都 是 有用 之 材 ； 运送 树木 的 货车 、 拖拉机 ， 南来北往 。

Output: a syntactic parsing tree of the sentence with appropriate constitute tag and POS tag annotations.

- [zj [fj [fj [dj 沿途/s ，/wP [dj 我们/rNP [vp 不时/d [vp 见到/v [np [np [vp [pp 因/p 更新/v] [vp 而/cC 伐倒/v]] 的 /uJDE 树木/n] ，/wP [np [vp [pp 因/p [vp 修/v 路/n]] [vp 需/vM 伐倒/v]] 的/uJDE 树木/n]]]]]]，/wP [vp 都 /d [vp 是/v [np 有用/a 之/uJDE 材 /n]]]] ；/wP [dj [np [vp 运送/v 树木 /n] 的/uJDE [np 货车/n 、/wD 拖拉 机/n]] ，/wP 南来北往/v]]。/wE]

We define a Chinese sentence as the Chinese word serials ending with period, question mark or exclamation mark in the Chinese text. Usually, a Chinese sentence can describe a complex situation with several inter-related events. It consists of several clauses separated by commas or semicolons to describe one or more detailed event content. We call these clauses as event description clauses.

We use the following example to explain the relationship between a Chinese sentence and

[1] Each bracketed constituent is annotated with constituent tag and head positions separated by '-'.
Constituent tags used in the sentence are: dj-simple sentence, vp-verb phrase, np-noun phrase, pp-preposition phrase.
POS tags used are: s-space noun, wP-comma, rNP-personal pronoun, d-adverb, v-verb, p-preposition, cC-conjunction, uJDE-particle, n-noun, vM-modality verb;

event description clauses.

- [沿途，我们见到因为更新而伐倒的树木，因为建筑需伐倒的树木]，[都是有用之材]；[运送树木的货车、拖拉机，南来北往]。 (1)

- [Along the way, we see the trees have been cut down for regeneration, and the trees needed to be cut for building]. [All of them are useful building material]. [We also see several freight trucks and tractors for carry away trees going south and north].

The sentence gives us several sequential situations through the vision changing along the author's journey way: Firstly, we see the trees that have been cut down. They are useful building material. Then, we see several trucks and tractors to carry away these trees. They are going south and north busily. All the above situations are described through three EDCs annotated with bracket pairs in the sentence.

Interestingly, in the corresponding English translation, the same situation is described through three English sentences with complete subject and predicate structures. They show difference event description characteristics of these two languages.

The Chinese author tends to describe a complex situation through a sentence. Many complex event relations are implicit in the structural sequences or semantic connections among the EDCs of the sentence. So many subjects or objects of an EDC can be easily omitted based on the adjacent contexts.

The English author tends to describe a complex situation through several sentences. Each sentence can give a complete description of an event through the subject and predicate structure. The event relations are directly set through the paragraph structures and conjunctions.

The distinction between Chinese sentence and EDC can make us focus on different evaluation emphasis in the CIPS-Bakeoff-2010 section.

For an EDC, we can focus on the parsing performance of event content recognition. So we design a special metric to evaluate the recall of the event recognition based on the syntactic parsing results.

For a sentence, we can focus on the parsing performance of event relation recognition. So we separate the simple and complex sentence constitutes and give different evaluation metrics for them.

Some detailed designations of the evaluation metrics can be found in section 4.

3 Data preparation

The evaluation data were extracted from Tsinghua Chinese Treebank (TCT) and PKU Chinese Treebank (PKU-CTB).

TCT (Zhou, 2004) adopted a new annotation scheme for Chinese Treebank. Under this scheme, every Chinese sentence will be annotated with a complete parse tree, where each non-terminal constituent is assigned with two tags. One is the syntactic constituent tag, such as noun phrase(np), verb phrase(vp), simple sentence(dj), complex sentence(fj), etc., which describes basic syntactic characteristics of a constituent in the parse tree. The other is the grammatical relation tag, which describes the internal structural relation of its sub-components, including the grammatical relations among different phrases and the event relations among different clauses. These two tag sets consist of 16 and 27 tags respectively.

Now we have two Chinese treebanks annotated under above scheme: (1) TCT version 1.0, which is a 1M words Chinese treebank covering a balanced collection of journalistic, literary, academic, and other documents; (2) TCT-2010, which consists of 100 journalistic annotated articles. The following is an annotated sentence under TCT scheme:

- [zj-XX [fj-LS [dj-ZW 我们/rN [vp-PO 问/v [dj-ZW [np-DZ 他/rN 自己/rN] [vp-PO 买/v 多少/m]]]] ，/， [dj-ZW 他/rN [vp-LW [vp-PO 凑近/v [sp-DZ 记者/n 面前/s]] [vp-PO 伸出/v [np-DZ [mp-DZ 4 /m 个/qN] 指头/n]]]]] 。/。] [2] (2)

PKU-CTB (Zhan et al., 2006) adopted a traditional syntactic annotation scheme. They annotated Chinese sentences with syntactic constitu-

---

[2] Some grammatical relation tags used in the sentence are as follows: LS—complex timing event relation, ZW—subject-predicate relation, DZ—modifier-head relation, PO—predicate-object relation.

ent and head position tags in a complete parse tree. The tag set consists of 22 constituent tags. Because every content word is directly annotated with suitable constituent tag, there are many unary phrases in PKU-CTB annotated sentences. Its current annotation scale is 881,771 Chinese words, 55264 sentences. The following is an annotated sentence under PKU-CTB scheme:

- (zj (!fj (!fj (!dj (np (vp (!v (建筑)) !np (!n (公司))) !vp (!vp (!v (进)) np (!n (区)))) wco (，) dj (np (ap (!b (有关)) !np (!n (部门))) !vp (dp (!d (先)) !vp (!vp (!vp (!v (送)) v (上)) np (qp (mp (!rm (这)) !q (些)) !np (np (!n (法规性)) !np (!n (文件))))))))) wco (，) vp (c (然后) !vp (!v (有) np (ap (!b (专门)) !np (!n (队伍))) vp (!vp (!v (进行)) vp (!vp (!v (监督)) vp (!v (检查)))))))) wfs (。)))[3] (3)

Due to the different annotation schemes and formats used in these two treebanks, we proposed the following strategies to build the gold-standard data set for Task 2-1 and Task 2-2:

1) Unify POS tag set

The PKU-CTB has 97 POS tags, and TCT has 70 POS tags. After analyzing these POS tags, we found most of them have same meanings. So we designed a unified POS tag set with 58 intersected tags. All the POS tags used in PKU-CTB and TCT can be automatically mapped to this unified tag set.

2) Transform PKU-CTB annotations

Firstly, we mapped the POS tags into the unified tag set, and transformed the word and POS tag format into TCT's format. Then, we deleted all unary constituents in PKU-CTB parse trees and transferred the constituent structures and tags into TCT's constituent tags. Finally, we manually proofread the transformed parse trees to modify some constituent structures that are inconsistent with TCT annotation scheme. About 5% constituents are modified.

3) Extract EDCs and event annotations from TCT

Based on the detailed grammatical relation tags annotated in TCT, we can easily extract each EDC for a TCT sentence (Zhou and Zhu, 2009). Then, we proposed an algorithm to extract different event constructions in each EDC and build a large scale Chinese event bank. It can be used as a gold-standard data to evaluation the event recognition performance of an automatic syntactic parser in Task 2-1.

An event construction is an event chunk serial controlled by an event target verb. It is a basic unit to describe event content. For example, for the first EDC extracted from the above sentence (1), we can obtain the follow four event constructions for the event target verb '见到', '伐倒', '修', and '伐倒'.

- [D-sp 沿途/s-@] ， /wP [S-np 我们/rNP-@] [D-dp 不时/d-@] [P-vp-Tgt 见到/v-@] [O-np 因/p 更新/v 而/cC 伐倒/v 的/uJDE 树木/n-@ ， /wP 因/p 修/v 路/n 需/vM 伐倒/v 的/uJDE 树木/n-@][4]
- [D-pp 因/p 更新/v-@] [P-vp-Tgt 需/vM 伐倒/v-@] 的/uJDE [H-np 树木/n-@] …
- … 因/p [P-vp-Tgt 修/v-@] [O-np 路/n-@] 需/vM 伐倒/v 的/uJDE 树木/n
- … [D-pp 因/p 修/v-@ 路/n] [P-vp-Tgt 需/vM 伐倒/v-@]的/uJDE [H-np 树木/n-@]

4) Obtain TCT constituent structure trees

We can easily select all syntactic constituent tags annotated in TCT sentences to build the gold-standard parsing trees for Task 2-2.

We mainly used the journalistic and academic texts annotated in TCT and PKU-CTB to build different training and test set for task 2-1 and 2-2. Table 1 summarizes current building status of these gold-standard data sets.

[3] The PKU-CTB uses the similar POS and constituent tags with TCT scheme. The exclamation symbol '!' is used to annotate the head of each constituent in the parse tree.

[4] Each event chunk is annotated with bracket pairs with functional and constituent tags. Some functional tags used in the EDCs are as follows: D—adverbial, S—subject, P—predicate, O—object. The constituent tags are same with that ones used in above parse tree. The head of each chunk is indicated through '-@'.

Data set	Source	Genre	Methods
2-1, TR	TCT ver1.0	News, Academy	POS unification, EDC and event extraction
2-1, TS	TCT-2010	News	POS unification, EDC and event extraction
2-2, TR	TCT ver1.0	News, Academy	POS unification, Parse tree extraction
2-2, TS	PKU-CTB	Academy	POS unification, annotation transformation

Table 1 Gold-standard data building status (TR=Training data, TS=Test data)

We selected all news and academic texts annotated in TCT ver1.0 to form the training set of Task 2-1 and 2-2. 1000 EDCs extracted from TCT-2010 were selected as the test set of Task 2-1. These sentences are extracted from the People's Daily corpus with the same source of TCT ver1.0. 1000 sentences extracted from PKU-CTB were selected as the test set of Task 2-2. Most of them are extracted from the technical reports or popular science articles. They have much more technical terms than the encyclopedic articles used in TCT ver1.0. Table 2 shows the basic statistics of all the training and test sets in Task 2.

Data set	Word Sum	Sent. Sum	Average Length
2-1, TR	425619	37219	11.44
2-1, TS	9182	1000	9.18
2-2, TR	481061	17529	27.44
2-2, TS	26381	1000	26.38

Table 2 Basic statistics of Task 2

4 Evaluation metrics

For Task 2-1, we designed three kinds of evaluation metrics:

1) POS accuracy (POS-A)

This metri is used to evaluate the performance of automatic POS tagging. Its computation formula is as follows:

- POS accuracy = (sum of words with correct POS tags) / (sum of words in gold-standard sentences) * 100%

The correctness criteria of POS tagging is as follows:

✧ The automatically assigned POS tag is same with the gold-standard one.

2) Constituent parsing evaluation

We selected three commonly-used metrics to evaluation the performance of constituent parsing: labeled precision, recall, and F1-score. Their computation formulas are as follows:

- Precision = (sum of correctly labeled constituents) / (sum of parsed constituents) * 100%
- Recall = (sum of correctly labeled constituents) / (sum of gold-standard constituents) *100%
- F1-score = 2*P*R / (P+R)

Two correctness criteria are used for constituent parsing evaluation:

✧ 'B+C' criteria: the boundaries and syntactic tags of the automatically parsed constituents must be same with the gold-standard ones.

✧ 'B+C+H' criteria: the boundaries, syntactic tags and head positions of the automatically parsed constituents must be same with the gold-standard ones.

3) Event recognition evaluation

We only considered the recognition recall of each event construction annotated in the event bank, due to the current parsing status of Task 2-1 output. For each event target verb annotated in the event bank, we computed their Micro and Macro average recognition recall. The computation formulas are as follows:

- Micro Recall = (sum of all correctly recognized event constructions) / (sum of all gold standard event constructions) * 100%
- Macro Recall = (sum of Micro-R of each event target verb) / (sum of event target verbs in gold-standard set)

The correctness criteria of event recognition should consider following two matching conditions:

Condition 1: Each event chunk in a gold-standard event construction should have a corresponding constituent in the automatic parse tree. For the single-word chunk, the automatically assigned POS tag should be same with the gold standard one. For the multiword chunk, the boundary, syntactic tag and head positions of the automatically parsed constituent should be same with the gold-standard ones. Meanwhile, the corresponding constituents should have the same layout sequences with the gold standard event construction.

Condition 2: All event-chunk-corresponding constituents should have a common ancestor node in the parse tree. One of the left and right boundaries of the ancestor node should be same with the left and right boundaries of the corresponding event construction.

For Task 2-2, we design two kinds of evaluation metrics:

1) POS accuracy (POS-A)

This index is used to evaluate the performance of automatic POS tagging. Its formula and correctness criteria are same with the above definitions of Task 2-1.

2) Constituent parsing evaluation

To evaluate the parsing performance of event relation recognition in complex Chinese sentences, we firstly divided all parsed constituents into following two parts:

- Constituent of complex sentence (C_S), whose tag is 'fj';
- Constituents in simple sentence (S_S), whose tags are belong to the tag set {dj, vp, ap, np, sp, tp, mp, mbar, dp, pp, bp}.

Then we computed the labeled precision, recall and F1-socre of these two parts and obtain the arithmetic mean of these two F1-score as the final ranking index. Their computation formulas of each part are as follows:

- Precision = (sum of correctly labeled constituents in one part) / (sum of parsed constituents in the part) * 100%
- Recall = (sum of correctly labeled constituents in one part) / (sum of gold-standard constituents in the part) *100%
- F1-score = 2*P*R / (P+R)
- Total F1-Score = (C_S F1 + S_S F1) / 2

We use the above 'B+C' correctness criteria for constituent evaluation in Task 2-2.

ID	Participants	Task 2-1			Task 2-2		
		TPI	Open	close	TPI	open	Close
01	School of Computer Sci. and Tech., Harbin Institute of Technology	Y			Y		1
02	Knowledge Engineering Research Center, Shenyang Aerospace Univ.	Y		3	Y		2
03	Dalian University of Technology	Y		1	Y		1
04	National Laboratory of Pattern Recognition Institute of Automation, Chinese Academy of Science	Y	2	2	Y	4	2
05	Beijing University of Posts and Telecommunications	Y		2	Y		
06	University of Science and Technology of China	Y			Y		
07	Dept. of Computer Science and Technology, Shanghai Jiao Tong University,	Y		3	Y		3
08	Soochow University	Y			Y		
09	Harbin Institute of Technology	Y		1	Y		
10	German Research Center for Artificial Intelligence	Y	1	1	Y	1	
11	China Center for Information Industry Development	N			Y	1	
12	City University of Hong Kong	Y			Y		
13	National Central University	Y			Y		
Total		12	3	13	13	6	9

Table 3 Result submission data of all participants in Task 2. (TPI=Take Part In)

5 Evaluation results

The Task 2 of CIPS-Bakeoff-2010 attracted 13 participants. Almost all of them took part in the two subtasks: Task 2-1 and 2-2. Only one participant took part in the Task 2-2 subtask alone.

Among them, 9 participants submitted parsing results. In Task 2-1, we received 16 parsing results, including 13 close track systems and 3 open track systems. In Task 2-2, we received 15 parsing results, including 9 close track systems and 6 open track systems. Table 3 shows the submission information of all participants of Task 2.

5.1 Task 2-1 analysis

We evaluated the parsing performance of EDC on the constituent and event level respectively. The constituent parsing evaluation only considers the parsing performance of one single constituent. The event recognition evaluation will consider the recognition performance of a complete event construction. So it can provide more useful reference information for event extraction application.

Table 5 and Table 6 show the evaluation results of constituent parsing in the close and open tracks respectively. In the close track, the best F1-score under 'B+C' criteria is 85.39%, while the best F1 score under 'B+C+H' criteria is 83.66%. Compared with the evaluation results of the task 5 in CIPS-ParEval-2009 under the similar training and test conditions (Zhou and Li, 2009), the performance of head identification is improved about 2%. Table 4 shows the detailed comparison data.

Rank	ID	'B+C'	'B+C+H'	POS-A
09-1	08	87.22	83.70	Gold
09-2	15	86.25	81.75	Gold
10-1	02	85.39	83.66	93.96
10-2	04	84.36	82.51	91.84

Table 4 F1 scores of the Top-2 single-model close-track systems in the ParsEval-2009 and ParsEval-2010.

Table 7 and Table 8 show the evaluation results of event recognition in the close and open tracks respectively. When we consider the complete event constructions contained in a parse tree, the best Macro-Recall is only about 71%. There are still lots of room to improve in the future.

ID	Sys-ID	Model	'B+C'			'B+C+H'			POS-A	Rank
			P	R	F1	P	R	F1		
02	SAU01	Single	85.42	85.35	85.39	83.69	83.63	83.66	93.96	1
02	SAU02	Single	85.02	85.11	85.06	83.21	83.31	83.26	93.96	2
04	a	Single	84.40	84.32	84.36	82.55	82.47	82.51	91.84	3
04	b	Single	83.79	83.74	83.76	81.82	81.78	81.80	91.67	4
10	DFKI_C	Single	82.93	82.85	82.89	80.54	80.46	80.50	81.99	5
02	SAU03	Single	80.28	79.31	79.79	78.55	77.61	78.08	93.93	6
07	b	Single	78.61	78.76	78.69	76.61	76.75	76.68	92.77	7
07	c	Single	77.78	78.13	77.96	75.78	76.13	75.95	92.77	8
05	BUPT	Single	74.86	76.05	75.45	71.06	72.20	71.63	87.00	9
05	BUPT	Multiple	74.48	75.64	75.05	70.72	71.81	71.26	87.00	10
03	DLUT	Single	71.42	71.19	71.30	69.22	69.00	69.11	86.69	11
09	InsunP	Single	70.69	70.48	70.58	67.07	66.87	66.97	77.87	12
07	a	Single	9.09	12.51	10.53	7.17	9.88	8.31	7.02	13

Table 5 Constituent parsing evaluation results of Task 2-1 (Close Track), ranked with 'B+C+H'- F1

ID	Sys-ID	Model	'B+C'			'B+C+H'			POS-A	Rank
			P	R	F1	P	R	F1		
04	a	Single	86.07	86.08	86.08	84.27	84.28	84.27	92.51	1
04	b	Single	83.79	83.74	83.76	81.82	81.78	81.80	91.67	2
10	DFKI_C	Single	82.37	83.05	82.71	79.99	80.65	80.32	81.87	3

Table 6 Constituent parsing evaluation results of Task 2-1 (Open Track), ranked with 'B+C+H'- F1

ID	Sys-ID	Model	Micro-R	Macro-R	POS-A	Rank
02	SAU01	Single	72.47	71.53	93.96	1
02	SAU02	Single	72.93	70.71	93.96	2
04	a	Single	67.37	65.05	91.84	3
04	b	Single	67.17	64.23	91.67	4
02	SAU03	Single	63.73	63.54	93.93	5
07	c	Single	63.14	62.48	92.77	6
07	b	Single	62.74	62.47	92.77	7
10	DFKI_C	Single	55.99	53.58	81.99	8
03	DLUT	Single	51.75	53.33	86.69	9
05	BUPT	Single	53.08	48.82	87.00	10
05	BUPT	Multiple	52.88	48.75	87.00	11
09	InsunP	Single	43.15	43.14	77.87	12
07	a	Single	1.13	0.79	7.02	13

Table 7 Event recognition evaluation results of Task 2-1 (Close Track), ranked with Macro-R

ID	Sys-ID	Model	Micro-R	Macro-R	POS-A	Rank
04	a	Single	70.62	69.33	92.51	1
04	b	Single	67.17	64.23	91.67	2
10	DFKI_C	Single	54.47	52.25	81.87	3

Table 8 Event recognition evaluation results of Task 2-1 (Open Track), ranked with Macro-R

5.2 Task 2-2 analysis

Table 9 and Table 10 show the evaluation results of constituent parsing in the close and open tracks of Task 2-2 respectively. In each track, the F1-score of the complex sentence recognition is about 5-6% lower than that of the constituents in simple sentences. It indicates the difficultness of event relation recognition in real world Chinese sentences. Some new features need to be explored for them.

Almost all the parsing performances of the systems in the open track are better than that ones in the close track. It indicates some outside language resources may useful for parsing performance improvement. Compared with the commonly-used English Treebank PTB with about 1M words, our current annotated data may be not enough to train a good Chinese parser. We may need to collect more useful treebank data in the future evaluation tasks.

The F1-scores of constituent parsing in simple sentences of Task 2-2 are still about 5-6% lower than that of EDC constituents under 'B+C' criteria in Task 2-1. It indicates some lower level errors may be propagated to up-level constituents during complex sentence parsing. How to restrict the error propagation chains is an interesting issue need to be explored.

5.3 POS tagging analysis

The best POS accuracy in Task 2-1 is 93.96%, approaching to the state-of-art performance of the Task 1 in CIPS-ParsEval-2009, under similar training and test conditions. But the POS accuracy in Task 2-2 is about 3-4% lower than it. A possible reason is that there are lots of unknown words in the test data of Task 2-2. Most of them are technical terms outside the training data lexicon. How to deal with the unknown words is still an open challenge for POS tagging.

6 Conclusions

The paper introduced the task designing ideas, data preparation methods, evaluation metrics and results of the second Chinese syntactic parsing evaluation jointed with SIGHAN Bakeoff tasks.

Some new contributions of the evaluation are as follows:

1) Set a new metric to evaluate the event construction recognition performance in the constituent parsing tree;

ID	Sys-ID	Model	Constituents in S_S			C_S constituent			Total	POS-A	Rank
			P	R	F1	P	R	F1	F1		
04	b	Single	77.79	77.47	77.63	69.55	76.50	72.86	75.24	88.79	1
04	a	Single	77.91	77.54	77.73	68.47	76.90	72.44	75.08	88.95	2
O2	SAU01	Single	78.64	78.73	78.69	70.22	71.62	70.91	74.80	91.05	3
O2	SAU02	Single	78.46	78.34	78.40	69.48	72.42	70.92	74.66	91.03	4
03	DLUT	Single	61.67	59.75	60.69	65.27	67.31	66.27	63.48	79.67	5
01	CHP	Single	70.20	69.64	69.92	53.95	59.47	56.58	63.25	89.62	6
07	b	Single	55.33	59.57	57.37	6.25	0.64	1.16	29.26	89.01	7
07	c	Single	52.57	57.69	55.01	7.47	1.68	2.74	28.88	89.01	8
07	a	Single	0.71	1.00	0.83	0.00	0.00	0.00	0.42	1.39	9

Table 9 Constituent parsing evaluation results of Task 2-2 (Close Track), ranked with Tot-F1 (S_S=simple sentence, C_S=complex sentence)

ID	Sys-ID	Model	Constituents in S_S			C_S constituent			Total	POS-A	Rank
			P	R	F1	P	R	F1	F1		
04	d	Single	80.04	79.68	79.86	70.11	76.50	73.17	76.51	89.59	1
04	a	Single	80.27	79.99	80.13	70.36	75.54	72.86	76.50	89.69	2
04	c	Single	80.25	79.95	80.10	70.40	75.30	72.77	76.44	89.78	3
04	b	Single	80.02	79.68	79.85	69.82	75.62	72.60	76.22	89.75	4
10	DFKI_C	Single	79.37	79.27	79.32	71.06	73.22	72.13	75.72	81.23	5
11*	CCID	Single	/	/	/	/	/	/	/	/	/

Table 10 Constituent parsing evaluation results of Task 2-2 (Open Track), ranked with Tot-F1 (S_S=simple sentence, C_S=complex sentence) There are some data format errors in the submitted results of CCID system (ID=11)

2) Set a separated metric to evaluate the event relation recognition performance in complex Chinese sentence.

Through this evaluation, we found:

1) The event construction recognition in a Chinese EDC is still a challenge. Some new techniques and machine learning models need to be explored for this task.
2) Compared with about 90% F1-score of the state-of-art English parser, the 75% F1-score of current Chinese parser is still on its primitive stage. There is a long way to go in the future.
3) The event relation recognition in real world complex Chinese sentences is a difficult problem. Some new features and methods need to be explored for it.

They lay good foundations for the new task designation in the future evaluation round.

Acknowledgements

Thanks Li Yemei for her hard work to organize the evaluation. Thanks Li Yanjiao and Li Yumei for their hard work to prepare the test data for the evaluation. Thanks Zhu Muhua for making the evaluation tools and processing all the submitted data. Thanks all participants of the evaluation.

The work was also supported by the research projects of National Science Foundation of China (Grant No. 60573185, 60873173) and National 863 High-Tech research projects (Grant No. 2007AA01Z173).

References

E. Black, S. Abney, et al. 1991. A Procedure for Quantitatively Comparing the Syntactic Coverage of English Grammars. In *Speech and natural language: proceedings of a workshop, held at Pacific Grove, California*, page 306.

E. Charniak and M. Johnson. 2005. Coarse-to-fine nbest parsing and MaxEnt discriminative reranking. In *Proc. of the 43rd Annual Meeting on Association for Computational Linguistics*, page 180.

S. Clark and J.R. Curran. 2007. Wide-coverage efficient statistical parsing with CCG and log-linear models. *Computational Linguistics*, 33(4):493–552.

D. Klein and C. Manning. 2003. Accurate Unlexicalized Parsing. In *Proc. of ACL-03.*

M. Collins. 2003. Head-driven statistical models for natural language parsing. *Computational linguistics*, 29(4):589–637.

J. Hockenmaier and M. Steedman. 2007. CCGbank: a corpus of CCG derivations and dependency structures extracted from the Penn Treebank. *Computational Linguistics*, 33(3):355–396.

R. Levy and C. Manning. (2003). Is it harder to parse Chinese, or the Chinese Treebank? In *Proc. of ACL-03.*

J. Li, G. Zhou, and H.T. Ng. 2010. Joint Syntactic and Semantic Parsing of Chinese. In *Proc. of the 48th Annual Meeting of the Association for Computational Linguistics*, pages 1108–1117.

R. McDonald, F. Pereira, K. Ribarov, and J. Hajic. 2005. Non-projective dependency parsing using spanning tree algorithms. In *Proc. of HLT/EMNLP*, pages 523–530.

Mitchell P.Marcus, Mary Ann Marcinkiewicz, and Beatrice Santorini. 1993. Building a Large Annotated Corpus of English: The Penn Treebank, *Computational Linguistics,* 19(2): 313-330

J. Nivre, J. Hall, J. Nilsson, el.al. 2007. Malt-Parser: A language-independent system for data driven dependency parsing. *Natural Language Engineering*, 13(02):95–135.

S. Petrov and D. Klein. 2007. Improved inference for unlexicalized parsing. In *Proc. of NAACL HLT 2007*, pages 404–411.

N. Xue, F. Chiou, and M. Palmer. 2002. Building a large-scale annotated Chinese corpus. In *Proc. of COLING-2002.*

Zhan Weidong, Chang Baobao, Dui Huiming, Zhang Huarui. 2006. Recent Developments in Chinese Corpus Research. *Presented in The 13th NIJL International Symposium, Language Corpora: Their Compliation and Application. Tokyo, Japan.*

Zhou Qiang, 2004. Chinese Treebank Annotation Scheme. *Journal of Chinese Information*, 18(4):1-8.

Zhou Qiang, Li Yuemei. 2009. Evaluation report of CIPS-ParsEval-2009. In *Proc. of First Workshop on Chinese Syntactic Parsing Evaluation, Beijing China.*

Zhou Qiang, Zhu Jingbo. 2009. Evaluation tasks and data preparation of CIPS-ParsEval-2009, http://www.ncmmsc.org/ CIPS-ParsEval-20

Discriminative Parse Reranking for Chinese with Homogeneous and Heterogeneous Annotations

Weiwei Sun[†‡] and **Rui Wang**[†] and **Yi Zhang**[†‡]
[†]Department of Computational Linguistics, Saarland University
[‡]German Research Center for Artificial Intelligence (DFKI)
D-66123, Saarbrücken, Germany
{wsun, rwang, yzhang}@coli.uni-saarland.de

Abstract

Discriminative parse reranking has been shown to be an effective technique to improve the generative parsing models. In this paper, we present a series of experiments on parsing the Tsinghua Chinese Treebank with hierarchically split-merge grammars and reranked with a perceptron-based discriminative model. In addition to the homogeneous annotation on TCT, we also incorporate the PCTB-based parsing result as heterogeneous annotation into the reranking feature model. The reranking model achieved 1.12% absolute improvement on F1 over the Berkeley parser on a development set. The head labels in Task 2.1 are annotated with a sequence labeling model. The system achieved 80.32 (B+C+H F1) in CIPS-SIGHAN-2010 Task 2.1 (Open Track) and 76.11 (Overall F1) in Task 2.2 (Open Track)[1].

1 Introduction

The data-driven approach to syntactic analysis of natural language has undergone revolutionary development in the last 15 years, ever since the first few large scale syntactically annotated corpora, i.e. treebanks, became publicly available in the mid-90s of the last century. One and a half decades later, treebanks remain to be an expensive type of language resources and only available for a small number of languages. The main issue that hinders large treebank development projects is the difficulties in creating a complete and consistent annotation guideline which then constitutes the very basis for sustainable parallel annotation and quality assurance. While traditional linguistic studies typically focus on either isolated language phenomena or limited interaction among a small groups of phenomena, the annotation scheme in treebanking project requires full coverage of language use in the source media, and proper treatment with an uniformed annotation format. Such high demand from the practical application of linguistic theory has given rise to a countless number of attempts and variations in the formalization frameworks. While the harsh natural selection set the bar high and many attempts failed to even reach the actual annotation phase, a handful highly competent grammar frameworks have given birth to several large scale treebanks.

The co-existence of multiple treebanks with heterogeneous annotation presents a new challenge to the consumers of such resources. The immediately relevant task is the automated syntactic analysis, or parsing. While many state-of-the-art statistical parsing systems are not bound to specific treebank annotation (assuming the formalism is predetermined independently), almost all of them assume homogeneous annotation in the training corpus. Therefore, such treebanks can not be simply put together when training the parser. One approach would be to convert them into an uniformed representation, although such conversion is usually difficult and by its nature error-

[1]This result is achieved with a bug-fixed version of the system and does not correspond to the numbers in the original evaluation report.

prune. The differences in annotations constitute different generative stories: i.e., when the parsing models are viewed as mechanisms to produce structured sentences, each treebank model will associate its own structure with the surface string independently. On the other hand, if the discriminative view is adopted, it is possible to use annotations in different treebanks as indication of goodness of the tree in the original annotation.

In this paper, we present a series of experiments to improve the Chinese parsing accuracy on the Tsinghua Chinese Treebank. First, we use coarse-to-fine parsing with hierarchically split-merge generative grammars to obtain a list of candidate trees in TCT annotation. A discriminative parse selection model is then used to rerank the list of candidates. The reranking model is trained with both homogeneous (TCT) and heterogeneous (PCTB) data. A sequence labeling system is used to annotate the heads in Task 2-1.

The remaining part of the paper is organized as follows. Section 2 reviews the relevant previous study on generative split-merge parsing and discriminative reranking models. Section 3 describes the work flow of our system participated in the CIPS-SIGHAN-2010 bake-off Task 2. Section 4 describes the detailed settings for the evaluation and the empirical results. Section 5 concludes the paper.

2 Background

Statistical constituent-based parsing is popularized through the decade-long competition on parsing the Wall Street Journal sections of the English Penn Treebank. While the evaluation setup has for long seen its limitation (a frustratingly low of 2% overall improvement throughout a decade of research), the value of newly proposed parsing methods along the way has clearly much more profound merits than the seemly trivial increase in evaluation figures. In this section we review two effective techniques in constituent-based statistical parsing, and their potential benefits in parsing Chinese.

Comparing with many other languages, statistical parsing for Chinese has reached early success, due to the fact that the language has relatively fixed word order and extremely poor inflectional morphology. Both facts allow the PCFG-based statistical modeling to perform well. On the other hand, the much higher ambiguity between basic word categories like nouns and verbs makes Chinese parsing interestingly different from the situation of English.

The type of treebank annotations also affects the performance of the parsing models. Taking the Penn Chinese Treebank (PCTB; Xue et al. (2005)) and Tsinghua Chinese Treebank (TCT; Zhou (2004)) as examples, PCTB is annotated with a much more detailed set of phrase categories, while TCT uses a more fine-grained POS tagset. The asymmetry in the annotation information is partially due to the difference of linguistic treatment. But more importantly, it shows that both treebanks have the potential of being refined with more detailed classification, on either phrasal or word categories. One data-driven approach to derive more fine-grained annotation is the hierarchically split-merge parsing (Petrov et al., 2006; Petrov and Klein, 2007), which induces subcategories from coarse-grained annotations through an expectation maximization procedure. In combination with the coarse-to-fine parsing strategy, efficient inference can be done with a cascade of grammars of different granularity. Such parsing models have reached (close to) state-of-the-art performance for many languages including Chinese and English.

Another effective technique to improve parsing results is discriminative reranking (Charniak and Johnson, 2005; Collins and Koo, 2005). While the generative models compose candidate parse trees, a discriminative reranker reorders the list of candidates in favor of those trees which maximizes the properties of being a good analysis. Such extra model refines the original scores assigned by the generative model by focusing its decisions on the fine details among already "good" candidates. Due to this nature, the set of features in the reranker focus on those global (and potentially long distance) properties which are difficult to model with the generative model. Also, since it is not necessary for the reranker to generate the candidate trees, one can easily integrate additional external information to help adjust the ranking of the analysis. In the following section, we will de-

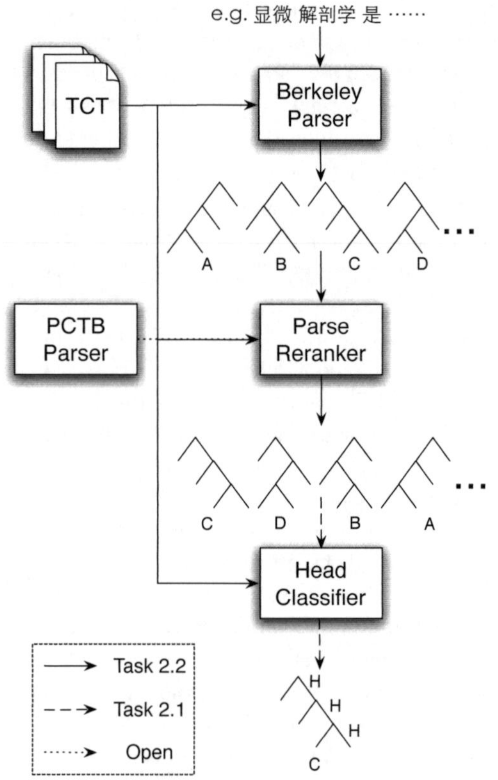

Figure 1: Workflow of the System

scribe the reranking model we developed for the CIPS-SIGHAN-2010 parsing tasks. We will also show how the heterogeneous parsing results can be integrated through the reranker to further improve the performance of the system.

3 System Description

In this section, we will present our approach in detail. The whole system consists of three main components, the Berkeley Parser, the Parse Reranker, and the Head Classifier. The workflow is shown in Figure 1. Firstly, we use the Berkeley Parser trained on the TCT to parse the input sentence and obtain a list of possible parses; then, all the parses[2] will be re-ranked by the Parse Reranker; and finally, the Head Classifer will annotate the head information for each constituent on the best parse tree. For parse reranking, we can extract features either from TCT-style parses or together with the PCTB-style parse of the same sentence. For example, we can check whether the boundary predictions given by the TCT parser are agreed by the PCTB parser. Since the PCTB parser is trained on a different treebank from TCT, our reranking model can be seen as a method to use a heterogenous resource. The best parse tree given by the Parse Reranker will be the result for Task 2.2; and the final output of the system will be the result for Task 2.1. Since we have already mentioned the Berkeley Parser in the related work, we will focus on the other two modules in the rest of this section.

[2]In practice, we only take the top n parses. We have different n values in the experiment settings, and n is up to 50.

Algorithm 1: The *Perptron* learning procedure.

input : Data $\{(\mathbf{x}_t, y_t), t = 1, 2, ..., m\}$
Initialize: $\mathbf{w} \leftarrow (0, ..., 0)$
for $i = 1, 2, ..., I$ **do**
  for $t =$ SHUFFLE $(1, ..., m)$ **do**
    $y_t^* = \arg\max_{y \in \mathrm{GEN}_n^{\mathrm{best}}(\mathbf{x}_t)} \mathbf{w}^\top \Phi(\mathbf{x}_t, y)$
    if $y_t^* \neq y_t$ **then**
      $\mathbf{w} \leftarrow \mathbf{w} + (\Phi(\mathbf{x}_t, y_t) - \Phi(\mathbf{x}_t, y_t^*))$
    end
  end
  $\mathbf{w}_i \leftarrow \mathbf{w}$
end
return $\mathbf{aw} = \frac{1}{I}\sum_{i=1}^{I} \mathbf{w}_i$

3.1 Parse Reranker

We follow Collins and Koo (2005)'s discriminative reranking model to score possible parse trees of each sentence given by the Berkeley Parser.

Previous research on English shows that structured perceptron (Collins, 2002) is one of the strongest machine learning algorithms for parse reranking (Collins and Duffy, 2002; Gao et al., 2007). In our system, we use the averaged perceptron algorithm to do parameter estimation. Algorithm 1 illustrates the learning procedure. The parameter vector $\mathbf{w}$ is initialized to $(0, ..., 0)$. The learner processes all the instances (t is from 1 to n) in each iteration (i). If current hypothesis ($\mathbf{w}$)

fails to predict $\mathbf{x}_t$, the learner update $\mathbf{w}$ through calculating the difference between $\Phi(\mathbf{x}_t, y_t^*)$ and $\Phi(\mathbf{x}_t, y_t)$. At the end of each iteration, the learner save the current model as $\mathbf{w} + i$, and finally all these models will be added up to get $\mathbf{aw}$.

3.2 Features

We use an example to show the features we extract in Figure 2.

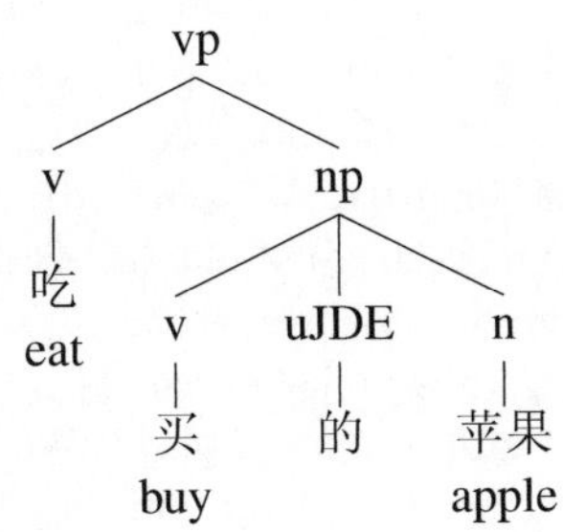

Figure 2: An Example

Rules The context-free rule itself: $\mathrm{np} \rightarrow \mathrm{v} + \mathrm{uJDE} + \mathrm{np}$.

Grandparent Rules Same as the Rules, but also including the nonterminal above the rule: $\mathrm{vp}(\mathrm{np} \rightarrow \mathrm{v} + \mathrm{uJDE} + \mathrm{np})$

Bigrams Pairs of nonterminals from the left to right of the the rule. The example rule would contribute the bigrams $\mathrm{np}(\mathrm{STOP}, \mathrm{v})$, $\mathrm{np}(\mathrm{v}, \mathrm{uJDE})$, $\mathrm{np}(\mathrm{uJDE}, \mathrm{np})$ and $\mathrm{np}(\mathrm{np}, \mathrm{STOP})$.

Grandparent Bigrams Same as Bigrams, but also including the nonterminal above the bigrams. For instance, $\mathrm{vp}(\mathrm{np}(\mathrm{STOP}, \mathrm{v}))$

Lexical Bigrams Same as Bigrams, but with the lexical heads of the two nonterminals also included. For instance, np(STOP,买).

Trigrams All trigrams within the rule. The example rule would contribute the trigrams $\mathrm{np}(\mathrm{STOP}, \mathrm{STOP}, \mathrm{v})$, $\mathrm{np}(\mathrm{STOP}, \mathrm{v}, \mathrm{uJDE})$, $\mathrm{np}(\mathrm{v}, \mathrm{uJDE}, \mathrm{np})$, $\mathrm{np}(\mathrm{uJDE}, \mathrm{np}, \mathrm{STOP})$ and $\mathrm{np}(\mathrm{np}, \mathrm{STOP}, \mathrm{STOP})$.

Combination of Boundary Words and Rules The first word and the rule (i.e. 买+($\mathrm{np} \rightarrow \mathrm{v} + \mathrm{uJDE} + \mathrm{np}$)), the last word and the rule one word before and the rule, one word after and the rule, the first word, the last word and the rule, and the first word's POS, last word's POS and the rule.

Combination of Boundary Words and Phrasal Category : Same as combination of boundary words and rules, but substitute the rule with the category of current phrases.

Two level Rules Same as Rules, but also including the entire rule above the rule: $\mathrm{vp} \rightarrow \mathrm{v} + (\mathrm{np} \rightarrow \mathrm{v} + \mathrm{uJDE} + \mathrm{np})$

Original Rank : The logarithm of the original rank of n-best candidates.

Affixation features In order to better handle unknown words, we also extract morphological features: character n-gram prefixes and suffixes for n up to 3. For example, for word/tag pair 自然环境/n, we add the following features: (prefix1,自,n), (prefix2,自然,n), (prefix3,自然环,n), (suffix1,境,n), (suffix2,环境,n), (suffix3,然环境,n).

Apart from training the reranking model using the same dataset (i.e. the TCT), we can also use another treebank (e.g. the PCTB). Although they have quite different annotations as well as the data source, it would still be interesting to see whether a heterogenous resource is helpful with the parse reranking.

Consist Category If a phrase is also analyzed as one phrase by the PCTB parser, both the TCT and PCTB categories are used as two individual features. The combination of the two categories are also used.

Inconsist Category If a phrase is not analyzed as one phrase by the PCTB parser, the TCT category is used as a feature.

Number of Consist and Inconsist phrases The two number are used as two individual featuers. We also use the ratio of the number of consist phrases and inconsist phrase (we add 0.1 to each number for smoothing), the ratio of the number of consist/inconsist phrases and the length of the current sentence.

POS Tags For each word, the combination of TCT and PCTB POS tags (with or without word content) are used.

3.3 Head Classifier

Following (Song and Kit, 2009), we apply a sequence tagging method to find head constituents. We suggest readers to refer to the original paper for details of the method. However, since the feature set is different, we give the discription of them in this paper. To predict whether current phrase is a head phrase of its parent, we use the same example above (Figure 2) for convenience. If we consider np as our current phrase, the following features are extracted,

Rules The generative rule, $\mathrm{vp} \rightarrow \mathrm{v} + (\mathrm{np})$.

Category of the Current Phrase and its Parent np, vp, and $(\mathrm{np}, \mathrm{vp})$.

Bigrams and Trigrams $(\mathrm{v}, \mathrm{np})$, $(\mathrm{np}, \mathrm{STOP})$, $(\mathrm{STOP}, \mathrm{v}, \mathrm{np})$, and $(\mathrm{np}, \mathrm{STOP}, \mathrm{STOP})$.

Parent Bigrams and Trigrams $\mathrm{vp}(\mathrm{v}, \mathrm{np})$, $\mathrm{vp}(\mathrm{np}, \mathrm{STOP})$, $\mathrm{vp}(\mathrm{STOP}, \mathrm{v}, \mathrm{np})$, $\mathrm{vp}(\mathrm{np}, \mathrm{STOP}, \mathrm{STOP})$.

Lexical Unigram The first word 买, the last word 苹果, and together with the parent, (vp,买) and (vp,苹果)

4 Evaluation

4.1 Datasets

The dataset used in the CIPS-ParsEval-2010 evaluation is converted from the Tsinghua Chinese Treebank (TCT). There are two subtasks: (1) event description sub-sentence analysis and (2) complete sentence parsing. On the assumption that the boundaries and relations between these event description units are determined separately, the first task aims to identify the local fine-grained syntactic structures. The goal of the second task is to evaluate the performance of the automatic parsers on complete sentences in real texts. The training dataset is a mixture of several genres, including newspaper texts, encyclopedic texts and novel texts.

The annotation in the dataset is different to the other frequently used Chinese treebank (i.e. PCTB) Whereas TCT annotation strongly reflects early descriptive linguistics, PCTB draws primarily on Government-Binding (GB) theory from 1980s. PCTB annotation differs from TCT annotation from many perspectives:

- TCT and PCTB have different segmentation standards.
- TCT is somehow branching-rich annotation, while PCTB annotation is category-rich. Specifically the topological tree structures is more detailed in TCT, and there are not many flat structures. However constituents are detailed classified, namely the number of phrasal categories is small. On the contrary, though flat structures are very common in PCTB, the categorization of phrases is fine-grained. In addition, PCTB contains functional information. Function tags appended to constituent labels are used to indicate additional syntactic or semantic information.
- TCT contains head indices, making head identification of each constituent an important goal of task 1.
- Following the GB theory, PCTB assume there are *movement*s, so there are empty category annotation. Because of different theoretical foundations, there are different explanations for a series of linguistic phenomena such as the usage of function word "的".

In the reranking experiments, we also use a parser trained on PCTB to provide more syntactic clues.

4.2 Setting

In order to gain a representative set of training data, we use cross-validation scheme described in (Collins, 2000). The dataset is a mixture of three genres. We equally split every genre data into 10 subsets, and collect three subset of different genres as one fold of the whole data. In this way, we can divide the whole data into 10 balanced subsets. For each fold data, a complement parser is trained using all other data to produce multiple hypotheses for each sentence. This cross-validation

n	1	2	5	10	20	30	40	50
F1	79.97	81.62	83.51	84.63	85.59	86.07	86.38	86.60

Table 1: Upper bound of f-score as a function of number n of n-best parses.

scheme can prevent the initial model from being unrealistically "good" on the training sentences. We use the first 9 folds as training data and the last fold as development data for the following experiments. For the final submission of the evaluation task, we re-train a reranking model using all 10 folds data. All reranking models are trained with 30 iterations.

For parsing experiments, we use the Berkeley parser[3]. All parsers are trained with 5 iterations of split, merge, smooth. To produce PCTB-style analysis, we train the Berkeley parse with PCTB 5.0 data that contains 18804 sentences and 508764 words. For the evaluation of development experiments, we used the EVALB tool[4] for evaluation, and used labeled recall (LR), labeled precision (LP) and F1 score (which is the harmonic mean of LR and LP) to measure accuracy.

For the head classification, we use SVM^{hmm}[5], an implementation of structural SVMs for sequence tagging. The main setting of learning parameter is C that trades off margin size and training error. In our experiments, the head classification is not sensitive to this parameter and we set it to 1 for all experiments reported. For the kernel function setting, we use the simplest linear kernel.

4.3 Results

4.3.1 Upper Bound of Reranking

The upper bound of n-best parse reranking is shown in Table 1. From the 1-best result we see that the base accuracy of the parser is 79.97. 2-best and 10-best show promising oracle-rate improvements. After that things start to slow down, and we achieve an oracle rate of 86.60 at 50-best.

4.3.2 Reranking Using Homogeneous Data

Table 2 summarizes the performance of the basic reranking model. It is evaluated on short sentences (less than 40 words) from the development data of the task 2. When 40 reranking candidates are used, the model gives a 0.76% absolute improvement over the basic Berkeley parser.

	POS(%)	LP(%)	LR(%)	F1
Baseline	93.59	85.60	85.36	85.48
$n = 2$	93.66	85.84	85.54	85.69
$n = 5$	93.62	86.04	85.73	85.88
$n = 10$	93.66	86.22	85.85	86.04
$n = 20$	93.70	86.19	85.87	86.03
$n = 30$	93.70	86.32	86.00	86.16
$n = 40$	93.76	86.40	86.09	86.24
$n = 50$	93.73	86.10	85.81	85.96

Table 2: Reranking performance with different number of parse candidates on the sentences that contain no more than 40 words in the development data.

4.3.3 Reranking Using Heterogeneous Data

Table 3 summarizes the reranking performance using PCTB data. It is also evaluated on short sentences of the task 2. When 30 reranking candidates are used, the model gives a 1.12% absolute improvement over the Berkeley parser. Comparison of Table 2 and 3 shows an improvement by using heterogeneous data.

	POS(%)	LP(%)	LR(%)	F1
$n = 2$	93.70	85.98	85.67	85.82
$n = 5$	93.75	86.52	86.19	86.35
$n = 10$	93.77	86.64	86.29	86.47
$n = 20$	93.79	86.71	86.34	86.53
$n = 30$	93.80	86.72	86.48	86.60
$n = 40$	93.80	86.54	86.22	86.38
$n = 50$	93.89	86.73	86.41	86.57

Table 3: Reranking performance with different number of parse candidates on the sentences that contain no more than 40 words in the development data.

[3] http://code.google.com/p/berkeleyparser/

[4] http://nlp.cs.nyu.edu/evalb/

[5] http://www.cs.cornell.edu/People/tj/svm_light/svm_hmm.html

Task 1	"B+C"-P	"B+C"-R	"B+C"-F1	"B+C+H"-P	"B+C+H"-R	"B+C+H"-F1	POS
Old data	82.37	83.05	82.71	79.99	80.65	80.32	81.87

Table 4: Final results of task 1.

Task 2	dj-P	dj-R	dj-F1	fj-P	fj-R	fj-F1	Avg.	POS
Old data	79.37	79.27	79.32	71.06	73.22	72.13	75.72	81.23
New data	79.60	79.13	79.36	70.01	75.94	72.85	76.11	89.05

Table 5: Final results of task 2.

4.3.4 Head Classification

The head classification performance is evaluated using gold-standard syntactic trees. For each constituent in a gold parse tree, a structured classifier is trained to predict whether it is a head constituent of its parent. Table 6 shows the overall performance of head classification. We can see that the head classification can achieve a high performance.

P(%)	R(%)	$F_{\beta=1}$
98.59%	98.20%	98.39

Table 6: Head classification performance with gold trees on the development data.

4.3.5 Final Result

Table 4 and 5 summarize the final results. Here we use the reranking model with heterogeneous data. The second line of Table 5 shows the offical final results. In this submission, we trained a model using an old version of training data. Note that, the standard of POS tags of the "old" version is different from the latest version which is also used as test data. For example, the name of some tags are changed. The third line of Table 4[6] shows the results predicted by the newest data[7]. This result is comparable to other systems.

5 Conclusion

In this paper, we described our participation of the CIPS-SIGHAN-2010 parsing task. The generative coarse-to-fine parsing model is integrated with a discriminative parse reranking model, as well as a head classifier based on sequence labeling. We use the perceptron algorithm to train the reranking models and experiment with both homogenous and heterogenous data. The results show improvements over the baseline in both cases.

[6]There are two sentences that are not parsed by the Berkeley parser. We use a simple strategy to solve this problem: We first roughly segment the sentence according to punctuation; Then the parsed sub-sentences are merged as a single *zj*.

[7]We would like to thank the organizer to re-test our new submission.

Acknowledgments

The first author is supported by the German Academic Exchange Service (DAAD). The second author is supported by the PIRE scholarship program; the third author thanks DFKI and the Cluster of Excellence on Multimodal Computing and Interaction for their support of the work.

References

Charniak, E. and M Johnson. 2005. oarse-to-fine n-best parsing and maxent discriminative reranking. In *Proceedings of ACL*, pages 173–180.

Collins, Michael and Nigel Duffy. 2002. New ranking algorithms for parsing and tagging: Kernels over discrete structures, and the voted perceptron. In *Proceedings of 40th Annual Meeting of the Association for Computational Linguistics*, pages 263–270, Philadelphia, Pennsylvania, USA, July. Association for Computational Linguistics.

Collins, Michael and Terry Koo. 2005. Discriminative reranking for natural language parsing. In *Computational Linguistics*, volume 31(1), pages 25–69.

Collins, Michael. 2000. Discriminative reranking for natural language parsing. In *Computational Linguistics*, pages 175–182. Morgan Kaufmann.

Collins, Michael. 2002. Discriminative training methods for hidden markov models: theory and experiments with perceptron algorithms. In *EMNLP '02:*

Proceedings of the ACL-02 conference on Empirical methods in natural language processing, pages 1–8, Morristown, NJ, USA. Association for Computational Linguistics.

Gao, Jianfeng, Galen Andrew, Mark Johnson, and Kristina Toutanova. 2007. A comparative study of parameter estimation methods for statistical natural language processing. In *Proceedings of the 45th Annual Meeting of the Association of Computational Linguistics*, pages 824–831, Prague, Czech Republic, June. Association for Computational Linguistics.

Petrov, S. and D. Klein. 2007. Improved inference for unlexicalized parsing. In *Proceedings of HLT-NAACL-2007*, Rochester, NY, USA, April.

Petrov, Slav, Leon Barrett, Romain Thibaux, and Dan Klein. 2006. Learning accurate, compact, and interpretable tree annotation. In *Proceedings of the 21st International Conference on Computational Linguistics and 44th Annual Meeting of the Association for Computational Linguistics*, pages 433–440, Sydney, Australia, July. Association for Computational Linguistics.

Song, Yan and Chunyu Kit. 2009. Pcfg parsing with crf tagging for head recognition. In *Proceedings of the CIPS-ParsEval-2009*.

Xue, Nianwen, Fei Xia, Fu-Dong Chiou, and Martha Palmer. 2005. The penn chinese treebank: Phrase structure annotation of a large corpus. *Natural Language Engineering*, 11(2):207–238.

Zhou, Qiang. 2004. Annotation scheme for chinese treebank (in chinese). *Journal of Chinese Information Processing*, 18(4):1–8.

The SAU Report for the 1st CIPS-SIGHAN-ParsEval-2010

Qiaoli Zhou **Wenjing Lang** **Yingying Wang** **Yan Wang** **Dongfeng Cai**

Knowledge Engineering Research Center,Shenyang Aerospace University,Shenyang,China

Qiaoli_z@yahoo.com.cn

Abstract

This paper presents our work for participation in the 2010 CIPS-SIGHAN evaluation on two tasks which are Event Description Sub-sentence (EDSs) Analysis and Complete Sentence (CS) Parsing in Chinese Parsing. The paper describes the implementation of our system as well as the results we have achieved and the analysis.

1 Introduction

The paper describes the parsing system of SAU in 1st CLPS-SIGHAN evaluation task 2. We participate in two tasks - EDS Analysis and CS Parsing. The testing set only provides segmentation results, therefore, we divide our system into the following subsystems: (1) Part-of-Speech (POS) tagging system, we mainly make use of Conditional Random Fields (CRFs) model for POS tagging; (2) parsing system, the paper adopts divide-and-conquer strategy to parsing, which uses CCRFs model for parsing and adopts searching algorithm to build trees in decoding; (3) head recognition system, which also makes use of CCRFs model.

The rest of the paper is organized as follows: Section 2 describes the POS tagging system; Section 3 describes the structure of our parsing system; Section 4 describes head recognition system in parsing tree; Section 5 presents the results of our system and the analysis; Section 6 concludes the paper.

2 Part-of-Speech Tagging

We use CRFs model and post-processing method for POS tagging. In the first step, we tag POS based on CRFs. The second step is the post-processing after tagging, which is correcting by using dictionary drawn from training set. The system architecture of POS tagging is shown in Figure 1.

2.1 Features

Feature selection significantly influences the performance of CRFs. We use the following features in our system.

Atom Template
word(-2) , word(-1) , word(0) , word(1) , word(2) prefix(word (0)) ,suffix(word(0)) includeDot1(word (0)) includeDot2(word (0))
Complex Template
word(-1)& word(0) ， word(0)& word(1) word(0)& prefix(word (0)) word(0)& suffix(word(0)) word(0)& includeDot1(word (0)) word(0)& includeDot2(word (0))

Table 1: Feature templates used in POS tagger. word(i) represents the ith word, prefix(word (i)) represents the first character of the ith word, suffix(word (i)) represents the last character of the ith word, ncludeDot1(word (i)) represents the ith word containing '· ' or not, and includeDot2(word (i)) represnts the ith word containing '.' or not.

2.2 Post-processing

The post-processing module adopts the following processing by analyzing the errors from tagging result based on CRFs. We firstly need to build two dictionaries which are single class word dictionary and ambiguity word dictionary before the post-processing. The single class word dictionary and ambiguity word dictionary are built by drawing from training set.

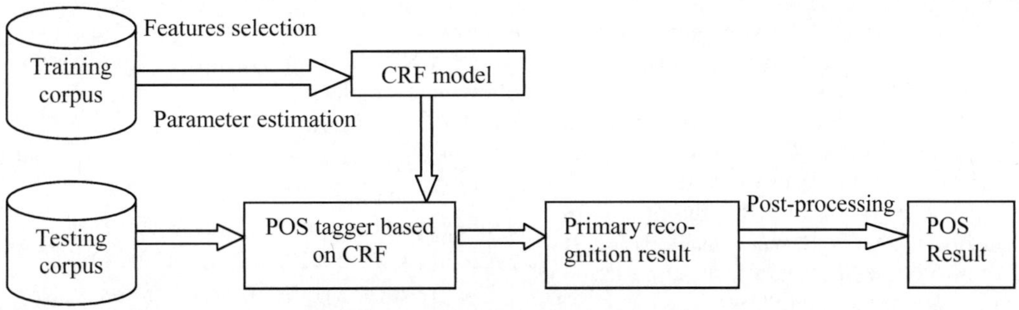

Figure 1: System architecture of POS tagging

The single class word is the word having single POS in training set, and the ambiguity word is the word having multi POS in training set. Besides, we build rules for words with distinctive features aiming at correcting errors, such as "的", numbers and English characters, etc.

Figure 2 shows the post-processing step after POS tagging by CRFs model. As shown in Figure 2, we respectively post-process single class words and ambiguity words according to CRF score.

(1) Single class word processing module

The post-processing of single class words consults the single class word dictionary and CRFs score. When the score from CRFs is higher than 0.9, we take the POS from CRFs as the final POS; otherwise, POS of the word is corrected by the POS in the single class word dictionary.

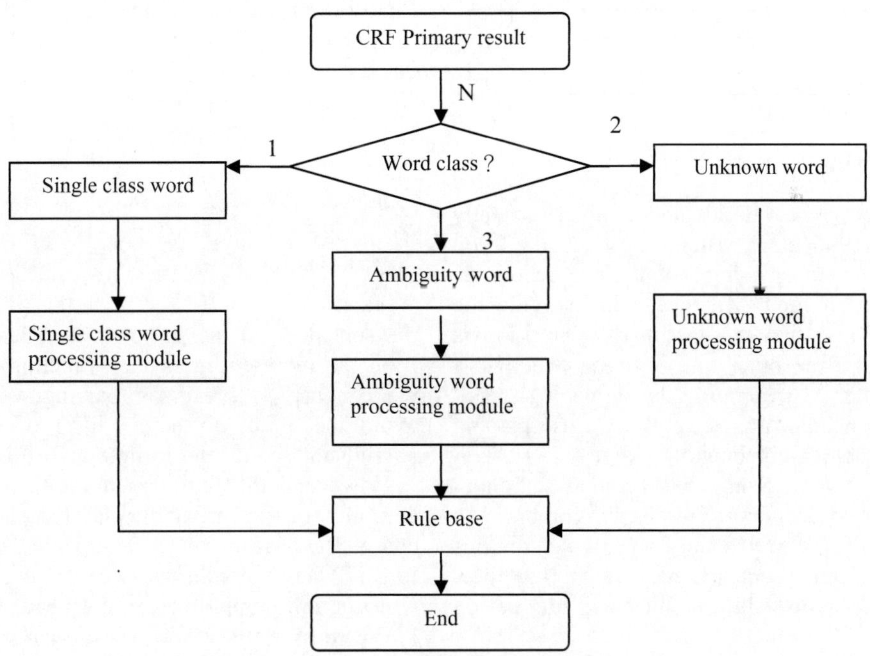

Figure2: Post-processing architecture after CRF labeling

(2) Ambiguity word processing module

The post-processing of ambiguity words consults the ambiguity word dictionary and CRFs score. When the POS from CRFs belongs to the POS of the word in the ambiguity word dictionary, we take the POS from CRFs as the final POS; otherwise, we examine the score of CRF, if the score is less than 0.4, the final POS of the word is the POS who has the highest score (has highest frequency), or else taking POS from CRF as the final POS.

(3) Unknown word processing module

The unknown words are the words not in training set. By analyzing the examples, we find that there are great deals of person names, location names, organization names and numbers, etc. And the words have characteristics when building word, therefore, we set up rules for processing.

2.3 Experiment results

Table 2 shows the comparative experimental results of POS tagging using two methods.

Method	EDSs precision	CS precision
CRF	92.83%	89.42%
CRF + post-processing	93.96%	91.05%

Table 2: Comparative POS tagging results

3 Parsing system

The paper uses divide-and-conquer strategy (Shiuan 1996 et al., Braun 2000 et al., Lyon 1997 et al.)for parsing. Firstly, we recognize MNP for an input sentence, which divide the sentence into two kinds of parts. One kind is MNPs, and the other one is frame which is a new sentence generating by replacing MNP using its head word. Secondly, we use parsing approach based on chunking (Abney, 1991, Erik Tjong and Kim Sang, 2001) and a searching algorithm in decoding. Thirdly, we combine the parsing trees of MNPs and frame, which obtains the full parsing tree of the original sentence. Figure 3 shows the architecture of paring system.

3.1 MNP recognition

Maximal Noun Phrase (MNP) is the noun phrase which is not contained by any other noun phrases. We use Berkeley parser (2009 1.0) for MNP recognition. We first use Berkeley parser to parse sentences after POS tagging, and then we tag MNPs from the parsing results. As the following example:

Berkeley parser result: dj[中国/nS vp[重视/v vp[发展/v np[pp[与/p np[欧洲/nS 国家/n]] 的/uJDE 关系/n]]]]

MNP recognition result: 中国/nS 重视/v 发展/v np[与/p 欧洲/nS 国家/n 的/uJDE 关系/n]

The results of MNP recognition EDSs analysis and CS parsing are as table3:

	P	R	F
EDSs	85.3202%	85.998%	85.6578%
CS	77.7102%	79.2782%	78.4864%

Table 3: Results of MNP recognition

3.2 Head recognition of MNP and generation of frame

In this paper, the new sentence in which MNPs are replaced by their head word is defined as the sentence's frame. The head of MNPs is identified after MNP recognition and then they are used to replace the original MNP, and finally the sentence's frame is formed. We use the rules to recognize the head of MNP. Usually, the last word of MNP is the head of the phrase, which can represent the MNP in function. For example: "[该/r 学派/n] 同样/ad 主张/v 消除/v [干预/v 造成/v 的/u 阻碍/n]。" In this sentence" 该/r学派/n" and " 干预/v 造成/v 的/u 阻碍/n" are MNPs. If we omit the modifier in MNP, for example "[学派/n] 同样/ad 主张/v 消除/v [阻碍/n]。", the meaning of the sentence will not be changed. Because the head can represent the syntax function of MNP, we can use the head for parsing, which can avoid the effect of the modifier of MNP on parsing and reduce the complexity of parsing.

However, the components of MNP are complicated, not all of the last word of MNP can be the head of MNP. The paper shows that if MNP has parentheses, we can use the last word before parentheses as the head. When the last word of MNP is "等", we use the second last word as the head.

3.3 Chunking with CRFs

The accuracy of chunk parsing is highly dependent on the accuracy of each level of

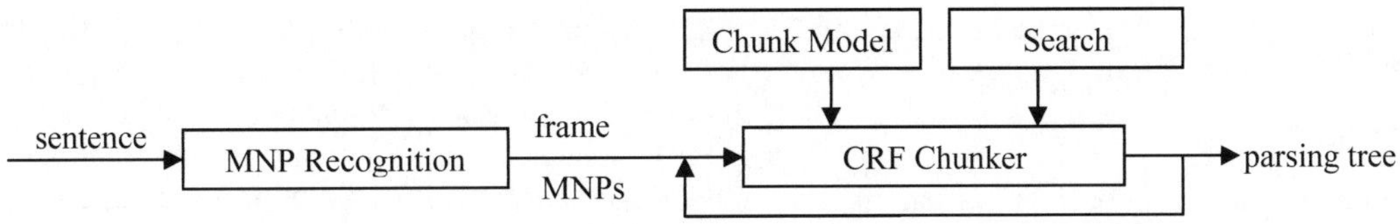

Figure3: Parsing system architecture

chunking. This section describes our approach to the chunking task. A common approach to the chunking problem is to convert the problem into a sequence tagging task by using the "BIEO" (B for beginning, I for inside, E for ending, and O for outside) representation.

This representation enables us to use the linear chain CRF model to perform chunking, since the task is simply assigning appropriate labels to sequence.

3.3.1 Features

Table 4 shows feature templates used in the whole levels of chunking. In the whole levels of chunking, we can use a rich set of features because the chunker has access to the information about the partial trees that have been already created (Yoshimasa et al., 2009). It uses the words and POS tags around the edges of the covered by the current non-terminal symbol.

Word Unigrams	$W_{-2}, W_{-1}, W_0, W_1, W_2$
Word Bigrams	$W_{-2}W_{-1}, W_{-1}W_0, W_0W_1, W_1W_2, W_0W_{-2}, W_0W_2$
Word Trigrams	$W_0W_{-1}W_{-2}, W_0W_1W_2$
POS Unigrams	$P_{-3}, P_{-2}, P_{-1}, P_0, P_1, P_2, P_3$
POS Bigrams	$P_{-3}P_{-2}, P_{-2}P_{-1}, P_{-1}P_0, P_0P_1, P_1P_2, P_2P_3, P_0P_{-2}, P_0P_2$
POS Trigrams	$P_{-3}P_{-2}P_{-1}, P_{-2}P_{-1}P_0, P_{-1}P_0P_1, P_0P_1P_2, P_1P_2P_3$
Word & POS	$W_0P_0, W_0P_{-1}, W_0P_1$
Word & WordCount	W_0C_0
Word & FirstWord	$W_0F_0, W_{-1}F_0$
Word & LastWord	W_0L_0, W_1L_0
Word & Symbol	W_0S_0

Table 4: Feature templates used in parsing system. W represents a word, P represents the part-of-speech of the word, C represents the sum of the chunk containing the word, F represents the first word of the chunk containing the word, L represents the last word of the chunk containing the word, S represents that the word is a non-terminal symbol or not. W_j is the current word; W_{j-1} is the word preceding W_j, W_{j+1} is the word following W_j.

3.4 Searching for the Best Parse

The probability for an entire parsing tree is computed as the product of the probabilities output by the individual CRF chunkers:

$$score = \prod_{i=0}^{h} p(y_i / x_i)$$

We use a searching algorithm to find the highest probability derivation. CRF can score each chunker result by A* search algorithm, therefore, we use the score as the probability of each chunker. We do not give pseudo code, but the basic idea is as figure 4.

```
inti parser(sent)
Parse(sent, 1, 0)

function Parse(sent, m, n)
 if sent is chunked as a complete sentence
   return m
 H = Chunking(sent, m/n)
  for h∈H do
  r = m * h.probability
    if r>n then
      sent2 = Update(sent, h)
      s = Parse(sent2, r, n)
      if s>n then n = s
  return n
function Chunking(sent, t)
perform chunking with a CRF chunker and
return a set of chunking hypotheses whose
probabilities are greater than t.
function Update(sent, h)
 update sequence sent according to chunking
hypothesis h and return the updated sequence.
```

Figure 4: Searching algorithm for the best parse

It is straightforward to introduce beam search in this search algorithm—we simply limit the number of hypotheses generated by the CRF chunker. We examine how the width of the beam affects the parsing performance in the experiments. We experiment beam width and we adopt the beam width of 4 at last.

3.5 Head Finding

Head finding is a post process after parsing in our system. The paper uses method combining statistics and rules to find head. The selected statistical method is CRF model. The first step is to train a CRF classifier to classify each context-free production into several categories. Then a rule-based method is used to post process the identification results and gets the final recognition results. The rule-based post-processing module mainly uses rule base and case base to carry out post-processing.

3.6 Head finding based on CRFs

The head finding procedure proceeds in the bottom-up fashion, so that the head words of productions in lower layers could be used as features for the productions of higher layers (Xiao chen et al. 2009).

Atom template	Definition
CurPhraseTag	The label of the current word
LCh_Word	The left most child
RCh_Word	The right most child
LCh_Pos	The POS of the left most child
MCh_Pos	The POS of the middle child
RCh_Pos	The POS of the right most child
NumCh	The number of children
CurPhraseTag ± 1	The labels of the former phrase and the latter

Table 5: Atom templates for Head finding

Complex Template
CurPhraseTag/ NumCh, CurPhraseTag/ LCh_Word, CurPhraseTag/LCh_Pos, CurPhraseTag/LCh_Pos/RCh_Pos, CurPhraseTag/NumCh/LCh_Pos/ RCh_Pos, CurPhraseTag/NumCh/LCh_Word/LCh_Pos/MCh_Pos/RCh_Word/RCh_Pos, LCh_Word/LCh_Pos, CurPhraseTag/MCh_Pos, NumCh/LCh_Pos/ MCh_Pos/ RCh_Pos, CurPhraseTag/ NumCh/ MCh_Pos, CurPhraseTag/LCh_Word/LCh_Pos/MCh_Pos/RCh_Word/RCh_Pos, LCh_Word/ LCh_Pos, LCh_Pos/ MCh_Pos, CurPhraseTag/NumCh, RCh_Word/RCh_Pos, NumCh/LCh_Word/LCh_Pos/MCh_Pos/RCh_Word/RCh_Pos

Table 6: Complex templates for Head finding

The atom templates are not sufficient for labeling context; therefore, we use some complex templates by combining the upper atom templates for more effectively describing context. When the feature function is fixed, the atom templates in complex templates are instantiated, which will generate features.

The final feature templates are composed of the atom templates and the complex templates. The feature templates of the head recognition in phrases contain 24 types.

3.7 Head Finding based on rules

Through the analysis of error examples, we found that some CRFs recognition results are clearly inconsistent with the actual situation; we can use rules to correct these errors, thus forming a rule base. Example-base is a chunk-based library built through analysis and processing on the training corpus. The Example-base is composed of all the bottom chunk and high-level chunk in training corpus. High-level phrases are the bottom chunk replaced by heads.

3.8 Experiment results of head finding

Table 7 shows the comparative experiment results of head recognition.

	Total Num	Wrong Num	Precision
CRFs	7035	93	98.68%
CRFs + rule-base+ case-base	7035	74	98.95%

Table7: Comparative results of head recognition

4 Experiment of parsing system

We perform experiments on the training set and testing set of Tsinghua Treebank provided by CIPS-SIGHAN-ParsEval-2010. For the direct influence of parsing result by the length of sentence, we count the length distribution of corpus.

Table 8 shows that the length of training set and testing set of EDSs is mostly less than 20 words. The length of training set of CS is evenly distributed, while the length of testing set is between 30 and 40 words.

The paper adopts divide-and-conquer strategy to parsing; therefore, we conduct the comparative experiment of MNP parsing and frame parsing. In addition, the results of MNP parsing and frame parsing depend on the length largely, so we list the length distribution of MNP and frame of EDSs and CS as table 9 and table 10.

length	EDSs		CS	
	training set	testing set	training set	testing set
[0, 10)	50.68%	64.30%	10.59%	0
[10,20)	37.27%	29.50%	27.55%	0
[20,30)	8.64%	5.40%	26.37%	79.9%
[30,40)	2.31%	0.60%	16.63%	20.1%
40≤	1.10%	0.20%	18.86%	0

Table 8: Length distribution of EDSs and CS

We define Simple MNP (SMNP) whose length is less than 5 words and Complete MNP (CMNP) whose length is more than 5 words.

length	EDSs		CS	
	training set	testing set	training set	testing set
[0,5)	55.30%	62.46%	55.42%	59.45%
[5,10)	32.66%	29.69%	32.57%	30.77%
[10,20)	10.03%	6.75%	10.03%	8.65%
20≤	2.00%	1.09%	1.98%	1.12%

Table 9: Length distribution of MNP

Table 9 shows the length distribution of MNP in training set and testing set of sub-sentence is consistent in basic, but the SMNP distribution of EDSs is 3.01% less than CS, which illuminates the complexity of MNP in CS is higher than in EDSs.

length	EDSs		CS	
	training set	testing set	training set	testing set
[0,5)	45.84%	47.20%	10.17%	1.00%
[5, 10)	43.58%	44.00%	24.14%	10.80%
[10, 20)	9.98%	8.70%	41.31%	62.20%
20≤	0.60%	0.10%	24.38%	26.00%

Table 10: Length distribution of frame

Table 10 shows the length distribution of frame in training set and testing set of EDSs is consistent in basic, while the CS is non-consistent. For the frame whose length is less than 5 words, the frame length distribution of training set is 9.17% higher than the testing set; for the frame whose length is more than 5 words and less than 10 words, the training set is 7.65% lower than testing; and for the frame whose length is between 10 words and 20 words, the testing set is 20.09% higher compared with the training set. From another aspect, in testing set, CS is 46.2% lower compared with EDSs for frame whose length is less than 5. Therefore, the complexity of frame in CS is higher than in EDSs.

As shown in Table 8, 9 and 10, the length distribution of testing set shows that the paring unit length of EDSs is reduced to less than 10 from less than 20 in original sentence and CS is reduced to less than 20 from between 30 and 40 after dividing an original sentence into MNPs parts and frame part. The above data indicate the divide-and-conquer strategy reduces the complexity of sentences significantly.

We can conclude that the parsing result of CS is lower than EDSs from Table 11, which is due to the higher complexity of MNP and frame in CS compared with EDSs from the results of Table 9 and Table 10. In addition, we obtain about 1% improvement compared with Berkeley parser in MNP and Frame parsing result in EDSs from Table 11 and Table 12, which indicates that our method is effective for short length parsing units. In particular, Table 12 shows that our result is 1.8% higher than Berkeley parser in the frame parsing of CS. Due to the non-consistent frame length distribution of training set and testing set in CS from Table 10, we find that Berkeley parser largely depends on training set compared with our method.

To more fairly compare the performance of our proposed method, the comparative results are shown as Table 13, the first one (Model01) is combination method of MNP pre-processing and chunk-based, and the chunk-based result which adopts CCRFs method with searching algorithm; the second one (Berkeley) is the parsing result of Berkeley parser; the third one (Model02) also is combination method of MNP pre-processing and chunk-based, and the chunk-based result which adopts CCRFs method only; and the lase one (Model03) is the chunk-based result which adopts CCRFs method with searching algorithm.

	method	P	R	F
EDSs	Berkeley	87.5746%	87.8365%	87.7053%
	Proposed Method	88.5752%	88.6341%	88.6047%
CS	Berkeley	84.4755%	84.9182%	84.6963%
	Proposed Method	84.7535%	85.046%	84.8995%

Table 11: Comparative results of MNP parsing

	method	P	R	F
EDSs	Berkeley	91.3411%	91.1823%	91.2617%
	Proposed Method	92.4669%	92.0765%	92.2713%
CS	Berkeley	85.4388%	85.3023%	85.3705%
	Proposed Method	87.3357%	87.0357%	87.1854%

Table12: Comparative results of Frame parsing

	P	R	F
Model 01	85.42%	85.35%	**85.39%**
Berkeley	84.56%	84.62%	84.59%
Models 02	85.31%	85.30%	85.31%
Models 03	83.99%	83.77%	83.88%

Table13: Comparative results of EDSs

	dj constituent			fj constituent			overall F
	P	R	P	R	F	F	F
Model 01	78.64%	78.73%	78.69%	70.22%	71.62%	70.91%	**74.80%**
Berkeley	78.37%	78.16%	78.26%	69.43%	72.42%	70.89%	74.58%
Models 02	78.18%	78.30%	78.24%	70.20%	70.98%	70.59%	74.41%
Models 03	77.38%	77.41%	77.39%	70.39%	70.01%	70.24%	73.82%

Table14: Comparative results of CS

From Table 13, we can see that Model01 performance in EDSs is improved by 0.08% than Model02, and the searching algorithm helps little in EDSs analysis. From Table 14, we can see that Model01 performance in CS is improved by 0.4% than Model02, better than Berkeley parser result with search algorism. Overall, in EDSs analysis, Model01 performance is improved by 0.8% than Berkeley parser, and in overall F-measure of CS, Model01 performance is 0.22% higher than Berkeley parser. From Table 13 and 14, We can see that Model01 performance in EDSs is improved by 1.51% than Model03 and the Model01 in CS is improved by 0.98% than Model03, and the MNP pre-processing helps.

5 Conclusions

We participate in two tasks - EDS Analysis and CS Parsing in CLPS-SIGHAN- ParsEval-2010. We use divide-and-conquer strategy for parsing and a chunking-based discriminative approach to full parsing by using CRF for chunking. As we all know, CRF is effective for chunking task. However, the chunking result in the current level is based on the upper level in the chunking-based parsing approach, which will enhance ambiguity problems when the input of the current level contains non-terminal symbols, therefore, the features used in chunking is crucial. This paper, for effectively using the information of partial trees that have been already created, keeps the terminal symbols in the node containing non-terminal symbols for features. Our experiments show that these features are effective for ambiguity problems.

We suppose that MNP pre-processing before statistical model can significantly simplify the analysis of complex sentences, which will have more satisfatory results compared with using statistical model singly. The current results show that the MNP pre-processing does simplify the complex sentences. However, the performance of MNP recognition and the parsing of MNP need to be improved, which will be our next work.

References

Yoshimasa Tsuruoka, Jun'ichi Tsujii, Sophia Anaiakou. 2009. Fast Full Parsing by Linear-Chain Conditional Random Fields. In *Proceedings of EACL'09,* pages 790-798.

Xiao chen, Changning Huang, Mu li, Chunyu Kit. 2009. Better Parser Combination. In *CIPS-ParsEval-2009,* pages 81-90.

Abney, S.. 1991. Parsing by chunks, Principle-Based Parsing, Kluwer Academic Publishers.

Erik Tjong, Kim Sang. 2000. Transforming a chunker to a parser. In J.Veenstra W.daelemans, K Sima' an and J. Zavrek, editors, *Computational Linguistics in the Netherlands 2000,* Rodopi, page 177-188.

P.L. Shiuan, C.T.H. Ann. 1996. A Divided-and-Conquer Strategy for Parsing. In *Proc. of the ACL/SIGPARSE 5th International Workshop on Parsing Technologies.* Santa Cruz, USA, 1996, pages 57-66

C. Braun, G. Neumann, J, Piskorski. 2000. A Divide-and-Conquer Strategy for Shallow Parsing of German Free Texts. In *Proc. of ANLP-2000.* Seattle, Washington, 2000, pages 239-246.

C.Lyon, B.Dickerson. 1997. Reducing the Complexity of Parsing by a Method of Decomposition International Workshop on Parsing Technology, 1997, pages 215-222.

Qiaoli Zhou, Xin Liu, Xiaona Ren, Wenjing Lang, Dongfeng Cai. 2009. Statistical parsing based on Maximal Noun Phrase pre-processing. In *CIPS-ParsEval-2209.*

P.L. Shiuan, C.T.H. Ann. A Divide-and-Conquer Strategy for Parsing. In: Proc. of the ACL/SIGPARSE 5th International Workshop on Parsing Technologies. Santa Cruz, USA, 1996. 57-66.

C. Braun, G. Neumann, J. Piskorski. A Divide-and-Conquer Strategy for Shallow Parsing of German Free Texts. In: Proc. of ANLP-2000. Seattle, Washington, 2000. 239-246.

C. Lyon, B. Dickerson. Reducing the Complexity of Parsing by a Method of Decomposition. International Workshop on Parsing Technology. 1997. 215-222.

Dependency Parser for Chinese Constituent Parsing *

Xuezhe Ma, Xiaotian Zhang, Hai Zhao, Bao-Liang Lu
[1]Center for Brain-Like Computing and Machine Intelligence
Department of Computer Science and Engineering, Shanghai Jiao Tong University
[2]MOE-Microsoft Key Laboratory for Intelligent Computing and Intelligent Systems
Shanghai Jiao Tong University, 800 Dong Chuan Rd., Shanghai 200240, China
{xuezhe.ma,xtian.zh}@gmail.com, {zhaohai,blu}@cs.sjtu.edu.cn

Abstract

This paper presents our work for participation in the 2010 CIPS-ParsEval shared task on Chinese syntactic constituent tree parsing. We use dependency parsers for this constituent parsing task based on a formal dependency-constituent transformation method which converts dependency to constituent structures using a machine learning approach. A conditional random fields (CRF) tagger is adopted for head information recognition. Our experiments shows that acceptable parsing and head tagging results are obtained on our approaches.

1 Introduction

Constituent parsing is a challenging but useful task aiming at analyzing the constituent structure of a sentence. Recently, it is widely adopted by the popular applications of natural language processing techniques, such as machine translation (Ding and Palmer, 2005), synonym generation (Shinyama et al., 2002), relation extraction (Culotta and Sorensen, 2004) and lexical resource augmentation (Snow et al., 2004). A great deal of researches have been conducted on this topic with promising progress (Magerman, 1995; Collins, 1999; Charniak, 2000; Charniak and Johnson, 2005; Sagae and Lavie, 2006; Petrov and Klein, 2007; Finkel et al., 2008; Huang, 2008).

Recently, several effective dependency parsing algorithms has been developed and shows excellent performance in the responding parsing tasks (McDonald, 2006; Nivre and Scholz, 2004). Since graph structures of dependency and constituent parsing over a sentence are strongly related, they should be benefited from each other. It is true that constituent parsing may be smoothly altered to fit dependency parsing. However, due to the inconvenience from dependency to constituent structure, it is not so easy to adopt the latter for the former. This means that most of these popular and effective dependency parsing models can not be directly extended to constituents parsing. This paper proposes an formal method for such a conversion which adoptively solves the problem of ambiguity. Based on the proposed method, a dependency parsing algorithm can be used to solve tasks of constituent parsing.

A part of Tsinghua Chinese Treebank (TCT) (Zhou, 2004; Zhou, 2007; Chen et al., 2008) is used as the training and test data for the 2010 CIPS-ParsEval shared task. Being different from the annotation scheme of the Penn Chinese Treebank (CTB), the TCT has another annotation scheme, which combines both the constituent tree structure and the head information of each constituent. Specifically, there can be always multiple heads in a constituent. For the 2010 CIPS-ParsEval shared task, only segmented sentences are given in test data without part-of-speech (POS) tags, a POS tagger is required for this task. Therefore, we divide our system into three major cascade stages, namely POS tagging, constituent parsing and head information recognition, which are connected as a pipeline of processing. For the POS tagging, we adopt the SVMTool tagger (Gimenez and Marquez, 2004); for the constituent parsing, we use the Maximum Spanning Tree (MST) (McDonald, 2006) parser combined with a dependencies-to-constituents conversion; and for the head information recognition, we apply a sequence labeling method to label head information.

Section 2 presents the POS tagger in our approach. The details of our parsing method is presented in section 3. The head information recognition is described in section 4. The data and experimental results are shown in section 5. The last section is the conclusion and future work.

2 POS Tagging

The SVMTool tagger (Gimenez and Marquez, 2004) is used as our POS tagging tool for the first stage. It is a POS tagger based on SVM classifier, written in Perl. It can be trained on standardized collection of hand POS-tagged sentences. It uses SVM-Light[1] toolkit as the

*This work is partially supported by the National Natural Science Foundation of China (Grant No. 60903119, Grant No. 60773090 and Grant No. 90820018), the National Basic Research Program of China (Grant No. 2009CB320901), and the National High-Tech Research Program of China (Grant No.2008AA02Z315).

[1]http://www.cs.cornell.edu/People/tj/svm_light/.

implementation of SVM classifier and achieves 97.2% accuracy on the Penn English Treebank. We test the accuracy of the SVMTool tagger on the development set of the TCT (see section 5.1) and achieve accuracy of 94.98%.

3 Parsing Constituents Using Dependency Parsing Algorithms

3.1 Convert Dependencies to Constituents

The conversion from constituent to dependency structures is straightforward with some specific rules based on linguistic theory. However, there is not an effective method which can accurately accomplish the opposite transformation, from the dependency structures back into constituent ones due to the existence of ambiguity introduced by the former transformation.

Aimed at the above difficulty, our solution is to introduce a formal dependency structure and a machine learning method so that the ambiguity from dependency structures to constituent structures can be dealt with automatically.

3.1.1 Binarization

We first transform constituent trees into the form that all productions for all subtrees are either unary or binary, before converting them to dependency structures. Due to the binarization, the target constituent trees of the conversion from dependency back to constituent structures are binary branching.

This binarization is done by the left-factoring approach described in (Charniak et al., 1998; Petrov and Klein, 2008), which converts each production with n children, where $n > 2$, into $n - 1$ binary productions. Additional non-terminal nodes introduced in this conversion must be clearly marked. Transforming the binary branching trees into arbitrary branching trees is accomplished by using the reverse process.

3.1.2 Using Binary Classifier

We train a classifier to decide which dependency edges should be transformed first at each step of conversion automatically. After the binarization described in the previous section, only one dependency edge should be transformed at each step. Therefore the classifier only need to decide which dependency edge should be transformed at each step during the conversion.

As a result of the projective property of constituent structures, this problem only happens in the cases that modifiers are at both sides of their heads. And for these cases that one head has multiple modifiers, only the leftmost or the rightmost dependency edge could be transformed first. Therefore, a binary classifier is always enough for the disambiguation at each step.

1.	Word form of the parent
2.	Part-of-speech (POS) tag of the parent
3.	Word form of the leftmost child
4.	POS tag of the leftmost child
5.	Dependency label of the leftmost child
6.	Word form of the rightmost child
7.	POS tag of the rightmost child
8.	Dependency label of the rightmost child
9.	Distance between the leftmost child and the parent
10.	Distance between the rightmost child and the parent

Table 1: Features used for conversion classifier.

Support Vector Machine (SVM) is adopted as the learning algorithm for the binary classifier and the features are in Table 1.

3.1.3 Convert Constituent Labels

The rest problem is that we should restore the label for each constituent when dependency structure trees are again converted to constituent structures. The problem is solved by storing constituent labels as labels of dependency types. The label for each constituent is just used as the label dependency type for each dependency edge.

The conversion method is tested on the development, too. Constituent trees are firstly converted into dependency structures using the head rules described in (Li and Zhou, 2009). Then, we transform those trees back to constituent structure using our conversion method and use the PARSEVAL (Black et al., 1991) measures to evaluate the performance of the conversion method. Our conversion method obtains 99.76% precision and 99.76% recall, which is a great performance.

3.2 Dependency Parser for Constituent Parsing

Based on the proposed conversion method, dependency parsing algorithms can be used for constituent parsing. This can be done by firstly transforming training data from constituents into dependencies and extract training instances to train a binary classifier for dependency-constituent conversion, then training a dependency parser using the transformed training data. On the test step, parse the test data using the dependency parser and convert output dependencies to constituents using the binary classifier trained in advance. In addition, since our conversion method needs dependency types, labeled dependency parsing algorithms are always required.

1.	Constituent label of the constituent
2.	Constituent label of each child of the constituent.
3.	Wether it is a terminal for each child of the constituent
4.	The leftmost word in the sentence of each child of the constituent.
5.	The leftmost word in the sentence of each child of the constituent.

Table 2: CRF features for head information recognition.

1.	Word form and POS tag of the parent.
2.	Word form and POS tag of each child.
3.	POS tag of the leftmost child of each child.
4.	POS tag of the rightmost child of each child.
5.	Dependency label between the parent and its parent

Table 3: CRF features for dependency type labeling.

4 Head Information Recognition

Since head information of each constituent is always determined by the syntactic label of its own and the categories of the constituents in subtrees, the order and relations between the productions of each constituent strongly affects the head information labeling. It is natural to apply a sequential labeling strategy to tackle this problem. The linear chain CRF model is adopted for the head information labeling, and the implementation of CRF model we used is the 0.53 version of the CRF++ toolkit[2]. We assume that head information is independent between different constituents, which could decrease the length of sequence to be labeled for the CRF model.

We use a binary tag set to determine whether a constituent is a head, e.g. H for a head, O for a non-head, which is the same as (Song and Kit, 2009). The features in Table 2 are used for CRF model.

To test our CRF tagger, we remove all head information from the development set, and use the CRF tagger to retrieve the head. The result strongly proves its effectiveness by showing an accuracy of 99.52%.

5 Experiments

All experiments reported here were performed on a Core 2 Quad 2.83Ghz CPU with 8GB of RAM.

5.1 Data

There are 37,219 short sentences in official released training data for the first sub-task and 17,744 long sentences for the second sub-task (for the second sub-task, one line in the training data set may contain more than one sentence). We split one eighth of the data as our development set. On the other hand, there are both 1,000 sentences in released test data for the first and second sub-tasks.

5.2 Constituent Parsing

As mentioned in section 3, constituent parsing is done by using a dependency parser combined with our conversion method. We choose the second order maximum spanning tree parser with k-best online large-margin learning algorithm (Crammer and Singer, 2003; Crammer et al., 2003). The MST parser we use is in the form of an open source program implemented in C++[3].

The features used for MST parser is the same as (McDonald, 2006). Both the single-stage and two-stage dependency type labeling approaches are applied in our experiments. For the two-stage dependency type labeling, The linear chain CRF model is adopted instead of the first-order Markov model used in (McDonald, 2006). The features in Table 3 are used for CRF model. It takes about 7 hours for training the MST parser, and about 24 hours for training the CRF model.

As mentioned in section 3.1.2, SVM is adopted as the learning algorithm for the binary classifier. There are about 40,000 training instances in the first sub-task and about 80,000 in the second sub-task. Development sets are used for tuning parameter C of SVM and the training time of the SVM classifier for the first and second sub-task is about 8 and 24 hours, respectively. However, the conversion from dependencies to constituents is extremely fast. Converting more than 2,000 trees takes less than 1 second.

To transform the constituent trees in training set into dependency structures, we use the head rules of (Li and Zhou, 2009).

5.3 Results

The evaluation metrics used in 2010 CIPS-ParsEval shared task is shown in following:

1. syntactic parsing

$$\textbf{Precision} = \frac{\text{number of correct constituents in proposed parse}}{\text{number of constituents in proposed parse}}$$

$$\textbf{Recall} = \frac{\text{number of correct constituents in proposed parse}}{\text{number of constituents in standard parse}}$$

$$\textbf{F1} = \frac{\text{2*Precision*Recall}}{\text{Precision+Recall}}$$

[2]The CRF++ toolkit is publicly available from `http://crfpp.sourceforge.net/`.

[3]The Max-MSTParser is publicly available from `http://max-mstparser.sourceforge.net/`.

	without head			with head		
	Precision	Recall	F1	Precision	Recall	F1
single-stage	77.78	78.13	77.96	75.78	76.13	75.95
two-stage	78.61	78.76	78.69	76.61	76.75	76.68

Table 4: Official scores of syntactic parsing. single-stage and two-stage are for single-stage and two-stage dependency type labeling approached, respectively.

	Micro-R	Macro-R
single-stage	62.74	62.47
two-stage	63.14	62.48

Table 5: Official scores of event recognition

The correctness of syntactic constituents is judged based on the following two criteria:

(a) the boundary, the POS tags of all the words in the constituent and the constituent type label should match that of the constituent in the gold standard data.

(b) the boundary, the POS tags of all the words in the constituent, the constituent type label and head child index of the constituent should match that of the constituent in the gold standard data. (if the constituent contains more than one head child index, at least one of them should be correct.)

2. event pattern recognition

$$\textbf{Micro-R} = \frac{\text{number of all correct events in proposed parse}}{\text{number of all events in standard parse}}$$

$$\textbf{Macro-R} = \frac{\text{sum of recall of different target verbs}}{\text{number of target verbs}}$$

Here the event pattern of a sentence is defined to be the sequence of event blocks controlled by the target verb in a sentence. The criteria for judging the correctness of event pattern recognition is:

- the event pattern should be completely consistent with gold standard data (information of each event block should completely match and the order of event blocks should also consistent).

There are both two submissions for the first and second sub-tasks. One is using the single-stage dependency type labeling and the other is two-stage. Since there are some mistakes in our models for the second sub-task, the results of our submissions are unexpectedly poor and are not shown in this paper. All the results in this paper is reported by the official organizer of the 2010 CIPS-ParsEval shared task.

The accuracy of POS tagging on the official test data is 92.77%. The results of syntactic parsing for the first sub-task is shown in Table 4. And results of event recognition is shown in Table 5.

From the Table 4 and 5, we can see that our system achieves acceptable parsing and head tagging results, and the results of event recognition is also reasonably high.

5.4 Comparison with Previous Works

We comparison our approach with previous works of 2009 CIPS-ParsEval shared task. The data set and evaluation measures of 2009 CIPS-ParsEval shared task, which are quite different from that of 2010 CIPS-ParsEval shared task, are used in this experiment for the comparison purpose. Table 6 shows the comparison.

We compare our method with several main parsers on the official data set of 2009 CIPS-ParsEval shared task. All these results are evaluated with official evaluation tool by the 2009 CIPS-ParsEval shared task. Bikel's parser[4] (Bikel, 2004) in Table 6 is a implementation of Collins' head-driven statistical model (Collins, 2003). The Stanford parser[5] is based on the factored model described in (Klein and Manning, 2002). The Charniak's parser[6] is based on the parsing model described in (Charniak, 2000). Berkeley parser[7] is based on unlexicalized parsing model described in (Petrov and Klein, 2007). According to Table 6, the performance of our method is better than all the four parsers described above. Chen et al. (2009) and Jiang et al. (2009) both make use of combination of multiple parsers and achieve considerably high performance.

[4] `http://www.cis.upenn.edu/~dbikel/software.html`

[5] `http://nlp.stanford.edu/software/lex-parser.shtml/`

[6] `ftp://ftp.cs.brown.edu/pub/nlparser/`

[7] `http://nlp.cs.berkeley.edu/Main.html`

	F1
Bikel's parser	81.8
Stanford parser	83.3
Charniak's parser	83.9
Berkeley parser	85.2
this paper	**85.6**
Jiang et al (2009).	87.2
Chen et al (2009).	88.8

Table 6: Comparison with previous works

6 Conclusion

This paper describes our approaches for the parsing task in CIPS-ParsEval 2010 shared task. A pipeline system is used to solve the POS tagging, constituent parsing and head information recognition. SVMTool tagger is used for the POS tagging. For constituent parsing, we proposes a conversion based method, which can use dependency parsers for constituent parsing. MST parser is chosen as our dependency parser. A CRF tagger is used for head information recognition. The official scores indicate that our system obtains acceptable results on constituent parsing and high performance on head information tagging.

One of future work should apply parser combination and reranking approaches to leverage this in producing more accurate parsers.

References

Bikel, Daniel M. 2004. Intricacies of collins parsing model. *Computational Linguistics*, 30(4):480–511.

Black, Ezra W., Steven P. Abney, Daniel P. Flickinger, Cluadia Gdaniec, Ralph Grishman, Philio Harrison, Donald Hindle, Robert J.P. Inqria, Frederick Jelinek, Judith L. Klavans, Mark Y. Liberman, Mitchell P. Marcus, Salim Roukos, and B Santorini. 1991. A procedure for quantitatively comparing the syntactic coverage of english grammars. In *Proceedings of the February 1991 DARPA Speech and Natural Language Workshop*.

Charniak, Eugene and Mark Johnson. 2005. Coarse-to-fine-grained n-best parsing and discriminative reranking. In *Proceedings of the 43rd ACLL*, pages 132–139.

Charniak, Eugene, Sharon Goldwater, and Mark Johnson. 1998. Edge-based best-first chart parsing. In *Proceedings of the Sixth Workshop on Very Large Corpora*.

Charniak, Eugene. 2000. A maximum-entropy-inspired parser. In *Proceedings of NAACL*, pages 132–139, seattle, WA.

Chen, Yi, Qiang Zhou, and Hang Yu. 2008. Analysis of the hierarchical Chinese funcitional chunk bank. *Journal of Chinese Information Processing*, 22(3):24–31.

Chen, Xiao, Changning Huang, Mu Li, and Chunyu Kit. 2009. Better parser combination. In *CIPS-ParsEval-2009 shared task*.

Collins, Michael. 1999. *Head-Driven Statistical Models for Natural Language Parsing*. Ph.D. thesis, University of Pennsylvania.

Collins, Michael. 2003. Head-driven statistical models for natural language parsing. *Computational Linguistics*, 29(4):589–637.

Crammer, Koby and Yoram Singer. 2003. Ultraconservative online algorithms for multiclass problems. *Journal of Machine Learining*.

Crammer, Koby, Ofer Dekel, Joseph Keshet, Shai Shalev-Shwartz, and Yoram Singer. 2003. Online passive aggressive algorithms. In *Proceedings of NIPS*.

Culotta, Aron and Jeffrey Sorensen. 2004. Dependency tree kernels for relation extraction. In *Proceedings of ACL*.

Ding, Yuan and Martha Palmer. 2005. Machine translation using probabilistic synchronous dependency insertion grammars. In *Proceedings of ACL*.

Finkel, Jenny Rose, Alex Kleeman, and Christopher D. Manning. 2008. Efficient, feature-based, conditional random field parsing. pages 959–967, The Ohio State University, Columbus, Ohio, USA.

Gimenez and Marquez. 2004. Svmtool: A general POS tagger generator based on support vector machines. In *Proceedings of the 4th International Conference of Language Resources and Evaluation*, Lisbon, Portugal.

Huang, Liang. 2008. Forest reranking: Discriminative parsing with non-local features. In *Proceedings of ACL/HLT*.

Jiang, Wenbin, Hao Xiong, and Qun Liu. 2009. Mutipath shift-reduce parsing with online training. In *CIPS-ParsEval-2009 shared task*.

Klein, Dan and Christopher Manning. 2002. Fast exact inference with a factored model for natural language parsing. In *In Advances in NIPS 2002*, pages 3–10.

Li, Junhui and Guodong Zhou. 2009. Soochow university report for the 1st china workshop on syntactic parsing. In *CIPS-ParsEval-2009 shared task*.

Magerman, David M. 1995. Statistical decision-tree models for parsing. In *Proceedings of ACL*, pages 276–283, MIT, Cambridge, Massachusetts, USA.

McDonald, Ryan. 2006. *Discriminative Learning Spanning Tree Algorithm for Dependency Parsing*. Ph.D. thesis, University of Pennsylvania.

Nivre, Joakim and Mario Scholz. 2004. Deterministic dependency parsing of english text. In *Proceedings of the 20th international conference on Computational Linguistics (COLING-2004)*, pages 64–70, Geneva, Switzerland, August 23rd-27th.

Petrov, Slav and Dan Klein. 2007. Improved inference for unlexicalized parsing. In *Proceedings of HLT/NAACL*, pages 404–411, Rochester, New York.

Petrov, Slav and Dan Klein. 2008. Discriminative log-linear grammars with latent variables. In *Proceedings of NIPS 20*.

Sagae, Kenji and Alon Lavie. 2006. A best-first probabilistic shift-reduce parser. In *Proceedings of COLING/ACL*, pages 689–691, Sydney, Australia.

Shinyama, Yusuke, Satoshi Sekine, and Kiyoshi Sudo. 2002. Automatic paraphrase acquisition from news articles. In *HLT-2002*.

Snow, Rion, Daniel Jurafsky, and Andrew Y. Ng. 2004. Learning syntactic patterns for automatic hypernym discovery. In *Proceedings of NIPS*.

Song, Yan and Chunyu Kit. 2009. PCFG parsing with crf tagging for head recognition. In *CIPS-ParsEval-2009 shared task*.

Zhou, Qiang. 2004. Annotation scheme for Chinese treebank. *Journal of Chinese Information Processing*, 18(4):1–8.

Zhou, Qiang. 2007. Base chuck scheme for the Chinese language. *Journal of Chinese Information Processing*, 21(3):21–27.

Technical Report of the CCID System for the 2th Evaluation on Chinese Parsing

Guangfan Sun
China Center for Information Industry Development, Beijing, 100044
morgan2001_sun@163.com

Abstract

This paper gives an overview of China Center for Information Industry Development(CCID) participating in the 2th Evaluation on Chinese parsing. CCID has taken part in the subtask of the analysis of complete sentences. The system participating in the above Evaluation is a rule-based Chinese parser, and its basic information is described in the paper, and its experimental situation for the Evaluation has been analyzed.

1 Introduction

Parsing is one of key issues in natural language processing, and its main task is to automatically identify the syntactic structure of sentences (syntactic units and their syntactic relations between units). The study of parsing is of critical importance for machine translation, natural language understanding, information extraction and automatic summarization of natural language processing systems. Syntactic analysis methods include methods of use of corpus annotation information in syntactic analysis and the rule-based methods such as: Shift-Reduce Parsing and Chart Parsing technology to study the Chinese syntactic structure[1]. In this paper, the Chinese parser which China Electronic Information Industry Development (CCID) uses to participate in the 2th Evaluation on Chinese Parsing is described.

2 System

The Chinese parser which CCID uses to participate in the 2th Evaluation on Chinese Parsing serves as a component of a practical Chinese-English machine translation system, and uses rule-based method, and uses statistical approach for unknown word recognition. The Chinese parser includes the following three modules: 1) Chinese word segmenting, 2) Chinese POS tagging, 3) Chinese parsing. The form of rules in the Chinese parser is production rule. The rules include general rules and specific rules. The general rules are indexed by POS or phrase types, and specific rules are indexed by Chinese word or Chinese phrase. There are multi-passes during Chinese parsing, and the result of the parsing of a Chinese sentence is a Chinese syntactic tree. The CCID's Chinese parser includes 1,930,000 entries in the basic dictionaries and 6,000 rules in knowledge base. Parts of speech and syntactic elements of the output of the CCID's Chinese parser are marked by its own set of markup symbols, and these markup symbols are mapped to parts of speech tags and syntactic component tags defined by CIPS-ParsEval-2009 by a conversion function. The CCID's tag set is mainly same as the set of CIPS-ParsEval-2009 except the used tag characters. For example, in the CCID's tag set, the tag of noun phrase is NP, and the tag of verb phrase is VP, and the tag of preposition phrase is IP; for the tags in CIPS-ParsEval-2009, the tag of noun phrase is np, and the tag of verb phrase is vp, and the tag of preposition phrase is pp.

3 Experiment

CCID participated in the 2th Evaluation on Chinese Parsing, and timely submitted parsing output of test sentences of the syntactic analysis. The Test Group returned to a very unfortunate message: "find that the results presented in the original segmentation of data are automatically merged, so can not give the appropriate evaluation of data."

Here are two specific examples:

Original input 1:

1 显微 解剖学 是 用 光学 显微镜 和 电子 显微镜 等 显微镜 来 观察 细胞 、 组织 或 器官 等 的 构造 、 形态 的 分支 学科 ， 它 也 叫做 组织学 。

Parsing output 1:

1 [zj [dj [dj [np 显微解剖学/n] [vp [pp 用/p [np [np [np 光学显微镜/n] 和/c [np 电子显微镜/n]] 等/uO [np 显微镜/n]]] [vp [vp 观察/v] [np [np [np [np [np 细胞/n] 、/wD [np 组织/n] 或/c [np 器官/n]] 等/uO] 的/uJDE [np 构造/n]] 、/wD [np [np 形态/n] 的/uJDE [np 分支学科/n]]]]]]] ，/wP [dj 它/r [vp [vp [dp 也/d] [vp 叫做/v]] [np 组织学/n]]]] 。/wE]

Original input 183:

183 除此而外 ， 发作性 室上性 心动 过速 、 快速 心房 颤动 、 心房 扑动 等 ， 虽 属 快速性 心律 失常 ， 有时 也 必须 进行 心电图 监护 。

Parsing output 183:

183 [zj [dj [dp [dp 除此而外/d] ，/wP] [dj [np [np [np [ap 发作性/a 室上性/a] [np 心动过速/n]] 、/wD [np [ap 快速/a] [np 心房颤动/n]] 、/wD [np 心房扑动/n]] 等/uO] [pp 虽/c [dj [np [np 属/n] [np 快速性心律失常/n]] [vp [dp 有时/d] [vp [dp 也/d] [vp [vp 必须/vM [vp 进行/v]] [np 心电图监护/n]]]]]]]] 。/wE]

Reasons for these phenomena are: "显微解剖学"、"光学显微镜"、"电子显微镜"、"心动过速"、"心房颤动"、"心房扑动"、"快速性心律失常"、"心电图监护" and some other entries have already existed as separate entries in the basic dictionaries of the CCID's Chinese parser. In parsing, these entries act as separate entries and the results also show up as separate entries. This occurs because of the larger basic dictionary(1.93 million entries), and these entries have the corresponding English translations on the expression. For a practical Chinese parser, a large number of phrases that already exist in the basic vocabularies can reduce the burden of parsing, and are useful for improving the success rate of Chinese syntactic analysis. But this adds extra burden to evaluation programs. When participating in the next Chinese parsing evaluation, some phrases that have existed in the basic dictionaries of Chinese parser will be divided to further analyze their internal syntactic structures to facilitate the evaluation process.

After receiving the notice that a re-evaluation can be done by the Evaluation Group to help CCID to evaluate the effectiveness of the modification of the parsing model, the following steps are carried out for the convenience of the evaluation programs:

1) Compare all words in the test task with CCID's Chinese parser, and find out the information for the words from CCID's Chinese parser, and delete all other words from the Chinese parser to avoid the situation that some Chinese words are combined when parsing.
2) Modify parsing rules that contain operations of deleting words to avoid the deletion of Chinese words in the parsing results.
3) Re-parse Chinese sentences in the test task.
4) Submit the result of the parsing to the Evaluation Group to evaluate.

The re-evaluation result is as the following:

Performance Report for Task 2-2
pos accuracy: 72.98% (19253/26381)
average of F1 of dj_sum and fj: 26.87 (%)

Label	#Auto	#Gold	#Correct
dj	3826	2290	1156
vp	5954	7397	3090
ap	532	432	267
np	5778	5199	3478
sp	0	433	0
tp	0	381	0
mp	443	614	341
mbar	47	45	29
dp	782	65	42
pp	1263	1191	546
bp	0	1	0
total	18625	18048	8949

Label	Precision	Recall	F1
dj	30.21	50.48	37.80
vp	51.90	41.77	46.29
ap	50.19	61.81	55.39
np	60.19	66.90	63.37
sp	0.00	0.00	0.00
tp	0.00	0.00	0.00
mp	76.98	55.54	64.52
mbar	61.70	64.44	63.04
dp	5.37	64.62	9.92
pp	43.23	45.84	44.50
bp	0.00	0.00	0.00
total	48.05	49.58	48.80

Label	#Auto	#Gold	#Correct
fj	450	1251	42

Label	Precision	Recall	F1
fj	9.33(%)	3.36(%)	4.94(%)

4 Discussion

Chinese parsing is an important basic research for Chinese information processing research, and gets the attention of many researchers. Current research focuses on the research on syntactic knowledge acquisition based on the corpus, and its goal is to use statistical methods from a good tree bank annotation to learn the parsing needed knowledge, and the trained parser also promotes the work of automatic/semi-automatic annotation to corpus. Statistical methods have an advantage for fine-grained knowledge of the language than the rule method, and can automatically learn knowledge from the annotated corpus, and is attractive and worthy of research.

Meanwhile, many Chinese parsers that have the background for the practical application use the rule-based approach, and, in addition to the accumulation of knowledge in the process of manual knowledge acquisition, also use statistical methods to help get the phrases from the corpus, and also include the translation equivalents acquired automatically for machine translation. An important direction of development for these systems is to find ways to learn a lot of phrase knowledge from the corpus, which can greatly reduce the difficulties encountered in the ambiguity resolution to improve the accuracy of syntactic analysis. For Chinese-English machine translation system, the difficulty will be significantly lower after adding a large number of phrases and their translation to the system, and as a result, some syntactic structure ambiguities are eliminated, and many phrases are translated as a whole and the readability of the translation also are improved.

An important development trend of natural language processing is that corpus is considered as processing objects and sources of knowledge acquisition. Rule approach has proven to be difficult to the task of processing large-scale real corpus, so the researchers turn to the help of statistical methods, and many experiments prove that statistical methods indeed have made great progress. But the statistical method has its inherent shortcomings, and statistical methods alone can hardly reach expectations of the perfect goal of natural language processing. Thus, Many researchers begin to explore ways of combination of statistical methods and rules, and have made some progress, but there is still a long way to go from the ultimate goal of natural language processing (computer can fully understand the nature of human language). The current trend of integration of empiricism and rationalism in natural language processing is a significant phenomenon, and its development will produce a lot of valuable results, and natural language processing research and applications will benefit from it.

The CCID's future research will focus on methods of automatically extracting knowledge of Chinese phrases and their translations. These methods will be mainly statistical methods, combining with some of the rules means to facilitate access to single-language knowledge and improve the correct translation rate. Progress of the research in this regard will be helpful for our practical machine translation system to improve the quality of translation. At the same time, it has a direct role in improving the quality of Chinese parser.

The paper is funded by National Natural Science Foundation of China, and the project number is: 60872118.

References

Feng Zhiwei. 2004. *The Research on Machine Translation. China Translation and Publishing Corporation.* China Translation and Publishing Corporation. Beijing, China

Zhong Chengqing. 2008. *Statistical Natural Language Processing.* Tsinghua University Press. Beijing, China

Zhao Tiejun, etc. 2000. *Principles of Machine Translation.* Harbin Institute of Technology Press. Harbin, China

Sun Guangfan, Song Jinping, Yuan Qi. 2006. *Design of bi-directional English-Chinese machine translation systems based on hybrid strategy*, Journal of Chinese Information Processing, Beijing, China.

Li Xing. 2005. *The Research on Chinese Parsing*, Master thesis, Chinese Academy of Sciences, Beijing, China.

Lu Junzhi, Chen Xiaohe, Wang Dongbo, Chen Feng. 2008. *Chinese Parsing Algorithm Based on Grammatical Function Matching*, Computer Engineering and Applications, Beijing, China.

CRF tagging for head recognition based on Stanford parser

Yong Cheng, Chengjie Sun, Bingquan Liu, Lei Lin
Harbin Institute of Technology
{ycheng, cjsun, linl,liubq}@insun.hit.edu.cn

Abstract

Chinese parsing has received more and more attention, and in this paper, we use toolkit to perform parsing on the data of Tsinghua Chinese Treebank (TCT) used in CIPS, and we use Conditional Random Fields (CRFs) to train specific model for the head recognition. At last, we compare different results on different POS results.

1 Introduction

In the past decade, Chinese parsing has received more and more attention, it is the core of Chinese information processing technology, and it is also the cornerstone for deep understanding of Chinese.

Parsing is to identify automatically syntactic units in the sentence and give the relationship between these units. It is based on a given grammar. The results of parsing are usually structured syntax tree. For example, the parsing result of sentence "中国是多民族国家" is as following.

```
(ROOT
  (dj (nS 中国)
    (vp (v 是)
      (np
        (np (m 多) (n 民族))
          (n 国家)))))
```

With the development of Chinese economy, Chinese information processing has become a worldwide hot spot, and parsing is an essential task. However, parsing is a recognized research problem, and it is so difficult to meet the urgent needs of industrial applications in accuracy, robustness, speed. So the study of Chinese grammar and syntax analysis algorithm are still the focus of Chinese information processing.

In all the parsing technology research, English parsing research is the most in-depth, and there are three main aspects of research in statistical parsing, they are parsing model, parsing algorithm, and corpus construction. As for the parsing model, currently there are four commonly used parsing models, PCFG model [1], the model based on historical, Hierarchical model of progressive, head-driven model [2].

Since parsing is mostly a data driven process, its performance is determined by the amount of data in a Treebank on which a parser is trained. Much more data for English than for any other languages have been available so far. Thus most researches on parsing are concentrated on English. It is unrealistic to directly apply any existing parser trained on an English Treebank for Chinese sentences. But the methodology is, without doubt, highly applicable. Even for those corpora with special format and information integrated some modification and enhancement on a well-performed parser to fit the special structure for the data could help to obtain a good performance.

This paper presents our solution for the shared Task 2 of CIPS2010-Chinese Parsing. We exploit an existing powerful parser, Stanford parser, which has showed its effectiveness on English, with necessary modifications for parsing Chinese for the shared task. Since the corpus used in CIPS is from TCT, and the sentence contains the head-word information, but for the Stanford parser, it can't recognize the head constituents. So we apply a sequence tagging method to label head constituents based on the data extracted from the TCT corpus, In section 2 and section 3, we will present the

Table 1. Training data with different formats

Parsing model	1.(ROOT (np-0-2 (n 货币学派) (cC 及其) (np-0-1 (n 政策) (n 主张)))) 2.(ROOT (vp-1 (pp-1 (p 对) (np-0-2 (np-1 (n 金融) (n 政策)) (cC 以及) (np-2 (a 类似) (uJDE 的) (np-1 (n 宏观) (np-1 (n 经济) (n 政策)))))) (vp-1 (d 必须) (vp-1 (d 重新) (v 估价)))))
POS model	1. 中国/nS 传统/a 医学/n 2.中国/nS 是/vC 多/a 民族/n 国家/n ，/wP 中华/nR 民族/n 是/vC ５０/m 多/m 个/qN 民族/n 的/uJDE 总称/n 。/wE
Head-recognition model	a O n np 0 n a O np 1 nS O np np 0 np nS O np 1

details of our approach, and In section 4, we present the details of experiment.

2 Parsing

Since English parsing has made many achievements, so we investigated some statistical parsing models designed for English. There are three open source constituent parsers, Stanford parser [3], Berkeley parser [4] and Bikel's parser [5]. Bikel's parser is an implementation of Collins' head-driven statistical model [6]. The Stanford parser is based on the factored model described in [7]. Berkeley parser is based on unlexicalized parsing model, as described in [8].

All the three parsers are claimed to be multilingual parsers but only accept training data in UPenn Treebank format. To adapt these parsers to Tsinghua Chinese Treebank (TCT) used in CIP, we firstly transform the TCT training data into UPenn format. Then, some slight modifications have been made to the three parsers. So that they could fulfill the needs in our task.

In our work, we use Stanford parser to train our model by change the training data to three parts with different formats, one for training parsing model, one for training POS model, and the last for training head-recognition model. Table 1 shows the three different forms.

3 Head recognition

Head recognition is to find the head word in a clause, for example, 'np-1' express that in the clause, the word with index '1' is the key word.

To recognize the head constituents, and extra step is needed since Stanford parsing could not provide a straight forward way for this. Consider that head constituents are always determined by their syntactic symbol and their neighbors, whose order and relations strongly affects the head labeling. Like chunking [9], it is natural to apply a sequence labeling strategy to tackle this problem. We adopt the linear-chain CRF [10], one of the most successful sequence labeling framework so far, for the head recognition is this stage.

4 Experiment

4.1 Data

The training data is from Tsinghua Chinese Treebank (TCT), and our task is to perform full parsing on them. There are 37218 lines in official released training data, As the Table 1 show; we change the data into three parts for different models.

The testing data doesn't contain POS labels, and there are 1000 lines in official released testing data.

Table 2. Different POS tagging results

	original	new
pos accuracy	80.40	94.82

4.2 Models training

4.2.1 Parsing model training

As for training parsing model with Stanford parser, since there are little parameters need to set, so we directly use the Stanford parser to train a model without any parameter setting.

4.2.2 POS model training

In this session of the evaluation, POS tagging is no longer as a separate task, so we have to train our own POS tagging model. In the evaluation process, we didn't fully consider the POS tagging results' impact on the overall results, so we didn't train the POS model specially, we directly use the POS function in Stanford parser toolkit. This has led to relatively poor results in POS tagging, and it also affects the overall parsing result. After the evaluation, we train a specific model to improve the POS tagging results. As the table 1 shows, we extract training data from the original corpus and adopt the linear-chain CRF to train a POS tagging model. Table 2 shows the original POS tagging results and new results.

4.2.3 Head recognition model training

As the table 1 shows, we extract specific training data from original corpus.

Table 3. Training data formats for Head-recognition

original corpus	1.[vp-0 减少/v [np-1 财政/n 收入/n]]
temp corpus	1.[np-1 财政/n 收入/n] 2.[vp-0 减少/v [np-1 财政/n 收入/n]]
final corpus	n O n np 0 n n O np 1 v O np vp 1 np v O vp 0

Table 4. Statistics the frequency of the words in each clause

number of word	statistics number
< 1	160
2	50834
3	12592
4	56
5	664
>5	360

And for head-word recognition, since the adjacent clause has little effect on the recognition of head-word, so we set the clause as the smallest unit. We chose CRF to train our model. However, for getting the proper format of data for training in CRF, We have to do further processing on the data. As the table 3 shows, the final data set word as the unit.

For example, the line 'n O np vp 1', the meaning from beginning to end is POS or clause mark of current word or clause, POS or clause mark of previous word, POS or clause mark of latter word, the clause mark of current word, and the last mean that if current word or clause is headword 1 represents YES, 0 represents NO.

4.4 Result and Conclusion

As we mention before, in evaluation, we didn't train specific POS tagging model, So we re-train our pos model, and the new results is shown in table 6, it can be seen that, with the increase of POS result, there is a corresponding increase in the overall results.

Table 5. Performance of head recognition and the template for model training

Boundary + Constituent	70.58
Boundary + Constituent + Head	66.97
template	U00:%x[0,0] U01:%x[-1,0] U02:%x[1,0] U04:%x[0,0]/%x[-1,0] U05:%x[0,0]/%x[1,0] U06:%x[-1,0]/%x[1,0]

Table 6. Overall results on different POS results

	POS	Boundary + Constituent
original	80.40	67.00
new	94.82	74.28

Through our evaluation results, we can see that it is not appropriate to directly use English parser toolkit to process Chinese. And it is urgent to development parsing model based on the characteristics of Chinese.

References

[1] T. L. Booth and R. A. Thompson. Applying Probability Measures to Abstract Languages. IEEE Transactions on Computers, 1973, C-22(5):422-450.

[2] M. Collins. Three Generative, Lexicalised Models for Statistical Parsing. In Proceedings of the 35th annual meeting of the association for computational linguistics.

[3] http://nlp.stanford.edu/software/lex-parser.html

[4] http://code.google.com/p/berkeleyparser

[5] http://www.cis.upenn.edu/~dbikel/download

[6] Michael Collins. 1999. Head-Driven Statistical Models for Natural Language Parsing. Ph.D. thesis. University of Pennsylvania.

[7] Dan Klein and Christopher D. Manning Accurate unlixicalized parsing. In Proceedings of the 41st Annual Meeting on Association for Computational Linguistics.

[8] S Petrov and D Klein. Improved inference for unlexicalized parsing. In Proceedings of NAACL HLT 2007.

[9] Fei Sha and Fernando Pereira. 2003. Shallow parsing with conditional random fields. In Proceedings of HLT-NAACL 2003, pages 213-220, Edmonton. Canada.

[10] John Lafferty. Andrew McCallum. And Fernando Pereira. 2001. Conditional random fields: Probabilistic models for segmenting and labeling sequence data. In Proceedings of ICML 2001, pages 282-289, Williams College, Williamstown, MA, USA.

Treebank Conversion based Self-training Strategy for Parsing

Zhiguo Wang and **Chengqing Zong**
National Laboratory of Pattern Recognition
Institute of Automation, Chinese Academy of Sciences
{zgwang, cqzong}@nlpr.ia.ac.cn

Abstract

In this paper, we propose a novel self-training strategy for parsing which is based on Treebank conversion (SSPTC). In SSPTC, we make full use of the strong points of Treebank conversion and self-training, and offset their weaknesses with each other. To provide good parse selection strategies which are needed in self-training, we score the automatically generated parse trees with parse trees in source Treebank as a reference. To maintain the constituency between source Treebank and conversion Treebank which is needed in Treebank conversion, we get the conversion trees with the help of self-training. In our experiments, SSPTC strategy is utilized to parse Tsinghua Chinese Treebank with the help of Penn Chinese Treebank. The results significantly outperform the baseline parser.

1 Introduction

Syntax parsing is one of the most fundamental tasks in natural language processing (NLP) and has attracted extensive attention during the past few decades. In statistical area, according to the type of data used in training stage, the parsing approaches can be classified into three categories: supervised, semi-supervised and unsupervised. In supervised parsing approach, a high-performance parser can be built when given sufficient labeled data (Charniak, 2000; Collins, 2003; Henderson, 2004). The semi-supervised approach utilizes some labeled data to annotate unlabeled data, then uses the annotated data to improve original model, e.g., self-training (McClosky et al., 2006) and co-training (Hwa et al., 2003). In unsupervised parsing, the labeled data was not employed and all annotations and grammars are discovered automatically from unlabeled data.

State-of-the-art supervised parsers (Charniak, 2000; Collins, 2003; Henderson, 2004) require large amounts of manually annotated training data, such as the Penn Treebank (Marcus et al., 1993), to achieve high performance. However, it is quite costly and time-consuming to create high quality labeled data. So it becomes a key bottleneck for supervised approach to acquire sufficient labeled training data. Self-training is an effective strategy to overcome this shortage. It tries to enlarge the training set with automatically annotated unlabeled data and trains a parser with the enlarged training set.

During the last few decades, many Treebanks annotated with different grammar formalisms are released (Zhou, 2004; Xue et al., 2005). Although they are annotated with different schemes, they have some linguistic consistency in some extent. Intuitively, we can convert Treebank annotated with one grammar formalisms into another Treebank annotated with grammar formalism that we are interested in. For simplicity, we call the first source Treebank, and the second target Treebank. And we call this strategy as Treebank conversion.

Although both self-training and Treebank conversion can overcome the limitation of labeled data shortage for supervised parsing in some extent, they all have drawbacks. For self-training, the quality of automatically annotated unlabeled data will affect the performance of semi-supervised parsers highly. For example, McClosky et al. (2006) shows that when the parser-best list is used for self-training, the parsing performance isn't improved, but after using reranker-best list, the retrained parser achieves an absolute 1.1% improvement. For Treebank conversion, different types among Treebanks make the converting procedure very complicated, and it is very hard to get a conversion Treebank constituent with target Treebank.

To overcome the limitations mentioned above, we propose a Treebank conversion based self-training strategy for parsing, which tries to combine self-training and Treebank conversion together.

Remainder of this paper is organized as follows. In Section 2, we introduce some related work. Section 3 describes details of our SSPTC strategy. In Section 4, we propose a head finding method for Task21 in CLP2010. The experiments and analysis is given in Section 5. The last section draws conclusions and describes the future work.

2 Related Work

With the development of statistical parsing approaches, large scale corpus has become an indispensable resource. Because of the limited amount of existing labeled training data and the hardness of constructing corpus, many strategies have been proposed and experimented to overcome the contradiction.

Self-training is one of the most successful strategies. McClosky et al. (2006) shows that self-training effectively improves the accuracy of English parsing. First, they trained a two-stage reranking parser(Charniak and Johnson, 2005) using Penn Treebank (PTB)(Marcus et al., 1993) and parsed 1,750k unlabeled sentences from North American News Text corpus (NANC). Then they combined the labeled NANC sentences with PTB together as training set and retrained the first stage of the parser. The final result got a 1.1% improvement over the previous best parser for section 23 of the Penn Treebank. Huang and Harper (2009) combined self-training into a PCFG-LA based parser both for English and Chinese. Experimental result showed that self-training contributed 0.83% absolute improvement using only 210k unlabeled sentences with a single generative parser. For the Chinese parsing, self-training contributed 1.03% absolute improvement.

Treebank Conversion is another potential strategy to reuse existing source Treebanks for the study of target grammar parsing. Wang et al. (1994) proposed a Treebank conversion algorithm for corpus sharing. They employed a parser with target grammar formalism to get *N*-best parse list for each sentence in source Treebank, selected the best conversion tree from the list using their algorithm, then inserted the conversion trees into training set, and finally retrained the parser with the enlarged training set. Experimental result shows their algorithm is effective. Collins et al. (1999) performed statistical constituency parsing of Czech on a Treebank that was converted from the Prague Dependency Treebank under the guidance of conversion rules and heuristic rules, and the final performance was also improved. Xia and Palmer (2001) proposed three methods to convert dependency trees into phrase structure trees with some hand-written heuristic rules. For acquisition of better conversion rules, Xia et al. (2008) proposed a method to automatically extract conversion rules from a target Treebank. Niu et al. (2009) tried to exploit heterogeneous Treebanks for parsing. They proposed a grammar formalism conversion algorithm to convert dependency formalism Treebank into phrase structure formalism, and did phrase structure parsing with the conversion trees. Their experiments are done in Chinese parsing, and the final performance is improved indeed.

In summary, from the existing work we are confident that the strategies of self-training and Treebank conversion are effective to improve the performance of parser.

3 Our Strategy

3.1 Parsing Algorithm

Although self-training and Treebank Conversion are effective for training set enlarging, they all have drawbacks. Self-training needs some parse selection strategies to select higher quality parsers. Treebank Conversion needs us to maintain the consistency between conversed Treebank and target Treebank. On the other hand, self-training strategy provides us a good idea to get annotated trees consistent with target grammar formalism, and the parse trees in source side provide a reference for higher quality parsers selecting. So we can combine self-training and Treebank Conversion together, use self-training strategy to get converted candidates for sentences in source Treebank, and select higher quality parses according to trees in source Treebank. We call this strategy Treebank

Conversion based Self-training, and show more details in Algorithm 1.

In Algorithm 1, target Treebank T_t and source Treebank T_s are input first (line 1). Then T_t is split into two parts: training set T_{train} and development set T_{dev} (line 3). And we train an

Algorithm 1

1: **Input**: T_t and T_s
2: ▷ initialize
3: $\{T_{train}, T_{dev}\} \leftarrow Split(T_t)$
4: $Parser_0 \leftarrow Train(T_{train}, T_{dev})$
5: ▷ *Iter* iterations
6: **for** $i \leftarrow 1 \dots Iter$ **do**
7: $T^i_{s\to t} \leftarrow \phi$
8: **for** $k \leftarrow 1 \dots N$ **do**
9: $ParseList_k \leftarrow Nbest(Parser_{i-1}, s_k)$
10: $\hat{p}_k = \arg\max_{p_j \in ParseList_k} Score(p_{s,k}, p_j)$
11: $T^i_{s\to t} \leftarrow \hat{p}_k$
12: $Parser_i \leftarrow Train(T_{train}, T_{dev}, T^i_{s\to t})$
13: **return** $Parser_{Iter}$

initial parser with T_{train} and T_{dev} in line 4. From line 6 to line 12, we train parsers with SSPTC strategy *Iter* times iteratively. Let $T^i_{s\to t}$ be the automatically converted Treebank from source Treebank to target Treebank grammar formalism during the *i*-th iteration. From line 8 to line 11, we try to get a conversion tree with target grammar for each of the *N* sentences in source Treebank. We get *N*-best parse list $ParseList_k$ for sentence s_k with $Parser_{i-1}$ (line 9), select the parse $\hat{p}_k$ with the highest score from $ParseList_k$ (line 10), and insert it into $T^i_{s\to t}$ (line 11). This procedure runs iteratively until all the trees in source Treebank have been converted, finally, we train a new parser $Parser_i$ with T_{train}, T_{dev} and $T^i_{s\to t}$ (line 12).

3.2 Parse selection

In line 10 of Algorithm 1, we select the highest quality parse $\hat{p}_k$ from $ParseList_k$ according to function $Score(p_s, p_{s\to t})$, where p_s denotes a tree in source Treebank and $p_{s\to t}$ denotes a conversion tree with target Treebank grammar formalism for p_s. $Score(p_s, p_{s\to t})$ compares $p_{s\to t}$ with p_s and computes a score for $p_{s\to t}$ taken p_s as a reference. According to the idea proposed in Wang et al. (1994), we use the number of aligned constituents in the source and target trees to construct $Score(p_s, p_{s\to t})$. We propose two types of $Score(p_s, p_{s\to t})$ as follows.

(1) Unlabeled aligned constituents F1 score (UAF)

First, we define a constituent as *tag[i,j]*, which represents a non-terminal node labeled with *tag* and spanning words from positions *i* to *j* of the input sentence. A non-terminal node in $p_{s\to t}$ aligns with a non-terminal node in p_s when they span the same words. If two nodes are aligned, we call them an aligned constituent and denote the aligned relationship as $tag_s[i,j] \Leftrightarrow tag_t[i,j]$. For example in Figure 1, there are three aligned constituents between the source Treebank tree and the conversion tree, and we can denote them as $IP_s[0,7] \Leftrightarrow dj_t[0,7]$, $NR_s[0,2] \Leftrightarrow sp_t[0,2]$ and $NR_s[2,6] \Leftrightarrow np_t[2,6]$, respectively.

When given p_s and $p_{s\to t}$, we can easily collect all the aligned constituents. So we define Unlabeled aligned constituents Precision (UAP) and Unlabeled aligned constituents Recall (UAR) as follows.

$$UAP = \frac{\sum_{i,j} Count(tag_s[i,j] \Leftrightarrow tag_t[i,j])}{\sum_{i,j} Count(tag_t[i,j])}$$

$$UAR = \frac{\sum_{i,j} Count(tag_s[i,j] \Leftrightarrow tag_t[i,j])}{\sum_{i,j} Count(tag_s[i,j])}$$

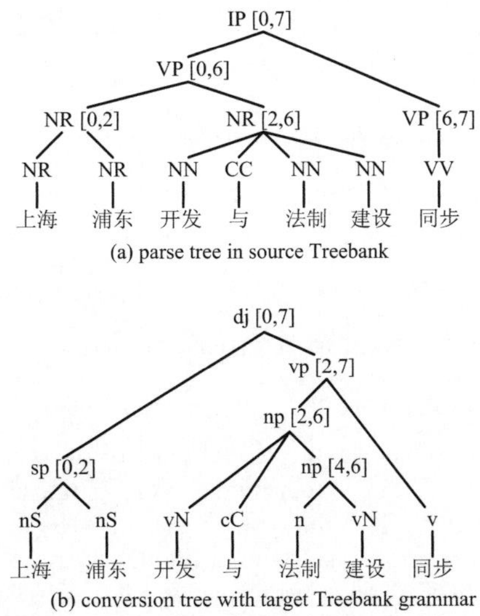

Figure 1: source tree and its conversion tree with target grammar formalism

Then Unlabeled aligned constituents F1 score (UAF) is defined as:

$$Score(p_s, p_{s\to t}) = \frac{2 \times UAP \times UAR}{UAP + UAR}$$
$$= \frac{2 \times \sum_{i,j} Count(tag_s[i,j] \Leftrightarrow tag_t[i,j])}{\sum_{i,j} (Count(tag_s[i,j]) + Count(tag_t[i,j]))} \quad (1)$$

(2) Labeled aligned constituents F1 score (LAF)

In the last subsection, we define $Score(p_s, p_{s\to t})$ according to UAF. In fact, the tags of constituents bring us much information to score conversion trees. So we define $Score(p_s, p_{s\to t})$ with Labeled aligned constituents F1 score (LAF) in this subsection.

Because the annotation schemes are different, constituent tags in source Treebank may be much more different from target Treebank. The number of such tags may be drastically different and the mapping may not be one-to-one. To eliminate the contradiction, we assume that each tag in source Treebank can be converted into every tag in target Treebank with various probabilities. So there is a converting matrix representing the converting probabilities, and we can calculate the converting matrix through source Treebank and *N*-best conversion trees.

Given the source Treebank and N-best conversion trees, first we align all the constituents, then collect all the aligned tags and compute the converting probability as the following equation.

$$p(tag_s \to tag_t) = \frac{Count(tag_s \Leftrightarrow tag_t)}{Count(tag_s)} \quad (2)$$

Finally, we modify UAF computed by equation (1) into LAF as below.

$$Score(p_s, p_{s\to t}) = \frac{2 \times \sum_{i,j} (1 + \gamma \times p(tag_s \to tag_t)) \times Count(tag_s[i,j] \Leftrightarrow tag_t[i,j])}{\sum_{i,j} (Count(tag_s[i,j]) + Count(tag_t[i,j]))} \quad (3)$$

In equation (3), γ is a tunable variable, which is used to weight the converting probability. Especially, LAF will be transferred into UAF when γ=0.

3.3 Corpus weighting technique

In line 12 of Algorithm 1, we train a new parser with target Treebank and conversion trees. However, the errors in automatically conversion trees are unavoidable and they would limit the accuracy of the self-trained model. So we have to take some measures to weight the gold target Treebank and the automatically conversion trees. McClosky et al. (2006) and Niu et al. (2009) take the strategy that duplicates the gold Treebank data many times. However, this strategy isn't suitable for PCFG-LA parser[1] (Matsuzaki et al., 2005; Petrov et al., 2006), because PCFG-LA employs an EM algorithm in training stage, so duplicating gold Treebank would increase the training time tremendously. Instead, according to Huang and Harper (2009), we weight the posterior probabilities computed for the gold and automatically converted trees to balance their importance.

Let $count(A \to \beta \mid t)$ be the count of rule $A \to \beta$ in a parse tree t. T_t and $T_{s\to t}$ are the sets of target Treebank and automatically converted trees from source Treebank respectively. The posterior probability of rule $A \to \beta$ (with weighting parameter α) can be expressed as:

[1] We will use BerkeleyParser as our baseline parser, which is a PCFG-LA based parser.

Feature templates
The label of the current constituent;
The label of the left most child, the middle child and the right most child;
The head word of the left most child, the middle child and the right most child;
The POS tag of the head word of the left most child, the middle child and the right most child;
Bigram of label, head word and POS tag of head word of the children: L/M, M/R;
Trigram of label, head word and POS tag of head word of the children: L/M/R;
The number of children;

Table 1: Feature Templates for Head Finding

$$p(A \rightarrow \beta) = \frac{\sum_{t \in T_t} Count(A \rightarrow \beta \mid t) + \alpha \sum_{t \in T_{s \rightarrow t}} Count(A \rightarrow \beta \mid t)}{\sum_{\beta} (\sum_{t \in T_t} Count(A \rightarrow \beta \mid t) + \alpha \sum_{t \in T_{s \rightarrow t}} Count(A \rightarrow \beta \mid t))} \quad (4)$$

4 Head Finding

In Task21 of CLP2010, we are required to find heads for each constituent. Our method is to make head finding as a post procedure after parsing.

We treat head finding problem as a classification problem, which is to classify each context-free production into categories labelled with their heads. For example, there are three types of heads: -0, -0-2 and -2 for $\text{vp} \rightarrow \text{vp wP vp}$, so we try to classify this production into categories labelled with -0, -0-2 and -2. First, we scan the train set and collect all the heads for each context-free production. Then we train a Maxent classifier to classify each context-free production into categories. We take the same feature templates for the classification as Chen et al. (2009) did, which is described in Table 1.

The head finding procedure proceeds in a bottom-up fashion, so that we can make use of heads of productions in lower layers as features for classification of the higher layers.

To evaluate the accuracy of our head finding method, we randomly select a development set, remove all head information and use our Maxent classifier to retrieve the heads. Experimental results show the accuracy has reached 98.28%. However, the final performance would drop much when the parse trees are generated automatically. Because the automatically generated parse trees would bring many errors, and the post procedure of head finding can't correct the errors.

5 Experiments and Analysis

5.1 Data Preparation

In order to evaluate the effectiveness of our approach, we do experiments for Chinese parsing using Tsinghua Chinese Treebank (TCTB) on target side and Penn Chinese Treebank (PCTB) on source side. We divide the training portion of the Tsinghua Chinese Treebank provided by CLP2010 into three parts as follows: 500 trees are randomly extracted as development set, another 500 as validating set and the rest trees are taken as training set. For trees in PCTB, all the empty-node and function tag information are removed. All the ParseVal measures reported in this paper are evaluated by the EVALB tool[2].

5.2 Experiments

In order to get a good final accuracy, we choose BerkeleyParser [3], which is a state-of-the-art unlexicalized parser, and train a model with the training set as our baseline. The F1 score of validating set parsed by baseline parser is 85.72%. In the following of this subsection, we try to combine our strategies into the baseline parser and evaluate the effectiveness. Because mult-time iterations can't improve parsing performance tremendously but cost much time during our experiments, we take *Iter*=1 here.

(1) Corpus weighting experiment

To evaluate the corpus weighting strategy, we take sentences (ignore the tree structure) in PCTB as unlabeled data, and train a parser with self-training strategy. F1 scores of validating set varying with α in equation (4) are shown in Figure 2. From Figure 2, we find that the F1 score varies with α, and reaches 86.46%

[2] http://nlp.cs.nyu.edu/evalb/

[3] http://code.google.com/p/berkeleyparser/

when α =1. The 0.74 absolute improvement comparing with the baseline certifies the effectiveness of our corpus weighting strategy.

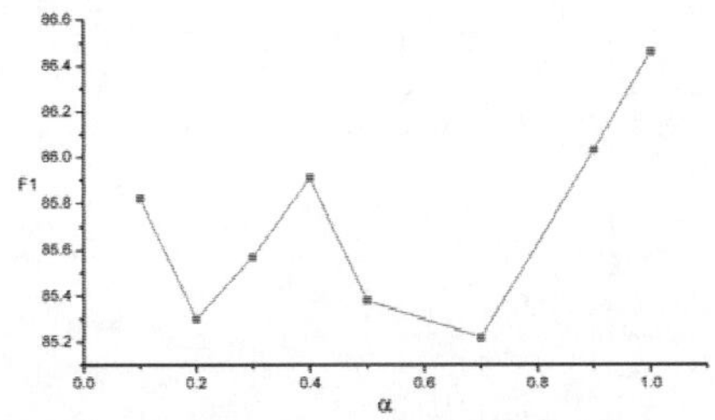

Figure 2: F1 score of self-training

(2) Parse selection experiments

In this subsection we evaluate our parse selection strategies with the help of PCTB. According to Algorithm 1, we train an initial parser with training set and development set. Then we generate 50-best parses list with the initial parser for each sentence in PCTB, and select a higher-score parse for each sentence through our parse selection strategies to build a conversion Treebank. Finally, we retrain a parser with training set and the conversion Treebank with the help of corpus weighting strategy.

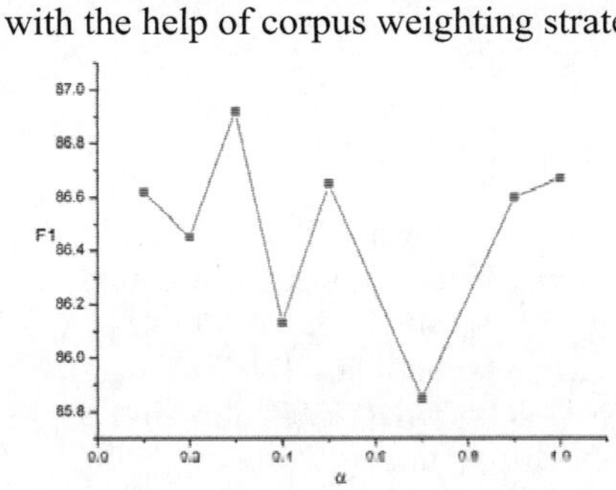

Figure 3: F1 score of UAF strategy

Figure 3 shows F1 scores of validating set using UAF to select higher quality parses. When α =0.3, F1 score reaches 86.92%. The improvement over baseline is 1.2 percentage points. Comparing with the highest F1 score of self-training, we got 0.46 more improvement. So our parse selection strategy with UAF is effective.

Because the highest F1 score is at the point α =0.3 in Figure 3, we choose α =0.3 to evaluating LAF strategy. Figure 4 shows F1 scores on validating set using LAF. The highest F1 score is 87.44% at the point γ =6, and it gets 1.72 percentage points improvement over baseline. Comparing with UAF, LAF gets 0.52 more improvement. So we can conclude that the parse selection strategy with LAF is much more effective.

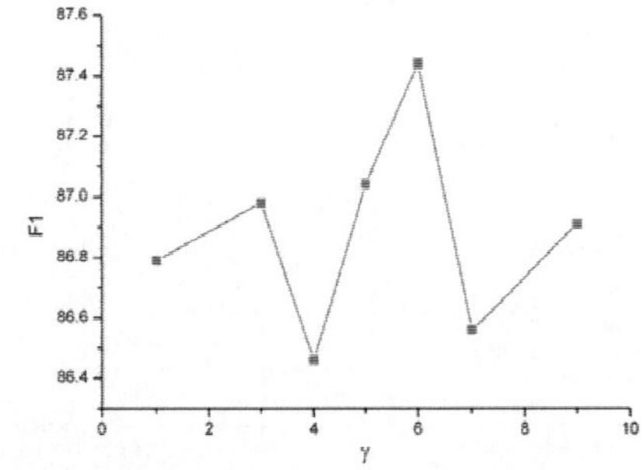

Figure 4: F1 score of LAF strategy

5.3 Discussion

Table 2 reports the highest performances of various strategies. From the table we can easily find that all strategies outperform the baseline parser. Corpus weighting experiment tells us that balancing the importance of gold target Treebank and conversion trees is helpful for the final performance. Using UAF to select conversion trees can get more improvement than self-training which just selects the best-first trees. This fact proves that our SSPTC strategy is reasonable and effective. Making use of LAF, we get more improvement than UAF. It tells us that exploiting source Treebank deeply can bring us more useful knowledge which is helpful to develop high-performance parser.

Strategy	F1 score
Baseline	85.72%
Corpus weighting	86.46%
UAF	86.92%
LAF	87.44%

Table 2: F1 scores of various strategies

6 Experiments for Task 2 of CLP2010

Task 2 of CLP2010 includes two sub-tasks: sub-sentence parsing and complete sentence parsing. For each sub-task, there are two tracks: closed track and open track. To accomplish tasks in closed track, we make use of our baseline parser shown in section 5 and train it with different parameters and data set. For open track, we make use of our SSPTC strategy and train it with different parameters and data set. We tuned the parameters on the development set and selected

Sub-task	Track	ID	Parser	Parameters	Train data
Sub-task 1	Closed	a	Berkeley	--	TS
		b	Berkeley	--	TS && VS
	Open	a	SSPTC	$\alpha = 0.3$ $\gamma = 5$	TS && PTCB
		b	SSPTC	$\alpha = 0.3$ $\gamma = 5$	TS && VS && PTCB
Sub-task 2	Closed	a	Berkeley	--	TS
		b	Berkeley	--	TS && VS
	Open	a	SSPTC	$\alpha = 0.3$ $\gamma = 6$	TS && PTCB
		b	SSPTC	$\alpha = 0.3$ $\gamma = 5$	TS && VS && PTCB
		c	SSPTC	$\alpha = 0.3$ $\gamma = 5$	TS && PTCB
		d	SSPTC	$\alpha = 0.3$ $\gamma = 3$	TS && PTCB

Table 3: The configurations of our systems. The abbreviations in the last column mean training set(TS) and validating set(VS) explaining in section 5.1.

some configurations which achieve higher performance on the development set(more details have been shown in section 5). The final parameters and training data of our systems are shown in Table 3[4]. We also make use of the approach explained in section 4 for the head finding procedure.

The parsing results of our systems on the test set can be found on the official ranking report. Our systems training with SSPTC strategy bring us an amazing performance which outperforms other systems in both the two sub-tasks.

7 Conclusion and Future work

In this paper, we propose a novel self-training strategy for parsing which is based on Treebank conversion. Benefiting from SSPTC strategy, we have gotten higher quality parse trees with the help of source Treebank, and gotten conversion Treebank with target Treebank grammar formalism simply and consistently. The parsing results on validating set show SSPTC is effective. We apply SSPTC to the test set of Task 2 in CLP2010, and get 1.27[5] percentage points improvement over baseline parser using the parameters tuned on validating set.

All the delightful results tell us that SSPTC is a promoting strategy for parsing. However, there is much knowledge in source Treebank remained to further exploit, e.g. the POS tags in source Treebank is a good resource to improve the POS tagging accuracy of target Treebank. So, in the next step we will exploit source Treebank deeply and try to get more knowledge from it for parsing.

Acknowledgement

The research work has been partially funded by the Natural Science Foundation of China under Grant No. 6097 5053, 90820303 and 60736014, the National Key Technology R&D Program under Grant No. 2006BAH03B02, the Hi-Tech Research and Development Program ("863" Program) of China under Grant No. 2006AA010108-4, and also supported by the China-Singapore Institute of Digital Media (CSIDM) project under grant No. CSIDM-200804.

References

Eugene Charniak, 2000. A maximum-entropy-inspired parser. In NAACL-2000

Eugene Charniak and Mark Johnson, 2005. Coarse-to-fine n-best parsing and MaxEnt discriminative reranking. In ACL-05.

Xiao Chen, Changning Huang, Mu Li and Chunyu Kit, 2009. Better Parser Combination. In CIPS.

[4] The parsing result for system b in open track of sub-task1 has been submitted mistakenly, so the figures of this system on the official ranking report have no reference value.

[5] The F1 score of baseline parser is 75.24%, and it reaches 76.51% using TCBS strategy.

Michael Collins, 2003. Head-driven statistical models for natural language parsing. Computational Linguistics, 29 (4). pages 589-637.

M Collins, J Hajic, L Ramshaw and C Tillman, 1999. A statistical parser for Czech. In ACL-99. J Henderson, 2004. Discriminative training of a neural network statistical parser.

Zhongqiang Huang and Mary Harper, 2009. Self-Training PCFG grammars with latent annotations across languages. ACL-09.

R Hwa, M Osborne, A Sarkar and M Steedman, 2003. Corrected co-training for statistical parsers. Citeseer.

MP Marcus, B Santorini and MA Marcinkiewicz, 1993. Building a large annotated corpus of English: The Penn Treebank. Computational Linguistics, 19 (2). pages 313-330.

Takuya Matsuzaki, Yusuke Miyao and Jun'ichi Tsujii, 2005. Probabilistic CFG with latent annotations. In ACL-05.

David McClosky, Eugene Charniak and Mark Johnson, 2006. Effective self-training for parsing. In ACL-06.

Zheng-Yu Niu, Haifeng Wang and Hua Wu, 2009. Exploiting heterogeneous treebanks for parsing. In ACL-09, pages 46-54.

Slav Petrov, Leon Barrett, Romain Thibaux and Dan Klein, 2006. Learning accurate, compact, and interpretable tree annotation. In ACL-06.

Jong-Nae Wang, Jing-Shin Chang and Keh-Yih Su, 1994. An automatic treebank conversion algorithm for corpus sharing. In ACL-94.

Fei Xia and Martha Palmer, 2001. Converting dependency structures to phrase structures. In The 1st Human Language Technology Conference (HLT-2001).

Fei Xia, Owen Rambow, Rajesh Bhatt, Martha Palmer and Dipti Misra Sharma, 2008. Towards a multi-representational treebank. Proc. of the 7th Int'lWorkshop on Treebanks and Linguistic Theories (TLT-7). pages 207-238.

Qiang Zhou, 2004. Annotation Scheme for Chinese Treebank. Journal of Chinese Information Processing, 18 (004).

A Chinese LPCFG Parser with Hybrid Character Information

Wenzhi Xu, Chaobo Sun and Caixia Yuan
School of Computer,
Beijing University of Posts and Telecommunications,
Beijing, 100876 China
{ earl808, sunchaobo}@gmail.com
yuancx@bupt.edu.cn

Abstract

We present a new probabilistic model based on the lexical PCFG model, which can easily utilize the Chinese character information to solve the lexical information sparseness in lexical PCFG model. We discuss in particular some important features that can improve the parsing performance, and describe the strategy of modifying original label structure to reduce the label ambiguities. Final experiment demonstrates that the character information and label modification improve the parsing performance.

1 Introduction

Parsing is an important and fundamental task in natural language processing. The challenge of Chinese parser has been the focus of attention in recent years, and many different kinds of Chinese parsing models are investigated. (Bikel, 2000) adopts Head-Driven model to parse Chinese. (Levy, 2003) analyzes the difficulties of Chinese parsing through comparing the differences between Chinese and English. (Wang, 2006) utilizes shift-reduce approach, dramatically improved the decoding speed of parsing. All these research adopted the same models which are also used in English parser – the models based on the words.

However, there is a big difference between English and Chinese: the expressing unit in English is word, while character is the smallest unit in Chinese. Due to difficulties of word segmentation, especially for different segmenting criteria, many researchers explored parsing Chinese based on characters. The parser of (Luo, 2003) received sentence as input and conducted word segmentation and syntactic parsing at the same time, but they did not utilize the character information in generating subtree; (Zhao, 2009)'s dependency parsing tree totally abandoned the word concept, so the dependency relations are the relations between characters.

We combine both word and character information to gain better performance of parsing. Although the criteria of segmentation are difficult to be unified, different criteria conflict only within the phrases which have little influence on the structure between phrases. So we still use word as our basic unit of parsing. Although word has been proved to be effective in head-driven parser (Collins,1999), the data of word dependence is very sparse. While it is worthy to note that words with similar concept always share the same characters in Chinese. For instance, "科学家(scientist)", "历史学家(historian)", etc., share the same character "家(expert)", since they belong to the same concept "expert in a certain field". So the problem of word sparseness can be solved by combining the character information to some extent.

Throughout this paper, we use TCT Treebank (Zhou, 2004) as experimental data. TCT mainly consists of binary trees, with a few of multi-branch and single-branch trees. Thus, we first transfer all trees to binary trees. Then we use Lexical-PCFG model to exploit the word and character information, and Maximum Entropy Model to calculate the probability of induced trees as (Charinak, 2000). Finally we use CKY-based decoder.

In the following section, we will introduce how to utilize character information in our parsing model and the other features in detail. Section 3 gives experiment results and analysis, which show improvement of our parsing approach. Section 4 presents the conclusion and future work.

2 Lexical PCFG model

2.1 Model Introduction

Starting from the Lexical-PCFG model (Model 2 in Collins, 1999), we propose a new generative process which can conveniently exploit the character information and other features.

Assume P is the label of parent, H is the head child of the rule, and $L1, ..., Ln$ and $R1, ..., Rn$ is the left and right modifiers of H. Then the rule of Lexical-PCFG (LPCFG) can be written as:

$$P(hw, ht) \rightarrow L_n(lw_n, lt_n)...L_1(lw_1, lt_1)H(hw, ht) R_1(rw_1, rt_1)...R_n(rw_n, rt_n), \quad (1)$$

where (hw, ht) represents the head word and head tag of head child, $(lw1, lt1), ..., (lwn, ltn)$ and $(rw1, rt1), ..., (rwn, rtn)$ are the head words and head tags of left and right modifiers, and parent node P's head word and tag are the same as that of H.

As mentioned above, our trees are all binary trees. In this case, the LPCFG can be written as:

$$P(hw, ht) \rightarrow H(hw, ht)R(rw, rt), \quad (2)$$

$$P(hw, ht) \rightarrow L(lw, lt)H(hw, ht). \quad (3)$$

Formula 2 and 3 represent that the head child is the left or right child respectively. The probability of the rule is conditioned on the head words and tags of head and its modified children, which is specified as:

$$Pr(P, L, H|hw, ht, lw, lt), \quad (4)$$

and

$$Pr(P, R, H|hw, ht, rw, rt). \quad (5)$$

To calculate these probabilities, we rewrite Equation 4 and 5 by three factors in 6 and 7 using the chain rule.

$$Pr(P, R, H|hw, ht, lw, lt) = Pr_d(P - DIR|hw, ht, lw, lt) * Pr_h(H|P, hw, ht) *Pr_m(L - DIR|P, H, hw, ht), \quad (6)$$

$$Pr(P, R, H|hw, ht, rw, rt) = Pr_d(P - DIR|hw, ht, rw, rt) * Pr_h(H|P, hw, ht) *Pr_m(R - DIR|P, H, hw, ht). \quad (7)$$

in which, DIR=LEFT/RIGHT. DIR in P-DIR is used to discriminate different positions of head child, DIR in L-DIR and R-DIR are used to represent different positions of modifiers.

The calculation processes of Equation 6 and 7 can be interpreted by following generative process. Firstly, the head words and tags of children generate the parent and the head position (the first probability in Equation 6 and 7). We define this probability as the word dependency probability Pr_d: if two words (or characters in words) always appear together in the training data, this probability will be large (< 1); if two words (or characters in words) do not have any dependence in the training data, this probability will be approximately equal to $1/|Y|$, where $|Y|$ is the predicted number of the Pr_d. The second probability generates the head child label (defined as the head child probability Pr_h), we hold that the head word and tag of modifier do not provide information to determine the head child label, so we omit them. The third one produces the modifier label, which is defined as the modifier probability Pr_m, and evaluates the dependency relation between modifier and the head child. We also omit the influence of the head word and tag of modifier.

For example, assume there is a tree as shown in Figure 1. For the rule "vp $\rightarrow$ v np", head child of parent vp and np are the left child v and right child n respectively, so "组织(organize)" and "专家(expert)" are the head word of vp and np. Thus the LPCFG rule is "vp(组织,v) $\rightarrow$ v(组织,v)

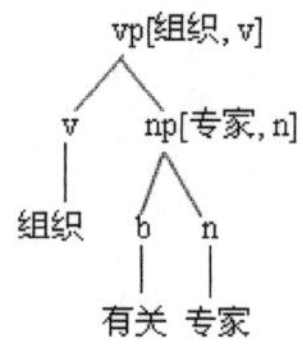

Figure 1: Tree representation of LPCFG rule.

np(专家,n)". The probability can be written as: $Pr_d(vp\text{-LEFT} \mid$ 组织$,v,$专家$,n) * Pr_h(v|vp,$组织$,v) * Pr_m(np\text{-RIGHT} \mid vp, v,$ 组织$,v)$.

2.2 Probability Model and Feature Set

We use Maximum Entropy (ME) Model to compute probabilities of candidate trees. ME model estimate parameters that would maximize the entropy over distributions, meanwhile satisfy certain constraints. These constraints will force the model to reflect characteristic of training data. With the feature function, Maximum Entropy can exploit kinds of features flexibly, some of which are very important to improve the performance of tasks at hand. ME model has been applied successfully in many tasks, such as parser (Charniak, 2000; Luo, 2003), POS tagging (Ratnaparkhi,1996), etc. In our experiment, we use Maxent toolkit developped by Zhang (Zhang, 2004), which uses the LBFGS algorithm for parameter estimation. Details of the model and toolkit can be seen in (Berger, 1996; Zhang, 2004).

Our features consist of four parts: basic features, character features, context features and overlapping features of character and context. Basic features are traditional LPCFG features, including head word, head tag and the label. We extract the first and last characters of a word as the Character features, of course for a single character word the first and last character are the same. Context features are defined as the previous and following POS tags of the current subtree, and these features utilize the information outside of the subtree very well without increasing the complexity of parsing decoder. Overlapping features are the combinations of character features and context features.

Take Chinese sentence "委员会/n 由/p 农业部/n 组织/v 有关/b 专家/n 组建/v 完成/v (Committee is composed of experts organized by the Ministry of Agriculture)" for example, the corresponding rule is "vp(组织,v) → v(组织,v) np(专家,n)", the feature template of the example sentence is shown in Table 1.

When applying the character information, it is worthwhile to note that character is always combined with the POS tag of the word since the sense of single character varies as word's POS tag changes. For example, the sense of "爱(love)" in verb "爱护(care and protect)" and noun "爱情(love)" is different. Of course the sense discussed here is reflected in the dependency of words: "爱护(care and protect)" can be followed by some nouns which are objects, while "爱情(love)" can not.

For the multi-branch tree, (Collins,1999) calculates the probability of the left or right modifier with a feature which represent whether there are modifiers between current modifier and the head child (distance feature). But in the situation of binary tree, it is obvious that current modifier is unlikely to follow other modifiers. Since the representation of binary tree conforms to the X-bar theory of Chomsky, we can modify the head child label to get this non-local information in binary tree. For instance, a multi-branche tree rule "vp1 → pp d vp2" corresponding to these two binary tree rules: "vp3 → pp vp4" and "vp4 → d vp5" (the index numbers of the vb here stand for different vp). So when we calculate the probability of pp with the multi-branch situations, d lies between pp and vp2. While in binary tree situation, we cannot catch this information between pp and vp4. However, we can modify vp4 to vp-LEFT, which means there is a modifier at the left child of vp4, then we get the similar effect in (Collins, 1999). We call this as the head position labeling.

2.3 Label splitting and Head Position Modifying

(Klein, 2003) improves the performance of parser via splitting the POS tag in corpus. We split the non-terminal label using the same approaches (assuming the POS tag is terminal label). The need of label splitting is that the corpus does not sufficiently consider different situations and treat them

Table 1: Feature templates and symbol explanation.

	Pr_d (vp-LEFT)		Pr_h (v)		Pr_m (np-RIGHT)	
basic	lw rw	组织专家	p	vp	p h	vp v
feature	lw lt rw rt	组织v 专家n	p hw	vp 组织	p h hw	vp v组织
			p hw ht	vp 组织v	p h hw ht	vp v 组织v
			p ht	vp v	p h ht	vp v v
char.	lw frc rt	组织专n	p fhc ht	vp 组v	p h fhc ht	vp v 组v
feature	other combinations	···	p lhc ht	vp 织v	p h lhc ht	vp v 织v
	flc lt frc rt	组v 专n				
	other combinations	···				
context	lw rw pt1 at1	组织专家n v	p pt1	vp n	p h pt1	vp v n
feature	lw lt rw rt pt1 at1	组织v 专家n n v	p pt1 pt2	vp n p	p h pt1 pt2	vp v n p
			p at1	vp v	p h at1	vp v v
			p at1 at2	vp v v	p h at1 at2	vp v v v
			p pt1 at1	vp n v	p h pt1 at1	vp v n v
			p hw pt1 at1	vp 组织v n	p h hw pt1 at1	vp v组织v n
overlap	lw frc rt pt1 at1	组织专n n v	p fhc ht pt1 at1	vp 组v n v	p h fhc ht pt1 at1	vp v 组v n v
feature	other combinations	...	p lhc ht pt1 at1	vp 织v n v	p h lhc ht pt1 at1	vp v 织v n v
	flc lt frc rt pt1 at1	组v 专n n v				
	other combinations	...				

Symbol Explanation	
frc lrc	the first and last characters of the head word of the right child
pt at	previous and following POS tag of current subtree, number indicates the position
flc llc	the first and last characters of the head word of the left child
fhc lhc	the first and last characters of the head word

as the same label which results in ambiguity. Furthermore, in our experiment, the corpus that we adopt is binary tree. Though the rule set in binary tree is closed, it brings stronger independent assumption (Jonson,1998). Thus splitting the label can make the node label represent more information from descendants. Just like the intuition of head position labeling, this is also one method to utilize the non-local information. We mainly consider these modifying as follows.

First of all, we split the label vp. There are three kinds of verb phrases: the first one is that there is modifier ahead (such as advp); the second phrase consists of an object; while the third one has the form of two verbs or verb plus an auxiliary word. The formal two situations can not follow any object any more (some double-object verb phrase may be continued to contain object, but their POS label is different with common verb), the vp in last situation can be followed by object (there maybe actually no object). If we do not discriminate these situations, it will be easy to result in dividing the object into two objects during parsing test, just as shown in Figure 2. However, if we modify vp in the third situation into vb, then this difference can be discriminated well. We take a simple statistics as an example to illustrate the sense. Assume our object is np, rule "vp → vp np" appears for 5,284 times in corpus before modifying, while it present only 166 times after modifying.

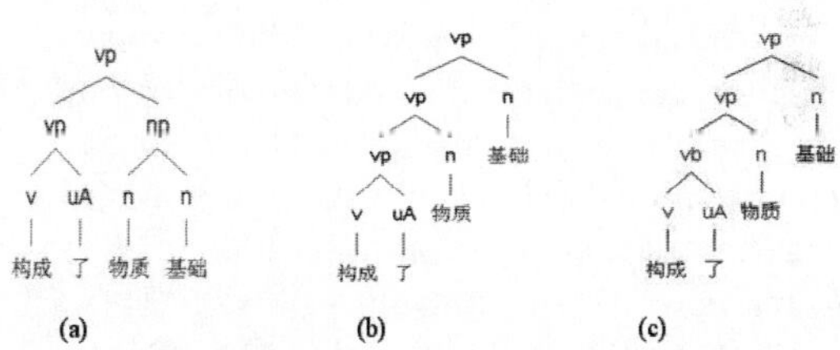

Figure 2: Parsing Result Example: (a) is a correct tree, (b) is a wrong one, while the probability may be not small enough, (c) is also wrong, but the probability is very small due to the symbol vb.

Secondly, we also split the np tag. We notice that a noun phrase, which consists of non-noun (phrase) modifier (such as ADJP, PP) and a noun (phrase), is always the final noun phrase but rarely part of another noun phrase. So we transform the np, which has the non-noun (phrase) modifier, to nm. From the statistics of corpus, we find rule "np $\rightarrow$ np n" occurs for 4,502 times, while "np $\rightarrow$ nm n" only appears 826 times.

Finally, we change the head position of preposition phrase. The head position of preposition phrases in corpus mostly is the phrase behind the preposition, but we found the grammar of preposition phrase is much related to the preposition. Take the preposition "以(by)" and "对(to)" as example, these two prepositions occur for 755 and 1,300 times respectively. In our corpus, 98.7% of preposition phrases with 以(by)" are the modifiers of verb phrases, while only 57.2% of phrases with "对(to)" appear as the modifiers of verb phrases, and the remaining 42.8% are the modifiers of noun phrases.

3 Experiment Result and Analysis

Our experiments are conducted on the TCT corpus, which is used as the standard data of the CIPS-SIGHAN Parser 2010 bakeoff. We omit the sentences with length 1 during training and testing. Performance on the test corpus is evaluated with the standard measures from (SIGHAN REPORT, 2010).

We submit two results for the parsing bakeoff: one is single model we described in Section 2, another is reranking model, which is an attempt to apply a perceptron algorithm to rerank the 50-best result produced by the ME model.[1] Table 2 shows the result of our parser compared with the top one in this bakeoff. Since the parser we built is strictly dependent on the POS tags, the precision of POS tagging has a harsh effect on the overall parsing performance.

The performance of the rerank model is lightly lower than that of the single model. The most likely reason is that the features we count on are far from enough, and the informative features proved to be useful in (Charniak and Johnson, 2003) are not yet included in our discriminative ranker. Besides, the rank model we used is a simple perceptron learner, more delicated model, such as ME model used in (Charniak and Johnson,

Table 3: Results of different features with no limit sentence length.

feature set	LR	LP	F	CB	0CB	2CB
basic	80.19	79.61	79.90	1.20	56.10	83.49
+ch	81.91	81.38.	81.65	1.10	58.34	84.95
+cont	85.53	85.34	85.44	0.83	65.62	88.86
+ch + cont	86.17	85.94	86.06	0.80	66.61	89.62
+ch + cont + ol	86.34	86.13	86.24	0.79	66.65	89.81
+ch + cont + ol + cwd	86.47	86.26	86.37	0.78	66.73	89.87
+ch + cont + ol + cwd + cm	87.03	86.77	86.90	0.75	67.06	90.36
+ch + cont + ol + cwd + cm + hpl	87.20	86.94	87.07	0.74	67.43	90.40

ch=character feature, cont=context feature
ol=overlap feature, cwd=coordinate word dependence
cm=corpus modifying, hpl= head position label

2003), might improve the result.

In order to make clear how different features effect the parser performance, we conducted experiments on the TCT data provided by CIPS-ParEval-2009 for Chinese parser bakeoff [2], since the sentences in CIPSParEval-2009 are given with head words and gold-standard POS tags. The results of our parser are given in Table 3. From Table 3 we can see that character features bring the improvement of F score for 1.75 compared with the basic features (line 2 vs line 3), and for 0.8 after adding the context features (line 4 vs line 6). These results show that character features can improve the model with basic features very well. After applying the context features, character features can still bring improvement, which states that character features can solve the ambiguities that can not be solved by the context features.

One likely reason why character information is helpful is that the character can partly represent the meaning of word and can partly resolve the sparseness problem of word dependence as been observed in the work of (Kang, 2005). Kang calculated the statistics for 50,000 double characters words and divided the methods of constructing word into 8 types according to the relations of meaning between word and characters:

(1) A+B=A=B (2) A+B=A
(3) A+B=B (4) A+B=C
(5) A+B=A+B (6) A+B=A+B+D
(7) A+B=A+D (8) A+B=D+B

A and B stand for the meaning of the two characters which are used to construct the word. C is a totally new meaning and D represents an ad-

[1] More details can be found in (Charniak and Johnson, 2003; Huang, 2008). The features we used include ParentRule, RightBranch, Rule, Heads, WProj described in (Charniak and Johnson, 2003).

[2] http://www.ncmmsc.org/CIPS-ParsEval-2009/index.asp, the first workshop on Chinese Syntactic Parsing Evaluation, November, 2009.

Table 2: Results of different features with no limit sentence length.

	"B+C"-P	"B+C"-R	"B+C"-F1	"B+C+H"-P	"B+C+H"-R	"B+C+H"-F1	POS-P
Top one	85.42	85.35	85.39	83.69	83.63	83.66	93.96
Single	74.86	76.05	75.45	71.06	72.20	71.63	87.00
Rerank	74.48	75.64	75.05	70.72	71.81	71.26	87.00

Table 4: The relation between the meaning of words and characters.

type	1	2	3	4	5	6	7	8
word number	4035	1031	297	4201	14455	23562	2780	1886
rate(%)	7.71	1.97	0.57	8.02	27.60	44.99	5.31	3.60

ditional meaning. The expression after the first "=" is the meaning of the word, and the symbol "+" indicates the melding of meaning. For example, A+B=A+D indicates that the word retains the meaning of character A, and adds new meaning D. The distribution of each type in the dataset is shown in Table 4. From Table 4 we can see that type 4, i.e., there are no relation between characters and word, occupies only 8.02%. This data proves that the word inherits the meaning from the characters which are used to construct the word. However, the relations are really complicated. For example, some words only inherit the meaning of formal characters and others of the last characters. This might be the reason why character information does not have very obvious effect as expected.

In our parsing model, context features are really helpful to the parsing accuracy. Different with the decision method in (Rantnaparkhi, 1999) and (Wang, 2006), and reranking in (Collins, 2000) which all can utilize the context of current subtree very well (not only the POS tag), the CYK decoding algorithm restricts our context features. However, we can conveniently exploit the POS tags around the current subtree without increasing the complexity of decoding and thus improve the performance.

Commonly, each subtree has only one head word. However, we notice that the two head words of two coordinate children are equivalent, as illustrated in Figure 3. We assume that the parent node of these two children is A and the two head word are all the head words of A. When A is the child of the parent node B, all the head words in A can be dependent with the other head

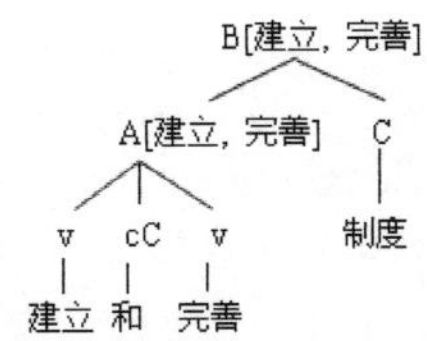

Figure 3: Example of dependence between coordinate words.

words of another child C. When A is still the head child of B, the head words of B are also the same as A. Then we can extract more word dependence data. For example, A have two head words "建立(construct)" and "完善(complete)", and "制度(rule)" is the head word of C, then we consider that "建立(construct)" and "完善(complete)" are all dependent with "制度(rule)". Meanwhile, A is also the head child of B, and the head words of B are also "建立(construct)" and "完善(complete)". During the decoding, we choose the most probable dependence as the dependence probability of B. From the result, we can see that this strategy yields 0.17 improvements in the F score.

Label splitting can also improve the performance. However, modifying the labels need much linguistic knowledge and manual work. (Petrov, 2006) proposed an automated splitting and merging method. As an attempt, we tested the effectiveness of it in our parser empirically. When tested on the TCT data provided by CIPS-ParsEval-2009 for Chinese parser, bakeoff the label spitting improve the F1 measure from 0.864 to 0.869.

4 Conclusion and Future Work

This paper presents a new lexical PCFG model, which can synthetically exploit the word and character information. The results of experiment prove the effectiveness of character information.

Also our model can utilize the context features and some non-local features which can dramatically improve the performance.

In future work, we need improve the decoding algorithm to exploit more complex features. As the parser we build is greatly dependent on the preprocessing result of word segmentation, POS tagging and head labeling, a critical direction of future work is to do word-segmentation, POS tagging, head detection and parsing in a unified framework. Besides, as for the K-best reranking, we should take into account more informative features and more powerful reranking model.

Acknowledgment

This research has been partially supported by the National Science Foundation of China (NO. NSFC90920006). We also thank Xiaojie Wang, Huixing Jiang, Jiashen Sun and Bichuan Zhang for useful discussion of this work.

References

A.L. Beger, S. A. D Pietra, and V.J.D Pietra. 1996. A maximum entropy approach to natural language processing. *Computational Linguistics*, 39–71.

D.M. Bikel and D. Chiang. 2000. Two statistical parsing models applied to the Chinese Treebank. *In Proceedings of the Second Chinese Language Processing Workshop*, 1–6.

E. Charniak. 2000. A maximum-entropy-inspired parser. *In Proceedings of the 1st NAACL*, Seattle, WA, 132–139.

E. Charniak. 1997. Statistical parsing with a context-free grammar and word statistics. *In Proceddings of the Fourteenth National Conference on Artificial Intelligence*, Menlo Park, CA. 598–603.

X. Chen, C.N. Huang, M. Li, and C.Y. Kit. 2009. Better Parser Combination. *In CIPS ParsEval*, Beijing, China. 81–90.

M. Collins. 1999. *Head-Driven Statistical Models for Natural Language Parsing.* Ph.D. Dissertation, University of Pennsylvania.

M. Collins. 2000. Discriminative reranking for natural language parsing. *In Proceedings of ICML 2000*, 175–182.

S.Y. Kang, X.X. Xu, and M.S. Sun. 2005. The Research on the Modern Chinese Semantic Word-Formation. *Journal of Chinese Language and Computing*, 103–112.

D. Klein and C. Manning. 2003. Accurate unlexicalized parsing. *In Proceedings of ACL 2003*, 423–430.

L. Huang. 2008. Forest Reranking: Discriminative Parsing with Non-Local Features. *In Proceedings of ACL 2008*, 586–594.

D. Klein and C.D. Manning. 2003. Accurate unlexicalized parsing. *In Proceedings of ACL 2003*, 423–430.

E. Charniak and M. Johnson. 2005. Coarse-to-fine n-best parsing and MaxEnt discriminative reranking. *In Proceedings of ACL 2005*, 173–180.

R. Levy and C.D. Manning. 2003. Is it harder to parse Chinese, or the Chinese Treebank? *In Proceedings of ACL 2003*, 439–446.

X.Q. Luo. 2003. A maximum entropy Chinese character-based parser. *In Proceedings of EMNLP 2003*, 192–199.

M. Johnson. 1998. PCFG models of linguistic tree representations. *Computational Linguistics*, 613–632.

S. Petrov, L. Barrett, R. Thibaux, and D. Klein. 2006. Learning accurate, compact, and interpretable tree annotation. *In Proceedings of ACL 2006*, 433–440.

A. Ratnaparkhi. 1996. A maximum entropy part-of-speech tagger. *In Proceedings of EMNLP 1996*, 133–142.

A. Ratnaparkhi. 1999. Learning to parse natural language with maximum entropy models. *Machine Learning*, 503–512.

M.W. Wang, K. Sagae, and T. Mitamura. 2006. A Fast, Accurate Deterministic Parser for Chinese. *In Proceedings of ACL 2006*, 425–432.

L. Zhang. 2004. *Reference Manual.* Maximum Entropy Modeling Toolkit for Python and C++.

H. Zhao. 2009. Character-Level Dependencies in Chinese: Usefulness and Learning. *In Proceedings of 12th ECACL 2009*, 879–887.

SIGHAN REPORT. 2010. SIGHAN REPORT ON TASK2. *In Proceedings of CIPS-SIGHAN 2010*, Beijing, China.

Q. Zhou. 2004. Annotation Scheme for Chinese Treebank. *Journal of Chinese Information Processing*, 1–8.

Complete Syntactic Analysis Based on Multi-level Chunking

ZhiPeng Jiang and **Yu Zhao** and **Yi Guan** and
Chao Li and **Sheng Li**
School of Computer Science and Technology,
Harbin Institute of Technology,
150001, Harbin, China
xyf-3456@163.com; woshizhaoy@gmail.com
guanyi@hit.edu.cn; beyondlee2008@yahoo.cn
lisheng@hit.edu.cn

Abstract

This paper describes a complete syntactic analysis system based on multi-level chunking. On the basis of the correct sequences of Chinese words provided by CLP2010, the system firstly has a Part-of-speech (POS) tagging with Conditional Random Fields (CRFs), and then does the base chunking and complex chunking with Maximum Entropy (ME), and finally generates a complete syntactic analysis tree. The system took part in the Complete Sentence Parsing Track of the Task 2 Chinese Parsing in CLP2010, achieved the F-1 measure of 63.25% on the overall analysis, ranked the sixth; POS accuracy rate of 89.62%, ranked the third.

1 Introduction

Chunk is a group of adjacent words which belong to the same s-projection set in a sentence, whose syntactic structure is actually a tree (Abney, 1991), but apart from the root node, all other nodes are leaf nodes. Complete syntactic analysis requires a series of analyzing processes, eventually to get a full parsing tree. Parsing by chunks is proved to be feasible (Abney, 1994).

The concept of chunking was first proposed by Abney in 1991, who defined chunks in terms of major heads, and parsed by chunks in 1994 (Abney, 1994). An additional chunk tag set {B, I, O} was added to chunking (Ramshaw and Marcus, 1995), which limited dependencies between elements in a chunk, changed chunking into a question of sequenced tags, to promote the development of chunking. Chunking algorithm was extended to the bottom-up parser, which is trained and tested on the Wall Street Journal (WSJ) part of the Penn Treebank (Marcus, Santorini and Marcinkiewicz 1993), and achieved a performance of 80.49% F-measure, the results show that it performed better than a standard probabilistic context-free grammar, and can improve performance by adding the information of parent node (Sang, 2000).

On Chinese parsing, Maximum Entropy Model was first used to have a POS tagging and chunking, and then a full parsing tree was generated (Fung, 2004), training and testing in the Penn Chinese Treebank, which achieved 79.56% F-measure. The parsing process was divided into POS tagging, base chunking and complex chunking, having a POS tagging and chunking on a given sentence, and then looping the process of complex chunking up to identify the root node (Li and Zhou, 2009). This parsing method is the basis of this paper. In addition, we have the existing Chinese chunking system in laboratory, which ranked first in Task 2: Chinese Base Chunking of CIPS-ParsEval-2009, so we try to apply chunking to complete syntactic analysis in CLP2010, to achieve better results.

We will describe the POS tagging based on CRFs in Section 2, including CRFs, feature template selection and empirical results. Multi-level chunking based on ME will be expounded in Section 3, including ME, MEMM, base chunking and complex chunking. Finally, we will summarize our work in Section 4.

2 POS Tagging Based on CRFs

2.1 Conditional Random Fields

X is a random variable over data sequences to be labeled, and Y is a random variable over corresponding label sequences. All components Y_i of Y are assumed to range over a finite label alphabet. For example, X might range over natural language sentences and Y range over part-of-speech tags of those sentences, a finite label alphabet is the set of possible part-of-speech tags (Lafferty and McCallum and Pereira, 2001). CRFs is represented by the local feature vector f and the corresponding weight vector, f is divided into the state feature s (y, x, i) and transfer feature t (y, y', x, i), where y and y' are possible POS tags, x is the current input sentence, i is the position of current term (Jiang and Guan and Wang, 2006). Formalized as follows:

$$s(y, x, i) = s(y_i, x, i) \quad (1)$$

$$t(y,x,i) = \begin{cases} t(y_{i-1}, y_i, x, i) & i > 1 \\ 0 & i = 1 \end{cases} \quad (2)$$

By the local feature of the formula (1) and (2), the global features of x and y:

$$F(y,x) = \sum_i f(y,x,i) \quad (3)$$

At this point of (X, Y), the conditional probability distribution of CRFs:

$$p_\lambda(Y \mid X) = \frac{\exp(\lambda \cdot F(Y,X))}{Z_\lambda(X)} \quad (4)$$

where $Z_\lambda(x) = \sum_y \exp(\lambda \cdot F(y,x))$ is a factor for normalizing. For the input sentence x, the best sequence of POS tagging:

$$y^* = \arg\max_y p_\lambda(y \mid x)$$

2.2 Feature Template Selection

We use the template as a baseline which is taken by Yang (2009) in CIPS-ParsEval-2009, directly testing the performance, whose accuracy was 93.52%. On this basis, we adjust the feature template through the experiment, and improve the tagging accuracy of unknown words by introducing rules, in the same corpus for training and testing, accuracy is to 93.89%. Adjusted feature template is shown in Table 1, in which the term pre is the first character in current word, suf is the last character of current word, num is the number of characters of current word, pos_{-1} is the tagging results of the previous word.

Table 1: feature template

feature template
$w_2, w_1, w_0, w_{-1}, w_{-2}, w_{+1}w_0, w_0w_{-1}, pre_0, pre_0w_0, suf_0, w_0suf_0$, num, pos_{-1}

2.3 Empirical Results and Analysis

We divide the training data provided by CLP2010 into five folds, the first four of which are train corpus, the last one is test corpus, on which we use the CRF++ toolkit for training and testing. Tagging results with different features are shown in table 2.

Table 2: tagging results with different features

Model	Explain	Accuracy
CRF	baseline	93.52%
CRF1	add w_{-1}, pos_{-1}	93.58%
CRF2	add num	93.66%
CRF3	add num, w_{-1}, pos_{-1}	93.68%
CRF4	add num, rules	93.80%
CRF5	add num, w_{-1}, pos_{-1}, rules	93.89%

Tagging results show that the number of character and POS information can be added to improve the accuracy of tagging, but in CLP2010, the tagging accuracy is only 89.62%, on the one hand it may be caused by differences of corpus, on the other hand it may be due to that we don't use all the features of CRFs but remove the features which appear one time in order to reduce the training time.

3 Multi-level Chunking Based on ME

3.1 Maximum Entropy Models and Maximum Entropy Markov Models

Maximum entropy model is mainly used to estimate the unknown probability distribution whose entropy is the maximum under some existing conditions. Suppose h is the observations of context, t is tag, the conditional probability p (t | h) can be expressed as:

$$P(t \mid h) = \frac{\exp(\sum_i \lambda_i f_i(t,h))}{Z(h)}$$

where f_i is the feature of model, $Z(h) = \sum_t \exp(\sum_i \lambda_i f_i(t,h))$ is a factor for normalizing. λ_i is weigh of feature f_i, training is the process of seeking the value of λ_i.

Maximum entropy Markov model is the serialized form of Maximum entropy model (McCallum and Freitag and Pereira, 2000), for example, transition probabilities and emission probabilities are merged into a single conditional probability function $P(t_i \mid t_{i-1}, h)$ in binary Maximum entropy Markov model, $P(t_i \mid t_{i-1}, h)$ is turned to $p(t \mid h)$ to be solved by adding features which can express previously tagging information (Li and Sun and Guan, 2009).

3.2 Base Chunking

Following the method of multi-level chunking, we first do the base chunking on the sentences which are through the POS tagging, then loop the process of complex chunking until they can't be merged. We use the existing Chinese base chunking system to do base chunking in laboratory, which marks boundaries and composition information of chunk with MEMM, and achieved 93.196% F-measure in Task 2: Chinese Base Chunking of CIPS-ParsEval -2009. The input and output of base chunking are as follows:

Input：中国/nS 传统/a 医学/n 是/v 中华/nR 民族/n 在/p 长期/n 的/uJDE 医疗/n 、/wD 生活/n 实践/vN 中/f ，/wP 不断/d 积累/v ，/wP 反复/d 总结/v 而/c 逐渐/d 形成/v 的/uJDE 具有/v 独特/a 理论/n 风格/n 的/uJDE 医学/n 体系/n 。/wE

Output：中国/nS [np 传统/a 医学/n] 是/v [np 中华/nR 民族/n] 在/p 长期/n 的/uJDE [np 医疗/n 、/wD 生活/n] 实践/vN 中/f ，/wP [vp 不断/d 积累/v] ，/wP [vp 反复/d 总结/v] 而/c [vp 逐渐/d 形成/v] 的/uJDE 具有/v [np 独特/a 理论/n] 风格/n 的/uJDE [np 医学/n 体系/n] 。/wE

3.3 Complex Chunking

We take the sentences which are through POS tagging and base chunking as input, using Li's tagging method and feature template. Categories of complex chunk include xx_Start, xx_Middle, xx_End and Other, where xx is a category of arbitrary chunk. The process of complex chunking is shown as follows:

Step 1: input the sentences which are through POS tagging and base chunking, for example:

中国/nS [np 传统/a 医学/n] 的/uJDE [np 发生/vN 发展/vN] 及/c [np 学术/n 特点/n]

Step 2: if there are some category tags in the sentence, then turn a series of tags to brackets, for instance, if continuous cells are marked as xx_Start, xx_Middle, ..., xx_Middle, xx_End, then the combination of continuous cells is a complex chunk xx;

Step 3: determine the head words with the set of rules, and compress the sentence:

中国/nS [np 医学/n] 的/uJDE [np 发展/vN] 及/c [np 特点/n]

Step 4: if the sentence can be merged, mark the sentence with ME, then return step 2, else the analysis process ends:

中国/nS@np_Start [np 医学/n]@np_End 的/uJDE@Other [np 发展/vN]@np_Start 及/c@np_Middle [np 特点/n]@np_End

At last, the output is:

[np [np 中国/nS [np 传统/a 医学/n]] 的/uJDE [np [np 发生/vN 发展/vN] 及/c [np 学术/n 特点/n]]]

Following the above method, we first use the Viterbi decoding, but in the decoding process we encountered two problems:

1. Similar to the label xx_Start, whose back is only xx_Middle or xx_End, so the probability of xx_Start label turning to Other is 0, But, if only using ME to predict, the probability may not be 0.
2. Viterbi decoding can't solve that all the labels of predicted results are Other, if all labels are Other, they can't be merged, this result doesn't make sense.

Solution:

For the first question, we add the initial transfer matrix and the end transfer matrix in decoding process, that is, the corresponding xx_Middle or xx_End of xx_Start is seted to 1 in the transfer matrix, the others are marked as 0, matrix multiplication is taken during the state transition. It can effectively avoid errors caused by probability to improve accuracy.

To rule out the second question, we use heuristic search approach to decode, and exclude all Other labels with the above matrix. In addition, we defined another ME classifier to do some pruning in the decoding process, the features of ME classifier are POS, the head word, the POS of head word. The pseudo-code of Heuristic search is:

```
While searching priority queue is not empty
    Take the node with the greatest priority in the
        queue;
    If the node's depth = length of the chunking
        results
            Searching is over, reverse the search-
                ing path to get searching results;
    Else
            Compute the probability of all candi-
                date children nodes according to
                the current probability;
            Record searching path;
            Press it into the priority queue;
```

In addition, we found that some punctuation at the end of a sentence can't be merged, probably due to sparseness of data, according to that the tone punctuation (period, exclamation mark, question mark) at the end of the sentence can be added to implement a complete sentence (zj) (Zhou, 2004), we carried out a separate deal with this situation, directly add punctuation at the end of the sentence, to form a sentence.

In training data provided by CLP2010 in subtask: Complete Sentence Parsing, the head words aren't marked. We can't use the statistical method to determine the head words, but only by rules. We take Li's rule set as baseline, but the rule set was used to supplement the statistical methods, so some head words don't appear in the rule set, resulting in many head words are marked as NULL, for this situation, we add some rules through experiment, Table 3 lists some additional rules.

Table 3: increasing part of rules

parent	head words
vp	vp, vB, vSB, vM, vJY, vC, v
ap	a, b, d
mp	qN, qV, qC, q
dj	vp, dj, ap, v, fj
dlc	vp
mbar	m, mp

3.4 Empirical Results and Analysis

We take the corpus which are through correct POS tagging and base chunking for training and testing, it is divided into five folds, the first four as training corpus, the last one as testing corpus, using the existing ME toolkit to train and test model in laboratory. Table 4 shows the results on Viterbi decoding and Heuristic Search method, where head words are determined by rules.

Table 4: results with different decoding

Decoding	Accuracy	Recall	Fmeasure
Viterbi	84.87%	84.47%	84.67%
Heuristic Search	85.62%	85.19%	85.40%

The system participated in the Complete Sentence Parsing of CLP2010, results are shown in Table 5 below. Because we can't determine the head words by statistical method on the corpus provided by CLP2010, resulting in the accuracy decreasing, creating a great impact on results.

Table 5: the track results

Training mode	Model use	F-measure	POS Accuracy
Closed	Single	63.25%	89.62%

4 Conclusions

In this paper, we use CRFs to have a POS tagging, and increase the tagging accuracy by adjusting the feature template; multi-level chunking is applied to complete syntactic analysis, we do the base chunking with MEMM to recognize boundaries and components, and make the complex chunking with ME to generate a full parsing tree; on decoding, we add transfer matrix to improve performance, and remove some features with a ME classifier to reduce training time.

As the training data are temporarily changed, our system's training on the Event Description Sub-sentence Analysis of CLP2010 isn't completed, and head words are marked in the training corpus of this task, so our next step will be to complete training and testing of this task, compare the existing evaluation results, and use ME classifier to determine head words, analyze impact of head words on system. On the POS tagging, we will retain all features to train and compare tagging results.

Acknowledgement

We would like to thank XingJun Xu and BenYang Li for their valuable advice to our work in Complete Sentence Parsing of CLP2010. We also thank JunHui Li, XiaoRui Yang and HaiLong Cao for paving the way for our work.

References

S. Abney (1991) Parsing by Chunks. Kluwer Academic Publishers, Dordrecht, 257-278

Lance A. Ramshaw, Mitchell P. Marcus (1995) Text Chunking Using Transformation-Based Learning. In Proceeding of the Third ACL Workshop on Very Large Corpora, USA, 87-88

Erik F. Tjong Kim Sang (2001) Transforming a Chunker to a Parser. Computational Linguistics in the Netherlands 2000, 6-8

YongSheng Yang, BenFeng Chen (2004) A Maximum-Entropy Chinese Parser Augmented by Transformation-Based Learning. ACM Transactions on Asian Language Information Processing, 4-8

John Lafferty, Andrew McCallum, and Fernando Pereira (2001) Conditional Random Fields: Probabilistic Models for Segmenting and Labeling Sequence Data. Proceedings of the Eighteenth International Conference on Machine Learning, 282-289

Junhui Li, Guodong Zhou (2009) Soochow University Report for the 1st China Workshop on Syntactic Parsing. CIPS-ParsEval-2009, 5-8

Wei Jiang, Yi Guan, and Xiaolong Wang (2006) Conditional Random Fields Based POS Tagging.Computer Engineering and Applications, 14-15

Xiaorui Yang, Bingquan Liu, Chengjie Sun, and Lei Lin (2009) InsunPOS: a CRF-based POS Tagging System. CIPS-ParsEval-2009, 4-6

A. McCallum, D. Freitag, and F. Pereira (2000) Maximum Entropy Markov Models for Information Extraction and Segmentation. Proceedings of ICML-2000, Stanford University, USA, 591-598

Chao Li, Jian Sun, Yi Guan, Xingjun Xu, Lei Hou, and Sheng Li (2009) Chinese Chunking With Maximum Entropy Models. CIPS-ParsEval-2009, 2-4

Qiang Zhou (2004) Annotation Scheme for Chinese Treebank. Journal of Chinese Information Processing, 4-5

The Chinese Persons Name Disambiguation Evaluation: Exploration of Personal Name Disambiguation in Chinese News

Ying Chen*, Peng Jin†, Wenjie Li‡, Chu-Ren Huang‡

* China Agricultural University
chenying3176@gmail.com

†Leshan Teachers' College
jandp@pku.edu.cn

‡The Hong Kong Polytechnic University
cswjli@comp.polyu.edu.hk
churenhuang@gmail.com

Abstract

Personal name disambiguation becomes hot as it provides a way to incorporate semantic understanding into information retrieval. In this campaign, we explore Chinese personal name disambiguation in news. In order to examine how well disambiguation technologies work, we concentrate on news articles, which is well-formatted and whose genre is well-studied. We then design a diagnosis test to explore the impact of Chinese word segmentation to personal name disambiguation.

1 Introduction

Incorporating semantic understanding technologies from the field of NLP becomes one of further directions for information retrieval. Among them, named entity disambiguation, which intends to use state-of-the-art named entity processing to enhance a search engine, is a hot research issue. Because of the popularity of personal names in queries, more efforts are put on personal name disambiguation. The personal name disambiguation used both in Web Personal Search (WePS[1]) and our campaign is defined as follow. Given documents containing a personal name in interest, the task is to cluster them according to which entity the name in a document refers to.

WePS, which explores English personal name disambiguation, has been held twice (Artiles et al., 2007, 2009). Compared to the one in English, personal name disambiguation in Chinese has special issues, such as Chinese text processing and Chinese personal naming system. Therefore, we hold Chinese personal name disambiguation (CPND) to explore those problems. In this campaign, we mainly examine the relationships between Chinese word segmentation and Chinese personal name disambiguation.

Moreover, from our experiences in WePS (Chen et al., 2007, 2009), we notice that webpages are so noisy that text pre-processing that extracts useful text for disambiguation needs much effort. In fact, text pre-processing for webpages is rather complicated, such as deleting of HTML tags, the detection of JavaScript codes and so on. Therefore, the final system performance in the WePS campaign sometimes does not reflect the disambiguation power of the system, and instead it shows the comprehensive result of text pre-processing as well as disambiguation. In order to focus on personal name disambiguation, we choose news documents in CPND.

The paper is organized as follows. Section 2 describes our formal test including datasets and evaluation. Section 3 introduces the diagnosis test, which explores the impact of Chinese word segmentation to personal name disambiguation. Section 4 describes our campaign, and Section 5 presents the results of the participating systems. Finally, Section 6 concludes our main findings in this campaign.

[1] http://nlp.uned.es/weps/

2 The Formal Test

2.1 Datasets

To avoid the difficulty to clean a webpage, we choose news articles in this campaign. Given a full name in Chinese, we search the character-based personal name string in all documents of Chinese Gigaword Corpus, a large Chinese news collection. If a document contains the name, it is belonged to the dataset of this name. To ensure the popularity of a personal name, we keep only a personal name whose corresponding dataset comprises more than 100 documents. In addition, if there are more than 300 documents in that dataset, we randomly select 300 articles to annotate. Finally, there are totally 58 personal names and 12,534 news articles used in our data, where 32 names are in the development data and 26 names are in the test data, as shown Appendix Table 4 and 5 separately.

From Table 4 and 5, we can find that the ambiguity (the document number per cluster) distribution is much different between the development data and the test data. In fact, the ambiguity varies with a personal name in interest, such as the popularity of the name in the given corpus, the celebrity degree of the name, and so on.

2.2 Evaluation

In WePS, Artiles et al. (2009) made an intensive study of clustering evaluation metrics, and found that B-Cubed metric is an appropriate evaluation approach. Moreover, in order to handle overlapping clusters (i.e. a personal name in a document refers to more than one person entity in reality), we extend B-Cubed metric as Table 1, where $S = \{S_1, S_2, \ldots\}$ is a system clustering and $R = \{R_1, R_2, \ldots\}$ is a gold-standard clustering. The final performance of a system clustering for a personal name is the F score ($\alpha = 0.5$), and the final performance of a system is the Mac F score, the average of the F scores of all personal names.

Moreover, Artiles et al. (2009) also discuss three cheat systems: one-in-one, all-in-one, and the hybrid cheat system. One-in-one assigns each document into a cluster, and in contrast, all-in-one put all documents into one cluster. The hybrid cheat system just incorporates all clusters both in one-in-one and all-in-one clustering. Although the hybrid cheat system can achieve fairly good performance, it is not useful for real applications. In the formal test, these three systems serve as the baseline.

	Formula
Precision	$\dfrac{\sum_{S_i \in S} \sum_{d \in S_i} \max_{R_j \in R; d \in R_j} \frac{\lvert S_i \cap R_j \rvert}{\lvert S_i \rvert}}{\sum_{S_i \in S} \lvert S_i \rvert}$
Recall	$\dfrac{\sum_{R_i \in R} \sum_{d \in R_i} \max_{S_j \in S; d \in S_j} \frac{\lvert R_i \cap S_j \rvert}{\lvert R_i \rvert}}{\sum_{R_i \in R} \lvert R_i \rvert}$

Table 1: the formula of the modified B-cubed metrics

3 The Diagnosis Test

Because of no word delimiter, Chinese text processing often needs to do Chinese word segmentation first. In order to explore the relationship between personal name disambiguation and word segmentation, we provide a diagnosis data which attempts to examine the impact of word segmentation to disambiguation.

Firstly, for each personal name, its corresponding dataset will be manually divided into three groups as follows. The disambiguation system then runs for each group of documents. The three clustering outputs are merged into the final clustering for that personal name.

(1) Exactly matching: news articles containing personal names that exactly match the query personal name.

(2) Partially matching: news articles containing personal names that are super-strings of the query personal name. For instance, an article that has a person named with "高军田" (*Gao Jun* Tian) is retrieved for the query personal name "高军" (Gao Jun).

(3) Discarded: news articles containing character sequences that match the query personal name string and however in fact are not a personal name. For instance, an article that has the string "最高军事法

院" (Zui *Gao Jun* Shi Fa Yuan: supreme military court) is also retrieved for the personal name "高军" (Gao Jun).

This diagnosis test is designed to simulate the realistic scenario where Chinese word segmentation works before personal name disambiguation. If a Chinese word segmenter works perfectly, a word-based matching can be used to retrieve the documents containing a personal name, and articles in Groups (2) and (3) should not be returned. The personal name disambiguation task that is limited to the documents in Group (1) should be simpler.

Moreover, in this diagnosis test, we propose a baseline based on the gold-standard word segmentation as follows, namely the word-segment system.

1) All articles in the "exactly matching" group are merged into a cluster, and all articles in the "discarded" group are merged into a cluster.
2) In the "partially matching" group, entities exactly sharing the same personal name are merged into a cluster. For example, all articles containing "高军田" (Gao Jun Tian) are merged into a cluster, and all articles containing 高军华" (Gao Jun Hua) are merged into another cluster.

4 Campaign Design

4.1 The Participants

The task of Chinese personal name disambiguation in news has attracted the participation of 10 teams. As a team can submit at most 2 results, there are 17 submissions from the 10 teams in the formal test, and there are 11 submissions from 7 teams in the diagnosis.

4.2 System descriptions

Regarding system architecture, all systems are based on clustering, and most of them comprise two components: feature extraction and clustering. However, NEU-1 and HITSZ_CITYU develop a different clustering, which in fact is a cascaded clustering. Taking the advantage of the properties of a news article, both systems first divide the dataset for a personal name into two groups according to whether the person in question is a reporter of the news. They then choose a different strategy to make further clustering for each group.

In terms of feature extraction, we find that all systems except SoochowHY use word segmentation as pre-processing. Moreover, most systems choose named entity detection to enhance their feature extraction. In addition, character-based bigrams are also used in some systems. In Appendix Table 6, we give the summary of word segmentation and named entity detection used in the participating systems.

Regarding clustering algorithms, agglomerative hierarchical clustering is popular in the submissions. Moreover, we find that weight learning is very crucial for similarity matrix, which has a big impact to the final clustering performance. Besides the popular Boolean and TFIDF weighting schemes, SoochowHY and NEU-2 use different weighting learning. NEU-2 manually assigns weights to different kinds of features. SoochowHY develops an algorithm that iteratively learns a weight for a character-based n-gram.

5 Results

We first provide the performances of the formal test, and make some analysis. We then present and discuss the performances of the diagnosis test.

5.1 Results of the Formal test

For the formal test, we show the performances of 11 submissions from 10 teams in Table 2. For each team, we keep only the better result except the NEU team because they use different technologies in their two submissions (NEU_1 and NEU_2).

From Table 2, we first observe that 7 submissions perform better than the hybrid cheat system. In contrast, in Artiles et al. (2009), only 3 teams can beat the hybrid system. From our analysis, this may attribute to the following facts.

1) Personal name disambiguation on Chinese may be easier than the one on English. For example, one of key issues in personal name disambiguation is to capture the occurrences of a query name in text. However, various personal name expressions, such as the use of

	Precision	Recall	Macro F
NEU_1	95.76	88.37	91.47
NEU_2	95.08	88.62	91.15
HITSZ_CITYU	83.99	93.29	87.42
ICL_1	83.68	92.23	86.94
DLUT_1	82.69	91.33	86.36
BUPT_1	80.33	94.52	85.79
XMU	90.55	84.88	85.72
Hybrid cheat system	73.48	100	82.37
HIT_ITNLP_2	91.08	62.75	71.03
BIT	80.2	68.75	68.4
ALL_IN_ONE	52.54	100	61.74
BUPT_pris02	72.39	58.35	57.68
SoochowHY_2	84.51	44.17	51.42
ONE_IN_ONE	94.42	14.41	21.07

Table 2: The B-Cubed performances of the formal test

	Precision	Recall	Macro F
NEU_1	95.6	89.74	92.14
NEU_2	94.53	89.99	91.66
XMU	89.84	89.84	89.08
ICL_1	84.53	93.42	87.96
BUPT_1	80.43	95.41	86.18
Word_segment system	71.11	100	80.92
BUPT_pris01	77.91	75.09	74.25
BIT	94.62	63.32	72.48
SoochowHY	87.22	58.52	61.85

Table 3: The B-Cubed performances of the diagnosis test

middle names in English, cause many problems during recognizing of the occurrences of a personal name in interest.

2) We works on news articles, which have less noisy information compared to webpages used in Artiles et al. (2009). More efforts are put on the exploration directly on disambiguation, not on text pre-processing. Furthermore, most of systems extract features based on some popular NLP techniques, such as Chinese word segmentation, named entity recognition and POS tagger. As those tools usually are developed based on news corpora, they should extract high-quality features for disambiguation in our task.

We then notice that the NEU team achieves the best performance. From their system description, we find that they make some special processing just for this task. For example, they develop a personal name recognition system to detect the occurrences of a query name in a news article, and a cascaded clustering for different kinds of persons.

5.2 Results of the Diagnosis test

We present the performances of 8 submissions for the diagnosis test from 7 teams in Table 3 as the format of Table 2. Meanwhile, we use the word-segment system as the baseline.

Comparing Table 2 and 3, we first find that the word-segment system has a lower performance than the hybrid cheat system although the word-segment system is more useful for real applications. This implies the importance to develop an appropriate evaluation method for clustering. From Table 3, five submissions achieve better performances than the word-segment system.

Given the gold-standard word segmentation on personal names in the diagnosis test, from Table 3, our total impression is that the top systems take less advantages, and the bottom systems take more. This indicates that bottom systems suffer from their low-quality word segmentation and named entity detection. For example, BUPT_pris01 increases ~22% F score (from 52.81% to 74.25%).

6 Conclusions

This campaign follows the work of WePS, and explores Chinese personal name disambiguation on news. We examine two issues: one is for Chinese word segmentation, and the other is noisy information. As Chinese word segmentation usually is a pre-processing for most NLP processing, we investigate the impact of word segmentation to disambiguation. To avoid noisy information for disambiguation, such as HTML tags in webpage used in WePS, we choose news article to work on so that we can capture how good the state-of-the-art disambiguation technique is.

References

Artiles, Javier, Julio Gonzalo and Satoshi Sekine.2007. The SemEval-2007 WePS Evaluation: Establishing a benchmark for the Web People Search Task. In Proceedings of *Semeval 2007, Association for Computational Linguistics*.

Artiles, Javier, Julio Gonzalo and Satoshi Sekine. 2009. WePS 2 Evaluation Campaign: overview of the Web People Search Clustering Task. In *2nd Web People Search Evaluation Workshop (WePS 2009), 18th WWW Conference*.

Bagga, Amit and Breck Baldwin.1998. Entity-based Cross-document Co-referencing Using the Vector Space Model. In Proceedings of *the 17th International Conference on Computational Linguistics*.

Chen, Ying and James H. Martin. 2007. CU-COMSEM: Exploring Rich Features for Unsupervised Web Personal Name Disambiguation. In Proceedings of *Semeval 2007, Association for Computational Linguistics*.

Chen, Ying, Sophia Yat Mei Lee and Chu-Ren Huang. 2009. PolyUHK: A Robust Information Extraction System for Web Personal Names. In *2nd Web People Search Evaluation Workshop (WePS 2009), 18th WWW Conference*.

Appendix

name	document #	cluster #	document # per cluster
赵伟	155	37	4.19
高明	301	42	7.17
高军	300	5	60
高伟	105	30	3.5
郭伟	156	42	3.71
朱建军	350	15	23.33
杨伟	269	70	3.84
何涛	257	8	32.13
王华	211	109	1.94
马杰	177	36	4.92
罗杰	358	165	2.17
黄海	300	20	15
徐明	140	57	2.46
刘海	300	27	11.11
孙海	296	73	4.05
黄明	135	75	1.8
郭勇	297	14	21.21
唐海	110	24	4.58
孙明	207	68	3.04

何海	131	26	5.04
郭华	145	22	6.59
孙涛	164	15	10.93
张建军	247	20	12.35
杨波	173	34	5.09
张志强	171	21	8.14
梁伟	170	34	5
胡明	195	32	6.09
林海	301	22	13.68
李刚	318	76	4.18
李军	234	117	2
胡刚	134	9	14.89
马强	123	7	17.57
	6930	1352	5.13

Table 4: The training data distribution

name	document #	cluster #	document # per cluster
刘俊	190	96	1.99
郭超	191	5	38.2
罗毅	258	16	16.13
王建民	224	32	7
王晓东	118	29	4.07
赵颖	239	21	11.38
王峰	208	43	4.84
李建民	201	17	11.82
黄志红	317	3	105.67
杨永强	151	6	25.17
何文	188	61	3.08
李学军	200	2	100
李燕	213	69	3.09
刘洪波	182	5	36.4
林鹏	278	11	25.27
周雷	180	4	45
徐金平	286	1	286
李玲	206	38	5.42
孙平	193	16	12.06
吴小军	172	9	19.11
朱芳	174	5	34.8
张民	299	39	7.67
刘丽	233	90	2.59
高峰	300	13	23.08
朱洪	141	25	5.64

王永康	262	13	20.15
	5604	669	8.38

Table5: The test data distribution

	Word segmentation	Named Entity
NEU	Name: Neucsp Source: 1998 People's Daily	Name: in-house
HITSZ_CITYU		
ICL	Name: LTP F score: 96.5% Source: 2nd SIGHAN	Name: LTP
DLUT		
BUPT	Name: in-house F score: 96.5% Source: SIGHAN 2010	
XMU	Name: in-house Source: 1998 People's Daily F score: 97.8%	
HIT_ITNLP	Name: IRLAS Source: 1998 People's Daily F score: 97.4%	Name: IRLAS
BIT	Name: ICTCLAS2010 Precision: ~97% Source: 1998 People's Daily	Name: ICTCLAS2010
BUPT_pris	Name: LTP	Name: LTP
SoochowHY	None	None

Table 6: The summary of word segmentation and named entity detection used in the participants

* LTP(Language Technology Platform)

A Multi-stage Clustering Framework for Chinese Personal Name Disambiguation

Huizhen Wang, Haibo Ding, Yingchao Shi, Ji Ma, Xiao Zhou, Jingbo Zhu
Natural Language Processing Laboratory,
Northeatern University
Shenyang, Liaoning, China
{wanghuizhen|zhujingbo@mail.neu.edu.cn
{dinghb|shiyc|maji}@mail.neu.edu.cn

Abstract

This paper presents our systems for the participation of Chinese Personal Name Disambiguation task in the CIPS-SIGHAN 2010. We submitted two different systems for this task, and both of them all achieve the best performance. This paper introduces the multi-stage clustering framework and some key techniques used in our systems, and demonstrates experimental results on evaluation data. Finally, we further discuss some interesting issues found during the development of the system.

1 Introduction

Personal name disambiguation (PND) is very important for web search and potentially other natural language applications such as question answering. CIPS-SIGHAN bakeoffs provide a platform to evaluate the effectiveness of various methods on Chinese PND task.

Different from English PND, word segmentation techniques are needed for Chinese PND tasks. In practice, person names are highly ambiguous because different people may have the same name, and the same name can be written in different ways. It's an n-to-n mapping of person names to the specific people. There are two main challenges on Chinese PND: the first one is how to correctly recognize personal names in the text, and the other is how to distinguish different persons who have the same name. For address these challenges, we designed a rule-based combination technique to improve NER performance and propose a multi-stage clustering framework for Chinese PND. We participated in the bakeoff of the Chinese PND task, on the test set and the diagnosis test set, our two systems are ranked at the 1st and 2nd position.

The rest of this paper is organized as follows. In Section 2, we first give the key features and techniques used in our two systems. In Section 3, experimental results on the evaluation test data demonstrated that our methods are effective to disambiguate the personal name, and discussions on some issues we found during the development of the system are given. In Section 4, we conclude our work.

2 System Description

In this section, we describe the framework of our systems in more detail, involving data preprocessing, *discard*-class document identification, feature definition, clustering algorithms, and sub-system combination.

2.1 Data Preprocessing

There are around 100-300 news articles per personal name in the evaluation corpus. Each article is stored in the form of XML and encoded in UTF-8. At first, each news article should be preprocessed as follows:

- Use a publicly available Chinese encoding Converter tool to convert each news article from UTF-8 coding into GB[1];
- Remove all XML tags;
- Process Chinese word segmentation, part-of-speech (POS) tagging and name entity recognition (NER);

The performance of word segmentation and NER tools generally affect the effectiveness of our Chinese PND systems. During system de-

[1] http://www.mandarintools.com/

veloping process, we found that the publicly available NER systems obtain unsatisfactory performance on evaluation data. To address this challenge, we propose a new rule-based combination technique to improve NER performance. In our combination framework, two different NER systems are utilized, including a CRF-based NER system and our laboratory's NER system (Yao et al.,2002). The latter was implemented based on the maximum matching principle and some linguistic post-preprocessing rules. Since both two NER systems adopt different technical frameworks, it is possible to achieve a better performance by means of system combination techniques.

The basic idea of our combination method is to first simply combine the results produced by both NER systems, and further utilize some heuristic post-processing rules to refine NE identification results. To achieve this goal, we first investigate error types caused by both NER systems, and design some post-preprocessing rules to correct errors or select the appropriate NER results from disagreements. Notice that such rules are learned from sample data (i.e., training set), not from test set. Experimental results demonstrate satisfactory NER performance by introducing these heuristic refinement rules as follows:

- **Conjunction Rules**. Two NEs separated by a conjunction (such as "和","或","与", "、") belong to the same type, e.g., "高明/adj.和/吴倩莲/person". Such a conjunction rule can help NER systems make a consistent prediction on both NEs, e.g., "高明/person" and "高峰/person".
- **Professional Title Rules**. Professional title words such as "主任" are strong indicators of person names, e.g., "主任/李刚". Such a rule can be written in the form of "*professional_title+person_name*".
- **Suffix Rules**. If an identified person name is followed by a suffix of another type of named entities such as location, it is not a true person name, for example, "阿萨姆邦德马杰/person 镇/的/居民". Since "镇" is a suffix of a location name. "阿萨姆邦德马杰/person 镇/location-suffix" should be revised to be a new location name, namely "阿萨姆邦德马杰镇/location".
- **Foreign Person Name Rules**. Two identified person names connected by a dot are merged into a single foreign person name, e.g., "菲/. /罗杰斯" => "菲. 罗杰斯"
- **Chinese Surname Rules**. Surnames are very important for Chinese person name identification. However, some common surnames can be single words depending upon the context, for example, the Chinese word "张" can be either a surname or a quantifier. To tackle this problem, some post-processing rules for "张, 段, 高, 刘, 赵" are designed in our system.
- **Query-Dependent Rules.** Given a query person name *A*, if the string *AB* occurring in the current document has been identified as a single person name many times in other documents, our system would tend to segment *AB* as a single person name rather than as *A/B*. For example, if "郭伟明" was identified as a true person name more than one time in other documents, in such a case, "议员/郭伟/明/表示/"=> "议员/郭伟明/person 表示/"

Incorporating these above post-processing rules, our NER system based on heuristic post-processing rules shows 98.89% precision of NER on training set.

2.2 Discard-Class Document Identification

Seen from evaluation data, there are a lot of documents belonging to a specific class, referred to as *discard*-class. In the discard-class, the query person name occurring in the document is not a true person name. For example, a query word "黄海" is a famous ocean name not a person name in the sentence "三江飘流分别可达日本海、<u>**黄海**</u>和鄂霍茨克海". In such a case, the corresponding document is considered as discard-class. Along this line, actually the discard-class document identification is very simple task. If a document does not contain a true person name that is the same as the query or contains the query, it is a discard-class document.

2.3 Feature Definition

To identify different types of person name and for the PND purpose, some effective binary features are defined to construct the document representation as feature vectors as follows:

- **Personal attributes**: involving professional title, affiliation, location, co-occurrence person name and organization related to the given query.
- **NE-type Features**: collecting all NEs occurring in the context of the given query. There are two kinds of NE-type features used in our systems, local features and global features. The global features are defined with respect to the whole document while the local features are extracted only from the two or three adjacent sentences for the given query.
- **BOW-type features**: constructing the context feature vector based on bag-of-word model. Similarly, there are local and global BOW-type features with respect to the context considered.

2.4 A Multi-stage Clustering Framework

Seen from the training set, 36% of person names indicate journalists, 10% are sportsmen, and the remaining are common person names. Based on such observations, it is necessary to utilize different methodology to PND on different types of person names, for example, because the most effective information to distinguish different journalists are the reports' location and colleagues, instead of the whole document content. To achieve a satisfactory PND performance, in our system we design three different modules for analyzing journalist, sportsman and common person name, respectively.

2.4.1 PND on the Journalist Class

In our system, some regular expressions are designed to determine whether a person name is a journalist or not. For example:

- 新华社/ni */ns */t */t 消息|电/n (/w .* [《/w */ni 》/w]* query name/nh .*)/w
- (/w .*query name/nh .*)/w
- [*/nh]* query name/nh [*/nh]
- 记者|编辑/n [*/nh]* query name/nh [*/nh]*

To disambiguate on the journalist class, our system utilizes a rule-based clustering technique distinguish different journalists. For each document containing the query person name as journalists, we first extract the organization and the location occurring in the local context of the query. Two such documents can be put into the same cluster if they contain the same organization or location names, otherwise not. In our system, a location dictionary containing province-city information extracted from Wikipedia is used to identify location name. For example: 辽宁省 (沈阳 大连 铁岭 鞍山 ...), 河北(石家庄 唐山 秦皇岛 邯郸 邢台...). Based on this dictionary, it is very easy to map a city to its corresponding province.

2.4.2 PND on the Sportsman Class

Like done in PND on the journalist class, we also use rule-based clustering techniques for disambiguating sportsman class. The major difference is to utilize topic features for PND on the sportsman class. If the topic of the given document is sports, this document can be considered as sportsman class. The key is to how to automatically identify the topic of the document containing the query. To address this challenge, we adopt a domain knowledge based technique for document topic identification. The basic idea is to utilize a domain knowledge dictionary NEUKD developed by our lab, which contains more than 600,000 domain associated terms and the corresponding domain features. Some domain associated terms defined in NEUKD are shown in Table 1.

Domain associated term	Domain feature concept
足球队(football team)	Football, Sports
自行车队 (cycling team)	Traffic, Sports, cycling
中国象棋 (Chinese chess)	Sports, Chinese chess
执白(white side)	Sports, the game of go
芝加哥公牛 (Chicago bulls)	Sports, basketball

Table 1: Six examples defined in the NEUKD

In the domain knowledge based topic identification algorithm, all domain associated terms occurring in the given document are first mapped into domain features such as *football*, *basketball* or *cycling*. The most frequent domain feature is considered as the most likely topic. See Zhu and Chen (2005) for details.

Two documents with the same topic can be grouped into the same cluster.

Person name	Document no.	sports
杨波	081	篮球
杨波	094	射箭
杨波	098	射箭
杨波	100	射箭

Table 2: Examples of PND on Sportsman Class

2.4.3 Multi-Stage Clustering Framework

We proposed a multi-stage clustering framework for PND on common person name class, as shown In Figure 1.

In the multi-stage clustering framework, the first-stage is to adopt strict rule-based hard clustering algorithm using the feature set of personal attributes. The second-stage is to implement constrained hierarchical agglomerative clustering using NE-type local features. The third-stage is to design hierarchical agglomerative clustering using BOW-type global features. By combining those above techniques, we submitted the first system named NEU_1.

2.4.4 The second system

Besides, we also submitted another PND system named NEU_2 by using the single-link hierarchical agglomerative clustering algorithm in which the distance of two clusters is the cosine similarity of their most similar members (Masaki et al., 2009, Duda et al., 2004). The difference between our two submission systems NEU_1 and NEU_2 is the feature weighting method. The motivation of feature weighting method used in NEU_2 is to assume that words surrounding the query person name in the given document are more important features than those far away from it, and person name and location names occurring in the context are more discriminative features than common words for PND purpose. Along this line, in the feature weighting scheme used in NEU_2, for each feature extracted from the sentence containing the query person name, the weight of a word-type feature with the POS of "ns", "ni" or "nh " is assigned as 3, Otherwise 1.5; For the features extracted from other sentences, the weight of a word with the POS of "ns"or "nh " is set to be 2, the ones of "ni" POS is set to 1.5, otherwise 1.0.

Algorithm 1: Multi-stage Clustering Framework
Input: a person name *pn*, and its related document set D={d_1, d_2, ..., d_m} in which each document d_i contains the person name *pn*;
Output: clustering results C={C_1,C_2, …,C_n}, where $\bigcup_i C_i = C$ and $C_i \cap C_j = \Phi$

For each $d_i \in D$ do
  $S_i = \{s|pn \in s, s \in d_i\}$;
  $ORG_i=\{t|t \in s, s \in S_i, POS(t)= ni\}$;
  $PER_i=\{t|t \in s, s \in S_i, POS(t)=nh\}$;
  $L_{di} = \{t|t \in s, s \in S_i \}$; //local feature set
  $G_{di} = \{t|t \in d_i\}$; //global feature set
  $C_i = \{d_i\}$;
End for
Stage 1: Strict rules-based clustering
Begin
  For each $C_i \in C$ do
   If $ORG_i \cap ORG_j \neq \Phi$ or
    $|PER_i \cap PER_j| \geq 2$
   Then $C_i = C_i \cup C_j$;
    $ORG_i = ORG_i \cup ORG_j$;
    $PER_i = PER_i \cup PER_j$;
    Remove C_j from C ;
  End for
End
Stage 2: Constrained hierarchical agglomerative clustering algorithm using local features
Begin
  Set each c ∈C as an initial cluster;
  do
   $$[C_i, C_j] = \arg\max_{C_i, C_j \in C} sim(C_i, C_j)$$
   $$sim(C_i, C_j) = \max_{d_x \in C_i, d_y \in C_j} sim(d_x, d_y) = \max_{d_x \in C_i, d_y \in C_j} \cos(L_{d_x}, L_{d_y})$$
   $C_i = C_i \cup C_j$;
   Remove C_j from C ;
  until $sim(C_i,C_j) < \theta$.
End
Stage 3: Constrained hierarchical agglomerative clustering algorithm using global features, i.e., utilize the same algorithm used in stage 2 by considering the global feature set G for cosine-based similarity calculation instead of the local feature set L.

Figure 1: Multi-stage Clustering Framework

2.5 Final Result Generation

As discussed above, there are many modules for PND on Chinese person name. In our NEU_1, the final results are produced by combining outputs of discard-class document clustering, journalist-class clustering, sportsman-class clustering and multi-stage clustering modules. In NEU-2 system, the outputs of discard-class document clustering, journalist-class clustering, sportsman-class clustering and single-link clustering modules are combined to generate the final results.

3 Evaluation

3.1 Experimental Settings

- Training data: containing about 30 Chinese person names, and a set of about 100-300 news articles are provided for each person name.
- Test data: similar to the training data, and containing 26 unseen Chinese personal names, provided by the SIGHAN organizer.
- Performance evaluation metrics (Artiles et al., 2009): B_Cubed and P_IP metrics.

3.2 Results

Table 3 shows the performance of our two submission systems NEU_1 and NEU_2 on the test set of Sighan2010 Chinese personal name disambiguation task.

System No.	B_Cubed			P_IP		
	P	R	F	P	IP	F
NEU_1	**95.76**	88.37	**91.47**	**96.99**	92.58	**94.56**
NEU_2	95.08	88.62	91.15	96.73	92.73	94.46

Table 3: Results on the test data

NEU-1 system was implemented by the multi-stage clustering framework that uses single-link clustering method. In this framework, there are two threshold parameters θ and μ. Both threshold parameters are tuned from training data sets.

After the formal evaluation, the organizer provided a diagnosis test designed to explore the relationship between Chinese word segmentation and personal name disambiguation. In the diagnosis test, the personal name disambiguation task was simplified and limited to the documents in which the personal name is tagged correctly. The performance of our two systems on the diagnosis test set of Sighan2010 Chinese personal name disambiguation task are shown in Table 4.

System no.	B_Cubed			P_IP		
	P	R	F	P	IP	F
NEU_1	**95.6**	89.74	**92.14**	**96.83**	93.62	**95.03**
NEU_2	94.53	89.99	91.66	96.41	93.8	94.9

Table 4: Results of the diagnosis test on test data

As shown in the Table 3 and Table 4, NEU-1 system achieves the highest precision and F values on the test data and the diagnosis test data.

3.3 Discussion

We propose a multi-stage clustering framework for Chinese personal name disambiguation. The evaluation results demonstrate that the features and key techniques our systems adopt are effective. Our systems achieve the best performance in this competition. However, our recall values are not unsatisfactory. In such a case, there is still much room for improvement. Observed from experimental results, some interesting issues are worth being discussed and addressed in our future work as follows:

(1) For PND on some personal names, the document topic information seems not effective. For example, the personal name "郭华(Guo Hua)" in training set represent one shooter and one billiards player. The PND system based on traditional clustering method can not effectively work in such a case due to the same sports topic. To solve this problem, one solution is to sufficiently combine the personal attributes and document topic information for PND on this person name.

(2) For the journalist-class personal names, global BOW-type features are not effective in this case as different persons can report on the same or similar events. For example, there are four different journalists named "朱建军(Zhu Jianjun)" in the training set, involving different locations such as Beijing, Zhengzhou, Xining or Guangzhou. We can distinguish them in terms of the location they are working in.

(3) We found that some documents in the training set only contain lists of news title and the news reporter. In this case, we can not discriminate the persons with respect to the location of entire news. It's worth studying some effective solution to address this challenge in our future work.

(4) Seen from the experimental results, some personal names such as "李刚(Li gang)" are wrong identified because this person is associated with multiple professional titles and affiliates. In this case, the use of exact matching methods can not yield satisfactory results. For example, the query name "李刚(Li gang)" in the documents 274 and 275 is the president of "中国对外文化交流协会(China International Culture Association)" while in the documents 202, 225 and 228, he is the director of "文化部对外文化联络局(Bureau of External Cultural Relations of Chinese Ministry of Culture)". To group both cases into the same cluster, it's worth mining the relations and underlying semantic relations between entities to achieve this goal.

4 Conclusion

This paper presents our two Chinese personal name disambiguation systems in which various constrained hierarchical agglomerative clustering algorithms using local or global features are adopted. The bakeoff results show that our systems achieve the best performance. In the future, we will pay more attention on the personal attribute extraction and unsupervised learning approaches for Chinese personal name disambiguation.

5 Acknowledgements

This work was supported in part by the National Science Foundation of China (60873091) and the Fundamental Research Funds for the Central Universities.

References

Artiles, Javier, Julio Gonzalo and Satoshi Sekine. 2009. "WePS 2 Evaluation Campaign: overview of the Web People Search Clustering Task," In 2nd Web People Search Evaluation Workshop (WePS 2009), 18th WWW Conference.

Duda, Richard O., Peter E.Hart, and David G.Stork. 2004. Pattern Classification. China Machine Press.

Masaki, Ikeda, Shingo Ono, Issei Sato, Minoru Yoshida, and Hiroshi Nakagawa. 2009. Person Name Disambiguation on the Web by TwoStage Clustering. In 2nd Web People Search Evaluation Workshop (WePS 2009), 18th WWW Conference.

Yao, Tianshun, Zhu Jingbo , Zhang Li, Yang Ying. Nov. 2002. Natural Language Processing , Second Edition, Tsinghua press.

Zhu, Jingbo and Wenliang Chen. 2005. Some Studies on Chinese Domain Knowledge Dictionary and Its Application to Text Classification. In Proc. of SIGHAN4.

Combine Person Name and Person Identity Recognition and Document Clustering for Chinese Person Name Disambiguation

Ruifeng Xu[1,2],Jun Xu[1],Xiangying Dai[1]
Harbin Institute of Technology,
Shenzhen Postgraduate School, China
{xuruifeng.hitsz;hit.xujun;
mi-chealdai}@gmail.com

Chunyu Kit[2]
[2]City University of Hong Kong,
Hong Kong, China
ctckit@cityu.edu.hk

Abstract

This paper presents the HITSZ_CITYU system in the CIPS-SIGHAN bakeoff 2010 Task 3, Chinese person name disambiguation. This system incorporates person name string recognition, person identity string recognition and an agglomerative hierarchical clustering for grouping the documents to each identical person. Firstly, for the given name index string, three segmentors are applied to segment the sentences having the index string into Chinese words, respectively. Their outputs are compared and analyzed. An unsupervised clustering is applied here to help the personal name recognition. The document set is then divided into subsets according to each recognized person name string. Next, the system identifies/extracts the person identity string from the sentences based on lexicon and heuristic rules. By incorporating the recognized person identity string, person name, organization name and contextual content words as features, an agglomerative hierarchical clustering is applied to group the similar documents in the document subsets to obtain the final person name disambiguation results. Evaluations show that the proposed system, which incorporates extraction and clustering technique, achieves encouraging recall and good overall performance.

1 Introduction

Many people may have the same name which leads to lots of ambiguities in text, especially for some common person names. This problem puzzles many information retrieval and natural language processing tasks. The person name ambiguity problem becomes more serious in Chinese text. Firstly, Chinese names normally consist of two to four characters. It means that for a two-character person name, it has only one character as surname to distinguish from other person names with the same family name. It leads to thousands of people have the same common name, such 王刚 and 李明. Secondly, some three-character or four-character person name may have one two-character person name as its substring such as 王明 and 王明树, which leads to more ambiguities. Thirdly, some Chinese person name string has the sense beyond the person name. For example, a common Chinese name, 高峰 has a sense of "*Peak*". Thus, the role of a string as person name or normal word must be determined. Finally, Chinese text is written in continuous character strings without word gap. It leads to the problem that some person names may be segmented into wrong forms.

In the recent years, there have been many researches on person name disambiguation (Fleischman and Hovy 2004; Li et al. 2004; Niu et al. 2004; Bekkerman and McCallum 2005; Chen and Martin 2007; Song et al. 2009). To promote the research in this area, Web People Search (WePS and WePS2) provides a standard evaluation, which focuses on information extraction of personal named-entities in Web data (Artiles et al., 2007; Artiles et al., 2009; Sekine and Artiles, 2009). Generally speaking, both cluster-based techniques which cluster documents corresponding to one person with similar contexts, global features and document features (Han et al. 2004; Pedersen et al. 2005; Elmacioglu et al. 2007; Pedersen and Anagha 2007; Rao et al. 2007) and information extraction based techniques which recognizes/extracts the description features of one person name (Heyl and Neumann 2007; Chen et al. 2009) are adopted. Considering that these evaluations are only applied to English text, CIPS-SIGHAN 2010 bakeoff proposed the first evaluation campaign on Chinese person name disambiguation. In this evaluation, corresponding to given index person name string, the systems are required to recognize each identical person having the index string as substring and classify the document corresponding to each identical person into a group.

This paper presents the design and implementation of HITSZ_CITYU system in this bakeoff. This system incorporates both recognition/extract technique and clustering technique for person name disambiguation. It consists of two major components. Firstly, by incorporating word segmentation, named entity recognition, and unsupervised clustering, the system recognize the person name string in the document and then classify the documents into subsets corresponding to the person name. Secondly, for the documents having the same person name string, the system identifies the person identify string, other person name, organization name and contextual context words as features. An agglomerative hierarchical clustering algorithm is applied to cluster the documents to each identical person. In this way, the documents corresponding to each identical person are grouped, i.e. the person name ambiguities are removed. The evaluation results show that the HITSZ_CITYU system achieved 0.8399(B-Cubed)/0.8853(P-IP) precisions and 0.9329(B-Cubed)/0.9578(P-IP) recall, respectively. The overall F1 performance 0.8742(B-Cubed)/0.915(P-IP) is ranked 2nd in ten participate teams. These results indicate that the proposed system incorporating both extraction and clustering techniques achieves satisfactory recall and overall performance.

The rest of this report is organized as follows. Section 2 describes and analyzes the task. Section 3 presents the word segmentation and person name recognition and Section 4 presents the person description extraction and document clustering. Section 5 gives and discusses the evaluation results. Finally, Section 6 concludes.

2 Task Description

CIPS-SIGHAN bakeoff on person name disambiguation is a clustering task. Corresponding to 26 person name query string, the systems are required to cluster the documents having the index string into multiple groups, which each group representing a separate entity.

HITSZ_CITYU system divided the whole task into two subtasks:

1. Person name recognition. It includes:

   1.1 Distinguish person name/ non person name in the document. For a given index string 高峰, in Example 1, 高峰 is a person name while in Example 2, 高峰 is a noun meaning "*peak*" rather than a person name.

   Example 1. 谈判专家、北京人民警察学院教授高峰说。(*Gaofeng, the Negotiator and professor of Beijing People's Police College, said*).

   Example 2. 这一数字上升至 11.83%的高峰值 (*This value raise to the peak value of 11.83%*).

   1.2 Recognize the exact person name, especially for three-character to four-character names. For a given index string, 李燕, a person name 李燕 should be identified in Example 3 while 李燕卿 should be identified from Example 4.

   Example 3. 中国一队的李燕是参赛女选手中身材最高的(*Li Yan from Chinese team one is the highest one in the female athletes participating this game*).

   Example 4. 战士李燕卿是个孤儿 (*The soldier Li YanQing is an orphan*)

2. Cluster the documents for each identical person. That is for each person recognized person name, cluster documents into groups while each group representing an individual person. For the non person names instances (such as Example 2), they are clustered into a *discarded* group. Meanwhile, the different person with the same name should be separated. For example, 李燕 in the Example 3 and Example 5 is a athlete and a painter, re-

spectively. These two sentences should be cluster into different groups.

Example 5. 参与主办这次画展的著名画家李燕说(*The famous painter Li Yan , who involved in hosting this exhibition, said that*)

3 Person Name Recognition

As discussed in Section 2, HITSZ_CITYU system firstly recognizes the person names from the text including distinguish the person name/ non-person name word and recognize the different person name having the name index string. In our study, we adopted three developed word segmentation and named entity recognition tools to generate the person name candidates. The three tools are:

1. Language Processing Toolkit from Intelligent Technology & Natural Language Processing Lab (ITNLP) of Harbin Institute of Technology (HIT). http://www.insun.hit.edu.cn/
2. ICTCLAS from Chinese Academy of Sciences. http://ictclas.org/
3. The Language Technology Platform from Information Retrieval Lab of Harbin Institute of Technology. http://ir.hit.edu.cn

We apply the three tools to segment and tag the documents into Chinese words. The recognized person name having the name index string will be labeled as */nr* while the index string is labeled as *discard* if it is no recognized as a person name even not a word. For the sentences having no name index string, we simply vote the word segmentation results by as the output. As for the sentences having name index string, we conduct further analysis on the word segmentation results.

1. For the cases that the matched string is recognized as person name and non-person name by different systems, respectively, we selected the recognized person name as the output. For example, in
   Example 6. 卫生福利及食物局局长**<u>杨永强</u>**赞扬谢婉雯工作尽心尽力 (*Secretary for Health, Welfare and Food, Yang Yongqiang commended the excellent work of Tse Wanwen*).
   the segmentation results by three segmentors are **<u>杨永强/nr |discarded|杨永强/nr</u>**, respectively. We select **<u>杨永强/nr</u>** as the output.
2. For the cases that three systems generate different person names, we further incorporating unsupervised clustering results for determination. Here, an agglomerative hierarchical clustering with high threshold is applied (the details of clustering will be presented in Section 4).
   Example 7. 朱芳勇闯三关 (*Zhufang overcome three barriers*)
   In this example, the word segmentation results are **<u>朱芳/nr, 朱芳勇/nr, 朱芳勇/nr</u>**, respectively. It is shown that there is a segmentation ambiguity here because both 朱芳 and 朱芳勇 are legal Chinese person names. Such kinds of ambiguity cannot be solved by segmentors individually. We further consider the clustering results. Since the Example 7 is clustered with the documents having the segmentation results of 朱芳, two votes (emphasize the clustering confidence) for 朱芳 are assigned. Thus, 朱芳 and 朱芳勇 obtained 3 votes and 2 votes in this case, respectively, and thus 朱芳 is selected as the output.
3. For cases that the different person name forms having the same votes, the longer person name is selected. In the following example,
   Example 8. 上海市教育委员会副主任张民选教授在论坛上表示 (*Prof. Zhang Mingxuan, the deputy director of Shanghai Municipal Education Commission, said at the forum*)
   The segmentation form of 张民 and 张民选 received the same votes, thus, the longer one 张民选 is selected as the output.

In this component, we applied three segmentors (normally using the local features only) with the help of clustering to (using both the local and global features) recognize person name in the text with high accuracy. It is important to ensure the recall performance of the final output. Noted, in order to ensure the high precision of clustering, we set a high similarity threshold here.

4 Person Name Disambiguation

4.1 Person Identity Recognition/Extraction

A person is distinguished by its associated attributes in which its identity description is essential. For example, a person name has the identity of 总统 *president* and 农民 *farmer*, respectively, tends to be two different persons. Therefore, in HITSZ_CITYU system, the person identity is extracted based on lexicon and heuristic rules before person name disambiguation.

We have an entity lexicon consisting of 85 suffixes and 248 prefix descriptor for persons as the initial lexicon. We further expand this lexicon through extracting frequently used entity words from Gigaword. Here, we segmented documents in Gigaword into word sequences. For each identified person name, we collect its neighboring nouns. The associations between the nouns and person name can be estimated by their χ^2 test value. For a candidate entity w_a and person name w_b, (here, w_b is corresponding to person name class with the label */nr*), the following 2-by-2 table shown the dependence of their occurrence.

Table 1 The co-occurrence of two words

	$x = w_a$	$x \neq w_a$
$y = w_b$	C_{11}	C_{12}
$y \neq w_b$	C_{21}	C_{22}

For w_a and w_b, χ^2 test (chi-square test) estimates the differences between observed and expected values as follows:

$$\chi^2 = \frac{N \cdot (C_{11}C_{22} - C_{12}C_{21})^2}{(C_{11}+C_{22})+(C_{11}+C_{21})+(C_{12}+C_{22})+(C_{21}+C_{22})} \quad (1)$$

where, N is the total number of words in the corpus. The nouns having the χ^2 value greater than a threshold are extracted as entity descriptors.

In person entity extraction subtask, for each sentence has the recognized person name, the system matches its neighboring nouns (-2 to +2 words surrounding the person name) with the entries in entity descriptor lexicon. The matched entity descriptors are extracted.

In this part, several heuristic rules are applied to handle some non-neighboring cases. Two example rules with cases are given below.

Example Rule 1. The prefix entity descriptor will be assigned to parallel person names with the split mark of "/" , "、 "and "和","与"(*and*).

中国选手龚跃春/王辉 (*Chinese players Gong Yuechun/Wang Hui*)->

选手 *player*-龚跃春 *Gong Yuechun*

选手 *player*-王辉 *Wang Hui*

Example Rule 2. The entity descriptor will be assigned to each person in the structure of parallel person name following "等(*etc.*)" and then a entity word.

刘炳森、陈大章、李燕、金鸿钧等书画家挥毫泼墨 (*The painter, Liu Bingsen, Chen Dazhang, Li Yan, Jin Hongjun, etc., paint a..*) ->

刘炳森 *Liu Bingsen* - 书画家 *painter*

陈大章 *Chen Dazhang* - 书画家 *painter*

李燕 *Li Yan* - 书画家 *painter*

金鸿钧 *Jin Hongjun* - 书画家 *painter*

Furthermore, the HITSZ_CITYU system applies several rules to identify a special kind of person entity, i.e. the reporter or author using structure information. For example, in the beginning or the end of a document, there is a person name in a bracket means this person and this name appear in the document for only once; such person name is regarded as the reporter or author. (记者金林鹏、石涛) –>金林鹏 *Jin Linpeng* - 记者 *reporter*

(金林鹏　李霁) –>金林鹏 *Jin Linpeng* - 记者 *reporter*

4.2 Clustering-based Person Name Disambiguation

For the document set corresponding to each given index person name, we firstly split the document set into: (1) Discarded subset, (2) Subset with different recognized person name. The subsets are further split into (2-1) the person is the author/reporter and (2-2) the person is not the author/reporter. The clustering techniques are then applied to group documents in each (2-2) subset into several clusters which each cluster is corresponding to each identical person.

In the Chinese Person Name Disambiguation task, the number of clusters contained in a subset is not pre-available. Thus, the clustering method which fixes the number of clusters, such as *k-nearest neighbor* (*k-NN*) is not applicable. Considering that Agglomerative Hierarchical Clustering (AHC) algorithm doesn't require the fixed number of cluster and it performs well in document categorization (Jain and Dubes 1988), it is adopted in HITSZ_CITYU system.

Preprocessing and Document Representation

Before representing documents, a series of procedures are adopted to preprocess these documents including stop word removal. Next, we select feature words for document clustering. Generally, paragraphs containing the target person name usually contain more person-related information, such as descriptor, occupation, affiliation, and partners. Therefore, larger weights should be assigned to these words. Furthermore, we further consider the appearance position of the features. Intuitively, local feature words with small distance are more important than the global features words with longer distance.

We implemented some experiments on the training data to verify our point. Table 2 and Table 3 show the clustering performance achieved using different combination of global features and local features as well as different similarity thresholds.

Table 2. Performance achieved on training set with different weights (similarity threshold 0.1)

Feature words	Precision	Recall	F-1
Paragraph	0.820	0.889	0.849
All	0.791	0.880	0.826
All+ Paragraph×1	0.791	0.904	0.839
All+ Paragraph×2	0.802	0.908	0.848
All+ Paragraph×3	0.824	0.909	0.860
All+ Paragraph×4	0.831	0.911	0.865
All+ Paragraph×5	0.839	0.910	0.869
All+ Paragraph×6	0.833	0.905	0.864
All+ Paragraph×7	0.838	0.904	0.867

Table 3. Performance achieved on training set with different weights (similarity threshold 0.15)

Feature words	Precision	Recall	F-1
Paragraph	0. 901	0.873	0.883
All	0.859	0.867	0.859
All+ Paragraph×1	0.875	0.887	0.877
All+ Paragraph×2	0.885	0.890	0.884
All+ Paragraph×3	0.889	0.887	0.885
All+ Paragraph×4	0.896	0.887	0.880
All+ Paragraph×5	0.906	0.882	0.891
All+ Paragraph×6	0.905	0.884	0.891
All+ Paragraph×7	0.910	0.882	0.893

In this two tables, "Paragraph" means that we only select words containing in paragraph which contains the person index name as feature words (which are the local features), and "All" means that we select all words but stop words in a document as feature words. "*All+ Paragraph×k*" means feature words consist of two parts, one part is obtained from "All", the other is gained from "Paragraph", at the same time, we assign the feature weights to the two parts, respectively. The feature weight coefficient of "All" is $1/(k+1)$, while the feature weight coefficient of "*All+ Paragraph×k*" is $k/(k+1)$.

It is shown that, the system perform best using appropriate feature weight coefficient distribution. Therefore, we select all words in the document (besides stop words) as global feature words and the words in paragraph having the index person name as local feature words. We then assign the corresponding empirical feature weight coefficient to the global/local features, respectively. A document is now represented as a vector of feature words as follows:

$$V(d) \rightarrow ((t_1, w_1(d)); (t_2, w_2(d)); \cdots (t_n, w_n(d))) \quad (2)$$

where, d is a document, t_i is a feature word, $w_i(d)$ is the feature weight of t_i in the document d. In this paper, we adopt a widely used weighting scheme, named Term Frequency with Inverse Document Frequency (TF-IDF). In addition, for each document, we need to normalize weights of features because documents have different lengths. The weight of word t_i in document d is shown as:

$$w_i(d) = \frac{tf_i(d) * \log(\frac{N}{df_i} + 0.05)}{\sqrt{\sum_{i=1}^{n} (tf_i(d) * \log(\frac{N}{df_i} + 0.05))^2}} \quad (3)$$

where $tf_i(d)$ means how many times word t_i occurs in the document d, df_i means how many documents contains word t_i, and N is the number of documents in the corpus.

Similarity Estimation

We use the cosine distance as similarity calculation function. After the normalization of weights of each document, the similarity between document d_1 and document d_2 is computed as:

$$sim(d_1, d_2) = \sum_{t_i \in d_1 \cap d_2} w_i(d_1) * w_i(d_2) \quad (4)$$

where t_i is the term which appears in document d_1 and document d_2 simultaneously, $w_i(d_1)$ and $w_i(d_1)$ are the weights of t_i in document d_1 and document d_2 respectively. If t_i does not appear in a document, the corresponding weight in the document is zero.

Agglomerative Hierarchical Clustering (AHC)

AHC is a bottom-up hierarchical clustering method. The framework of AHC is described as follows:

> Assign each document to a single cluster.
> Calculate all pair-wise similarities between clusters.
> Construct a distance matrix using the similarity values.
> Look for the pair of clusters with the largest similarity.
> Remove the pair from the matrix and merge them.
> Evaluate all similarities from this new cluster to all other clusters, and update the matrix.
> Repeat until the largest similarity in the matrix is smaller than some similarity criteria.

There are three methods to estimate the similarity between two different clusters during the cluster mergence: single link method, average link method and complete link method (Nallapati et al. 2004). The three methods define the similarity between two clusters c_1 and c_2 as follows:

Single link method: The similarity is the largest of all similarities of all pairs of documents between clusters c_1 and c_2 and defined as:

$$sim(c_1,c_2) = \max_{d_i \in c_1, d_j \in c_2} sim(d_i,d_j) \quad (5)$$

Average link method: The similarity is the average of the similarities of all pairs of documents between clusters c_1 and c_2 and defined as:

$$sim(c_1,c_2) = \frac{\sum_{d_i \in c_1} \sum_{d_j \in c_2} sim(d_i,d_j)}{|c_1| * |c_2|} \quad (6)$$

Complete link method: The similarity is the smallest of all similarities of all pairs of documents between clusters c_1 and c_2 and defined as:

$$sim(c_1,c_2) = \min_{d_i \in c_1, d_j \in c_2} sim(d_i,d_j) \quad (7)$$

where, d_i and d_j are the documents belongs to clusters c_1 and c_2, respectively.

We evaluated the AHC algorithm with the above three link methods. The achieved performance are given in Table 4. It is shown that the system performs best with the complete link method. Therefore, the complete link method is selected for the bakeoff testing.

Table 4. Performance achieved on training set with different link method

Similarity threshold	Link method	Precision	Recall	F1
0.1	Single link	0.048	1.000	0.089
0.1	Average link	0.839	0.910	0.869
0.1	Complete link	0.867	0.888	0.874
0.15	Single link	0.048	1.000	0.089
0.15	Average link	0.906	0.882	0.891
0.15	Complete link	0.923	0.868	0.891

5 Evaluations

The task organizer provides two set of evaluation criteria. They are purity-based score (usually used in IR), B-cubed score (used in WePS-2), respectively. The details of the evaluation criteria are given in the task overview.

The performance achieved by the top-3 systems are shown in Table 5.

Table 5. Performance of Top-3 Systems

	B-Cubed			P-IP		
System	Precision	Recall	F1	Precision	Recall	F1
NEU	**0.957**	0.883	**0.914**	**0.969**	0.925	**0.945**
HITSZ	0.839	**0.932**	0.874	0.885	**0.958**	0.915
DLUT	0.826	0.913	0.863	0.879	0.942	0.907

The evaluation results show that the HITSZ_CITYU system achieved overall F1 performance of 0.8742(B-Cubed)/ 0.915(P-IP), respectively.

It is also shown that HITSZ_CITYU achieves the highest the recall performance. It shows that the proposed system is good at split the document to different identical persons. Meanwhile, this system should improve the capacity on merge small clusters to enhance the precision and overall performance.

6 Conclusions

The presented HITSZ_CITYU system applies multi-segmentor and unsupervised clustering to achieve good accuracy on person name string recognition. The system then incorporates entity descriptor extraction, feature word extraction and agglomerative hierarchical clustering method for person name disambiguation. The achieved encouraging performance shown the high performance word segmentation/name recognition and extraction-based technique are helpful to improve the cluster-based person name disambiguation.

References

Andrea Heyl and Günter Neumann. DFKI2: An Information Extraction based Approach to People Disambiguation. Proceedings of ACL SEMEVAL 2007, 137-140, 2007.

Artiles, Javier, Julio Gonzalo and Satoshi Sekine, The SemEval-2007 WePS Evaluation: Establishing a benchmark for the Web People Search Task, Proceedings of Semeval 2007, Association for Computational Linguistics, 2007.

Artiles, Javier, Julio Gonzalo and Satoshi Sekine. "WePS 2 Evaluation Campaign: Overview of the Web People Search Clustering Task, In 2nd Web People Search Evaluation Workshop (WePS 2009), 18th WWW Conference, 2009

Bekkerman, Ron and McCallum, Andrew, Disambiguating Web Appearances of People in a Social Network, Proceedings of WWW2005, pp.463-470, 2005

Ergin Elmacioglu, Yee Fan Tan, Su Yan, Min-Yen Kan, and Dongwon Lee. PSNUS: Web People Name Disambiguation by Simple Clustering with Rich Features. Proceedings of ACL SEMEVAL 2007, 268-271, 2007.

Fei Song, Robin Cohen, Song Lin, Web People Search Based on Locality and Relative Similarity Measures, Proceedings of WWW 2009

Fleischman M. B. and Hovy E., Multi-document Person Name Resolution, Proceedings of ACL-42, Reference Resolution Workshop, 2004

Hui Han , Lee Giles , Hongyuan Zha , Cheng Li , Kostas Tsioutsiouliklis, Two Supervised Learning Approaches for Name Disambiguation in Author Citations, Proceedings of the 4th ACM/IEEE-CS joint conference on Digital libraries, 2004

Jain, A. K. and Dubes, R.C. Algorithms for Clustering Data, Prentice Hall, Upper Saddle River, N.J., 1988

Nallapati, R., Feng, A., Peng, F., Allan, J., Event Threading within News Topics, Proceedings of-CIKM 2004, pp. 446–453, 2004

Niu, Cheng, Wei Li, and Rohini K. Srihari,Weakly Supervised Learning for Cross-document Person Name Disambiguation Supported by Information Extraction, Proceedings of ACL 2004

Pedersen, Ted, Amruta Purandare, and Anagha Kulkarni, Name Discrimination by Clustering Similar Contexts, Proceedings of the Sixth International Conference on Intelligent Text Processing and Computational Linguistics, Mexico City, Mexico, 2005

Pedersen, Ted and Anagha Kulkarni, Unsupervised Discrimination of Person Names in Web Contexts, Proceedings of the Eighth International Conference on Intelligent Text Processing and Computational Linguistics, Mexico City, 2007.

Rao, Delip, Nikesh Garera and David Yarowsky, JHU1: An Unsupervised Approach to Person Name Disambiguation using Web Snippets, In Proceedings of ACL Semeval 2007

Sekine, Satoshi and Javier Artiles. WePS 2 Evaluation Campaign: overview of the Web People Search Attribute Extraction Task, Proceedings of 2nd Web People Search Evaluation Workshop (WePS 2009), 18th WWW Conference, 2009

Xin Li, Paul Morie, and Dan Roth, Robust Reading: Identification and Tracing of Ambiguous Names, Proceedings of NAACL,pp. 17-24, 2004.

Ying Chen, Sophia Yat Mei Lee, Chu-Ren Huang, PolyUHK: A Robust Information Extraction System for Web Personal Names, Proceedings of WWW 2009

Ying Chen and Martin J.H. CU-COMSEM: Exploring Rich Features for Unsupervised Web Personal Name Disambiguation, Proceedings of ACL Semeval 2007

A Pipeline Approach to Chinese Personal Name Disambiguation

Yang Song, Zhengyan He, Chen Chen, Houfeng Wang
Key Laboratory of Computational Linguistics (Peking University)
Ministry of Education,China
{ysong, hezhengyan, chenchen, wanghf}@pku.edu.cn

Abstract

In this paper, we describe our system for Chinese personal name disambiguation task in the first CIPS-SIGHAN joint conference on Chinese Language Processing(CLP2010). We use a pipeline approach, in which preprocessing, unrelated documents discarding, Chinese personal name extension and document clustering are performed separately. Chinese personal name extension is the most important part of the system. It uses two additional dictionaries to extract full personal names in Chinese text. And then document clustering is performed under different personal names. Experimental results show that our system can achieve good performances.

1 Introduction

Personal name search is one of the most important tasks for search engines. When a personal name query is given to a search engine, a list of related documents will be shown. But not all of the returned documents refer to the same person whom users want to find. For example, the query name "jordan" is submitted to a search engine, we can get a lot of documents containing "jordan". Some of them may refer to the computer scientist, others perhaps refer to the basketball player. For English, there have been three Web People Search (WePS[1]) evaluation campaigns on personal name disambiguation. But for Chinese, this is the first time. It encounters more challenge for Chinese personal name disambiguation. There are no word boundary in Chinese text, so it becomes difficult to recognize the full personal names from Chinese text. For example, a query name "高明" is given, but the full personal name from some documents may be an extension of "高明", like "高明光" or "高明珍", and so on. Meanwhile, "高明" can also be a common Chinese word. So we need to discard those documents which are not refered to any person related to the given query name.

To solve the above-mentioned problem, we explore a pipeline approach to Chinese personal name disambiguation. The overview of our system is illustrated in Figure 1. We split this task into four parts: preprocessing, unrelated documents discarding, Chinese personal name extension and document clustering. In preprocessing and unrelated documents discarding, we use word segmentation and part-of-speech tagging tools to process the given dataset and documents are discarded when the given query name is not tagged as a personal name or part of a personal name. After that we perform personal name extension in the documents for a given query name. When the query name has only two characters. We extend it to the left or right for one character. For example, we can extend "林鹏" to "金林鹏" or "林鹏飞". The purpose of extending the query name is to obtain the full personal name. In this way, we can get a lot of full personal names for a given query name from the documents. And then document clustering

[1]http://nlp.uned.es/weps/

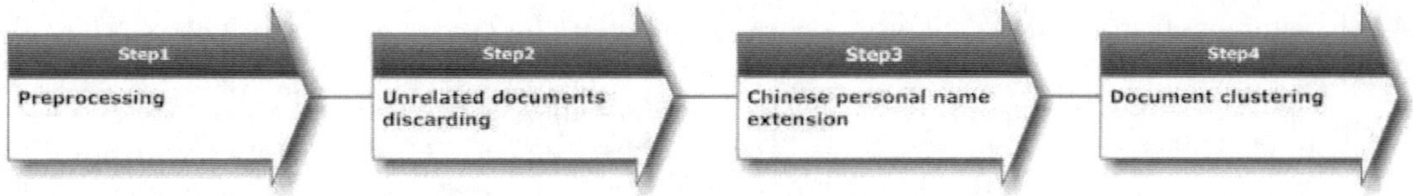

Figure 1: Overview of the System

is performed under different personal names. HAC (Hierarchical Agglomerative Clustering) is selected here. We represent documents with bag of words and solve the problem in vector space model, nouns, verbs, bigrams of nouns or verbs and named entities are selected as features. The feature weight value takes 0 or 1. In HAC, we use group-average link method as the distance measure and consine similarity as the similarity computing measure. The stopping criteria is dependent on a threshold which is obtained from training data. Our system produces pretty good results in the final evaluation.

The remainder of this paper is organized as follows. Section 2 introduces related work. Section 3 gives a detailed description about our pipeline approach. It includes preprocessing, unrelated documents discarding, Chinese personal name extension and document clustering. Section 4 presents the experimental results. The conclusions are given in Section 5.

2 Related Work

Several important studies have tried to solve the task introduced in the previous section. Most of them treated it as an clustering problem. Bagga & Baldwin (1998) first selected tokens from local context as features to perform intra-document coreference resolution. Mann & Yarowsky (2003) extracted local biographical information as features. Niu *et al.* (2004) used relation extraction results in addition to local context features and get a perfect results. Al-Kamha and Embley (2004) clustered search results with feature set including attributes, links and page similarities.

In recent years, this problem has attracted a great deal of attention from many research institutes. Ying Chen *et al.* (2009) used a Web 1T 5-gram corpus released by Google to extract additional features for clustering. Masaki Ikeda *et al.* (2009) proposed a two-stage clustering algorithm to improve the low recall values. In the first stage, some reliable features (like named entities) are used to connect documents about the same person. After that, the connected documents (document cluster) are used as a source from which new features (compound keyword features) are extracted. These new features are used in the second stage to make additional connections between documents. Their approach is to improve clusters step by step, where each step refines clusters conservatively. Han & Zhao (2009) presented a system named CASIANED to disambiguate personal names based on professional categorization. They first categorize different personal name appearances into a real world professional taxonomy, and then the personal name appearances are clustered into a single cluster. Chen Chen *et al.* (2009) explored a novel feature weight computing method in clustering. It is based on the pointwise mutual information between the ambiguous name and features. In their paper, they also develop a trade-off point based cluster stopping criteria which find the trade-off point between intra-cluster compactness and inter-cluster separation.

Our approach is based on Chinese personal name extension. We recognize the full personal names in Chinese text and perform document clustering under different personal names.

3 Methodology

In this section, we will explain preprocessing, unrelated documents discarding, Chinese personal name extension and document clustering in order.

3.1 Preprocessing

We use ltp-service[2] to process the given Chinese personal name disambiguation dataset (a detailed introduction to it will be given in section 4). Training data in the dataset contains 32 query names. There are 100-300 documents under every query name. All the documents are collected from Xinhua News Agency. They contain the exact same string as query names. Ltp-service is a web service interface for LTP[3](Language Technology Platform). LTP has integrated many Chinese processing modules, including word segmentation, part-of-speech tagging, named entity recognition, word sense disambiguation, and so on. Jun Lang *et al.* (2006) give a detailed introduction to LTP. Here we only use LTP to generate word segmentation, part-of-speech tagging and named entity recognition results for the given dataset.

3.2 Unrelated documents discarding

Under every query name, there are 100-300 documents. But not all of them are really related. For example, "高军" is a query name in training data. In corresponding documents, some are refered to real personal names like "高军" or "高军田". But others may be a substring of an expression such as "最高军事法院". These documents are needed to be filtered out. We use the preprocessing tool LTP to slove this problem. LTP can do word segmentation and part-of-speech tagging for us. For each document under a given query name, if the query name in the document is tagged as a personal name or part of some extended personal name, the document will be marked as undiscarded, otherwise the document will be discarded. Generally speaking, for the query name containing three characters, we don't need to discard any of the corresponding documents. But in practice, we find that for some query names, LTP always gives the invariable part-of-speech. For example, no matter what the context of "黄海" is, it is always tagged as a geographic name. So we use another preprocessing tool ICTCLAS[4]. Only when both of them mark one document as discarded, we discard the corresponding document.

[2]http://code.google.com/p/ltp-service/

[3]http://ir.hit.edu.cn/ltp/

3.3 Chinese personal name extension

After discarding unrelated documents, we need to recognize the full Chinese personal names. We hypothesize that the full Chinese personal name has not more than three characters (We don't consider the compound surnames here). So the query names containing only two Chinese characters are considered to extend. In our approach, we use two Chinese personal names dictionaries. One is a surname dictionary containing 423 one-character entries. We use it to do left extend for the query name. For example, the query name is "高明" and its left character in a document is "刘", we will extend it to full personal name "刘高明". The other is a non-ending Chinese character dictionary containing 64 characters which could not occur at the end of personal names. It is constructed by a personal title dictionary. We use every title's first character and some other special characters (such as numbers or punctuations) to constuct the dictionary. Some manual work has also been done to filter a few incorrect characters. Several examples of the two dictionaries are shown in Table 1.

Through the analysis of Xinhua News articles, we also find that nearly half of the documents under given query name actually refer to the reporters. And they often appear in the first or last brackets in the body of corresponding document. For example, "(通讯员刘国党、黄海生)" is a sentence containing query name "黄海". We use some simple but efficient rules to get full personal names for this case.

3.4 Document clustering

For every query name, we can get a list of full peronal names. For example, when the

[4]http://ictclas.org/

Table 1: Several Examples of the two Dictionaries

Dictionaries	Examples
Surnames	王, 张, 李, 陈, 刘, 杨, 黄, 吴, 周, 赵, 徐, 孙, 朱, 胡...
Non-ending Chinese characters	说, 的, 县, 市, 坐, 反, 讲, 跳, 牌, 各, 住, 在, 仍, 打...

query name is "郭勇", we can get the personal names like "郭勇民", "郭勇军", "郭勇勤", "郭勇孝". And then document clustering is performed under different personal names.

3.4.1 Features

We use bag of words to represent documents. Some representative words need to be chosen as features. LTP can give us POS tagging and NER results. We select all the nouns, verbs and named entities which appear in the same paragraph with given query name as features. Meanwhile, the bigrams of nouns or verbs are also selected. We take 0 or 1 for feature weight value. 0 represents that the feature doesn't appear in corresponding paragraphs, and 1 represents just the opposite. We find that this weighting scheme is more effective than TFIDF.

3.4.2 Clustering

All features are represented in vector space model. Every document is modeled as a vertex in the vector space. So every document can be seen as a feature vector. Before clustering, the similarity between documents is computed by cosine value of the angle between feature vectors. We use HAC to do document clustering. It is a bottom-up algorithm which treats each document as a singleton cluster at the outset and then successively merges (or agglomerates) pairs of clusters until all clusters have been merged into a single cluster that contains all documents. From our experience, single link and group-average link method seem to work better than complete link one. We use group-average link method in the final submission. The stopping criteria is a difficult problem for clustering. Here we use a threshold for terminating condition. So it is not necessary to determine the number of clusters beforehand. We select a threshold which produces the best performance in training data.

4 Experimental Results

The dataset for Chinese personal name disambiguation task contains training data and testing data. The training data contains 32 query names. Every query name folder contains 100-300 news articles. Given the query name, all the documents are retrived by character-based matching from a collection of Xinhua news documents in a time span of fourteen years. The testing data contains 25 query names. Two threshold values as terminating conditions are obtained from training data. They are 0.4 and 0.5. For evaluation, we use P-IP score and B-cubed score (Bagga and Baldwin, 1998). Table 2 & Table 3 show the official evaluation results.

Table 2: Official Results for P-IP score

Threshold	**P-IP**		
	P	**IP**	**F score**
0.4	88.32	94.9	91.15
0.5	91.3	91.77	91.18

Table 3: Official Results for B-Cubed score

Threshold	**B-Cubed**		
	Precision	**Recall**	**F score**
0.4	83.68	92.23	86.94
0.5	87.87	87.49	86.84

Besides the formal evaluation, the organizer also provide a diagnosis test designed to explore the relationship between Chinese word segmentation and personal name disambiguation. That means the query names in the documents are segmented correctly by manual work. Table 4 & Table 5 show the diagnosis results.

Table 4: Diagnosis Results for P-IP score

Threshold	P-IP		
	P	IP	F score
0.4	89.01	95.83	91.96
0.5	91.85	92.68	91.96

Table 5: Diagnosis Results for B-Cubed score

Threshold	B-Cubed		
	Precision	Recall	F score
0.4	84.53	93.42	87.96
0.5	88.59	88.59	87.8

The official results show that our method performs pretty good. The diagnosis results show that correct word segmentation can improve the evaluation results. But the improvement is rather limited. That is mainly because Chinese personal name extension is done well in our approach. So the diagnosis results don't gain much profit from query names' correct segmentation.

5 Conclusions

We describe our framework in this paper. First, we use LTP to do preprocessing for original dataset which comes from Xinhua news articles. LTP can produce good results for Chinese text processing. And then we use two additional dictionaries(one is Chinese surname dictionary, the other is Non-ending Chinese character dictionary) to do Chinese personal name extension. After that we perform document clustering under different personal names. Official evaluation results show that our method can achieve good performances.

In the future, we will attempt to use other features to represent corresponding persons in the documents. We will also investigate automatic terminating condition.

6 Acknowledgments

This research is supported by National Natural Science Foundation of Chinese (No.60973053) and Research Fund for the Doctoral Program of Higher Education of China (No.20090001110047).

References

J. Artiles, J. Gonzalo, and S. Sekine. 2009. *WePS 2 evaluation campaign: overview of the web people search clustering task.* In 2nd Web People Search Evaluation Workshop(WePS 2009), 18th WWW Conference.

Bagga and B. Baldwin. 1998. *Entity-based cross-document coreferencing using the vector space model.* In Proceedings of 17th International Conference on Computational Linguistics, 79–85.

Mann G. and D. Yarowsky. 2003. *Unsupervised personal name disambiguation.* In Proceedings of CoNLL-2003, 33–40, Edmonton, Canada.

C. Niu, W. Li, and R. K. Srihari. 2004. *Weakly Supervised Learning for Cross-document Person Name Disambiguation Supported by Information Extraction.* In Proceedings of ACL 2004.

Al-Kamha. R. and D. W. Embley. 2004. *Grouping search-engine returned citations for person-name queries.* In Proceedings of WIDM 2004, 96-103, Washington, DC, USA.

Ying Chen, Sophia Yat Mei Lee, and Chu-Ren Huang. 2009. *PolyUHK:A Robust Information Extraction System for Web Personal Names.* In 2nd Web People Search Evaluation Workshop(WePS 2009), 18th WWW Conference.

Masaki Ikeda, Shingo Ono, Issei Sato, Minoru Yoshida, and Hiroshi Nakagawa. 2009. *Person Name Disambiguation on the Web by Two-Stage Clustering.* In 2nd Web People Search Evaluation Workshop(WePS 2009), 18th WWW Conference.

Xianpei Han and Jun Zhao. 2009. *CASIANED: Web Personal Name Disambiguation Based on Professional Categorization.* In 2nd Web People Search Evaluation Workshop(WePS 2009), 18th WWW Conference.

Chen Chen, Junfeng Hu, and Houfeng Wang. 2009. *Clustering technique in multi-document personal name disambiguation.* In Proceedings of the ACL-IJCNLP 2009 Student Research Workshop, pages 88–95.

Jun Lang, Ting Liu, Huipeng Zhang and Sheng Li. 2006. *LTP: Language Technology Platform.* In Proceedings of SWCL 2006.

Bagga, Amit and B. Baldwin. 1998. *Algorithms for scoring co-reference chains.* In Proceedings of the First International Conference on Language Resources and Evaluation Workshop on Linguistic co-reference.

Chinese Personal Name Disambiguation:

Technical Report of Natural Language Processing Lab of Xiamen University

Xiang Zhu, Xiaodong Shi, Ningfeng Liu, YingMei Guo, Yidong Chen
Natural Language Processing Lab, Department of Cognitive Science, Xiamen University , Xiamen 361005
zhuxiang_sm@163.com,mandel@xmu.edu.cn,nffliu@gmail.com

Abstract

This report presents the work of our group in the Chinese personal name disambiguation workshop. We propose a system which uses a HAC algorithm to cluster the mentions referring to the same person with features extracted from the documents.

1 Introduction

Personal name disambiguation is actually a task to group those documents according to whether the given personal name appearing in that document refers to the same person in reality. It becomes an active research topic recently, and the evaluation campaign for the English personal name has been held twice.

Chinese personal name disambiguation is thought to be more challenging due to the need for word segmentation which could bring errors into the subsequent processes.

The most widely used method for personal name disambiguation is unsupervised clustering, we adopt a Hierarchical Agglomerative Clustering algorithm in our system, which is also the most popular clustering algorithm used by the teams of the second Web People Search Evaluation campaign.

The remaining part of this report is organized as follows. Section 2 introduces the document preprocessing. Section 3 describes the feature used for the clustering and the section 4 addresses the clustering algorithm. The workshop requests two different tests, a formal test, and a diagnosis test, we will discuss the difference between them with our system's result in section 5.

2 Document preprocessing

Different from the document preprocessing for English, we have to use a segmentation tool and a part-of-speech tagger to do some preprocessing work. For example, without the segmenting process, the documents only contain the string "最高军事法院" could be clustered when the query name is "高军", and we need the part-of-speech tagger to detect whether the Chinese word "黄海" stands for a personal name or a toponym.

Our experiments prove that the system is sensitive to the tools' performance, the different result between the formal test and the diagnosis test also proves this.

These tools are trained with the 90% data of The People's Daily published in Jan.1998,and tested with the others 10% data.

The performances of the tools are:

	Precision	Recall	F
seg	97.746%	97.793%	97.769%
tag	94.197%	94.242%	94.219%

Table 1: the performances of the tools

3 Extracted features

As mentioned previously, our goal is to group those documents. In our approach, each document is represented by a vector of features extracted from it automatically. We use three kinds of token-based features:

1) Nouns occur around the ambiguous personal name.

This kind of features is selected based on the idea that words around the ambiguous personal name are more relevant to it, and Nouns can provide a more diagnostic description of the person. We use a window to select the nouns.

2) Personal names (except the ambiguous personal name) and toponyms occur in the document.

It is intuitive that the identical person often associated with the same personal names and toponyms.

3) Words with high TFIDF value. In our final system, we use the ten words with highest TFIDF value.

This kind of features can reflect the theme of an article, an identical person often be mentioned in articles with the same theme.

Using these features simultaneously can alleviate the problem caused by spare data. The following table presents a quantitative analysis:

used features	highest F score on dev data
Feature 1	83.76
Feature 1,2	86.18
Feature 1,3	84.83
Feature 1,2,3	86.76

Table 2:analysis of features

These results are obtained by using a initial version of the preprocessing toools, and when we improve the performances of the tools, the highest F score increases from 86.76 to 89.61 .

The similarity between documents was measured with the cosine of feature vectors. When computing the similarity between two documents, we proposed a weighting method for the features as:

If the token occurs in the document, the weight will be 1, else 0.

We have tried another method that count the tokens' weight by its frequency, but experiments prove it is a less effective one, we can interpret it by this example:

If a word "教授" which refers to a person named " 李 明 " appears twice in one document while three times in another document, these two documents are very likely referring to the same person, but the latter weighting method decreases the similarity between them.

4 Clustering algorithm

A Hierarchical Agglomerative Clustering algorithm is adopted in our system, which determines the number of the cluster by a fixed similarity threshold learned from the train data. At each stage of the clustering, the two most similar clusters are merged into a new one, and other clusters' similarities with the new cluster is the larger one of their similarities with the two old clusters.

We have tried some other clustering methods such as modified k-means clustering with the same features, but the performances are worse.

A pre-judgment stage before clustering is useful in the experiment, which can be done as follow:

If two documents have the same triple tokens "token1 token2 PersonName" (token2 is tagged as noun), then they are classified to one cluster.

5 Result and discussion

The difference between the formal test and the diagnosis test is that the ambiguous personal name in each document have been told in the latter, but you have to find it in the former by yourself. The method we adopt to detect the ambiguous personal name in the formal test is to find the token which is tagged as personal name while contains the query name.

Our system's performances are:

B-Cubed	precision	Recall	F
Formal test	90.55	84.88	85.72
Diagnosis test	89.84	89.84	89.08

Table 3: the performances in the B-Cubed criterion

P-IP	P	IP	F
Formal test	93.3	89.22	89.9
Diagnosis test	92.77	93.33	92.71

Table 4: the performances in the P-IP criterion

From the results we can know that Chinese personal name disambiguation can be affected by the segmentation tool and the part-of-speech tagger.

References

Y. Chen, S. Y. M. Lee, and C.-R. Huang. Polyuhk: A robust information extraction system for web personal names. In 2nd Web People Search Evaluation Workshop (WePS 2009), 18th WWW Conference, 2009.

J. Gong and D. Oard. Determine the entity number in hierarchical clustering for web personal name disambiguation. In 2nd Web

People Search Evaluation Workshop (WePS 2009), 18th WWW Conference, 2009.

P. Kalmar and D. Freitag. Features for web person disambiguation. In 2nd Web People Search Evaluation Workshop (WePS 2009), 18th WWW Conference, 2009.

Chinese Personal Name Disambiguation Based on Person Modeling

Hua-Ping ZHANG[1] Zhi-Hua LIU[2] Qian MO[3] He-Yan HUANG[1]
[1] Beijing Institute of Technology, Beijing, P.R.C 100081
[2] North China University of Technology, P.R.C 100041
[3] Beijing Technology and Business University, Beijing, P.R.C 100048
Email: kevinzhang@bit.edu.cn

Abstract

This document presents the bakeoff results of Chinese personal name in the First CIPS-SIGHAN Joint Conference on Chinese Language Processing. The authors introduce the frame of person disambiguation system LJPD, which uses a new person model. LJPD was built in short time, and it is not given enough training and adjustment. Evaluation on LJPD shows that the precision is competitive, but the recall is very low. It has more space for further improvement.

1 Introduction

We participated in the First CIPS-SIGHAN Joint Conference on Chinese Language Processing. And have taken task 3: Chinese Personal Name disambiguation.

Chinese personal name disambiguation includes two stages: words are segmented to recognize Chinese personal name, and documents are clustered to disambiguate different person with the same personal name.

In our system, it involves the following steps:

1) Segmenting words and tagging the part-of-speech, and then recognizing Chinese personal name using ICTCLAS 2010 system[1].

2) Extracting personal feature to create the person attribution model on each document.

3) Generating initial clusters according to features in person model, and then clustering the initial clusters until the stop criteria is reached. The processing flow is illustrated in figure 1.

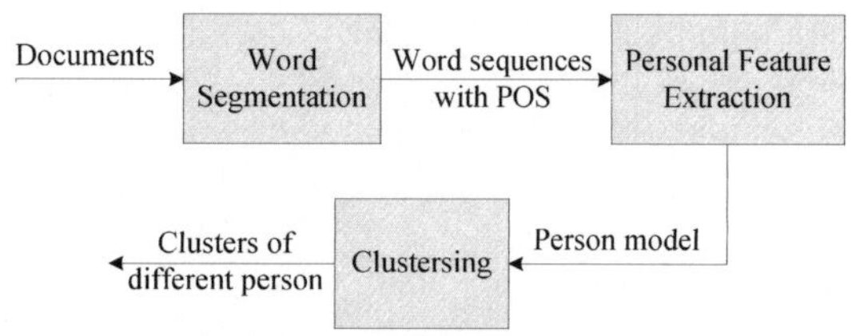

Figure 1 Step of Person Disambiguation

As illustrated in figure 1, the whole system addresses four problems: personal name recognition, anaphora resolution of personal name, person model creation and clustering.

2 Personal Name Recognition

Chinese personal name recognition is more difficult than English. Such difficulties usually combine with Chinese word segmentation. The set of Chinese personal name is infinite, and the rule of name construction is varied. Chinese personal name is often made up of a usual word, and has ambiguity with its context.

To solve the difficulties mentioned above, Chinese personal name recognition based on role tagging is given in [Zhang etc., 2002]. The approach is: tokens after segmentation are tagged using Viterbi algorithm with different roles according to their functions in the generation of Chinese personal name; the possible names are recognized after maximum pattern matching on the roles sequence [ZHANG, etc., 2002]. With this approach, the precision of ICTCLAS reaches 95.57% and the recall is 95.23% in an opening corpus which contains 1,108,049 words. In the corpus, the count of the personal name is 15,888. And ICTCLAS is a Chinese lexical analysis system witch combines part-of-speech

[1] It can be downloaded from http://hi.baidu.com/drkevinzhang

tagging, word segmentation, unknown words recognition. It can meet our requirements, so ICTCLAS provides personal name recognition in our system.

3 Anaphora Resolution of Personal Name

Anaphora is very common in natural language. Resolve this problem can help us get more information of the person from a document.

Anaphora resolution of personal name is an important part of anaphora resolution. At present, much advancement in anaphora resolution have occurred [Saliha 1998]. Anaphora resolution of personal pronouns is an especially complicate problem in anaphora resolution of personal name. In our system, we don't process this problem. The reason is that anaphora resolution of personal name will take side effect to personal name disambiguation unless its precision is definitely high. So we just process the anaphora of the first name or the second name. For example, "Jianmin Wang" in above context and "Professor Wang" will be resolved in our system.

4 Personal Model

We propose a person model to represent the person in the document:

$$\text{Person} = \{N, P, Q, R\}$$

where:

N is the collection of appellation of person, such as name, nickname, alias, and so on

P is the collection of the basic attributes of person

Q is the collection of the other attributes of person

R is the collection of the terms co-occurrence with person name, witch is called term field

In the system, we focused on seven attributes such as sex, nationality, birthday, native place, address, profession, family members and personal name, co-occurrence terms. In these features, name $\in$ N, {sex, nationality, birthday, native place} $\in$ P, {address, profession, family members} $\in$ Q, {co-occurrence term} $\in$ R. Table 1 is the examples of person model.

In view of the co-occurrence personal name is especially important for person disambiguation. We separate it as another field in R.

4.1 Attributes Feature

The components N, P and Q of person model are attributes feature. The dimension of these features for a person is different. For example, the sex of a person is constant in life, while his or her address may be different in different time. Take DOM to represent the dimension of the attributes features. Then:

$$DOM(N_i) = 1; (1 \leqslant i \leqslant n)$$
$$DOM(P_i) = 1; (1 \leqslant i \leqslant k)$$
$$DOM(Q_i) \geqslant 1; (1 \leqslant i \leqslant m)$$

For a person, N and P are constant in life. If one attribute of N or P between two persons is different, they are not the same person.

To get the attributes feature, we have three steps: First, segment word and tag part-of-speech for the input document. Second, we identify the triggering word which is defined as attributes value and the Max-Noun Phrase. The triggering words are identified by their POS and a hand-built triggering word thesaurus. At last, a classifier determines the attribute belongs to the left personal name or the right to the attribute. The classifier is trained by the corpus which is hand-tagged documents from internet.

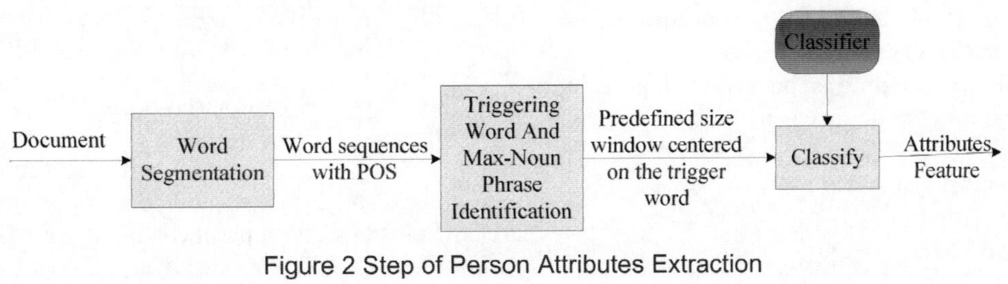

Figure 2 Step of Person Attributes Extraction

4.2 Term Field

In person model, R is the collection of the terms co-occurrence within person. We adopt Vector Space Model to represent these terms. The i-th term is represented by t_i, and its weight is represented by w_i, and the weight shows the importance of the term for the person.

$$R = (t_1, w_1; t_2, w_2; \ldots ; t_H, w_H)$$

To get the person's term field, we identify a scope witch these terms occurred. We consider three kinds of scope for term field: the total document, the paragraph where the personal name is present, sentence where the personal name is present. And then segment words and tag part-of-speech for these fragments. Next, filter out the attribute terms and filter by part-of-speech and leave only nouns, verb, adjective, adverb and name entry. Third, we make a stop word list, and filter out these stop terms. Last, according to the term's DF, filter out high frequency and low frequency terms, and only the terms witch DF is not lower than 2 and not higher than N/3(N is the total count of documents) are left.

In collection R, we have separated term field to co-occurrence personal name vector and co-occurrence common term vector. Because the two vectors have different affect to person disambiguation. This difference manifests in the different method to compute these weight. The common term's weight is computed by tf-idf algorithm:

$$w(t,\vec{d}) = \log(tf(t,\vec{d})+1)\times\log(N/n_t+1)$$

where:

$w(t,\vec{d})$ is the weight of term t in document $\vec{d}$

$tf(t,\vec{d})$ is the frequency of occurrence of t in $\vec{d}$

N is the total count of documents

n_t is the count of documents which contain term t

	sex	nationality	birthday	Native place	address	Family members	profession	Co-occurrence personal name	Co-occurrence terms field
Name1	男	汉	1949		北京		演员	...	......
Name2	女			山东		王红	教师	...	......
Name3	男	蒙			安徽		书记	...	......

Table 1 Examples of Person Model

The co-occurrence personal name's weight is computed below:

$$w(name,\vec{p}) = \log(nf(name,\vec{p})+1)\times\log(N'/n_{name}+1)$$

where:

$w(name,\vec{p})$ is the weight of co-occurrence name *name*

$nf(name,\vec{p})$ is the frequency of co-occurrence of *name* and person $\vec{p}$

name is the count of the co-occurrence of *name* and the other personal name

The similarity of term field between two persons is calculated by the angle cosine:

$$Sim(X,Y) = \cos(X,Y) = \frac{\sum_i x_i * y_i}{\sqrt{\sum_i x_i^2 * \sum_i y_i^2}}$$

5 Clustering

Person model "Person = {N, P, Q, R}" is multi-dimensional. First, we adopted two rules to generate original clusters:

Rule 1: For two persons whose name is same, if one of the birthday (accurate to month) or relative is matched, these two persons are the same person.

Rule 2: For two persons whose name is same, if one of the sex, nationality, native place or birthday is not matched, these two persons are different.

There are profession, co-occurrence personal name and co-occurrence common terms left. For two persons whose name is same, we apply rule 1 and 2 first. If both of the two rules are not activating, compute the similarity $Sim_{position}(X, Y)$, $cos_{name}(X, Y)$, $cos_{term}(X, Y)$. And then synthesize these three similarities.

Assume the three factors profession, co-occurrence personal name and co-occurrence common terms are independent, and adopt Stanford certainty theory to synthesize the three similarities. The Stanford certainty theory creates confidence measures and some simple rules for combing these confidences. Assume E1, E2, E2 are the Stanford certainty factors of event B, and CF represent the confidence, then the confidence of event B is :

$$CF(B) = CF(E1) + CF(E2) + CF(E3) - CF(E1)\times CF(E2) - CF(E1)\times CF(E3) - CF(E2)\times CF(E3) + CF(E1)\times CF(E2)\times CF(E3)$$

For example, if the confidence of the three factors for event B is respectively: 88%, 74%, 66%, then the confidence for event B is 88% + 74% + 66% − 88%x74% − 88%x66% − 76%x 66% + 88%x74%x66% = 98.93%.

To compute the confidence of the factors, we should get the threshold (represented by u_i) of the similarity for factors. If the similarity of the factor reaches the threshold, its confidence is 100%:

$$CF(E_i) = {sim_{E_i}}/{u_i} \qquad CF(E_i) \in [0,1]$$

The training method is: clustering training data according to the single factor, select the threshold with which the recall is higher with the premise that the precision is not lower than 98%. We get three thresholds 3, 0.5, 0.25 respectively for factor profession, co-occurrence personal name and co-occurrence common terms.

Overall, the algorithm takes two steps:

1) Adopt rule 1 and 2 to group the persons to the original clusters
2) Adopt agglomerative hierarchical clustering algorithm to clustering these original clusters.
   (1) Take each original cluster as a single cluster
   (2) Select two clusters which are most likelihood and merge to one cluster
   (3) If there is only one cluster or reaches stop criteria, exit. Else, go to step (2).

In the process of merging the clusters, we should merge the fragment of person. For term field vector, we simply compute the average of the term weights. For attribute feature, we adopt rule method to merge two clusters.

6 Task

We would introduce the operation of some different track in this section.

In formal test, we first get a query name and its all files. Then we segment these files and extract the related information of our person model and output to files. At last, we cluster these person models and output to result xml.

In the diagnosis test, the basic process is same to the formal test. The difference is that the element of clustering is changed to the subfolder of a real name. When all the subfolders are clustered for a query name, we merge the results to one xml file.

	B-Cubed			P-IP		
	precision	recall	F score	P	IP	F score
Formal test	80.2	68.75	68.4	86.12	76.37	77.54
Diagnosis test	94.62	63.32	72.48	96.44	72.78	80.85

Table 2 Evaluation result of Personal Disambiguation

7 Conclusion

Through the first bakeoff, we have learned much about the development in Chinese personal name recognition and person disambiguation. At the same time, we really find our problems during the evaluation. The bakeoff is interesting and helpful. We look forward to participate in forthcoming bakeoff.

References

ZHANG Hua-Ping, LIU Qun, YU Hong-Kui, CHENG Xue-Qi, BAI Shuo. *Chinese Named Entity Recognition Using Role Model.* International Journal of Computational Linguistics and Chinese language processing, 2003,Vol. 8 (2)

Azzam Saliha, Kevin Humphreys & Robert Gaizauskas. *Coreference resolution in a multilingual information extraction.* In the Proc. of the Workshop on Linguistic Coference. Granada, Spain.1998.

Yu Manquan. *Research on Knowledge Mining in Person Tracking*. Ph.D.Thesis of GUCAS. 2006

Jumping Distance based Chinese Person Name Disambiguation[1]

Yu Hong Fei Pei Yue-hui Yang Jian-min Yao Qiao-ming Zhu

School of Computer Science and Technology, Soochow University
No.1 Shizi street, Suzhou City, Jiansu Province, China
{hongy, 20094527004, 0727401137, jyao, qmzhu}@suda.edu.cn

Abstract

In this paper, we describe a Chinese person name disambiguation system for news articles and report the results obtained on the data set of the CLP 2010 Bakeoff-3[1]. The main task of the Bakeoff is to identify different persons from the news stories that contain the same person-name string. Compared to the traditional methods, two additional features are used in our system: 1) n-grams co-occurred with target name string; 2) Jumping distance among the n-grams. On the basis, we propose a two-stage clustering algorithm to improve the low recall.

1 Our Novel Try

For this task, we propose a Jumping-Distance based n-gram model (abbr. DJ n-gram) to describe the semantics of the closest contexts of the target person-name strings.

The generation of the DJ n-gram model mainly involves two steps. First, we mine the Jumping tree for the target string; second, we give the statistical description of the tree.

- Jumping Tree

Given a target string, we firstly extract the sentence where it locates as its closest context. Then we segment the sentence into n-grams(Chen et al. ,2009) (only Bi-gram and Tri-gram are used in this paper). For each n-gram, we regard it as the beginning of a jumping journey. And the places where we jump are the sentences which involve the n-gram. By the same way, we segment the sentences into n-grams which will be regarded as the new beginnings to open further jumping. The procedure will run iteratively until there are no sentences in the document (viz. the document which involves the target string) can be used to jump. Actually, we find there are only 3 jumps in average in our previous test and simultaneously 11 sentences in a document can be involved into the jumping journey. Thus, we can obtain a Jumping Tree where each jumping route from the initially n-gram (viz. the gram in the closes context) refer to a branch. And for each intermediate node, its child-nodes are the n-grams co-occurred with it in the same sentences.

The motivation to generate the Jumping Tree is to imitate the thinking model of human recognizing the word senses and semantics. In detail, for each intermediate node of the tree, its child-nodes all come from its closest contexts, especially the nodes co-occur with it in the same sentences which involve the real grammar and semantic relations. Thus the child-nodes normally provide the natural inference for its word sense. For example, given the string "SARS", we can deduce its sense from its child nodes "Severe", "Acute", "Respiratory" and "Syndromes" even if we see the string for the first time. On the basis, the procedure of inference run iteratively, that is, the tree always use the child nodes deduce the meaning of their father nodes then further ancestor nodes until the root. Thus the tree acts as a hierarchical understanding procedure. Additionally, the distances among nodes in the tree give the degree of semantic relation.

In the task of person-name disambiguation, we use the Jumping Tree to deduce the identities and backgrounds of a person. Each branch of the tree refers to a property of the person.

- Jumping-Distance based n-gram model

In this paper, we give a simple statistical model to describe the Jumping Tree. Given a node in the tree (viz. an n-gram), we record the

1 Supported by the National Natural Science Foundation of China under Grant No. 60970057, No.60873105.

steps jumping from the root to it, viz. the depth of the node in the tree. Then based on the priori-trained TFIDF value, we calculate the generation probability of the node as follows:

$$P = TF \cdot \frac{\alpha}{depth}$$

where the α denotes the smoothing factor.

In fact, we create more comprehensive models to describe the semantic correlations among the nodes in the Jumping Tree. The models well use the distances among the nodes in local Jumping Tree (viz. the tree generated based on the test document) and that normalized on the large-scale training data to calculate the probability of n-grams correboratively generate a semantics. They try to imitate the thinking model of human combine differents features to understand panoramic knowledge. In the task of name disambiguation, we can use the models to improve the distinguishment of different persons who have the same name. And we have illustrate the well effectiveness on the topic description and relevance measurement in other tasks, such as Link Detection. But we actually didn't use the models to perform the task of name diaambiguation this time with the aim to purely evaluate the usefulness of the Jumping Tree.

2 Systems

For the task of Chinese person name disambiguation, we submitted two systems as follows:

- System1

The system involves two main components: DJ-based name Identification error detection and DJ-based person name disambiguation.

The first component, viz. DJ-based name segmentation error detection, aims to distinguish the target string referring to person name from that referring to something else. Such as, the string "黄海" can be a person name "Hai Huang" but also a name of sea "the Yellow Sea". And the detection component focuses on obtaining the pure person name "Hai Huang".

The detection component firstly establish two classes of features which respectively describe the nature of human and that of things. Such as, the features "professor", "research", "honest" et al., can roughly be determined as the nature of human, and conversely the features "solid", "collapse", "deep" et al., can be that of things. For obtaining the features, we extract 10,000 documents that discuss person, eg. "Albert Einstein" and 6000 documents that discuss technology, science, geography, et.al., from Wikipedia[2]. For each document, we generate its Jumping Tree, and regard the nodes in the tree as the features. After that, we combine the weights of the same features and normalized the value by dividing that by the average weight in the specific class of features.

Based on the two classes of features, given a target string and the document where it occurs, the detection component firstly generate the Jumping Tree of the document, and then determines whether the string is person name or things by measuring the similarity of the tree to the classes of features. Here, we simply use the VSM and Cosine metric （Bagga and Baldwin, 1998） to obtain the similarity.

The second component, viz. DJ-based person name disambiguation, firstly generates the Jumping trees for all documents that involve specific person name. And a two-stage clustering algorithm is adopted to divide the documents and refer each cluster to a person. The first stage of the algorithm runs a strict division which focuses on obtaining high precision. The second stage performs a soft division which is used to improve recall. The two-stage clustering algorithm(Ikeda et al.,2009) initially obtains the optimal parameters that respectively refer to the maximum precision and recall based on training data, and then regards a statistical tradeoff as the final value of the parameters. Here, the Affinity Propagation clustering tools (Frey BJ and Dueck D, 2007) is in use.

- System2

The system is similar to the system1 except that it additionally involve Named Entity Identification (Artiles et.al,2009B; Popescu,O. and Magnini, B.,2007)before the two-stage clustering in the component of person name disambiguation. In detail, given a person name and the documents that it occurs in, the disambiguation component of System2 firstly adopt NER CRF++ toolkit[3] provided by MSRA to identify Named Entities(Chen et al., 2006) that involve the given name string, such as the entity "李高明" (viz. Gao-ming Li in English) when given the target name string "高明"(viz. Ming Gao in English). Thus the documents can be roughly divided into different clusters of Named Entities without name segmentation errors. After that, we additionally adopt the two-stage clustering algorithm to further divide each cluster. Thus we can deal with the issue of disambiguation without the interruption of name segmentation errors.

3 Data sets

- Training dataset: They contain about 30 Chinese personal names, and a document set of about 100-300 news articles from collection of Xinhua news documents in a time span of fourteen years are provided for each personal name.
- External dataset: Chinese Wikipedia[2] personal attribution (Cucerzan, 2007; Nguyen and Cao,2008).
- Test dataset: There are about 26 Chinese personal names, which are similar to train data sets.

4 Experiments

The systems that run on test dataset are evaluated by both B-Cubed (Bagga and Baldwin, 1998; Artiles et al.,2009A) and P-IP (Artiles et al., 2007 ;Artiles et al.,2009A). And the systems that run on training dataset were only evaluated by B-Cubed.

In experiments, we firstly evaluate the performance of name segmentation error detection on the training dataset. For comparison, we additionally perform another detection method which only using Name Entity Identifcation (NER CRF++ tools) to distinguish name-strings from the discarded ones. The results are shown in table 1. We can find that our error detection method can achieve more recall than NER, but lower precision.

Besides, we evaluate the performance of the two-stage clustering in the component of name disambiguation step by step. Four steps are in use to evaluate the first-stage clustering method as follows:

- DJ^2

This step look like to run the system1 mentionedin in section 3 which don't involve the prior-division of documents by using NER before the first-stage clustering in the component of name disambiguation. Especially it don't perform the second-stage clustering to improve the recall probability.

- DJ^2+NER

This step is similar to the step of DJ^2 mentioned above except that it perform the prior-divison of documents by using NER.

- NER+DJ

This step is also similar to the step of DJ^2 except that its name segmentation error detection performs by using the NER.

- NER^2+DJ

This step is similar to the step of NER+DJ except that it involve the treatment of prior-divison as that in DJ^2+NER.

The performances of the four steps are shown in table 2. We can find that all steps achieve poor recall. And the step of DJ^2 achieve the best F-score although it don't involve the prior-division. That is because NER is helpful to improve precision but not recall, as shown in table 1. Conversely, DJ^2 can avoid the bias caused by the procedure of greatly maximizing the precision.

	P	recall	F-score
DJ-based	0.62	0.81	0.70
NER-based	0.91	0.77	0.71

Table 1: Performance of name segmentation error detection

	P	IP	F-score
DJ^2	80.49	53.85	60.12
DJ^2+NER	88.56	51.30	59.02
NER+DJ	93.27	46.78	57.44
NER^2+DJ	97.79	42.13	55.47

Table 2: Performances of the-stage clustering

Additionally, another two steps are used to evluate the both two stages of clustering in name disambiguation. The steps are as follows:

- DJ^2+NER_2

This step is similar to the step of DJ^2+NER except that it additionally run the second-stage clustering to improve recall.

- NER^2+DJ_2

This step also run the second-stage clustering on the basis of NER^2+DJ.

The performances of the two step are shown in table 3. We can find that the F-scores both have been improved substantially. And the two steps still maintain the original distribution between precision and recall. That is, the DJ^2+NER_2, which has outperformance on recall in the name segmentation error detection, still maintain the higher recall at the second-stage clustering. And NER^2+DJ_2 also maintains higher precision. This illustrates that the clustering has no ability to remedy the shortcomings of NER in the prior-division.

	P	IP	F-score
DJ^2+NER_2	82.65	63.40	66.59
NER^2+DJ_2	87.71	60.45	66.23

Table 3: Performances of two-stage clustering

The test results of the two systems mentioned in section 3 are shown in the table 4. We also show the performances of each stage clustering as that on training dataset. We can find that the poor performance mainly come from the low recall, which illustrates that the DJ-based n-gram disambiguation is not robust.

	B-Cubed		
	precision	recall	F-Score
System1(one	85.26	28.43	37.74
System1(both	84.51	44.17	51.42
	P-IP		
	P	IP	F-Score
System2(one	88.4	39.47	50.52
System2(both	88.36	55.23	63.89

Table 4 :Test results

5.Conclusions

In this paper, we report a hybrid Chinese personal disambiguation system and a novel algorithm for extract useful global n-gram features from the context .Experiment showed that our algorithm performed high precision and poor recall. Furthermore, two-stage clustering can handl a change in the one-stage clustering algorithm, especially for recall score. In the future, we will investigate global new types of features to improve the recall score and local new types of features to improve the precision score. For instance, the location and organization besides the person in the named-entities. And we try to use Hierarchical Agglomerative Clustering algorithm to help raise the recall score.

References

Artiles J, J Gonzalo and S Sekine. 2007. The SemEval-2007 WePS Evaluation: "Establishing a benchmark for the Web People Search Task.", The SemEval-2007, 64-69, Association for Computational Linguistics.

Artiles Javier, Julio Gonzalo and Satoshi Sekine.2009A. "WePS 2 Evaluation Campaign: overview of the Web People Search Clustering Task," In 2nd Web People Search Evaluation Workshop (WePS 2009), 18th WWW Conference.

Artiles J, E Amig´o and J Gonzalo. 2009B.The Role of Named Entities in Web People Search. Proceedings of the 2009 Conference on Empirical Methods Natural Language Processing, 534–542,Singapore, August 2009.

Bagga A and Baldwin B. 1998. Entity-based cross-document coreferenceing using the Vector Space Model.Proceedings of the 17th international conference on computational linguistics. Volume 1, 79-85.

Chen,Ying., Sophia Yat., Mei Lee and Chu-Ren Huang. 2009. PolyUHK:A Roubust Information Extraction System for Web Personal Names In 2nd Web People Search Evaluation Workshop (WePS 2009), 18th WWW Conference.

Chen Wen-liang, Zhang Yu-jie. 2006. Chinese Named Entity Recognition with Conditional Random Fields. Proceedings of the Fifth SIGHAN Workshop on Chinese Language Processing.

Cucerzan, Silviu. 2007. Large scale named entity Disambiguation based on Wikipedia data. In The EMNLP-CoNLL-2007.

Frey BJ and Dueck D. 2007. Clustering by Passing Messages Between Data Points .science, 2007 - sciencemag.org.

Ikeda MS, Ono I, Sato MY and Nakagawa H. 2009. Person Name disambiguation on the Web by Two-Stage Clustering. In 2nd Web People Search Evaluation Workshop(WePS 2009),18th WWW Conference.

Popescu,O and Magnini, B. 2007. IRST-BP:Web People Search Using Name Entities.Proceeding s of the 4th International Workshop on Semantic Evaluations (SemEval-2007), 195-198, Prague June 2007. Association for Computational Linguistics.

Research of People Disambiguation by Combining Multiple knowledges

Erlei Ma
School of computer science and technology, harbin institute of technology
elma@insun.hit.edu.cn

Yuanchao Liu
School of computer science and technology, harbin institute of technology
ycliu@hit.edu.cn

Abstract

With the rapid development of Internet and many related technology, Web has become the main source of information. For many search engines, there are many different identities in the returned results of character information query. Thus the Research of People disambiguation is important. In this paper we attempt to solve this problem by combing different knowledge. As people usually have different kind of careers, so we first utilize this knowledge to classify people roughly. Then we use social context of people to identify different person. The experimental results show that these knowledge are helpful for people disambiguation.

1 Introduction

For the real world, many people share one name; this is a very common phenomenon. According to the third national census sample survey conducted by the State Language Committee in 1989, the duplicate names rate for single name was 67.7%, whereas that of double name was 32.4%.

There are two commonly used name disambiguation approach, one is based on the vector space model, and the other is based on social networks.

The first is text-based vector space clustering approach. An entity can be expressed as one vector which is formed according to the content word of the original document. And then the similarity is used to merge documents or classify documents.

The second method is based on social networks. The first step of the method is to build social networks, by analyze the relationship of different people. Generally if two people's name always occurs in same document or very near context ,they will have close relations, one of them will be helpful for disambiguate the other.

In this paper, we first use the domain of character's document to classify roughly, and then context information using social networking is considered again to disambiguate person's name again.

2 the principle of our system

Fig.1. shows the basic principle of our system. The basic steps are:

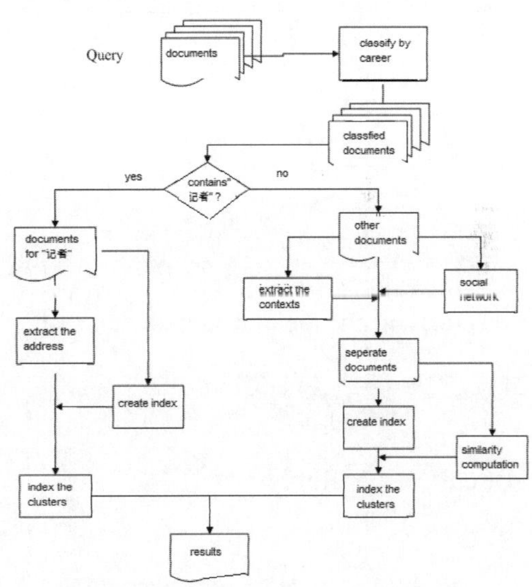

Fig.1. the general framework of our approach

1) documents with same people's name are input;
2) classify these documents into seven careers which include Cultural, administrative, military, science, education, sports, health, economic and etc;

3) Judge if the people are reporter in document, if yes; separate them according to their address.

4) Separate documents by using social networks. This is because different people usually have different social relations. Different social relations usually means different people and different identity. The social network of one people is gained by counting its co-occur frequency with other peoples.

3 experimental results

3.1 evaluation method

Here are the evaluation formula provided by SIGHAN 2010:

$$\text{Precision}_i = \frac{\sum_{S_i \in S} \max_{R_j \in R} |S_i \cap R_j|}{\sum_{S_i \in S} |S_i|} \quad (1)$$

$$\text{Recall}_i = \frac{\sum_{R_i \in R} \max_{S_j \in S} |R_i \cap S_j|}{\sum_{R_i \in R} |R_i|} \quad (2)$$

B-Cubed :

$$\text{Recall}_i = \frac{\sum_{R_i \in R} \sum_{d \in R_i} \max_{S_j \in S; d \in S_j} \frac{|R_i \cap S_j|}{|R_i|}}{\sum_{R_i \in R} |R_i|}$$

(3)

$$\text{Precision}_i = \frac{\sum_{S_i \in S} \sum_{d \in S_i} \max_{R_j \in R; d \in R_j} \frac{|S_i \cap R_j|}{|S_i|}}{\sum_{S_i \in S} |S_i|} \quad (4)$$

$$F-measure_i = \frac{2 \times Precision_i \times Recall_i}{Precision_i + Recall_i} \quad (5)$$

The overall precision and recall is as follows:

$$Precision = \frac{1}{n} \sum_{i=1}^{n} Precision_i \quad (6)$$

$$Recall = \frac{1}{n} \sum_{i=1}^{n} Recall_i \quad (7)$$

$$F-measure = \frac{1}{n} \sum_{i=1}^{n} F-measure_i \quad (8)$$

3.2 The performance of our system

By only utilizing the career domain knowledge, the performance is shown in table 1. Obviously the people in this division of the seven categories, the accuracy is low and the recall rates were high. The reasons include the following:

First, in he document pre-classification processing, the named entity recognition has not been carried out in the text dealing with the classification of the document. Some of them are not the people's name.

Second, different people may have same domain, thus the accuracy is adversely affected.

Table 1 . The performance after the first-step classification

	precision	recall	Fmeasure
B-Cube	28.78	99.97	44.69
P_IP	42.82	99.97	59.96

By adding the knowledge of social networks, the performance is shown in Fig.2-Fig.3.

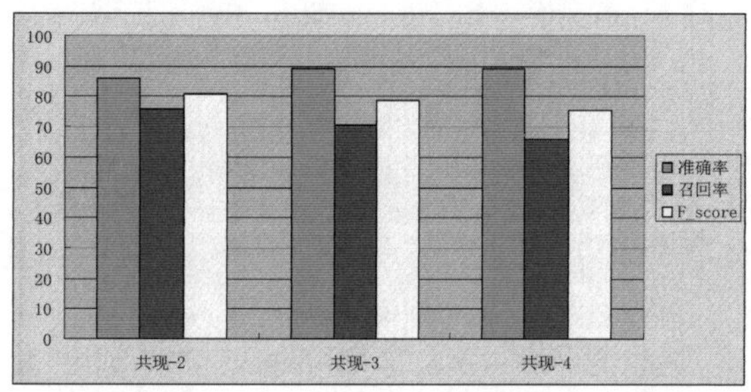

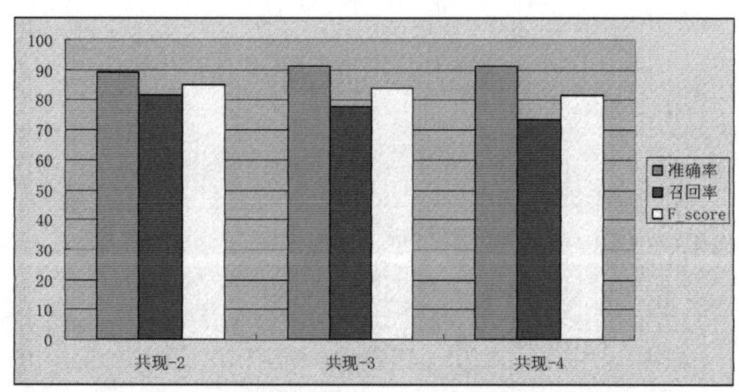

Fig.2 result of B-Cubed

Fig.3. result of P_IP

Clearly the experiment showed that after matching character society attribute information, the recall rate increased significantly, and the F value also have increased. .

4 Summaries

In this paper, we utilize two kind of knowledges: 1) people always have his own career; 2) people have his own social circle. We think these information will be more helpful for disambiguation. Thus we attempt to solve this problem by combing different knowledge. As people usually have different kind of careers, so we first utilize this knowledge to classify people roughly. Then we use social context of people to identify different person. In the future we wish to address the following aspects: 1) add and improve name recognition accuracy; 2) extract and select the useful context of person's name, which is the problem of information extraction; 3) recognize some kind of public people such as political leaders, famous singers and etc. to improve the effect of social networks.

References

[1]Amit Bagga and Breck Baldwin.Entity Based Cross-Document Coreferencing Using the Vector Space Model In Proceedings of the 36th Annual Meeting of the Association for Computational Linguistics and the 17th International Conference on Computational Linguistics(COLING-ACL'98),1998 :79-85.

[2] Gideon S. Mann and David Yarowsky. Unsupervised Personal Name Disambiguation In Proceedings of the seventh conference on Natural language learning at HLT-NAACL, 2003: 33-40.

[3] Bollegala, D., Y. Matsuo, M. Ishizuka. Disambiguating Personal Names on the Web Using Automatically Extracted Key Phrases. In: Gerhard Brewka, Silvia Coradeschi, Anna Perini, Paolo Traverso, eds. Proc. of the 17th European Conference on Artificial Intelligence. Riva del Garda, Italy: IOS Press, 2006:553-557

[4] Bekkerman, Ron, Andrew McCallum. Disambiguating Web Appearances of People in a Social Network. In: Allan Ellis, Tatsuya Hagino , eds. Proc. of the 14th international conference on World Wide Web. Chiba, Japan: ACM Press, 2005:463-470

[5] Javier Artiles, Julio Gonzalo, Satoshi Sekine. The SemEval-2007 WePS Evaluation: Establishing a benchmark for the Web People Search Task. IN: Proceedings of the 4th International Workshop on Semantic Evaluations (SemEval-2007),2007: 64–69

[6] Malin, Bradley. Unsupervised Name Disambiguation via Social Network Similarity. In: Hillol Kargupta, Jaideep Srivastava, Chandrika Kamath, Arnold Goodman, eds. Proc. of the Workshop on Link Analysis, Counterterrorism, and Security, in conjunction with the SIAM International Conference on Data Mining. Newport Beach, California, USA: SIAM, 2005:93-102

[7] Nahm, U. Y. and Mooney, R. J.; Text Mining with Information Extraction. In Proceedings of the AAAI 2002 Spring Symposium on Mining Answers from Texts and Knowledge Bases, Stanford, CA, March 2002: 60-67.

[8] Yang, Y., and Jan O. Pedersen. A comparative study on Feature Selection in Text Categorization. Proceedings of the Fourteenth International Conference on Machine Learning Table of Contents, 1997: 412-420.

DLUT: Chinese Personal Name Disambiguation with Rich Features

Dongliang Wang
Department of Computer Science and Engineering, Dalian University of Technology
wdl129@163.com

Degen Huang
Department of Computer Science and Engineering, Dalian University of Technology
huangdg@dlut.edu.cn

Abstract

In this paper we describe a person clustering system for a given document set and report the results we have obtained on the test set of Chinese personal name (CPN) disambiguation task of CIPS-SIGHAN 2010. This task consists of clustering a set of Xinhua news documents that mention an ambiguous CPN according to named entity in reality. Several features including named entities (NE) and common nouns generated from the documents and a variety of rules are employed in our system. This system achieves F = 86.36% with B_Cubed scoring metrics and F = 90.78% with purity_based metrics.

1 Introduction

As the amount of web information expands at an ever more rapid pace, extraction of information for specific named entity is more and more important. Usually there are named-entity ambiguity in web data, for example more than one person use a same name, therefore it is difficult to decide which document refers to a specific named entity.

The goal of CPN disambiguation is to clustering input Xinhua news corpus by the entity each document refers to. The new documents which span a time of fourteen years are extracted on web.

As description of CPN disambiguation task of CIPS-SIGHAN 2010, Chinese personal name disambiguation is potentially more challenging due to the need for word segmentation, which could introduce errors that can in large part be avoided in the English task.

In this paper we employ a CPN disambiguation system that extracts NE and common nouns from the input corpus as features, and then computes the similarity of each two documents in the corpus based on feature vector. Hierarchical Agglomerative Clustering (HAC) algorithm (AK Jain et al., 1999) is used to implement clustering.

After a great deal of analysis of news corpus, we constitute several rules, the experiments show that these rules can improve the result of this task.

The remainder of this paper is organized as follows. Section 2 introduces the preprocessing of test corpus, and in section 3 we present the methodology of our system. In section 4 we present the experimental results and give a conclusion in section 5.

2 Preprocessing

In this step, we mainly complete the works as follows.

Firstly, corpuses including a given name string are in different files, one document one file. In order to convenient for processing, we combine these documents into one file, distinguish them with document id.

Secondly, some news corpuses have several subtitles but usually only part of them including focused name string, the others are noise of disambiguate of focused named entity, for example a news about sports may contain several subtitles about basketball, swimming, race and so on. These noises are removed from the corpus by us.

Lastly, there is a lack of date-line in a few documents; in general, these data-lines are recognized as part of text, they can be recognized through simple matching method. Because data-lines have consistent format as "新华社**月*日电".

3 Methodology

The system follows a procedure include: word segmentation, the detection of ambiguous objects, feature extractions, computation of document similarity and clustering.

First, the text is segmented by a word segmentation system explored by Luo and Huang (2009). The second step is extract all features from segmented text, all features are put into two feature vectors: NE vector and common noun vector. Then we will compute the distance between corresponding vectors of each two documents, the standard SoftTFIDF (Chen and Martin, 2007) are employed to compute the distance between two feature vectors. Lastly, we use the HAC algorithm for clustering of documents.

3.1 Word Segmentation

Word segmentation is a base and difficult work of natural language processing (NLP) and a precondition of feature extraction. In this paper, the word segmentation system explored by Luo and Huang (2009) are employed to do this work.

This system training on the corpus of 2000's "People's Daily". In addition, this system can recognize named entities including personal name, location name and organization name. We can extract these NEs by part-of-speech (POS) directly.

3.2 The Detection of Ambiguous Entities

Given a name string, the documents can be divided into three groups:

(1) Documents which contain names that are exactly match the query name string.

(2) Documents which contain names that have a substring exactly match the query name string.

(3) Documents which contain the query name string that is not personal name.

After word segmentation, all personal names are labeled by system, when we find one personal name or its substring match the query name string; we will cluster this document according to the name. If we failure all over the document, it's considered that this document belong to category (3), it will be discarded.

The ambiguous personal name in a document may refer to multiple entities, for example a news about party of namesakes, but this is a very small probability event, so we assume that all mentions in one document refers to the same entity, viz. "one person one document".

Although we assume that "one person one document", the same personal name may occur more than once. Some times the word segmentation system will give the same personal name different labels in one document, for example a personal name "杨永强" may be recognized as "杨永" and "杨永强" in different sentence in one document. Suppose that $P_1, P_2, \dots, P_n$ are recognized names that match the query name string, $T_1, T_2, \dots, T_n$ are the corresponding occur times. We use the following method to ensure the final needed personal name:

(1) If $T_i > T_j$ for $j = 1, 2, \dots, i\text{-}1, i+1, \dots, n$, P_i is selected as the final needed personal name, else go to step (2).

(2) Define $S = \{ T_1, T_2, \dots, T_n \}$, $E_1 = \{T_{11}, T_{12}, \dots, T_{1m}\}$, $E_2 = S - E1$ satisfying $T_{11} = T_{12} = \dots = T_{1m}$, $E_1 \subseteq S$ and $T_i > T_j$ ($T_i \in E_1$, $T_j \in E_2$). F_i shows the word before P_i and B_i after P_i. For each $T_i \in E_1$, connect F_i, T_i and B_i into a new string named R_i, we can get $R = \{R_{11}, R_{12}, \dots, R_{1m}\}$ corresponding to E1, the longest common substring of R are considered the final needed personal name.

3.3 Features

We define local sentence as sentences which contain the query name string, the features extracted from local sentences named local features. Otherwise, all sentences except local sentences in a document are named global sentences; the features extracted from global sentences are global features. The reason to distinguish them is because they have different contribution to similarity computation. Local features are generally considered more important than global features, therefore a high weight should be given to local features.

Named entities are important information about focused name. In this paper, NEs include personal names, location names and organization names. Location name and organization name usually indicate the region and department of focused name, and personal names usually have high co-occurrence rate, for example "邓亚萍" and "高军" are two names of table tennis players, so they always appear in a same news document about table tennis. The NE features which have been tagged by segmentation system can be extracted from the document directly.

We also consider the features of common nouns. Semantically independent common nouns such as person's job and person's hobby etc usually include some useful information about the ambiguous object. We attempt to capture these noun features and use them as elements in feature vector.

Location names in data-line. The location name in the data-line indicates the place the news had occurred, if two documents have the same date-line location name, and then there is a good chance that these two documents refer the same person.

Appellation of query name. Appellation usually demonstrate a person's identity, for example, if the appellation of the query name is "记者", it shows that he or she is a journalist. As location names in data-line, if two query names have the same appellation, the possibility of them refer to the same person increased. The word segmentation system doesn't clearly marked out appellation but marked as common noun. In generally, appellations appear neighbor in front of name, so we collect the common nouns neighbor front of query names as their appellations.

So far, we have developed four feature vectors: local NE vector, local common noun vector, global NE vector and global common noun vector. Given feature vectors, we need to find a way to learn the similarity matrix. In this paper, we choose the standard TF-IDF method to calculate the similarity matrix. Location name in date-line and appellation of query name will be used in rule method without similarity calculation.

3.4 Similarity Matrix

Given a pair of feature vectors consisting of NEs or common nouns, we need to choose a similarity scheme to calculate the similarity matrix. The standard TF-IDF method is introduced here, then a little change for Chinese string.

Standard TF-IDF: Given a pair of vector S and T, S = (s1, s2, …, sn), T = (t1, t2, …, tm). Here, si (i = 1, …, n) and tj (j = 1, …, m) are NE or common noun. We define:

$$CLOSE(\theta;S;T)= \{w; w\in S, \exists v\in T, dist(w,v)>\theta\} \quad (1)$$

Where dist(w;v) is the Jaro-Winkler distance function (Winkler, 1999), which will be introduced later.

$$D(w;T)=\max_{v\in T} dist(w;v) \quad (2)$$

Then the standard TF-IDF SoftTFIDF is computed as:

$$SoftTFIDF(S,T)= \sum_{w\in CLOSE(\theta;S;T)} V(w,S)*V(w,T)*D(w,T) \quad (3)$$

$$V(w,S)=\frac{V'(w,S)}{\sqrt{\sum_{w\in S} V'(w,S)^2}} \quad (4)$$

$$V'(w,S)=\log(TF_{w,S}+1)*\log(IDF_w) \quad (5)$$

Where $TF_{w,S}$ is the frequency of substring w in S, and IDF_w is the inverse of the fraction of documents in the corpus that contain w. Suppose N_t is total number of documents, N_w is total number of documents which contain w. Then IDF_w computed as:

$$IDF_\omega=\frac{N_t}{N_w} \quad (6)$$

The Jaro-Winkler distance Jw of two given strings s1 and s2 as shown in formula (7), l is the length of common prefix at the start of the string up to a maximum of 4 characters, p is a constant scaling factor for how much the score is adjusted upwards for having common prefixes, the value for p is 0.1.

$$d_w=d_j+lp(1-d_j) \quad (7)$$

$$d_j=(\frac{m}{|s1|}+\frac{m}{|s2|}+\frac{m-t}{m}) \quad (8)$$

In formula (8) m is the number of matching characters, t is the number of transpositions. In order to be consistent with the English strings, a Chinese character is seen as two English characters.

Corresponding to four feature vectors, we can calculate the four similarities: S(gNE), S(gCN), S(lNE), S(lCN). The similarity between two documents (DS) is computed as:

$$DS= \lambda*\frac{S(lNE)+S(gNE)}{2}+(1-\lambda)*\frac{S(lCN)+S(gCN)}{2} \quad (9)$$

As time is tight, we just give λ a value of 0.8 with out experiment because we consider NEs have stronger instructions.

3.5 Clustering

Clustering is a key work of this task, it is very important to choose a clustering algorithm. Here we use HAC algorithm to do clustering. HAC algorithm is an unsupervised clustering algorithm, which can be described as follows:

(1) Initialization. Every document is regarded as a separate class.

(2) Repetition. Computing the similarity of each of the two classes, merge the two classes whose similarity are the highest and higher than the threshold value of δ into a new class.

(3) Termination. Repeat step (2) until all classes don't satisfy the clustering condition.

Suppose document class F = $\{f_1, f_2, \ldots, f_n\}$ and K = $\{k_1, k_2, \ldots, k_m\}$, f_i and k_j are documents in class F and class K, then the similarity between F and K is:

$$S(J,K) = \frac{\sum_{i,j} S(f_i,k_j)}{m*n} \quad (9)$$

If two documents have different query name, obviously they refer to different person, only documents which have same query name will be clustered. Before clustering, several rules are afforded to improve the clustering condition. These rules are generally applicable to news corpus.

(1) If two documents have the same query name and both of them are reporter, and both date-lines have the same location name, then combine the two documents into one class.

(2) If two documents have the same query name and another same personal name, then combine the two documents into one class.

(3) If two documents have the same query name and both date-lines have the same location name, then double the similarity, else halve the similarity.

(4) If two documents have the same query name and both personal names have the same appellation, then double the similarity, else halve the similarity.

4 Evaluation

In order to prove the validity of the rule approach, a group of experiments are performed on the train set of Chinese personal name disambiguation task of CIPS-SIGHAN 2010. The result is shown in Table 1. R1 is the result without rules, and R2 shows the accuracy after adding the rules.

The system performance on the test set of CPN disambiguation task of CIPS-SIGHAN 2010 is F = 90.78% evaluated with P_IP evaluation, and F = 86.36% with B_Cubed evaluation. The accuracy is shown in Table 2.

B_Cubed	Precision	Recall	F
R1	70.56	86.77	74.74
R2	78.05	84.99	79.60
P_IP	Purity	Inverse Purity	F
R1	77.22	90.48	81.20
R2	82.92	88.30	84.29

Table 1. Experimental results for system with rules and without rules on training set

B_Cubed	Precision	Recall	F
	82.96	91.33	86.36
P_IP	Purity	Inverse Purity	F
	87.94	94.21	90.78

Table 2. The results on test set

5 Conclusion

We described our system that disambiguates Chinese personal names in Xinhua corpus. We mainly focus on extracting rich features from documents and computing the similarity of each two documents. Several rules are introduced to improve the accuracy and have proved effective.

References

Anil K. Jain, M. Narasimha Murty, and Patrick J. Flynn. 1999. Data clustering: A review. ACM Computing Surveys, 31(3): 264-323.

Bradley Malin. 2005. *Unsupervised Name Disambiguation via Network Similarity.* In proceedings SIAM Conference on Data Mining, 2005.

Chen Ying, James Martin. 2007. *CU-COMSEM: Exploring Rich Features for Unsupervised Web Personal Name Disambiguation.* In proceedings of Semeval 2007, Association for Computational Linguistics, 2007.

Chen Ying, Sophia Y. M. Lee and Churen Huang. 2009. *PolyUHK:A Robust Information Extraction System for Web Personal Names.* In proceedings of Semeval 2009, Association for Computational Linguistics, 2009.

Gusfield, Dan. 1997. *Algorithms on Strings, Trees and Sequences*. Cambridge University Press, Cambridge, UK

Javier Artiles, J. Gonzalo and S. Sekine. WePS2 Evaluation Campaign: Overview of the Web People Search Clustering Task. In proceedings of Semeval 2009, Association for Computational Linguistics, 2009.

Luo Yanyan, Degen Huang. 2009. *Chinese word segmentation based on the marginal probabilities Generated by CRFs*. Journal of Chinese Information Processing, 23(5): 3-8.

Octavian Popescu, B. Magnini. 2007. *IRST-BP: Web People Search Using Name Entities.* In proceedings of Semeval 2007, Association for Computational Linguistics, 2007.

William E. Winkler. 1999. The state of record linkage and current research problems. Statistics of Income Division, Internal Revenue Service Publication R99/04.

Person Name Disambiguation based on Topic Model

Jiashen Sun, Tianmin Wang and Li Li
Center of Intelligence Science and Technology
Beijing University of Posts and Telecommunications
b.bigart911@gmail.com,
tianmin180@sina.com, wbg111@126.com

Xing Wu
School of Computer
Beijing University of Posts and
Telecommunications
wuxing-6@163.com

Abstract

In this paper we describe our participation in the SIGHAN 2010 Task-3 (Person Name Disambiguation) and detail our approaches. Person Name Disambiguation is typically viewed as an unsupervised clustering problem where the aim is to partition a name's contexts into different clusters, each representing a real world people. The key point of Clustering is the similarity measure of context, which depends upon the features selection and representation. Two clustering algorithms, HAC and DBSCAN, are investigated in our system. The experiments show that the topic features learned by LDA outperforms token features and more robust.

1 Introduction

Most current web searches relate to person names. A study of the query log of the AllTheWeb and Altavista search sites gives an idea of the relevance of the people search task: 11-17% of the queries were composed of a person name with additional terms and 4% were identified simply as person names (Spink et al., 2004).

However, there is a high level of ambiguity where multiple individuals share the same name and thus the harvesting and the retrieval of relevant information becomes more difficult. This ambiguity has recently become an active research topic and, simultaneously, a relevant application domain for Web search services. Zoominfo.com, Spock.com and 123people.com are examples of sites which perform web people search, although with limited disambiguation capabilities (Artiles et al., 2009).

This issue directed current researchers towards the definition of a new task called Web People Search (WePS) or Personal Name Disambiguation (PND). The key assumption underlying the task is that the context surrounding an ambiguous person name is indicative of its ascription. The goal of the clustering task was to group web pages containing the target person's name, so that pages referring to the same individual are assigned to the same cluster. For this purpose a large dataset was collected and manually annotated.

Moreover, because of the ambiguity in word segmentation in Chinese, person name detection is necessary, which is subtask of Named Entity Recognition (NER). NER is one of difficulties of the study of natural language processing, of which the main task is to identify person names, place names, organization names, number, time words, money and other entities. The main difficulties of Chinese person name entity recognition are embodied in the following points: 1) the diversity of names form; 2) the Chinese character within names form words with each; 3) names and their context form words; 4) translation of foreign names require special considerations.

In this paper we describe our system and approach in the SIGHAN 2010 task-3 (Person Name Disambiguation). A novel Bayesian approach is adopt in our system, which formalizes the disambiguation problem in a generative model. For each ambiguous name we first draw a distribution over person, and then generate context words according to this distribution. It is thus assumed that different persons will correspond to distinct lexical distributions. In this framework, Person Name Disambiguation postulates that the observed data (contexts) are explicitly intended to communicate a latent topic distribution corresponding to real world people.

The remainder of this paper is structured as follows. We first present an overview of related work (Section 2) and then describe our system which consists of NER and clustering in more details (Sections 3 and 4). Section 5 describes the resources and evaluation results in our experiments. We discuss our results and conclude our work in Section 6.

2 Related Work

The most commonly used feature is the bag of words in local or global context of the ambiguous name (Ikeda et al., 2009; Romano et al., 2009). Because the given corpus is often not large enough to learn the realistic probabilities or weights for those features, traditional algorithm such as vector-based techniques used in large-scale text will lead to data sparseness.

In recent years, more and more important studies have attempted to overcome the problem to get a better (semantic) similarity measures. A lot of features such as syntactic chunks, named entities, dependency parses, semantic role labels, etc., were employed. However, these features need many NLP preprocessing (Chen, 2009). Many studies show that they can achieve state-of-the-art performances only with lightweight features. Pedersen et al. (2005) present SenseClusters which represents the instances to be clustered using second order co–occurrence vectors. Kozareva (2008) focuses on the resolution of the web people search problem through the integration of domain information, which can represent relationship between contexts and is learned from WordNet. PoBOC clustering (Cleuziou et al., 2004) is used which builds a weighted graph with weights being the similarity among the objects.

Another way is to utilize universal data repositories as external knowledge sources (Rao et al., 2007; Kalmar and Blume, 2007; Pedersen and Kulkarni; 2007) in order to give more realistic frequency for a proper name or measure whether a bigram is a collocation.

Phan et al. (2008) presents a general framework for building classifiers that deal with short and sparse text and Web segments by making the most of hidden topics discovered from large-scale data collections. Samuel Brody et al. (2009) adopt a novel Bayesian approach and formalize the word sense induction problem in a generative model.

Previous work using the WePS1 (Artiles et al., 2007) or WePS2 data set (Artiles et al., 2009) shows that standard document clustering methods can deliver excellent performance if similarity measure is enough good to represent relationship of context.

The study in Chinese PND is still in its infancy. Person Name detection is often necessary in Chinese. At present, the main technology of person name recognition is used statistical models, and the hybrid approach. Liu et al. (2000) designed a Chinese person name recognition system based on statistical methods, using samples of names from the text corpus and the real amount of statistical data to improve the system performance, while the shortcoming is that samples of name database are too small, resulting in low recall. Li et al. (2006) use the combination of the boundary templates and local statistics to recognize Chinese person name, the recognition process is to use the boundary with the frequency of template to identify potential names, and to recognize the results spread to the entire article in order to recall missing names caused by sparse data.

3 Person Name Recognition

In this section, we focus on Conditional Random Fields (CRFs) algorithm to establish the appropriate language model. Given of the input text, we may detect the potential person names in the text fragments, and then take various features into account to recognize of Chinese person names.

Conditional Random Fields as a sequence learning method has been successfully applied in many NLP tasks. More details of the its principle can be referred in (Lafferty, McCallum, and Pereira, 2001; Wallach, 2004). We here will focus on how to apply CRFs in our person name recognition task.

3.1 CRFs-based name recognition

CRFs is used to get potential names as the first stage name recognition outcome. To avoid the interference that caused by word segmentation errors, we use single Chinese character information rather than word as discriminative features for CRFs learning model.

We use BIEO label strategy to transfer the name recognition as a sequence learning task. The label set includes: B-Nr (Begin, the initial character of name), I-Nr (In, the middle character of name), E-Nr(End, the end character of name) and O (Other, other characters that aren't name).

3.2 Rule-based Correction

After labeling the potential names by CRFs model, we apply a set of rules to boost recognition result, which has been proved to be the key to improve Chinese name recognition.

The error of the potential names outcome by CRFs model is mainly divided into the following categories: the initial character of name is not recognized, the middle character of name is not recognized, the end character of name is not recognized, and their combinations of those three errors. The other two extreme errors, including non-name recognition for the anchor name, and the name is not recognized as potential names.

In the stage of rule-based correction, we first conduct word segmentation for the text. The segmentation process is also realized with the method of CRFs, without using dictionaries and other external knowledge. The detailed description is beyond this paper, which can be accessible in the paper (Lafferty, McCallum, and Pereira, 2001). The only thing we should note is that part of the error in such segmentation result obtained in this way can be corrected through the introduction of an external dictionary.

For each potential name, and we examine it from the following two aspects:

1) It is reasonable to use the word in a person name, including checking the surname and the character used in names;

2) The left and right borders are correct. Check the left and right sides of the cutting unit can be added to the names, including the words used before names, the words used behind names and the surname and character used in names.

4 Clustering

4.1 Features

The clustering features we used can be divided into two types, one is token features, including word (after stop-word removal), uni-character and bi-character, the other is topic features, which is topic-based distribution of global or window context learned by LDA (Latent Dirichlet Allocation) model.

4.1.1 Token-based Features

Simple token-based features are used in almost every disambiguation system. Here, we extract three kinds of tokens: words, uni-char and bi-char occurring in a given document.

Then, each token in each feature vector is weighed by using a tf-idf weighting and entropy weighting schemes defined as follows.

tf-idf weighting:

$$a_{ik} = f_{ik} \bullet \log(\frac{N}{n_i})$$

entropy weighting:

$$a_{ik} = \log(f_{ik} + 1.0) \bullet \left(1 + \frac{1}{\log(N)} \sum_{j=1}^{N} \left[\frac{f_{ij}}{n_i} \log(\frac{f_{ij}}{n_i})\right]\right)$$

where f_{ik} is the frequency of term i in document k, N is the number of document in corpus, n_i is the frequency of term i in corpus. So,

$$\frac{1}{\log(N)} \sum_{j=1}^{N} \left[\frac{f_{ij}}{n_i} \log(\frac{f_{ij}}{n_i})\right]$$

is the average uncertainty or entropy of term i. Entropy weighting is based on information theoretic ideas and is the most sophisticated weighting scheme.

4.1.2 Features Selection

In this Section, we give a brief introduction on two effective unsupervised feature selection methods, DF and global tf-idf.

DF (Document frequency) is the number of documents in which a term occurs in a dataset. It is the simplest criterion for term selection and easily scales to a large dataset with linear computation complexity. It is a simple but effective feature selection method for text categorization (Yang & Pedersen, 1997).

We introduce a new feature selection method called "global tf-idf" that takes the term weight into account. Because DF assumes that each term is of same importance in different documents, it is easily biased by those common terms which have high document frequency but uniform distribution over different classes. Global tf-idf is proposed to deal with this problem:

$$g_i = \sum_{k=1}^{N} tfidf_{ik}$$

4.1.3 Latent Dirichlet Allocation (LDA)

Our work is related to Latent Dirichlet Allocation (LDA, Blei et al. 2003), a probabilistic generative model of text generation. LDA models each document using a mixture over K topics, which are in turn characterized as distributions over words. The main motivation is that the task, fail to achieve high accuracy due to the data sparseness.

LDA is a generative graphical model as shown in Figure 1. It can be used to model and discover underlying topic structures of any kind of discrete data in which text is a typical example. LDA was developed based on an assumption of document generation process depicted in both Figure 1 and Table 1.

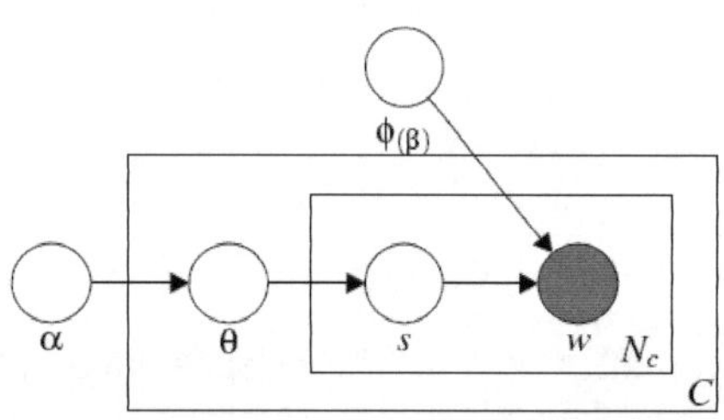

Figure 1 Generation Process for LDA

4.1.4 LDA Estimation with Gibbs Sampling

Estimating parameters for LDA by directly and exactly maximizing the likelihood of the whole data collection is intractable. The solution to this is to use approximate estimation methods like Gibbs Sampling (Griffiths and Steyvers, 2004).

Here, we only show the most important formula that is used for topic sampling for words. After finishing Gibbs Sampling, two matrices Φ and Θ are computed as follows.

$$\varphi_{k,t} = \frac{n_k^{(t)} + \beta_t}{\sum_{v=1}^{V} n_k^{(v)} + \beta_v}$$

$$\vartheta_{m,k} = \frac{n_m^{(k)} + \alpha_k}{\sum_{j=1}^{K} n_m^{(j)} + \alpha_j}$$

where Θ is the latent topic distribution corresponding to real world people.

Table 1: Generation process for LDA

for all topics $k \in [1, K]$ **do**
sample mixture components $\vec{\varphi}_k \sim Dir(\vec{\beta})$
end for
for all documents $m \in [1, M]$ **do**
sample mixture proportion $\vec{\vartheta}_m \sim Dir(\vec{\alpha})$
sample document length $N_m \sim Poiss(\xi)$
for all words $n \in [1, N_m]$ **do**
sample topic index $z_{m,n} \sim Mult(\vec{\vartheta}_m)$
sample term for word $w_{m,n} \sim Mult(\vec{\varphi}_{z_{m,n}})$
end for
end for
Parameters and variables:
• M: the total number of documents
• K: the number of (hidden/latent) topics
• V: vocabulary size
• $\vec{\alpha}, \vec{\beta}$: Dirichlet parameters
• $\vec{\vartheta}_m$: topic distribution for document m
• $\Theta = \{\vec{\vartheta}_m\}_{m=1}^{M}$: a $M \times K$ matrix
• $\vec{\varphi}_k$: word distribution for topic k
• $\Phi = \{\vec{\varphi}_k\}_{k=1}^{K}$: a $K \times V$ matrix
• N_m: the length of document m
• $z_{m,n}$: topic index of nth word in document m
• $w_{m,n}$: a particular word for word placeholder [m, n]

4.1.5 Topic-based Features

Through the observation for the given corpus, many key information, like occupation, affiliation, mentor, location, and so on, in many cases, around the target name. So, both local and global context are choose to doing topic analysis. Finally, the latent topic distributions are topic-based representation of context.

4.2 Clustering

Our system trusts the result of Person Name detection absolutely, so contexts need to do clustering only if they refer to persons with the same name. We experimented with two different classical clustering methods: HAC and DBSCAN.

4.2.1 HAC

At the heart of hierarchical clustering lies the definition of similarity between clusters, which based on similarity between individual documents. In my system, a linear combination of similarity based on both local and global context is employed:

$$sim = \alpha \cdot sim_{global} + (1-\alpha) sim_{local}$$

where, the general similarity between two features-vector of documents di and dj is defined as the cosine similarity:

$$sim(d_i, d_j) = \frac{d_i \bullet d_j}{|d_i||d_j|}$$

We will now refine this algorithm for the different similarity measures of single-link, complete-link, group-average and centroid clustering when clustering two smaller clusters together. In our approach we used an overall similarity stopping threshold.

4.2.2 DBSCAN

In this section, we present the algorithm DBSCAN (Density Based Spatial Clustering of Applications with Noise) (Ester et al., 1996) (Table 2) which is designed to discover the clusters and the noise in a spatial database.

Table 2 Algorithm of DBSCAN

Arbitrary select a point p
Retrieve all points density-reachable from p wrt Eps and MinPts.
If p is a core point, a cluster is formed.
If p is a border point, no points are density-reachable from p and DBSCAN visits the next point of the database.
Continue the process until all of the points

5 Experiments and Results Analysis

We run all experiments on SIGHAN 2010 training and test corpus.

5.1 Preprocessing and Person Name Recognition

Firstly, a word segmentation tool based on CRF is used in each document. Then, person name recognition is processing. The training data for word segmentation and PNR is People's Daily in January, 1998 and the whole 2000, respectively.

5.2 Feature Space

Our experiments used five types of feature (uni-char, bi-char, word and topic in local and global), two feature weighting methods (tf-idf and entropy) and two feature selection methods (DF and global tf-idf).

5.3 Model Selection in LDA

Our model is conditioned on the Dirichlet hyperparameters α and β, the number of topic K and iterations. The value for the α was set to 0.2, which was optimized in tuning experiment used training datasets. The β was set to 0.1, which is often considered optimal in LDA-related models (Griffiths and Steyvers, 2004). The K was set to 200. The Gibbs sampler was run for 1,000 iterations.

5.4 Clustering Results and Analysis

Since the parameter setting for the clustering system is very important, we focus only on the B-cubed scoring (Artiles et al., 2009), and acquire an overall optimal fixed stop-threshold from the training data, and then use it in test data. In this section, we report our results evaluated by the clustering scoring provided by SIGNAN 2010 evaluation, which includes both the B-cubed scoring and the purity-based scoring.

Table 3 and 4 demonstrate the performance (F scores) of our system in different features representation and clustering for the training data of the SIGNAN 2010. In Table 3, the numbers in parentheses are MinPts and Eps respectively, and stop-threshold in Table 4. As shown in Table 3, DBSCAN isn't suitable for this task, and the results are very sensitive to parameters. So we didn't submit DBSCAN-based results.

Table 4 shows that the best averaged F-scores for PND are based on topic model, which meet our initial assumptions, and result based on merging local and global information is a bit better than both local and global information independently. Also, the results based on topic model are the most robust because the F-score of variation is slightly with stop-threshold changing. Conversely, the results based on token are not like this. As the performance of segmentation is not very satisfactory, results based on word are worst, even worse than uni-char-based. In addition, it is found that global tf-idf is better than DF, which is the simplest unsupervised feature selection method. Entropy weighting is more effective than tf-idf weighting.

Table 5 shows that the evaluation results in test data on SIGHAN 2010, and the last two lines are results in diagnosis test. We are in fifth place. The evaluation results (F-score) of Person Name Recognition in training data is 0.965.

Features	FS	Weighting	B-Cubed			P-IP		
			precision	recall	F	P	IP	F
word (0.19)	DF	tf-idf	79.05	79.68	76.49	83.25	85.84	82.72
word (0.2)			80.99	75.72	75.54	84.67	83.08	82.2
word (0.3)		entropy	78.8	80.71	77.42	83.13	86.62	83.58
word (0.25)	global tf-idf	tf-idf	80.79	83.1	80.53	84.88	88.32	85.79
word (0.23)			79.45	84.49	79.66	83.76	89.25	85.08
uni-char (0.43)	DF	tf-idf	76.47	85.46	78.77	81.7	90.05	84.45
uni-char (0.5)			82.34	75.97	77	86.11	83.54	83.78
uni-char (0.48)			80.42	79.44	78.01	84.53	86.17	84.26
bi-char (0.35)			88.3	67.75	75.34	89.96	77.38	82.44
bi-char (0.315)			81.84	81.58	80.54	85.72	87.17	85.8
local topic (0.6)			78.76	86.8	80.63	83.27	91.16	85.88
global topic (0.4)			77.92	88.72	81.04	82.67	92.64	86.26
global topic (0.7)			80.54	88.43	83.55	84.76	92.55	88.02
merged topic (0.63)			81.39	87.82	83.88	85.42	91.94	88.21

Table 3 Performance of HAC

	B-Cubed			P-IP		
MinPts and Eps	precision	recall	F	P	IP	F
2 0.9	64.15	95.84	74.19	71.95	97.36	80.97
2 0.4	71.34	62.25	63.95	76.56	71.94	72.59
3 0.9	64.15	95.88	74.2	71.95	97.37	80.97
6 0.95	64.12	96.55	74.44	71.92	97.79	81.12

Table 4 Performance of DBSCAN

B-Cubed			P-IP		
precision	recall	F	P	IP	F
80.33	94.52	85.79	85.1	96.46	89.77
80.56	92.56	85.29	85.34	95.19	89.5
80.43	95.41	86.18	85.07	97.06	89.96
80.82	93.41	85.77	85.62	95.76	89.91

Table 5 Evaluation Results in test data

6 Discussion and Future Work

In this paper, we present implementation of our systems for SIGHAN-2010 PND bekeoff,.The experiments show that the topic features learned by LDA outperform token features and exhibit good robustness.

However, in our system, only given data is exploited. We are going to collect a very large external data as universal dataset to train topic model, and then do clustering on both a small set of training data and a rich set of hidden topics discovered from universal dataset. The universal dataset can be snippets returned by search engine or Wikipedia queried by target name and some keywords, and so on.

We built our PDN system on the result of person name recognition. However, it is not appropriate to toally trust the result of Person Name detection. So an algorithm that can correct NER mistakes should be investigated in future work..

Moreover, Cluster Ensemble system can ensure the result to be more robust and accurate accordingly, which is another direction of future work..

Acknowledgments

This research has been partially supported by the National Science Foundation of China (NO. NSFC90920006). We also thank Xiaojie Wang, Caixia Yuan and Huixing Jiang for useful discussion of this work.

References

Spink, B. Jansen, and J. Pedersen. 2004. Searching for people on web search engines. *Journal of Documentation*, 60:266 -278.

Javier Artiles, Julio Gonzalo, and Satoshi Sekine. 2009. Weps 2 evaluation campaign: overview of the web people search clustering task. In *WePS 2 Evaluation Workshop. WWW Conference.*

Javier Artiles, Julio Gonzalo, and Satoshi Sekine. 2007. The semeval-2007 weps evaluation: Establishing a benchmark for the web people search task. In *Proceedings of the Fourth International Workshop on Semantic Evaluations (SemEval-2007).* ACL.

M. Ikeda, S. Ono, I. Sato, M. Yoshida, and H. Nakagawa. 2009. Person name disambiguation on the web by twostage clustering. In *2nd Web People Search Evaluation Workshop (WePS 2009), 18th WWW Conference.*

L. Romano, K. Buza, C. Giuliano, and L. Schmidt-Thieme. 2009. Person name disambiguation on the web by twostage clustering. In *2nd Web People Search Evaluation Workshop (WePS 2009), 18th WWW Conference.*

Y. Chen, S. Y. M. Lee, and C.-R. Huang. 2009. Polyuhk: A robust information extraction system for web personal names. In *2nd Web People Search Evaluation Workshop (WePS 2009), 18th WWW Conference.*

Z. Kozareva, R. Moraliyski, and G. Dias. 2008. Web people search with domain ranking. In *TSD '08: Proceedings of the 11th international conference on Text, Speech and Dialogue,* 133-140, Berlin, Heidelberg.

Pedersen, Ted, Amruta Purandare, and Anagha Kulkarni. 2005. Name Discrimination by Clustering Similar Contexts. In *Proceedings of the Sixth International Conference on Intelligent Text Processing and Computational Linguistics, Mexico City, Mexico.*

G. Cleuziou, L. Martin, and C. Vrain. 2004. Poboc: an overlapping clustering algorithm. application to rule-based classification and textual data, 440-444.

Kalmar, Paul and Matthias Blume. 2007. FICO: Web Person Disambiguation Via Weighted Similarity of Entity Contexts. In *Proceedings of the Fourth International Workshop on Semantic Evaluations (SemEval-2007).* ACL.

Rao, Delip, Nikesh Garera and David Yarowsky. 2007. JHU1 : An Unsupervised Approach to Person Name Disambiguation using Web Snippets. In *Proceedings of the Fourth International Workshop on Semantic Evaluations (SemEval-2007).* ACL.

Pedersen, Ted and Anagha Kulkarni. 2007. Unsupervised Discrimination of Person Names in Web Contexts. In *Proceedings of the Eighth International Conference on Intelligent Text Processing and Computational Linguistics, Mexico City, Mexico.*

Phan, X., Nguyen, L. and Horiguchi. 2008. Learning to Classify Short and Sparse Test & Web with Hidden Topics from large-scale

Data collection. In *Proceedings of 17th International World Wide Web Conference. (Beijing, China, April 21-25, 2008)*. ACM Press, New York, NY, 91-100.

Samuel Brody and Mirella Lapata. 2009. Bayesian word sense induction In *Proceedings of the 12th Conference of the European Chapter of the Association for Computational Linguistics*, 103-111.

Sun et al. 1995. Identifying Chinese Names in Unrestricted Texts (in Chinese). In *Journal of Chinese Information Processing*, 9(2):16-27.

Liu et al. 2000. Statistical Chinese Person Names Identification (in Chinese). In *Journal of Chinese Information Processing*, 14(3):16-24.

Huang et al. 2001. Identification of Chinese Names Based on Statistics (in Chinese). In *Journal of Chinese Information Processing*, 15(2):31-37.

Li et al. 2006. Chinese Name Recognition Based on Boundary Templates and Local Frequency (in Chinese). In *Journal of Chinese Information Processing*, 20(5):44-50.

Mao et al. 2007. Recognizing Chinese Person Names Based on Hybrid Models (in Chinese). In *Journal of Chinese Information Processing*, 21(2):22-27.

J. Lafferty, A. McCallum, and F. Pereira. 2001. Conditional random fields: Probabilistic models for segmenting and labeling sequence data. In *Proc. ICML-01*, 282-289, 2001.

Wallach, Hanna. 2004. Conditional random fields: An introduction. Technical report, University of Pennsylvania, Department of Computer and Information Science.

Yang, Y. and Pedersen, J. O. 1997. A comparative study on feature selection in text categorization. In *Proceedings of ICML-97, 14th International Conference on Machine Learning (Nashville, US, 1997)*, 412–420.

Martin Ester, Hans-Peter Kriegel, Jörg Sander, Xiaowei Xu. 1996. A density-based algorithm for discovering clusters in large spatial databases with noise. In *Proceedings of the Second International Conference on Knowledge Discovery and Data Mining (KDD-96)*. AAAI Press. 226-231.

Blei, David M., Andrew Y. Ng, and Michael I. Jordan. 2003. Latent dirichlet allocation. In *J. Machine Learn. Res. 3*, 993-1022.

T. Griffiths and M. Steyvers. 2004. Finding scientific topics. In *The National Academy of Sciences*, 101:5228-5235.

PRIS at Chinese Language Processing

--Chinese Personal Name Disambiguation

Jiayue Zhang, Yichao Cai, Si Li, Weiran Xu, Jun Guo
School of Information and Communication Engineering
Beijing Universit of Posts and Telecommunications
jyz0706@gmail.com

Abstract

The more Chinese language materials come out, the more we have to focus on the "same personal name" problem. In our personal name disambiguation system, the hierarchical agglomerative clustering is applied, and named entity is used as feature for document similarity calculation. We propose a two-stage strategy in which the first stage involves word segmentation and named entity recognition (NER) for feature extraction, and the second stage focuses on clustering.

1 Introduction

World Wide Web (WWW) search engines have become widely used in recent years to retrieve information about real-world entities such as people. Web person search is one of the most frequent search types on the web search engine. As the sheer amount of web information expands at an ever more rapid pace, the named-entity ambiguity problem becomes more and more serious in many fields, such as information integration, cross-document co-reference, and question answering. It is crucial to develop methodologies that can efficiently disambiguate the ambiguous names form any given set of data.

There have been two recent Web People Search (WePS) evaluation campaigns [1] on personal name disambiguation using data from English language web pages. Previous researches on name disambiguation mainly employ clustering algorithms which disambiguates ambiguous names in a given document collection through clustering them into different reference entities. However, Chinese personal name disambiguation is potentially more challenging due to the need for word segmentation, which could introduce errors that can in large part be avoided in the English task.

There are four tasks in Chinese Language Processing of the CIPS-SIGHAN Joint Conference, and we participate in the Chinese Personal Name Disambiguation task. To accomplish this task, we focused on solving two main problems which are word segmentation and duplicate names distinguishment. To distinguish duplicate names, the system adopts named entity recognition and clustering strategy. For word segmentation and NER, we applied a sharing platform named LTP designed by Harbin Institute of Technology [2].This tagger identifies and labels names of locations, organizations, people, time, date, numbers and proper nouns in the input text.

The paper is organized as follows. Section 2 introduces our feature extractions along with their corresponding similarity matrix learning. In Section 3, we analyze the performance of our system. Finally, we draw some conclusions.

2 Methodology

Our approach follows a common architecture for named-entity disambiguation: the detection of ambiguous objects, feature extractions and their corresponding similarity matrix learning, and clustering. The framework of overall processing is shown in Figure 1.

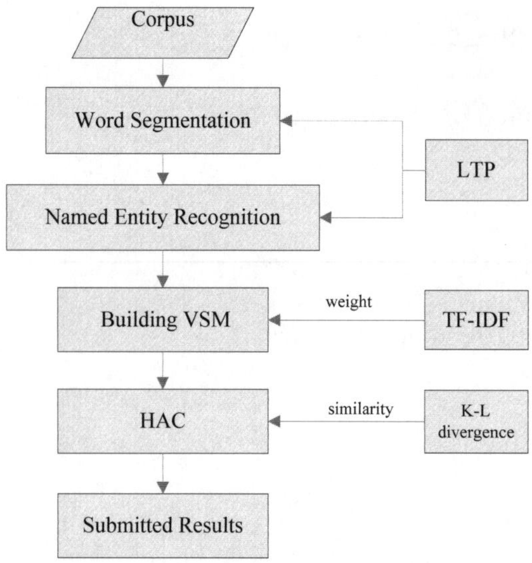

Figure 1. System Framework

2.1 The detection of ambiguous objects

Since it is common for a single document to contain one or more mentions of the ambiguous personal name, that is to say, the personal name may appear several times in one document, there is a need to define the object to be disambiguated. Here, we adopt the policy of "one person per document" (all mentions of the ambiguous personal name in one document are assumed to refer to the same personal entity in reality) as in [3] [4] [5]. Therefore, an object is defined as a single entity with the ambiguous personal name in a given document. This definition of the object (document-level object) might be not comprehensive, because the mentions of the ambiguous personal name in a document may refer to multiple entities, but we found that this is a rare case (most of those cases occur in genealogy web pages). On the other hand, the document-level object can include much information derived from that document, so that it can be represented by features [6].

For a given ambiguous personal name, word segmentation is applied first. Then we try to extract all mentions of the ambiguous personal name. Take the given personal name "高军" for example, first, the exact match of the name is extracted. Secondly, mentions that are super-strings of the given name like "高军田"is also extracted . Finally , mentions that contain character sequences but not a personal name like "最高军事法院" is ignored.

Given this definition of an object, we define a target entity as an entity that includes a mention of the ambiguous personal name.

2.2 Feature extraction and similarity matrix learning

Most of the previous work ([3] [4] [5]) used token information in the given documents. In this paper, we follow and extend their work especially for a web corpus. Furthermore, compared to a token, a phrase contains more information for named-entity disambiguation. Therefore, we explore both token and phrase-based information in this paper. Finally, there are two kinds of feature vectors developed in our system, token-based and phrase-based. The token-based feature vector is composed of tokens, and the phrase-based feature is composed of phrases. The two feature vectors are combined into a unified feature vector in which tf-idf strategy is used for similarity calculation.

2.2.1 Named Entity Features

From the results and papers of various teams participating WePS, NEs have been shown to be effective features in person name disambiguation, so we used NEs as features in this study. Through observation, we found that two different individuals can be identified by their corresponding NEs, especially by location, organization name and some proper nouns. Hence, in our study, we only extracted person, location, organization name and proper noun as feature from the output of LTP, while time, date and numbers are discarded. However, location and organization name have many proper nouns related weakly to a certain person. Therefore, terms having high-document-frequency in training data sets are removed from test data.

2.2.2 Similarity matrix learning

After NE extraction, we applied the vector space model to the calculation of similarities between features. In the model, tf-idf is used as the weight of the feature, which is defined in Eq. (1).

$$TF-IDF: w_{ij} = (\frac{freq_{ij}}{MaxFreq_{ij}}) \times \log\frac{N}{n_i} \quad (1)$$

Here, w_{ij} is the weight of term (or phrase) t_i in document d_j, $freq_{ij}$ is the frequency of t_i in d_j, $MaxFreq_{ij}$ is the frequency of the term (or phrase) whose frequency is the most in d_j, N is the number of documents under one given name, and n_i is the number of documents which has term (or phrase) t_i.

In this study, the similarities based on features described above were calculated using K-L divergence defined as Eq. (2).

$$D_{KL}(P \| Q) = \sum_i P(i) \log\frac{P(i)}{Q(i)} \quad (2)$$

P and Q denote the vector of a document respectively. K-L divergence between two vectors shows the distance of two related documents. The smaller the value of K-L divergence of two vectors becomes, the closer the two documents are. In order to prevent the zero denominator, we applied Dirichlet smoothing, i.e. , the zero element in the vector will be replaced by 0.00001.

2.3 Clustering

Clustering is the key part for our personal name disambiguation system. This task is viewed as an unsupervised hard clustering problem. First, we view the problem as unsupervised, using the distributed training data for parameter validation, to optimally tune the parameters in the clustering algorithm. Secondly, we observed that the majority of the input documents reference a single individual. Hence, we view the problem as hard clustering, assigning input document to exactly one individual, so that the produced clusters do not overlap.

In our system, hierarchical agglomerative clustering (HAC) is used as a clustering method. It builds up a hierarchy of groups by continuously merging the two most similar groups. Each of these groups starts as a single item, in this case an individual document. In each iteration this method calculates the distances between every pair of groups, and the closest ones are merged together to form a new group. The vector of the new group is the average of the original pair. This is repeated until there is only one group. This process is shown in Fig. 2.

We used a threshold for selecting cluster. So it is not necessary to determine the number of clusters beforehand. We view the whole group as a binary tree, every node which is not a leaf has two children, left child and right child, and has a record of the distance between the two children. We traverse the tree from the root, if the distance between the pair of children which form the cluster is larger than the threshold, then move down to check the distance of its left child, then right child. The process will continue until the distance between two children is less than the threshold. When the process comes to an end, all the leaves under the node will be considered to be in the same cluster. The selecting process will continue until all the leaves are assigned to a cluster. The threshold is tuned using the distributed training data.

The whole process mainly consists of two phases, the first phase is clustering all the single items into one group, and the second is selecting cluster down along the tree from the root. This strategy has a major disadvantage which is the new node is the average of its children. Hence, with the merger of nodes going on, the distance between different groups becomes smaller and smaller, which makes the boundaries between different clusters blur. This is probably the main reason that leads to the unsatisfactory results.

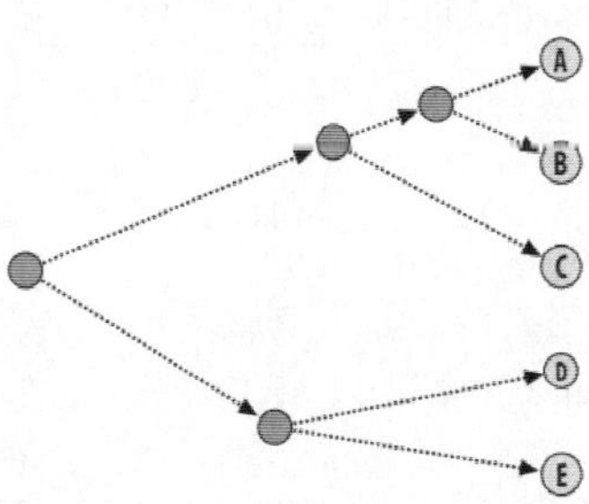

Figure 2 visualization of hierarchical clustering

3 Performance

Since there is no correct answer of test data received, we present the performance of our system of training data. There are two results gotten from the distributed evaluation in Table 1: one is evaluated with B-Cubed, and the other with P_IP. Both scores indicate that personal name disambiguation needs more effort.

Table 1 The performance of training data

	prici-sion	recall	F_score
B-Cubed	71.83	62.88	56.98
	purity	In-verse purity	F_score
P_IP	76.43	67.71	62.76

4 Conclusion

In this report, we describe a system for the Chinese Personal Name Disambiguation task, applying a two-stage clustering model. Because this is our first time attending this kind of task, there are many aspects not having been taken into account. Therefore, improving system performance becomes motivation for us to work on it continuously. In future work, we'll focus on improving the clustering algorithm and proper feature extraction.

References

J. Artiles, J. Gonzalo and S. Sekine. WePS 2 Evaluation Campaign: overview of the Web People Search Clustering Task. In 2nd Web People Search Evaluation Workshop (WePS 2009). In 18th WWW Conference, 2009.

http://ir.hit.edu.cn/

A. Bagga and B. Baldwin. 1998. Entity–based Cross–document Co–referencing Using the Vector Space Model. In 17th COLING.

C. H. Gooi and J. Allan. 2004. Cross-Document Coreference on a Large Scale Corpus.NAACL

T. Pedersen, A. Purandare and A. Kulkarni. 2005. Name Discrimination by Clustering Similar Contexts. In Proc. of the Sixth International Conference on Intelligent Text Processing and Computational Linguistics, page 226-237. Mexico City, Mexico.

Y. Chen and J. H. Martin. CU-COMSEM: Exploring Rich Features for Unsupervised Web Personal Name Disambiguation. In WWW Conference, 2007.

M. Ikeda, S. Ono, I. Sato, M. Yoshida and H. Nakagawa. Person Name Disambiguation on the Web by TwoStage Clustering. In 18th WWW Conference, 2009.

E. Elmacioglu, Y. F. Tan, S.Yan, M. Y. Kan and D. W. Lee. Web People Name Disambiguation by Simple Clustering with Rich Features. In WWW Conference, 2007.

Overview of the Chinese Word Sense Induction Task at CLP2010

Le Sun
Institute of Software
Chinese Academy of Sciences
sunle@iscas.ac.cn

Zhenzhong Zhang
Institute of Software, Graduate University Chinese Academy of Sciences
zhenzhong@nfs.iscas.ac.cn

Qiang Dong
Canada Keentime Inc.
dongqiang@keenage.com

Abstract

In this paper, we describe the Chinese word sense induction task at CLP2010. Seventeen teams participated in this task and nineteen system results were submitted. All participant systems are evaluated on a dataset containing 100 target words and 5000 instances using the standard cluster evaluation. We will describe the participating systems and the evaluation results, and then find the most suitable method by comparing the different Chinese word sense induction systems.

1 Introduction

Word Sense Disambiguation (WSD) is an important task in natural language proceeding research and is critical to many applications which require language understanding. In traditional evaluations, the supervised methods usually can achieve a better WSD performance than the unsupervised methods. But the supervised WSD methods have some drawbacks: Firstly, they need large annotated dataset which is expensive to manually annotate (Agirre and Aitor, 2007). Secondly, the supervised WSD methods are based on the "fixed-list of senses" paradigm, i.e., the senses of a target word are represented as a closed list coming from a manually constructed dictionary (Agirre et al., 2006). Such a "Fixed-list of senses" paradigm suffers from the lack of explicit and topic relations between word senses, are usually cannot reflect the exact context of the target word (Veronis, 2004). Furthermore, because the "fixed-list of senses" paradigm make the fix granularity assumption of the senses distinction, it may not be suitable in different situations (Samuel and Mirella, 2009). Thirdly, since most supervised WSD methods assign senses based on dictionaries or other lexical resources, it will be difficult to adapt them to new domains or languages when such resources are scare (Samuel and Mirella, 2009).

To overcome the deficiencies of the supervised WSD methods, many unsupervised WSD methods have been developed in recent years, which can induce word senses directly from the unannotated dataset, i.e., Word Sense Induction (WSI). In this sense, WSI could be treat as a clustering task, which groups the instances of the target word according to their contextual similarity, with each resulting cluster corresponding to a specific "word sense" or "word use" of the target word (in the task of WSI, the term "word use" is more suitable than "word sense"(Agirre and Aitor, 2007)).

Although traditional clustering techniques can be directly employed in WSI, in recent years some new methods have been proposed to enhance the WSI performance, such as the Bayesian approach (Samuel and Mirella, 2009) and the collocation graph approach (Ioannis and Suresh, 2008). Both the traditional and the new methods can achieve a good performance in the task of English word sense induction. However, the methods work well in English may not be suitable for Chinese due to the difference between Chinese and English. So it is both important and critical to provide a standard testbed for the task of Chinese word sense induction (CWSI), in order to compare the performance of different Chinese WSI methods and find the methods which are suitable for the Chinese word sense induction task.

In this paper, we describe the Chinese word sense induction task at CLP2010. The goal of this task is to provide a standard testbed for Chinese WSI task. By comparing the different Chinese WSI methods, we can find the suitable methods for the Chinese word sense induction task.

This paper is organized as follow. Section 2 describes the evaluation dataset in detail. Section 3 demonstrates the evaluation criteria. Section 3 describes the participated systems and their results. The conclusions are drawn in section 4.

2 Dataset

Two datasets are provided to the participants: the trial dataset and the test dataset.

The trial dataset contains 50 Chinese words, and for each Chinese word, a set of 50 word instances are provided. All word instances are extracted from the Web and the newspapers like the Xinhua newspaper and the Renmin newspaper, and the HowNet senses of target words were manually annotated (Dong). Figure 1 shows an example of the trial data without hand-annotated tag. Figure 2 shows an example of the trial data with hand-annotated tag. In Figure 1, the tag "snum=2" indicates that the target word "杜鹃" has two different senses in this dataset. In each instance, the target word is marked between the tag "<head>" and the tag "</head>". In Figure 2, all instances between the tag "<sense s=S0>" and the tag "</sense>" are belong to the same sense class.

```
<lexelt item="杜鹃" snum="2">
<instance id="0001">
……三清山的<head>杜鹃</head>花野性十足……
</instance>
<instance id="0002">
……听那<head>杜鹃</head>在林中轻啼：不如归去……
</instance>
<instance id="0003">
……这首诗以<head>杜鹃</head>的啼鸣衬托人民的反抗情绪……
</instance>
<instance id="0004">
……红土地上漫山遍野绽放的<head>杜鹃</head>……
</instance>
......
```

Figure 1: Example of the trial data without hand-annotated tag.

The case of the test dataset is similar to the trial dataset, but with little different in the number of target words. The test dataset contains 100 target words (22 Chinese words containing one Chinese character and 78 Chinese words containing two or more Chinese ideographs). Figure 3 shows an example of a system's output. In Figure 3, the first column represents the identifiers of target word, the second column represents the identifiers of instances, and the third column represents the identifiers of the resulting clusters and their weight (1.0 by default) generated by Chinese WSI systems.

```
<lexelt item="杜鹃">
<sense s="S0">
<instance id="0001">
……三清山的<head>杜鹃</head>花野性十足……
</instance>
<instance id="0004">
……红土地上漫山遍野绽放的<head>杜鹃</head>……
</instance>
......
</sense>
<sense s="S1">
<instance id="0002">
……听那<head>杜鹃</head>在林中轻啼：不如归去……
</instance>
<instance id="0003">
……这首诗以<head>杜鹃</head>的啼鸣衬托人民的反抗情绪……
</instance>
......
</sense>
......
```

Figure 2: Example of the trial data with hand-annotated tag.

```
杜鹃   0001   s0
杜鹃   0002   s1/1.0  s0/0.0
杜鹃   0003   s1
杜鹃   0004   s0
......
```

Figure 3: Example of the output format.

3 Evaluation Metric

As described in Section 1, WSI could be conceptualized as a clustering problem. So we can measure the performance of WSI systems using the standard cluster evaluation metrics. As the same as Zhao and Karypis(2005), we use the FScore measure as the primary measure for assessing different WSI methods. The FScore is used in a similar way as at Information Retrieval field.

In this case, the results of the WSI systems are treated as clusters of instances and the gold standard senses are classes. Then the precision of a class with respect to a cluster is defined as the number of their mutual instances divided by the total cluster size, and the recall of a class with respect to a cluster is defined as the number of their mutual instances divided by the total class size. The detailed definition is as bellows.

Let the size of a particular class s_r is n_r, the size of a particular cluster h_j is n_j and the size of their common instances set is $n_{r,j}$.,then the precision can be defined as:

$$P(s_r, h_j) = \frac{n_{r,j}}{n_j}$$

The recall can be defined as:

$$R(s_r, h_j) = \frac{n_{r,j}}{n_r}$$

Then FScore of this class and cluster is defined to be:

$$F(s_r, h_j) = \frac{2 \times P(s_r, h_j) \times R(s_r, h_j)}{P(s_r, h_j) + R(s_r, h_j)}$$

The FScore of a class s_r, $F(s_r)$, is the maximum $F(s_r, h_j)$ value attained by any cluster, and it is defined as:

$$F(s_r) = \max_{h_j}(F(s_r, h_j))$$

Finally, the FScore of the entire clustering solution is defined as the weighted average FScore of all class:

$$FScore = \sum_{r=1}^{q} \frac{n_r \times F(s_r)}{n}$$

where q is the number of classes and n is the size of the instance set for particular target word. Table 1 shows an example of a contingency table of classes and clusters, which can be used to calculate FScore.

	Cluster 1	Cluster 2
Class 1	100	500
Class 2	400	200

Table 1: A contingency table of classes and clusters

Using this contingency table, we can calculate the FScore of this example is 0.7483. It is easy to know the FScore of a perfect clustering solution will be equal to one, where each cluster has exactly the same instances as one of the classes, and vice versa. This means that the higher the FScore, the better the clustering performance.

Purity and entropy (Zhao and Karypis, 2005) are also used to measure the performance of the clustering solution. Compared to FScore, they have some disadvantages. FScore uses two complementary concepts, precision and recall, to assess the quality of a clustering solution. Precision indicates the degree of the instances that make up a cluster, which belong to a single class. On the other hand, recall indicates the degree of the instances that make up a class, which belong to a single cluster. But purity and entropy only consider one factor and discard another. So we use FScore measure to assess a clustering solution.

For the sake of completeness, we also employ the V-Measure to assess different clustering solutions. V-Measure assesses a cluster solution by considering its homogeneity and its completeness (Rosenberg and Hirschberg, 2007). Homogeneity measures the degree that each cluster contains data points which belong to a single Gold Standard class. And completeness measures the degree that each Gold Standard class contains data points assigned to a single cluster (Rosenberg and Hirschberg, 2007). In general, the larger the V-Measure, the better the clustering performance. More details can be referred to (Rosenberg and Hirschberg, 2007).

4 Results

In this section we describe the participant systems and present their results.

Since the size of test data may not be large enough to distinguish word senses, participants were provided the total number of the target word's senses. And participants were also allowed to use extra resources without hand-annotated.

4.1 Participant teams and systems

There were 17 teams registered for the WSI task and 12 teams submitted their results. Totally 19 participant system results were submitted (One was submitted after the deadline). 10 teams submitted their technical reports. Table 2 demonstrates the statistics of the participant information.

The methods used by the participated systems were described as follows:

FDU: This system first extracted the triplets for target word in each instance and got the intersection of all related words of these triplets using Baidu web search engine. Then the triplets and their corresponding intersections were used to construct feature vectors of the target word's instances. After that, sequential Information

Bottleneck algorithm was used to group instances into clusters.

BUPT: Three clustering algorithms- the k-means algorithm, the Expectation-maximization algorithm and the Locally Adaptive Clustering algorithm were employed to cluster instances, where all instances were represented using some combined features. In the end the Group-average agglomerative clustering was used to cluster the consensus matrix M, which was obtained from the

Name of Participant Team	Result	Report
Natural Language Processing Laboratory at Northeastern University (NEU)	√	√
Beijing University of Posts and Telecommunications (BUPT)	√	√
Beijing Institute of Technology (BIT)	√	
Shanghai Jiao Tong University (SJTU)		
Laboratory of Intelligent Information Processing and Application Institutional at Leshan Teachers' College (LSTC)	√	√
Natural Language Processing Laboratory at Soochow University (SCU)	√	√
Fudan University (FDU)	√	√
Institute of Computational Linguistics at Peking University 1 (PKU1)	√	√
Beijing University of Information Science and Technology (BUIST)	√	
Tsinghua University Research Institute of Information Technology, Speech and Language Technologies R&D Center (THU)		
Information Retrieval Laboratory at Dalian University of Technology (DLUT)	√	√
Institute of Computational Linguistics at Peking University 2 (PKU2)	√	√
City University of HK (CTU)		
Institute of Software Chinese Academy of Sciences (ISCAS)	√	√
Cognitive Science Department at Xiamen University (XMU)	√	√
Harbin Institute of Technology Shenzhen Graduate School (HITSZGS)		
National Taipei University of Technology (NTUT)		

Table 2: The registered teams. " √ " means that the team submitted the result or the report.

adjacency matrices of the individual clusters generated by the three single clustering algorithms mentioned above.

LSTC: This team extracted the five neighbor words and their POSs around the target word as features. Then the k-means algorithm was used to cluster the instances of each target word.

NEU: The "Global collocation" and the "local collocation" were extracted as features. A constraint hierarchical clustering algorithm was used to cluster the instances of each target word.

XMU: The neighbor words of the target word were extracted as features and TongYiCi CiLin[1] was employed to measure the similarity between instances. The word instances are clustered using the improved hierarchical clustering algorithm based on parts of speech.

DLUT: This team used the information gain to determine the size of the feature window. TongYiCi CiLin was used to solve the data sparseness problem. The word instances are clustered using an improvement k-means algorithm where k-initial centers were selected based on maximum distance.

ISCAS: This team employed k-means clustering algorithm to cluster the second order co-occurrence vectors of contextual words. TongYiCi CiLin and singular value decomposition method were used to solve the problem of data sparseness. Please note that this system was submitted by the organizers. The organizers have taken great care in order to

[1] http://www.ir-lab.org/

guaranty all participants are under the same conditions.

PKU2: This team used local tokens, local bigram feature and topical feature to represent words as vectors. Spectral clustering method was used to cluster the instances of each target word.

PKU1: This team extracted three types of features to represent instances as feature vectors. Then the clustering was done by using k-means algorithm.

SCU: All words except stop words in instances were extracted to produce the feature vectors, based on which the similarity matrix were generated. After that, the spectral clustering algorithm was applied to group instances into clusters.

4.2 Official Results

In this section we present the official results of the participant systems (ISCAS* was submitted by organizers; BUIST** was submitted after the deadline). We also provide the result of a baseline -- 1c1w, which group all instances of a target word into a single cluster.

Table 3 shows the FScore of the main systems submitted by participant teams on the test dataset. Table 4 shows the FScore and V-Measure of all participant systems. Systems were ranked according to their FScore.

Systems	Rank	FScore
BUPT_mainsys	1	**0.7933**
PKU1_main_system	2	**0.7812**
FDU	3	**0.7788**
DLUT_main_system	4	**0.7729**
PKU2	5	**0.7598**
ISCAS*	6	**0.7209**
SCU	7	**0.7108**
NEU_WSI_1	8	**0.6715**
XMU	9	**0.6534**
BIT	10	**0.6366**
1c1w	11	**0.6147**
BUIST**	12	**0.5972**
LSTC	13	**0.5789**

Table 3: FScore of main systems on the test dataset including one baseline -1c1w.

Systems	Rank	FScore	V-Measure
BUPT_mainsys	1	**0.7933**	0.4628
BUPT_LAC	2	0.7895	0.4538
BUPT_EM	3	0.7855	0.4356
BUPT_kmeans	4	0.7849	0.4472
PKU1_main_system	5	0.7812	0.4300
FDU	6	0.7788	0.4196
DLUT_main_system	7	0.7729	**0.5032**
PKU1_agglo	8	0.7651	0.4096
PKU2	9	0.7598	0.4078
ISCAS*	10	0.7209	0.3174
SCU	11	0.7108	0.3131
NEU_WSI_1	12	0.6715	0.2331
XMU	13	0.6534	0.1954
NEU_WSI_0	14	0.6520	0.1947
BIT	15	0.6366	0.1713
1c1w	16	0.6147	0.0
DLUT_RUN2	17	0.6067	0.1192
BUIST**	18	0.5972	0.1014
DLUT_RUN3	19	0.5882	0.0906
LSTC	20	0.5789	0.0535

Table 4: FScore and V-Measure of all systems, including one baseline.

From the results shown in Table 3 and 4, we can see that:

1) As described in section 4.1, most systems use traditional clustering methods. For example, the teams using the k-means algorithm contain BUPT, LSTC, PKU1, DLUT and ISCAS. The teams using the spectral clustering algorithm contain SCU and PKU2. The team XMU and NEU use hierarchical clustering algorithm. The results shows that if provided with the number of target word senses, traditional methods can achieve a good performance. But we also notice that even the same method can have a different performance. This seems to indicate that features which are predictive of word senses are important to the task of CWSI.
2) Most systems outperform the 1c1w baseline, which indicates these systems are able to induce correct senses of target words to some extent.

3) The rank of FScore is much the same as that of V-Measure but with little difference. This may be because that the two evaluation measures both assess quality of a clustering solution by considering two different aspects, where precision corresponds to homogeneity and recall corresponds to completeness. But when assessing the quality of a clustering solution, the FScore only considers the contributions from the classes which are most similar to the clusters while the V-Measure considers the contributions from all classes.

Systems	Characters	Words
BUPT_mainsys	0.6307	0.8392
BUPT_LAC	0.6298	0.8346
BUPT_EM	0.6191	0.8324
BUPT_kmeans	0.6104	0.8341
PKU1_main_system	0.6291	0.8240
FDU	0.6964	0.8020
DLUT_main_system	0.5178	0.8448
PKU1_agglo	0.5946	0.8132
PKU2	0.6157	0.8004
ISCAS*	0.5639	0.7651
SCU	0.5715	0.7501
NEU_WSI_1	0.5786	0.6977
XMU	0.5290	0.6885
NEU_WSI_0	0.5439	0.6825
BIT	0.5328	0.6659
DLUT_RUN2	0.5196	0.6313
BUIST**	0.5022	0.6240
DLUT_RUN3	0.5066	0.6113
LSTC	0.4648	0.6110
1c1w	0.4611	0.6581

Table 5: FScore of all systems on the dataset only containing either single characters or words respectively.

A Chinese word can be constituted by single or multiple Chinese characters. Senses of Chinese characters are usually determined by the words containing the character. In order to compare the WSI performance on different granularity of words, we add 22 Chinese characters into the test corpus. Table 5 shows the results of the participant systems correspondingly on the corpus which only contains the 22 Chinese characters and the corpus which only contains the 78 Chinese words.

From Table 5, we can see that:

1) The FScore of systems on the corpus only containing single characters is significantly lower than that on the corpus only containing words. We believe this is because: 1) The Single Chinese characters usually contains more senses than Chinese words; 2) Their senses are not determined directly by their contexts but by the words containing them. Compared to the number of instances, the number of words containing the single character is large. So it is difficult to distinguish different senses of single characters because of the data sparseness.
2) We noticed that all systems outperform the 1c1w baseline on the corpus only containing single characters but there are some systems' FScore are lower than the baseline on the corpus only containing words. It may be because the large number of characters' senses and the FScore favored the words which have small number of senses.

5 Conclusions

In this paper we describe the design and the results of CLP2010 back-off task 4-Chinese word sense induction task. 17 teams registered to this task and 12 teams submitted their results. In total there were 19 participant systems (One of them was submitted after the deadline). And 10 teams submitted their technical reports. All systems are evaluated on a corpus containing 100 target words and 5000 instances using FScore measure and V-Measure. Participants are also provided with the number of senses and allowed to use resources without hand-annotated.

The evaluation results have shown that most of the participant systems achieve a better performance than the 1c1w baseline. We also notice that it is more difficult to distinguish senses of Chinese characters than words. For future work, in order to test the performances of Chinese word sense induction systems under different conditions, corpus from different fields will be constructed and the number of target word senses will not be provided and will leave as an open task to the participant systems.

Acknowledgments

This work has been partially funded by National Natural Science Foundation of China under grant #60773027, #60736044 and #90920010 and by "863" Key Projects #2006AA010108, "863" Projects #2008AA01Z145. We would like to thank Dr. Han Xianpei and Zhang Weiru for their detailed comments. We also want to thank the annotators for their hard work on preparing the trial and test dataset.

References

Andrew Rosenberg and Julia Hirschberg. 2007. V-Measure: A conditional entropy-based external cluster evaluation measure. In Proceedings of the 2007 Joint Conference on Empirical Methods in Natural Language Processing and Computational Natural Language Learning (EMNLP-CoNLL), pages 410–420.

Eneko Agirre, David Mart´ınez, Oier L´opez de Lacalle,and Aitor Soroa. 2006. *Two graph-based algorithms for state-of-the-art WSD.* In Proceedings of the 2006 Conference on Empirical Methods in Natural Language Processing, pages 585–593, Sydney, Australia.

Eneko Agirre and Aitor Soroa. 2007. *Semeval-2007 task2: Evaluating word sense induction and discrimination systems.* In Proceedings of SemEval-2007. Association for Computational Llinguistics, pages 7-12, Prague.

Ioannis P. Klapaftis and Suresh Manandhar, 2008. *Word Sense Induction Using Graphs of Collocations.* In Proceeding of the 2008 conference on 18th European Conference on Artificial Intelligence, Pages: 298-302.

Jean. V´eronis. 2004. *Hyperlex: lexical cartography for information retrieval. Computer Speech & Language*,18(3):223.252.

Samuel Brody and Mirella Lapata, 2009. *Bayesian word sense induction.* In Proceedings of the 12th Conference of the European Chapter of the Association for Computational Linguistics, pages 103-111, Athens, Greece.

Ying Zhao and George Karypis. 2005. *Hierarchical clustering algorithms for document datasets.* Data Mining and Knowledge Discovery,10(2):141.168.

Zhendong Dong, *http://www.keenage.com/zhiwang/e_zhiwang.html*

Chinese Word Sense Induction with Basic Clustering Algorithms

Yuxiang Jia[1,2], Shiwen Yu[1], Zhengyan Chen[3]
[1]Key Laboratory of Computational Linguistics, Ministry of Education, China
[2]College of Information and Engineering, Zhengzhou University, Zhengzhou, China
[3]Department of Information Technology, Henan Institute of Education, Zhengzhou, China
{yxjia,yusw}@pku.edu.cn chenzhengyan1981@163.com

Abstract

Word Sense Induction (WSI) is an important topic in natural langage processing area. For the bakeoff task Chinese Word Sense Induction (CWSI), this paper proposes two systems using basic clustering algorithms, k-means and agglomerative clustering. Experimental results show that k-means achieves a better performance. Based only on the data provided by the task organizers, the two systems get FScores of 0.7812 and 0.7651 respectively.

1 Introduction

Word Sense Induction (WSI) or Word Sense Discrimination is a task of automatically discovering word senses from un-annotated text. It is distinct from Word Sense Disambiguation (WSD) where the senses are assumed to be known and the aim is to decide the right meaning of the target word in context. WSD generally requires the use of large-scale manually annotated lexical resources, while WSI can overcome this limitation. Furthermore, automatically induced word senses can improve performance on many natural language processing tasks such as information retrieval (Uzuner et al., 1999), information extraction (Chai and Biermann, 1999) and machine translation (Vickrey et al., 2005).

WSI is typically treated as a clustering problem. The input is instances of the ambiguous word with their accompanying contexts and the output is a grouping of these instances into classes corresponding to the induced senses. In other words, contexts that are grouped together in the same class represent a specific word sense.

The task can be formally defined as a two stage process, feature selection and word clustering. The first stage determines which context features to consider when comparing similarity between words, while the second stage apply some process that clusters similar words using the selected features. So the simplest approaches to WSI involve the use of basic word co-occurrence features and application of classical clustering algorithms, more sophisticated techniques improve performance by introducing new context features, novel clustering algorithms, or both. (Denkowski, 2009) makes a comprehensive survey of techniques for unsupervised word sense induction.

Two tasks on English Word Sense Induction were held on SemEval2007 (Agirre and Soroa, 2007) and SemEval2010 (Manandhar and Klapaftis, 2010) respectively, which greatly promote the research of English WSI.

However, the study on Chinese Word Sense Induction (CWSI) is inadequate (Zhu, 2009), and Chinese word senses have their own characteristics. The methods that work well in English may not work well in Chinese. So, as an exploration, this paper proposes simple approaches utilizing basic features and basic clustering algorithms, such as partitional method k-means and hierarchical agglomerative method.

The rest of this paper is organized as follows. Section 2 briefly introduces the basic clustering algorithms. Section 3 describes the feature set. Section 4 gives experimental details and analysis. Conclusions and future work are given in Section 5.

2 Clustering Algorithms

Partitional clustering and hierarchical clustering are the two basic types of clustering algorithms.

Partitional clustering partitions a given dataset into a set of clusters without any explicit structure, while hierarchical clustering creates a hierarchy of clusters.

The k-means algorithm is the most notable partitional clustering method. It takes a simple two step iterative process, data assignment and relocation of means, to divide the dataset into a specified number of clusters, *k*.

Hierarchical clustering algorithms are either top-down or bottom-up. Bottom-up algorithms treat each instance as a singleton cluster at the beginning and then successively merge pairs of clusters until all clusters have been merged into a single cluster. Bottom-up clustering is also called hierarchical agglomerative clustering, which is more popular than top-down clustering.

We use k-means and agglomerative algorithms for the CWSI task, and compare the performances of the two algorithms.

Estimating the number of the induced clusters, *k*, is difficult for general clustering problems. But in CWSI, it is simplified because the sense number of the target word is given beforehand.

CLUTO (Karypis, 2003), a clustering toolkit, is used for implementation. The similarity between objects is computed using cosine function. The criterion functions for k-means and agglomerative algorithms are I2 and UPGMA respectively. Biased agglomerative approach is chosen in stead of the traditional agglomerative approach.

3 Feature Set

For each target word, instances are extracted from the XML data file. Then the encoding of the instance file is transformed from UTF-8 to GB2312. Word segmentation and part-of-speech tagging is finished with the tool ICTCLAS[1]. Then the following three types of features are extracted:

1. The part-of-speech of the target word
2. Words before and after the target word within window of size 3 with position information
3. Unordered single words in all the contextual sentences without the target word, punctuations and symbols of the part-of-speech "nx" (Each word is only counted once, which is different from the word frequency in the bag-of-words model)

The target word is not necessarily a segmented word. Their relations are as follows:

1. The target word is a segmented word.

E.g. 别/d 打/v 我/r 电话/n

Don't dial my phone.

The target word is "打" (dial) and the segmented word is also "打" (dial). So they match.

2. The target word is inside of a segmented word.

E.g.同/p 媒体/n 打交道/v

deal with media

The target word is "打" (deal), but the segmented word is "打交道" (deal with). Then we split the segmented word and specify the part-of-speech of the target word as "1".

3. The target word is the combination of two segmented words.

E.g. 发/v 动/v "/w 文化大革命/nz "/w

launching the "Culture Revolution"

The target word is "发动" (launching), but it is split into two segmented words "发" (start) and "动" (move). Then we combine the two segmented words and specify the part-of-speech of the target word as "2".

4. The target word is split into two segmented words.

E.g. 刮/v 起/v 了/u 东/j 北风/n

blow up northeast wind

The target word is "东北", but it is segmented into two words "东" (east) and "北风" (north wind). In this case, we specify the postion of first segmented word as the position of the target word and the part-of-speech of the target word as "3".

If the target word occurs more than once in an instance, we consider the first occurrence.

4 Experiments

4.1 Data Sets

Two data sets are provided. The trial set contains 50 target words and 50 examples for each target word. The test set consists of 100 new target word and 50 examples for each target word. Both data sets are collected from the internet.

Table 1 shows the distribution of sense numbers of the target words in the two data sets. We can see that two sense words dominate and three

[1]http://ictclas.org/

sense words are the second majority. The word "打" (beat) in the trial set has 21 senses.

Table 1. Distribution of sense numbers

sense number	2	3	4	6	7	8	21
trial set	39	9	1	0	0	0	1
test set	77	10	7	4	1	1	0

Table 2. Distribution of relations between target words and segmented words

relation type	1	2	3	4	Total
trial set	2314	105	68	12	2499
test set	4031	710	212	47	5000

As is shown in table 2, the total instance number in the trial set is 2499 because there is a target word has only 49 instances. About 7.4% of the instances in the trial set and 19.38% of the instances in the test set have mismatched target words and segmented words (with relation types 2, 3 and 4).

4.2 Evaluation Metrics

The official performance metric for the CWSI task is *FScore* (Zhao and Karypis, 2005). Given a particular class C_i of size n_i and a cluster S_r of size n_r, suppose n_r^i examples in the class C_i belong to S_r. The F value of this class and cluster is defined to be:

$$F(C_i, S_r) = \frac{2 * P(C_i, S_r) * R(C_i, S_r)}{P(C_i, S_r) + R(C_i, S_r)},$$

where $P(C_i, S_r) = \frac{n_r^i}{n_r}$ is the precision value and $R(C_i, S_r) = \frac{n_r^i}{n_i}$ is the recall value defined for class C_i and cluster S_r. The *FScore* of class C_i is the maximum F value attained at any cluster, that is

$$FScore(C_i) = \max_{S_r} F(C_i, S_r)$$

and the *FScore* of the entire clustering solution is

$$FScore = \sum_{i=1}^{c} \frac{n_i}{n} FScore(C_i)$$

where c is the number of classes and n is the size of the clustering solution.

Another two metrics, *Entropy* and *Purity* (Zhao and Karypis, 2001), are also employed in this paper to measure our system performance. *Entropy* measures how the various classes of word senses are distributed within each cluster, while *Purity* measures the extent to which each cluster contained word senses from primarily one class. The entropy of cluster S_r is defined as

$$E(S_r) = -\frac{1}{\log c} \sum_{i=1}^{c} \frac{n_r^i}{n_r} \log \frac{n_r^i}{n_r}$$

The entropy of the entire clustering solution is then defined to be the sum of the individual cluster entropies weighted according to the cluster size. That is

$$Entropy = \sum_{r=1}^{k} \frac{n_r}{n} E(S_r)$$

The purity of a cluster is defined to be

$$P(S_r) = \frac{1}{n_r} \max_i (n_r^i),$$

which is the fraction of the overall cluster size that the largest class of examples assigned to that cluster represents. The overall purity of the clustering solution is obtained as a weighted sum of the individual cluster purities and is given by

$$Purity = \sum_{r=1}^{k} \frac{n_r}{n} P(S_r)$$

In general, the larger the values of *FScore* and *Purity*, the better the clustering solution is. The smaller the *Entropy* values, the better the clustering solution is.

The above three metrics are defined to evaluate the result of a single target word. Macro average metrics are used to evaluate the overall performance of all the target words.

4.3 Results

The overall performance on the trial data is shown in table 3. From the Macro Average Entropy and Macro Average Purity, we can see that k-means works better than agglomerative method. The detailed results of the k-means system are shown in table 4.

Table 3. Result comparison on the trial data

	Entropy	Purity
k-means	0.4858	0.8288
agglomerative	0.5328	0.8020

Table 4. Detailed results of k-means system

TargetWord	SenseNum	Entropy	Purity
反射	2	0.855	0.72
翻身	2	0.692	0.78
发展	2	0.377	0.92
发动	3	0.207	0.94
扼杀	2	0.833	0.7
断气	2	0	1
断交	2	0.592	0.82
杜鹃	2	0.245	0.959
动力	2	0.116	0.98
东西	3	0.396	0.82
东方	2	0.201	0.96
东北	2	0.201	0.96
调动	3	0.181	0.9
导师	2	0.122	0.98
单纯	2	0.327	0.92
大人	2	0.653	0.82
大气	2	0	1
大陆	2	0.855	0.72
大军	2	0.5	0.8
打气	2	0.312	0.92
打破	2	0.519	0.86
打开	3	0.534	0.72
打断	2	0.846	0.7
打	21	0.264	0.48
戳穿	2	0.521	0.88
春秋	3	0	1
初二	2	0.76	0.78
出口	3	0.205	0.92
冲撞	2	0.854	0.72
冲洗	2	0.449	0.9
充电	2	0.467	0.9
吃饭	2	0.881	0.7
澄清	2	0.402	0.92
程序	2	0.39	0.92
草包	2	0.793	0.76
参加	2	0.904	0.68
采购	2	0.943	0.64
材料	3	0.548	0.74
哺育	2	0.583	0.86
补贴	2	0.999	0.52
病毒	2	0.242	0.96
标兵	2	0.75	0.74
便宜	3	0.464	0.84
比重	2	0.181	0.96
背离	2	0.672	0.78
报销	2	0.471	0.82
保管	3	0.543	0.7
保安	2	0.347	0.9
把握	4	0.508	0.66
暗淡	2	0.583	0.86

The official results on the test set are shown in table 5. Our k-means system and agglomerative system rank 5 and 8 respectively among all the 18 systems.

Table 5. System ranking

Rank	FScore	Rank	FScore
1	0.7933	6	0.7788
2	0.7895	7	0.7729
3	0.7855	8*	0.7651
4	0.7849	9	0.7598
5*	0.7812	18	0.5789

5 Conclusions and Future Work

This paper tries to build basic systems for Chinese Word Sense Induction (CWSI) task. Basic clustering algorithms including k-means and agglomerative methods are studied. No extra language resources are used except the data given by the task organizers.

To improve the performance of CWSI systems, we will introduce new features and study novel clustering algorithms. We will also investigate the bakeoff data sets to find some more characteristics of Chinese word senses.

Acknowledgements

The authors are grateful to the organizers of the Word Sense Induction task for their hard work to provide such a good research platform. The work in this paper is supported by grants from the National Natural Science Foundation of China (No.60773173, No.60970083).

References

D. Vickrey, L. Biewald, M. Teyssler, and D. Koller. 2005. Word sense disambiguation for machine translation. In *Proceedings of HLT/EMNLP2005*, pp. 771-778.

E. Agirre and A. Soroa. 2007. Semeval-2007 task 02: Evaluating word sense induction and discrimination systems. In *Proceedings of SemEval2007*, pp. 7-12.

G. Karypis. 2002. CLUTO - a clustering toolkit. *Technical Report 02-017, Dept. of Computer Science, University of Minnesota*. Available at http://www.cs.umn.edu˜cluto.

H. Zhu. 2009. Research into Automatic Word Sense Discrimination on Chinese. *PhD Dissertation of Peking University*.

J. Y. Chai and A. W. Biermann. 1999. The use of word sense disambiguation in an information extraction system. *In Proceedings of AAAI/IAAI1999*, pp. 850-855.

M. Denkowski. 2009. A Survey of Techniques for Unsupervised Word Sense Induction. *Language & Statistics II Literature Review*.

O. Uzuner, B. Katz, and D. Yuret. 1999. Word sense disambiguation for information retrieval. In *Proceedings of AAAI/IAAI1999*, pp.985.

S. Manandhar and I. P. Klapaftis. 2010. SemEval-2010 Task 14: Evaluation Setting forWord Sense Induction &Disambiguation Systems. In *Proceedings of SemEval2010*, pp. 117-122.

Y. Zhao and G. Karypis. 2005. Hierarchical clustering algorithms for document datasets. *Data Mining and Knowledge Discovery*, 10(2):141–168.

Y. Zhao and G. Karypis. 2001. Criterion functions for document clustering: Experiments and analysis. *Technical Report 01–40, Dept. of Computer Science, University of Minnesota.* Available at http://cs.umn.edu/˜karypis/publications.

Triplet-Based Chinese Word Sense Induction

Zhao Liu	Xipeng Qiu	Xuanjing Huang
School of Computer Science	School of Computer Science	School of Computer Science
Fudan University	Fudan University	Fudan University
Shanghai, China	Shanghai, China	Shanghai, China
ZLiu.fd@gmail.com	xpqiu@fudan.edu.cn	xjhuang@fudan.edu.cn

Abstract

This paper describes the implementation of our system at CLP 2010 bake-off of Chinese word sense induction. We first extract the triplets for the target word in each sentence, then use the intersection of all related words of these triplets from the Internet. We use the related word to construct feature vectors for the sentence. At last we discriminate the word senses by clustering the sentences. Our system achieved 77.88% F-score under the official evaluation.

1 Introduction

The goal of the CLP 2010 bake-off of Chinese word sense induction is to automatically discriminate the senses of Chinese target words by the use of only un-annotated data.

The use of word senses instead of word forms has been shown to improve performance in information retrieval, information extraction and machine translation. Word Sense Disambiguation generally requires the use of large-scale manually annotated lexical resources. Word Sense Induction can overcome this limitation, and it has become one of the most important topics in current computational linguistics research.

In this paper we introduce a method to solve the problem of Chinese word sense induction.For this task, Firstly we constructed triplets containing the target word in every instance, then searched the intersection of all the three words from the Internet with web searching engine and constructed feature vectors.Then we clustered the vectors with the sIB clustering algorithm and at last discriminated the word senses.

This paper is organized as following: firstly we introduce the related works. Then we talk about the methods in features selection and clustering. The method of evaluation and the result of our system is following. At last we discuss the improvement and the weakness of our system.

2 Related Works

Sense induction is typically treated as a clustering problem, by considering their co-occurring contexts, the instances of a target word are partitioned into classes. Previous methods have used the first or second order co-occurrence (Pedersen and Bruce, 1997; Schütze, 1998), parts of speech, and local collocations (Niu et al., 2007). The size of context window is also various, it can be as small as only two words before and after the target words. It may be the sentence where the target word is in. Or it will be 20 surrounding words on either side of the target words and even more words.

After every instance of the target word is represented as a feature vector, it will be the input of the clustering methods. Many clustering methods have been used in the task of word sense induction. For example, k-means and agglomerative clustering (Schütze, 1998). sIB (Sequential Information Bottleneck) a variation of Information Bottleneck is applied in (Niu et al., 2007). In (Dorow and

Widdows, 2003) Graph-based clustering algorithm is employed that in a graph a node represents a noun and two nodes have an edge between them if they co-occur in list more than a given number of times. A generative model based on LDA is proposed in (Brody and Lapata, 2009).

In our method, we use the triplets (Bordag, 2006) and their intersections from the Internet to construct the feature vectors then sIB is used as the clustering method.

3 Feature Selection

Our method select the features of the words similar to (Bordag, 2006) is also using the triplets. In Chinese there are no natural separators between the words as English, so the first step in Chinese language processing is often the Chinese word segmentation. In our system we use the FudanNLP toolkit[1] to split the words.

At the first stage, we split the instance of the target word and filter out the numbers, English words and stop words from it. So we get a sequence of the words. Then we select two words before the target and another two words after it. If there are no words before or after then leave it empty. After that we enumerate two words from the selected four words to construct a triplets together with the target words. So we can get several triplets for every instance of the target. Because the faulty of Chinese word segmentation and some special target word for example a single Chinese character as a word, there are some errors finding the position of the target words. If the word is a single Chinese character and the toolkit combine it with other Chinese characters to be a word, we will use that word as the target instead of the character to construct the triplets.

The second stage is obtaining corpus from the Internet. For every triplet we search the three words sequence in it with a pair of double quotation marks in Baidu web searching engine[2]. It gives the snippets of the webs which have all the three words in it. We select the first 50 snippets of each triplets. If the number of the snippets is less than 50, we will ignore that triplet. For some rare words the snippets searched from the Internet for all the triplets of the instance is less than 50. In that situation we will search the target word and another one co-occurring word in the searching engine to achieve enough snippets as features. After searching the triplets we select the first three triplets (or doublets) with largest amount of the webs searched by the searching engine. For every instance there are three or less triplets (or doublets) and we have obtained many snippets for them. After segmenting and filtering these snippets we use the bag of words from them as the feature for this instance.

The last stage of feature selection is to construct the feature vector for every instances containing the target word. In the previous stage we get a bag of words for each instance. For all the instances of one target word we make a statistic of the frequence of each word in the bags. In our system we select the words whose frequence is more than 50 as the dimensions for the feature vectors. From the tests we find that when this thread varies from 50 to 120 the result of our system is nearly the same, but outside that bound the result will become rather bad. So we use 50 as the thread. After constructing the dimension of that target word, we can get a feature vector for each instance that at each dimension the number is the frequence of that word occurs in that position.

We obtain the feature vectors for the target words by employing these three stage. The following work is clustering these vector to get the classes of the word senses.

4 The Clustering Algorithm

There are many classical clustering methods such as k-means, EM and so on. In (Niu et al., 2007) they applied the sIB (Slonim et al., 2002) clustering algorithm at SemEval-2007 for task 2 and it achieved a quite good result. And at first this algorithm is also introduced

[1]`http://code.google.com/p/fudannlp/`

[2]`http://www.baidu.com`

for the unsupervised document classification problem. So we use the sIB algorithm for clustering the feature vectors in our system.

Unlike the situation in (Niu et al., 2007), the number of the sense classes is provided in CLP2010 task 4. So we can apply the sIB algorithm directly without the sense number estimation procedure in that paper. sIB algorithm is a variant of the information bottleneck method.

Let d represent a document, and w represent a feature word, $d \in D$,$w \in F$. Given the joint distribution $p(d,w)$, the document clustering problem is formulated as looking for a compact representation T for D, which reserves as much information as possible about F. T is the document clustering solution. For solving this optimization problem, sIB algorithm was proposed in (Slonim et al., 2002), which found a local maximum of $I(T,F)$ by: given a initial partition T, iteratively drawing a $d \in D$ out of its cluster $t(d)$, $t \in T$, and merging it into t^{new} such that $t^{new} = argmax_{t \in T}\mathbf{d}(d,t)$. $\mathbf{d}(d,t)$ is the change of $I(T,F)$ due to merging d into cluster t^{new}, which is given by

$$\mathbf{d}(d,t) = (p(d)+p(t))JS(p(w|d),p(w|t)). \quad (1)$$

$JS(p,q)$ is the Jensen-Shannon divergence, which is defined as

$$JS(p,q) = \pi_p D_{KL}(p||\overline{p}) + \pi_q D_{KL}(q||\overline{p}), \quad (2)$$

$$D_{KL}(p||\overline{p}) = \sum_y p\log\frac{p}{\overline{p}}, \quad (3)$$

$$D_{KL}(q||\overline{p}) = \sum_y q\log\frac{q}{\overline{p}}, \quad (4)$$

$$\{p,q\} \equiv \{p(w|d),p(w|t)\}, \quad (5)$$

$$\{\pi_p,\pi_q\} \equiv \{\frac{p(d)}{p(d)+p(t)},\frac{p(t)}{p(d)+p(t)}\}, \quad (6)$$

$$\overline{p} = \pi_p p(w|d) + \pi_q p(w|t). \quad (7)$$

In our system we use the sIB algorithm in the Weka 3.5.8 cluster package to cluster the feature vectors obtained in the previous section. The detailed description of the sIB algorithm in weka can refer to the website [3]. And the parameters for this Weka class is that: the number of clusters is the number of senses provided by the task, the random number seed is zero and the other parameters like maximum number of iteration and so on is set as default.

5 CLP 2010 Bake-Off of Chinese Word Sense Induction

5.1 Evaluation Measure

The evaluation measure is described as following:

We consider the gold standard as a solution to the clustering problem. All examples tagged with a given sense in the gold standard form a class. For the system output, the clusters are formed by instances assigned to the same sense tag (the sense tag with the highest weight for that instance). We will compare clusters output by the system with the classes in the gold standard and compute F-score as usual. F-score is computed with the formula below.

Suppose C_r is a class of the gold standard, and S_i is a cluster of the system generated, then

1. $F-score(C_r,S_i) = \frac{2*P*R}{P+R}$
2. P =the number of correctly labeled examples for a cluster/total cluster size
3. R =the number of correctly labeled examples for a cluster/total class size

Then for a given class C_r,

$$FScore(C_r) = \max_{S_i}(F-score(C_r,S_i)) \quad (8)$$

Then

$$FScore = \sum_{r=1}^{c}\frac{n_r}{n}FScore(C_r) \quad (9)$$

[3]http://pacific.mpi-cbg.de/javadoc/Weka/clusterers/sIB.html

Where c is total number of classes, n_r is the size of class C_r , and n is the total size.

5.2 DataSet

The data set includes 100 ambiguous Chinese words and for every word it provided 50 instances. Besides that they also provided a sample test set of 2500 examples of 50 target words with the answers to illustrate the data format.

Besides the sIB algorithm we also apply the k-means and EM algorithm to cluster the feature vectors. These algorithms are separately using the simpleKMeans class and the EM class in the Weka 3.5.8 cluster package. Except the number of clusters set as the given number of senses and number of seeds set as zero, all other parameters are set as default. For the given sample test set with answers the result is illustrated in the Table 1 below.

algorithm	F-score
k-means	0.7025
EM	0.7286
sIB	0.8132

Table 1: Results of three clustering algorithms

From Table 1 we can see the sIB clustering algorithm improves the result of the Chinese word sense induction evidently.

In the real test data test containing 100 ambiguous Chinese words, our system achieves a F-score 0.7788 ranking 6th among the 18 systems submitted. The best F-score of these 18 systems is 0.7933 and the average of them is 0.7128.

5.3 Discussion

In our system we only use the local collocations and the co-occurrences of the target words. But the words distance for the target word in the same sentence and the parts of speech of the neighboring word together with the target word is also important in this task.

In our experiment we used the parts of speech for the target word and each word before and after it achieved by the Chinese word segmentation system as part of the features vectors for clustering. With a proper weight on each POS dimension in the feature vectors, the F score for some word in the given sample test set with answers improved evidently. For example the Chinese word "便宜", the F score of it was developed from 0.5983 to 0.7573. But because of the fault of the segmentation system and other reasons F score of other words fell and the speed of the system was rather slower than before, we gave up this improvement finally.

Without the words distance for the target word in the same sentence the feature vectors maybe lack some information useful. So if we can calculate the correlation between the target word and other words, we will use these word sufficiently. However because of quantity of the Internet corpus is unknown, we didn't find the proper method to weigh the correlation.

From the previous section we find that the F score for the real test data test is lower than that for the sample test set. It is mainly because there are more single Chinese characters (as words) in the real test data set. Our system does not process these characters specially. For most of the Chinese characters we can't judge their correct senses only from the context where they appear. Their meaning always depends on the collocations with the other Chinese characters with which they become a Chinese word. However our system discriminates the senses of them only referring to the context of them, it can't judge the meaning of these Chinese characters properly. Maybe the best way is to search them in the dictionary.

However our system does not always have a very poor performance for any single Chinese character (as a word). The result is quite good for some Chinese characters. For example the Chinese character "谷" which has three meaning: valley, millet and a family name, the precision (P) of our system is 0.760. But for most of single Chinese characters such as "服" and "公", it is so bad that the result in the sample test worked rather better than the real test.

In Chinese the former character "谷" tends to express a complete meaning and the other characters in the word which they combine often modify it such as the characters "山" and "稻" in the word "山谷" and "稻谷". So this character can have a relatively high correlation with the words around and our system can deal with such characters like it. Unfortunately most characters need other characters to represent a complete meaning as the the latter "服" and "公" so they almost have no correlation with the words around but with those characters in the word in which they occur. But our system only uses the context features and even doesn't do any special process about these single Chinese characters. Therefore our system can not address those characters appropriately and we need to find a proper method to solve it, using a dictionary may be a choice.

This method works better for nouns and adjectives (in the sample test data set there are only 4 adjectives), but for verbs F score falls a little, illustrated in the Table 2 below.

POS	F-score
nouns	0.8473
adjectives	0.8543
verbs	0.7921

Table 2: Results of each POS in the sample test data set

Only using the local collocations in our system the F score is achieve above 80% (in the sample test), it demonstrates to some extent the information of collocations is so important that we should pay more attention to it.

6 Conclusion

The triplet-based Chinese word sense induction method is fitted to the task of Chinese word sense induction and obtain rather good result. But for some single characters word and some verbs, this method is not appropriate enough. In the future work, we will improve the method with more reasonable triplet selection strategies.

Acknowledgments

This work was (partially) funded by 863 Program (No. 2009AA01A346), 973 Program (No. 2010CB327906), and Shanghai Science and Technology Development Funds (No. 08511500302).

References

Bordag, S. 2006. Word sense induction: Triplet-based clustering and automatic evaluation. *Proceedings of EACL-06. Trento.*

Brody, S. and M. Lapata. 2009. Bayesian word sense induction. In *Proceedings of the 12th Conference of the European Chapter of the Association for Computational Linguistics*, pages 103–111. Association for Computational Linguistics.

Dorow, B. and D. Widdows. 2003. Discovering corpus-specific word senses. In *Proceedings of the tenth conference on European chapter of the Association for Computational Linguistics-Volume 2*, pages 79–82. Association for Computational Linguistics.

Niu, Z.Y., D.H. Ji, and C.L. Tan. 2007. I2r: Three systems for word sense discrimination, chinese word sense disambiguation, and english word sense disambiguation. In *Proceedings of the 4th International Workshop on Semantic Evaluations*, pages 177–182. Association for Computational Linguistics.

Pedersen, T. and R. Bruce. 1997. Distinguishing word senses in untagged text. In *Proceedings of the Second Conference on Empirical Methods in Natural Language Processing*, volume 2, pages 197–207.

Schütze, H. 1998. Automatic word sense discrimination. *Computational Linguistics*, 24(1):97–123.

Slonim, N., N. Friedman, and N. Tishby. 2002. Unsupervised document classification using sequential information maximization. In *Proceedings of the 25th annual international ACM SIGIR conference on Research and development in information retrieval*, pages 129–136. ACM.

Word Sense Induction using Cluster Ensemble

Bichuan Zhang, Jiashen Sun

Center of Intelligence Science and Technology

Lingjia Deng, Yun Huang, Jianri Li, Zhongwan Liu, Pujun Zuo

School of Computer

Beijing University of Posts and Telecommunications, Beijing, 100876 China

Abstract

In this paper, we describe the implementation of an unsupervised learning method for Chinese word sense induction in CIPS-SIGHAN-2010 bakeoff. We present three individual clustering algorithms and the ensemble of them, and discuss in particular different approaches to represent text and select features. Our main system based on cluster ensemble achieves 79.33% in F-score, the best result of this WSI task. Our experiments also demonstrate the versatility and effectiveness of the proposed model on data sparseness problems.

1 Introduction

Word Sense Induction (WSI) is a particular task of computational linguistics which consists in automatically discovering the correct sense for each instance of a given ambiguous word (Pinto , 2007). This problem is closely related to Word Sense Disambiguation (WSD), however, in WSD the aim is to tag each ambiguous word in a text with one of the senses known as prior, whereas in WSI the aim is to induce the different senses of that word.

The object of the sense induction task of CIPS-SIGHAN-2010 was to cluster 5,000 instances of 100 different words into senses or classes. The task data consisted of the combination of the test and training data (minus the sense tags) from the Chinese lexical sample task. Each instance is a context of several sentences which contains an occurrence of a given word that serves as the target of sense induction.

The accuracy of the corpus-based algorithms for WSD is usually proportional to the amount of hand-tagged data available, but the construction of that kind of training data is often difficult for real applications. WSI overcomes this drawback by using clustering algorithms which do not need training data in order to determine the possible sense for a given ambiguous word.

This paper describes an ensemble-based unsupervised system for induction and classification. Given a set of data to be classified, the system clusters the data by individual clusters, then operates cluster ensemble to ensure the result to be robust and accurate accordingly.

The paper is organized as follows. Section 2 gives an description of the general framework of our system. Sections 3 and 4 present in more detail the implementation of feature set and cluster algorithms used for the task, respectively. Section 5 presents the results obtained, and Section 6 draws conclusions and some interesting future work.

2 Methodology in Sense Induction Task

Sense induction is typically treated as an unsupervised clustering problem. The input to the clustering algorithm are instances of the ambiguous word with their accompanying contexts (represented by co-occurrence vectors) and the output is a grouping of these instances into classes corresponding to the induced senses. In other words, contexts that are grouped together in the same class represent a specific word sense.

In this task, an instance to be clustered is represented as a bag of tokens or characters that co–occur with the target word. To exploit the diversity of features, besides the co–occurrence matrix, we invoke the n-gram such as bi-grams that occur in the contexts. For assigning a weight for each term in each instance, a number of alternatives to tf-idf and entropy have been investigated.

This representation raises one severe problem: the high dimensionality of the feature space and the inherent data sparseness.

Obviously, a single document has a sparse vector over the set of all terms. The performance of clustering algorithms will decline dramatically due to the problems of high dimensionality and data sparseness. Therefore it is highly desirable to reduce the feature space dimensionality. We used two techniques to deal with this problem: feature selection and feature combination.

Feature selection is a process that chooses a subset from the original feature set according to some criterion. The selected feature retains original physical meaning and provides a better understanding for the data and learning process. Depending on whether the class label information is required, feature selection can be either unsupervised or supervised. For WSI should be an unsupervised fashion, the correlation of each feature with the class label is computed by distance, information dependence, or consistency measures.

Feature combination is a process that combines multiple complementary features based on different aspects extracted at the selection step, and forms a new set of features.

The methods mentioned above are not directly targeted to clustering instances; in this paper we introduce three cluster algorithms: (a) EM algorithms (Dempster et al., 1977; McLachlan and Krishnan, 1997), (b) K-means (MacQueen, 1967), and (c) LAC (Locally Adaptive Clustering) (Domeniconi et al., 2004), and one cluster ensemble method to incorporate three results together to represent the target patterns and conduct sense clustering.

We conduct multiple experiments to assess different methods for feature selection and feature combination on real unsupervised WSI problems, and make analysis through three facets: (a) to what extent feature selection can improve the clustering quality, (b) how much width of the smallest window that contains all the co–occurrence context can be reduced without losing useful information in text clustering, and (c) what index weighting methods should be applied to sense clustering. Besides the feature exploitation, we studied in more detail the performance of cluster ensemble method.

3 Feature Extraction

3.1 Preprocessing

Each training or test instance for WSI task contains up to a few sentences as the surrounding context of the target word *w*, and the number of the sense of *w* is provided. We assume that the surrounding context of a target *w* is informative to determine the sense of it. Therefore a stream of induction methods can be designed by exploiting the context features for WSI.

In our experiment, we consider both tokens (after word segmentation) and characters (without word segmentation) in the surrounding context of target word *w* as discriminative features, and these tokens or characters can be in different sentences from instances of *w*. Tokens in the list of stop words and tokens with only one character (such as punctuation symbols) are removed from the feature sets. All remaining terms are gathered to constitute the feature space of *w*.

Since the long dependency property, the word sense could be relying on the context far away from it. From this point, it seems that more features will bring more accurate induction, and all linguistic cues should be incorporated into the model. However, more features are involved, more serious sparseness happens. Therefore, it is important to find a sound trade-off between the scale and the representativeness of features. We use the sample data provided by the CIPS-SIGHAN as a development data to find a genetic parameter to confine the context scale. Let ω be the width of the smallest window in an instance *d* that contains terms near the target word, measured in the number of words in the window. In cases where the terms in the window do not contain all of the informative terms, we can set ω to be some enormous number (ω < the length of sentence). Such proximity-weighted scoring functions are a departure from pure cosine similarity and closer to the "soft conjunctive" semantics.

Token or character is the most straightforward basic term to be used to represent an instance. For WSI, in many cases a term is a meaningful unit with little ambiguity even without considering context. In this case the bag-of-terms representation is in fact a bag-of-words, therefore N-gram model can be used to exploit such meaningful units. An n-gram is a sequence of *n* consecutive characters (or tokens) in an instance. The advantages of n-grams are: they are language independent, robust against errors in instance, and they capture information about phrases. We performed experiments to show that for WSI, n-gram features perform significantly better than the flat features.

There exists many approaches to weight features in text computing (Aas and Eikvil, 1999).

A simple approach is TF (term frequency) using the frequency of the word in the document. The schemes take into account the frequency of the word throughout all documents in the collection. A well known variant of TF measure is TF-IDF weighting which assigns the weight to word i in document k in proportion to the number of occurrences of the word in the document, and in inverse proportion to the number of documents in the collection for which the word occurs at least once.

$$a_{ik} = f_{ik} * \log(\frac{N}{n_i})$$

Another approach is Entropy weighting, Entropy weighting is based on information theoretic ideas and is the most sophisticated weighting scheme. It has been proved more effective than word frequency weighting in text representing. In the entropy weighting scheme, the weight for word i in document k is given by a_{ik}.

$$a_{ik} = \log(f_{ik} + 1.0) * \left(1 + \frac{1}{\log(N)} \sum_{j=1}^{N} \left[\frac{f_{ij}}{n_i} \log(\frac{f_{ij}}{n_i})\right]\right)$$

Re-parameterization is the process of constructing new features as combinations or transformations of the original features. We investigated Latent Semantic Indexing (LSI) method in our research and produce a term-document matrix for each target word. LSI is based on the assumption that there is some underlying or latent structure in the pattern of word usage across documents, and that statistical techniques can be used to estimate this structure. However, it is against the primitive goal of the LSI weighting that LSI performs slightly poorer compared with the TF, TF-IDF and entropy. The most likely reason may is that the feature space we construct is far from high-dimension, while feature the LSI omitted may be of help for specific sense induction.

3.2 Feature Selection

A simple features election method used here is frequency thresholding. Instance frequency is the number of instance to be clustered in which a term occurs. We compute the instance frequency for each unique term in the training corpus and remove from the feature space those terms whose instance frequency was less than some predetermined threshold (in our experiment, the threshold is 5). The basic assumption is that rare terms are either non-informative for category prediction, or not influential in global performance. The assumption of instance frequency threshold is more straightforward that of LSI, and in either case, removal of rare terms reduces the dimensionality of the feature space. Improvement in cluster accuracy is also possible if rare terms happen to be noise terms.

Frequency threshold is the simplest technique for feature space reduction. It easily scales to sparse data, with a computational complexity approximately linear in the number of training documents. However, it is usually considered an ad hoc approach to improve efficiency, not a principled criterion for selecting predictive features. Also, frequency threshold is typically not used for aggressive term removal because of a widely received assumption in information retrieval. That is, low instance frequency terms are assumed to be relatively informative and therefore should not be removed aggressively. We will re-examine this assumption with respect to WSI tasks in experiments.

Information gain (IG) is another feature felection can be easily applied to clustering and frequently employed as a term-goodness criterion in the field of machine learning. It measures the number of bits of information obtained for cluster prediction by knowing the presence or absence of a term in an instance.

Since WSI should be conducted in an unsupervised fashion, that is, the labels are not provided, the IG method can not be directly used for WSI task. But IG can be used to find which kind of features we consider in Section 3.1 are most informative feature among all the feature set. We take the training samples as the development data to seek for the cues of most informative feature. For each unique term we compute the information gain and selecte from the feature space those terms whose information gain is more than some predetermined threshold. The computation includes the estimation of the conditional probabilities of a cluster given a term and the entropy computations in the definition.

$$\begin{aligned} \mathrm{IG(t)} = & -\sum\nolimits_{\mathrm{i=1}}^{\mathrm{m}} p(c_i)\log p(c_i) \\ & + p(t)\sum\nolimits_{\mathrm{i=1}}^{\mathrm{m}} p(c_i \mid \mathrm{t})\log p(c_i \mid \mathrm{t}) \\ & + p(\overline{t})\sum\nolimits_{\mathrm{i=1}}^{\mathrm{m}} p(c_i \mid \overline{t})\log p(c_i \mid \overline{t}) \end{aligned}$$

where t is the token under consideration, c_i is the corresponding cluster.This definition is more general than the one employed in binary classification models. We use the more general form because WSI task have a feature sparse problem, and we need to measure the goodness of a feature selection method globally with respect to all clusters on average.

3.3 Feature combination

Combining all features selected by different feature set can improve the performance of a WSI system. In the selection step, we find the feature that best distinguishes the sense classes, and iteratively search additional features which in combination with other chosen features improve word sense class discrimination. This process stops once the maximal evaluation criterion is achieved.

We are trying to disply an empirical comparison of representative feature combination methods. We hold that particular cluster support specific datasets; a test with such combination of cluster algorithm and feature set may wrongly show a high accuracy rate unless a variety of clusterers are chosen and many statistically different feature sets are used. Also, as different feature selection methods have a different bias in selecting features, similar to that of different clusterers, it is not fair to use certain combinations of methods and clusterers, and try to generalize from the results that some feature selection methods are better than others without considering the clusterer.

This problem is challenging because the instances belonging to the same sense class usually have high intraclass variability. To overcome the problem of variability, one strategy is to design feature combination method which are highly invariant to the variations present within the sense classes. Invariance is an improvement, but it is clear that none of the feature combination method will have the same discriminative power for all clusterers.

For example, features based on global window might perform well when instances are shot, whereas a feature weighting method for this task should be invariant to the all the WSI corpus. Therefore it is widely accepted that, instead of using a single feature type for all target words it is better to adaptively combine a set of diverse and complementary features. In our experiment, we use several combination of features in multiple views, that is, uni-gram/bi-gram, global/window, and tfidf/entropy – in order to discriminate each combination best from all other clusters.

4 Cluster

There are two main issues in designing cluster ensembles: (a) the design of the individual "clusterers" so that they form potentially an accurate ensemble, and (b) the way the outputs of the clusterers are combined to obtain the final partition, called the consensus function. In some ensemble design methods the two issues are merged into a single design procedure, e.g., when one clusterer is added at a time and the overall partition is updated accordingly (called the direct or greedy approach).

In this task we consider the two tasks separately, and investigate three powerful cluster methods and corresponding consensus functions.

4.1 EM algorithm

Expectation-maximization algorithm, or EM algorithm (Dempster et al., 1977; McLachlan and Krishnan, 1997) is an elegant and powerful method for finding maximum likelihood solutions for models with latent variables.

Given a joint distribution $p(\mathrm{X},\mathrm{Z}\mid\theta)$ over observed variables X and latent variables Z, governed by parameters θ, the goal is to maximize the likelihood function $p(\mathrm{X}\mid\theta)$ with respect to θ.

1. Choose an initial setting for the parameters θ^{old};

2. E step Evaluate $p(\mathrm{Z}\mid\mathrm{X},\theta^{old})$;

3. M step Evaluate θ^{new} given by

$$\theta^{new} = \underset{\theta}{\operatorname{argmax}}\, \vartheta(\theta,\theta^{old});$$

where $\vartheta(\theta,\theta^{old}) = \sum_{z} p(\mathrm{Z}|\mathrm{X},\theta^{old}) \ln p(\mathrm{X},\mathrm{Z}|\theta)$

4. Check for convergence of either the log likelihood or the parameter values. If the convergence criterion is not satisfied, then let

$$\theta^{old} \leftarrow \theta^{new}$$

and return to step 2.

4.2 K-means

K-means clustering (MacQueen, 1967) is a method commonly used to automatically partition a data set into k groups. It proceeds by selecting k initial cluster centers and then iteratively refining them as follows:

1. Each instance d_i is assigned to its closest cluster center.

2. Each cluster center C_j is updated to be the mean of its constituent instances.

The algorithm converges when there is no further change in assignment of instances to clusters. In this work, we initialize the clusters using instances chosen at random from the data set. The data sets we used are composed of numeric feature, for numeric features, we use a Euclidean distance metric.

4.3 LAC

Domeniconi et al.(2004) proposed an Locally Adaptive Clustering algorithm (LAC), which discovers clusters in subspaces spanned by different combinations of dimensions via local weightings of features. Dimensions along which data are loosely correlated receive a small weight, which has the effect of elongating distances along that dimension. Features along which data are strongly correlated receive a large weight, which has the effect of constricting distances along that dimension. Thus the learned weights perform a directional local reshaping of distances which allows a better separation of clusters, and therefore the discovery of different patterns in different subspaces of the original input space.

The clustering result of LAC depends on two input parameters. The first one is common to all clustering algorithms: the number of clusters k to be discovered in the data. The second one (called h) controls the strength of the incentive to cluster on more features. The setting of h is particularly difficult, since no domain knowledge for its tuning is likely to be available. Thus, it would be convenient if the clustering process automatically determined the relevant subspaces.

4.4 Cluster Ensemble

Cluster ensembles offer a solution to challenges inherent to clustering arising from its ill-posed nature. Cluster ensembles can provide robust and stable solutions by leveraging the consensus across multiple clustering results, while averaging out emergent spurious structures that arise due to the various biases to which each participating algorithm is tuned.

Kuncheva et al. (2006) has shown Cluster ensembles to be a robust and accurate alternative to single clustering runs. In the work of Kuncheva et al. (2006), 24 methods for designing cluster ensembles are compared using 24 data sets, both artificial and real. Both diversity within the ensemble and accuracy of the individual clusterers are important factors, although not straightforwardly related to the ensemble accuracy.

The consensus function aggregates the outputs of the Individual clusterers into a single partition. Many consensus functions use the consensus matrix obtained from the adjacency matrices of the individual clusterers. Let N be the number of objects in the data set. The adjacency matrix for clusterer k is an N by N matrix with entry $(i, j) = 1$ if objects i and j are placed in the same cluster by clusterer k, and $(i, j) = 0$, otherwise. The overall consensus matrix, M, is the average of the adjacency matrices of the clusterers. Its (i, j) entry gives the proportion of clusterers which put i and j in the same cluster.

Here the overall consensus matrix, *M*, can be interpreted as similarity between the objects or the "data". It appears that the clear winner in the consensus function "competition" is using the consensus matrix as data. Therefore, the consensus functions used in the WSI task invoke the approach whereby the consensus matrix M is used as data (features). Each object is represented by N features, i.e., the j-the feature for object i is the (i, j) entry of *M*.

Then we use Group-average agglomerative clustering (GAAC) to be the consensus functions clustering the *M* matrix.

5 Analysis

First, we conducte an ideal case experiment on the training samples provided by CIPS-SIGHAN 2010, to see whether good terms can help sense clustering. Specifically, we applied supervised feature selection methods to choose the best feature combinations driven by performance improving on the training features. Then, we executed the word sense induction task using features under the prefered feature combinations and compare the various clustering results output by three individual cluster.

We then designe cluster ensemble method with results on three clusters, distributed as *M* data consensus matrix.

5.1 Soundex for Feature

We apply feature selection and feature combination to instances in the preprocessing of K-means, EM and LAC. The effectiveness of a combination method is evaluated using the performance of the cluster algorithm on the preprocessed WSI. We use the standard definition of recall and precision as F-score (Zhao and Karypis, 2005) to evaluate the clustering result.

As described in Section 3, selection methods are included in this study, each of which uses a term-goodness criterion threshold to achieve a desired degree from the full feature set of WSI corpus.

Table 2 shows The F-score figures for the different combinations of knowledge sources and learning algorithms for the training data set. The feature columns correspond to:

(i) tfidf: tf-idf weighting
(ii) entro: Entropy weighting
(iii) bi: bi-gram representation
(iv) uni: uni-gram representation
(v) global: using all the terms in the instance
(vi) winXX: using only terms in the surrounding context, and the width of the window is the figure followed by.

As shown in Table 2, the best averaged F-score for WSI (without combination) is obtained by global_entro by maintaining a very consistent result for three cluster algorithm. That is, the feature weighting method will dominate the F-score. On the other hand, we should combine uni_global_entro and bi_global_entro to improve the cluster performance:

(vii) combine: combining all two feature (uni and bi) with the at the rate of the ratio followed by.

From these figures, we found the following points. First, feature selection can improve the clustering performance when a certain terms are combined. For example, any feature combination methods can achieve about 5% improvement. Second, as can be seen from Table 1, the best performances yielded at the combination ratio of 8:2. As can be seen, when more bi-gram terms are added, the performances of combination methods drop obviously. In order to find out the reason, we compared the terms selected at different ratio. After analysis, we found that Chinese word senses have their own characteristics, unigram language model is suitable for WSI in Chinese; also, in WSI task, informative term may be in the entire instance but not appear closest to the target word, the language model and the width of window is much more important than the feature weighting for feature selection. Since entropy weighting perform better than tf-idf weighting, tf-idf weighting can be removed with an improvement in clustering performance on the training dataset. Hence, it is obvious that combination methods are much better than single feature set when processing WSI, and we chose combine_uni_bi_entro_8:2, i.e., the top 80%

Feature	k-means	LAC	EM	average
combine_uni_bi_entro_8:2	0.817375775	0.819315654	0.811188742	0.81596
combine_uni_bi_entro_9:1	0.812858111	0.817265352	0.81510355	0.815075
combine_uni_bi_entro_7:3	0.805319576	0.817909374	0.819887132	0.814372
combine_uni_bi_entro_1:1	0.810324177	0.81397143	0.812962625	0.812419
combine_uni_bi_entro_6:4	0.806647971	0.815069965	0.810440791	0.811945
combine_uni_bi_entro_1:9	0.810576944	0.811287122	0.813785918	0.811883
combine_uni_bi_entro_4:6	0.810475113	0.810512846	0.811584054	0.810857
combine_uni_bi_entro_3:7	0.809265111	0.811142052	0.811340668	0.810582
combine_uni_bi_entro_2:8	0.811090379	0.804433939	0.813767918	0.809764
uni_global_entro	0.765063808	0.75954835	0.746212504	0.756942
uni_global_tfidf	0.765011785	0.757537564	0.745006996	0.755852
uni_win30_tfidf	0.764949578	0.757424304	0.744497086	0.755624
uni_win40_tfidf	0.764772672	0.755702292	0.744319609	0.754932
uni_win30_entro	0.764286757	0.755514592	0.742825875	0.754209
uni_win40_tfidf	0.763994795	0.75954835	0.742747114	0.75543
bi_global_entro	0.740026161	0.731310077	0.71651859	0.729285
bi_global_tfidf	0.739555095	0.731264758	0.716031966	0.728951
bi_win30_entro	0.737209909	0.729711844	0.714498518	0.72714
bi_win40_entro	0.715230191	0.713987571	0.699644178	0.709621
bi_win40_tfidf	0.714031488	0.710282928	0.697201196	0.707172
bi_win30_ tfidf	0.740026161	0.731310077	0.71651859	0.729285

Table 1: Feature selection for our system.

uni-gram features and top 20% features as the final clustering features.

5.2 The cluster ensembles

As described in Section 5.1, we use two language models (uni-gram and bi-gram), 4 types of the context window (20, 30, 40 and global) and 2 feature weighting methods (tf-idf and entropy), also, 10 combined feature set and 3 cluster algorithm is introduced; in the other word, we have at least 78 result, that is 78 consensus matrix interpreted as “data” to be aggregated. Thus we can evaluate the statistical significance of the difference among any ensemble methods on any cluster result set.

To compare all ensemble methods, we group the result sets (out of 78) into different feature representation scheme. Significant difference for a given feature representation methods, the ensemble result is observed to check weather cluster ensembles can be more accurate than single feature set and to find out which method appears to be the best choice for the WSI task.

Table 2 shows the ensembles examined in our experiment. The feature columns correspond to different group of result set, for example, bi_tfidf indicates bi-gram model and tf-idf feature weighting methods are selected, all the 3 cluster results on win20, win30, win 40 and global feature sets (12 consensus matrix) are aggregated; complex_entro indicates that all the feature representation methods selecting entropy weighting are chosen.

Results show that the best performance is the group in which all the outputs of all the clusterers are combined (the top row in Table 2).

Feature	F1-score	Scale
complex	0.827566232	78
complex_entro	0.823006644	24
complex_nocomb	0.822970703	48
complex_global	0.821960768	12
uni_complex	0.821931155	24
uni_ entro	0.821931155	15
uni_global	0.821817211	6
complex_combine	0.819456935	30
uni_ tfidf	0.811631894	12
complex_tfidf	0.806807226	24
complex_entro	0.806063712	24
bi_complex	0.801211134	24
bi_entro	0.794939656	12
bi_global	0.788673134	6
bi_tfidf	0.788170215	12

Table 2: Ensemble designs sorted by the total index of performance

5.3 CIPS-SIGHAN WSI Performance

The goal of this task is to promote the exchange of ideas among participants and improve the performance of Chinese WSI systems. The input consists of 100 target words, each target word having a set of contexts where the word appears. The goal is to automatically induce the senses each word has, and cluster the contexts accordingly. The evaluation measures provided is F-Score measure. In order to improve the overall performance, we used two techniques: feature combination and Cluster Ensemble.

We chose combinomg global size of window, entropy weighting, uni-garm and bi-gram at the ratio of 8:2 as the final feature extraction method. Three powerful cluster algorithms, EM, K-means and LAC recieve these features as input, and in our main system all the outputs of all the clusterers are combined to process cluster ensemble. In Table 3 we show four results obtained by three individual clusters and one ensemble of them.

Our main system has outperformed the other systems achieving 79.33%. Performance for LAC is 78.95%, 0.4% lower the best system. For EM our F-sore is 78.55%, which is around 0.8% lower than the best system, the similar result ia also observed for K-means. The results of our system are ranked in the top 4 place and obviously better the other systems.

Name	F1-score	Rank
BUPT_mainsys	0.7933	1
BUPT_LAC	0.7895	2
BUPT_EM	0.7855	3
BUPT_kmeans	0.7849	4

Table 3: Evaluation (F-score performance)

6 Conclusions

In this paper, we described the implementation of our systems that participated in word sense induction task at CIPS-SIGHAN-2010 bakeoff. Our ensemble model achieved 79.33% in F-score, 78.95% for LAC, 78.55% for EM and 78.49% for K-means. The result proved that our system had the ability to fully exploit the informative feature in senses and the ensemble clusters enhance this advantage.

One direction of future work is to exploit more semantic cues for word sense distribution. Furthermore, in order to represent the short context of the target word, we should investigate more powerful model and external knowledge to expand its linguistic environments.

Acknowledgement

This research has been partially supported by the National Science Foundation of China (NO. NSFC90920006). We also thank Xiaojie Wang, Caixia Yuan and Huixing Jiang for useful discussion of this work.

References

D. Pinto, P. Rosso, and H. Jim´enez-Salazar. *UPV-SI: Word sense induction using self term expansion.* In Proc. of the 4th International Workshop on Semantic Evaluations - SemEval 2007. Association for Computational Linguistics, 2007. pp. 430-433.

Yiming Yang and Jan O. Pedersen. *A Comparative Study on Feature Selection in Text Categorization.* In Proceedings of the 14th International Conference on Machine Learning (ICML), 1997. pp. 412-420.

Salton, Gerard, and Chris Buckley. 1987. *Term weighting approaches in automatic text retrieval.* Technical report, Cornell University, Ithaca, NY, USA.

S. Dumais, *Improving the retrieval of information from external sources*, Behavior Research Methods, Instruments, & Computers, 1991, 23:229-236.

M. W. Berry, S. T. Dumais, and G. W. O'Brien, *Using linear algebra for intelligent information retrieval*, SIAM Rev., 1995, 37:573-595

MacQueen, J. B. (1967). *Some methods for classification and analysis of multivariate observations.* Proceedings of the Fifth Symposium on Math, Statistics, and Probability, Berkeley, CA: University of California Press. pp. 281 297.

Dempster,A.P., Laird,N.M and Rubin,D.B. (1977) *Maximum likelihood from incomplete data via the EM algorithm.* J. Roy. Statist. Soc. B, 39, 1-38.

MCLACHLAN, G., AND KRISHNAN, T. 1997. *The EM algorithm and extensions.* Wiley series in probability and statistics. JohnWiley & Sons.

Y. Zhao and G. Karypis. 2002. *Evaluation of hierarchical clustering algorithms for document datasets.* In Proceedings of the 11th Conference of Information and Knowledge Management (CIKM), pp. 515-524.

K. Aas and L. Eikvil. *Text categorisation: A survey.* Technical Report 941, Norwegian Computing Center, June 1999.

C. Domeniconi, D. Papadopoulos, D. Gunopulos, and S. Ma. *Subspace clustering of high dimensional data.* SIAM International Conference on Data Mining, 2004.

Kuncheva, L.I., Hadjitodorov, S.T., and Todorova, L.P. *Experimental Comparison of Cluster Ensemble Methods*, The 9th International Conference on Information Fusion, 2006.

LSTC System for Chinese Word Sense Induction

Peng Jin, Yihao Zhang, Rui Sun
Laboratory of Intelligent Information Processing and Application
Leshan Teachers' College
jandp@pku.edu.cn,yhaozhang@163.com,dram_218@163.com

Abstract

This paper presents the Chinese word sense Induction system of Leshan Teachers' College. The system participates in the Chinese word sense Induction of task 4 in Back offs organized by the Chinese Information Processing Society of China (CIPS) and SIGHAN. The system extracts neighbor words and their POSs centered in the target words and selected the best one of four cluster algorithms: Simple KMeans, EM, Farthest First and Hierarchical Cluster based on training data. We obtained the F-Score of 60.5% on the training data otherwise the F-Score is 57.89% on the test data provided by organizers.

1. Introduction

Automatically obtain the intended sense of polysemous words according to its context has been shown to improve performance in information retrieval、information extraction and machine translation. There are two ways to resolve this problem in view of machine learning, one is supervised classification and the other is unsupervised classification i.e. clustering. The former is word sense disambiguation (WSD) which relies on large scale, high quality manually annotated sense corpus, but building a sense-annotated corpus is a time-consuming and expensive project. Even the corpus were constructed, the system trained from this corpus show the low performance on different domain test corpus. The later is word sense induction (WSI) which needs not any training data, and it has become one of the most important topics in current computational linguistics.

Chinese Information Processing Society of China (CIPS) and SIGHAN organized a task is intended to promote the research on Chinese WSI. We built a WSI system named LSTC-WSI system for this task. This system tried four cluster algorithms, i.e. Simple KMeans、EM、Farthest First and Hierarchical Cluster implemented by weak 3.7.1 [6], and found Simple KMeans compete the other three ones according to their performances on training data. Finally, the results returned by Simple KMeans were submitted.

2. Features Selection

Following the feature selection in word sense disambiguation, we extract neighbor words and their POSs centered in the target words. Word segmented and POS-tag tool adapted Chinese Lexical Analysis System developed by Institute of Computing Technology. No other resource is used in the system. The window size of the context is set to 5 around the ambiguous word. The neighbor words which occur only once were removed. Each sample is represented as a vector, and feature form is binary: if it occurs in is 1 otherwise is 0.

3. Clusters Algorithms

Four cluster algorithms were tried in our system. I will introduce them simply in the next respectively.

K-means clustering [1] is one of the simplest unsupervised learning algorithms that solve the well known clustering problem. The main idea is to define *k* centroids, one for each cluster. These centroids should be placed in a cunning way because of different location causes different result. So, the better choice is to place them as much as possible far away from each other.

EM algorithm[2] is a method for finding maximum likelihood estimates of parameters in statistical models, where the model depends on unobserved latent variables. EM is an iterative method which alternates between performing an expectation (E) step, which computes the expectation of the log-likelihood evaluated using the current estimate for the latent variables, and maximization (M) step, which computes parameters maximizing the expected log likelihood found on the E step.

The Farthest First algorithm [3] is an implementation of the "Farthest First Traversal Algorithm" by Hochbaum and Shmoys (1985). It finds fast, approximate clusters and may be useful as an initialiser for k-means.

A hierarchical clustering [4] is the guarantee that for every k, the induced k clustering has cost at most eight times that of the optimal k-clustering. A hierarchical clustering of n data points is a recursive partitioning of the data into 2, 3, 4, . . . and finally n, clusters. Each intermediate clustering is made more fine-grained by dividing one of its clusters.

4. Development

4.1 Evaluation method

We consider the gold standard as a solution to the clustering problem. All examples tagged with a given sense in the gold standard form a class. For the system output, the clusters are formed by instances assigned to the same sense tag. We will compare clusters output by the system with the classes in the gold standard and compute F-score as usual [5]. F-score is computed with the formula below.

Suppose C_r is a class of the gold standard, and S_i is a cluster of the system generated, then

$$F-Score(C_r, S_i) = 2 * P * R / (P + R) \quad (1)$$

$$p = \frac{\text{the number of correctly labeled examples for a cluster}}{\text{total cluster size}}$$

$$R = \frac{\text{the number of correctly labeled examples for a cluster}}{\text{total cluster size}}$$

Then for a given class Cr,

$$F-score(C_r) = \max_{S_i}(F-score(C_r, S_i))$$

$$F-Score = \sum_{r=1}^{c} \frac{nr}{n} FScore(C_r) \quad (2)$$

where *c* is total number of classes, n_r is the size of class C_r, and n is the total size. Participants will be required to induce the senses of the target word using only the dataset provided by the organizers.

4.2 Data Set

The organizers provide 50 Chinese training data of SIGHAN2010-WSI-SampleData. The training data contain 50 Chinese words; each word has 50 example sentences, and gives each word the total number of sense. The total number of sense is ranging from 2 to 21, but more cases are 2. In order to facilitate the team participating in the contest to do experiment, the organizers also provide answer to each word.

In order to evaluating the system's performance of all participating team, the organizers provide 100 test word and each word have 50 example sentences, the system of each participating team need to run out the results which the organizers need.

4.3 System Setup

We developed the LSTC-WSI system based on Weka. Firstly, we implemented the evaluation algorithm described in section 4.1. Then, the instances were represented as vectors according to the feature selection. Thirdly, four cluster algorithms from Weka were tried and set different thresholds for feature frequency. Because of paper length constraints, we could not list all the experience data we get. Table 1 listed system performance when frequency threshold set two and without POS information.

Table 1: The Performance on test data

Target word	Simple Kmeans	EM	Farthest First	Hierar chical
暗淡	0.618	0.680	0.538	0.649
把握	0.404	0.365	0.400	0.327
保安	0.711	0.557	0.672	0.636
保管	0.626	0.700	0.536	0.570
报销	0.571	0.555	0.572	0.573
背离	0.789	0.596	0.680	0.548
比重	0.704	0.617	0.704	0.682
便宜	0.568	0.495	0.461	0.583
标兵	0.5679	0.679	0.625	0.688
病毒	0.601	0.590	0.648	0.603
补贴	0.578	0.554	0.662	0.616
哺育	0.621	0.537	0.615	0.627
材料	0.560	0.429	0.466	0.527
采购	0.627	0.537	0.643	0.603
参加	0.610	0.538	0.643	0.638
草包	0.643	0.607	0.648	0.632
程序	0.615	0.545	0.662	0.603
澄清	0.621	0.616	0.615	0.658
吃饭	0.538	0.583	0.569	0.609
冲洗	0.603	0.540	0.632	0.569
冲撞	0.653	0.557	0.657	0.603
充电	0.627	0.622	0.652	0.690
出口	0.421	0.438	0.454	0.453
初二	0.609	0.528	0.583	0.627
春秋	0.634	0.667	0.486	0.652
戳穿	0.574	0.546	0.577	0.584
打	0.462	0.429	0.518	0.501
打断	0.661	0.584	0.584	0.602
打开	0.430	0.501	0.549	0.418
打破	0.596	0.644	0.647	0.654
打气	0.614	0.580	0.672	0.708
大军	0.666	0.600	0.615	0.595
大陆	0.638	0.590	0.540	0.678
大气	0.841	0.734	0.662	0.618
大人	0.613	0.562	0.670	0.568
单纯	0.635	0.617	0.646	0.649
导师	0.603	0.594	0.615	0.577
东北	0.644	0.635	0.661	0.560
东方	0.599	0.595	0.624	0.638
东西	0.588	0.575	0.587	0.508
动力	0.699	0.723	0.673	0.643
杜鹃	0.585	0.596	0.666	0.603
断交	0.643	0.639	0.666	0.656
断气	0.624	0.537	0.663	0.608
扼杀	0.632	0.525	0.629	0.617
发动	0.451	0.472	0.490	0.477
发展	0.613	0.625	0.6723	0.625
翻身	0.601	0.640	0.646	0.661
反射	0.591	0.585	0.663	0.639
调动	0.536	0.505	0.477	0.532

We tried two ways for feature selection: the frequency of features and neighbor words' POS were taken into account or not. Table 2 shows the average performance on the test data via varying the parameter setting. Observing the results returned by Hierarchical cluster is very imbalance, we set the options "-L WARD" in order to balance the number.

Table 2: The Average Performance of 50 Training Data

Features	Simple Kmeans	EM	Farthest First	Hierar chical
Word, Windows 5	0.555	0.566	0.607	0.558
Word, Windows 5, Frequency 1	0.583	0.567	0.599	0.582
Word, Windows 5, Frequency 2	0.605	0.575	0.605	0.598
Word, Windows 5, Frequency 3	0.598	0.590	0.600	0.599
Word+POSs, Windows 5	0.562	0.582	0.618	0.569
Word+POSs, Windows 5, Frequency 1	0.589	0.580	0.610	0.594
Word+POSs, Windows 5, Frequency 2	0.589	0.580	0.610	0.594

Compared with the average performance of the 50 test data, we find the performance is best[1] when considering word only and setting the frequency is two at the same time simple KMeans was adapted. So, we use the same parameters setting and clustered the test data by simple KMeans. As table 2 shows, the F-Score is 60.5% on training data. But on test data, our system's F-Score is 57.89% officially evaluated by task organizers.

5. Conclusion and Future Works

Four cluster algorithms are tried for Chinese word sense induction: Simple KMeans, EM, Farthest First and Hierarchical Cluster. We construct different feature spaces and select out the best combination of cluster and feature space. Finally, we apply the best system to the test data.

In the future, we will look for better cluster algorithms for word sense induction. Furthermore, we observe that it is different from word sense disambiguation, different part of speech will cause the polysemy. We will make use of this character to improve our system.

Acknowledgements

This work is supported by the Open Projects Program of Key Laboratory of Computational Linguistics(Peking University), Ministry of Education, Grant No. KLCL-1002. This work is also supported by Leshan Teachers' College, Grant No. Z1046.

References

[1] Dekang Lin, Xiaoyun Wu. Phrase Clustering for Discriminative Learning. Proceedings of ACL ,2009.

[2]Neal R, & Hinton G. A view of the EM algorithm that justifies incremental, sparse, and other variants. Learning in Graphical Models, 89, 355–368.

[3] Jon Gibson, Firat Tekiner, Peter Halfpenny. NCeSS Project: Data Mining for Social Scientists. Research Computing Services, University of Manchester, U.K.

[4] Sanjoy Dasgupta, Philip M. Long. Performance guarantees for hierarchical clustering. Journal of Computer and System Sciences, 555–569, 2005.

[5] Eneko Agirre, Aitor Soroa. Semeval-2007 Task 02:Evaluating Word Sense Induction and Discrimination Systems. Proceedings of SemEval-2007, pages 7–12, 2007.

[6] http://www.cs.waikato.ac.nz/ml/weka/

[1] Although "Farthest First" got the highest score, the results of "Farthest First" are too imbalance.

NEUNLPLab Chinese Word Sense Induction System for SIGHAN Bakeoff 2010

Hao Zhang **Tong Xiao** **Jingbo Zhu**

1. Key Laboratory of Medical Image Computing (Northeastern University), Ministry of Education

2. Natural Language Processing Laboratory, Northeastern University

zhanghao1216@gmail.com

{xiaotong, zhujingbo}@mail.neu.edu.cn

Abstract

This paper describes a character-based Chinese word sense induction (WSI) system for the International Chinese Language Processing Bakeoff 2010. By computing the longest common substrings between any two contexts of the ambiguous word, our system extracts collocations as features and does not depend on any extra tools, such as Chinese word segmenters. We also design a constrained clustering algorithm for this task. Experiemental results show that our system could achieve 69.88 scores of *FScore* on the development data set of SIGHAN Bakeoff 2010.

1 Introduction

The goal of word sense induction (WSI) is to group occurrences containing a given ambiguous word into clusters with respect to sense. Most researchers take the problem of word sense induction as a clustering problem. Pantel & Lin (2002) clustered words on the basis of the distances of their co-occurrence vectors, and used global clustering as a solution. Neill (2002) used local clustering, and determined the senses of a given word by clustering its close associations.

In this paper, we propose a simple but effective method to extract collocations as features from texts without pre-segmentations, and design a constrained clustering algorithm to address the issue of Chinese word sense induction. By using our collocation extraction method, our Chinese WSI system is independent of any extra natural language processing tools, such as Chinese word segmenters. On the development set of SIGHAN 2010 WSI task, the experimental results show that our system could achieve 69.88 scores of *FScore*. In addition, the official results show that the performance of our system is 67.15 scores of *FScore* on the test set of SIGHAN Bakeoff 2010.

The rest of this paper is organized as follows. In Section 2, we present the task description of Chinese word sense induction. In Section 3, we first give an overview of our Chinese WSI system, and then propose our feature extraction method and constrained clustering algorithm. In Section 4, we describe the evaluation method and show the experimental results on the development and test data sets of the Bakeoff 2010. In Section 5, we conclude our work.

2 Task Description

Given the number of senses *S* and occurrences of the ambiguous word *w*, a word sense induction system is supposed to cluster the occurrences into *S* clusters, with each cluster representing a sense of the ambiguous word *w*. For example, suppose that there are some sentences containing the ambiguous word "暗淡" (gloomy), and the sense number *S* is 2, the job of WSI system is to cluster these sentences into 2 clusters, with each cluster representing a sense of "暗淡". Based on this task description, it is obvious to regard the problem of WSI as a clustering problem.

Figures 1-2 shows example input and output of our WSI system , where there are 6 sentences and 2 resulting clusters. In Figure 1, the first column are the identifiers of sentences containing the word "暗淡", and the second column are part of the sentences. In Figure 2, the first column represents the identifiers of sentences, and the second column represents the identifiers of clusters generated by our Chinese WSI system.

0001 ...同时，经济增长<head>暗淡</head>也前所未有地激起...
0002 ...因而对未来的命运感到前途<head>暗淡</head>、渺茫...
0003 ...考生可能目光<head>暗淡</head>，双眉紧皱...
0004 ...第三季度就业形势趋于<head>暗淡</head>，就业人数...
0005 ...灯光显得有点<head>暗淡</head>，路面看上去黑乎乎的...
0006 ...离开了网络单调无趣，目光<head>暗淡</head>冷漠...

Figure 1 Part of input of word "暗淡" for our WSI system

0001	C1
0002	C0
0003	C1
0004	C0
0005	C0
0006	C1

Figure 2 Output of our WSI system for word "暗淡"

3 NEU Chinese WSI System

3.1 System overview

Our Chinese word sense induction system is built based on clustering work-frame. There are four major modules in the system, including *data pre-processing*, *feature extraction*, *clustering* and *data post-processing* modules. The architecture of our Chinese WSI system is illustrated in Figure 3.

3.2 Feature extraction

Since there is no separators in Chinese like "space" in English to mark word boundaries, most Chinese natural language processing applications need to first apply a Chinese word segmenter to segment Chinese sentences. In our Chinese word sense induction system, we extract collocations from sentences containing the ambiguous word as features. To extract collocations, we might first segment the sentences into word sequences, and then conduct feature extraction on the word-segmented corpus. However, errors might be induced in the procedure due to unavoidable incorrect segmentation results. Addressing this issue, we propose a method to directly extract collocations from sentences without pre-segmentations.

In our method, we extract two kinds of collocations, namely "global collocation" and "local collocation". Here global collocations are defined to be the words (or character sequences) that frequently co-occur with the ambiguous word, and local collocations are defined to be the characters adjacent to the ambiguous word[1].

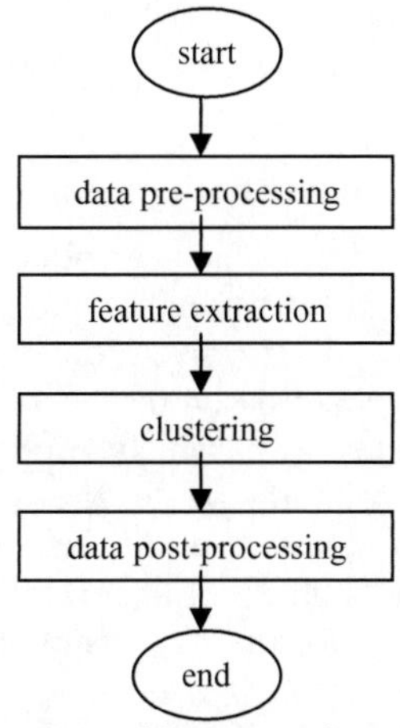

Figure 3 Architecture of our system

To extract global collocations, we first compute all the longest common substrings between any two of the sentences containing the ambiguous word to form the set of candidate global collocations. For each candidate global collocation, we count the number of sentences containing it. We then reduce the size of the candidate set by eliminating candidates which contain only one character or functional words. We also remove the candidate with other candidates as its substrings. Finally, we eliminate the candidates whose count of the number of sentences is below a certain threshold. The threshold equals to two in our experiments. We regard the candidates after the above processing as global collocations for WSI.

To extract local collocations, we simply extract one character on both left and right sides of the ambiguous word to form the set of candidate local collocations. We then refine the candidate set by eliminating candidates which are functional words or whose frequency is below a certain threshold. The threshold is set to two in our experiments.

After extracting global collocations and local collocations, we put them together to form the

[1] Definitions of global collocation and local collocation might be different from those in other papers.

final set of collocations and use them as features of our system. For each collocation (or feature), we compute the list of indices of sentences that containing the collocation. Thus, every element of the set of collocations has the data structure of pair of "key" and "value", where "key" is the collocation itself, and the "value" is the list of indices.

3.3 Clustering algorithm

We find that the high-confidence collocation is a very good indicator to distinguish the senses of an ambiguous word. However, the traditional clustering methods are based on the vector representations of features, which probably decreases the effect of dominant features (i.e. high-confidence collocations). To alleviate the problem, a nice way is to incorporate collocations into the clustering process as constraints. Motivated by this idea, we design a constrained clustering algorithm. In this algorithm, we could ensure that some occurrences of the ambiguous word *must* be in one cluster and some *must not* be in one cluster. The input for our constrained clustering algorithm is the set of collocations described in the previous section and the process of our clustering algorithm is shown in Table 1. Here the notation starting with character "C" represents a collocation, and the notations of "*Sin*" and "*Srlt*" represent the collocation set and the result set, respectively.

Every element in the result set *Srlt* is regarded as one cluster for a given ambigous word, and the list of the element records the indices of the sentences belonging to the cluster.

4 Evaluation of Our System

The evaluation method is *F-score* which is provided within the Bakeoff 2010 (Zhao and Karypis, 2005). Suppose *Cr* is a class of the gold standard, and *Si* is a cluster of our system generated. *FScore* is computed with the formulas below.

$$F-score(Cr,Si) = 2*P*R/(P+R) \quad (1)$$

$$FScore(Cr) = \max_{Si}(F-score(Cr,Si)) \quad (2)$$

$$FScore = \sum_{r=1}^{c} \frac{nr}{n} FScore(Cr) \quad (3)$$

We evaluate our Chinese word sense induction system on the development data set and the test data set of the Bakeoff 2010. The details of the development data set and the test data set are summarized in Table 2.

For comparison, we develop a baseline system that also uses the collocations as features and clustering based on the vector representations of features. On the development data set, we test our system and compare it with the baseline system. The performance of our Chinese WSI system and the baseline system are shown in Table 3. From Table 3, we see that using our constrained clustering algorithm is better than using the traditional hierarchical clustering methods by 7.06 scores of *FScore* for our Chinese WSI system. It indicates that our constrained clustering algorithm could avoid reducing the effect of

```
Input:      collocation set Sin
while there is available collocation Ci in the input set Sin
    for each collocation Ct in the set Sin
        if Ct not equals to Ci, and Ct is available
            if list of Ct has intersection with that of Ci, or Ct and Ci have a
            meaningful substring (word or character), compose list of Ct into
            list of Ci, and mark Ct to be unavailable
            end if
        end if
    end for
    store Ci and its list into result set Srlt, and mark Ci to be unavailable
end while
if there are available collocations in the input set Sin
    if the size of result set Srlt does not satisfy the given cluster number, devide the
    rest collocations in Sin evenly into the rest clusters, and append their lists to
    their own clusters' lists respectively
    else add the rest collocations into the last cluster, and append their list to the list of
    the last cluster
    end if
end if
return the result set Srlt
Output:     result set Srlt
```

Table 1 Constrained clustering algorithm

high-confidence features (i.e. high-confidence collocations) and lead to better clustering results. This conclusion is also ensured by the comparison between our constrained clustering algorithm and the traditional K-means clustering algorithm.

In addition, our system achieves 67.15 scores of *FScore* on the test data set reported by the SIGHAN Bakeoff 2010.

data	descriptions
Dev set	containing 50 ambiguous words, about 50 sentences for each ambiguous word
Test set	containing 100 ambiguous words, about 50 sentences for each ambiguous word

Table 2 Data sets of SIGHAN Bakeoff 2010

clustering methods	*FScore* of our system (%)
traditional hierarchical clustering	62.82
traditional K-means clustering	62.48
our constrained clustering	69.88

Table 3 System performance on dev set of Bakeoff 2010 using different clustering methods

5 Conclusions

In this paper, we propose a collocation extraction method and a constrained clustering algorithm for Chinese WSI task. By using the collocation extraction method and the clustering algorithm, our Chinese word sense induction system is independent of any extra tools. When tested on the test data set of the Bakeoff 2010, our system achieves 67.15 scores of *FScore*.

References

Vickrey, David, Luke Biewald, Marc Teyssler, and Daphne Koller. 2005. *Word-sense disambiguation for machine translation*. In Proceedings of the conference on Human Language Technology and Empirical Methods in Natural Language Processing, Morristown, NJ, USA, pages 771-778.

Yarowsky, David. 1995. *Unsupervised word sense disambiguation rivaling supervised methods*. In Proceedings of 33rd Meeting of the Association for Computational Linguistics, Cambridge, MA, 189-196.

Schutze, Hinrich. 1998. *Automatic word sense discrimination*. Computational Linguistics, Montreal, Canada, 24(1):97–123.

Ng, Hwee Tou, Hian Beng Lee. 1996. *Integrating Multiple Knowledge Sources to Disambiguate Word Sense: An Exemplar-Based Approach*. In Proceedings of the 34th Meeting of the Association for Computational Linguistics, California, USA, pages 40-47.

Daniel, Neill. 2002. *Fully Automatic Word Sense Induction by Semantic Clustering*. In Computer Speech, Cambridge University, Master's Thesis.

Pantel, Patrick, Dekang Lin. 2002. *Discovering word senses from text*. In Proceedings of ACM SIGKDD, Edmonton, 613-619.

Rapp, Reinhard. 2004. *A Practical Solution to the Problem of Automatic Word Sense Induction*. In Proceedings of the 42nd Meeting of the Association for Computational Linguistics, Barcelona, Spain.

Zhao, Ying, George Karypis. 2005. *Hierarchical Clustering Algorithms for Document Datasets*. Data Mining and Knowledge Discovery, 10:141-168.

Chinese Word Sense Induction based on Hierarchical Clustering Algorithm

Ke Cai, Xiaodong Shi, Yidong Chen，Zhehuang Huang, Yan Gao
Cognitive Science Department, Xiamen University, Xiamen, 361005, China

Abstract

Sense induction seeks to automatically identify word senses of polysemous words encountered in a corpus. Unsupervised word sense induction can be viewed as a clustering problem. In this paper, we used the Hierarchical Clustering Algorithm as the classifier for word sense induction. Experiments show the system can achieve 72% F-score about train-corpus and 65% F-score about test-corpus.

1. Introduction

Word sense induction is a central problem in many natural language processing tasks such as information extraction, information retrieval, and machine translation [Vickrey et al., 2005].

Clp 2010 launches totally 4 tasks for evaluation exercise, these are: Chinese word segmentation, Chinese parsing, Chinese Personal Name disambiguation and Chinese Word Sense Induction. We participated in task 4, which is Chinese Word Sense Induction..

Because the contents surround an ambiguous word is related to its meaning, we solve the sense problem by grouping the instances of the target word into the supposed number of clusters according to the similarity of contexts of the instance. In this paper we used the hierarchical clustering algorithm to accomplish the problem.

The task can be defined as two stage process: Feature selection and word clustering. Researchers have proposed much approach to the sense induction task which involved the use of basic word co-occurrence features and application of classical clustering algorithms.

Because the meanings of unknown words can be inferred from the contexts in which they appear, Pantel and Lin (2002) map the senses to WordNet. More recently, the mapping has been used to test the system on publicly available benchmarks (Purandare and Pedersen, 2004; Niu et al., 2005).

However, this approach does not generalize to multiple-sense words. Each sense of a polysemous word can appear in a different context, there have been many attempts in recent years to apply classical clustering algorithms to this problem.

Clustering algorithms have been employed ranging from k-means (Purandare and Pedersen, 2004), to agglomerative clustering (Sch¨utze, 1998), and the Information Bottleneck (Niu et al., 2007). Senses are induced by identifying highly dense subgraphs (hubs) in the co-occurrence graph (V´eronis, 2004).The sIB algorithm was used to estimate cluster structure, which measures the similarity of contexts of instances according to the similarity of their feature conditional distribution(Slonim, et al.,2002). Each algorithm treats words as feature vectors, using the same similarity function based on context information.

The remainder of this paper is organized as follows. In section 2 the Featured set and word similarity definition is introduced. The hierarchical clustering algorithm is presented in section 3. Section 4 provides the experimental results and conclusion is drawn in section 5.

2. Feature Selection and Word Similarity Definition

2.1 Feature Selection

A feature set is used designed to capture both immediate local context in our experiment, wider context and syntactic context. Specifically, we experimented with several feature categories: ±5-word window (5w), ±3-word window (3w), part-of speech n-grams and dependency relations. These features have been widely adopted in various word sense induction algorithms. The overall best scores are achieved with local (5 words) context windows.

. 2.2 Similarity Definition

We treat the context words as feature vectors, using the same similarity function. Suppose $C_i(w_{i1}, w_{i2} \cdots w_{in})$ is the contexts set of sentence S_i, and $C_j(w_{j1}, w_{j2} \cdots w_{jn})$ is the contexts set of sentence S_j.

Then we defined $sim(S_i, S_j) = \sum_{\substack{W_{jk} \in C_i \\ W_{jl} \in C_j}} w_{kl} sim(w_{ik}, w_{jl})$, here w_{kl} is variable weight,

Where $sim(w_{ik}, w_{jl}) = \dfrac{\beta}{dis(w_{ik}, w_{jl}) + \beta}$, β is an adjustable parameter with a value of 1.2, and

$Dis(w_{ik}, w_{jl})$ is the path length between w_{ik} and w_{jl} based on the semantic tree structure used for TongYiCi CiLin (同义词词林).

3. The Hierarchical Clustering Algorithm Used In Word Sense Induction

Sense induction is viewed as an unsupervised clustering problem where to group a word's contexts into different classes, each representing a word sense. In this paper, we use the bottom-up clumping approach, which begin with n singleton clusters and successively merge clusters to produce the other ones.

Table1: Hierarchical Clustering Algorithm:

1. initialize number of senses n 、 number of clusters m

   and clusters $C_i(w_{i1}, w_{i2} \cdots), i = 1, 2 \cdots m$

2. Set $k = n$
3. Set $k = k - 1$

4. Find the nearest clusters C_i and C_j , Merge C_i and C_j

5. If $k > m$, go to step 3, otherwise go to step 6;

6. return m clusters

The merging of the two clusters in step 4 simply corresponds to adding an edge between the nearest pair of nodes in C_i and C_j. To find the nearest clusters, the following clustering similarity function is used:

$$sim(S_i, S_j) = \sum_{\substack{W_{jk} \in C_i \\ W_{jl} \in C_j}} w_{kl} sim(w_{ik}, w_{jl}) .$$

Our model incorporates features based on lexical information and parts of speech. So we propose a improved hierarchical clustering algorithm based on parts of speech.

Table2: improved algorithm based on parts of speech.

---

1. initialize number of senses n 、 number of clusters m

   and clusters $C_i(w_{i1}, w_{i2} \cdots), i = 1, 2 \cdots m$

2. Part of Speech Tagging on the corpus

3. Divided n senses into nn classes base on the information of parts of speech.

4. If $nn = m$, return m clusters

5. If $nn < m$, invoke hierarchical clustering algorithm in different classes, merge clusters into m cluster.

6. if $nn > m$, invoke hierarchical clustering algorithm in different tagging, merge clusters into m cluster.

7. return m clusters

---

4. Experimental Results

The test data includes totally 100 ambiguous Chinese words, every word have 50 untagged instances. Table3 show the best/worst/average F-Score of our system about train-corpus and test-corpus.

	Best word	Worst word	All words
Train-corpus	0.98	0.5	0.73
Test-corpus	------	-----	0.65

Table 3 Model performance with deferent corpus

Table 4 shows the performance of our model about train-corpus when using 3w and 5w word windows, which represent more immediate, local context.

	Best word	Worst word	All words
3w(±3-word window)	0.98	0.5	0.73
5w(±5-word window)	0.92	0.52	0.72

Table 4 Model performance with deferent windows

Table 5 summarizes the F-score in our system about train-corpus when using deferent similarity definition.

	Best word	Worst word	All words
This article	0.98	0.5	0.73
Qun LIU	0.99	0.59	0.78

Table 5 Model performance with deferent similarity definition

Experimental results show that the Hierarchical Clustering Algorithm can be applied to sense induction. Considering words to be feature vectors and applying clustering algorithm can improve accuracy of the task. A significant gap still exists between the results of these techniques and the gold standard of manually compiled word sense dictionaries.

5. Conclusions

Sense induction is treated as an unsupervised clustering problem. In this paper we adopt hierarchical clustering algorithm to accomplish the problem. Generate context words according to this distribution of key words and formalize the induction problem in a generative mode. Experiments show the system can achieved 72% F-score about train-corpus and 65% F-score about test-corpus. The basic cluster algorithm can sorts the word sense into clusters corresponding to the context.

References

Boyd-Graber, Jordan, David Blei, and Xiaojin Zhu. 2007.A topic model for word sense disambiguation. In Proceedings of the EMNLP-CoNLL. Prague, Czech Republic,pages 1024–1033.

David Vickrey, Luke Biewald, Marc Teyssler, and Daphne Koller. Word-sense disambiguation for machine translation. In Proceedings of the conference on Human Language Technology and Empirical Methods in Natural Language Processing, page

771-778, 2005.

Qun LIU , Sujian LI. Word Similarity Computing Based on How-net. Computational Linguistics and Chinese Language Processing

Niu, Zheng-Yu, Dong-Hong Ji, and Chew-Lim Tan. 2007. I2r: Three systems for word sense discrimination, chineseword sense disambiguation, and english word sense disambiguation. In Proceedings of the Fourth International Workshop on Semantic Evaluations (SemEval-2007). Association for Computational Linguistics, Prague, Czech Republic, pages 177–182.

Niu, Z.Y., Ji, D.H., & Tan, C.L. 2005. Word Sense Disambiguation Using Label Propagation Based Semi-Supervised Learning. Proceedings of the 43rd Annual Meeting of the Association for Computational Linguistics.

Pantel, Patrick and Dekang Lin. 2002. Discovering word senses from text. In Proceedings of the 8th KDD. New York, NY, pages 613–619.

Pedersen, Ted. 2007. Umnd2 : Senseclusters applied to the sense induction task of senseval-4. In Proceedings of SemEval-2007. Prague, Czech Republic, pages 394–397.

Purandare, Amruta and Ted Pedersen. 2004. Word sense discrimination by clustering contexts in vector and similarity spaces. In Proceedings of the CoNLL. Boston, MA, pages 41–48

V'eronis, Jean. 2004. Hyperlex: lexical cartography for information retrieval. Computer Speech & Language. 18(3):223–252.

ISCAS: A System for Chinese Word Sense Induction Based on K-means Algorithm

Zhenzhong Zhang* **Le Sun†** **Wenbo Li†**

*Institute of Software, Graduate University
Chinese Academy of Sciences
zhenzhong@nfs.iscas.ac.cn

†Institute of Software
Chinese Academy of Sciences
{sunle,wenbo02}@iscas.ac.cn

Abstract

This paper presents an unsupervised method for automatic Chinese word sense induction. The algorithm is based on clustering the similar words according to the contexts in which they occur. First, the target word which needs to be disambiguated is represented as the vector of its contexts. Then, reconstruct the matrix constituted by the vectors of target words through singular value decomposition (SVD) method, and use the vectors to cluster the similar words. Our system participants in CLP2010 back off task4-Chinese word sense induction.

1 Introduction

It has been shown that using word senses instead of surface word forms could improve performance on many nature language processing tasks such as information extraction (Joyce and Alan, 1999), information retrieval (Ozlem et al., 1999) and machine translation (David et al., 2005). Historically, word senses are represented as a fixed-list of definitions coming from a manually complied dictionary. However, there seem to be some disadvantages associated with such fixed-list of senses paradigm. Since dictionaries usually contain general definitions and lack explicit semantic, they can't reflect the exact content of the context where the target word appears. Another disadvantage is that the granularity of sense distinctions is fixed, so it may not be entirely suitable for different applications.

In order to overcome these limitations, some techniques like word sense induction (WSI) have been proposed for discovering words' senses automatically from the unannotated corpus. The word sense induction algorithms are usually base on the Distributional Hypothesis, proposed by (Zellig, 1954), which showed that words with similar meanings appear in similar contexts (Michael, 2009). And the hypothesis is also popularized with the phrase "a word characterized by the company it keeps" (John, 1957). This concept shows us a method to automatically discover senses of words by clustering the target words with similar contexts (Lin, 1998). The word sense induction can be regarded as an unsupervised clustering problem. First, select some features to be used when comparing similarity between words. Second, represent disambiguated words as vectors of selected features according to target words' contexts. Third, cluster the similar words using the vectors. But compared with European languages such as English, Chinese language has its own characteristics. For example, Chinese ideographs have senses while the English alphabets don't have. So the methods which work well in English may not be entirely suitable for Chinese.

This paper proposes a method for Chinese word sense induction, which contains two stage processes: features selecting and context clustering. Chinese ideographs and Chinese words which have two or more Chinese ideographs are used different strategies when selecting features. The vectors of target word's instances are put together to constitute a matrix, whose row is instances and column is features. Reconstruct the matrix through singular value decomposition to get a new vector for each instance. Then, K-means clustering algorithm is employed to cluster the vectors of disambiguated words' contexts. Each cluster to which some instances belong to identifies a sense of corresponding target word.

Our system participants in CLP2010 back off task4 - Chinese word sense induction.

The remainder of this paper is organized as follows. Section 2 presents the Chinese word senses induction algorithm. Section 3 presents the evaluation sheme and the results of our system. Section 4 gives some discussions and conclusions.

2 Chinese Word Senses Induction

This section will present the strategies of selecting features for disambiguated Chinese words and k-means algorithm for clustering vectors of the contexts.

2.1 Features Selection

Since the input instances of target words are unstructured, it's necessary to select features and transform them into structured format to fit the automatic clustering algorithm. Following the example in (Ted, 2007), words are chosen as features to represent the contexts where target words appear. A word *w* in the context of the target word can be represented as a vector whose *ith* component is the average of the calculated conditional probabilities of *w* and w_j.

The target words are usually removed from the corpus in the task of English word sense induction. But Chinese language is very different from European languages such as English. Chinese ideographs usually have meanings of their own while English alphabets don't have. In Chinese word senses induction tasks, the target word may be a Chinese word which could have one or more Chinese ideographs or a Chinese ideograph. And the meaning of Chinese ideographs is determined by the Chinese word where it appears. The following example shows us this case.

- 我国依靠推广超级稻累计增产稻*谷* 162 亿公斤。
- 在木化石园附件的一处山*谷*，是大佛寺近期增加的五百罗汉堂。

In this example, the target word is Chinese ideograph "谷" displayed in italic in the contexts. In the first context, its meaning is paddy which is determined by the Chinese word "稻谷", and similarly in the second context its meaning is valley determined by "山谷". Since the meaning of the Chinese ideograph "谷" is determined by the word where it appears, it may not be appropriate to remove it from the contexts simply while the others of the word are left. Different strategies are employed to remove target words. If the target word contains two or more Chinese ideographs, it will be removed from the context. Otherwise it will be kept.

To solve the problem of data sparseness, we extracted extra 100 instances for each target word from Sogou Data and also used the thesauruses (TongYiCi CiLin of HIT) to reduce the dimensionality of the word space (feature space). Two filtering heuristics are applied when selecting features. The first one is the minimum frequency p_1 of words, and the second one is the maximum frequency p_2 of words.

Each selected word (feature) should be assigned a weight, which indicates the relative frequency of two co-occurring words. Using conditional probabilities for weighting for object/verb and subject/verb pairs is better than point-wise mutual information (Philipp et al., 2005). So we used conditional probabilities for weighting words pairs. Let $num_{i,j}$ denote the number of the instances where the word i and word j co-occur, and num_i denote the number of the instances in which the word i appears. Then the *jth* component of the vector of the word i can be calculated using the following equation.

$$w_{i,j} = \frac{p(j \mid i) + p(i \mid j)}{2}$$

Where

$$p(i \mid j) = \frac{num_{i,j}}{num_j}$$

The contexts of each target word are represented as the centroid of the vectors of the words occurring in the target contexts. Figure 1 shows an example of context vector, where the Chinese word "果实" co-occurs with Chinese words "水果"and "种子".

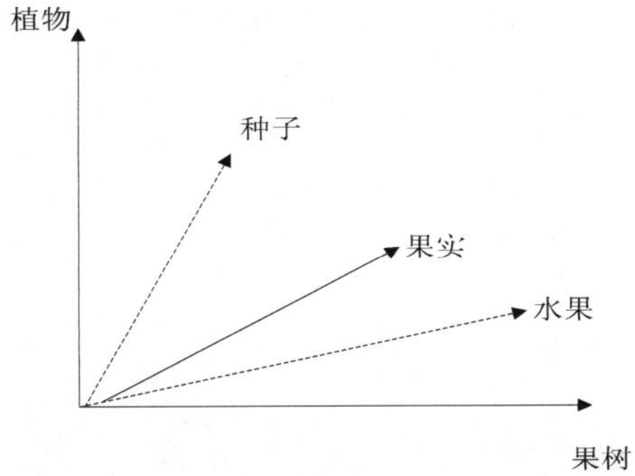

Figure 1: An example of a context vector for "果实", calculated as the centroid of vectors of "种子" and "水果".

2.2 Clustering Algorithm

K-means algorithm is applied to cluster the vectors of the target word. It assigns each element to one of K clusters according to which centroid the element is close to by the similarity function. The cosine function is used to measure the similarity between two vectors V and W:

$$sim(V,W) = \frac{V \bullet W}{|V| \times |W|} = \frac{\sum_{i=1}^{n} V_i W_i}{\sqrt{\sum_{i=1}^{n} V_i^2 \sum_{i=1}^{n} W_i^2}}$$

where n is the number of features in each vector. Before clustering the vectors of instances, we put together the vectors of instances in the corpus and obtain a co-occurrence matrix of instances and words. Singular value decomposition is applied to reduce the dimensionality of the resulting multidimensional space and finds the major axes of variation in the word space (Golub and Van Loan, 1989). After the reduction, the similarity between two instances can be measured using the cosine function mentioned as above between the corresponding vectors. The clustering algorithm stops when the centroid of each cluster does not change or the iteration of the algorithm exceed a user-defined threshold p_3. And the number of the clusters is determined by the corpus where the target word appears. Each cluster to which some instances belong represents one senses of the target word represented by the vector.

We also employed a graph-based clustering algorithm -Chinese Whispers (CW) (Chris, 2006) to deal with the task of Chinese WSI. CW does not require any input parameters and has a good performance in WSI (Chris, 2006). For more details about CW algorithm please refer to (Chris, 2006). We first constructed a graph, whose vertexes were instances of target word and edges' weight was the similarity of the corresponding two vertexes. Then we removed the edges with minimum weight until the percentage of the kept edges' sum respect the total was below a threshold p_4. CW algorithm was employed to cluster the graph and each clusters represented a sense of target word.

3 Evaluation

This section presents the evaluation scheme, set of parameters and the result of our system.

3.1 Evaluation Scheme

We use standard cluster evaluation methods to measure the performance of our WSI system. Following the former practice (Zhao and Karypis, 2005), we consider the FScore measure for assessing WSI methods. The FScore is used in a similar fashion to Information Retrieval exercises.

Let we assume that the size of a particular class s_r is n_r, the size of a particular cluster h_j is n_j and the size of their common instances set is $n_{r,j}$. The precision can be calculated as follow:

$$P(s_r, h_j) = \frac{n_{r,j}}{n_j}$$

The recall value can be defined as:

$$R(s_r, h_j) = \frac{n_{r,j}}{n_r}$$

Then FScore of this class and cluster is defined to be:

$$F(s_r, h_j) = \frac{2 \times P(s_r, h_j) \times R(s_r, h_j)}{P(s_r, h_j) + R(s_r, h_j)}$$

The FScore of class s_r, $F(s_r)$, is the maximum $F(s_r, h_j)$ value attained by any cluster, and it is defined as:

$$F(s_r) = \max_{h_j}(F(s_r, h_j))$$

Finally, the FScore of the entire clustering solution is defined as the weighted average FScore of each class:

$$FScore = \sum_{r=1}^{q} \frac{n_r \times F(s_r)}{n}$$

Where q is the number of classes and n is the total number of the instances where target word appears.

3.2 Tuning the Parameters

We tune the parameters of our system on the training data. But because of time restrictions, we do not optimize these parameters. The maximum frequency of a word (p_2) and the maximum number of the K-means' iteration (p_3) are tuned on the training data. The minimum frequency of a word (p_1) was set to two following our intuition. The last parameter K -the number of the clusters is determined by the test data in which the target word appears. When tuning parameters, we first fixed the parameter p_3 and found the best value of parameter p_2, which could lead to the best performance. The results have been shown in Table 1 and Table 2.

Parameters	FScore
P_3=300,p_2=35	0.7502
P_3=400,p_2=40	0.7523
P_3=500,p_2=40	**0.7582**

Table 1: The results of K-means with SVD

Parameters	FScore
P_3=300,p_2=40	0.7454
P_3=400,p_2=40	**0.7493**
P_3=500,p_2=45	0.7404

Table 2: The results of K-means

The performance of CW algorithm is shown in Table 3. The parameter p_4 is a threshold for pruning graph as describing in section 2.2.

Parameter	FScore
P_4=0.55	0.6325
P_4=0.6	0.6321
P_4=0.65	0.6278
P_4=0.7	**0.6393**
P_4=0.75	0.6289
P_4=0.8	0.6345
P_4=0.85	0.6326
P_4=0.9	0.6342
P_4=0.95	0.6355

Table 3: The results of CW.

The result shows that the K-means algorithm has a better performance than CW. That may because CW can't use the information of the number of clusters, but K-means could. Another problem for CW is that the size of corpus is small and the constructed graph can't reflect the inherent relation between the instances.

Based on the result of experiments, we employed K-means algorithm for our system and the parameters is shown in Table 4.

Parameters	Value
P_1: Minimum frequency of a word	2
P_2: Maximum frequency of a word	40
P_3: Maximum number of K-means iteration	500
K: the number of the cluster	-

Table 4: Parameters for the system. The last parameter K is provided by the test data.

3.3 Result

Our system participants in the CLP2010 back-off task4 and disambiguate 100 target words, total 5000 instances. The F-score of our system on the test data is 0.7209 against the F-score 0.7933 of the best system.

4 Conclusion

We have presented a model for Chinese word sense induction. Different strategies are applied to deal with Chinese ideographs and Chinese words that contain two or more Chinese ideographs. After selecting the features –words, singular value decomposition is used to find the major axes of variation in the feature space and reconstruct the vector of each context. Then we employ k-means cluster algorithm to cluster the vectors of contexts. Result shows that our system is able to induce correct senses. One drawback of our system is that it overlooks the infrequent senses because of lacking enough data. And our system only uses the information of word co-occurrences. So in the future we would like to integrate different kinds of information such as topical information, syntactic information and semantic information, and see if we could get a better result.

Acknowledgement

This work has been partially funded by National Natural Science Foundation of China under grant #60773027, #60736044 and #90920010 and by "863" Key Projects #2006AA010108, "863" Projects #2008AA01Z145. We would like to thank anonymous reviewers for their detailed comments.

References

Chris Biemann, 2006. *Chinese whispers - an efficient graph clustering algorithm and its application to natural language processing problems,* In Proceedings of TextGraphs, pp. 73–80, New York, USA.

David Vickrey, Luke Biewald, Marc Teyssley, and Daphne Koller. 2005. *Word-sense disambiguation for machine translation.* In Proceedings of the conference on Human Language Technology and Empirical Methods in Natural Language Processing, pages 771-778, Vancouver, British Columbia, Canada

Dekang Lin. 1998. *Automatic retrieval and clustering of similar words.* In Proceedings of the 17th international conference on Computational linguistics, volume 2, pages 768-774, Montreal, Quebec, Canada

Golub, G. H. and Van Loan, C. F. 1989. *Matrix Computations.* The John Hopkins University Press, Baltimore, MD

John, R., Firth. 1957. *A Synopsis of Linguistic Theory 1930-1955*, pages 1-32.

Joyce Yue Chai and Alan W. Biermann. 1999. *The use of word sense disambiguation in an information extraction system.* In Proceedings of the sixteenth national conference on Artificial intelligence and the eleventh Innovative applications of artificial intelligence conference innovative applications of artificial intelligence, pages 850-855, Orlando, Florida, United States.

Michael Denkowski. 2009. *A Survey of Techniques for Unsupervised Word Sense Induction.*

Ozlem Uzuner, Boris Katz, and Deniz Yuret. 1999. *Word sense disambiguation for information retrieval.* In Proceedings of the sixteenth national conference on Artificial intelligence and the eleventh Innovative applications of artificial intelligence conference innovative applications of artificial intelligence, page 985, Orlando, Florida, United States.

Philipp Cimiano, Andreas Hotho, and Steffen Staab, 2005. *Learning concept hierarchies from text corpora using formal concept analysis,* Journal of Artificial Intelligence Research (JAIR), 24, 305–339.

Ted Pedersen, 2007. *Umnd2: Senseclusters applied to the sense induction task of senseval-4.* In Proceedings of the Fourth International Workshop on Semantic Evaluations, pages 394–397, Prague, Czech Republic.

Zellig Harris. 1954. *Distributional Structure*, pages 146-162.

Ying Zhao and George Karypis. 2005. *Hierarchical clustering algorithms for document datasets.* Data Mining and Knowledge Discovery, 10(2):141.168.

Soochow University: Description and Analysis of the Chinese Word Sense Induction System for CLP2010

Hua Xu Bing Liu Longhua Qian[*] Guodong Zhou
Natural Language Processing Lab
School of Computer Science and Technology
Soochow University, Suzhou, China 215006
Email:
{20094227034,20084227065055,qianlonghua,gdzhou}@suda.edu.cn

Abstract

Recent studies on word sense induction (WSI) mainly concentrate on European languages, Chinese word sense induction is becoming popular as it presents a new challenge to WSI. In this paper, we propose a feature-based approach using the spectral clustering algorithm to this problem. We also compare various clustering algorithms and similarity metrics. Experimental results show that our system achieves promising performance in F-score.

1 Introduction

Word sense induction (WSI) is an open problem of natural language processing (NLP), which governs the process of automatic discovery of the possible senses of a word. WSI is similar to word sense disambiguation (WSD) both in methods employed and in problem encountered. In the procedure of WSD, the senses are assumed to be known and the task focuses on choosing the correct one for an ambiguous word in a context. The main difference between them is that the task of WSD generally requires large-scale manually annotated lexical resources while WSI does not. As WSI doesn't rely on the manually annotated corpus, it has become one of the most important topics in current NLP research (Pantel and Lin, 2002; Neill, 2002; Rapp, 2003). Typically, the input to a WSI algorithm is a target word to be disambiguated. The task of WSI is to distinguish which target words share the same meaning when they appear in different contexts. Such result can be at the very least used as empirically grounded suggestions for lexicographers or as input for WSD algorithm. Other possible uses include automatic thesaurus or ontology construction, machine translation or information retrieval. Compared with European languages, the study of WSI in Chinese is scarce. Furthermore, as Chinese has its special writing style and Chinese word senses have their own characteristics, the methods that work well in English may not perform effectively in Chinese and the usefulness of WSI in real-world applications has yet to be tested and proved.

The core idea behind word sense induction is that contextual information provides important cues regarding a word's meaning. The idea dates back to (at least) Firth (1957) ("You shall know a word by the company it keeps"), and underlies most WSD and lexicon acquisition work to date. For example, when the adverb phrase occurring prior to the ambiguous word "把握" , then the target word is more likely to be a verb and the meaning of which is "to hold something"; Otherwise, if an adjective phrase locates in the same position, then it probably means "confidence" in English. Thus, the words surrounds the target word are main contributor to sense induction.

The bake off task 4 on WSI in the first CIPS-SIGHAN Joint Conference on Chinese Language Processing (CLP2010) is intended to promote the exchange of ideas among participants and improve the performance of Chinese WSI systems. Generally, our WSI system also adopts a clustering algorithm to group the contexts of a target word. Differently, after generat-

[*] Corresponding author

ing feature vectors of words, we compute a similarity matrix with each cell denoting the similarity between two contexts. Furthermore, the set of similarity values of a context with other contexts is viewed as another kind of feature vector, which we refer to as similarity vector. Both feature vectors and similarity vectors can be separately used as the input to clustering algorithms. Experimental results show our system achieves good performances on the development dataset as well as on the final test dataset provided by the CLP2010.

2 System Description

This section sequentially describes the architecture of our WSI system and its main components.

2.1 System Architecture

Figure 1 shows the architecture of our WSI system. The first step is to preprocess the raw dataset for feature extraction. After that, we extract "bag of words" from the sentence containing a target word (feature extraction) and transform them into high-dimension vectors (feature vector generation). Then, similarities of every two vectors could be computed based on the feature vectors (similarity measurement). the similarities of an instance can be viewed as another vector—similarity vector. Both feature vectors and similarity vectors can be served as the input for clustering algorithms. Finally, we perform three clustering algorithms, namely, k-means, HAC and spectral clustering.

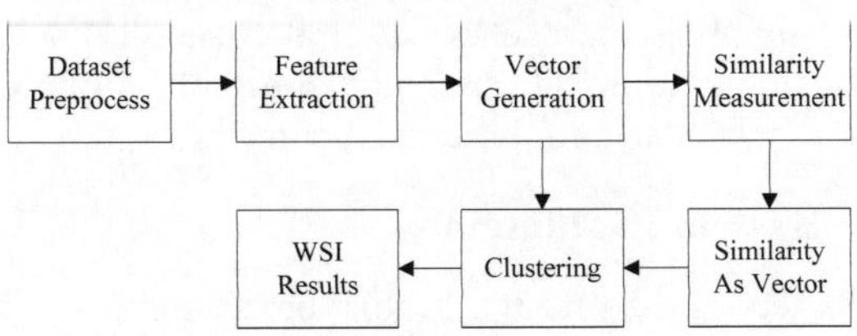

Figure 1 Architecture of our Chinese WSI system

2.2 Feature Engineering

In the task of WSI, the target words with their topical context are first transformed into multi-dimensional vectors with various features, and then applying clustering algorithm to detect the relevance of each other.

Corpus Preprocessing

For each raw file, we first extract each sentence embedded in the tag `<instance>`, including the `<head>` and `</head>` tags which are used to identify the ambiguous word. Then, we put all the sentences related to one target word into a file, ordered by their instance IDs. The next step is word segmentation, which segments each sentence into a sequence of Chinese words and is unique for Chinese WSI. Here, we use the software from Hylanda[1] since it is ready to use and considered an efficient word segmentation tool. Finally, since we retain the `<head>` tag in the sentence, the `<head>` and `</head>` tags are usually separated after word segmentation, thus we have to restore them in order to correctly locate the target word during the process of feature extraction.

Feature Extraction

After word segmentation, for a context of a particular word, we extract all the words around it in the sentence and build a feature vector based on a "bag-of-words" Boolean model. "Bag-of-words" means that we don't consider the order of words. Meanwhile, in the Boolean model, each word in the context is used to generate a feature. This feature will be set to 1 if the word appears in the context or 0 if it does not. Finally, we get a number of feature vectors, each of them corresponds to an instance of the target word. One problem with this feature-based method is that, since the size of word set may be huge, the dimension is also very high, which might lead to data sparsity problem.

Similarity measurement

One commonly used metric for similarity measurement is cosine similarity, which measures the angle between two feature vectors in a high-dimensional space. Formally, the cosine similarity can be computed as follows:

$$\cos ine\ similarity < \mathbf{x}, \mathbf{y} > = \frac{\mathbf{x} \cdot \mathbf{y}}{|\mathbf{x}| \cdot |\mathbf{y}|}$$

where $\mathbf{x}$, $\mathbf{y}$ are two vectors in the vector space and $|\mathbf{x}|$, $|\mathbf{y}|$ are the lengths of $\mathbf{x}$, $\mathbf{y}$ respectively.

[1] http://www.hylanda.com/

Some clustering algorithms takes feature vectors as the input and use cosine similarity as the similarity measurement between two vectors. This may lead to performance degradation due to data sparsity in feature vectors. To avoid this problem, we compute the similarities of every two vectors and generate an $N*N$ similarity matrix, where N is the number of all the instances containing the ambiguous word. Generally, N is usually much smaller than the dimension size and may alleviate the data sparsity problem. Moreover, we view every row of this matrix (i.e., an ordered set of similarities of an instance with other instances) as another kind of feature vector. In other words, each instance itself is regarded as a feature, and the similarity with this instance reflects the weight of the feature. We call this vector similarity vector, which we believe will more properly represent the instance and achieve promising performance.

2.3 Clustering Algorithm

Clustering is a very popular technique which aims to partition a dataset into such subgroups that samples in the same group share more similarities than those from different groups. Our system explores various cluster algorithms for Chinese WSI, including K-means, hierarchical agglomerative clustering (HAC), and spectral clustering (SC).

K-means (KM)

K-means is a very popular method for general clustering used to automatically partition a data set into k groups. K-means works by assigning multidimensional vectors to one of K clusters, where K is given as a priori. The aim of the algorithm is to minimize the variance of the vectors assigned to each cluster.

K-means proceeds by selecting k initial cluster centers and then iteratively refining them as follows:

(1) Choose k cluster centers to coincide with k randomly-chosen patterns or k randomly defined points.

(2) Assign each pattern to the closest cluster center.

(3) Recompute the cluster centers using the current cluster memberships.

(4) If a convergence criterion is not met, go to step 2.

Hierarchical Agglomerative Clustering (HAC)

Different from K-means, hierarchical clustering creates a hierarchy of clusters which can be represented in a tree structure called a dendrogram. The root of the tree consists of a single cluster containing all objects, and the leaves correspond to individual object.

Typically, hierarchical agglomerative clustering (HAC) starts at the leaves and successively merges two clusters together as long as they have the shortest distance among all the pair-wise distances between any two clusters.

Given a specified number of clusters, the key problem is to determine where to cut the hierarchical tree into clusters. In this paper, we generate the final flat cluster structures greedily by maximizing the equal distribution of instances among different clusters.

Spectral Clustering (SC)

Spectral clustering refers to a class of techniques which rely on the eigen-structure of a similarity matrix to partition points into disjoint clusters with points in the same cluster having high similarity and points in different clusters having low similarity.

Compared to the "traditional algorithms" such as K-means or single linkage, spectral clustering has many fundamental advantages. Results obtained by spectral clustering often outperform the traditional approaches, spectral clustering is very simple to implement and can be solved efficiently by standard linear algebra methods.

3 System Evaluation

This section reports the evaluation dataset and system performance for our feature-based Chinese WSI system.

3.1 Dataset and Evaluation Metrics

We use the CLP2010 bake off task 4 sample dataset as our development dataset. There are 2500 examples containing 50 target words and each word has 50 sentences with different meanings. The exact meanings of the target words are blind, only the number of the meanings is provided in the data. We compute the system performance with the sample dataset because it contains the answers of each candidate meaning. The test dataset provided by the CLP2010 is similar to the sample dataset. It contains 100 target words and 5000 instances in total. However, it doesn't provide the answers.

The F-score measurement is the same as Zhao and Karypis (2005). Given a particular class L_r of size n_r and a particular cluster S_i of size n_i, suppose n_{ir} in the cluster S_i belong to L_r, then the F value of this class and cluster is defined to be

$$F(L_r, S_i) = \frac{2 \times R(L_r, S_i) \times P(L_r, S_i)}{R(L_r, S_i) + P(L_r, S_i)}$$

$$R(L_r, S_i) = n_{ir} / n_r$$

$$P(L_r, S_i) = n_{ir} / n_i$$

where $R(L_r, S_i)$ is the recall value and $P(L_r, S_i)$ is the precision value. The F-score of class L_r is the maximum F value and F-score value follow:

$$F\text{-}score(L_r) = \max_{S_i} F(L_r, S_i)$$

$$F - score = \sum_{r=1}^{c} \frac{n_r}{n} F - score(L_r)$$

where c is the total number of classes and n is the total size.

3.2 Experiment Results

Table 1 reports the F-score of our feature-based Chinese WSI for different feature sets with various window sizes using K-means clustering. Since there are different results for each run of K-means clustering algorithm, we perform 20 trials and compute their average as the final results. The columns denote different window size *n*, that is, the *n* words before and after the target word are extracted as features. Particularly, the size of infinity (∞) means that all the words in the sentence except the target word are considered. The rows represent various combinations of feature sets and similarity measurements, currently, four of which are considered as follows:

F-All: all the words are considered as features and from them feature vectors are constructed.

F-Stop: the top 150 most frequently occurring words in the total "word bags" of the corpus are regarded as stop words and thus removed from the feature set. Feature vectors are then formed from these words.

S-All: the feature set and the feature vector are the same as those of F-All, but instead the similarity vector is used for clustering (c.f. Section 2.2).

S-Stop: the feature set and the feature vector are the same as those of F-Stop, but instead the similarity vector is used for clustering.

Feature/ Similarity	3	7	10	∞
F-All	0.5949	0.6199	0.6320	0.6575
F-Stop	0.6384	0.6500	0.6493	0.6428
S-All	0.5856	0.6044	0.6186	0.6843
S-Stop	**0.6532**	**0.6696**	**0.6804**	**0.7320**

Table 1 Experimental results for different feature sets with different window sizes using K-means clustering

This table shows that S-Stop achieves the best performance of 0.7320 in F-score. This suggests that for K-means clustering, Chinese WSI can benefit much from removing stop words and adopting similarity vector. It also shows that:

- As the window size increases, the performance is almost consistently enhanced. This indicates that all the words in the sentence more or less help disambiguate the target word.
- Removing stop words consistently improves the F-score for both similarity metrics. This means some high frequent words do not help discriminate the meaning of the target words, and further work on feature selection is thus encouraged.
- Similarity vector consistently outperforms feature vector for stop-removed features, but not so for all-words features. This may be due to the fact that, when the window size is limited, the influence of frequently occurring stop words is relatively high, thus the similarity vector misrepresent the context of the target word. On the contrary, when stop words are removed or the context is wide, the similarity vector can better reflect the target word's context, leading to better performance.

In order to intuitively explain why the similarity vector is more discriminative than the feature vector, we take two sentences containing the Chinese word “把握” (hold, grasp) as an example (Figure 2). These two sentences have few common words, so clustering via feature vectors puts them into different classes. However, since the similarities of these two feature vectors with other feature vectors are much similar, clustering via similarity vectors group them into the same class.

<lexelt item="把握" snum="4">
<instance id="0012">
当一个人有了跳槽想法后，很自然他（她）确需要找到一个合适的时机。实际上，<head>把握</head>“时”和“机”都非常重要。
</instance>
<instance id="0015">
无论是在球场上还是学习中，现在的李纵横都表现得非常自信，“人生要懂得<head>把握</head>机会，一次机会或许可以使你的一生发生转变，然而这样的前提就是参与。”
</instance>
</lexelt>

Figure 2 An example from the dataset

According to the conclusion of the above experiments, it is better to include all the words except stop words in the sentence as the features in the subsequent experiment. Table 2 lists the results using various clustering algorithms with this same experimental setting. It shows that the spectral clustering algorithm achieves the best performance of 0.7692 in F-score for Chinese WSI using the S-All setup. Additionally, there are some interesting findings:

- Although SC performs best, KM with similarity vectors achieves comparable results of 0.7320 units in F-score, slightly lower than that of SC.
- HAC performs worst among all clustering algorithms. An observation reveals that this algorithm always groups the instances into highly skewed clusters, i.e., one or two clusters are extremely large while others usually have only one instance in each cluster.
- It is surprising that S-All slightly outperforms F-All by only 0.0006 units in F-score. The truth is that, as discussed in the first experiment, KM using F-All doesn't consider instance density while S-All does. On the contrary, SC identifies the eign-structure in the instance space and thus already considers the density information, therefore S-All will not significantly improve the performance.

Feature/ Similarity	KM	HAC	SC
F-All	0.6428	0.6280	0.7686
S-All	0.7320	0.6332	**0.7692**

Table 2 Experiments results using different clustering algorithms

3.3 Final System Performance

For the CLP2010 task 4 test dataset which contains 100 target words and 5000 instances in total, we first extract all the words except stop words in a sentence containing the target word, then produce the feature vector for each context and generate the similarity matrix, finally we perform the spectral cluster algorithm. Probably because the distribution of the target word in the test dataset is different from that in the development dataset, the F-score of our system on the test dataset is 0.7108, about 0.05 units lower than that we got on the sample dataset.

4 Conclusions and Future Work

In our Chinese WSI system, we extract all the words except stop words in the sentence, construct feature vectors and similarity vectors, and apply the spectral clustering algorithm to this problem. Experimental results show that our simple and efficient system achieve a promising result. Moreover, we also compare various clustering algorithms and similarity metrics. We find that although the spectral clustering algorithm outperforms other clustering algorithms, the K-means clustering with similarity vectors can also achieve comparable results.

For future work, we will incorporate more linguistic features, such as base chunking, parse tree feature as well as dependency information into our system to further improve the performance.

Acknowledgement

This research is supported by Project 60873150, 60970056 and 90920004 under the National Natural Science Foundation of China. We would also like to thank other contributors in the NLP lab at Soochow University.

References

Jain A, Murty M. 1999.Flynn P. *Data clustering : A Review* [J]. ACM Computing Surveys,1999,31 (3) :2642323

F. Bach and M. Jordan.2004. *Learning spectral clustering.* In Proc. of NIPS-16. MIT Press, 2004.

Samuel Brody and Mirella Lapata. 2009. *Bayesian word sense induction.* In Proceedings of the 12th Conference of the European Chapter of the ACL (EACL 2009), pages 103–111.

Neill, D. B. 2002. *Fully Automatic Word Sense Induction by Semantic Clustering.* Cambridge University, Master's Thesis, M.Phil. in Computer Speech.

Agirre, E. and Soroa, A. 2007. *Semeval-2007 task 02: Evaluating word sense induction and discrimination systems.* In Proceedings of the 4th International Workshop on Semantic Evaluations:7-12

Ioannis P. Klapaftis and Suresh Manandhar. 2008. *Word sense induction using graphs of collocations.* In Proceedings of the 18th European Conference On Artificial Intelligence (ECAI-2008), Patras, Greece, July. IOS Press.

Kannan, R., Vempala, S and Vetta, A. 2004. *On clusterings: Good, bad and spectral.* J. ACM, 51(3), 497–515.

Reinhard Rapp.2004. *A practical solution to the problem of automatic word sense induction.* Proceedings of the ACL 2004 on Interactive poster and demonstration sessions, p.26-es, July 21-26, 2004, Barcelona, Spain

Bordag, S. 2006. *Word sense induction: Triplet-based clustering and automatic evaluation.* In Proceedings of the 11th Conference of the European Chapter of the Association for Computational Linguistics (EACL, Trento, Italy). 137--144.

Ying Zhao, and George Karypis.2005. *Hierarchical Clustering Algorithms for Document Datasets.* Data Mining and Knowledge Discovery, 10, 141–168.

K-means and Graph-based Approaches for Chinese Word Sense Induction Task

Lisha Wang **Yanzhao Dou** **Xiaoling Sun** **Hongfei Lin**
Computer Science Department
Dalian University of Technology
{lisawang0110,yanzhaodou}@gmail.com
xlsun@mail.dlut.edu.cn hflin@dlut.edu.cn

Abstract

This paper details our experiments carried out at Word Sense Induction task. For the foreign language (especially English), there have been many studies of word sense induction (WSI), and the approaches and the techniques are more and more mature. However, the study of Chinese WSI is just getting started, and there has not been a better way to solve the problems encountered. WSI can be divided into two categories: supervised manner and unsupervised manner. But in the light of the high cost of supervised manner, we introduce novel solutions to automatic and unsupervised WSI. In this paper, we propose two different systems. The first one is called K-means-based Chinese word sense induction in an unsupervised manner while the second one is graph-based Chinese word sense induction. In the experiments, the first system has achieved a 0.7729 Fscore on average while the second one has achieved a 0.6067 Fscore.

1 Introduction

No matter in which kind of language, ambiguous terms always exist, Chinese is also not exceptional. According to statistics, although the percent of ambiguous terms in Chinese dictionary is only about 14.8%, the frequency of them is up to 42% in Chinese corpora. This phenomenon shows that the number of ambiguous terms is small in natural language, but their frequency is extremely high. Therefore, the key step in natural language processing (NLP) is to identify the specific meaning of a given target word according to its context. In this task, the input to a WSI algorithm is the sentences including the same ambiguous term, and our task is to cluster these sentences into different categories according to the meanings of this ambiguous term in every sentence. The study of WSI is earlier abroad and there has been a set of well-developed theories by now. However, the start of studying Chinese WSI is later and we need to find a better and appropriate way for Chinese WSI. In this paper, we develop two different systems. The first one is based on K-means algorithm which optimizes the initial centers and a Chinese thesaurus - TongYiCi CiLin is used to solve the problem of sparseness of a sentence's vector. The second one is a combination approach of graph-based clustering and K-means algorithm. We choose Chinese Whisper as the graph-based clustering approach.

2 K-means-based Chinese WSI in an Unsupervised Manner

Since the number of total meanings of an ambiguous term has been given in this task, our goal is to cluster those sentences which contain the same ambiguous term in an unsupervised manner. In this condition our primary problem is the selection of a suitable clustering method.

Clustering algorithms are generally divided into two categories, namely partitioning clustering algorithm and hierarchical clustering algorithm. Partitioning clustering algorithm is usually selected when the number of final clusters is known. Consequently, we need to input a parameter K as the number. Typical partitioning clustering algorithm contains K-means, K-medoids, CLARANS and so on. Among them, K-means clustering algorithm is widely used and relatively simple. Hierarchical clustering algorithms are not required to input any parameters, which is their advantage compared to partitioning clustering algorithms. Typical hierarchical clustering algorithms contain BIRCH algorithm, DBSCAN algorithm, CURE algorithm and so on.

Considering the characters of WSI (e.g. the total number of a target word's sense has been given in advance), we should select partitioning clustering algorithm. In addition, considering the quality, the performance, and the degree of difficulty while being implemented among all kinds of partitioning clustering algorithms, we finally decide to use k-means algorithm, but we have improved it in order to obtain better clustering performance.

2.1 Traditional K-means Algorithm

The process of traditional K-means algorithm is as follows:

Input: the number of clusters (k) and n-data objects.

Output: k-clusters. The clusters should satisfy the following requirements: the objects in the same cluster have higher similarity, while the objects in different clusters have lower similarity.

The process steps:

(1) Choose k-objects randomly as initial cluster centers;
(2) Repeat;
(3) Compute each object's distance to each cluster's center, then object is assigned to the most similar cluster;
(4) Update the center of each cluster;
(5) Until the changes of all clusters' centers are smaller than a given threshold.

2.2 The Advantages and Disadvantages of Traditional K-means Algorithm

The greatest advantage of traditional K-means algorithm is comparatively simple. In addition, its implementation is quick, effective and does not need a high cost. However, from the idea and processes as illustrated, we can see that the traditional K-means algorithm has two disadvantages: (1) an over-reliance on the selection of initial points. If the selection is improper (e.g. just select some points in the same cluster as the initial points), the result will be poor. (2) the clustering results are sensitive to "noise" and isolated points. Small amounts of such data can greatly decrease the precision.

2.3 Maximum Distance-based Selection of the Initial Centers

Given the above considerations, this paper introduces a maximum distance-based selection of the initial centers.

The selection of initial centers has a great impact on the result in traditional K-means clustering algorithm. If the selection is more appropriate, then the result will be more reasonable, while the convergence rate will be faster. So we hope that the initial centers should be dispersed as far as possible, not be placed in a particular one or limited several clusters. The best selection should be that K-initial points belong to K-different clusters. In order to achieve this goal, we use the maximum distance. Specific method is processed as follows: Firstly, select an arbitrary point as the first cluster's center from the n-data objects, and then calculate its distance to the remaining (n-1) data objects, to find out the farthest point away from it as the second cluster's initial center. Secondly, calculate the distances of the remaining (n-2) data objects to both the clusters' center, compute the average of the two values, and then select the point with the maximum average value as the initial cluster center of the third. We repeat this process until find out K-initial points.

From Figure 1 we can see that the result of improved algorithm is much better than traditional K-means algorithm.

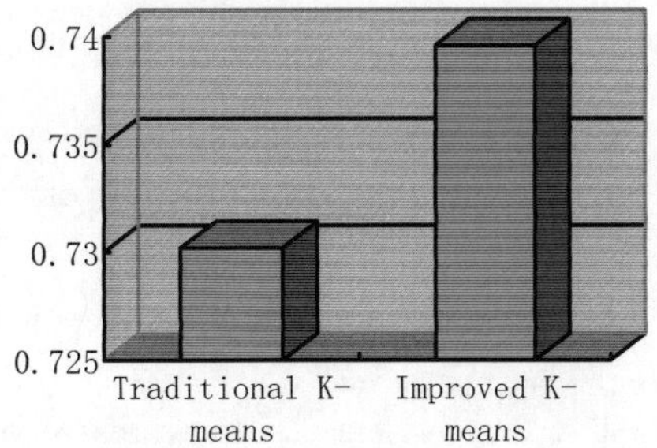

Figure 1: The results of traditional K-means algorithm and improved K-means algorithm.

2.4 The Context of the Target Words

During the process of WSI, we believe that the specific meaning of an ambiguous term is determined by its context, that is to say, those target words with similar context should have similar meaning in theory. So the first step we have to do is to establish all sentences' context around a target word (we have carried out Chinese word segmentation and stop word filtering to these sentences). As the K-means algorithm can only handle numerical data, we change the context into numerical format and then represent it using VSM. But how to determine the window size of the context is necessary to be further discussed.

In this paper, we use the information gain proposed by Lu et al. to achieve the goal of determining the window size. We count out 3000 high frequency words from the given test set in this task, every word as a class, and then calculate the statistical uncertainty of the whole system (entropy), namely H (D) in equation (3); The next step is to calculate the uncertainty of the whole system on the premise of knowing relative position, namely the $\Sigma_{v\in Vp}P(v)\times H(D|v)$ in equation (3); Difference between the two values is just the amount of information on the entire system provided by this relative position. The amount of information (i.e. information gain) is the weight of this position in the whole system. In this way we can determine the windows size by the weight.

$$IG_p=H(D)-\Sigma_{v\in Vp}P(v)\times H\ (D\mid v) \quad (1)$$

where

$$H(D)=-\Sigma_{d\in D}P(d)\times\log_2 P(d) \quad (2)$$

$$P(d)=\frac{|fre(d)|}{\sum_i|fre(d_i)|} \quad (3)$$

$\sum_i|fre(d_i)|$ is the sum of frequency of the 3,000 high frequency words appearing in the corpus; $|fre(d)|$ is the occurrence frequency of term d in the corpus.

We first separately select eight words before and after the target word in a sentence to constitute the context, expressed as the following form:

<wd_{-8}, wd_{-7}, wd_{-6}, wd_{-5}, wd_{-4}, wd_{-3}, wd_{-2}, wd_{-1} , ***focus-word***, wd_{+1}, wd_{+2}, wd_{+3}, wd_{+4}, wd_{+5}, wd_{+6}, wd_{+7}, wd_{+8}>

Table 1 Information gain of every position of context

Left context		Right context	
Position	Information gain	Position	Information gain
wd−1	3.979 875	wd+1	4.005 737
wd−2	2.800 943	wd+2	2.931 834
wd−3	2.183 287	wd+3	2.287 020
wd−4	1.709 504	wd+4	1.810 530
wd−5	1.361 637	wd+5	1.437 952
wd−6	1.074 606	wd+6	1.137 979
wd−7	0.304 546	wd+7	0.821 330
wd−8	0.298 992	wd+8	0.419 472

The amount of information provided by each position is presented in Table 1. According to the information gain in this table we can draw a conclusion: the closer a term to the target word, the more greatly it contributes to its meaning, and the ability to describe the target word's meaning decreases with the term's distance increasing to the focus-word. Because those words whose distance to the target word is more than 6 words contribute less to the meaning of the target word, we separately select at most 6 words before and after the target word as context.

2.5 Sparsity Problem

For those sentences containing the same target word we can respectively establish their context, and then merge the same words in those context to form a n-dimension space .Then we establish the vector model for each sentence. We have experimented with two different methods to represent weight in the vector: one is TF*IDF which is conventional and widely used in practice and the other one is Boolean. However, from Figure 2 we can see that the result of Boolean method is better. Analyzing the reasons, we can infer that the decisive role of a word to the target word is relevant whether the word appears or not, and has nothing to do with the times of appearance. Consequently, we select Boolean method to represent weight in the vector: if a word in the space appears in this sentence, the weight of this position in sentence's vector is 1, otherwise is 0.

Now we find a problem which should be solved: vector sparsity problem. In a few hundreds dimension vector space, a sentence contains only several limited words, thus the vector is highly sparse. As we analyzed, there are two main causes: 1). The length of a sentence is too short, so the number of words contained by it is few. 2). When merging those words in the context of a target word, we don't take into account the semantic similarity between them. We know that if the vector is too sparse, the result will have large errors, even two sentences which should have belonged to the same class are divided into different clusters.

We can not solve the problem caused by the first factor, but we can improve the second one. In this paper we introduce TongYiCi CiLin from HIT to compress the vector's dimension.

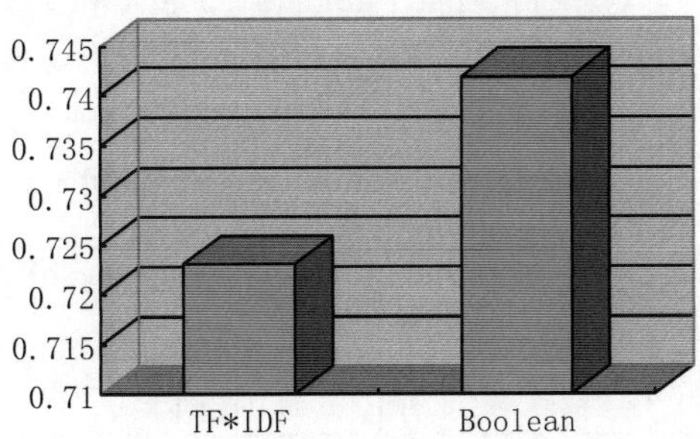

Figure 2: The results of two different methods to represent weight in the vector. Here we have selected improved K-means algorithm to optimize the initial centers.

2.6 Experiments

The whole process of experiment is as follows:

(1) Segment all sentences and filter stop-words for a given data set;
(2) Extract respectively six words before and after the focus-word from those sentences containing the same target words, and then use TongYiCi CiLin to merge these words into a lower n-dimension space;
(3) Establish the vector model for each sentence in this space;
(4) Cluster those sentences containing the same target words with maximum distance-based K-means algorithm proposed in this paper.

This experimental method is based on the following assumption: the similarity of target words' context determines the similarity of their meanings. In the framework of this assumption, we construct the context vector of each sentence, and then cluster those sentences containing the same target word.

In the experimental result, we have achieved 0.7729 Fscore on 100 ambiguous words.

3 Graph-based Chinese Word Sense Induction

In this system, we use a combination of graph-based clustering and K-means algorithm. At first we use Chinese Whisper to cluster the words in the corpus and the clustering result can be considered as an artificial synonyms dictionary. Secondly we construct corpus vectors using different methods, and now the vector dimension is decreased to the number of clusters. At last we cluster the vectors with the help of K-means algorithm.

3.1 Chinese Whisper Method

Many researches on WSI are based on word co-occurrence. The approach proposed by Chris Biemann has a wide range of applications, including language separation, acquisition of word class, word sense induction and so on. Chinese Whisper, which comes from a game called "Chinese Whisper", is a method used for graph clustering and its process is as follows:

(1) All nodes belong to different classes at the beginning;
(2) The nodes are processed for a small number of iterations and inherit the strongest class in the local neighborhoods. The sum of edge weights is maximal in this class.
(3) While updating a vertex i, each class, e.g. cl, receives a score equal to the weight of edge (i, j), here j has been assigned to cl. The maximum score determines the strongest class. If there are more than 2 strongest classes, only one is chosen randomly.
(4) While clustering, there are two important parameters to select: convergence constant and the iterations. From this we can see that this method has a great flexibility on parameter selection, and its clustering result is totally determined by the parameters.

In Chris Biemann's paper, using Chinese Whisper, his experiment about WSI based on British National Corpus (BNC) achieved 92.2% precision in adjective, 90% precision in noun, and 77.6% precision in verbs. Ioannis P.

Klapaftis and Suresh Manandhar use Chinese Whisper method for clustering and their experiment based on BNC achieved 81.1% FScore after trying 72 different parameters.

3.2 Graph Construction

When we construct the graph, every word is considered as a node in the graph and the weight of edge eij is measured by co-cocurence times of word i and word j. However, if we just use this method to construct the graph, the graph is very sparse. We use some methods proposed by IP Klapaftis to add new edges:

(1) Associate a vertex vector VC_i containing the vertices, which share an edge with vertex i in the graph.
(2) Calculate the similarity between each vertex vector VC_i and each vertex vector VC_j, here we use Jaccard similarity coefficient (JC) as a similarity measure:

$$JC(VC_i, VC_j) = \frac{|VC_i \cap VC_j|}{|VC_i \cup VC_j|} \quad (4)$$

Two nodes c_i and c_j are mutually similar if c_i is the most similar node to c_j and the other way round.
(3) Two mutually similar nodes c_i and c_j are clustered with the result that an occurrence of a node ck with one of c_i, c_j is also counted as an occurrence with the other node.

3.3 Experiments

K-means algorithm has a good performance for small corpus, but when the corpus size is too big, vector dimension will increase rapidly. So At first we use Chinese Whisper to cluster the words in the corpus after preprocessing, such as splitting the sentences, filtering stopwords and selecting context. Secondly we construct corpus vectors with VSM, and now the vector dimension is decreased to the number of clusters. At last we cluster the vectors using K-means algorithm analogous to the first system.

The choice of parameters is an important factor in Chinese Whisper and different parameters will result in different clusters. In this experiment we use batch process method in order to select the best parameters on training set. We select a group of parameters: convergence constant is from 0 to 1 and the step length is 0.1; iterations is from 1 to 30 and the step length is 1, which depends on the size of corpus. The process of experiment is as follows:

(1) Get a pair of parameters from the parameter group, cluster the corpus using Chinese Whisper, and then remove this pair of parameter from the parameter group.
(2) Construct vectors using the result of step (1).
(3) Cluster the vectors using K-means.
(4) The results are as the following two tables. From table 2 and table 3 we can see that if we use JC method to add new edges, the precision has a great improvement.

In the experimental result, we have achieved 0.6067 Fscore on 100 ambiguous words with the parameters: 0.8 and 12.

Table 2 Experimental results without using JC method

converge constance	iterations	precision (Boolean)
0.1	11	0.6119
0.1	15	0.6175
0.3	15	0.6210
0.5	15	0.6188

Table 3 Experimental results using JC method

converge constance	iterations	precision (Boolean)
0.6	17	0.6211
0.6	15	0.6251
0.7	11	0.6261
0.7	15	0.6287
0.8	12	0.6391
0.9	14	0.6192
1.0	16	0.6389
1.0	15	0.6300

4 Conclusion

In this paper, we propose two different systems for the task of Chinese WSI.

The result of the first system which is based on an improved K-means algorithm shows the proposed idea is feasible, and the precision is guaranteed. However, some problems still exist and need further to be resolved:

(1) The extended particle size of a word's synonym while using TongYiCi CiLin. If particle size is too large, the "noise" affects

the accuracy of the result; If particle size is too small, time complexity of the algorithm will increase drastically.

(2) The selection of initial centers in K-means algorithm remains to be further optimized. In addition to avoid the selected initial centers placing in one or several clusters, the problem of "noise" and isolated data need to be considered.

(3) The instability of this method. While we have got better results on most of ambiguous terms, but for those words with very many meanings, the induction effect is not so good. The reasons should be further analyzed and the solutions should be found out.

The result of the second system which is based on graph clustering shows that this method has a good performance in decreasing vector dimension. However, the number of clusters is too small, which made the performance of K-means algorithm poor.

Chinese Whisper has a good performance in WSI, but this is the first time to combine it with K-means together, thus there are lots of problems to be solved. As we have investigated, some methods can be used to improve the performance in the future work:

(1) Use a pair of words as a vertex of the graph instead of using a single word.

(2) Instead of using co-occurrence times as the weight of an edge, we can use conditional probability.

(3) Constrain words pair which can filter out some "noise", i.e. only use those words whose co-occurrence times is greater than a given value threshold.

Acknowledgments

This work is supported by grant from the Natural Science Foundation of China (No.60673039 and 60973068), the National High Tech Research and Development Plan of China (No.2006AA01Z151), National Social Science Foundation of China (No.08BTQ025), the Project Sponsored by the Scientific Research Foundation for the Returned Overseas Chinese Scholars, State Education Ministry and The Research Fund for the Doctoral Program of Higher Education (No.20090041110002).

References

Lu Song, Bai Shuo, and Huang Xiong. 2002. An Unsupervised Approach to Word Sense Disambiguation Based on Sense-Words in Vector Space Model. *Journal of Software*, 13(06): 1082-1089.

Stefan Bordag. 2004. Word Sense Induction: Triplet-Based Clustering and Automatic Evaluation. *In: Proceedings of HLT-NAACL, Workshop on Computational Lexical Semantics*, pages 137-144, Boston, Massachusetts.

Ioannis P.Klapaftis and Suresh Manandhar. 2008. Word Sense Induction Using Graphs of Collocations. *In: Proceedings of the 2008 conference on ECAI 2008: 18th European Conference on Artificial Intelligence, Frontiers in Artificial Intelligence and Applications*, pages 298-302, United Kingdom.

Chris Biemann. 2006. Chinese Whispers - an Efficient Graph Clustering Algorithm and its Application to Natural Language Processing Problems. *In: Proceedings of the HLT-NAACL 2006 Workshop on Textgraphs*, New York, USA.

Applying Spectral Clustering for Chinese Word Sense Induction

Zhengyan He, Yang Song, Houfeng Wang
Key Laboratory of Computational Linguistics (Peking University)
Ministry of Education,China
{hezhengyan, ysong, wanghf}@pku.edu.cn

Abstract

Sense Induction is the process of identifying the word sense given its context, often treated as a clustering task. This paper explores the use of spectral cluster method which incorporates word features and n-gram features to determine which cluster the word belongs to, each cluster represents one sense in the given document set.

1 Introduction

Word Sense Induction(WSI) is defined as the process of identifying different senses of a target word in a given context in an unsupervised method. It's different from word sense disambiguation(WSD) in that senses in WSD are assumed to be known. The disadvantage of WSD is that it derives the senses of word from existing dictionaries or other corpus and the senses cannot be extended to other domains. WSI can overcome this problem as it can automatically derive word senses from the given document set, or a specific domain.

Many different approaches based on co-occurence have been proposed so far. Bordag (2006) proposes an approach that uses triplets of co-occurences. The most significant co-occurences of target word are used to build triplets that consist of the target word and its two co-occurences. Then intersection built from the co-occurence list of each word in the triplet is used as feature vector. After merging similar triplets that have more than 80% overlapping words, clustering is performed on the triplets. Triplets with fewer than 4 intersection words are removed in order to reduce noise.

LDA model has also been applied to WSI (Brody and Lapata, 2009). Brody proposes a method that treats document and topics in LDA as word context and senses respectively. The process of generating the context words is as follows: first generate sense from a multinomial distribution given context, then generate context words given sense. They also derive a layered model to incorporate different kind of features and use Gibbs sampling method to solve the problem.

Graph-based methods become popular recently. These methods use the co-occurence graph of context words to obtain sense clusters based on sub-graph density. Markov clustering(MCL) has been used to identify dense regions of graph (Agirre and Soroa, 2007).

Spectral clustering performs well on problems in which points cluster based on shape. The method is that first compute the Laplace matrix of the affinity matrix, then reform the data points by stacking the largest eigenvectors of the Laplace matrix in columns, finally cluster the new data points using a more simple clustering method like k-means (Ng et al., 2001).

2 Methodology

Our approach follows a common cluster model that represents the given context as a word vector and later uses a spectral clustering method to group each instance in its own cluster.

Different types of polysemy may arise and the most significant distinction may be the syntactic classes of the word and the conceptually different senses (Bordag, 2006). Thus we must extract the features able to distinguish these differences. They are:

Local tokens: the word occuring in the window -3 – +3;

Local bigram feature: bigram within -5 – +5 Chinese character range;

The above two features model the syntactic usage of a specific sense of a Chinese word.

Topical or conceptual feature: the content words (pos-tagged as noun, verb, adjective) within the given sentence. As the sentence in the training set seems generally short, a short window may not contains enough infomation.

We represent the words in a 0-1 vector according to their existence in a given sentence. Then the similarity measure between two given sentences is derived from their cosine similarity. We find that it is difficult to define the relative importance of different types of features in order to combine them in one vector space, and find that ignoring weight achieve better result. Brody (2009) achieves this in LDA model through a layered model with different probability of feature given sense.

Later we use a spectral clustering method from R kernlab package (Karatzoglou et al., 2004) which implements the algorithm described in (Ng et al., 2001). Instead of using the Gaussian kernel matrix as the similarity matrix we use the cosine similarity derived above.

One observation is that instances with the same target word sense often appear in the same context. However, for some verb in Chinese, it is often the case that one sense relates to a concrete object while the other relates to a more broad and abstract concept and the context varies considerably. Simple word co-occurence cannot define a good similarity measure to group these cases into one cluster. We must consider semantic relatedness measures between contexts.

3 Performance

Our system performs well on the training set. Two methods are used to evaluate the performance under different features.

method	precision	recall	F-score
Purity-based	81.11	83.19	81.99
B-cubed	74.41	76.51	75.33

Table 1: The performance of training set

Our system finally gets a F-score of 0.7598 on the test set.

4 Conclusion

Our experiment in the Chinese word sense induction task performs good with respect to the relative small corpus(only the training set). But only considering token co-occurence cannot achieve better result. Moreover, it is difficult to define a similarity measure solely based on lexicon infomation with no regard to semantic relatedness. Finally, combining different types of features seems to be another challenge in our model.

5 Acknowledgments

This research is supported by National Natural Science Foundation of Chinese (No.9092001).

References

Agirre, Eneko and Aitor Soroa. 2007. Ubc-as: a graph based unsupervised system for induction and classification. In *SemEval '07: Proceedings of the 4th International Workshop on Semantic Evaluations*, pages 346–349, Morristown, NJ, USA. Association for Computational Linguistics.

Bordag, Stefan. 2006. Word sense induction: Triplet-based clustering and automatic evaluation. In *EACL*. The Association for Computer Linguistics.

Brody, Samuel and Mirella Lapata. 2009. Bayesian word sense induction. In *EACL*, pages 103–111. The Association for Computer Linguistics.

Karatzoglou, Alexandros, Alex Smola, Kurt Hornik, and Achim Zeileis. 2004. kernlab – an S4 package for kernel methods in R. *Journal of Statistical Software*, 11(9):1–20.

Ng, Andrew Y., Michael I. Jordan, and Yair Weiss. 2001. On spectral clustering: Analysis and an algorithm. In *Advances in Neural Information Processing Systems 14*, pages 849–856. MIT Press.

Author Index

Association for Computational Linguistics
209 N. Eighth Street
Stroudsburg, Pennsylvania 18360

CURRAN ASSOCIATES INC
proceedings
.com